Political Campaign Communication

Communication, Media, and Politics
Series Editor
Robert E. Denton, Jr., Virginia Tech

This series features a range of work dealing with the role and function of communication in the realm of politics, broadly defined. Including general academic books and texts for use in graduate and advanced undergraduate courses, the series encompasses humanistic, critical, historical, and empirical studies in political communication in the United States. Primary subject areas include campaigns and elections, media, and political institutions. *Communication, Media, and Politics* books will be of interest to students, teachers, and scholars of political communication from the disciplines of communication, rhetorical studies, political science, journalism, and political sociology.

Recent Titles in the Series

Reelpolitik II: Political Ideologies in '50s and '60s Films
    Beverly Merrill Kelley
New Frontiers in International Communication Theory
    Edited by Mehdi Semati
News Narratives and News Framing: Constructing Political Reality
    Karen S. Johnson-Cartee
Leading Ladies of the White House: Communication Strategies of Notable Twentieth-Century First Ladies
    Edited by Molly Meijer Wertheimer
Entertaining Politics: New Political Television and Civic Culture
    Jeffrey P. Jones
Presidential Candidate Images
    Edited by Kenneth L. Hacker
Bring 'Em On: Media and Politics in the Iraq War
    Edited by Lee Artz and Yahya R. Kamalipour
The Talk of the Party: Political Labels, Symbolic Capital, and American Life
    Sharon E. Jarvis
The 2004 Presidential Campaign: A Communication Perspective
    Edited by Robert E. Denton, Jr.
Women's Political Discourse: A 21st-Century Perspective
    Molly A. Mayhead and Brenda DeVore Marshall
Making Sense of Political Ideology: The Power of Language in Democracy
    Bernard L. Brock, Mark E. Huglen, James F. Klumpp, and Sharon Howell
Transforming Conflict: Communication and Ethnopolitical Conflict
    Donald G. Ellis
Towel Snapping the Press: Bush's Journey from Locker-Room Antics to Message Control
    James E. Mueller
The Internet Election: Perspectives on the Web in Campaign 2004
    Edited by Andrew Paul Williams and John C. Tedesco
Center Stage: Media and the Performance of American Politics
    Gary C. Woodward
Bush's War: Media Bias and Justifications for War in a Terrorist Age
    Jim A. Kuypers
Mediating the Vote: The Changing Media Landscape in U.S. Presidential Campaigns
    Michael Pfau, J. Brian Houston, and Shane M. Semmler
Message Control: How News Is Made on the Campaign Trail
    Elizabeth A. Skewes

Political Campaign Communication

Principles and Practices

Sixth Edition

Judith S. Trent and Robert V. Friedenberg

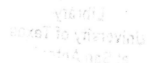

ROWMAN & LITTLEFIELD PUBLISHERS, INC.
Lanham • Boulder • New York • Toronto • Plymouth, UK

ROWMAN & LITTLEFIELD PUBLISHERS, INC.

Published in the United States of America
by Rowman & Littlefield Publishers, Inc.
A wholly owned subsidiary of The Rowman & Littlefield Publishing Group, Inc.
4501 Forbes Boulevard, Suite 200, Lanham, Maryland 20706
www.rowmanlittlefield.com

Estover Road, Plymouth PL6 7PY, United Kingdom

British Library Cataloguing in Publication Information Available

Library of Congress Cataloging-in-Publication Data

Trent, Judith S.
  Political campaign communication : principles and practices / Judith S. Trent
and Robert V. Friedenberg. — 6th ed.
      p. cm. — (Communication, media, and politics)
  Includes bibliographical references and index.
  ISBN-13: 978-0-7425-5302-6 (cloth : alk. paper)
  ISBN-10: 0-7425-5302-7 (cloth : alk. paper)
  ISBN-13: 978-0-7425-5303-3 (pbk. : alk. paper)
  ISBN-10: 0-7425-5303-5 (pbk. : alk. paper)
  1. Political campaigns. 2. Communication in politics. I. Friedenberg, Robert V.
II. Title.
  JF1001.T73 2008
  324.7'3—dc22
                                                                    2007001032

Printed in the United States of America

♾™ The paper used in this publication meets the minimum requirements of
American National Standard for Information Sciences—Permanence of Paper
for Printed Library Materials, ANSI/NISO Z39.48-1992.

To Jimmie Douglas Trent
and the memory of
Aaron and Florence Friedenberg

Contents

Preface   xi

Part I: Principles of Political Campaign Communication

1 Communication and Political Campaigns: A Prologue   3
     Importance of Political Campaigns   3
     Changes in the Political Campaign   5
     Decline of Political Parties   5
     Finance Reforms   7
     Political Action Committees   9
     Technology   13
     Technology in the First Decade of the Twenty-first Century   14
     Communication and Political Campaigns   16
     Organization and Preview of Chapters   17
     Notes   20

2 Communicative Functions of Political Campaigns   22
     First Political Stage: Surfacing   22
     Second Political Stage: Primaries   38
     Third Political Stage: Nominating Conventions   51
     Fourth Political Stage: The General Election   66
     Conclusion   68
     Notes   68

3 Communicative Styles and Strategies of Political Campaigns   72
     Preliminary Considerations   73
     Styles and Strategies of Campaigns   86

| | Conclusion | 117 |
| | Notes | 118 |

4	Communicative Mass Channels of Political Campaigning	122
	Early Studies	125
	Contemporary Studies	133
	Conclusion	146
	Notes	150

5	Communicative Types and Functions of Televised Political Advertising	154
	Historical Development	155
	Types and Functions of Political Ads	161
	Televised Attack Advertising When the Candidate Is a Woman	171
	A Final Question: Do Televised Attack Ads Work?	181
	Conclusion	182
	Notes	183

Part II: Practices of Political Campaign Communication

6	Public Speaking in Political Campaigns	191
	The Decision to Speak	191
	The Speech	199
	Political Speechwriting	207
	Surrogate Speakers	217
	Conclusion	221
	Notes	221

7	Recurring Forms of Political Campaign Communication	226
	Announcement Speeches	227
	Acceptance Addresses	238
	News Conferences	253
	Apologias	265
	Conclusion	272
	Notes	272

8	Debates in Political Campaigns	277
	History of Political Debates	280
	Deciding Whether to Debate	285
	Applying the Conditions Requisite for Political Debates	287
	Political Debate Strategies	293
	Effects of Political Debates	304
	Conclusion	314
	Notes	315

9   Interpersonal Communication in Political Campaigns   322
    Interpersonal Communication between Candidates
        and Voters   324
    Interpersonal Communication between the Candidate and
        Prospective Financial Contributors   334
    Interpersonal Communication between Voters   341
    Interpersonal Communication among Voters, Mass
        Media, and Voting Behavior   343
    Interpersonal Communication and Getting Out The
        Vote Efforts   345
    Conclusion   349
    Notes   349

10 Advertising in Political Campaigns   353
    Developing a Master Plan for Political Advertising   354
    Basic Considerations in the Selection of Political
        Advertising Media   357
    Campaign Advertising Strategies   378
    Media and Other Types of Political Consultants   382
    Functions of Political Consultants   386
    Conclusion   391
    Notes   391

11 The Internet and Political Campaigns   399
    Content of Candidate Websites   399
    Functions of Candidate Websites   402
    The Breadth and Future of the Internet and Internet Tools
        in Elective Politics   408
    Conclusion   412
    Notes   412

Political Campaign Communication: An Epilogue   415

Selected Bibliography   423

Index   427

About the Authors   435

Preface

When the first edition of this book was published in 1983, it was the first book-length study of election campaigns that utilized the principles and practices of speech communication to examine elective politics. While we certainly drew on other disciplines and acknowledged the merit of much of the material they contributed to the study of election campaigns, we argued that communication was the epistemological base of political campaigns. Consequently, we wrote from a speech communication perspective. We have been extremely gratified by the reception that our first five editions received. We continue to believe that the use of the principles and practices of speech communication as a means of examining elective politics contributes appreciably to our knowledge of the electoral process.

If there is any one theme of this book, it is that we view political campaigns as communication phenomena, and, in the following pages, we have examined those communication principles and practices central to election campaigns. We have sought to offer readers a realistic understanding of the strategic and tactical communication choices candidates and their managers must make as they wage the campaign. To that end, the five chapters in Part I have been edited and updated to reflect what occurred in the 2004 and 2006 campaigns as well as to consider the early stage of the 2008 campaign. Similarly, the first five chapters in Part II have been edited and updated to reflect recent election campaigns and any changes resulting from them. Additionally, a new chapter on the use of the Internet has been added.

This was a collaborative effort. We examined drafts of each chapter and shared equally in the writing of the epilogue and various editing chores. Chapters 1 through 5 were written primarily by Juddi, and chapters 6 through 10 were written primarily by Bob. Chapter 11 was jointly written. Both share any of the successes or shortcomings of this volume.

We wish to acknowledge many people for their aid in producing this book. Particularly helpful to both authors were our colleagues, students, staffs, and libraries of our home institutions, the University of Cincinnati and Miami (Ohio) University. The staff at Rowman & Littlefield was uniformly helpful and pleasant. We also want to thank Amber K. Erickson for preparing the index while under considerable time pressure.

In addition, Juddi would like to thank Amber K. Erickson for her professional and dedicated help in preparing the manuscript and providing consistently reliable research help, the many University of Cincinnati students in her political communication classes, Communication Department colleagues, and political communication colleagues across the country who provided valuable comments about the fifth edition. Most important, she would like to thank Jimmie for his constant support throughout this and all other endeavors.

Moreover, Bob would like to acknowledge the consistently excellent support he has received from the Miami University Libraries. He would also like to acknowledge the *Journal of American Forensic Association* (*JAFA*) for permission to use portions of two articles he originally wrote for *JAFA*. He thanks as well his many Miami University political communication students for their helpful comments on the previous editions. Finally, and most important, he would like to acknowledge the wonderful support he received throughout the writing of every edition of this book from his wife, Emmy.

I

PRINCIPLES OF POLITICAL CAMPAIGN COMMUNICATION

1

~

Communication and Political Campaigns: A Prologue

It has become fashionable to criticize our electoral system. Campaigns are too long and too expensive. Candidates are dishonest, concerned only with the image they project, and speak only in sound bites. Voters are bored with the process, are distrustful of government and politicians, and frequently do not vote. Although we express these and other complaints, elections, and the political campaigns that are a part of them, are vital to us in at least three different but complementary senses.

IMPORTANCE OF POLITICAL CAMPAIGNS

Elections are important because they allow us freedom to actively participate in selecting our leaders. They are the core of democracy. Nowhere in the world are more people more freely engaged in active, responsible participation in the choice of leadership than in the United States. Whether the election will determine the occupants of two seats on the city council or one chair in the Oval Office of the White House, the political election campaign is an essential element of a democratic system.

Elections provide us with the opportunity to determine how our own interests can best be served. We may, for example, try to decide which board of education candidate does not favor increasing our property taxes. We might also ask whether the Republican candidate for governor sees the need to create jobs as the state's top priority or whether the Democratic challenger running for Congress supports increasing money for education and public transportation. Once we feel enough questions

3

have been answered, we must decide how actively to participate in the campaign. Will we try to ignore it? Will we work for the candidate or political party we favor? Will we vote? Any decision contributes to our self-development and expression.

Not only do elections give opportunities for quiet decision making or overt participation in determining who will govern; they also provide the legitimacy with which to govern. The winners of elections receive a general acceptance of their right to power. No matter how large or small the margin of victory, the candidate who receives the necessary votes has been granted a legitimacy quite distinct from power. Any election can give the winner power. Only a democratic election will provide the sense of "rightness" or even "genuineness" necessary to govern or be governed. We may no longer "like" the president for whom we voted two years ago, but we recognize that he has a legitimate claim to the office until the next election. The president, like all other candidates we elect, can only be "overthrown" as a consequence of the next election.

Thus, in pragmatic ways, our electoral system is important to us. No less significant are the symbolic aspects of election campaigns. The British historian J. H. Plumb maintained that there are two histories: the actual series of events that once occurred and the ideal series we affirm and hold in memory. In other words, the past is composed not only of historical "fact" but of what is "made" of history. It is, in the largest sense, the collective memory—the national myth—that unites us as a people. Not only do elections provide leaders and grant them authority to govern; they also add to our memory or image of the electoral process and thus give proof that the system is a good one. The fact that we have elections, that leaders are not overthrown by revolution, that citizens freely discuss and participate in the selection process, or that the Constitution "worked" during the Watergate crisis of the 1970s grants support for the belief that the American Dream is real and that this country really is destined to be the mighty keeper of liberty. All the fanfare and excitement of the political campaign—be it bands and parades, buttons and billboards, speeches and rallies, television ads and debates, or Internet chat rooms and home pages—are important for the reinforcement provided about the rightness of what we do and the way we do it.

Now, all of this is to tell you that the subject matter of this book is worthwhile. Although aspects of our electoral system may need repair from time to time, the process and the product are worth the effort. While the value of elections has remained constant, the manner in which they are conducted has changed enormously in recent years. As a matter of fact, the political campaign has undergone such a radical transformation that those principles and practices accepted by practitioners and theorists even fifteen years ago are in many respects largely irrelevant today. Thus, before we can describe and analyze any of the dimensions of campaign communication in the chapters that follow, we must examine those changes that, to the greatest extent, comprise the essence of the new politics. Four of them will be discussed in the following order: (1) the decline in the influence of political parties, (2) electoral financing legislation, (3) political action committees, and (4) technological advancements.

CHANGES IN THE POLITICAL CAMPAIGN

The legendary party bosses once determined who would run for political office. In national and state politics, these people were often called king-makers, who from the sanctity of the so-called smoke-filled rooms at nominating conventions handpicked "their" candidate to be the party nominee. In local politics, especially in the large cities, party bosses, through a system that combined the disposition of jobs with political favors, support, and even protection, controlled the votes, the party, and thus the selection of all candidates.

DECLINE OF POLITICAL PARTIES

Undoubtedly, the most significant change in presidential politics occurred when, in 1976, the reform rules adopted by the Democratic Party and, to a lesser extent, the Republican Party forced changes in state laws regarding delegate selection. Under party rules adopted before the 1976 campaign, the caucus convention procedure was wide open for participation by everyone, and any candidate who could inspire a following had a chance to win delegates. By changing the process of delegate selection, political reformers aided in reshaping the presidential nominating system. In 1968, there were only fifteen primaries, in which less than 40 percent of the delegates were chosen. In 1976, however, 77 percent of the delegates at the Democratic Convention had come from thirty primary states, reducing the strength of delegates from caucus states to 704 of the 3,008 delegates. In 2000, there were eighty-nine primaries and caucuses that determined the choices of the majority of the 4,338 delegates to the Democratic Convention and the majority of the 2,066 delegates to the Republican Convention. And in 2004, there were eighty primaries and caucuses (by late spring a number of states cancelled their plans for a primary because they are expensive to run and it was absolutely clear that Senator John Kerry would be the nominee of the Democratic Party and that President George W. Bush would be the nominee of the Republican Party) that led to the selection of 4,322 delegates to the Democratic National Convention and 2,509 delegates to the Republican National Convention.

Clearly, then, the reform rules changed the nature of the presidential nominating system by transferring power from party officials to citizens who voted in state primary elections. In fact, by 1982, two years before the 1984 campaign, some Democrats were so concerned about the shift in power that the party accepted a plan proposed by its Commission on Presidential Nominations to return a little of the clout from citizen activists to elected officials by adding 548 (or 14 percent) uncommitted members of Congress, governors, mayors, and party officials to its 3,675 delegates. For its 2000 national nominating convention, the Democratic Party once again increased the number of uncommitted delegates—this time to eight hundred—maintaining, however, the principle that the vast majority (82 percent) of delegates would be determined by primary and caucus voters.

The result is that the change in rules and the proliferation of primaries have weakened political parties, the traditional vehicle for building coalitions and forging consensus. In the past, candidates had to work their way up through party ranks and appeal to party bosses, but, since 1960, successful candidates at all levels have often ignored the party regulars, built their own organizations, and taken their campaigns directly to the people. As presidential chronicler and political journalist Theodore H. White reflected, "the old bosses are long gone and with them the old parties. In their place has grown a new breed of young professionals whose working skills in the new politics would make the old boys look like stumblebums."[1]

While for our purposes it is unnecessary to trace the fall of the political bosses from "kingmaker" to "stumblebum," it is important to realize that citizens feel little allegiance to political parties. Each year since the mid-1960s, the results of the election studies conducted by the Center for Political Studies at the University of Michigan have shown that fewer and fewer voters identify themselves as Republicans or Democrats, while more and more call themselves Independents. In 1964, approximately 24 percent of the population eligible to vote labeled themselves as Independents. Thirty years later, in 1994, the Center for Political Studies reported that 35 percent identified themselves as Independent Democrats, Independent Independents, and Independent Republicans. In the 2000 election, according to the Gallup Poll, 38 percent of the electorate identified with neither the Republican nor the Democratic Party; 34 percent were Democrats and 28 percent Republican. Unfortunately, the rise in the number of Americans who self-identify as Independents has occurred at the same time voter turnout has declined in elections. Furthermore, respect for the parties as institutions that represent the public has also decreased.

FINANCE REFORMS

The decline in party identification and influence is not the only element that has altered the nature of the election campaign. Closely related are the reforms in financing that, although initially affecting only presidential candidates, have had some effect at all levels.

The Federal Election Campaign Act of 1974 and the amendment to it in 1976 changed much of the character of presidential campaigning, particularly in the early portion of the electoral cycle. The act provided for voluntary income tax checkoffs, and the U.S. Treasury used the money to provide matching grants to presidential candidates who had raised $5,000 in amounts of $250 or less, from citizens in at least twenty states. The maximum any individual could give a candidate was $1,000. But the Supreme Court ruled in 1976 that this ceiling could not prevent individuals or committees from spending unlimited amounts of money in support of a candidate so long as the effort was separate from the candidate's campaign, without any consultation or coordination. Suddenly, "running for president" became a possibility for people who were not wealthy. In fact, in the three elections that immediately followed passage of the act, thirty-six people were serious enough as presidential contenders to have qualified for federal matching funds. Two of the thirty-six candidates who qualified, Marion G. (Pat) Robertson in 1988 and John Connally in 1980, refused to use the funds, thereby freeing their campaigns from having to impose spending limits during the primary elections. In the 1996 presidential campaign, two Republican hopefuls, Malcolm S. (Steve) Forbes Jr. and Maurice (Morry) Manning Taylor Jr., spent their own money on their campaigns, as did Independent candidate H. Ross Perot. And during the presidential primaries in 2000, the front-running Republican hopeful, Texas governor George W. Bush, did not accept federal matching funds during the early stages of the election cycle.

Not only has the finance law resulted in generating more participation; it has also forced presidential hopefuls to establish themselves among small donors in a number of states. Contenders can no longer rely on the traditional "fat cats" who financed favored candidates in the past.

In spite of the limits imposed by legislation, campaigns during the 1980s and 1990s became more and more expensive. For example, in the 1980 election, candidates for Congress spent $228.8 million, which was well over the 1978 amount of $192.2 million; in the 1984 election, presidential hopefuls spent over $325 million, or double what was spent by those who sought the presidency in 1980; and spending on the total 1984 campaign (local, state, and national) reached $1.8 billion, a 50 percent increase over that spent for the total campaign in 1980. During the 1990s, costs continued their upward climb, so that by 1996 the total spending on all political campaigns exceeded $2.2 billion. And in the first years of the new millennium, costs continued to skyrocket. For example, by the time the ballots had been counted in November 2001, the 108th mayor of New York City, Michael R. Bloomberg, had spent over $73 million of his own money on his campaign. In preparing for the congressional elections of 2002, at least fifteen candidates from both major parties had each banked more than $2 million by December 31, 2001—almost eleven months before election day.

Advertising has become a major factor in rising campaign costs. For example, in the 2000 presidential election campaign, Republican candidate George W. Bush spent $134 million on television advertising during the general election campaign, spending more money on televised ads than any candidate for the presidency had ever spent (42 percent more than President Bill Clinton had spent in his 1996 reelection campaign). For the first time in political history, the spending of the two major political parties exceeded the amount spent by the candidates themselves. Republicans spent $71 million ($20 million on preconvention and $51 million on their postconvention ads), and the Democrats spent $61 million ($28 million for preconvention and $33 million on postconvention ads). Overall, Vice President Al Gore spent $45 million of his federal campaign dollars on television.[2]

Not only do candidates continue to spend vast amounts of money; they often find that they can raise it themselves. For example, in the 2004 presidential election, incumbent President George W. Bush's campaign raised $367,228,801, while Senator John Kerry's campaign raised almost half a billion dollars just during the primaries, and, even as the nonincumbent in the general election, Senator Kerry raised another $326,236,288.[3] Raising and spending large amounts of money is not confined to presidential candidates. In the 2005 Cincinnati mayoral race, candidates did not even have to rely solely on local contributors. Over half of the campaign money raised by the front-runners, David Pepper and Mark L. Mallory, came from outside Cincinnati—even as far away as California and Colorado.[4] For example, Mallory's outside-of-Cincinnati contributions were 60 percent of his money total, while 46.6 percent of Pepper's contributions were from non-Cincinnati supporters.[5] Mallory and Pepper combined raised 72 percent more than the two leading mayoral candidates of 2001.[6] As of May 2006, Hamilton County, Ohio, incumbent commissioner Phil Heimlich had raised almost $400,000 since January of that year to keep his job.[7]

Thus, for many who run even for mayor, governor, and Congress, the ability to raise money has been the most important effect of the reforms. It has widened the electoral process by bypassing the political parties. Candidates run their own campaigns and frequently hire their own professionals to raise funds—often completely independent of party support or discipline. In turn, raising money has become more challenging because individual voters who view themselves as political independents are contributing to specific candidates and causes and not to political parties.

Beginning in the mid-1980s and continuing until 2002, seventeen challenges (congressional battles) were made to existing campaign finance laws. Each challenge or legislative effort died because Republicans and Democrats could reach no compromise in Congress. However, in March 2002, Congress approved and President Bush signed a bill that did bring some change to the campaign finance system. Sponsored by John McCain and Russell Feingold in the United States Senate and Christopher Shays and Martin Meehan in the United States House of Representatives, the most prominent features of the legislation were its "ban on unlimited 'soft money' donations to the national political parties (typically five- and six-figure donations made by corporations, unions and individuals)" and its ban on using "soft money to buy 'issue ads' within 60 days of an election or 30 days of a primary."[8] According to the dictates of the Bipartisan Campaign Reform Act, in the 2004 election, individual citizens were permitted to contribute $2,000 to the campaigns of presidential or congressional candidates (a $1,000 increase over the 1974 legislation). And although many in Congress believed the 2002 reform legislation to be flawed, President Bush signed it anyway, arguing that it "improved the current system overall."[9] However, the reality was that individual contributions (not corporate) were greater than they had ever been: President Bush raised $271,814,020 in individual contributions, 74 percent of the total funds he raised. Senator Kerry was not far behind, raising $225,283,370 in individual contributions, 69 percent of his total funds.[10] Thus, two factors—the decline of the influence of political parties and campaign finance legislation—have combined to change contemporary political campaigns.

POLITICAL ACTION COMMITTEES

There is, however, a third and related element that has also altered the way in which campaigns are waged—political action committees (PACs) or single-issue groups.

Pressure groups have existed since the founding of the republic. Over the years, the efforts of some of these groups have brought about important changes, such as the abolitionists who helped eliminate slavery and the suffragettes who helped give women the right to vote. However, in recent years, pressure groups have become so powerful and so numerous that their efforts to influence legislation and elections have had a dramatic impact on electoral politics. Their campaigns for or against proposed legislation have often served to fragment the political system, and their efforts to affect the election of specific candidates have contributed to the declining influence of political parties.

Although by definition the single-issue or pressure groups are small, they have nonetheless become increasingly powerful. By the 1980 election, pollsters estimated that one in four voters was willing to vote against politicians for their position on a single issue, and the issues themselves affected 10 to 15 percent of the general electorate. While the issue around which the groups coalesce vary all the way from import quotas to environmental control, it is the so-called emotional or passionate issues such as abortion, gun control, prayer in school, and sexual preference that attract the most attention and motivate groups to spring into action quickly if they feel that a proposed bill or even an individual legislator threatens their interests. They concentrate on the grassroots, pressuring city councils and state legislators, while simultaneously bombarding members of Congress with telephone calls, telegrams, letters, and personal visits; heckling during public appearances, or letting them know that, without support for the issue, the PAC will work to defeat them in the next election.

In 1950, there were fewer than two thousand lobbyists in Washington. However, by the 1978 elections, pressure groups had proliferated to such an extent that fifteen thousand lobbyists were based just on Capitol Hill to work for the interests of over five hundred corporate lobbies, sixty-one working on Japan's interests, fifty-three minority group lobbies, thirty-four social welfare lobbies, thirty-three women's lobbies, thirty-one lobbies for environmental interests, twenty-one lobbies for religious interests, fifteen lobbies for the aging, ten for Israel, six for population control, and twelve for gun-related issues.[11] According to the 1990 *American Lobbyists Directory*, there were more than sixty-five thousand individual lobbyists and thirty thousand organizational lobbyists. Although some of these groups had been around for a long time, by 2000 they had formed 4,449 PACs and were much more aggressive in their attempts to influence legislation than they had been in the past.

Through the use of computerized mailing lists that identify supporters, many PACs have been able to raise large sums of money that have been spent not only to lobby for their specific issue but to defeat legislators who have not supported them and to elect others who have. The PACs' ability to do this is directly related to the election law reforms we have already discussed. When Congress limited individual campaign donations to $1,000 per candidate, per race, it simultaneously permitted corporations, unions, and other groups to become involved in making direct political contributions to candidates if they established political action committees. While companies were prohibited from contributing corporate funds, through their PACs they were able to solicit voluntary contributions from employees and stockholders and then give up to $5,000 to candidates for their primary and for their general election campaign. In the 2004 presidential campaign, individual contributions were limited to $2,000, and voluntary contributions of corporations, unions, and other groups through their PACs were limited to $10,000. Thus, although a congressional candidate who was oriented toward business could still receive tens of thousands of dollars in so-called soft money from dozens of corporate PACs, and a union-oriented candidate was able to receive tens of thousands of dollars from union PACs, it had to come from multiple groups (PACs).

In the primary and caucus period of the 2004 campaign, President Bush and his Democratic opponent Senator John Kerry of Massachusetts accepted no federal funds so that they could raise and use unlimited amounts of soft money. All told, about $300 million of unregulated soft money found its way to both national parties in 2004. However, this was down from the $500 million raised in the 2000 presidential election cycle—a likely result of the 2002 Bipartisan Campaign Reform Act. In fact, during the 2003–2004 election cycle, PAC contributions were down nearly 50 percent from the 1999–2000 election cycle.[12] Two of the top PACs for the 2003–2004 election cycle were the National Association of Realtors, which spent $3.7 million, and Laborers Union, which contributed $2.6 million.[13] The ability of the PACs to raise money to contribute to the campaigns of "friendly" incumbents and "promising" challengers cannot be taken lightly. It is an ability that has been proven in every election since the election law reforms. For example, EMILY's List (which stands for Early Money Is Like Yeast, because it makes the dough rise) provided $6,717,970 to the campaigns of forty-two pro-choice Democratic women during the 1996 election cycle. In fact, EMILY's List was the largest funder of U.S. congressional candidates in 1992 and again in 1996. In addition to funding political candidates, EMILY's List runs TV ads for candidates it supports, staffs campaigns, and provides strategic advice.[14]

The majority of PAC money goes to incumbents, although, in recent election cycles, contributions to challengers have been on the rise. In 1988, PACs contributed $66 million to congressional incumbents and only $7 million to those who challenged their seats. However, in 1992, and again in 1996, although PACs contributed far more to incumbents than to challengers, total contributions to incumbents somewhat decreased. In 1996, for example, 84 percent of the PAC contributions were channeled to incumbents, while in 1998 PACs contributed 65 percent of their total contributions to incumbents.[15] The 2004 presidential election was no different. Incumbent President Bush saw PAC contributions of $2,917,017 while his opponent Senator Kerry received a much smaller amount in PAC contributions, totaling only $141,918.[16] In spite of the fact that PACs have increased their contributions to challengers, they continue to contribute more to incumbents. The reason for this obvious disparity is that PACs understand that incumbents are far more likely to win elections than are newcomers.

Just as the PACs work toward specific candidates' success, so can they work for their defeat. For example, in 1980, the National Conservative Political Action Committee (NCPAC) targeted five prominent liberal Democratic senators for defeat and ran an extensive media campaign against each. All five—George McGovern of South Dakota, Warren Magnuson of Washington, Frank Church of Idaho, Birch Bayh of Indiana, and John Culver of Iowa—were beaten, and, because of its financial involvement and the publicity generated by announcing its campaigns against the senators, NCPAC received much of the credit or blame. In 1991, a group of young adults concerned about the nation's economic and social future who called themselves the Third Millennium rated and ranked congresspersons on their commitment to the nation's long-term prosperity. "The lawmakers were ranked by their votes on 10 issues with implications for the circumstances of citizens in the 21st century, ranging from the federal budget to housing policy and grazing fees, and from economic development to national service and savings and loan bailouts."[17] From those scorecards, the group categorized the politicians into lists of Third Millennium's friends and enemies and directed its money accordingly.

Perhaps the most interesting development regarding PACs and presidential politics occurred in 2004 with the appearance and breathtaking efficiency of organizations that became known as 527s. One such group, MoveOn.org, was created by Joan Blades and Wes Boyd in 1998 at the time of the President Clinton impeachment movement. Frustrated with the partisan politics in Washington, Blades and Boyd started the liberal MoveOn as an online petition to stop what they saw as a "ridiculous waste of our nation's focus" with the impeachment hearings.[18] During the 2004 presidential campaign, MoveOn maintained its liberal origins by focusing on raising money from individual citizens for the purpose of defeating the right wing and electing moderates and progressives. As of 2004, MoveOn.org raised $11 million for eighty-one candidates from over three hundred thousand donors.[19] Since 2004, MoveOn has helped to "bring ordinary people back into politics" by "building electronic advocacy groups" as a way of democratic participation.[20] It provides an outlet for more than two million online participants. In 2004, there were not only politically liberal 527s but many conservative ones as well. For example, the group Progress for America spent over $35 million to reelect Bush.[21] As of February 2006, the group launched a TV ad campaign aimed at "boosting public opinion about the war on Iraq on the eve of the 2006 election."[22]

Thus, it would make little sense to discuss contemporary political campaigns without acknowledging the effect of political action committees. They have become an important element because they breach party lines and make uncompromising, all-or-nothing demands on legislators and candidates. They care little for party loyalties, legislative voting records, or a candidate's overall philosophy or platform. They view every legislative roll call and every election as a major test of their cause. And, as we just noted, their zealotry allows them to be highly successful in raising money. In fact, from 1989 through the 2004 election cycle, the contributing top one hundred PACs (primarily corporations and unions) gave more than $1 billion to federal candidates and political parties.[23] Thus, in spite of the fact that the primary source of funds for political elections remains private citizens, the large-scale entrance of single-issue groups into the electoral process has contributed mightily to the changed nature of the electoral process for many statewide and national elections.

TECHNOLOGY

Perhaps the most obvious transformation in political campaigns has been in the area of technology. Although the additions of radio in the 1920s and television in the 1950s brought with them a number of alterations to U.S. political campaigns, as technological advancements, they were only the beginning. Today, campaigns from the county to national level rely on a number of devices sophisticated enough to have hardly even been envisioned in a campaign as contemporary as Jimmy Carter's in 1976. In so doing, their nature as well as the people who run them have changed. For example, in statewide as well as presidential campaigns, the old electoral map on the headquarters wall showing in what districts the voters live has been supplemented with a map of the major media markets. The new map decides how and where the candidate travels, carves new political regions around the interstate television centers, and pinpoints with a computer's help the exact demographic audiences who should serve as the targets of the candidate's campaign. Specialists, not county or state party leaders, now conduct campaigns for the candidates. The specialists who understand the media map can appreciate the intricacies of demographic target selection or the even newer geodemographics. Today's candidates for state legislature, governor, Congress, and president pick their media consultant almost before they do anything else. In fact, as Sidney Blumenthal writes in his book *The Permanent Campaign*, early in the contest, candidates are often viewed as successful or not successful by the person they are able to hire to run their campaign.[24] The bigger the name of the consultant, the more serious a contender the candidate is considered to be.

Not only have the media consultants taken over the modern political campaign; they are assisted by other specialists—in media advertising, in public opinion polling, in direct mail fund-raising, in street and telephone canvassing, and even in ethnic analysis. As White once wrote, everything has changed, including the vocabulary. Anyone who has the direct ear of the candidate is now called a "strategist," the old-fashioned hatchet man out on the hustings is now styled a "surrogate,"[25] and a sudden rise in the public opinion polls conducted by the candidate's polling specialist shows "momentum." Thus, the sophisticated use of modern technology has brought significant alterations to political campaign communication. When these changes occurred is not really important. Whether they began in 1952 when Dwight Eisenhower first brought television commercial spots to presidential campaigns, in 1960 when John Kennedy became the first presidential candidate to use his own polling specialist, in 1972 when George McGovern pioneered mass direct mail fund-raising, in 1980 when Jimmy Carter campaigned by conference phone calls to voters in Iowa and New Hampshire, in 1984 when Ronald Reagan used satellite transmissions to appear at fund-raisers and rallies, in 1988 when a number of presidential hopefuls used videotapes to deliver their message to voters in the early primary states, in 1992 when former California governor Edmund G. (Jerry) Brown introduced his 800 telephone number for fundraising and answering questions, in 1996 when candidates rushed to establish a presence on the Internet, or even in the 2000 presidential campaign when the Republican National Committee created Victory 2000 (a voter activation campaign, which used recorded one-minute phone calls from candidates, prominent party supporters, and volunteers and mailings to focus on issues that were believed to be important to voters), the result is the same. Technology has changed the manner in which candidates run for office.

TECHNOLOGY IN THE FIRST DECADE
OF THE TWENTY-FIRST CENTURY

Technology played a significant role in most presidential election campaigns, but by the 2000–2004 election cycles, the use of both old and new technology was even more intensified. Talk television and radio, which first played a prominent role in national political campaigns in 1992 and 1996, had become a fixture by 2000–2004. Television advertising was once again a major component of candidates' campaigns. In fact, the two major party candidates, Kerry and Bush spent over $600 million on advertising during the general election.[26] This figure was more than 200 percent of the advertising dollars spent in the 2000 presidential election.

New technological advances helped candidates and parties reach large numbers of people in short periods of time. Some of the most innovative technological campaigning occurred on the Internet. For example, the Bush campaign incorporated an Internet pop-up ad banner that allowed viewers to calculate how the Bush tax plan would affect them, and Senator McCain discussed his personal war stories on his website. With the escalating cost of campaigning, the Internet has been increasingly utilized because it is cost-effective and has high visibility, creating public awareness and support for presidential candidates and their platforms. It also is an effective way to raise campaign money. For example, in the 2000 presidential campaign Ralph Nader, the candidate of the Green Party, relied on the Web for fund-raising. He collected $7 million in a year, but Senator John McCain raised $6 million "in a few months, using the Internet during his primary."[27] However, it was former governor of Vermont Howard Dean who raised a record $15 million online through mostly individual contributions, just in the third quarter of 2003.[28]

Indeed, the Internet's potential began to be realized in the 2000 campaign when a variety of online services were developed by the candidates, parties, news media, and groups of all kinds. By campaign 2004, for example, the websites of many candidates used features such as online voter registration, online volunteer sign-up, online fund-raising, and video biographies. Not only did the websites use these features, but candidates frequently referred voters to their campaign websites in speeches. Presidential candidate Senator John Kerry often suggested that voters go to his site for more information on his views. They also had current news from the campaign trail, excerpts from speeches and public appearances, and media reports on the candidate and the television ads the campaign was running. In the future, voters can expect technology to become even more prominent in campaigns.

In addition to the widespread use of candidates' websites, web logs or blogs began to have an impact in the 2004 and 2006 campaigns. Political blogs were pioneered with the first major liberal blog of MyDD in 2001.[29] Since then, blogs have been responsible for giving unknown candidates a start and helping to ignite political movement around the country. This type of campaigning is now called "netroots" and is growing faster every year with more and more blogs being created by more and more bloggers and larger numbers of people interacting through them.[30]

In short, advances in technology as well as the advent of the single-issue group, the election law reforms, and the decline in the influence of political parties have combined to transform the nature and manner of our electoral system. Whether we like it or not, one significant result of these changes has been that we can scarcely avoid taking part in the campaign process. Those who choose not to participate directly become involved at some level even if it is only to explain to friends why they are refusing to respond to a candidate's telephone survey, or why they are turning off the television to avoid political programs and advertisements. "We must actively choose not to be active; hence we are participating symbolically even if not actually" because the political campaign is ubiquitous.[31] Somebody is always seeking elective office, and the "somebodies" are no longer strangers but your neighbor, the clerk in the store, or the mother of your best friend. The modern campaign knows no season. It seems that as one ends another begins. Candidates start running for office months and even years in advance of the primary election. Thus, campaigns are now an unavoidable part of our environment, forcing us to become consumers of political communication.

COMMUNICATION AND POLITICAL CAMPAIGNS

The major argument of this book is that political election campaigns are campaigns of communication. Certainly, numerous forms or combinations of economic, sociological, psychological, and historical features are crucial to or reflective of the electoral process. However, the core of each campaign is communication. This is not to argue that a variety of economic and situational needs, power relationships, and a whole host of additional elements and demands do not affect the campaign process or outcome, but rather to say that all of these other factors become important in the electoral system principally through the offices of communication. It is communication that occupies the area between the goals or aspirations of the candidate and the behavior of the electorate, just as it serves as the bridge between the dreams or hopes of the voter and the actions of the candidate. It is through communication that a political campaign begins. Individuals verbally announce their intention to run, and posters and billboards nonverbally announce that election time has begun. During the campaign, candidates and their staffs debate, appear on television, answer call-in questions on radio and television talk shows, prepare and present messages for media commercials, take part in parades and rallies, wear funny hats, submit to media interviews, write letters and position papers, and speak at all forms of public gatherings. They kiss babies, shake hands at factory gates and supermarkets, prepare and distribute literature, produce campaign videotapes and e-mail newsletters, wear campaign buttons, and establish phone banks to solicit money, workers, and votes. In addition, countless hours are spent during the campaign trying to raise enough money to buy radio and television time or computerized lists of voters. All of this effort is for the single purpose of communicating with the electorate, the media, and each other. And when the time comes, it is through communication that the campaign draws to a close. Candidates verbally concede defeat or extol victory, and the posters and billboards are taken down, announcing nonverbally that one campaign is over, even as another begins.

Hence, communication is the means by which the campaign begins, proceeds, and concludes. It is, as we suggested, the epistemological base. Without it, there is no political campaign. It is, therefore, not enough to approach the study of political campaign communication by analyzing the demographic characteristics or the attitudes of the electorate, although the information provided by such work is significant for our overall understanding of the phenomenon. It is also not enough to examine political campaign communication by studying only psychological construct theory or even the relationship and effect of the mass media on the campaign, in spite of the fact that each explains much about the contemporary electoral process. What is needed is a study that provides a communication perspective of a communication event or series of events—the political election campaign. Although you will find references to the works of political scientists, historians, and psychologists, as well as political journalists, we have drawn primarily on the work generated by scholars in communication.

In exploring such theoretical concerns as agenda setting, uses and gratifications, targeting, gatekeeping, and information diffusion, positioning and repositioning, functionalism, and legitimizing, or even in analyzing the pragmatic details of planning, organizing, and presenting speeches, television ads, debates, or fund-raising appeals, we have been guided by one question: What is it that we ought to study as political campaign communication? Our answers are contained in the subject areas we examine in the following chapters.

ORGANIZATION AND PREVIEW OF CHAPTERS

This book has two sections. Chapters 2 through 5 analyze important principles and theoretical concerns of political campaign communication, while chapters 6 through 10 examine the crucial practices of contemporary political campaign communication. Although this distinction is designed to help you better understand the phenomenon, in the real world of political campaigns, principles and practices blend. As you read the section on principles, keep in mind that, in political campaigns, principles often generate practices, and practices often generate principles. For example, in chapter 2 when we discuss the principles involved in an individual's surfacing as a viable candidate, principles cannot be meaningfully presented without examining the practices of many individuals who have surfaced. In turn, those practices have subsequently generated many of the principles. Similarly, in chapter 6 when we discuss the practices of political speechwriters, we cannot readily examine them without developing some of the principles that speechwriters utilize. Thus, artificial as the distinction is, it does provide us with a pedagogically useful organizational framework from which to view political campaign communication.

Following this introductory chapter, the next four chapters focus on principles of political campaign communication. *Political communication* is a broad term. It has been used to describe the communication involved in winning elections, governing a nation, reporting on governmental activity, gathering and determining public opinion, lobbying, and socializing people into a nation. We have deliberately chosen to narrow the term and focus not on political communication but rather on political campaign communication. We do not deny the validity of studying other forms of political communication. However, in a democratic society, to govern one must first win an election. To report on governmental activity, there must first be an elected government about which to report. To lobby, there must first be elected officials to be persuaded. To gather and determine public opinion about candidates and their progress, there must first be a campaign. And to socialize people so that they accept cultural norms, elected officials must first help set the norms. In other words, we believe that political campaign communication is the root of all other forms of political communication. It is undoubtedly for this reason that political campaign communication has been the focus of far more scholarly and popular journalistic inquiry than any other form of political communication. In addition, the number of elaborately planned and professionally implemented campaigns is growing each election year. Thus, it is particularly appropriate to limit our examination of political communication to political campaigns.

Chapter 2 examines the four stages of a political campaign, discussing the many pragmatic and symbolic functions provided by communicative acts to the electorate, the candidates, and the media.

Chapter 3 analyzes the communicative strategies and styles that incumbents and challengers have used in U.S. elections from 1789 to the present. In addition, a third style, one popularized by the two campaigns of Ronald Reagan and the 2000 campaign of Al Gore, is examined.

Chapter 4 presents an examination of the means or channels used in contemporary political campaigns. Theoretical approaches used to study the effect of mass media on political campaigns are discussed.

Chapter 5 considers the communicative types and functions of televised political advertising. In addition, the way in which women appear to use televised attack advertising in their campaigns is examined.

At the conclusion of these four chapters, many of the principles associated with political campaign communication will have been explored. We hope that, by the end of Part I, our readers will have an appreciation of the theoretical basis of campaign communication from the vantage point of a consumer, but we also hope that campaign communication principles will be understood from the vantage point of the user, one actively involved in campaigning for public office. We are aware that readers majoring in such fields as speech communication, mass communication, political science, and public relations may anticipate being involved in political campaigns professionally. Many other readers may also participate in campaigns, if not professionally, at least as highly interested citizens concerned with their communities. We believe that Part I can provide a valuable understanding of the principles of campaign communication from any vantage point that readers choose to follow in the future. Part II focuses on the practices of political campaign communication. In this section, we will discuss five of the most common communication events in contemporary political campaigns.

Chapter 6 examines public speaking in campaigns. It explains how political candidates decide where and when to speak, how they develop speeches, and how they utilize speechwriters and surrogate speakers.

Chapter 7 also focuses on public speaking in political campaigns. But whereas chapter 6 concentrates on the normal day-to-day public speaking that characterizes campaigns, chapter 7 examines forms of speeches that occur in most campaigns, are unique unto themselves, and are not day-to-day occurrences. Portions of the chapter deal with announcement speeches, press conferences, speeches of apologia, and acceptance speeches. Each of these forms takes place in virtually every campaign. The purposes and strategies involved in each genre are presented.

Chapter 8 deals with political debates. Debates are often the most anticipated and most publicized communication activity engaged in by candidates. The chapter presents a history of political debating and then discusses the factors that motivate candidates to accept or reject the opportunity to debate, the strategies that are used, and the effect of political debates.

Chapter 9 examines interpersonal communication in political campaigns. Three interpersonal communication situations, typical of all campaigns, are analyzed in light of current interpersonal communication theory.

Chapter 10 discusses the advantages and disadvantages of a variety of media used for political advertising in campaigns. It also discusses the key players in political advertising, the consultants.

Chapter 11 concludes the section on practices by examining the use of the Internet in contemporary campaigns. It also considers the future of Internet campaigning.

We find the study of political campaign communication to be fascinating and believe that some of our enthusiasm for the subject is apparent in the following pages. We hope readers come away from this book not only better informed but also with renewed understanding and interest in a political system that, although abused and attacked in recent years, does not depend on coercion or force but derives its strength from the fact that it relies on human communication, largely as manifested in political campaigns, as a major means of decision making.

NOTES

1. Theodore H. White, "The Search for President," *Boston Globe*, February 24, 1980, A1.

2. L. Patrick Devlin, "Contrasts in Presidential Campaign Commercials of 2000," *American Behavioral Scientist* 44 (2001): 2338–69.

3. Federal Election Commission Reports.

4. Gregory Korte, "The Battle for the Buck: Mallory, Pepper Getting Most of Their Money from Out of Town," *Cincinnati Enquirer*, September 29, 2005, A1, A14.

5. Korte, "The Battle for the Buck."

6. Korte, "The Battle for the Buck."

7. Kimball Perry, "Heimlich Campaign Raises $400,000," *Cincinnati Enquirer*, April 23, 2006, B3.

8. *Cincinnati Enquirer*, March 2002.

9. *Cincinnati Enquirer*, March 2002.

10. Federal Election Commission Reports, July 21, 2005.

11. Leslie Wayne, "Challengers to Incumbents Are Fighting Uphill Battle," *New York Times*, November 11, 1998, A26.

12. Charles Johnson, "Political Parties See Drop in Soft Money," *Helena Independent Record*, September 28, 2005.

13. Federal Election Commission Reports, July 21, 2005.

14. *Washington Post*, April/May 2002.

15. "Single Issue Politics," *Newsweek*, November 6, 1978, 49.

16. Federal Election Commission Reports.

17. "Generation X Advocacy Groups 11 Legislators 'Enemies,'" *Cincinnati Enquirer*, February 20, 1994, A1.

18. www.MoveOn.org/about.

19. www.MoveOn.org/about.

20. www.MoveOn.org/about.

21. Holly Bailey, "Politics," *Newsweek*, February 20, 2006, 10.

22. Bailey, "Politics."

23. "Biggest Donors Have Given More Than $1 Billion," *Cincinnati Enquirer*, October 23, 2002, A8.

24. Sidney Blumenthal, *The Permanent Campaign: Inside the World of Elite Political Operatives* (Boston: Beacon, 1980).

25. White, "The Search for President."

26. Pat Devlin, "Contrasts in Presidential Campaign Commercials of 2004," *The American Behavioral Scientist* 49(2): 281–313.

27. Devlin, "Contrasts in Presidential Campaign Commercials of 2000."

28. Danielle R. Wiese and Bruce E. Gronbeck, "Campaign 2004 Developments in Cyber-politics," in *The 2004 Presidential Campaign: A Communication Perspective*, ed. Robert E. Denton, Jr., 217–35 (Lanham, Md.: Rowman & Littlefield, 2005).

29. David Weigel, "Blogging Down the Money Trail," *Campaigns and Elections* (October/November 2005): 19–22.

30. Weigel, "Blogging Down the Money Trail."

31. Bruce E. Gronbeck, "The Functions of Presidential Campaigning," *Communication Monographs* 45 (1978): 271.

2

~

Communicative Functions of Political Campaigns

One of the ways to examine political campaigns is to analyze their communicative functions—that is, to investigate what functions the various forms or acts of campaign communication provide to the electorate and to the candidates themselves.[1] Many of these functions are instrumental or pragmatic in that they make specific tangible contributions. Others are consummatory or symbolic in nature; they fulfill ritualistic expectations or requirements. Both are discussed in this chapter.

The modern political campaign passes through relatively discrete stages, which can be categorized as preprimary, primary, convention, and general election. This chapter is organized and divided analogous to the campaign itself; the different functions are discussed in terms of these four specific stages. It is important to remember that each stage, although discrete, has a direct relationship to and bearing on all that follow. In other words, the functions of each stage affect the entire campaign.

FIRST POLITICAL STAGE: SURFACING

Although the first or preprimary stage has been called the "winnowing period,"[2] we have labeled it "surfacing" because this term more completely conceptualizes those communication activities that occur. *Surfacing* was originally labeled and defined as "the series of predictable and specifically timed rhetorical transactions which serve consummatory and instrumental functions during the preprimary phase of the campaign."[3] It would be difficult to set an exact time limit on the first stage, because it can vary from candidate to candidate and election to election. Political hopefuls must assess their visibility and credibility as well as determine their financial backing and organizational strength. Predictable rhetorical activities (the verbal and nonverbal communication acts) during the surfacing stage include building a political organization in each city, district, state, or region (depending on the geographic scope encompassed by the office being sought), speaking to many different kinds of public gatherings in an attempt to capture attention (media attention for state and national campaigns), conducting public opinion polls to assess visibility or to determine potential issues for which stances will later have to be devised, putting together an organizational structure and campaign blueprint, and raising money. These activities take time whether an individual is running for mayor or for president. As one woman who was elected to a seat on her city council told us, "I didn't just start campaigning. I started planning in January for the November election. And this involved an organized plan—contracting for billboards, purchasing material for signs, mapping out financing and finding volunteers for sign lettering and door-to-door canvassing."[4] A gubernatorial contender, who announced his candidacy thirteen months before a Democratic primary in Ohio, justified his early start by saying that his campaign could not be tied to traditional timetables because he had to let people know who he was and what his ideas were so that voters would know that alternatives existed to the "same old names."

If surfacing takes months for city council and gubernatorial candidates, it appears to take even longer for presidential contenders. For example, Vice President George H. W. Bush was an early participant in the first stage of the 1988 presidential campaign. Thirty months before the New Hampshire primary, Bush announced the formation of a 476-member national steering committee composed of Republicans from all fifty states. Similarly, in 1989, three years before the 1992 campaign, Senator Bill Bradley began taking public speaking lessons and building a national fund-raising base, two sure signs of "presidential fever." In 1990, two years and eight months before the 1992 presidential election, Georgia senator Sam Nunn was certainly at least thinking about a run for the White House. He resigned from a golf club that does not allow women as members or even as guests and told friends that he would announce his decision about running two weeks after the 1990 congressional election.[5] Most interesting in 1990, however, was the fact that two years before the 1992 general election, some of the most likely Democratic presidential contenders called press conferences, not to announce that they would be candidates for president but to explain that they would *not* be entering the race.

It was not that Democrats such as House majority leader Richard Gephardt, Senate majority leader George Mitchell, or Senators Albert

Gore Jr. and John (Jay) Rockefeller IV had no desire to retake the White House. It was just that they believed the incumbent president could not be defeated. In January 1991, thirteen months before the Iowa caucus and the New Hampshire primary, George H. W. Bush, as commander in chief, and therefore one of the heroes of Desert Storm (the Persian Gulf War that had been played out on American television), had one of the highest approval ratings ever recorded for a sitting president. A *Washington Post*/ABC News poll[6] found that 90 percent of Americans surveyed approved of his handling of the war, and a *USA Today* survey indicated that 91 percent of those polled approved of the job he was doing as president.[7] Thus, those who might have run surfaced early but became frightened by the popularity of the incumbent and declined.

In preparation for the 1996 presidential campaign, at least six Republican hopefuls were showing up at all manner of public events in New Hampshire shortly after President Clinton was inaugurated in January 1993. By May 1993, C-Span had already resumed its campaign program *Road to the White House*.[8] By June 1994, a relatively obscure Republican governor, Carroll Campbell Jr. of South Carolina, who said he had been planning a 1996 presidential bid by raising money and making trips to Iowa and New Hampshire, announced that he had changed his mind. Considering the two-year campaign that would have faced him, he said "financial considerations had helped him decide to abandon the quest."[9] And on June 25, 1994, according to leaders in the Iowa Republican Party, a straw poll of potential Republican contenders won by Senator Robert Dole was the "unofficial kick-off for the 1996 presidential campaign."[10]

The presidential campaign of 2000 began in May 1997, thirty-one months before any caucus/primary votes would be counted. And at one time or another, as many as thirty individuals (representing the Republican, Democratic, Reform, and Green Parties) let it be known that they were at least considering a run for the presidency. Although half of these potential candidates never really materialized, fifteen of them did for at least some period of time during the surfacing stage.

One of the most unusual aspects of the earliest stage in campaign 2000 was the appearance of several "glamour" or "celebrity" contenders. For example, Hollywood actor Warren Beatty announced in August 1999 (after all of the potential Democratic contenders except Vice President Gore and former New Jersey senator Bill Bradley had dropped out) that he might consider running for president and that he was offended by the effect money had had on American politics. By the end of August, Beatty had a presidential website, and it was rumored that he had been in conversation with professional organizers and a media manager. In September 1999, billionaire Donald Trump publicly acknowledged that he was considering running for the nomination of the Reform Party in 2000.

Trump claimed he was eager to challenge Pat Buchanan (who was, at that time, in the process of leaving the Republican Party to pursue the nomination of the Reform Party). Finally, although nothing concrete ever came of it, actress Cybil Shepherd was said to be considering a run.

The presidential campaign of 2004, like most of its predecessors, had any number of unofficial beginnings. It could have begun in early spring 2001 when Democratic senators Joseph Lieberman of Connecticut, John Kerry of Massachusetts, and Richard Gephardt of Missouri began spending weekends meeting party activists in key early primary states. Or it could have had its start when Senator John Edwards of North Carolina donated a number of computers to the Iowa Democratic Party (Iowa is the traditional home of the first presidential primary). Although most, if not all, public campaigning ceased for five months in the aftermath of the terrorists attacks on the Pentagon in Washington, D.C., and the twin towers of the World Trade Center in New York City on September 11, 2001, by late February 2002, eight Democrats (and later nine) were once again in pursuit of their party's presidential nomination. One of them, the Reverend Al Sharpton, said that the Democratic Party is moving too far to the right and told his campaign audiences that "it's time to move the party back away from reactionary behavior, from being a Republican in donkey clothes. There's nothing more humorous than to see an elephant dressed up like a donkey."[11] In April 2002, Al Gore, the 2000 nominee of the Democratic Party, broke his self-imposed silence about George W. Bush and announced that he had "had it" with the Bush administration's handling of the "environment, the economy and underlying values."[12] By May 2002, Vermont governor Howard Dean had filed candidacy papers with the Federal Election Commission.

However, one of the biggest surprises during the early surfacing period of the 2004 campaign was the unexpected announcement of former vice president Gore on December 15, 2002, that he would not seek the nomination of the Democratic Party. In explaining his decision, Gore said, "I don't think it's the right thing for me to do," because it "would inevitably involve a focus on the past that would in some measure distract from the focus on the future that I think all campaigns have to be about."[13] Gore's announcement startled many in his political party and in the media because it had been preceded by three weeks of intensive media exposure as Gore and his wife, Tipper, "traveled" the networks promoting their book on families and a collection of photos entitled *Joined at the Heart*. Moreover, the night before the withdrawal of his candidacy, he hosted NBC's *Saturday Night Live*.

Given the increasing length of the surfacing stage over the years, it is perhaps not surprising that by January 2006 more than twenty-two Republican and Democratic governors, ex-governors, and current and former members of U.S. Congress were regularly "testing the waters" in the early primary states and creating national websites in preparation for a possible run for president in 2008. For example, Arizona senator John McCain, who has said that even a discussion this early is preposterous, was "busily cobbling together a web of candidates to be precinct committee officers" in the states of Washington and Michigan.[14] McCain also began an "intensive courtship of Bush's financial and political networks."[15] In December 2005, McCain traveled through "the heart of Bush country," which put him in front of many of Bush's biggest supporters in Texas.[16] Former North Carolina senator and Democratic vice-presidential candidate John Edwards is keeping his name in the ring. In 2005, he became the director of the University of North Carolina's Center on Poverty, Work and Opportunity, and established his own nonprofit group, One America Committee. These organizations keep him in the public eye, giving speeches as early as the winter of 2005 in New Hampshire, New York City, Oklahoma, and Tennessee.[17] Edwards has said, however, that running for president is not his first priority. Similarly, although he denied that he would absolutely run for president, Nebraska senator Chuck Hagel was in the public eye a full two years before the election. In February 2006, he was on the cover of the *New York Times Magazine*, and was featured in an article talking about his presidential ambitions. In addition, he also made an appearance on NBC's *Meet the Press* in the winter of 2006, and spent time in the northern part of Minnesota, an area that many consider the next battleground state. These are just a few of the many examples of early surfacing that occurred for the 2008 presidential election.

It is important to understand that one of the reasons for extensive surfacing for 2008 was because there was no incumbent, thus leaving the field open for many. More examples include the 2006 President's Day weekend, which became what one reporter called "would-be President's Day."[18] Senators John McCain and Evan Bayh traveled to South Florida, an area with many Hispanic voters and generous financial supporters. Senator Hillary Rodham Clinton also spent time in Florida that weekend, hosting a Florida Democratic fundraising event in Tampa,[19] while Kansas senator Sam Brownback has raised money, and attended fundraisers in Houston, policy events in Atlanta, and delivered the keynote address at an Arizona "right to life" dinner.[20] Tennessee senator and Senate majority leader Bill Frist was another who demonstrated early interest in the White House. He toured a California border crossing and detention facility and raised money in California, for the state's Republican candidates. In other words, both Democrats and Republicans were out of the gates early for the 2008 presidential election.

Although it is impossible to place a definite time structure on the first stage, we have listed some of the important rhetorical activities the period demands. Thus, surfacing begins with candidates' initial efforts to create an interest and image of themselves as candidates and extends through a variety of public rhetorical transactions prior to the first primary election.

But not only do we know what is typically demanded of the candidate during the first stage; we also have some idea of the characteristic functions served by the communication acts of the surfacing period. Although these can vary with the level of office sought (just as the time period does), we have observed seven functions that appear to be important in all political campaigns.

Demonstrating Fitness for Office

The first function is to provide an indication of a candidate's fitness for office—the "caliber" of the individual. During the campaign, especially the earliest portions when public images of potential candidates are beginning to be formed, the electorate draws inferences from campaign actions about how a particular contender would behave as mayor, or governor, or even president.

The electorate does not want elected officials who are viewed as dishonest, dull, unjust, immoral, corrupt, incompetent, or slick—or even those who are the brunt of television hosts David Letterman's, Jay Leno's, and John Stewart's late-night jokes. In other words, U.S. voters have some preconceptions about people who run for public office. Generally, successful candidates will be perceived as trustworthy, intelligent, or competent enough to do the job; compassionate; articulate; poised; and honorable. The higher the office, the more judgmental voters become. For example, voters expect those candidates who run for or serve as our chief executive to be of "presidential timber"—to possess special qualities not always found to the same degree in all people. And although there is not a one-to-one relationship between the two, campaign actions are taken as symbolic of actions as president. We do not want presidents who hit their heads on helicopter doors, fall down steps, mispronounce words, or are attacked by "killer rabbits." These are behaviors that cause a candidate to be characterized as "clumsy," "dumb," or a "loser," as Gerald Ford and Jimmy Carter were labeled during the surfacing period of the 1976 and 1980 campaigns. As a matter of fact, perhaps conditioned by the negative perceptions of Ford's and Carter's actions, voters' assessments of many of the 1988, 1992, 1996, and 2000 presidential hopefuls were sometimes harsh. For example, in 1988, before his confrontation with CBS News anchor Dan Rather, then–vice president George H. W. Bush was perceived (in spite of his valor in World War II) as being a "wimp, a tinny-voiced preppy" who didn't possess the toughness to be president.[21] In 1992, Senator Tom Harkin came to be viewed (in spite of his championing of the poor, ethnics, and laborers) as mean to the people around him, especially those who waited on him. In 1996, former vice president J. Danforth (Dan) Quayle was perceived to lack the intelligence to be president. Also in 1996, Republican presidential hopeful Phil Gramm was considered nasty, negative, and "charismatically challenged."[22] And during the 2000 surfacing period, Malcolm (Steve) Forbes Jr. tried a second time to appeal to Republican primary voters, but all he got for his efforts were statements such as "he looks like a geek" or "he looks like a turtle."[23]

Potential presidents are not supposed to be considered wimps or mean people, but neither should reference to them produce laughter. This was the problem with the general perception of Dan Quayle during his vice presidential campaigns and as an early presidential hopeful in the 2000 election. There have been few other national political figures who have been the brunt of so many "dumb" jokes—jokes that were frequently the result of his own misstatements. Among the many infamous Quayle quotes is one made during a speech to the United Negro College Fund when he said, "What a waste it is to lose one's mind or not to have a mind is very wasteful."[24] What he meant to say, of course, is that "a mind is a terrible thing to waste." Whatever the ultimate judgment, certainly one function of the preprimary period is to provide an indication of a candidate's fitness for office.

Humor, of course, long a part of presidential politics, has seldom been demonstrated more than during the 2000 presidential campaign. There were frequent jabs at front-runners Governor George W. Bush and Vice President Al Gore from late-night talk show hosts Jay Leno and David Letterman. In addition, the television show *Saturday Night Live* created its "versions" of the contenders, ridiculing them on live television with actors who looked and spoke like the vice president and governor. Bush was mocked for his mangling of words (specifically his term "strategery") and Gore for his concept of "the lock box" (in reference to his assurance that nothing would happen to Social Security funding if he became president).

Initiating Political Rituals

A second communication function of the surfacing stage is that it initiates the ritualistic activities important to our political system. In his book *The Symbolic Uses of Politics*, social scientist Murray Edelman discusses the idea of U.S. political campaigns as traditional, rule-governed rituals and then describes rituals as a kind of motor activity that involves its participants symbolically in a common enterprise.[25] While each of the stages of the campaign demands certain rituals, none is more clearly defined than the activities surrounding the preprimary announcement speech. (Although the announcement speech itself is discussed in chapter 7, here we consider its ritualistic aspects.)

When candidates decide to enter the political arena formally, they must perform certain protocols because they are expected. For example, a press conference is called, the candidate is surrounded by family and friends while announcing the decision to run for office, and then the candidate embarks immediately on a campaign swing through the district, state, or nation. The candidate may only be announcing a campaign for the mayor's office, but there are expectations concerning how it is done. However, to capture the full flavor of the announcement ritual, we need to examine it at the presidential level.

The 1996 ritual began on February 24, 1995, when Senator Phil Gramm became the first officially announced candidate for the Republican presidential nomination. Surrounded by cadets and flags, Gramm made his announcement at Texas A&M, where years earlier he had been a professor of economics.

Former Secretary of Education Lamar Alexander returned to his hometown of Maryville, Tennessee, to deliver his announcement speech on February 28, 1995. Wearing his signature statement red plaid shirt and surrounded by townspeople, Alexander presented himself as a Washington outsider. His announcement concluded with his ragtime band playing a chorus of "Rocky Top."

Senator Robert Dole went home to Russell, Kansas, and delivered his announcement address on April 10, 1995. Amid a shower of balloons, he positioned himself as seasoned and experienced, yet someone who was able to change and keep up with the times. In campaign 2000, the candidates were not always ruled by the traditional symbolic "process." For example, Republican contender Elizabeth Dole never even made an official speech announcing her intention to run for the GOP presidential nomination, although, ironically, she did give a formal speech withdrawing her candidacy. Texas governor George W. Bush gave a speech on June 12, 1999, in Cedar Springs, Iowa, in which he said he would later announce that he would be a candidate for the Republican presidential nomination. Democratic candidate Al Gore did, however, provide an example of a traditional announcement speech. He returned to his hometown of Carthage, Tennessee, was introduced by his daughter, and was surrounded by family, friends, and local community supporters in front of the Smith County courthouse (where he had initiated every political campaign of his career). The theme of his speech was the American family, and, probably in an attempt to distance himself from the Clinton administration, he proclaimed that he would take the values of his faith and family to the presidency. However, none of the 1996 or 2000 candidates matched the detailed pageantry of Marion G. (Pat) Robertson's formal "beg me to run" announcement in the 1988 campaign.

During the summer of 1985, Robertson let the media know that people were asking him to run for president. By October 1985, he "allowed as how" he was considering a run for the presidency and was praying about it, seeking God's counsel. Apparently, his prayers were answered a few weeks later when he formed an exploratory committee and founded a think tank called the National Perspectives Institute. On September 17, 1986, Robertson went to Constitution Hall in Washington and on closed-circuit television, in a three-hour production of trumpet fanfare and patriotic song, announced that if three million registered voters signed petitions "telling me that they will pray—that they will work—that they will give toward my election, then I will run."[26] He set a deadline of one year for a show of support that would include the signatures of three million voters on petitions and raise $3 million by mid-1987. Clearly, one communicative function of the surfacing stage is that it initiates the ritual vital to U.S. politics.

Thus far in discussing the preprimary period, we have been focusing on what has been termed "consummatory functions of campaigning." These functions are essentially symbolic in nature—functions that seem to be rooted more deeply in the heart or soul rather than in the mind of the electorate. In other words, as communication scholar Bruce E. Gronbeck has written, "campaigning creates second-level or metapolitical images, personae, myths, associations, and social-psychological reactions which may even be detached or at least distinct from particular candidates, issues, and offices."[27]

Thus, communication during the first stage plays two symbolic but important roles: It provides an indication of a candidate's fitness for office, and it initiates the ritual we have come to expect in political campaigns. However, there are five additional contributions provided by the communication acts and symbols during the surfacing period. These functions are related to the pragmatic aspects of the campaign and have thus been labeled "instrumental."

Learning about a Candidate

The first of these instrumental functions is that the electorate begins to have some knowledge about a candidate's goals, potential programs, or initial stands on issues. During the surfacing period, in an attempt to determine whether and with whom their campaign has any appeal, candidates must speak at countless neighborhood coffees, potluck dinners, and service club meetings. During these appearances, they often have to answer questions about why they are running for office as well as state their positions on specific issues important to those attending the gathering. Answers may at first be sketchy, but as the frequency of the speaking occasions and the perceived receptivity of the audiences increase, so does the candidate's confidence. Statements about political goals and aspirations as well as positions on issues become refined. What was in the beginning somewhat tentative now becomes more definite as the candidate proceeds to formulate statements of philosophy apparently acceptable to most potential constituents. For example, when Congresswoman Elizabeth Holtzman decided to enter the 1980 New York senatorial race, she began scheduling a number of appearances throughout the state months before the primary. Countless efforts were made not only to expand her visibility from one congressional district to the whole state but also to let the electorate know what her positions were on issues wider than those facing her current constituents.

During the eight years in which Holtzman had been a member of the House of Representatives, she had demonstrated an ability to work for the fairly narrow concerns of her Kings County constituents. But with the decision to move from the House to the Senate, the congresswoman had to establish her understanding of and commitment to problems and issues facing a larger and more diverse audience. The surfacing period provided Holtzman the opportunity not only to determine what the issues were but to formulate positions that could be and were used during the second or primary stage of her campaign for the United States Senate.

Developing Voter Expectations of a Candidate's Style

Closely related is the second instrumental function: Voter expectation regarding a candidate's administrative and personal style begins to be established. For example, candidates who have well-organized and disciplined staffs provide some knowledge about the kind of administration they might have if they are elected. Even in a campaign for a seat on the local school board, those candidates who right from the beginning appear to be operating from a precise plan or blueprint with regard to where and when they will canvass the district, or distribute literature, or speak at neighborhood coffees provide voters with information regarding the level of organization and efficiency it might be reasonable to expect if and when they are elected to the school board.

The personal style of a candidate is also revealed during the early days of a campaign. Perhaps one of the most interesting examples occurred during the preprimary period of the 1980 presidential campaign. Before Edward Kennedy began his pursuit of the presidency, he, like his brothers before him, had been perceived as an excellent speaker, a master of the art of campaigning and campaign rhetoric. Thus, the expectations of the public were high—so high that it is unlikely that any candidate could have lived up to the dimensions of the Kennedy mystique. But in the first few ventures away from Washington and Boston, the senator fell far short. He read his speeches (he always had, but no one ever seemed to have noticed before), mispronounced words, seldom looked up from manuscripts to establish eye contact with his audience, stumbled frequently using vocal pauses or qualifiers such as "uh" or "ah," appeared confused in answers to questions on material and issues he should have known, rambled, and appeared unable to speak without constant reliance on manuscripts and specially prepared charts. Deficiencies were exaggerated because of high expectations, but the point is that the surfacing period is important for its revelations of a candidate's personal and administrative style.

Determining Main Campaign Issues

The third instrumental function of surfacing is that it aids in determining what the dominant theme or issues of the campaign will be. The early candidates set the rhetorical agenda for the campaign. As they crisscross the country, state, congressional district, or even the city, they begin to come to grips with the issues on people's minds, begin to address themselves to those issues, and, as we noted earlier, begin to formulate "solutions" to problems that seem to be compatible with popular perception. In national or statewide elections, the media repeat a candidate's statements and thus aid in translating the problems and positions into national or state issues. In local campaigns, candidates often determine the problems by word of mouth rather than the media.

A friend of ours who ran for a seat on a city council had a fairly direct method of determining the issues on voters' minds. Instead of polling, which he could not afford, or public appearances before various groups, which he wished to avoid until the announcement of his candidacy, he simply began attending weekly meetings of the city council nine months before the election. In this way, he had some guidance in selecting issues for his campaign because he was able to learn on a firsthand basis which issues were important or controversial enough to be discussed in council meetings.

Thus, the surfacing stage is important because the rhetorical agenda begins to be established. If these early concerns are widespread enough, they can become the dominant issues in succeeding stages of the campaign. And those candidates who surface early help determine what will be the agenda.

The surfacing stage in 2004 was like most others. During their campaigning in New Hampshire and other early primary/caucus stages, candidates became aware of issues on voters' minds and began to formulate agendas to match popular concerns. Incumbent George W. Bush focused on the global concerns of terrorism and national security. Democratic hopeful Missouri senator Richard Gephardt chose the domestic issue of health care, calling for a universal health insurance plan that would insure all workers through a government subsidized program through their employers.[28] Vermont governor Howard Dean also focused on the need of health care for American workers, while Dennis Kucinich, also a Democratic contender, combined both global and domestic issues, calling for an immediate pull-out from Iraq, the North Atlantic Free Trade Agreement, and the World Trade Organization in order to protect American jobs.

Selecting Serious Contenders

The first stage is also important because it begins the process of selecting front-runners or separating the serious contenders from the not so serious. Becoming a serious candidate during the surfacing period involves obtaining visibility. Even in small races, much less in state or national contests, obtaining visibility requires persuading the media that one is a viable enough candidate to deserve attention.

Almost from the beginning, at least in state and national contests, the media strongly influence who will be considered a major candidate. Despite the fact that John McCain would not, at least publicly, state that he was considering a run for the presidency until after his reelection campaign for the Senate in November 1998, he still had the full attention of the media, largely because of his status as a decorated military hero. Lamar Alexander and Steve Forbes were the earliest surfacers for the 2000 election cycle (each had been campaigning for five years—since losing their 1996 bids for the nomination of the Republican Party). Despite their efforts, Alexander never generated any degree of public or media enthusiasm, and Forbes, even after coming in second in the Iowa caucus, was, nonetheless, destined to remain a "back bencher" until he left the race.

Visibility during the surfacing period is often the initial reaction of the media to a candidate's past or present self. This has been illustrated a number of times when people who have achieved national recognition in the nonpolitical arena have decided to run for public office and the media have, in a relatively short period of time, turned them into serious candidates. Consider the cases of Senator John Glenn (one of the first U.S. astronauts); Senator Bill Bradley (a former All American and All Pro basketball player, and a Rhodes scholar); California mayors Clint Eastwood and Sonny Bono (a famous actor and singer, respectively); former governor of California Ronald Reagan (a movie actor and television host); and a Republican candidate for governor of California in the 2003 recall election,

Arnold Schwarzenegger (a bodybuilder who became a movie star). This was demonstrated, for example, during the surfacing period of the 1988 presidential campaign when Gary Hart and the Reverend Jesse Jackson, because of previous roles, were selected by the media as serious presidential contenders and thus accorded early and extensive coverage. To a lesser extent, this had also been a factor affecting Governor Jerry Brown and Senator Edward Kennedy during the surfacing period in 1980. However, in 1980, neither the past nor current positions of Brown and Kennedy were as important in generating visibility as was the fact that each was challenging his party's incumbent. Intraparty challenges such as theirs in 1980, Ronald Reagan's in 1976, Eugene McCarthy's in 1968, and Pat Buchanan's in 1992 normally attract media attention.

Who candidates are and their current position also aid in determining initial visibility. For example, George H. W. Bush and Robert Dole were considered the leading contenders during the early stage of the 1988 presidential campaign because of their respective positions as vice president and Senate minority leader. The capability of some jobs to generate visibility was also demonstrated by two people who held powerful positions outside the federal government during the surfacing period of 1988. In fact, Mario M. Cuomo, governor of New York, and Lee Iacocca, chairman of the board and chief executive officer of the Chrysler Corporation, received so much attention from the national media regarding their presidential prospects that each had to call a press conference to announce he was not then a candidate and would not be a presidential candidate. Conversely, Pat Robertson, Alexander Haig, Bruce Babbitt, and Pierre DuPont were not thought of as serious candidates by the media because they did not have current or powerful positions in government.

A second run for the presidential nomination can foster high visibility, as exemplified by Senator Robert Dole's campaign during the 1996 presidential election. As Senate majority leader and previous presidential hopeful, he had national visibility that no other Republican contender could match. In fact, as early as December 1993, a public opinion poll proclaimed him the leading Republican candidate.[29] And in campaign 2000, Al Gore as the sitting vice president had unlimited national visibility, was strongly favored by opinion polls, and was therefore, almost automatically, declared the leading Democratic candidate. Similarly, John McCain enjoyed national name recognition, and George W. Bush rapidly achieved national visibility due, in part, to being the son of a former U.S. president, governor of a major state, and because he raised much more money earlier than any of the other contenders ($23 million by June 1999).

Quite apart from persuading the media that one is a front-runner based on roles and present positions, a candidate may also emerge from the surfacing period as a possible leading contender by successful grassroots organizing and fund-raising. Acquiring sufficient money to generate the momentum necessary to do well in the primary stage has always been and continues to be important for local, state, and congressional candidates. But with the advent of the`campaign-financing laws, motivating enough support to raise the money to qualify for federal matching funds has become crucial to presidential contenders.

Becoming a front-runner because of early grassroots organizing and successful fund-raising helps explain the initial successes of presidential contenders such as Jimmy Carter in 1976, Michael Dukakis in 1988, and Bill Clinton in 1992. Not one of them had been considered a serious candidate by the media prior to the first or second competition. Each used the surfacing period to gather the strength necessary to do well in the first contests (Iowa and New Hampshire) and thus forced the media to acknowledge them as serious presidential candidates.

On the other hand, not using the surfacing period to become a front-runner through grassroots organizing and fund-raising in the early primary/caucus stages helps explain the initial losses experienced by numerous contenders in the 1996 and 2000 campaigns.

Indiana senator Richard Lugar announced his intention to run on April 19, 1995, with only a "bottoms-up" operation in Iowa and New Hampshire. He had no established campaign operation in any of the early primary states. And since he began many months behind the other contenders, he did not have any big-name political support, because they were already committed to other candidates. In addition, he had raised only $4 million compared to the $20 to $25 million that the "leading" contenders collected. On top of all of this, Lugar's announcement to run was "all but drowned out in the press by the Oklahoma City bombing that very day."[30] Not surprisingly, on March 7, 1996, Lugar withdrew from the race, having finished no better than fifth in any of the first eight primaries.

Similarly, on March 29, 1995, when Patrick J. Buchanan announced that he would run for the presidency, he did so without first raising the money or organizing a campaign that could effectively carry him through the 1996 primaries and caucuses. A veteran of the 1992 primaries, he had been unsuccessful in overthrowing the sitting president of his own party (although he had weakened Bush enough to help make him vulnerable to the Democratic attack during the general election). Throughout his candidacy, Buchanan operated with a minimal budget. The campaign did not have a pollster, and Buchanan did his own speechwriting and fund-raising, just as he had done in 1992. By the end of February, Buchanan had to abort a plan to challenge Robert Dole in North and South Dakota, because resources had to be directed to the Arizona and South Carolina primaries.

Steve Forbes Jr. announced his candidacy for the Republican nomination on September 23, 1995. Although he planned to finance his campaign with his own fortune, he lacked organizational support and placed fourth in the February 12 caucus. He eventually had more success, but, by the time of "Junior Tuesday" and the New York primary, the race came down to Dole's organizational support and Forbes's money. Clearly there were other dimensions, but the organization of the Dole campaign in each of the primary/caucus states was the dominating factor.

Without much question, one of campaign 2000's most glaring examples of someone who should have known more than he apparently did about the importance of early surfacing was Utah senator Orrin Hatch. The senator formally entered the competition for the Republican nomination on July 1, 1999, without having done anything to prepare the ground for his candidacy. Unlike most of the other Republican hopefuls who had been actively campaigning (surfacing) for at least two years, Hatch had done little. In fact, he acknowledged starting late and therefore being way behind when he told a reporter, "Let's face it, most people don't even know I'm in the race. I found that some of my closest friends in California didn't know it."[31] Hatch withdrew from the race on January 24, 2000, having raised only $2.5 million from fifteen thousand contributors.

John McCain was another Republican contender who surfaced late. In fact, he spent less time in preparing for a presidential run than had any other of the Republican contenders except Hatch. In July 1998, McCain said that he would not seriously consider running for the presidency until after his reelection campaign for the Senate in November 1998. True to his word, he skipped the Iowa caucus totally and, after his reelection to the Senate, began a serious campaign for the Republican nomination in New Hampshire in early 1999.

Elizabeth Dole stepped down as president of the American Red Cross in January 1999 to contend for the Republican presidential nomination. However, her informal declaration was late (she never officially entered the race and, as we noted earlier, never gave a formal announcement speech), and she was seriously behind most of her competitors in fundraising and organizing a campaign in the early primary states. Although Dole had the advantages of immediate national name recognition, the mystique of being the first truly viable female presidential candidate, and presumably the fund-raising contacts of her husband, Senator Robert Dole, with her late start, she was able to raise only $3.5 million (compared with the more than $60 million Bush had raised by October 1999). Thus, in October 1999, before any primary or caucus votes had been cast, Dole withdrew from the campaign.

If surfacing has ever been difficult for candidates to negotiate, by the time of the preprimary stage of the 2004 campaign, it became almost impossible—at least for those presidential hopefuls not well known or well financed. For example, Florida senator Bob Graham had a difficult time raising awareness of his campaign. He entered the race late, in May of 2003, and only managed to raise $1.5 million, much less than his opponents. Despite being behind, Senator Graham and his family made appearances at numerous auto races with his "Bob Graham for President" NASCAR truck and singing his campaign song "You've Got a Friend in Bob Graham."[32] However, he was never able to catch up to those who surfaced earlier and raised more money.

In preparation for 2004, the chair of the Democratic National Committee (DNC), Terry McAuliffe, urged states to hold early caucuses and primaries, in the hope that the Democratic nominee would be known by late February 2004, if not sooner. Because the war against terrorism pushed the popularity of President George W. Bush to historical highs, the DNC chair argued that the president would be a tough opponent in 2004 and that Democrats needed to decide who would challenge him early. His plan, which was agreed to by the DNC and state Democratic Parties, called for Iowa to start the season with its caucuses on Monday, January 19, 2004, followed by the New Hampshire primary on Tuesday, January 27.

Establishing Candidate–Media Relationships

The final communicative function of the surfacing stage is that the media and the candidates get to know one another. While this function is often not vital for local campaigns, it can be important in congressional and state races, and it is absolutely crucial in presidential campaigns. It is in these contests where we can most completely understand the significance of the function to the entire campaign.

At each stage of the campaign, the relationships between candidates and the media who cover them are vital not only to the candidate but to the individual media representative. The candidate needs the visibility that only the media can provide, and the media need information that only access to the candidate or immediate campaign staff can provide. It is not, especially in the preprimary period, the adversarial relationship as is commonly pictured. As one analyst who studied the candidate–media relations of the 1976 Carter campaign summarizes:

> A symbiosis of the goals of journalists and those who manage campaigns provides for a good deal of mutually beneficial interaction. On the one hand, news reporting organizations certainly define the presidential race as a story which must be covered . . . and are willing to expend considerable resources in news gathering. . . . Presidential candidate organizations, on the other hand, seek to use the news reporting process as a relatively inexpensive means of communicating with voters and political activists. Campaigns, therefore, are happy to facilitate journalists in the conduct of their work.[33]

Relationships can be established during the surfacing stage because there are few media representatives assigned to cover a specific candidate and because the candidate has a skeleton traveling staff—perhaps only the campaign director and candidate. Contact is informal; candidates and staff are accessible. It is a time for finding out details and learning enough about one another to know who can be counted on when or whether the candidate's campaign begins to gather momentum. Conditions change from the first stage to the second, and it is the surfacing period that allows media and candidate to get to know one another. The importance of the relationship is, first, that it provides the opportunity for local media–candidate interaction, which is not always available after candidates find they can get national exposure and, second, that it gives both candidate and national media representatives a contact to be used later. In other words, the reporter soon discovers who on the staff will have the "real" story or lead, and the candidate's people know not only who they can trust but which reporter has the best chance of getting stories in print or on the air.

Similarly, candidates themselves frequently try to establish relationships with a few of the major political journalists. Throughout the early stages of the 1992 campaign, Clinton, for example, sought the advice of writers his staff referred to as the "new breed of journalists," columnists such as E. J. Dionne Jr. of the *New York Times*.[34] In other words, it is a reciprocal relationship and a significant function of surfacing.

These, then, are the necessary functions served by communicative acts during the first political stage. The period is crucial because of the functions it provides. Candidates who announce late and thus do not participate in surfacing activities or those who fail to use the period wisely have little success and frequently do not even advance to the second stage.

SECOND POLITICAL STAGE: PRIMARIES

Primary elections are, at any level, "America's most original contribution to the art of democracy."[35] Under the primary system, voters who make up the political party determine who the party's candidates will be. Although the system varies from state to state, generally, primaries provide for a full-fledged intraparty election with the purpose of choosing a single candidate from each party to run in the general election. Direct primary elections, unlike the presidential primary, normally have a degree of finality in that the winning candidate is automatically placed on the November ballot. But in instances in which a number of candidates are competing for the same office, it is often necessary to have a second or runoff primary because one candidate usually does not capture a majority of votes in the first election. In the case of the presidential primary, even after all of the state elections have been held, the party nominees still have not been chosen. The national nominating convention (the third political stage) officially selects the candidate. Thus, in presidential campaigns, primary elections are only one phase of the nominating process, not the final act or choice.

There are almost as many variations of primaries as there are states. For example, Wisconsin for many years had what was known as the most "pure" of the open primaries because voters could vote in any primary (it was not necessary to be preregistered and vote as a Republican or as a Democrat and vote only in that party's primary) and have their vote remain secret. Registration took place on primary day, and crossover voting was the norm. Connecticut, on the other extreme, only began holding full-fledged presidential preference primaries in the 1980s. For many years, the state allowed party leaders to choose its statewide candidates without fighting it out in primary elections.

Not only are there different forms of state primaries; some states do not even hold direct primaries but operate under the caucus system to determine nominees. To further complicate the process, the political parties within one state may vary in terms of their selection procedure. For example, in 1980 Michigan Republicans stayed with the direct primary, while Michigan Democrats switched to a caucus system after they were unsuccessful in their efforts to get the legislature to change the state's law to prevent or inhibit crossover voting. By the time of the 1988 presidential election, however, it was the Michigan Republicans who changed the process. In an attempt to play a significant role in determining the presidential nominee, Republicans established a multitiered delegate selection process that began with party precinct elections on August 5, 1986.

Although Michigan Republicans were clearly hoping to replace Iowa's influence in 1988, Iowa remains one of the two best-known caucuses or primaries because since 1976 it has so frequently been the first real presidential testing ground for candidates of both political parties. In 1996, the Iowa caucus began the night of February 12, in living rooms, schools, church basements, and firehouses. Democrats and Republicans gathered by precinct to elect delegates to county conventions who in turn chose delegates to state conventions and finally to the national conventions. The whole process took until June. In 1992, the Iowa caucus played little or no role in the presidential campaign because Iowa's senior senator, Tom Harkin, was pretty much assured the backing of the Iowa Democratic Party. However, in 1996 and again in 2000 and 2004, the Iowa caucus resumed some of its former importance in the process because the contenders who ultimately began to lead the pack had done well in Iowa. In fact, Senator John Kerry's unexpected win in Iowa made him the front-runner for the remainder of the primary stage, while Howard Dean, the former governor of Vermont, who had been leading in the precaucus polls ended up in third place and for all intents and purposes (especially after the so-called "Dean Scream") suspended much of his presidential bid.

Interestingly, Maine has essentially the same system as Iowa, but timing and precedence have given the Iowa caucuses inordinate importance. In spite of the fact that local and state nominees are not selected at the precinct level and although proportionately fewer national nominating convention delegates for either party come from Iowa, the candidates who won the precinct caucuses in 1976 through 2004 received enormous publicity boosts from the national media.

Many professional politicians and party leaders hate the primary stage of a campaign because a genuine primary is a fight within the family of the party—a fight that can turn nasty as different factions within the family compete with each other to secure a place on the November ballot for their candidate. In addition, primaries can exhaust candidates, leaving them physically, emotionally, and financially drained just before the most important battle. Charges and countercharges of candidates and their staffs often provide the opposition party with ammunition they can use during the general election campaign. Moreover, beginning with the presidential primaries of 1980, another problem developed when the unit rule forced changes in strategy and thus made the presidential primary system even more detested by party leaders than it had been. Under the new rules, there could be no winner-take-all victory anywhere. Every state and every congressional district was forced to divide its delegates in proportion to the votes the candidates had won, and then candidates would "own" the delegate chosen in their name. In practical terms, it meant that no state was worth a candidate's full attention, yet no state could really be ignored. Each candidate had to campaign everywhere in each primary because, even in losing the state, the candidate could still get a substantial share of the delegates.

Finally, primaries use a lot of money—funds not only from contributors who might have been generous for the later campaign, but money that can be a drain on state and national resources in terms of matching funds. The total amount spent by the Democratic and Republican presidential candidates in the 1992 primaries and caucuses was approximately $153 million. In 1996 and again in 2000, the total spent by the candidates of both major parties during the primary and caucus season exceeded $390 million.[36] However, it was the 2004 presidential campaign that became the most expensive presidential campaign in the nation's history in that the candidates of both major parties spent over $490 million. It should be noted that much of the money spent by candidates in primary campaigns was raised online.

One reason inordinate amounts are spent on this stage of presidential campaigns is that there are so many primaries and they last so long. In 1996, for example, there were forty-three primaries and sixteen caucuses (not including the Alaska Republican Straw Ballot Caucus). They began on February 6 in Louisiana and did not conclude until June 14 when voters in New Mexico went to the polls. While the 1996 schedule was as drawn out as those of the previous six, it is important to note that the earliest major contests, Iowa and New Hampshire, frequently have more influence in selecting the eventual nominees than larger states simply because their caucus and primary are traditionally first. In 1996, much to the consternation of many Republican Party loyalists, Louisiana grabbed the lead as the first contest. However, not all candidates participated, for fear of upsetting party traditionalists.

Despite their size, Iowa and New Hampshire have frequently been able to exert an inordinate amount of influence because candidates have used the win to focus national attention on their campaign and build a momentum that has granted them front-runner status from the media. The idea is that the national surge of publicity provides a substantial "bounce" toward the nomination so that later, when states with large numbers of delegates go to the polls, the race is effectively over.

In the 2000 primaries, excessive front-loading continued. This included, for the first time, states such as California with the greatest number of delegates. In fact, although there were a total of eighty-nine caucuses and primaries (counting contests of both the Republican and Democratic Parties), and although they stretched from January 24 through June 6, the Super Tuesday contests accounted for nearly one-third of the 2,066 delegates to the Republican Convention and 4,338 to the Democratic Convention. Thus, when Bush and Gore won on Super Tuesday, March 7, 2000, the race for the nomination of both parties was effectively over, in spite of the fact that the primaries of a number of states, including eight states defined as the "Interior West," were ignored because their primaries occurred after Super Tuesday. Thus, issues important to those states and their citizens had not been a part of the presidential contenders' dialogue.

However, it was the 2004 frontloading that exacerbated the process. Terry McAuliffe, then chair of the DNC, and his allies on the Committee "quietly engineered a reworking of the primary and caucus schedule that all but guaranteed the fastest-starting and fastest-finishing nominating process in American political history."[37] Rule changes implemented by the DNC moved the Iowa caucus forward to January 17th, the New Hampshire primary forward to January 27th, created another "retail" primary in South Carolina, and thus moved the whole process forward by at least a month to have the party's candidate confirmed by the beginning of March.[38]

"With compression of the caucus/primary stage, McAuliffe envisioned a period of time between March and the Democratic National Convention in July when the Democratic and Republican nominees would be 'mano-a-mano' and, in his view, the sitting president would not have as much of an opportunity to upstage the Democratic candidate."[39] In an effort to do this, McAuliffe sought to change the Democratic caucus/primary schedule to avoid any lull between events. He had seen the Republican Party gain an advantage in 2000, by holding six primaries between February 1st and March 7th, while the Democrats held none. McAuliffe believed that this primary/caucus schedule had severely disadvantaged the Democratic Party in 2000 by forcing them out of the political spotlight for so long a period of time.[40] Under "his watch" that would not happen again.

Yet, for all of the problems with this second political stage, there are five functions that the communication acts and symbols of the period provide. While we do not want to suggest that primaries (particularly the presidential primary system) need no revision, we do believe these five functions are important to the entire political campaign process. The first relates directly to the candidates and the final four to the electorate.

A Source of Feedback for Candidates

For candidates, the primary season is a source of feedback from the voters about their campaigns, the organization they have put together, the competence of staffs, fund-raising efforts, and physical stamina—in other words, their strengths and weaknesses as campaigners. During the surfacing period, the candidates' only measures of how they are doing are the comments of the media and, in some cases, the results of polls. But the primaries provide direct feedback from the voters and thus a chance for repositioning in terms of stands on issues, themes, images, and overall campaign strategies. Obviously, for those candidates who have only one primary in which to compete (most local, state, and congressional contenders), either the feedback is of no use (except as it may account for defeat), or it is used to plan for the general election. For example, feedback from the first campaign of candidates such as John Glenn of Ohio, Lee Dreyfus of Wisconsin, and S. I. Hayakawa of California allowed them to reposition their public images from astronaut or academician to senator or governor. For presidential candidates, the early contests are direct sources of feedback that can be used immediately as preparations are made for campaigning in subsequent states.

There are times, of course, when repositioning does not work, as was the case in 1984 when John Glenn attempted to reposition his image from astronaut during the Iowa caucus to experienced statesman during the New Hampshire primary. But there are other times when it does. One of the most dramatic was the repositioning of Ronald Reagan's image and campaign strategy during the 1980 primaries.

As conceived originally by then–campaign manager John Sears, Reagan's 1980 quest for the presidency was to be a regal campaign, one in which Reagan would slowly but surely win the delegates necessary to assure the nomination. The front-runner campaign conceptualized by Sears would be characterized by an "above-the-battle" posture in which Reagan would campaign leisurely in each state by making only one or two appearances in any one day, not appear on forums or debates with his Republican rivals, honor his own already-famous "eleventh commandment" ("Thou shall not speak ill of other Republicans"), and be assisted with a well-planned and well-financed media campaign.

The strategy was tested in Iowa, the center of Reagan's so-called rural heartland. A week before the caucuses, Iowa newspapers talked about Reagan's failure to campaign in the state or even to appear with each of the other Republican candidates in the nationally televised forum sponsored by the *Des Moines Register*. Reagan's absence was noted throughout Iowa at countless fund-raising dinners or, as they are termed by politicians and the press, "cattle shows," where each of his Republican opponents made appearances and speeches. In fact, at some of these party functions, there were not even any signs of a Reagan campaign in the state—no campaign buttons, no posters, no candidate. By the time of the caucus, Reagan had spent only forty-one hours in the state, had avoided discussing the issues, and had made only one televised speech. It had been, as one newspaper headline proclaimed, a campaign that was "Invisible to Many." In defending this strategy, Sears said that "as a front-runner, Reagan could set the pace for the campaign, decide whether to give an event like the forum the prominence of his presence, and that the job of the other candidates was to make Reagan turn around and confront them."[41]

In contrast, one Republican, George Bush, had spent a full fifty-nine days campaigning in Iowa and had thoroughly extended his campaign organization throughout Iowa months in advance of the caucus. On January 21, it was clear that the effort had paid off when Bush upset front-runner Reagan and finished first among the Republican candidates.

Although we do not know Reagan's immediate private reaction to his Iowa upset, we do know that he must have accepted the caucus result as instructive feedback about his campaign strategy or image. By the following week, a "new" Reagan was campaigning in New Hampshire. This Reagan was talking about issues, riding a press bus, speaking at rallies throughout the state, appearing at all multicandidate Republican gatherings, participating in (in fact, pursuing vigorously) all opportunities to debate his Republican rivals, and using an expanded media campaign to present his view to New Englanders. Perhaps the clearest indication that Reagan had used feedback from Iowa Republicans to reposition his campaign strategy and thus his image came on election day in New Hampshire when he fired his press secretary, his operations director, and his manager, John Sears.

The effort to reposition or recast Bill Clinton's image was undertaken to solve the governor's "character" or "trust" problem and to put him in a better position to reach a national audience. It was called "The Manhattan Project."[42] Beginning with the Gennifer Flowers allegation of a twelve-year extramarital affair with Clinton and the Vietnam draft deferment issues during the New Hampshire through April primaries, the governor continually had to defend his character. During the New York primary, for example, Jerry Brown, his last remaining competitor, portrayed Clinton as morally and fiscally irresponsible[43] and a hypocrite who sought black support but played golf at a whites-only club in Arkansas,[44] and he referred to him as the "prince of sleaze."[45] It was also during the New York primary when the governor admitted that he had smoked (but never inhaled) marijuana while a student in England.

Although Clinton won New York and the other important April primaries and was assured the nomination, public opinion polls indicated that his negative rating had shot to 41 percent, that he was generally thought of as less trustworthy and less honest than President Bush, and that people had little understanding of him and why he felt he should be president.[46]

Thus, with the May and June primaries as well as the convention and general election still to come, Clinton's campaign staff knew it was important that they begin to let Americans know more about the governor as a man: his values, what he stood for, what he had done in Arkansas, and his disadvantaged childhood.

Consequently, they revised and made more specific the ideas in his basic stump speech and extended the campaign media reach to include not only the morning and evening television talk shows but MTV, where Clinton could advance his own themes in response to "soft" questions and directly answer viewers' questions.[47]

While doubts regarding the governor's character remained throughout the general election and into his presidency, clearly the attempt to reposition his image during the final two months of the primary period was successful. Public opinion polls indicated that Clinton's negative rating had begun to drop and he was moving ahead of both Ross Perot and President Bush.

Following his inauguration and the success of Republicans in the congressional elections of 1994 and early 1995, President Clinton again appeared to have little popular support. In fact, by summer 1994, polls showed his approval ratings to be dangerously low. In an effort to increase his credibility and viability, the president took steps to reposition or recast himself. For example, he studied Ronald Reagan videotapes with the idea of changing aspects of his rhetorical style, he merged his administration with his 1996 reelection effort, and he hired political adviser Richard Morris. Morris devised a three-prong strategy that came to be known as the Morris "triangulation" strategy. The president's position on issues moved so far to the center that Republicans (particularly the Republican presidential nominee) had little ideological space. For example, Clinton discussed the need for leadership through a "dynamic center" and proposed tax cut initiatives he termed a "middle class bill of rights."[48]

The second prong of the strategy began in July 1995, when Morris aired commercials in twenty key electoral states that attacked Republican congressional leadership (Bob Dole and Newt Gingrich) and the Republican Party for cutting programs important to large segments of the American electorate, such as Medicare. By fall 1995, the ads had aired in 30 percent of the nation's media markets.

Also during the surfacing period, the president began implementing the third part of the strategy, using popular, and thus safe, issues as talking points. For example, during his weekly radio addresses and on weekend trips to New Hampshire, he talked about the need for greater corporate responsibility, less violence in Hollywood, school uniforms, and drug use. The triangulation strategy was successful; the president's public approval polls went up, often ten to fifteen points, in primary states such as Pennsylvania, Florida, Michigan, Illinois, and Ohio.

A Source of Information for Voters

Important also are the functions provided to the electorate. Just as the primary campaign is valuable in giving candidates the feedback necessary for repositioning, so, too, can it offer voters the information necessary for cognitive adjustment or readjustment.

Images are rather easily acquired by voters during primaries. As candidates crisscross the city or the state speaking at all types of political receptions, coffees, rallies, or fund-raising events, voters have the opportunity to see and hear potential mayors, governors, or presidents. They can witness for themselves the candidate's habitual patterns of thinking and acting. They need no longer rely solely on earlier, perhaps inaccurate, accounts of a candidate's style or position on issues. A candidate for mayor does look and sound capable of coping with the city's striking sanitation and transportation workers. The Republican candidate for governor does have a plan for enticing major industry into the state. The nonincumbent candidate for city council is unable to answer a simple question about zoning ordinances. And the presidential candidate uses so many "ahs," "umhs," and "huhs" that it is impossible to understand responses to questions.

In other words, as the candidates seek all possible arenas of political talk during the primary stage of the campaign, voters can see on a first-hand basis just how candidates handle themselves verbally and nonverbally. The information they receive aids in determining or readjusting their opinions. As a matter of fact, political scientist Thomas E. Patterson has found that these early impressions gained during the primary stage tend to remain throughout the campaign.[49] From speeches and answers to audience questions, voters begin to have some information regarding the candidate's beliefs, attitudes, and value orientations. If Senator Richard Lugar was "everything a President should be" (his campaign slogan), why is it that his primary campaign never received any public or media attention? If former Tennessee governor Lamar Alexander was really the Washington outsider he claimed to be, how could his résumé, which included stints as an aide to a senator, as a president of the University of Tennessee, and as the secretary of education, be taken seriously? If Senator Bob Graham was, as he suggested, the "best prepared to lead and the most able to lead," why was he unable to gather any significant funding to support his presidential ambitions?[50] And if former General Wesley Clark really was a viable candidate for the presidency in 2004, how was it that much of the electorate was not sure just what he stood for? While it is true that voters liked and admired the general, throughout his brief campaign (particularly in the beginning), he rarely talked with the media (after all, he was the "celebrity" candidate). He appeared to be unable to build on his star power in terms of discussing issues and providing solutions to problems that voters expect in someone that would be president of the United States. Clearly, the general had relatively no experience with the multiplicity of issues that voters wanted him to discuss. Answers to these questions and countless others provide information about the candidates that allows voters to create what one communication theorist, Samuel L. Becker, has called a "mosaic model of communication," learning bits of information and then arranging those "bits" into a new or reinforced cognitive pattern.[51]

Citizen Involvement in the Political Process

The third function of the primary period is that it involves many citizens in the democratic process. Involvement in the political process can take a number of different forms. For example, a person can engage in *overt* political action by participating in such activities as raising money for candidates, preparing placards, canvassing door to door for a party or for a candidate, attending a rally or a neighborhood coffee or petition drive, distributing literature, licking envelopes, or voting.

While there are, of course, many other activities possible for those engaging in overt political action, involvement can also be at the *social interaction* level. By this we mean simply that politics gives people a variety of topics or issues for discussion at work, parties, or anyplace where people interact with one another. Involvement may be no more than talking with friends about whether or not a particular candidate is pro-choice or believes in "right to life," but social interaction is one form of involvement in the political process.

A third form of involvement is *parasocial* interaction. This is interaction not with other people but interaction with the messages provided by radio, television, newspapers, the candidate's website, brochures, and so on. In other words, it is arguing or agreeing with a negative political ad when it comes on your television set or in a candidate's speech that you read in their literature or in the evening newspaper.

Finally, involvement can be a matter of *self-reflection*—examination of your ideas or perceptions on economic or social priorities in light of the position or platform of a given candidate.[52]

Although the other political stages of the campaign do encourage forms of overt political action, social or parasocial interaction, and self-reflection, it is increasingly becoming the primary period where involvement is most intense because the sheer number of candidates and the attention given to the primaries by the media demand it. In his book on the role of the mass media in the 1976 presidential campaign, Patterson argues that one of the changes in contemporary campaigns is that public interest now peaks more quickly. In the election of 1940, for example, interest in the campaign did not peak until the general election stage, whereas interest in the 1976 campaign rose sharply in the early primaries. Patterson also found that interest in the campaign decreased during the later primaries, and so the overall interest of voters was no greater than it had been in 1940; it just peaked earlier.[53]

In 1988, the public was once again interested in the primary stage of the presidential campaign, and once again its interest peaked early and declined. The 1988 general election turnout (only 50.16 percent of the country's eligible voters cast ballots) was the lowest in sixty-four years, but the early primaries set voting records. In Iowa, for example, more than 233,000 people took part in the process of selecting a president. This figure was up from 200,000 in 1980, which was more than double the previous high of 88,000 set in 1968 when a desire to protest the Vietnam War drew thousands of supporters of former senator Eugene McCarthy to attend caucus meetings. And in New Hampshire, some 276,000 people cast ballots, surpassing the 1980 record of 261,000.

The 1996 election was much like the 1988 one had been in that the public was interested in the earliest of the competitions, and once again attention peaked early and declined by the later primaries. For example, the 1996 Iowa caucuses played their traditional role of narrowing the field of candidates. Only the top three finishers in Iowa—Senator Bob Dole, Patrick Buchanan, and former Tennessee governor Lamar Alexander—were viable contenders in the New Hampshire primary. Total Republican turnout for the Iowa caucuses was an estimated 96,451, while on the Democratic side, which saw President Clinton unopposed for his party's nomination, voter turnout was estimated at 50,000. For the 1996 New Hampshire primary, 301,380 people cast ballots. Although that figure was down from 1992, 44 percent of registered voters turned out for the 1996 New Hampshire primary, whereas in later primaries, such as New Jersey and New Mexico, voter turnout averaged about 20 percent.

In the 2000 election, data from Harvard's Joan Shorenstein Center on the Press, Politics, and Public Policy indicate that, although Americans were generally disengaged and uninformed about the presidential campaign, knowledge of the front-running contenders' positions on issues peaked during the early primaries and then began a gradual decrease.[54]

And in many respects, the election of 2004 did not differ significantly from its recent predecessors. For example, total Democratic turnout in the thirty primaries and caucuses through Super Tuesday was smaller in a number of states than either Democratic or Republican turnout in 2000 and, overall, the third lowest since 1960 (although the Democratic turnout in the Iowa caucuses was high, it was not a record; however the Democratic turnout in New Hampshire did set a Democratic record). In addition, at least five states canceled their primaries in favor of party-run caucuses to choose delegates to the national conventions because they were going to cost too much and served no purpose.[55] Why are citizens becoming involved in the primary stage of the campaign? Although there are no certain answers, participation has undoubtedly been strengthened for three important reasons. First, with the increased number of primaries, the public is growing more accustomed to them and the major changes they have contributed to the process of selecting a president over the last decade. People have discovered that presidential primaries are exciting, almost like a carnival, as ten or twelve presidential hopefuls, each with family, large contingents of Secret Service, and hundreds of national media representatives, descend on a state for three or four weeks during the winter or spring every fourth year. Even states such as Colorado that had never had or rarely had presidential primaries joined the swelling list by 1992.

Perhaps one reason for the excitement generated by the primaries is the direct personal contact with a potential president. Primary campaigning allows the candidate to meet individual voters. It is unlike the general election when the candidate is remote, isolated, and appears to exist only for the national media. The primaries, like the surfacing stage, are a time for interpersonal communication as candidates and citizens interact at dozens of small group gatherings throughout an individual state.

A second reason for increased involvement may be that a larger number of presidential candidates are actively campaigning and spending extraordinary sums of money in the primary states. For example, in Iowa the major candidates in 1988 spent record amounts on television and radio advertising, with most media budgets running to six figures. Each commercial for a candidate was also an advertisement, in a sense, for the caucuses themselves. The increased publicity given to the caucuses may have led a lot of Iowans to attend them out of curiosity. In New Hampshire in 1992, the Clinton campaign spent nearly $600,000 in the last few days of the primary to buy advertising to counter negative publicity from accusations that the governor had avoided the Vietnam draft and that he had had an extramarital affair. In the 1996 presidential campaign, television advertising began in Iowa and New Hampshire in June 1995, eight months before the first primary, with Lamar Alexander's sixty-second commercials. A month later, President Clinton and/or the DNC ran television ads in twelve states in twenty markets costing $2.4 million.[56] And, by the end of February 1996, with 92 percent of the primaries still in front of him, Senator Robert Dole, the leading Republican candidate, was nearing the $37 million mandated limit on spending imposed on candidates receiving federal matching funds during the primaries.[57] Not surprisingly, money spent by the leading candidates in the 2000 advertising campaign continued to escalate. In fact, Republican candidate Bush ultimately spent $28 million more than did his Democratic rival, Al Gore.[58]

Another explanation for the high levels of involvement in the second stage of the campaign is media coverage. The national media have also discovered the glamour, the excitement, the "gamelike" stakes of the presidential primary. Accordingly, each of the television network's evening news programs devotes substantial amounts of time to covering the candidates in Iowa, New Hampshire, Florida, or wherever the primary or caucus happens to be that week. In addition to regular news features, the primaries are highlighted by special programs such as the Tuesday night telecasts of primary election returns and interview programs such as *Meet the Press*. The media create "winners" and "losers," even though the "winner" may have won by only a few percentage points or maybe did not even win at all but did so much better than was expected or came so close to the "front-runner" that he is declared by the television commentators to have "won" the election. As Patterson argues, the media treat primary elections much as they do the general election—there must be a winner. Each primary is only incidentally treated as part of a larger nominating system.

Promises Made in Personalized Settings

There is, however, a fourth and closely related function of the primary period. As candidates campaign, regardless of what level of office is sought, they often make promises about what they will do if elected. Some promise little, others promise everything from lower taxes to increased morality, but few actually deliver once they take office. We believe that one of the important communication functions of primary campaigning is related to these promises made by candidates during the heat of the campaign.

As already observed, one characteristic of primary campaigns is that they are normally more personalized than the general election stage. That is, voters have more of an opportunity for direct interaction with candidates. Campaigning is personally oriented as candidates attend countless events at which the relatively small number of people present familiarize them with the problems important primarily to their specific neighborhood, city, or state. The voters try to elicit promises of help and assistance from the candidates if they are elected. Once the promise is given, we believe that there is more likelihood of promises being kept after the election because of the physical proximity in which they were articulated and the fact that they are given to a specific individual or small groups of individuals, not an amorphous large audience or an impersonal camera.

Determination of the True Front-Runners

Finally, we suggest a fifth function performed by the primary stage of the campaign. The voters have a chance to determine the "real" front-runners or leading contenders for the nomination. Throughout the surfacing period, the media label candidates as "possible winner," or "dark horse," or "a favorite," or even "front-runner." With the primary, voters have the opportunity to go over and above the media and actually select the nominees or at least give true meaning to the term *front-runner*. While we would not deny the influence the media have extended over the years in the self-fulfilling prophecy of their labels, there have still been a considerable number of instances when the voters, not the media, have determined the serious candidates.

Consider the 1976 presidential campaign in which the media, overanxious, perhaps, because the surfacing period had been so long, had a whole string of candidates they labeled front-runners at one time or another. The list included Senators Henry Jackson and Birch Bayh but never the former governor of Georgia, Jimmy Carter. The voters from Iowa and New Hampshire determined that Carter was a front-runner. The 1980 campaign was pretty much the same, as the media labeled candidates such as John Connally and Senator Howard Baker serious enough contenders to defeat front-runner Ronald Reagan. As it worked out, of course, the only Republican candidate who ever defeated Reagan in a primary was George H. W. Bush. The media had not even considered Bush a serious candidate until the voters from Iowa determined his front-runner status.

The reverse, of course, was true in the case of Senator Edward Kennedy. Prior to the first vote, the media gave the impression that Kennedy had already defeated President Carter. The voters, however, in Iowa and New Hampshire believed that the president was the Democratic front-runner and removed Kennedy from his preprimary position. In 1988, however, after Gary Hart withdrew from the race following the Donna Rice incident, the media were unable to decide on a serious Democratic candidate (calling the seven contenders "the seven dwarfs"). Apparently they decided to let voters determine who among the "dwarfs" was a front-runner. Voters in Iowa chose Gephardt; those in New Hampshire selected Dukakis; the voters on Super Tuesday decided on Gore. In 1992, after the media had referred to at least three of what they had labeled the Democratic "six pack" as front-runners (Kerry, Harkin, and Clinton), the voters in New Hampshire selected Paul Tsongas. And in 1996 and again in 2000, despite the prominence of the person supposed to be the leader, voters in New Hampshire selected Patrick Buchanan, not Robert Dole, in 1996 and John McCain, not George Bush, in 2000.

However, it was perhaps the 2004 campaign that most quickly determined who "would be on first." Vermont governor Howard Dean raised $7.5 million just in the spring of 2003, significantly more than any other candidate. However, he lost the Iowa caucus, actually coming in third to John Kerry and John Edwards. After Iowa, which determined Kerry as the front-runner, Dean's campaign all but dissolved with the Kerry momentum continuing into New Hampshire.

These, then, are the communication functions of the primary stage of the campaign. They are significant because the second stage is vital to our political system. The primary campaigns allow the people to determine who the candidates will be. During the primaries, the decision making is taken from the hands of political parties and media and given to the voters. The communication functions are crucial to the process.

THIRD POLITICAL STAGE: NOMINATING CONVENTIONS

Although a majority of citizens regularly tell pollsters that they would prefer some other method for nominating presidential candidates, the national party conventions remain as they have since their inception: the bodies that make official presidential and vice presidential nominations for the Republican and Democratic Parties. However, just as the first two political stages of the modern campaign have changed, so has the third. Where instrumental or pragmatic communicative functions were once the primary reason for holding party conventions, now the symbolic or ritualistic functions are, in most instances, the chief purposes. In other words, the convention stage is an important and distinct period in the four-step process because of the symbolic functions it provides.

From the time that the anti-Masons held the first national nominating convention in Baltimore in 1832 until the Democratic Convention in 1972, nominating conventions could be viewed as deliberative bodies—assemblies faced with difficult and important decisions to make in a few days. In addition to participating in the "required" political rituals of the day, delegates made decisions that often determined the success or failure of their political party during the coming election. In other words, the conventions served important pragmatic or instrumental functions in that the presidential and vice presidential nominees were selected, the platforms were determined, and even the tone or "battle posture" for the general election campaigns was established. In short, the convention met to make party decisions. For many years, decisions were made and the conventions were controlled by bosses and special interests. Some of those conventions nominated candidates of top quality such as Abraham Lincoln and Woodrow Wilson, and other conventions tapped candidates of dubious quality such as Franklin Pierce and Warren Harding. Whatever the caliber of the candidates nominated or the platform written, it is important to remember that the nominating conventions actually made party decisions; in other words, they served instrumental functions.

However, beginning in 1952 and strengthened by action taken for the 1972 Democratic Convention, at least three significant changes have occurred, thus shifting the communicative functions of conventions from instrumental to symbolic. While they have been discussed earlier, their impact on the third stage of the campaign has been so enormous that they should be understood with regard to the nominating conventions.

The first change was the introduction of television to the campaign. Although television did not bring the sights and sounds of the presidential contest to millions of people until the 1952 campaign, nonprint media had been involved in the nominating conventions for many years. In 1912, movies and phonograph records captured Woodrow Wilson's acceptance speech; in 1924, the acceptance speech of presidential nominee John Davis was broadcast over a network of fifteen radio stations; and by 1928, the influence of the medium was so pervasive that the time and date of Alfred Smith's acceptance speech were determined by the network of the 104 radio stations that were to broadcast the speech.

However, when television was first used during the 1952 primary campaigns, it contributed to the growth of public interest. Turnout jumped from less than five million primary voters in 1948 to almost thirteen million in 1952. The new medium brought a different dimension first to the primaries and then to the conventions by dramatizing suspense, conflict, and excitement, as well as projecting a visual image of the candidates that had never before been possible. Television gave the public a sense of involvement in the conventions, and, as many delegates and reporters covering the convention soon discovered, the television viewer could see more and know more of what was going on than could the persons who were on the floor of the convention hall.[59]

During the 1952 campaign, there were 108 television stations on the air, and, as one study of the election showed, the impact of the new medium was significant:

> The public went out of its way to watch the campaign on television. Only about 40 percent of the homes in the U.S. have televisions sets, but some 53 percent of the population saw TV programs on the campaign—a reflection of "television visiting." On the other hand, the campaign news and other material in newspapers, magazines and on the radio did not reach all of their respective audiences: more than 80 percent of the population take daily newspapers and have radios and more than 60 percent regularly read magazines, but in each case the number following the campaign in these media was smaller than the total audience. . . . In the nation as a whole, television, though available to only a minority of the people, led the other media in the number of persons who rated it most informative.[60]

As important as television's influence was in 1952, it can be seen as a mere shadow of what it was to become in all stages of subsequent campaigns, including the nominating conventions. In fact, by 1976 when electorate interest in that year's presidential contest was studied, it was discovered that television coverage of the conventions boosted voter interest and attention to the campaign, especially among those who were not strong political partisans.[61] Perhaps in response to electorate interest, coverage of the 1980 conventions was increased to the point that media representatives outnumbered delegates by four and five to one at the Republican and Democratic Conventions. As a matter of fact, according to the *New York Times*, the Democratic Convention included 3,381 delegates and 11,500 reporters, editors, camera operators, and broadcasters. And although the public appeared as bored with the 1980 conventions as it had been interested in those of 1976 (network ratings showed a sharp drop in the number of people watching the 1980 conventions as compared with four years earlier), the presence of television has, nonetheless, continued to increase. For example, the number of channels has drastically increased with new electronic technologies. Compared to the earlier coverage by the three networks (ABC, CBS, and NBC), the 1992 campaign was covered by five networks (ABC, NBC, CBS, PBS, and FOX), 1,500 television stations, and two cable networks. In 1996, coverage once again increased when the number of journalists at the Republican Convention climbed to over fifteen thousand, or seven journalists for each delegate. The 1996 campaign was also the first time that one of the political parties televised its own convention. Republicans donated $1.3 million to Pat Robertson's cable Family Channel to air their sessions, and they arranged for their own commentators. In spite of this increased coverage, however, viewership of the 1996 conventions was down nearly 40 percent from those of 1992.[62]

In the 2004 campaign, network coverage of the conventions reached an all-time low with the major networks of CBS, NBC, and ABC only showing three hours of coverage for each convention[63]—in other words they showed one hour, 10–11 p.m. for three nights. Network coverage affected the schedule of events at the conventions, with organizers putting their major speakers including the keynoter and the nomination acceptance speech during that hour. There were, however, a host of cable news networks covering the events, including CNN, Fox News, C-Span, and even Comedy Central. The cable networks gave viewers who wanted it another opportunity to get information and watch parts of the conventions the major networks did not cover.

Although fewer people appear to be viewing every televised convention activity (we should note, however that convention watching did not decline in 2004, but remained the same as it had been in 2000),[64] since 1952, the presence of television has restructured convention programming so that the party's "important" events occur during "prime time." To make certain that this happens, the convention chair often ignores the activities of the delegates on the convention floor and rushes through any official party business to make certain that those events planned to give the party the most favorable image (e.g., ecumenical prayers, civic greetings, performances by show business personalities, keynote and acceptance speeches, and controlled and planned "spontaneous" demonstrations for candidates) will be seen during the hours in which most people watch television. Whether this strategy fails (as, for example, it did in 1972 when George McGovern's acceptance speech began hours after most people had gone to bed or in 1980 when Congressman Morris Udall's keynote address started as the delegates were leaving Madison Square Garden for the night) or is successful, the convention proceedings become ritual with little or no pragmatic value.

Another effect of the presence of the television has been that convention participants have become almost more aware of media presence than of convention business and thus alter their behavior and interaction. As one critic of the 1980 Democratic Convention notes:

> The omni-present camera eye contributed to the funny hat, placard, banner and button syndromes. . . . At times, the television camera introduced an almost schizophrenic atmosphere as speakers addressed themselves to an unlistening, often chaotic arena audience, while really hoping that their individual performance would coincide with network coverage.[65]

The last and undoubtedly most significant effect has been that television covers only those events it decides are important, thereby altering the shape, structure, and activities of the convention. There were times during the 1980 conventions, for example, when the networks conducted interviews with relatives of the candidates while prominent convention participants were debating platform positions. In fact, so much "gatekeeping" was done by networks covering the Democratic Convention that one scholar estimated that television viewers saw less than half of the proceedings during those times when the networks were on the air. CBS, for example, made decisions about what to show or not to show viewers based on whether Walter Cronkite judged the event to be very exciting. During the 1984 conventions, NBC did not go to the podium for nearly an hour, preferring to present its own interviews rather than an address by Congressman Jack Kemp. An eighteen-minute film introducing President Reagan was carefully inserted into the convention schedule to assure airtime. However, only NBC and CNN showed the film in full. Thus, we believe communication analyst Gary Gumpert is correct when he writes that television has helped render the nominating conventions little more than "a series of arranged and controlled visual and auditory images."[66]

The second factor that has had a profound influence in changing the nature of the third political stage has been the reliance on primaries as the vehicle for selecting delegates to the national party conventions. As we discuss in the first chapter, the proliferation of primaries has contributed to the decline of the political parties, but now we want to emphasize that it has also changed the role of the national nominating convention from decision maker to "legitimizer." Perhaps this statement is explained best by taking a brief glance at the history of the presidential primary.

The presidential primary is a "uniquely American institution born, after decades of agitation, in the early twentieth century."[67] In the post–Civil War era, the party organizations in many states and cities came under the control of often corrupt political machines dominated by or allied with public utilities, railroads, and others who manipulated the convention system to suit their ends. In an effort to reform the system, the Populists and later the Progressives advocated the substitution of direct primary elections for party-nominating conventions. By 1917, all but four states had adopted the direct primary method of nomination for some or all offices filled by statewide election. However, the extension of primary elections from the local, state, and congressional levels to presidential politics was much more difficult.

In 1904, Florida held the first primary election for the choice of delegates to a national party convention, and, by 1916, presidential primaries were held in twenty-two states amid speculation that within a few years the national convention would be only an ornament for making official those decisions already arrived at by the electorate. Calculations such as these, however, were a few years premature because two decades after the first presidential primary had taken place, the movement came to a halt with the number of states stabilized at around fifteen. Turnout remained low, and there was little popular interest in them until the 1952 campaign when the entrance of television into the primary elections renewed voter enthusiasm and then again in 1956 when Senator Estes Kefauver became the first candidate to use the New Hampshire primary as a way to call attention to his campaign. Although the outcomes did not determine the parties' ultimate choices, they generated more interest than they had at any time since 1912.

Twenty years later, in 1972, a major incentive for the adoption of presidential primaries was provided when the Democratic Party's Commission on Party Structure and Delegate Selection to the Democratic National Committee, popularly known as the McGovern–Fraser Commission, sought to stop some of the injustices apparent to many liberals at the 1968 convention. The commission prepared eighteen guidelines intended to ensure that the state Democratic Parties' procedures for selecting delegates to the 1972 convention were open, fair, and timely. At least four other commissions followed McGovern–Fraser in the intervening years, and the guidelines have become so complex (to make certain that there is enough representation of minorities and women) that the state parties have found that they can best comply with them, and not disturb traditional ways of conducting other party business, by adopting a presidential primary law. Thus, the number of presidential primaries has proliferated. As primaries grew, so did the number of delegates pledged to a specific candidate, and since 1972 everyone has known before the conventions begin who the candidates would be (except in 1976 at the Republican Convention when Ford and Reagan fought down to the wire). The conventions no longer determine the candidates. Voters in those states holding presidential primaries have decided who will be nominated. The convention meets to legitimize the earlier selection.

The third factor that has influenced the changing nature of the convention stage has been the emergence of the campaign specialists who, with the consent of the candidates for whom they work, determine important aspects of the convention that were once the domain of delegate and party leaders. The consultants have planned the candidate's strategies through the first two stages for the precise purpose of winning the nomination. With the nomination secured before the convention even begins, the specialists now turn to "putting on the best show" possible, or what theorists Larry David Smith and Dan Nimmo describe as the orchestration of "cordial concurrence,"[68] for the television-viewing audience.

The party platform is negotiated in advance of the convention, with the staff of the candidate certain to be the nominee controlling the deliberations. If a spirited debate concerning a specific issue would enhance the "television show" or if, in the spirit of compromise, it becomes important to give the losing candidate and his supporters the chance to air a minority position, portions of the party's platform will be discussed during the convention itself. However, even when this has happened, as in the case of the "debate" on the MX missile at the 1980 Democratic Convention, the vast majority of the delegates paid no attention to the debaters. In fact, as one communication analyst who attended the convention notes:

> Signs against the MX popped up and down in the Garden: "X-rated Missiles Aren't Sexy," "NIX the MX," "MX-Missile Madness," "No MX—Nobody Wins World War III," "MX Says Have a Nice Doomsday," "Mighty Expensive," "MX Makes US the Target." Delegates wandered around talking to friends. There were many empty seats. The clear impression was of a ceremonial occasion rather than a deliberative one. . . . The debates served the symbolic function, though, of letting off steam for those who really did care.[69]

In other words, all real decisions regarding the convention are made by the candidate, based on the advice of consultants. The candidate, not the party leaders, determines the platform, the issues to be debated, the songs to be played, the identity of those who will speak from the podium during prime time, the name of the keynote speaker or speakers, and the content and length of the "spontaneous" demonstration. As one delegate to the 1980 Democratic Convention said, "We've turned over absolute control of the nominating process to the presidential candidates, and worse, to their staffs."[70]

Because of the influence generated by television coverage, presidential primaries, and campaign specialists, the overall function of the national nominating convention to the campaign has been altered. Gone is the once powerful role of decision maker. In its place is a new function. The primary significance of the modern nominating convention is symbolic-ritualistic—and as such, it serves four important communication functions, discussed next.

Reaffirming and Legitimizing the Electoral Process

The first function, and one of the most significant, is that convention ritu-als provide an opportunity for the legitimation and reaffirmation of the "rightness" of the American way or dream. The various communication acts and symbols of conventions (keynote speeches, nomination speeches, debates, demonstrations, state-by-state roll call balloting, official "greet-ings" from past party heroes, patriotic music, buttons, hats, placards, as well as nomination acceptance speeches) serve to renew our faith that U.S. citizens share not only a glorious tradition but a grand and proud future. In a sense, each convention can be viewed as a huge political rally where the candidate shares the spotlight with the democratic system that made success possible. When, for example, the presidential and vice presiden-tial nominees make their triumphant entrance to the speaker's platform the last night of the convention, their appearance reinforces the belief that citizens are bound together in a noble tradition. There have been instances when nominees have acknowledged the reciprocity of the relationship during the nomination acceptance speech. For example, in 2004, John Kerry said,

> And tonight we have an important message for those who question the pa-triotism of Americans who offer a better direction for our country. Before wrapping themselves in the flag and shutting their eyes to the truth and their ears, they should remember what America is really all about. They should remember the great idea of freedom for which so many have given their lives. Our purpose now is to reclaim our democracy itself. We are here to affirm that when Americans stand up and speak their minds and say America can do better, that is not a challenge to patriotism, it is the heart and soul of patriotism.
>
> You see that flag up there. We call her Old Glory. The Stars and Stripes for-ever. I fought under that flag, as did so many of those people who are here tonight and all across the country. That flag flew from the gun turret right be-hind my head. And it was shot through and through and tattered, but it never ceased to wave in the wind. It draped the caskets of men that I served with and friends I grew up with. For us that flag is the most powerful sym-bol of who we are and what we believe in. Our strength. Our diversity. Our love of country. All that makes America both great and good.

Certainly, conventions function to legitimize the selection of the candi-dates, the platform, and the unity of the party and its leaders. But in the largest sense, the communication rituals celebrate what is good about our system and thus ourselves. Convention sessions, for example, open and close with prayers (we are a spiritual and godly people). During the con-vention, former heroes are acknowledged (we have a sense of our roots), and countless speakers evoke selected elements of the American Dream (we believe that the United States is destined to become a mighty empire of liberty where everyone can share in the prosperity of society). On the final night, the selected candidates articulate their visions of a grand and more noble country (we value the traditions of reform and progress), while national songs provide periodic emotional climaxes (we have pride in and deep-seated feelings about our country).[71] The convention rituals are, in short, a kind of emotional/spiritual/patriotic catharsis in which we can, if necessary, lament current shortcomings within the party or the country while remaining proud of and faithful to our legacy.

In writing about conventions as legitimation rituals, one communication scholar found that typically the ritual has three steps: (1) It begins with a statement and demonstration of theme (traditionally the responsibility of keynote speakers); (2) it progresses to a clustering or gathering of stereotypical character types who are given convention time for speeches or "greetings" to the delegates (the hero or heroine, the also-rans or those who fought the good fight but lost in a noble cause and are now vindicated through history, and leaders representing the Right and Left and all divergent interest groups within the party); and (3) it culminates in the anointing of the nominee who symbolizes and enacts the convention's theme.

However, not only are there identifiable steps or phases in the convention ritual, but a variety of ritualistic forms are possible. For example, the 1984 Republican Convention explored the theme of "What's Right with This Country," by stressing that Americans were better off after four years of Republican control of the White House.[72]

Legitimizing the Party Nominee

Not only do the communicative acts of the convention serve to reaffirm our general commitment to the electoral process, but there is a second and closely related function. The convention provides legitimation for the party's nominees. When the struggle for nomination is long and intense (as it has been for presidential nominees since 1972), or when the selection has gone to a relative newcomer (as it did when the Democrats nominated Jimmy Carter in 1976, Michael Dukakis in 1988, and Bill Clinton in 1992), or even when the convention nominates nontraditional candidates (as the Democrats did with Geraldine Ferraro on the ticket as the vice presidential candidate in 1984), the ritual of the convention confirms or legitimizes the candidate as the party's nominee as a possible governor, senator, or even president of the United States. A person may have won primary after primary, but not until the convention delegates affirm selection through their votes at the convention can the candidate become the nominee.

With the act of confirmation comes added prestige and respect. The person is no longer just a candidate, but the nominee of a political party—something of an American icon. For example in 2004, Senator Kerry was presented as heroic and dedicated. With the first words of his acceptance speech he reminded Americans of the expectations and fulsome responsibilities of the American Presidency when he walked to the podium and saluted, saying, "I'm John Kerry and I'm reporting for duty." Democratic speaker and former Georgia senator Max Cleland, in introducing the Massachusetts senator, referred to Kerry's war record, giving an account of his experience serving with Kerry in Vietnam, saying that he was a "living testimony to his (Kerry's) leadership, his courage under fire, and his willingness to risk his life for his fellow Americans."[73] Incumbent Republican candidate President Bush was presented as a leader holding to his principles and not giving in to opinion polls or politics. Bush's leadership was presented as "rooted in the timeless values that have made America a unique and exulted nation: respect for individual rights; a deep commitment to freedom; [and] a desire to serve as a living example of the power of democracy."[74] In addition, the choice to hold the Republican Convention in New York City further helped to legitimize Bush, by referring to his work to rebuild and lead New York and the nation following the September 11, 2001 attacks.

Demonstrating Party Unity

The third function provided by the convention stage is that the party has a chance to show its unity. Whether the cohesion is more apparent than real, the convention is the time when wounds from the primary campaigns can be addressed and healed. Perhaps the importance of a unified party to the success of the approaching campaign can be understood by examining instances when the convention ritual has failed to produce cohesiveness.

In 1964, the Republican Convention that nominated Barry Goldwater appeared to repudiate Republicans whose political philosophies were more liberal than those of the conservatives who dominated the convention. The governor of New York, Nelson Rockefeller, who had been a contender for the nomination, was booed and not given the opportunity to finish a speech. When Goldwater included an endorsement of extremism in his acceptance speech, many liberals walked out of the convention. The Republican Party remained divided throughout the campaign, and Goldwater lost the election by one of the largest margins in the history of presidential politics. Similarly, in 1968 and again in 1972, the Democratic National Convention failed to unify and come together to support either Hubert Humphrey or George McGovern. Humphrey was tormented throughout the 1968 general election campaign by those in the Democratic Party who felt his nomination was a betrayal of party principle and a disfranchisement for liberals. McGovern, on the other hand, was never able to unify the traditional or "old-line" party leaders with his more youthful and/or liberal insurgents. In each case, the Democrats remained divided throughout the convention and general election campaign and lost in November.

Thus, even when tension below the surface is strained, the political parties strive for the appearance of unity during their conventions. At the 1976 Democratic Convention, for example, one communication analyst recalled that following Jimmy Carter's acceptance speech, party chairman Robert Strauss gathered all the party's candidates and factions on the speaker's platform as Martin Luther King Sr. delivered the benediction to the convention:

> King stunned the noisy delegates and galleries into silence, asking that they "cease walking, talking" and that "not a word be uttered unless that word is to God." In a rousing sermon that brought forth shouts of "Amen" from the audience, the father of Martin Luther King, Jr. cried: "Surely the Lord sent Jimmy Carter to come out and bring America back where she belongs. . . . As I close in prayer, let me tell you we must close ranks now. If there is any misunderstanding anywhere, if you haven't got a forgiving heart, get down on your knees. It is time for prayer." As Daddy King concluded, the delegates joined hands, linked arms, and slowly began to sing "We Shall Overcome Someday." The television cameras focused on the faces of the delegates, who wept and swayed as they achieved a cathartic moment of emotional release and affirmation.[75]

In a similar though less emotional manner, the Republicans and the Democrats in 1988 attempted to evoke images of unity in the closing moments of their conventions. Although the race for the 1988 Democratic nomination was filled with bitterness, particularly because of Jesse Jackson's feeling that neither the party nor the Dukakis staff was giving him the central role he felt he deserved, the victorious Michael Dukakis had Jackson join him at the speaker's podium after he had delivered his acceptance speech. Jackson was followed to the podium by others who had been opponents during the primary and caucus elections. In 1988, George H. W. Bush was joined at the podium following his address by those who had been opponents during the primary and caucus elections to sing "God Bless America." In the summer of 1992, the Democratic National Convention in New York was so positive and unifying, one journalist called it the "Lovefest in Madison Square Garden."[76]

From the beginning of the 1992 presidential campaign "season," Democratic National Chairman Ron Brown was determined that the party would be unified around a single candidate (as soon as the primaries and caucuses made clear who that person would be) and that the convention would reflect that unity:

> What Brown understood from the party's twelve years out of power and from the way the 1992 primaries and caucuses had played out was that his fellow Democrats were energized by the possibility of recapturing the White House. And, given the condition of the economy, they were not in a humor to argue endlessly over how many ideological nuances could be stuffed on the head of a pin. Brown was prepared to tolerate dissent but he was not willing to allow it to spoil his convention.[77]

Accordingly, Brown and the Clinton staff oversaw every detail of the convention. And Brown instituted a basic rule: People who had not endorsed the ticket would not be allowed to speak at the convention. Thus, days before the convention opened, Jerry Brown was the only scheduled speaker who had not endorsed the Clinton ticket. And although the former California governor was entitled to speak because his name was going to be put into nomination, Brown did not grant him a formal place on the program with the other defeated contenders, each of whom had endorsed Clinton. In addition, Brown devised and implemented a Wednesday evening schedule that minimized the media exposure this one last dissenter would receive.

In contrast, the Republican Convention in Houston was anything but a "lovefest." In fact, for the first time in many years, the convention exposed "significant fault lines"[78] in the Republican Party. The "mean-spirited" tone of the convention had been set by the GOP platform committee, which held its sessions in the days immediately preceding the opening of the convention. Although the committee had to develop a position on a variety of issues, it was the antiabortion plank, the opposition to legislation that recognized same-sex marriages, the support of home-based schools, and the charge that "elements within the media, the entertainment industry, academics and the Democratic Party are waging a guerrilla war against American values"[79] that set off the ideological sparks between the hard-line social issue conservatives who controlled the committee and the convention, and moderate Republicans.

In spite of the fact that the convention theme was "The American Spirit," not all of the major speakers reinforced it. For example, hardline conservatives such as Pat Buchanan, Pat Robertson, William Bennett, and Marilyn Quayle focused on the platform planks that appeared to exclude many Americans, even those in their own party who had more liberal philosophies. Their speeches were fiery condemnations of the "evils of liberalism"[80] with direct linkages to Bill Clinton, his wife, and Senator Edward Kennedy.

Despite the fact that on the last night of the convention all factions were together at the podium to symbolize unity, the overall impression for many Americans was that the Republican Party was disjointed and mean-spirited.[81]

The 2000 Democratic National Convention may forever be remembered because of the "serious" kiss that Al Gore gave his wife, Tipper, thanking her for introducing him so that he could formally accept the party's nomination on the final night of the convention. It may also be remembered because of the difficult task faced by the vice president—to separate himself from President Clinton's problems while simultaneously remaining close enough to share the achievements during the Clinton years. He solved the problem by announcing, "I stand here before you tonight as my own man," and "I want you to know me for who I truly am."

At the 2004 Republican and Democratic National Conventions, the appearance of party unity was again a predominant theme. The Democrats talked about equality, economic prosperity, and the protection of traditional American values. Republicans, meeting in New York City, emphasized the strength and vision of their nominee President George W. Bush, who had brought back New York City after the tragedy of the September 11, 2001 attacks. The Republicans also talked about how America was continuing to move in the right direction.

Introducing the Candidate's Campaign Themes and Issues

The fourth communication function served by nominating conventions is that they provide the public introduction of the candidate's rhetorical agenda for the general election campaign. Whether Republican or Democrat, the acceptance speeches of the nominees have frequently signaled the issues on which they plan to campaign (typically through the introduction of a specific slogan) and/or have announced an overall campaign style/plan they intend to follow (sometimes accomplished via a direct challenge to the opposition).

Franklin Roosevelt initiated the process of the nominee speaking to the delegates in person when in 1932 he flew from Albany, New York, to the Democratic Convention in Chicago. During his acceptance speech, he introduced the phrase the "New Deal," which became the slogan for his campaign and subsequent administration. In 1948, Harry Truman not only announced that the central issue in his campaign would be the "do-nothing Congress" but also explained that he was going to keep Congress in session during the summer to try and get some legislation from them. In 1960, Richard Nixon announced his intention to take the campaign to all fifty states, while John Kennedy introduced the "New

Frontier" as the slogan/theme for those issues important to his campaign. In 1976, while accepting the Republican nomination, President Gerald Ford announced his intention to debate, challenging his opponent to a face-to-face confrontation when he said, "This year the issues are on our side. I'm ready—I'm eager to go before the American People and debate the real issues face-to-face with Jimmy Carter."[82] In 1988, George H. W. Bush cited five major issues to draw a sharp distinction between his conservative agenda and Michael Dukakis's liberal agenda.[83] In 1992, Clinton defined the "New Covenant": "A solemn agreement between the people and their government based not simply on what each of us can take but what all of us must give to make America work again."[84] In 1996, Robert Dole advocated a revival of the nation's "old values" of family, duty, truth, and honor; and in 2000, George W. Bush talked about restoring dignity to the office of the president, and Al Gore argued for "the people, not the powerful."

In 2004, both the Democratic and Republican Conventions presented the major issues and themes of the campaign in a complex and multi-layered process throughout the four-day events. The Democrats vowed to have a positive convention. They were not going to attack Bush's character or leadership. They even went as far as to have "scrubbers" that approved all speeches delivered, forbidding any harsh attacks that could "alienate undecided and independent voters."[85] With this in mind, the major issues presented were that the team of Kerry and Edwards would "make healthcare affordable and accessible for all Americans, create and keep jobs in America, make us independent from Mideast oil, and restore America's respect in the world."[86]

The Democratic Convention hosted several popular Democratic figures as speakers, including former presidents Bill Clinton and Jimmy Carter, New York senator Hillary Rodham Clinton, and, most interestingly, a candidate for the United States Senate from Illinois, Barak Obama. Obama keynoted the convention, and used themes of party, political, and community unity, a "balance between government action and personal responsibility"[87] with America as a united family. The theme of American unity was reiterated the following day when vice-presidential candidate John Edwards spoke of building "one America," for "people who have lived the American Dream and . . . for most Americans who work hard and still struggle to make ends meet." Day four of the Democratic Convention was John Kerry's turn. His introduction was not done by a famous Democrat, but by his family and fellow soldiers from his Vietnam days in the Mekong Delta. This decision was made to reinforce the idea of Kerry as a fearless and courageous leader.

The 2004 Republican Convention was planned a bit differently. First, it was a month later, which provided speech writers and planners plenty of time to respond to what they believed had been missing links and stances on issues from the Democratic Convention. Second, the convention was in New York City, the place that had showcased the president's leadership on September 11, 2001. The location and timing was perfect for the Republicans because it provided the ultimate setting to champion their major issue, national security. Like the Democrats, unity was a theme at the Republican Convention, only this time it was that America "should be unified against terror and terrorists."[88] Arizona senator John McCain emphasized this in his convention speech, saying about the September 11th attacks, "We were not different races. We were not poor or rich. We were not Democrat or Republican, liberal or conservative. We were not two countries. We were Americans." McCain also stressed that national security and defense were the "greatest responsibility of the government."[89]

Republicans did not just stick with national security. They also, in day two of the convention, stressed the importance of domestic issues such as racial division, health care, and education. These issues were brought about by California governor Arnold Schwarzenegger. He gave a well-received speech, reminiscing at times about his own immigrant background, and called America "compassionate," "generous," "accepting," and "welcoming." He even called on immigrants to find their "Republican roots."

Unlike the Democrats, the Republicans did not vow to run a positive convention. Day three of the convention saw attacks on the Democratic Party and candidates John Kerry and John Edwards. The major player in this attack strategy was Georgia Democratic senator Zell Miller. His keynote address attacked the Democrats, saying that they were "motivated more by partisan politics than by national security." One attack was particularly blunt, with Miller saying, "no pair has been more wrong, more loudly, more often than the two senators from Massachusetts, Ted Kennedy and John Kerry." The attacks continued into Vice President Dick Cheney's speech, although not as harsh or strongly worded as Miller's had been. It was the president's speech on day four that brought the convention back to the triumphs and accomplishments of his administration. Bush stressed his role after September 11, and talked about the way in which his leadership skills had been tested and proven.

These, then, are the communication functions served by the third political stage of the campaign. As we have pointed out throughout our discussion of this stage, though the nominating convention serves only ritualistic functions, it is no less critical to the overall campaign than are the other stages. In fact, as we suggested earlier, a campaign that fails to get the most out of the ritual demanded during the nominating convention will proceed to the fourth stage with a potentially fatal handicap.

FOURTH POLITICAL STAGE: THE GENERAL ELECTION

"Electing time"[90] means speeches, parades, debates, bumper stickers, media commercials, band playing, doorbell ringing, posters, billboards, polling, sound bites, town hall meetings, direct mail fund-raising, call-in talk shows, and countless television spots. As we have discussed throughout this chapter, these acts and symbols are no longer reserved exclusively for the last stage, although they remain a significant and expected part. It is almost as if all has been in readiness—a type of dress rehearsal for this final and most important scene. Certainly, candidates may have been appearing and speaking at all manner of gatherings for many months. Thirty- and sixty-second television spots may have been interfering with television viewing since the primaries. Citizens may have even voted for their candidate in a primary or watched a part of one of the conventions on television. However, once the final stage begins, the campaign communication is at once more intense, less interpersonal, but more direct and certainly more important because the candidate who emerges will be the new mayor, governor, legislator, or president. It is precisely because of the importance of the general election stage that we must discuss briefly three communicative functions, which, although not unique to this stage, are nonetheless reflective of it.

Gaining Information

The first function is cognitive. The electorate voluntarily seeks or involuntarily learns of information about some feature of the election and/or the candidates. News regarding the campaign is so widespread during the fourth stage that additional or restructured information may be gained from something as simple as talking with a friend, watching the evening news, or reading a newspaper or magazine. Because so much information permeates the environment during the general election, the majority of the electorate possesses at least minimal knowledge about the election.

In recent years, people have been acquiring political knowledge from yet another source, the public opinion polls of the media. While syndicated polls during election years have been a regular feature of the press since the inception of modern public opinion polling in 1936, by the 1970s, news organizations began to serve as their own polling agencies. News-gathering organizations were not simply printing or broadcasting the findings of others; they were creating news on their own initiative with their own polls—often extending opinion soundings down to the local level.

The impact of this development is reflected in the results of a 1979 study by the National Research Council, which showed that, in two parallel surveys conducted during the heat of the 1976 campaign, only 16 percent of those interviewed failed to recall hearing something "in the news or in talking with friends" about "polls showing how candidates for office are doing."[91] Twenty years later, by the time of the general election stage of the 1996 campaign, virtually every major news organization was conducting some poll each week, thus providing a constant stream of information regarding the election.

Legitimizing the Political System

Communicative acts also serve a second function. The general election assigns legitimacy, the idea that the campaign process itself provides further proof that the system works.

In discussing the ritualistic functions of the nominating conventions, we discovered the importance of legitimation in affirming the candidate as the party's choice and the electoral system as superior. Legitimation is also an important function of the general election. As people stand in line to greet a candidate, put up posters for "their" candidate for city council, attend a rally, watch the presidential candidates debate, discuss with a friend the merits of one of the mayoral candidates, vote, or engage in any of the participatory activities typical of the final stage of the campaign, they symbolically reinforce the values for which the activities stand.[92] Thus, campaigning becomes a self-justifying activity that perpetuates two primal U.S. myths, according to Bruce Gronbeck:

> Acquiescence—providing a paradigmatic, "fail-safe" rationale for choosing leaders and fostering programs with particularly "American" bents, making it difficult for anyone to object to the process (for if you do, the system's ideological web reaches out, telling you to seek the desired change by participating—running for office, pressuring the parties, voicing your opinions in public forums); and, Quiescence—reasserting the values associated with campaigning and its outcomes (free-and-open decision-making, public accountability, habitual and even mandatory modes of campaigning, the two-party system), in order to remind a citizenry that it is "happy" and "content" with its electoral system; emphasizing the mores and ceremonial rituals associated with elections which make the country "devil-proof," invincible to attacks from within or without.[93]

Meeting Campaign Expectations

Finally, the fourth stage of the political campaign contributes to fulfilling our expectations regarding campaign rituals. We expect candidates to address themselves to society's problems; we expect debates, rallies, door-to-door volunteers, bumper stickers, buttons, continuous election specials and advertisements over radio and television, polls, and all manner of drama, excitement, and even pageantry. In other words, we have any number of expectations regarding political campaigns. While the previous stages also function to fulfill our "demands," the directness, intensity, and finality of the fourth stage emphasize our pleasure or displeasure with the way in which a particular election has or has not met our pragmatic or ritualistic expectations. If during the general election stage the candidates fail to address those issues of paramount importance to us, fail to debate each other, or even fail to provide for us any of the excitement or drama we normally expect, we may feel cheated. It is, in short, the climax of a political season—a time for decision and participation. It is electing time.

CONCLUSION

With the changes in election campaigns in recent years, countless proposals have been made to modify or alter each of the four political stages. While many of the suggestions might well prove beneficial, we hope that you can now better appreciate that our system is far from purposeless. The various verbal and nonverbal acts of communication provide a full range of instrumental and consummatory functions for the candidate and the electorate in each political stage. While some of the functions are perhaps more significant than others, taken together, they are justification enough for the routines and rituals that in this country comprise the political election campaign.

NOTES

1. Bruce E. Gronbeck, "The Functions of Presidential Campaigning," *Communication Monographs* 45 (November 1978): 268–80.

2. Donald R. Matthews, "Winnowing: The New Media and the 1976 Presidential Nominations," in *Race for the Presidency*, ed. James David Barber, 55–78 (Englewood Cliffs, N.J.: Prentice Hall, 1978).

3. Judith S. Trent, "Presidential Surfacing: The Ritualistic and Crucial First Act," *Communication Monographs* 45 (November 1978): 282.

4. The commentary is taken from an unpublished 1979 survey of all women officeholders in Ohio. Partial results of the survey were presented by Judith S. Trent at the 1979 convention in St. Louis of the Central States Communication Association.

5. Roland Evans and Robert Novak, "Sam Nunn Preparing to Run," *Cincinnati Enquirer*, April 10, 1990, A11.

6. David Von Drehle, "Restless in Bush Country: Once Reliable Michigan Voters Demonstrate Signs of Rebellion," *Washington Post*, August 16, 1992, A1.

7. David Yepsen, "Another Casualty of War: Democrats' 1992 Chances," *Cincinnati Enquirer*, March 10, 1991, A10.

8. Christine Gardner, "GOP Flocks to New Hampshire to Be Seen and Heard," *USA Today*, May 27, 1993, 4A.

9. "South Carolina Governor Ends Bid for Presidency," *New York Times*, June 5, 1994, A16.

10. Richard Berke, "Dole, Campaigning from Afar, Wins an Early Republican Straw Poll in Iowa," *New York Times*, June 26, 1994, A8.

11. B. Drummond Ayres Jr., "A Bronx Cheer in New Hampshire," *New York Times*, February, 24, 2002, 18.

12. Steven Thomma, "Gore Breaks His Silence, Criticizes President Bush," *Cincinnati Enquirer*, April 14, 2002, A12.

13. Will Lester, "Gore Says He's Out of 2004 Race," *Cincinnati Enquirer*, December 16, 2002, A1.

14. Peter Savodnik, "Two GOP Moves Would Hinder McCain Run," *The Hill*, January 31, 2006, 8.

15. Dan Balz, "Going A-Courting: McCain Woos Bush Loyalists for a Possible '08 Run," *The Washington Post National Weekend Edition*, February 20–26, 2006, 10.

16. Balz, "Going A-Courting.

17. Stuart Rothenberg, "Will the Second Time Be the Charm for John Edwards?" *Roll Call*, May 16, 2005, 8.

18. Alexander Bolton, "Maybe We Should Call It Would-be President's Day: Hopefuls for 2008 Head to Cash Hubs and Battleground," *The Hill*, February 22, 2006, 1, 6.

19. Bolton, "Maybe We Should Call It Would-be President's Day."

20. Bolton, "Maybe We Should Call It Would-be President's Day."

21. Michael Oreskes, "President Bush; He's a New Man Now, Thanks to the Press," *New York Times*, January 22, 1989.

22. Judith S. Trent, "The Beginning and the Early End," in *The 1996 Presidential Campaign: A Communication Perspective*, ed. Robert E. Denton Jr., 56 (Westport, Conn.: Praeger, 1998).

23. Carey Goldberg, "Remember Homely Abe, Forbes Says," *New York Times*, January 30, 2000, 20.

24. Jacob Weisberg, "Making Sure Black Minds Are Never Wasted," *Los Angeles Times*, November 15, 1992, 3.

25. Murray Edelman, *The Symbolic Uses of Politics* (Urbana: University of Illinois Press, 1964).

26. Dudley Clendinen, "Robertson Gets Conditions for Making a Run in 1988," *New York Times*, September 18, 1986, D1.

27. Gronbeck, "The Functions of Presidential Campaigning," 271.

28. Harold Meyerson, "Gephardt Goes Universal," *Washington Post National Weekly Edition*, May 5, 2003, 26.

29. Trent, "The Beginning and the Early End," 56.

30. Trent, "The Beginning and the Early End," 55.

31. David E. Rosenbaum, "Hatch Is the Latest to Dream a Senator's Dream," *New York Times*, October 3, 1999, 25.

32. Judith S. Trent, "Surfacing in 2004: The Democrats Emerge," in *The 2004 Presidential Campaign: A Communication Perspective*, ed. Robert E. Denton Jr., 1–28 (Lanham, Md.: Rowman & Littlefield, 2005).

33. F. Christopher Arterton, "The Media Politics of Presidential Campaigns: A Study of the Carter Nomination Drive," in *Race for the Presidency*, ed. James David Barber, 26 (Englewood Cliffs, N.J.: Prentice Hall, 1978).

34. Thomas Rosenstiel, *Strange Bedfellows* (New York: Hyperion, 1993), 51.

35. William R. Keech and Donald R. Matthews, *The Party's Choice* (Washington, D.C.: Brookings Institution, 1976), 91.

36. Trent, "The Beginning and the Early End," 65.

37. John Nichols, "Racing into 2004: The Primaries Are in Full Swing," *Nation*, February 17, 2003, 16–17.

38. Trent, "Surfacing in 2004."

39. Trent, "Surfacing in 2004."

40. William G. Mayer, ed., *The Making of the Presidential Candidates 2004* (New York: Rowman & Littlefield, 2004).

41. Adam Clymer, "Reagan's Fortunes in Iowa Caucuses Appear to Hang on His Organization," *New York Times*, January 13, 1980, A13.

42. Peter Goldman and Thomas Mathews, "Manhattan Project: 1992," *Newsweek*, Special Election Issue, November/December 1992, 40–41.

43. Jeffrey Schmalz, "Brown, in New York, Assails Clinton with a New Ferocity," *New York Times*, March 23, 1992, A1.

44. Gwen Ifill, "Bruised Clinton Tries to Regain New York Poise," *New York Times*, April 5, 1992, A1.

45. Ifill, "Bruised Clinton."

46. Goldman and Mathews, "Manhattan Project: 1992," 40–41.

47. Trent, "The Early Campaign," 59.

48. Trent, "The Beginning and the Early End," 61.

49. In studying the effects of the media on the 1976 presidential campaign, Patterson found that, even in the final stages of the campaign, intense partisanship and overtly partisan media communication did not override early impressions. In fact, in 80 percent of the cases analyzed by Patterson, he found that any single impression of a candidate held during the general election was related more closely to earlier impressions of the candidate than to partisanship. Those people who thought favorably of a candidate's background, personality, leadership, or positions before the conventions also thought favorably about the candidate in these areas after the conventions, regardless of partisan leanings. See Thomas E. Patterson, *The Mass Media Election* (New York: Praeger, 1980), 133–52.

50. Trent, "Surfacing in 2004."

51. Samuel L. Becker, "Rhetorical Studies for the Contemporary World," in *The Prospect of Rhetoric: Report of the National Developmental Project*, ed. Lloyd F. Bitzer and Edwin Black, 21–43 (Englewood Cliffs, N.J.: Prentice Hall, 1971).

52. Gronbeck talks about five classes of consummatory effects in "The Functions of Presidential Campaigning," 272. See also Jay G. Blumer and Elihu Katz, eds., *The Uses of Mass Communication* (Beverly Hills, Calif.: Sage, 1974). For further discussion of the uses and gratifications perspective, see Jay G. Blumer, "The Role of Theory in Uses and Gratifications Studies," *Communication Research* 6 (January 1979): 9–36.

53. Patterson, *The Mass Media Election*, 67–75.

54. Matthew Robert Kerbel, "The Media: Old Frames in a Time of Transition," in *The Elections of 2000*, ed. Michael Nelson, 113 (Washington, D.C.: CQ Press, 2001).

55. Robert Tanner, "The Presidential Primaries Shrink," *Cincinnati Enquirer*, November 10, 2003, 1.

56. Robert E. Denton Jr., "Communication Variables and Dynamics of the 1996 Presidential Campaign," in *The 1996 Presidential Campaign: A Communication Perspective*, ed. Denton, 22 (Westport, Conn.: Praeger, 1998).

57. Trent, "The Beginning and the Early End," 53.

58. L. Patrick Devlin, "Contrasts in Presidential Campaign Commercials of 2000," *American Behavioral Scientist* 44, no. 12 (August 2001): 2340.

59. David B. Valley, "Significant Characteristics of Democratic Presidential Nomination Acceptance Speeches," *Central States Speech Journal* 25 (Spring 1974): 56–62.

60. Samuel L. Becker and Elmer W. Lower, "Broadcasting in Presidential Campaigns," in *The Great Debates*, ed. Sidney Kraus, 25–55 (Bloomington: Indiana University Press, 1962).

61. Becker and Lower, "Broadcasting in Presidential Campaigns," 45.

62. Denton, "Communication Variables and Dynamics of the 1996 Presidential Campaign," 52.

63. Rachel L. Holloway, "Political Conventions of 2004: A Study in Character and Contrast," in *The 2004 Presidential Campaign*, ed. Robert E. Denton Jr., 29–73 (Lanham, Md.: Rowman & Littlefield, 2005).

64. Holloway, "Political Conventions of 2004."

65. Gary Gumpert, "The Critic in Search of a Convention or Diogenes in Madison Square Garden," *Exetasis* 6 (October 1980): 5.

66. Gumpert, "The Critic," 5.

67. Keech and Matthews, *The Party's Choice*, 92.

68. Robert E. Denton Jr., ed., *The 1992 Presidential Campaign: A Communication Perspective* (Westport, Conn.: Praeger, 1994), 87.

69. Kathleen Edgerton Kendall, "Fission and Fusion: Primaries and the Convention," paper presented at the Central State Speech Association, Chicago, 1981.

70. "Changing Times May Make Old-Style Conventions Obsolete," *Cincinnati Enquirer*, August 14, 1980, C3.

71. Kurt W. Ritter, "American Political Rhetoric and the Jeremiad Tradition: Presidential Nomination Acceptance Addresses, 1960–1976," *Central States Speech Journal* 31 (Fall 1980): 153–71.

72. "'What's Right with This Country' Is GOP Theme," *Cincinnati Enquirer*, August 20, 1984, A1.

73. Mary E. Stuckey, "One Nation (Pretty Darn) Divisible: National Identity in the 2004 Conventions," *Rhetoric and Public Affairs* 8, no. 4 (Winter 2005): 639–56.

74. Stuckey, "One Nation (Pretty Darn) Divisible."

75. Ritter, "American Political Rhetoric," 170.

76. Maureen Dowd, "OK on the Self-Realization; What about the Economy?" *New York Times*, July 27, 1992, A1.

77. Jack W. Germond and Jules Witcover, *Mad as Hell: Revolt at the Ballot Box, 1992* (New York: Warner, 1993), 337.

78. Germond and Witcover, *Mad as Hell*, 416.

79. Germond and Witcover, *Mad as Hell*, 408.

80. David M. Timmerman and Larry David Smith, "The 1992 Presidential Nominating Conventions: Cordial Concurrence Revisited," in *The 1992 Presidential Campaign*, ed. Denton, 70.

81. Timmerman and Smith, "The 1992 Presidential Nominating Conventions," 71.

82. When Ford issued his challenge to Carter, he was trailing badly in the polls and needed something to give a boost to his campaign. As Bitzer and Rueter point out, Ford chose a prime moment at the convention to announce his intention to debate. In his speech accepting the nomination, Ford was aggressive and confident, and, when he challenged Carter to a debate, the convention audience gave sustained applause. See Lloyd Bitzer and Theodore Rueter, *Carter vs. Ford: The Counterfeit Debates of 1976* (Madison: University of Wisconsin Press, 1980).

83. George Bush, "Acceptance Address, Republican National Convention, August 18, 1988," *New York Times*, August 19, 1988, A14.

84. "Clinton/Gore: 'New Covenant' for a New Generation," *Daily Report Card*, July 17, 1992, May 3, 1999; available at web.lexis.nexis.com/universe/.

85. Holloway, "Political Conventions of 2004."

86. Ryan Lizza, "Inside the Kerry Rewrite Operation," *New Republic*, August 9, 2004, 10.

87. Holloway, "Political Conventions of 2004."

88. Holloway, "Political Conventions of 2004."

89. Holloway, "Political Conventions of 2004."

90. This phrase is borrowed from Edwin Black, "Electing Time," *Quarterly Journal of Speech* 58 (April 1973): 125–29.

91. Albert E. Gollin, "Exploring the Liaison between Polling and the Press," *Public Opinion Quarterly* 44 (Winter 1980): 451.

92. Gronbeck, "Presidential Campaigning," 272.

93. Gronbeck, "Presidential Campaigning," 273.

3

∾

Communicative Styles and Strategies of Political Campaigns

One of the central imperatives of political campaign communication is the whole notion of the manner in which incumbents seek reelection and their challengers seek to replace them—in other words, the style and strategies used by candidates as they campaign. Campaign styles have undergone significant changes over the years. There have been, for example, elections when candidates campaigned by staying home and saying nothing. There have been others when the contenders "swung around the circle" on anything from trains to jets to riverboats to buses in an effort to draw attention to themselves and to be seen and heard by as many voters as possible. And we can each recall instances of campaigns that have been waged primarily by means of the mass media. In short, there has been no one way in which local, state, or national contenders have gone about the task of getting our vote. Strategies have been as varied and sometimes outrageous as those who have used them. Perhaps because of this, there has been relatively little systematic investigation or analysis of the communicative strategies and styles that have been, and continue to be, used by all manner of incumbents and challengers.

Thus, the subject of this chapter is the exploration of campaign styles. While it may be that readers are more interested in contemporary examples, the present is better understood when viewed from the perspective of the past. For this reason, examples from nineteenth- and early-twentieth-century campaigns have been incorporated, thereby providing a more complete catalog of the communication strategies important to all who have sought and those who will seek elective office.

Understanding of the material in this chapter is enhanced by an examination of three preliminary considerations that are important to the way in which candidates campaign. A consideration of the term *style* is first. Second is a discussion of political image and its role in developing campaign styles. Third is an exploration of the relationship of technological advancements to styles of campaigning.

PRELIMINARY CONSIDERATIONS

Style

For many years, style has been studied by scholars who are interested in the customs and rules governing the use of language, including the choice of words (figures of speech) and the way the words are arranged (syntactical patterns) in oral and written communication. Although controversy over its meaning occurred historically because some believed style was divorced from content and only a frill or ornamentation, the conception of style as the peculiar manner in which people express themselves by means of language has been generally accepted. In other words, style traditionally has been the province of those concerned with the correctness, beauty, or even workability of language—the investigation or analysis of the words and arrangements a speaker or writer chooses in preparing a message. Thus, one of the elements to be considered in the analysis of campaign style is the language that political candidates use as they campaign.

More recently, however, communication theorists have argued that style should not be limited to the language but ought to be considered a quality pervading all elements of an individual's communication. Considered in this way, style would include each of the nonverbal aspects of communication—including physical behavior, sound of the voice, body shape and movement, appearance, clothing, and choice of settings—that operate as symbols to create the meanings we infer from the transaction. In written messages, a number of symbols (in addition to language) create meaning, such as the quality, texture, size, and color of the paper and whether it is handwritten or typed for one particular person or printed and prepared for distribution to many. Thus, in election campaigns, style can be seen as a blend of what candidates say—in speeches, news conferences, websites, talk show interviews, advertisements, brochures, and so on—as well as their nonverbal political acts or behavior, such as kissing babies, wearing funny hats, shaking hands at rallies, waving at crowds from the motorcade, and their facial expressions and gestures while answering a question. It is what Bruce Gronbeck terms a question of "leadership style"—a combination of habitual modes of thought and action on which individuals perceive or judge a candidate.[1]

What does any of this have to do with our analysis of campaign styles and strategies? In this chapter, style is a manner of campaigning that can be recognized by the characteristics defining it and giving it form. We have termed these characteristics "communication strategies" and the styles "incumbency," "challenger," and the combined "incumbent/challenger." Certainly, in describing each of the styles we have been concerned with the traditional dimension of language; but as you have seen in the first two chapters, we believe strongly that political campaign communication is much more than just "talk." Thus, as the styles are explored, it will become obvious that many of the characteristics deal with nonverbal political behaviors as well as verbal.

Image and Campaign Style

Imagery plays an important role in the consideration of style. All candidates, whether they campaign using the strategies of incumbency or those of the challenger, must do and say whatever it is that will enhance voter perception of them. They are concerned, in other words, about their image.

Although widespread awareness regarding the significance of image creation to the political campaign did not occur until the early 1970s, it had been used for years. The first major image campaign took place in the presidential campaign of 1840 when the Whigs, after searching for a candidate they thought could defeat Martin Van Buren, found no one. So they invented a national hero, gave him a slogan, said he was champion of the ordinary citizen as well as a giant of the frontier, and elected a president.[2] When William Henry Harrison was "discovered" by the Whigs, he was sixty-seven years old, serving as clerk of courts of Hamilton County, Ohio, a long-retired army officer, and he had spent twelve years in Congress and three years as ambassador to Colombia.

While military and legislative experience must be considered reasonable credentials for a presidential challenger, Harrison's career had been distinctly undistinguished. The Whigs, however, billed Harrison as a legendary Indian fighter and maintained that he was known widely and fondly as "Old Tippecanoe." The Whig campaign ignored all issues, except those relating to the personality of their candidates, and gave image creation and "hype" a permanent place in presidential politics. When Democrats suggested that the aging Harrison might be content to spend his declining days in a log cabin "studying moral philosophy"—provided he had a barrel of hard cider at his side—the Whigs cleverly turned the attack into a reinforcement of Harrison's contrived image as a "common

man."[3] From then on, every Whig rally sported cider barrels and minia-
ture log cabins, and songs were written and sung celebrating Harrison's
humble tastes (the idea being that if logs and liquor were good enough for
the people, they were also good enough for the president). Lyrics from
one of the campaign songs best describe the image created by the Whigs:

> No ruffled shirt, no silken hose,
> No airs does Tip display;
> But like the "pitch of worth" he goes
> In homespun "hodding gray."
> Let Van from his coolers of silver drink wine
> And lounge on his cushioned setee,
> Our man on a buckeye bench can recline
> Content with hard cider is he![4]

Image campaigns did not end with the elevation of Old Tippecanoe to
the presidency. Instead, the place of imagery became entrenched in elective politics, especially in the area of campaign style, where specific strategies must be created and utilized to keep alive the perception of an incumbent or a challenger. The Harrison campaign's visual symbol of the
log cabin represents what has come to be called "image" advertising in
politics. As political analyst Wilcomb E. Washburn argues, "The modern-
day equivalent would be the 30-second television spot commercial."[5]
   The importance of imagery is evidenced each time we see yet another
television commercial of a candidate surrounded by family, talking
earnestly with a senior citizen, walking through a peanut field, or standing in front of a sea of flags. Television commercials that present candidates in such situations are clearly designed to build or maintain certain
perceptions of the candidate. Political images, however, are more complex than simply the strategies devised to present a candidate to voters.
Images should also be considered in terms of the impressions voters
have—what they believe to be true or untrue, desirable or undesirable
about the candidates and the campaign. As Kenneth E. Boulding writes
in his classic book, *The Image*, each of us possesses a store of subjective
knowledge about the world, a collection of ideas we believe to be true.
This knowledge constitutes our image.[6] While in recent years the work
of a number of researchers has served to broaden the perspective by
which scholars as well as practitioners view image, nonetheless, it is
generally understood that the strategies candidates use to construct a
public persona constitute an important area of political communication
inquiry. We believe, however, that, despite the importance of a candidate's role in the creation of a public perception, it is only part of the
equation. In his doctoral dissertation on the construction of image in television spot commercials, Allan Louden argues that image is "more than

the message projected by a candidate or even a picture created by a voter. Image is an evaluation negotiated and constructed by candidates and voters in a cooperative venture."[7] In other words, beliefs voters have about candidates are based on the interaction or interdependence of what candidates do and the evaluative responses voters have to it: a "transaction between a candidate and voter."[8] The view of image as a transaction, however, raises questions of balance or proportion between the strategies used by a candidate to create an image and the ideas already believed by the voter. Is one more important to the creation of persona than the other? Is one more likely to influence voter behavior than the other? Generally, researchers believe that one dimension does not necessarily play a more pivotal role than the other. People have some preconceived ideas regarding what a candidate's personal characteristics and behavior should be, and these ideas are continually measured against the reality of what an actual candidate says and does during the campaign. In this way, voters define the campaign for themselves—sorting through competing or contradictory messages. However, there are circumstances in which the balance between the idealized and actual can be disrupted. For example, the context in which the campaign occurs can become the dominating force—the Vietnam War during the 1972 election and the war on terror in 2004. In each instance, the images of the candidates were framed by an all-consuming event that in some instances overshadowed the candidates' strategies to build an image and in others overcame voters' preconceptions of the "ideal" candidate.

It is also possible that a single and dramatic campaign event can tip the scale one way or the other. During the surfacing period of the 1988 presidential campaign, Senator Gary Hart's alleged relationship with a Miami model, his challenge to the media to prove the relationship, the public accusation by reporters from the *Miami Herald*, and the subsequent intensity of national media attention completely overwhelmed anything else Hart said or did. No image strategies the senator might have utilized could have competed with public preconceptions about the way in which candidates who would be president should behave and the contrast of this with Hart's alleged behavior. And in 1984 when Geraldine Ferraro was nominated by the Democratic Party for vice president, we believe that there was very little the congresswoman could have said or done to have created a public persona favorable enough to refute the preconceptions of some Americans regarding the personal characteristics or attributes vice presidents are expected to possess. She, in fact, did not look or sound like—she did not resemble—a vice presidential nominee. Thus, for some voters the fact of Ferraro's gender created an imbalance between imaging determinants.

Even though imbalance regarding the way in which people organize their thoughts about politics can occur, nonetheless, a consistent finding after years of research indicates that we share a lot of beliefs about the personal qualities candidates ought to possess—especially presidential candidates. Moreover, these characteristics are strongly associated with voting preferences and, in most cases, dominate ideas (cognitions) about the candidates and the campaign.[9] These personal qualities or attributes tend to cluster around such leadership characteristics as competency, experience, trustworthiness, ability to be calm, cautiousness, decisiveness, and boldness[10] and closely related personality characteristics such as strength, honesty, fairness, open-mindedness, reliability, energy, and physical attractiveness.[11] Whether or not a candidate exists who embodies all of these attributes is almost immaterial in that we use the characteristics as a basis of comparison—a standard—by which to judge the acceptability of the flesh-and-blood women and men actually seeking our votes. As voters, we may ask ourselves whether the candidate campaigns as an incumbent should or whether the challenger fulfills our expectations.

Viewed from this perspective, the reason for two common campaign activities becomes clear. First, one of the most crucial tasks facing candidates, especially during the surfacing stage, is to determine just what attributes voters believe are ideal for the office sought. Second, campaign activities in later stages are designed to attempt to illustrate that the candidate possesses these qualities.

Although we know that voter assessment of a candidate's image is a significant factor in voting behavior (far more important, for example, than party identification) and that voters have a mental picture of an ideal candidate that they use as a gauge in evaluating actual candidates, it is less clear whether these characteristics vary among candidates and across election levels. In other words, are all candidates competing in the same race judged by the same preconceived attributes, and are the dimensions of "idealness" the same for candidates running for local offices as they are for those campaigning for president? While scholars studying the political campaigns of the 1970s into the twenty-first century have provided few absolutes, some evidence indicates that the relative importance of particular clusters of characteristics has remained fairly constant from presidential election to election. For example, in a study spanning across four New Hampshire presidential primary cycles, Judith Trent and colleagues found that most characteristics voters believe important for presidential candidates to possess (honesty, faithfulness to spouse, and moral integrity) remain constant. In 2000, as contrasted with 1996, the New Hampshire voters who were surveyed had some change of mind about the importance of just two characteristics: The capability to talk about problems facing the country was less important to them in 2000 than it had been in 1996, and interpersonal characteristics were more important than they had been in 1996.[12] However, in 2004 New Hampshire voters believed that the most important characteristics were, first, that the candidate be honest, second, that he or she talk about the nation's problems and, third, that he or she possess moral character.[13]

At this point, it is uncertain whether questions regarding preconceived image characteristics are important in local races where the attributes and idiosyncrasies of the candidates as well as their positions on the relevant issues are well known. However, in a study in 1998 of one of the image characteristics, physical attractiveness, in which subjects were told that the pictures they viewed were of candidates in local and congressional races, Jimmie Trent and coresearchers found that physical attractiveness on initial candidate selection was an asset. In every case, across race, gender, and age, subjects preferred the most physically attractive candidates.[14]

Obviously, further research is needed before we can say with any degree of certainty that voter expectations either do or do not vary across candidates and across election levels. One thing, though, is clear. The creation and maintenance of image, long a part of political campaigns, plays a dominant role because voters have a whole series of impressions regarding the behavior of those who seek elective office that they compare with a personal vision of an ideal candidate. And although other factors are important to the consideration of campaign style, it may well be that the extent to which a candidate is able to achieve these idealized expectations is the extent to which success can be achieved on election day.

Technology and Campaign Style

During the earliest period of our electoral system, the style of political campaigning was, at least in part, defined by the limits of our transportation system. This is one of the reasons that there were no national political campaigns as we think of them today. While it is true that in 1789 and again in 1792 George Washington had no opposition, it would have been difficult for him to conduct a national campaign even had it been necessary for him to do so. Travel was difficult, uncomfortable, and time-consuming. Even in 1800, when the Jeffersonian Democratic-Republicans launched the first activity that could be called a presidential campaign, it was not a national or even a regional effort. The rallies, parades, and leaflets were not nationally planned but the work of individual county and state political committees. The national road system, begun in Maryland in 1808, was the chief east-west artery, and it did not reach even the Ohio border until 1817. Commercial water travel started in 1807, but it took many days just to go from Pittsburgh to New York City. Therefore, the presidential election of 1824 was the first one in which any real mass campaigning took place. Friends of the three candidates (John Quincy Adams, Henry Clay, and Andrew Jackson) traveled within their own and neighboring states to campaign for the presidential contenders.

Although the Baltimore and Ohio Railroad began in 1829, it was 1853 before the tracks reached the Mississippi River and 1869 before the transcontinental railroad system was completed in Ogden, Utah. By 1854, although the transportation system had improved, it still took thirty hours to travel from Indianapolis to Cleveland by rail and twenty-four hours from Chicago to St. Louis. Thus, it is small wonder that 1840 was the first time a political party conducted a national campaign by sending speakers to then all twenty-six states or that 1860 was the first time a presidential candidate traveled throughout the north campaigning for his own election. Moreover, it was not until 1896, after railroads serviced most of the nation and automobile production had begun, that a presidential challenger, William Jennings Bryan, was able to "whirl" through twenty-one states, give six hundred speeches, and be seen by five million people.

Developments in the transportation network continued to affect the style of political campaigning. For example, the beginning of air travel in the 1920s allowed Franklin Roosevelt to fly to Chicago to accept the Democratic presidential nomination in 1932, just as the initiation of commercial jet service in 1959 afforded Richard Nixon and John Kennedy the opportunity to conduct "jet-stop" campaigns in 1960.

However, by the middle of the nineteenth century, a second factor had become important to the development of campaign style. With the invention of the telegraph in 1835, a communication network was able to transcend those of transportation because messages were able to move at the speed of electrical impulses rather than the speed of humans, horses, boats, or trains.[15] Moreover, the emergence of the telephone in 1876, wireless telegraph and the motion picture camera in 1895, commercial radio in 1920, and motion pictures with sound in 1927 allowed the public to "bypass the written word and extend communication senses and capabilities directly."[16] Communication scholar Frederick Williams has written that "speech and images could now span distances, be preserved in time, and be multiplied almost infinitely."[17]

Even the first advances in the communication network began to influence political campaigning. For example, one of the primary issues of the 1848 presidential campaign was the almost two-year war with Mexico. The Whigs selected one of the war's heroes, General Zachary Taylor, as their candidate. The principal reason the war could become important to the campaign was that the initiation of commercial telegraph service in 1844 and the subsequent founding of the Associated Press Wire Service had provided far more rapid news than the country had ever known. Citizens were aware of specific battles and vigorously applauded each victory over the Mexicans. In other words, the telegraph was able to inject the war into the campaign with an immediacy not known before.

By the campaign of 1884, the telegraph had so unified the nation's communication system that, as James G. Blaine unwittingly discovered, even one election eve gaffe could be telegraphed across the country and influence election returns. The day before the election, a Republican clergyman denounced the Democratic candidate, Grover Cleveland, by saying that his party was the party of "Rum, Romanism, and Rebellion." Republican candidate Blaine failed to disavow the statement and therefore lost the support of Irish Catholic voters. Another thousand votes in New York, a stronghold of Irish Catholics, would have elected him.

Although each early communication development had some influence on political campaigning, certainly the most dramatic were the changes brought about by radio. Beginning in 1921, when President Warren Harding first used the new medium to talk to the public, the radio became the nation's most important means of political communication. It remained so until the widespread use of television in 1952.[18] Radio had a direct effect on campaign style because it made the personal appearances of candidates less necessary by providing an option. For the first time, candidates (even unknown ones) could become public personalities without campaigning around the country. In 1924, William McAdoo, a contender for the Democratic presidential nomination, hoped to establish a radio station powerful enough to reach all parts of the country so that he would not have to travel around the nation making speeches.[19] Although McAdoo never put his plan into action, losing the nomination to John W. Davis, subsequent candidates did. In 1928, Republican contender Herbert Hoover undertook only a few public appearances. Rather, he made seven radio speeches the focal point of his campaign. In 1936, 1940, and 1944, incumbent Franklin Roosevelt used radio extensively so that he could reach the entire nation without traveling.[20]

Thus, the early achievements in electronic media had a profound effect on the manner of political campaigning. Although many innovations have occurred, those that have had some direct effect on campaign style include the beginning of scheduled television broadcasts in 1941, the first electronic computer in 1942, the beginning of color television in 1951, the introduction of portable video recorders in 1968, the widespread use of microelectronic chips in 1970, the perfected development of fiber-optic signal transmission in 1975, the popularity of home computers in 1980, the use of cable television in 1984, the widespread use of videocassettes and satellite transmissions in 1988,[21] the use of online computer networks and bulletin boards in 1992, the use of candidate listservs and online home pages in 1996, and the increased interactivity of candidates' websites with voters in 2000.

In 1999, the Missouri Republican Party, in an ultimately successful effort to elect Susan C. Phillips to the state House of Representatives, used Map Applications software to target three thousand voters with personal appeals via information received from public records, phone interviews, and computer-assisted surveys. In 2000, Hillary Rodham Clinton's New York senatorial campaign found a new way to get up-to-date information about constituents to the candidate and her speechwriters. Campaign volunteers called voters and requested their participation in answering a questionnaire regarding their views on selected issues and personal backgrounds. Participant responses were then faxed to a computer and recorded and then digitally sent to another computer to be sorted for an overnight report. The report about voters' positions as well as information regarding the success and weaknesses of the campaign were sent to the campaign staff. Thus, as Rodham Clinton campaigned, each day she had the most recent information possible about the issues important to each audience as well as some knowledge about "who they were" for each audience she addressed.

In the largest sense, television, as radio had done earlier, increased the number of campaign strategies available because candidates no longer had to be dependent on extensive national speaking tours to become well known to the public. A few nationwide television speeches, a series of well-executed and well-placed advertising spots, an appearance on one of the news/issues programs such as *Meet the Press*, campaign coverage on the evening network news broadcasts, and several appearances on the popular talk shows guaranteed public awareness. In addition, television, unlike radio, enhanced campaign swings by showing parts of them in evening news broadcasts. Although the candidate might go to one state or region of the country to campaign in person, millions of people across the country participated in the rally or parade by watching the pageantry from their own living rooms. Not only did a television campaign provide candidates with more exposure, but it also allowed for more flexibility in the management of physical and financial resources. Perhaps the essence of the mass media strategy of the late 1960s and the 1970s is explained best in a memorandum written by H. R. Haldeman (and interpreted by Theodore White), in which he outlined the plan for Richard Nixon's 1968 presidential campaign:

> Americans no longer gather in the streets to hear candidates; they gather at their television sets or where media assemble their attention. A candidate cannot storm the nation; at most he can see and let his voice be heard by no more than a million or two people in a Presidential year (the reach of the individual

campaigner doesn't add up to diddly-squat in votes). One minute or thirty seconds on the evening news shows of Messrs. Cronkite or Huntley/Brinkley will reach more people than ten months of barnstorming. One important favorable Washington column is worth more than two dozen press releases or position papers. News magazines like *Time* or *Newsweek*, picture magazines like *Life* and *Look* are media giants worth a hundred outdoor rallies. Therefore the candidate must not waste time storming the country, personally pleading for votes—no matter what he does, he can appear in newsprint or on television only once a day. The inner strength and vitality of the candidate must not be wasted; if you do more than one thing a day, you make a mistake. If you test a man's physical strength too far, you push him beyond the realm of good judgment; both candidate and the following press must be given time to stop, rest, reflect and write. The importance of old-style-outdoor campaigning now lies less in what the candidate tells the people than in what he learns from them with the important secondary value that outdoor exertions do provide the vital raw stuff for television cameras.[22]

Although 1968 was not the first time television had been used extensively in a campaign, it was the first time that a presidential candidate had planned his entire candidacy around the medium. Richard Nixon not only used technology to help him win an election but added an important dimension to campaign style—one that extended, in fact, to 1992 when Ross Perot became the nation's first true mass media presidential contender. Perot bypassed political parties, primaries, and traditional campaigning. Instead, he relied exclusively on television and computer technology.

In a similar fashion, the computer has made a profound impact on the manner of political campaigning since the 1980s. Its speed in information processing and its ability to allow web-based interaction between the candidates and voters in the 2000 and 2004 elections, as well as its ability to automate many of our methods of information analysis, have provided candidates with an invaluable resource in such traditional tasks as identifying and communicating with specific publics or raising funds.

Computer technology has also been enormously beneficial to the media. For example, on September 15, 1987, "The Presidential Campaign Hotline" went online. The hotline is a computer network that transmits campaign information each morning to subscribers (many of them are media outlets) for a monthly fee. The purpose of the service is to keep subscribers fully appraised of developments in the race for the White House, such as late-breaking news of events in the field; forwarding news stories, editorials, and columns from influential periodicals and local newspapers in battleground states; and up-to-the-minute analysis from assorted campaign experts. The hotline's practice of carrying daily reports from each presidential campaign press secretary has also created a unique opportunity for each campaign to determine and circulate its own interpretation of events (spin control) before such events have had the chance to make an impact on their own.[23] Thus, direct mail, instant voter prediction and analysis, and the campaign hotline are all part of the new politics facilitated by the computer.

But just as important as the past are the possibilities for the future—some of which have already been experienced in the campaigns of the 1990s and 2000s. Such communication technologies as the computer, cable television service, push-button telephones, videocassettes, and video disks have already or could completely change the nature of campaigns by allowing voters to interact with the candidate from their own living rooms. In other words, instead of a candidate simply stating a position on an issue to a mass audience during a television speech, debate, or interview, the candidate could ask a question and invite comments. Large numbers of viewers could press buttons on their television sets, phones, or computers and respond immediately to the candidate. This rapid and somewhat personal interaction might allow candidates the opportunity for repositioning their ideas and might also encourage voters to modify or change their beliefs regarding the candidate.[24]

Obviously, the effect on campaign style would be enormous. Incumbents and challengers alike could have the benefits of person-to-person campaigning without ever leaving the television studio or their office. In addition, the determination of public opinion on a given issue would no longer be subject to the intervention of a third party (e.g., pollsters or the press). Mass media campaigning would, in effect, become true two-way communication.

Although interactive television has not yet been a part of a candidate's communication strategy, by the 1988 presidential election, it had spilled over to elective politics. During the Democratic Iowa caucus debates, eighty-seven participants were linked to a computer by a small box with a dial. As they watched the candidates' debate, participants were asked to register continuously their feelings about the speakers by moving the dial on a rising scale of one to seven on traits such as leadership, speaking ability, experience, and qualifications.[25] By the midterm elections of 1994, congresspersons, state and local government officials, and the Democratic and Republican national committees were communicating on computerized bulletin boards. Online campaigning is inexpensive and extremely time-efficient. In addition, voters have direct access and interaction with representatives and candidates in cyberspace without the filter of the media.

In 1992 and 1996, and again in 2000, the major television networks (ABC, CBS, and NBC) cut their investment in covering the early campaign. As the data from a tracking study by the Center for Public Affairs illustrated, in the year 2000, the evening news programs of NBC, CBS, and

ABC together "ran 576 stories about the election over fifteen and a half hours of prime news time. During the comparable period in 1996 they had aired 737 stories over twenty-two and three-quarters hours."[26] Perhaps network coverage was reduced because of what appears to be a decline in public interest in network news programs. A 1998 survey from the Pew Research Center showed that the number of Americans who regularly watch the nightly news on ABC, CBS, and NBC declined from 60 percent in 1993 to 38 percent in 1998.[27]

The reduction in network coverage paved the way for a new kind of presidential campaign coverage in the 1990s and 2000s, one in which non-traditional popular culture media grew in importance. For candidates, the popular media formats presented opportunities not experienced in the past. For example, talk show hosts or citizens who called in asked questions that were much "softer" than those typically asked by the national media. Moreover, there were rarely follow-up questions, and, even when there were, no established journalist was there to push the candidate on evasions, contradictions, or half-truths.[28] There were also instances in presidential elections since 1992 in which small media operations set the agenda for major network news by printing a sensationalized story—for example, the allegations of Paula Jones that, while governor of Arkansas, Bill Clinton made unwanted sexual advances toward her first broke in the tabloids, or the report from a Maine television station during the last five days of the 2000 campaign that, when George W. Bush was thirty, he had been arrested while driving in Maine and had pleaded guilty to a misdemeanor charge of driving while intoxicated. And in 2004, both Republican and Democratic candidates had a brush with the tabloids. President Bush went under fire for his military record while Senator Kerry, according to the tabloids, did not appear to be the military hero he claimed to be. Such stories provoked candidate response and thus made coverage of the story "necessary" for the mainstream news media. It may well be that such mainstream news coverage of "interesting" versus "important" stories, as well as the increased dominance of popular culture media, has contributed to a growing public skepticism about the trustworthiness of the press. A 1998 *Newsweek* poll found that 42 percent of those surveyed believe only some of what they read and hear in the news media.[29] (Credibility is also an issue with the Internet in that 58 percent of Internet users believe most online information is accurate and reliable, whereas only one-third perceive half of the information as credible.)

One more difference regarding the use of media, which began in 1996 and continued in the 2000 and 2004 election campaigns, was that candidates came to recognize the potential of the local news stations. Beginning with New Hampshire, candidates did many of their satellite interviews with the anchors and reporters of local stations rather than with network commentators and journalists. They were able to do so because the networks could no longer control all of the pictures taken by their camera crews. For years, CBS, NBC, and ABC had refused to distribute pictures of national news events to their local stations until such pictures had first appeared in network newscasts. With the arrival of CNN, and later the Fox Network and MSNBC, this policy began to change. To make a profit, the cable networks started selling their pictures to local stations throughout the world.

Another technology that has made an impact on political campaigning is the proliferation of household videocassette recorders (VCRs). The practice of distributing campaign videos to provide primarily biographic information and to aid in fund-raising started with George H. W. Bush's 1980 effort in the Republican primaries. Beginning in the 1988 campaign and continuing through the 2000 campaign, each of the presidential hopefuls produced videos that were designed to introduce themselves to voters in the early primary and caucus states and to serve as vehicles for fund-raising. For example, Bob Dole's biographical video, entitled "Bob Dole: An American Hero," pictured his hometown, friends, and family members, as well as the struggles he endured, including his war wounds and his family's poverty. The biographical video used to introduce Al Gore for his acceptance speech at the 2000 Democratic Nominating Convention was composed primarily of pictures taken by his wife Tipper Gore. But as videos can be used to build a candidate's public persona, so, too, can they undo or destroy an opponent's credibility. This power was graphically demonstrated during the 1988 surfacing period when Senator Joseph Biden of Delaware, a Democratic presidential contender, "borrowed" a stirring soliloquy from British Labour Party leader Neil Kinnock without crediting him. Shortly after Biden gave the speech, the *New York Times* received an "attack video" showing the Biden and the Kinnock speeches back-to-back. The *Times* ran the story on page 1, and the video was shown on the evening newscasts. The video set in motion a chain of events that within eleven days drove Biden from the race.

The Internet is another technological innovation that is having a major influence on the way in which candidates seek our votes. And because it has become such an important new means of campaigning we discuss it in detail in chapter 11. Although it is impossible to know just what impact new technologies will ultimately have on political campaigns in the future, as we have seen before, innovations in transportation and communication have an infinite capacity to alter the strategies that candidates use to seek political office. As such, they are an important consideration in any examination of campaign style.

STYLES AND STRATEGIES OF CAMPAIGNS

Essentially, campaign styles are sets of communication strategies employed at times by all candidates, whether they run for president, mayor, governor, or legislator. Moreover, those who hold office may campaign in the manner of those who do not, just as those who challenge may adopt strategies of incumbency. In other words, those candidates who are incumbents are not restricted to a specific set of incumbency strategies any more than challengers are confined to a particular set of challenger strategies. In fact, candidates frequently combine strategies of one style with strategies of another so that there are times during the course of one contest where an individual contender may assume a rhetorical posture normally associated with incumbency campaigning and at other times may appear to be campaigning as a challenger. This combination may well be a result of the seasonless electoral process discussed in the first and second chapters. As candidates extend the length of the campaign, no one style is likely to remain appropriate for the duration. New events, as well as changes in conditions, force modification in the manner of pursuit. While in February an attack on the incumbent's economic policy might be appropriate, by August the situation may be different enough to make attack an inappropriate strategy. As such, it would be misleading to try to analyze style by only examining the practice of one candidate or one campaign. Styles (incumbency, challenger, and incumbent/challenger) are a product of whatever candidates and their staffs believe is needed at a particular time within the context of their particular campaign. Therefore, the best way to understand them is to determine the composition of each— that is, to catalog their strategies.

Incumbency Style

Incumbency campaigning in the United States is at least as old as the first presidential incumbent, George Washington, who ran for reelection in 1792. Its various strategies have been used by almost all who have sought election to any level of government. Given its longevity and frequent use, one might assume it would have been defined long ago and its characteristics carefully delineated. While that is not the case, incumbency has been considered a "symbolic resource"[30] and the "Rose Garden Strategy."[31] Although each idea is useful in attempting to understand what it is that candidates do and say when they appear to be "running as an incumbent," each is nonetheless incomplete. Incumbency campaigning is a blend of both symbolic and pragmatic communication strategies designed to make any candidate appear as both good enough for the office sought and possessing the office (an assumed incumbency stance). This is not an easy task. We know that image creation and maintenance take significant amounts of skill, time, and money.

But developing a credible incumbency style is well worth the effort. The results of countless elections indicate that incumbents tend to win. For example, during the twentieth century, only five presidents have lost their reelection bids; in the total history of our country 75 percent of incumbent presidents have been reelected.

Given this kind of success, it is not surprising that political scientist R. F. Fenno has suggested that incumbency is "a resource to be employed, an opportunity to be exploited."[32] The 2000 election stood out as yet another incredible year for incumbents. In the 2000 election cycle, 403 incumbents of the House of Representatives sought reelection, and all but nine won. In other words, incumbents enjoyed a 98 percent "success rate."[33] And in 2004, incumbents once again had a high success rate, including in the presidential election, with the win of the incumbent president, George W. Bush. In total, the 2004 election equaled that of 2000 with 98 percent of all incumbents winning their reelection bids.

With this understanding, we now consider the specific strategies that candidates employ when they seek the advantages of incumbency. The first four are symbolic in nature; the remaining eleven are pragmatic or instrumental.

Symbolic Strategies

In exploring the symbolic characteristics of incumbency campaigning, we are, in essence, discussing presidential candidates because there is no other elective office for which the public has the same kind of feelings. In one sense the presidency can be thought of as a focus of impressions and beliefs that exist in our mind—a kind of "collage of images, hopes, habits, and intentions shared by the nation who legitimizes the office and reacts to its occupants."[34] Viewed from a related perspective, when we speak of the presidency, we are dealing with the myth of the office, the image we have possessed since childhood of the one institution that stands for truth, honor, justice, and integrity. We have a conception of an individual and an office that in ennobling each other, ennoble us. Perhaps Theodore White described it best when he wrote:

Somewhere in American life there is at least one man who stands for law, the President. That faith surmounts all daily cynicism, all evidence or suspicion of wrong-doing by lesser leaders, all corruptions, all vulgarities, all the ugly compromises of daily striving and ambition. That faith holds that all men are created equal before the law and protected by it; and that no matter how the faith may be betrayed elsewhere, at one particular point—the Presidency—justice will be done beyond prejudice, beyond rancor, beyond the possibilities of a fix.[35]

People may debate the character, quality, and personality of the men who have filled the office, and public opinion polls may indicate dissatisfaction with the performance of an incumbent, but the presidency is, for most citizens, an idealized institution, headed by a single visible individual through whom it is possible to grasp a "cognitive handle" or an understanding of "political goings on."[36]

 In this context, then, the identity of a particular president is irrelevant; the concern is the office itself and the symbolic role it can play in a campaign.

Symbolic Trappings of the Office

The first strategy is the use of symbolic trappings to transmit the absolute strength and importance of the office. The presidency stands for power, and therefore incumbents take on the persona of the powerful. They are surrounded by large numbers of carefully trained and "important-looking" bodyguards who appear to anticipate their every move; their song (played when they enter or leave a public ceremony) is "Hail to the Chief"; incumbents are addressed by title, never by name; when they travel, a whole contingent of Secret Service, media reporters, technicians, and lesser governmental officials accompany them in a caravan of planes and limousines; their home, although the property of "the people," is heavily guarded and off limits to all who have no official business to conduct with them or their staff; incumbents can be in instant communication with the leader of any other country; they serve as commander in chief of all armed services; incumbents can command nationwide media time; and they are always close to a small black bag, the contents of which provide them the capability to blow up the world.

 Thus, it is little wonder that those who have campaigned against a president have objected to the continual and conscious use of devices that remind voters that they are seeing and hearing "the president," as opposed to "just another politician." For example, during the 1984 campaign, President Reagan changed the location of his televised press conferences. He stood before an open doorway in the East Room of the White House that reveals a long, elegant corridor. The cameras recorded a majestic setting and a stately exit that dramatized the importance of the office, and it served to remind the audience that they were listening to the president of the United States. During the Clinton years and the George W. Bush years countless bills have been signed into law in the Rose Garden of the White House with the president surrounded by admirers, legislators, and media.

Legitimacy of the Office

The second strategy involves not so much what incumbents do—that is, the use of specific tangible symbols to remind voters of their power—but an intangible tool that only they possess and about which their challengers cannot even object. The presidency stands for legitimacy, and therefore the person who holds the office is perceived as the natural and logical leader. In other words, no matter who the incumbent may be (or regardless of the incumbent's current rating in the public opinion polls), the president is accorded a kind of sociopolitical legitimacy—a public trust. As one theorist has argued, we place our faith and trust in the hands of our leaders because they project an image that seduces us into participating in the comforting illusion that, through rigid adherence to the constituted ideals of the society, they can guide us through whatever possible troubles the future might present.[37] Moreover, their position provides automatic legitimacy during a campaign in that they, unlike any of their opponents, are, from the beginning, considered legitimate candidates for the job.

Competency and the Office

The third strategy is also an intangible tool that comes with the office. The presidency stands for competency; therefore, the person who holds the office can easily convey that impression. To trust in the president's competence is to accept the incumbent as a symbol "that problems can be solved without a basic restructuring of social institutions and without the threat a radical reordering poses both to the contented and to the anxious."[38] In other words, when we attribute a sense of competency to the president, it provides us with reassurance that all can be right. We want to believe that the person who is president is capable (after all, we elected the president in the first place).

As a matter of fact, our feelings about the office itself are so strong that, whatever a specific president has done with regard to individual issues, a large number of people will always be supportive. For example, each year since World War II, every president has been ranked by U.S. citizens as one of the ten most admired persons in the world.[39] Perhaps a reason for this is, as Murray Edelman suggests, that "public issues fade from attention after a period in the limelight even when they are not 'solved' because they cannot remain dramatic and exciting for long and the media then have economic and psychological reasons to softpedal them."[40]

Goodwill is retained, for whatever reasons or in whatever manner. Our point is simply that any president possesses a sense of competency that none of his rivals can share. It is, of course, a distinct advantage of the office.

Charisma and the Office

The final symbolic strategy, like the first three, is dependent on the ability of the office to transfer its persona to the incumbent. However, this one is not an intangible resource in that it has had deliberate use since presidents began barnstorming the country for their own elections. The presidency stands for excitement, a kind of patriotic glamour, and therefore the person who holds the office takes on these characteristics. In no other way is the mystique of the presidency more visible than it is during a presidential campaign visit almost anywhere in the country. When the president comes to town (advance and security personnel have already been there for at least a week), roads are blocked, airports are closed, children are dismissed from school, bands play, television cameras and reporters are everywhere, hundreds or thousands of people converge along the streets or at the airport to greet the president; the very sight of the magnificent *Air Force One* produces a sense of awe, and, for a while, we are participants in a warm and patriotic festival. It matters little whether or not we plan to vote for the incumbent; regardless of how dull and unimaginative the president may have been before living in the White House, once there, the office itself envelops the president in its aura or charisma.

Although campaign tours were not undertaken by incumbents (at least during the election period) until Herbert Hoover paved the way, their symbolic power has not been lost on any of the presidents who have succeeded him. The reasons for their trips have been as varied as have been their modes of transportation. For example, in 1948, Harry Truman whistle-stopped his way across thirty-two thousand miles to blame what he termed the "do-nothing, good-for-nothing 80th Congress" for the nation's problems. In 1956, Dwight Eisenhower, in spite of two international crises, felt he had to undertake an extensive tour through the southern states to blunt his opponent's charges that he was too old and too sick to be president. In 1964, Lyndon Johnson barnstormed his way across the country, in part because he felt a psychological need to be "out with the people" and experience their warmth and acceptance of him. In 1976, Jimmy Carter boarded the paddlewheel riverboat *Delta Queen* and traveled the Ohio and Mississippi Rivers, campaigning at each stop, in an almost frantic effort to restore his popularity with voters. In 1984, Ronald Reagan whistle-stopped through several states riding the same presidential caboose Harry Truman rode in 1948. In 1992, over two thousand people turned out to shake hands with George H. W. Bush at a mall in Concord, New Hampshire, and to hear him explain why he should be reelected in spite of a depressed economy. In 1996, Bill Clinton's fourteen-bus caravan was greeted by a crowd of twenty-five thousand in Paducah, Kentucky, during a week-long trip that Clinton stated allowed him "to see the people I've been working for for four years."[41] In 2000, the sitting vice president and Democratic nominee, Al Gore, and his vice presidential nominee, Senator Joseph Lieberman, departed on a boat trip down the Mississippi River after the Democratic Nominating Convention. The purpose of their trip was to get a postconvention public opinion and media coverage boost by taking their campaign and new partnership to towns in Wisconsin, Iowa, and Missouri. Their trip emulated the Bush and Quayle boat trip to New Orleans after the 1988 Republican Nominating Convention. In 2004, Bush and Cheney did not tour together after the convention. Instead, President Bush met with then–Iraqi Prime Minister Iyad Allawi while Vice President Cheney spoke at campaign rallies and roundtable discussions around the Midwest.

For the most part, other incumbents have used campaign trips for the same reasons. They have known that the glamour and excitement, the drama and pageantry of a presidential visit will, even if just for a short time, transfer the charisma of the office to them. As such, the trips are well worth the effort.

Pragmatic Strategies

In turning to the pragmatic strategies of incumbency, it is important to note that they are more universal than are their symbolic counterparts because they can be and have been employed by candidates who are neither presidents nor, in some cases, even incumbents. Certainly, some strategies depend on the legitimate power that holding an office provides, but others have been used by candidates who only borrow the mantle or style of the incumbent.

Strategies that are examined in this section are the following:

- Creating pseudoevents to attract and control media attention
- Making appointments to state and federal jobs as well as appointments to state and national party committees
- Creating special city, state, or national task forces to investigate areas of public concern
- Appropriating federal funds/grants
- Consulting or negotiating with world leaders
- Manipulating the economy or other important domestic issues
- Endorsements by party and other important leaders
- Emphasizing accomplishments
- Creating and maintaining an "above the political trenches" posture
- Depending on surrogates for the campaign trail
- Interpreting and intensifying a foreign policy problem so that it becomes an international crisis

Creating Pseudoevents

As the use of public relations experts and publicists has increased in political campaigns, so, too, has the frequency of hyped or manufactured
news. Essentially, *pseudoevents* are defined as occurrences that differ from
"real" events in that they are planned, planted, or incited for the primary
purpose of being reported or reproduced.[42]

While all candidates use pseudoevents to try to capture media attention, incumbents have more success because they are in a better position
to create them. For example, a governor or state senator may be featured
on the evening television and radio news throughout the state because of
an announced "major" initiative in attracting a specific corporation to the
state and thus creating new jobs. A member of Congress may receive
headlines from appointment to a special committee or commission created by the president. Moreover, incumbents have many opportunities for
participation in ceremonious occasions—events that are sure to bring the
local media. The ceremonies can be as different as the groundbreaking for
a new government building to the announcement that a special day has
been set aside to honor the city's firefighters. But each can be hyped up
enough to guarantee publicity for the candidate.

However, not only do incumbents have more opportunities to attract
the attention of the media; they are better equipped to control the kind of
coverage they receive. Perhaps a politician whose experience provides
one of the best examples of what we mean is an ex-mayor of New York.
During his years as mayor, Edward I. Koch learned how to control the
New York media. He was seen on television virtually every evening; most
of the time it was as the leading participant in a special occasion or ceremony. (New York is a big city, and therefore many events can be important enough to make the mayor's attendance seem appropriate.) Equally
important was the way in which Koch controlled the kind of coverage he
received. During the 1985 Democratic mayoral primaries, the mayor's opponents issued frequent press statements attacking various administration programs. In response, Koch called press conferences on those days
to announce new initiatives city government was taking in such areas as
housing starts and education reforms or even to announce park dedica-
tions. According to Koch, "my own comments were getting covered in
long news stories, while the charges of my opponents were reduced to little metro briefs deep inside the paper. This is the power of incumbency."[43]

In 1996, the Clinton administration was successful in drawing favorable
and widely publicized coverage of presidential initiatives—initiatives
that had been frequently discussed by Republican candidates. Shortly after the 1994 election when the Democrats lost control of Congress, the
president and his staff identified issues congressional Republicans had

championed and began writing their own legislative proposals. Some of the proposals received daily media coverage. For example, within a two-day period, Clinton's announcements of initiatives to help schools and to track the illegal sale of guns made the front pages of *USA Today* and the *New York Times*, respectively. A month earlier, ABC reported on the president's announcement of a program to combat infectious diseases and his intention to "restate his belief" that cigarettes are addictive. The wide publicity received criticism from Senator Dole, whose campaign released a statement that Clinton and his aides were "getting away with refried beans and in some cases very thin gruel, and getting coverage that makes it seem like a full platter of policy."[44] Clinton, in other words, used the media exposure his incumbency guaranteed to seize the rhetorical agenda for the 1996 presidential campaign. However, his heir apparent in campaign 2000, Vice President Al Gore, threw away most of the incumbency strategies to which he was entitled because of his fear of being too closely associated to the scandals surrounding President Clinton. He, in fact, never even accepted the president's offer to speak for him in any state, including Arkansas, Tennessee, and Florida—places where Clinton was popular and states whose electoral college votes Gore and Lieberman eventually lost.

In 2003, President Bush staged a speech declaring the end of the active phase of the Iraq war on the USS Lincoln. The president flew onto the carrier in a navy plane wearing a pilot's jumpsuit, with a helmet under his arm. The event was covered by all media outlets and showcased how an incumbent president can use his office to draw attention to himself.

In short, incumbents have at their disposal the ability to create pseudo-events that not only generate media exposure but allow some measure of control over the coverage.

Making Appointments to Jobs and Committees

One of the most common yet powerful incumbency strategies revolves around the ability to appoint personal or political friends—or potential friends—to local, state, and federal jobs or to give them key positions on party committees. Although patronage has been condemned by reformers in both political parties, it continues largely because it is so advantageous to everyone concerned. First, it allows candidates (and is not limited to incumbents in that all contenders can hold out the "promise" of appointment) to reward those who have helped them in the past. Second, it creates potential friends or at least puts people in a position of gratitude. Third, and undoubtedly most significant, it places supporters in key positions that may well be important in later stages of the campaign or even in subsequent elections. As such, few candidates, from county commissioner to governor to president, have failed to use this strategy.

Creating Special Task Forces

Modern candidates understand the need not only to determine which issues are of concern to the voters in their city, district, or state but to speak to those concerns. One way to do this is to announce the formation of a special task force whose purpose is to investigate the issue/problem and make recommendations to the candidate regarding steps or actions to be taken in the future. The strategy is employed by incumbents as well as those who are not incumbents because the act of forming the task force is all that is really required to create the illusion that the candidate is concerned about the problem.

For example, during his first term, President George W. Bush formed a task force, headed by Vice President Cheney, with the purpose of developing a national energy policy. He also created a Drug Importation Task Force, as well as Task Forces on Education, Social Security, National Security, and Domestic Surveillance in the Fight against Terrorism.

The primary advantage of the strategy is that the candidate is perceived as a person who understands and cares about those issues important to a particular constituency. However, a second benefit is that the candidate is in the position to postpone taking a stand on a controversial issue—one that might create as many enemies as supporters. Thus, every election year seems to bring a plethora of specially created task forces composed of concerned community/state/national citizens who investigate topics as varied as mental health facilities and taxes for a new sewer system.

Appropriating Funds/Grants

Absolutely no incumbency strategy is less subtle or more powerful than appropriating special grants to "cooperative" (politically supportive) public officials for their cities and states. It is reserved only for incumbents (in that the strategy does not include promises for the future) and is viewed best at the presidential level, although it is certainly done at state and local levels as well.

Although every modern president since Franklin Roosevelt has had a prodigious amount of discretionary money to distribute in the form of federal grants, by the election of 1980, the amount totaled $80 billion. Like his predecessors, Jimmy Carter was determined to use it to aid him in the primaries—especially the early contests when the campaign of Edward Kennedy was still viewed as a threat. The money was employed to reward those public officials who announced their preference for the president, to gain a public endorsement where there had not been one, or to punish those who denied or withdrew support. For example, prior to the Illinois primary, Jane Byrne, mayor of Chicago, was told by the White House that U.S. Air Force facilities at O'Hare Field would be relocated to allow Chicago to expand its major airport. However, after the mayor announced her support of Senator Kennedy over the president, the secretary of transportation said that the cabinet had "lost confidence in Mayor Byrne, and would look for opportunities to deny transportation funds to Chicago and its mayor."[45]

Thus, the Carter White House went into the 1980 campaign determined to "grease" its way through the primaries. Florida (in advance of the Democratic straw primary) received a $1.1 billion loan guarantee to an electric cooperative, $29.9 billion in grants for public housing in various counties, and $31 million for housing projects for the elderly throughout the state. Prior to its primary, New Hampshire received funds for such projects as a four-lane highway from Manchester to Portsmouth and a special commuter train from Concord to Boston.[46] In 1992, President Bush made extensive use of his power to allocate funds. For example, government contracts were granted in states where jobs were affected. And after Hurricane Andrew swept through Florida, massive federal resources were promised to the disaster area. In 1996, President Clinton made extensive use of his power to allocate funds. For example, federal funds were provided to enlarge local police forces throughout the country. And, after Massachusetts suffered severe flooding from the "Great Rain of '96," it was immediately announced that funds would be made available by the government to those counties hit the hardest.

In the first term of George W. Bush's presidency, he allocated funds for several new programs and added funds for the continuation or extension of others. In 2002, Bush controversially asked for federal grant money for faith-based organizations (FBOs). Later in his first term, the president also supplied money for special education state grants, making money available for education and related services for 3- to 5-year-old children with disabilities. The 2003 budget included funds for the extension of the AmeriCorps program, funded early childhood care and education, and provided over $100 million for the Department of Homeland Security.

Is the appropriation of funds a successful incumbency strategy? While it is impossible to claim the effect of any one element in a phenomenon as complex as a primary election, President Carter soundly defeated Kennedy in New Hampshire and virtually annihilated him in the Florida and Illinois primaries. On the other hand, the emergency federal funds President Bush promised to Florida ultimately worked against him because Florida citizens said it was too little and arrived too late.

Consulting with World Leaders

While at first glance consultation with world leaders may appear to be a strategy possible for only presidential incumbents, the fact is that this strategy is employed by any number of governors and members of Congress as they attempt to build their credentials for reelection. Governors extend invitations to athletic teams or artists and may even negotiate with foreign business corporations and governments about the prospect of building a major factory in the state. Members of Congress take frequent junkets overseas in the effort to illustrate their power and importance to voters in their districts or states.

In addition to its use by incumbents, the strategy is employed by challengers who must also build credentials and convey a sense of their individual importance. Moreover, its use may be even more crucial for them because they do not possess the real authority or power of the incumbent. Thus, a meeting with foreign governmental leaders grants at least a sense of legitimacy because it illustrates acknowledgment and a kind of acceptance into an important and official group of leaders. For example, in 1992, challenger Bill Clinton met Russian president Boris Yeltsin to assure him of his support for the multibillion-dollar aid package for Russia that was then pending in Congress. Following the meeting, the governor described how the half-hour chat with the Russian leader was a meeting of the minds.[47] In 1998, in anticipation of the Iowa caucus for presidential campaign 2000, Republican hopeful Malcolm (Steve) Forbes Jr. brought former British prime minister Margaret Thatcher to Iowa to campaign by his side. In 2000, Elizabeth Dole, who was campaigning for the Republican nomination, had many international contacts, thanks to her husband's acquaintances during his years as Senate majority leader and as the 1996 Republican presidential nominee and her own years as president of the American Red Cross. In fact, to help demonstrate her international credentials, she traveled to Macedonia to hear "firsthand," she said, about the problems confronting the refugees. And in 2004, President George W. Bush frequently invited the media as he visited with other world leaders, particularly Russian president Vladimir Putin, Afghanistan president Hamid Karzai, and British prime minister Tony Blair. The alliance between Bush and Blair was particularly well documented with time spent together along with their wives. Each also verbalized support for the other during reelection campaigns.

While significant to congressional and gubernatorial candidates, a trip abroad—especially to Russia, China, or the Middle East—is virtually a prerequisite for potential presidential contenders, particularly those whose previous experiences have not included "official" foreign travel and consultation with government officials. At the very least, it allows them to work their trips into their discourse with such phrases as "in my meeting with the prime minister, I was told that . . . ." But even more important, the strategy provides those candidates who have absolutely no foreign policy experience the appearance of seeming to be a part of or involved in international affairs. As such, it is a useful strategy of the incumbency style.

Manipulating Important Domestic Issues

As a number of these strategies illustrate, incumbents have considerable power, which is, of course, one of the reasons they are difficult to defeat and challengers are so eager to assume their campaign style. However, the manipulation or management of important issues is one strategy that can be assumed only by the incumbent.

For example, throughout the years, the economy has been a primary area of presidential management. One way this has been done is timing economic benefits to specific groups within the electorate to ensure their vote in the election. Political scientist Frank Kessler has pointed to the following Social Security incident during the 1972 presidential campaign as a case in point:

> Checks went out in October 1972, one month before the elections, with the following memo enclosed and personally approved by President Nixon to each of the 24.7 million Social Security recipients: "Your social security payment has been increased by 20% starting with this month's check by a new statute enacted by Congress and signed into law by President Richard Nixon on July 1, 1972. The President also signed into law a provision which will allow your social security benefits to increase automatically as the cost of living goes up.[48]

In using this strategy, presidents have not limited themselves to economic manipulation; other issues have been managed. For example, President George H. W. Bush took a number of actions designed to win voter approval in 1992, including supporting the sale of F-15 fighters to Saudi Arabia in time to announce it to defense workers in Missouri,[49] signing a bill making carjacking a federal crime,[50] announcing to farmers a complicated plan for using corn-based ethanol fuel as an antidote for urban smog,[51] vetoing a bill that would regulate cable prices—saying that it benefited special interests rather than the public[52]—and retooling training programs that he said could be paid for without new taxes. And in 1996, in an effort to boost his campaign, President Clinton vetoed a bill that would have outlawed some late-term abortions,[53] signed legislation aimed at preventing gay marriages,[54] transferred U.S. Border Patrol agents from Texas to California (though illegal immigration is a major problem in both states),[55] vetoed bills that would place new limits on the ability of Americans to pursue civil court claims,[56] and signed a bill that increased the minimum wage.[57] In 2003, President George W. Bush signed the Medicare Prescription Drug Modernization Act, Partial Birth Abortion Ban Act of 2003, and the Patriot Act II among others in order to show voters that he was moving forward with his agenda.

Receiving Endorsements from Other Leaders

Although the growth of primaries has reduced their importance, endorsements are an attempt to identify and link the candidate with already-established, highly respected, and generally acknowledged leaders. The idea is that endorsement by respected leaders signifies that the candidate is already part of their group and should therefore also be thought of as a leader—in other words, credibility by association. Obviously, this perception can be crucial for a nonincumbent who wishes to adopt the incumbency style. It is, of course, equally significant for the incumbent because continued acceptance by other governmental or political leaders is one way of advancing the perception of a successful term of office. Similarly, candidates hope they receive no endorsements from individuals or groups who are not perceived positively by large segments of society because negative association is also possible. For example, during the 1960 presidential campaign, Richard Nixon was endorsed by the president of the Teamsters Union, Jimmy Hoffa. Because Hoffa was already thought of as a "racketeer" (or worse) by many citizens, it was an endorsement that Nixon tried to ignore. When reporters questioned John Kennedy about his reaction to Hoffa's endorsement of Nixon rather than himself, Kennedy responded humorously that he guessed he was just lucky, which of course reinforces our point.

Emphasizing Accomplishments

One of those strategies forming the core of the incumbency style is emphasizing accomplishments. Candidates must be able to demonstrate tangible accomplishments during their term of office if they are incumbents or in some related aspect of public service if they only assume the style. This is, of course, the reason that incumbents go to great lengths to list for voters all that they have done while in office. For example, during the 1992 presidential campaign, President Bush took credit for many of the events that happened in the world during his term of office, including the end of the Cold War.[58] In discussing United States foreign policy accomplishments, he said:

> Germany was unified. Central America was transformed through a policy based on free elections and reconciliation. The Soviet Union was dissolved peacefully and groundbreaking arms control agreements were reached. Iraq was defeated after the U.S. assembled an unprecedented international coalition to prosecute the war, opening the way for peace among the Arabs, Palestinians and Israelis.[59]

The strategy is simple as long as the deeds exist. The difficulty occurs when there have been few accomplishments or when major problems have arisen that overshadow positive contributions (taxes are higher than they were before the incumbent took office; inflation is worse; unemployment has not been reduced). When this happens, the strategy becomes more complex in that the incumbent must either deny that the current problems are important ones (normally an impossible task for even the most persuasive) or blame them on someone else—even on uncontrollable forces. Blaming someone, scapegoating, is the path normally chosen. Examples are as numerous as candidates. State legislators blame the governor, governors blame the federal government (especially Congress), presidents blame Congress, and, surprisingly enough, members of Congress often blame other congressional members. A case that aptly illustrates the practice of blaming others is the 1996 budget impasse that led to partial shutdowns of the federal government. President Clinton blamed the Republican majority of Congress for not compromising, and the Republicans blamed the president for their inability to reach agreement. A budget was finally agreed upon in April 1997, but by then the government had lost some $2 billion in uncollected taxes.[60]

The practice of casting blame elsewhere is certainly not a new variation of the accomplishment strategy. However, its most interesting use is by members of Congress, especially the House. Popular perceptions of Congress are not high. For example, in 1998, a Gallup Poll found that less than 45 percent of the public expressed confidence in the U.S. Congress and approved of the way they were doing their job.[61] In fact, surveys on congressional job approval and disapproval ratings have shown a trend of disapproval for decades. However, despite these feelings, congressional incumbents win the overwhelming majority of their elections. One of the reasons for this paradox is that, when individual representatives seek reelection, they disassociate themselves or even "run against" the institution of which they are a member. They talk about their accomplishments rather than those of Congress, and as two political communication scholars have noted, they play up the negative "myths" (Congress is a kind of shadowy process in which sinister figures operate) while projecting themselves as hardworking and honest people who work against evil.[62] In this way, then, even when genuine accomplishments may be few, scapegoating makes the strategy possible.

Creating an Image of Being above the Political Trenches

Another strategy that is at the center of incumbency style is the technique in which candidates try to create the image that they are somehow removed from politics. Essentially, the strategy is composed of any combination of the following three tactics (each designed to create the impression that the contender is a statesman rather than a politician):

- Appear to be aloof from the hurly-burly of political battle—the office has sought them, so they run because of a sense of love of country and duty.
- Fail to acknowledge publicly the existence of any opponent—candidates may have opponents, but statesmen do not.
- Sustain political silence (absolutely refrain from any personal campaign trips or confrontations with opponents, including not answering any charges or attacks or discussing partisan issues).[63]

While portions of this strategy are used by contemporary candidates, it has been around for a long time. As a matter of fact, its progenitor was George Washington. He did not have to create a nonpolitical or statesman image, because he was not a politician and he had been reluctant to become president. In spite of this, for candidates who were to follow (at least presidential candidates), he bequeathed a legacy of "being above politics," in a sense, conveying the attitude that being political would somehow "dirty" the office. Thus, for many years, the public picked presidents without ever seeing or hearing what their ideas or policies were—at least during the time in which they were candidates. With only two exceptions,[64] no major party candidates, even after formal nomination, personally solicited votes. They were not expected to (even after transportation networks improved), because the prevailing attitude was that the office must seek the person; that is, the appearance of modest reluctance—of being above politics—had to be maintained.

Stephen Douglas was the first to break the taboo in 1860 when he undertook announced campaign speaking tours around the country on behalf of his own candidacy. Although other Democratic candidates followed his example, none became president until Woodrow Wilson was elected in 1912. Republicans remembered Washington's example longer and eschewed mass campaigning (campaign speaking tours around the country on behalf of their own candidacy) until the 1932 campaign, when an incumbent was faced with a problem of such magnitude that he felt he had to travel the United States explaining why he should not be blamed for the Great Depression.

Thus, this strategy has a long history, and its use, in combination with the next two strategies, continues to play a central role in the development and maintenance of incumbency style.

Use of Surrogates on the Campaign Trail

This strategy is closely related to the last one in that it is possible for candidates to assume an above-politics posture because others are overtly campaigning for them while they stay home being nonpolitical. While the strategy is employed by a wide spectrum of candidates, it is the sophisticated use by presidential incumbents since the 1970s that allows us to see most clearly the technique at work.

In the 2004 presidential campaign, for example, both the incumbent Bush and the challenger Kerry used surrogates in their campaigns. For the first time in his political career, Bush's twenty-something twin daughters Jenna and Barbara traveled around the country focusing on college campuses and young voters in an effort to gain votes for their father. The twins also spoke on their father's behalf at the Republican National Convention in New York City. As well as his daughters, President Bush's parents, the former President Bush and first lady Barbara, also campaigned for their son. Like Bush, Kerry's children and step-children campaigned across the country and like the Bush twins the Kerry sons and daughters focused on young voters and college campuses.

In 1972, Richard Nixon also depended on the campaign tours of over forty-nine surrogates (including members of his family, cabinet officers, and other high-level government officials) while he stayed in the White House during most of the fall campaign against George McGovern. As a matter of fact, Nixon was so intent on creating the illusion of a hard-working, nonpolitical statesman that not only did he rarely take a political trip or make a speech in his own behalf, but when asked once by a reporter about his campaign, he cut off questioning with the remark "Let the political people talk on that."[65]

The use of surrogates did not end with Richard Nixon's election. As a matter of fact, it became more pronounced, especially when the media dubbed it the "Rose Garden" strategy during the stay-at-home period of Gerald Ford's campaign in 1976. What they meant was that for weeks on end, as part of a specifically designed plan, Ford did not leave the White House to campaign. Members of his family, his cabinet, and hundreds of Republican Party faithful were out on the hustings for him as he stayed close to the White House and acted "presidential." In addition, as part of the plan, the media were alerted several times each day to witness pseudoevents (the president's welcome to visiting dignitaries or his signature on legislation), most of which occurred in the area adjacent to the Oval Office, the Rose Garden (thus the name). During the midterm elections of 1982, the Republican National Committee developed a program called "Surrogate 82" in which all cabinet members were required to devote fifteen days to campaign activities.[66] But what is most interesting about surrogates and rose gardens is that the strategy is a direct descendant of the "Front Porch" campaigns used by Republicans many years earlier.

In 1888, the grandson of Old Tippecanoe, Benjamin Harrison, was the Republican candidate for president. The party believed it had lost the 1884 election because of the mistakes their candidate made. Therefore, it was decided that Harrison would campaign from his home in Indianapolis against the Democratic incumbent, giving rehearsed and dignified speeches to delegations of visitors who were invited to hear him speak while other party leaders toured the country on his behalf. In other words, the challenger would not only appear presidential but have little opportunity to err. Thus, when Harrison won, the Front Porch, or Rose Garden, strategy was born.

As is the case with most campaign strategies, success means repetition. So in 1896, Republicans went back to the porch with a new candidate and increased zest for a campaign style that was in stark contrast to the "swing around the circle" effort of the Democrats.

Although William McKinley never left his porch in Canton, Ohio, he nonetheless was part of a more vigorous campaign to return the White House to the Republicans than had been conducted for Harrison. Hundreds of visiting delegations were invited to visit his home and hear him speak. He gave as many as twelve carefully prepared speeches a day (each on a single issue specifically directed to the interests of the delegation), and copies were supplied to all major papers. Thus, while remaining at home, McKinley received daily nationwide press coverage—more, in fact, than did his opponent. In addition, 1,400 surrogates were sent out from party campaign headquarters to speak for him all across the country. With all this effort, McKinley defeated William Jennings Bryan.

In part because of their victories the first two times, Republicans returned to the porch for the 1920 election. While the Democratic candidate toured the country, the Republican managers sat Warren G. Harding on the front porch in Marion, Ohio (where day after day he delivered quiet and dignified platitudes about common sense and clean living), and then supplemented the porch performances with touring surrogates. Once again, the strategy worked as Democratic contender James Cox lost in the worst defeat a presidential candidate had known.

With this kind of success, it should now be easy to understand why front porches (currently called rose gardens) and surrogates have remained popular with modern presidential candidates.

Interpreting or Intensifying Foreign Policy Problems into International Crises

Although variations of the strategy of interpreting or intensifying foreign policy problems into international crises are employed by incumbents at all levels, it is most completely studied as it has been used by presidents. Its purpose is simple: to create enough of a crisis situation so that voters (either because of patriotism or not wanting to change leaders at the time of an emergency) will be motivated to rally around the president. There have been many instances when the technique has been successful. In 1964, when U.S. ships in the Gulf of Tonkin were fired upon, President Lyndon Johnson interrupted his "campaigning" to go on television, where he pledged that the United States would take rigorous defensive measures. In 1975, when a U.S. merchant ship, the *Mayaguez*, was captured by Cambodian forces, President Gerald Ford (who was about to make official his bid for reelection) used the situation to build his leadership or command credentials by ordering marines to bomb Cambodia until the *Mayaguez* crew was released. However, one of the most adept uses of the strategy occurred in the surfacing and primary stages of the 1980 campaign when President Jimmy Carter (who had two genuine foreign policy problems with the seizure of the U.S. embassy in Iran and the Soviet advances into Afghanistan) combined the use of surrogates, a nonpolitical image, and international crises to promote his renomination campaign.

Prior to the Iowa caucus and continuing through the Maine and New Hampshire primaries, Carter pledged that he would not personally campaign until the hostages in Tehran were released. Later, when the Soviets marched into Afghanistan, the president reinforced his earlier vow when he announced that, because "this is the most serious crisis since the last World War," he would be unable to leave the White House to campaign in person for reelection. In addition, when other candidates (notably Senator Edward Kennedy and Governor Jerry Brown) questioned the administration's handling of the "crisis," the president completed the strategy by suggesting that attacks on his policy were "damaging to our country and to the establishment of our principles and the maintenance of them, and the achievement of our goals to keep the peace and to get our hostages released."[67]

Until the very last round of the primaries, the president stuck to his pledge. He emerged only rarely from the White House or Camp David and left most comments on politics to his surrogates. Carter's use of incumbency strategies was eminently successful. While giving the appearance that he was too busy trying to solve the international crises to campaign for reelection, he was defeating his opponents in the Democratic primary elections. Twenty-four years later, President George W. Bush's most prominent strategy was reminding Americans of the tragedies that occurred on September 11th, and his "all out" response to it. Not only were there references to 9/11 in the president's speeches around the country, but his reelection campaign built TV commercials that showcased the president's leadership in responding to the fall of the World Trade Center in New York City.

Summary

These, then, are the strategies that comprise the incumbency style. There are, as we have seen, a large number of them—each somewhat different from, although often dependent on, the others and each potentially effective in the hands of candidates who understand and appreciate their power. Perhaps what is most startling about them is the extent to which they work. Normally, it takes enormous amounts of money, organization, and skill to defeat even somewhat inept incumbents. They have at their command not only the strategies we have examined but whatever privileges the office itself provides—including public awareness (visibility) and the opportunity to perform various popular and noncontroversial services for constituents. These strategies have repeatedly enabled incumbents to win reelections overwhelmingly and to win by larger margins than victorious nonincumbents. As we have said before, given all of the benefits, it is no wonder that candidates who are not incumbents often assume elements of the style.

Disadvantages to Incumbency Campaigning

But under what conditions can incumbents lose? In other words, are there burdens of the style as well as benefits? It seems to us that incumbency campaigning has at least four major disadvantages. First, and maybe most important, incumbents must run (at least in part) on their record. While they may cast blame elsewhere or minimize the scope or significance of problem areas within their administration, an effective challenger can make certain that the record of the incumbent (and shortcomings can be found in virtually all records) forms the core of the campaign rhetoric. The incumbent can be kept in a position of having to justify and explain—answering rather than charging, defending rather than attacking. Being forced to run on one's record can be a severe handicap, particularly in the hands of a skilled challenger.

The second and related burden faced by many incumbents is simply that the public may blame them for all problems—whether or not they were at fault. Incumbents are in the public eye, and, if the city sanitation workers refuse to pick up the garbage for a week or if the public transportation system is shut down because of weather, an accident, or striking employees, they are held accountable. At the very least, the question of competency or job effectiveness is raised in the public mind, waiting perhaps for the skilled challenger to capitalize on it.

The third disadvantage, although quite different from the first two, can be equally troublesome. The challenger is free to campaign, but incumbents must at least give the appearance of doing the job for which they have been elected. As campaign seasons become longer, this becomes more difficult. Incumbents often find it unnerving to go about the day-to-day task of administering a city, state, or nation while their opponents spend countless hours out on the hustings—garnering media attention with attacks against them and their policies. If they respond by indulging in overt campaigning, they are criticized for not doing their job. If they ignore it, they may well be accused of having no defense and being afraid to go out and face voters. In other words, it is a real damned if you do and damned if you don't situation.

Finally, because incumbents are at the center of media/public attention far more than their opponents, expectations are great regarding their "front-runner" status. If those expectations are not met, the incumbent is in trouble. Nowhere has this been more thoroughly illustrated than in presidential primary campaigns. Even when incumbents win, if they fail to meet some preconceived percentage set by the media or even by their own staffs, they have, at least in terms of media publicity, lost.

Thus, there are some burdens. Even the incumbency style does not guarantee election. With this in mind, we will now contrast the strategies of the incumbent style with those of the challenger, knowing that in each there are burdens as well as benefits.

Challenger Style

Challenger campaigning is not easy because the style demands a two-step process, the implementation of which requires not only a good deal of deliberate planning but also equal portions of skill and even luck. The style can be defined as a series of communication strategies designed to persuade voters that change is needed and that the challenger is the best person to bring about the change. While the kind of change can vary all the way from shifts in a whole economic system to personality characteristics desired in the officeholder, challengers must convince the electorate that some kind of alteration is necessary if they stand any chance for success.

However, the second part of the process is equally important; the voters must also be persuaded that the challenger is the candidate most likely to produce more desirable conditions or policies. Therefore, the complexity of the style is increased because not only must those who challenge call for change, but also they must simultaneously demonstrate their own capability in bringing about that change. As if all of this were not difficult enough, it is entirely possible that the success of the challenger may ultimately depend on the skill of the incumbent—whether or not the incumbent makes a major mistake in campaign strategy or becomes a victim of prevailing conditions. Thus, it is no understatement to maintain that the task facing most challengers is formidable.

In spite of the potential hazards or burdens, advocating change—the challenger campaign style—is not new. As a matter of fact, it probably got its start in the presidential campaign of 1800 when Jeffersonians distributed leaflets that asked, "Is it not time for a change?" Whenever it began, it has been used by many candidates who have sought elective office. Moreover, elements of the style have even been employed by incumbents such as Harry Truman and Gerald Ford, who felt it would be more beneficial to their candidacies to call for a change in Congress rather than only try to explain the present problems.

The strategies examined in this section include the following:

- Attacking the record of opponents
- Taking the offensive position on issues
- Calling for a change
- Emphasizing optimism for the future
- Speaking to traditional values rather than calling for value changes
- Appearing to represent the philosophical center of the political party
- Delegating personal or harsh attacks in an effort to control demagogic rhetoric

Attacking the Record

Just as running on the record of their accomplishments is a central strategy of incumbency, so, too, is attacking that same record a prime characteristic of the challenger style. As a matter of fact, the ability to criticize freely (and often in exaggerated terms) may well be one of the most important benefits the challenger possesses.[68]

When there is no incumbent, candidates attack the record of the current administration (if they do not represent the same political party) or even an opponent's record in a previous position. Whatever becomes the focus of criticism, the object is to attack—to create doubt in voters' minds regarding the incumbent's/opponent's ability—to stimulate public awareness of any problems that exist or to foster a sense of dissatisfaction and even unhappiness with the state of affairs generally.

In 1996, Senator Dole attacked President Clinton on a number of issues and tried to convince voters that problems existed that demanded attention. For example, Dole attacked Clinton's campaign for accepting large financial contributions from foreign business interests.[69] He also demanded that President Clinton forgo future pardons connected with Whitewater, the failed land deal in which Clinton had been accused of wrongdoing.[70] The problem for Dole was twofold. First, the president's campaign responded immediately by counterattacking; and second, voters appeared to have little interest in his attacks on the president. In the 2000 campaign, Vice President Gore (who, in his role as the sitting vice president, could have run as an incumbent but chose to attack as though he were the challenger) called Governor Bush's proposals a "risky scheme."[71] Not to be "outdone" by the attacks of his rival, Bush during his nominating acceptance address attacked the vice president by joking that if Gore had been around when Edison was testing the light bulb he would have called it a "risky anti-candle scheme."[72] And in 2004 Senator Kerry continually challenged President George W. Bush on his lack of an overall plan for Iraq as well as charging that the president had no plan for the health-care system.

Interestingly, attack is so much a part of challenger style that it frequently occurs even when the predominant public perception of the incumbent is that a credible job has been done. In this instance, the challenger may minimize the importance of the accomplishments, credit them to someone or something else (often another branch or level of government that happens to be controlled by their own party), never mention the accomplishments, or point out that in the years ahead accomplishments will be viewed as problems. Few challengers, however, have been as mean-spirited in their attacks on the incumbent as was Geoffrey Feiger during the 1998 Michigan primary when in his nonstop attack on the Republican incumbent, Governor John Engler, he called him "a cheater, a liar, and a coward . . . a man of mediocre intelligence who's never done anything in life but suck off the public trough."[73]

By whatever means various challengers go about it, their ability to attack existing records or policies is a crucial tool and integral to the overall style.

Taking the Offensive Position on Issues

Essentially, this strategy involves nothing more than taking the offensive position on issues important to the campaign—probing, questioning, challenging, attacking, but never presenting concrete solutions for problems.

It is the incumbent who has to defend unworkable solutions to insolvable problems; the challenger can limit rhetoric to developing problems, keeping the incumbent in a position where all actions have to be defended.[74] In a sense, it is part of a challenger's expected role—to criticize, attack, point out needs—generally guiding voters to begin thinking that the incumbent has been ineffective. Challengers are not expected to solve problems (they have had no chance as officeholders to do so). This is, of course, a major advantage (one of the relatively few), and those who abandon it often lose the election. As a matter of fact, the more detailed that challengers become in offering solutions, the more material they provide to be attacked themselves. In other words, when they drop the offensive, they have essentially traded places with incumbents, thus compounding their difficulties because, unlike incumbents, they lack the tools to solve problems. Thus, the strategy is simply to talk about what is wrong without suggesting any precise ways in which conditions can be righted.

History is replete with examples of successful challengers who used this strategy and won. In 1932, Franklin Roosevelt never divulged the contents of his "New Deal"; in 1952, Dwight Eisenhower never suggested how he would deal with the Korean conflict except to promise that he would personally go there and look it over; in 1960, John Kennedy never shared the details of the "New Frontier"; in 1968, Richard Nixon only said he had a plan regarding the war in Vietnam but never provided any clues regarding it; in 1976, Jimmy Carter seldom offered solutions more substantive than his love and admiration for the people; in 1980, Ronald Reagan never explained just how his supply-side economics would do all he claimed for it; and in 1992, Bill Clinton presented the necessity for economic reform, health-care reform, and welfare reform without providing clear details of the solutions he advocated. Clinton charged Bush with a failed economic policy and said the president had offered no plan to improve conditions. "Unlike our competitors, America has no natural economic strategy," he told employees in a manufacturing plant in Oregon. "Instead we have a series of unconnected, piecemeal efforts, and trickle-down economics. Under trickle-down economics, our manufacturing strength has trickled away."[75] At another time he said, "if you look at the last 12 years, we now have a chance to assess whether the theory has worked. In 1980, we had the highest wages in the world. Now we are 13th and dropping."[76] In 2000, George W. Bush never really explained how taxes could be cut while simultaneously maintaining the surplus in the federal government. And in 2004, John Kerry and his running mate John Edwards continually attacked the president's tax cuts, which they argued only helped America's most wealthy and called for an end to "the two Americas." In retrospect, it is unlikely that most of these challengers even knew how they might solve all of the problems they discussed once they were elected. Whether they did or did not, solutions were not offered, and the candidates managed to keep their offensive position on the issues while forcing their opponents to defend, justify, and offer plans.

Conversely, in 1964 and again in 1972, two challengers never seemed to understand the essential nature of the strategy. Barry Goldwater and George McGovern thought they had to present specific proposals on topics as varied as welfare and the way to fight wars. As the details of their plans became known, they were subjected to intensive analysis, debated, refuted by opponents and media, and finally rejected as absurd. Goldwater and McGovern not only lost their credibility as serious presidential candidates but lost an important advantage. Taking and keeping the right to attack without proposing solutions is a major challenger strategy that only the foolish abandon.

Calling for a Change

From the beginning of each campaign season, it becomes clear that many candidates announce that they are "willing" to run for office because they believe that a change is necessary. Whether it involves specific programs and policies, philosophical assumptions regarding the nature of government, or even modification in administrative style, calling for a change has become the dominant characteristic of those who challenge.

This strategy has been employed in various ways. For example, John Kennedy talked about the need to "get the country moving again"—a stylistic and substantive change from a passive attitude to aggressive, take-charge action. Jimmy Carter used a moralistic change—a return to honest, decent, and compassionate government. Ronald Reagan argued for economic as well as philosophical change, while Edward Kennedy gave, as his only reason for an intraparty challenge, the need for a change in the manner and style of presidential leadership. Perhaps one of the most specific uses of the strategy was exemplified by Senator John Glenn, who in the early months of the surfacing stage of the 1984 presidential campaign called for a change of direction in budgeting for basic research and technological development as well as a dramatic overhaul of the Social Security system. Conversely, the failure of Michael Dukakis to call for a change in 1988 was one of the reasons for his defeat. According to John Sasso, the chief strategist for Dukakis's presidential campaign, "the failure to establish a clear campaign theme and a compelling case for political change" was a mistake on their part.[77] In 1992, Clinton integrated talk of reform into his overall call for change. In June 1992, he told an audience, "When I got into this race, the President was at an historic high point in popularity. But I was convinced then and I am convinced now that this country needs profound change."[78] In 1996, Bob Dole asserted that the nation needed material, or economic, as well as moral change. In 2000, the Republican nominees George W. Bush and Dick Cheney asserted that the American military had been allowed to decline because funding to the Department of Defense had not increased significantly during the Clinton years. And in 2004, Senators Kerry and Edwards argued that changes were needed in our managing of Iraq.

Thus, regardless of how it is employed, the essence of challenger style must revolve around seeking change. If a change from existing conditions, incumbents, or administrations is unnecessary, then so, too, are challengers.

Emphasizing Optimism for the Future

While most candidates, regardless of the level of office sought, traditionally spend some time during the campaign talking about their vision or their optimism for the future, the strategy is particularly important for those who would challenge the status quo. After all, if existing conditions are so bad, can they ever be better? Thus, the task of the challenger is not only to attack but to hold out the promise of a better tomorrow—a day when wrongs will be righted, when justice will prevail, and when health, wealth, and happiness will be more than just vague illusions. In other words, challengers must assume a "rhetoric of optimism" as opposed to a "rhetoric of despair."[79]

This is not to suggest that candidates who employ the strategy dismiss the nation's needs from their discourse; rather, it is a question of emphasis. For example, in 1932, Franklin Roosevelt obviously acknowledged the problems caused by the economic depression, but the central focus of his campaign was hope for the future. John Kennedy talked about problems, but his emphasis was on the country's potential to get moving again; Ronald Reagan pledged that he would lead a crusade to make the United States great again; the commitment of George H. W. Bush to the spirit of volunteerism as a substitute for federal government programs was embodied in the phrases, first used in his nomination acceptance speech, "kinder, gentler nation" and "a thousand points of light"; and the focus of Bill Clinton's rhetoric was the creation of a government that efficiently works for people, for a change. In short, a part of the challenger style is reliance on the positive—emphasizing hope and faith in the future, an optimism that the nation's tomorrow will, in fact, be better than today.

Speaking to traditional values, even though the overall challenger style is dominated by a call for redirection or change, does not mean a redefinition of values. In fact, it is just the opposite. Successful challengers must reinforce majority values instead of attempting to forge new ones. In other words, they must have some understanding of the way in which people view themselves and their society—some understanding of the current tenets of the American Dream. In 1992, Bill Clinton

> used the challenger strategy of speaking to traditional values as both a defensive and as an offensive weapon. For example, he defended against direct attacks from Bush by saying, "I think the implication he has made that somehow Democrats are godless is deeply offensive to me . . . and to a lot of us who cherish our religious convictions and also respect America's tradition of religious diversity."[80]

While this strategy has been understood by challengers such as Richard Nixon, Jimmy Carter, Ronald Reagan, and George H. W. Bush, it may be more interesting to explain it by the example of one who did not. In 1972, before suffering the worst defeat in the history of presidential politics, Democratic challenger George McGovern seemed to have little comprehension of what most citizens wanted. He talked about massive or radical changes in welfare and tax reform, military spending and inflation, school busing, amnesty for those who had left the country rather than participate in the Vietnam War, and the need for more civil rights legislation. What McGovern failed to understand was that most citizens "were tired of social reforms, tired of the 'good-cause' people; that the majority preferred to live their own lives privately, unplagued by moralities, or war, or riots, or violence."[81] Middle-class citizens viewed McGovern as a candidate of an elitist upper class whose values they did not understand except to know that they angered and frightened them. Through his failure to speak to the dreams or visions of the electorate, McGovern abandoned an important strategy of the challenger style.

Appearing to Represent the Philosophical Center

Throughout our political history, successful challengers have been ideological representatives from the mainstream of the major parties, or they have tried to appear as though they were. While some may have been, on one or two issues, a bit to the right or left of the majority of the party, they have not been representatives of the outer or fringe groups. In most campaigns, the fringe groups eventually have compromised and supported their party's candidate, even though that candidate may have been more conservative or liberal than they would have preferred. In the presidential campaign of 1980 and even in 1984, Ronald Reagan, who had long been the champion of the ultraconservatives within the GOP, attempted to position himself closer to the ideological Republican middle once he had secured the nomination. In 1988, George H. W. Bush used the same strategy by repositioning himself on such issues as abortion. In 1996, Bill Clinton modified his stand on so many domestic issues, it was difficult, and frequently impossible, for his opponent to claim even traditional Republican positions. And in 2000, George W. Bush steadily moved to the philosophical center after his victories in the Super Tuesday primaries all but finalized his selection as the Republican nominee.

The only two major exceptions in contemporary presidential politics have been Barry Goldwater and George McGovern, each of whom, as the candidate of groups to the right and left of the centers of their two parties, did not try to reposition himself in the center of his respective party. Instead, each attempted to reform the ideological majority around the ideological minority. In so doing, they failed to employ a traditional challenger strategy.

While Goldwater and McGovern did not attempt to occupy a more central ideological ground, two nominees during the 1980s were blocked from using the strategy by their opponents. In 1984, Ronald Reagan was able to position Walter Mondale as a candidate of the extreme Democratic Left because of the former vice president's stand on increased taxes, social welfare issues, and defense spending and because of the endorsement of him by groups such as the National Organization of Women and the Gay Liberation Movement. Similarly, in 1988, George H. W. Bush, who for much of his political career had been perceived by conservative Republicans as too liberal, repositioned himself in the center and branded Michael Dukakis as a liberal even among Democrats. A liberal, according to the Bush definition, was someone who, like Governor Dukakis, was opposed to children saying the Pledge of Allegiance in school, was so soft on crime he let convicted murderers out of prison on weekend furloughs, and who did not support defense initiatives such as the MX missile—in other words, someone who was outside the mainstream of traditional American values. The label proved disastrous for Dukakis because the governor failed to reposition himself or to redefine the vice president's interpretation of a liberal.

In 1992, Bill Clinton did not allow himself to be defined by his opponents. From the surfacing period onward, he positioned himself as a "new kind of Democrat." As a matter of fact, he was one of the founding members of the Democratic Leadership Council—a group of Democrats recognized for its conservative to moderate position on many issues. However, in 1996, Republican challenger Bob Dole had a singular inability to define himself. In fact, it was his very lack of definition that allowed the incumbent and his fellow Democrats to maintain the hold on the ideological center and force Dole to the conservative Right, a position that he did not always fit.

Delegating Personal or Harsh Attacks

Although attack remains a central imperative of the challenger style, successful candidates (particularly in statewide or national races) do not themselves indulge in demagogic rhetoric. While smear tactics and political hatchet work have been a part of elective politics for years, wise challengers have left harsh or vitriolic language to running mates, surrogate speakers, or their television advertising and printed materials. The reason for delegating this kind of attack is, at least in part, related to the symbolic nature of the campaign itself. As we have mentioned earlier, campaigns are a symbolic representation of how candidates might behave if elected—a kind of vignette from which voters are able to transfer campaign performance into performance as officeholders. Thus, the challenger who likens the incumbent to Adolf Hitler, asserts that the president behaves like a reformed drunk, or argues that the incumbent is ignorant of foreign policy—as did George McGovern in 1972, Edward Kennedy in 1980, and Walter Mondale in 1984—is unwise.

Demagogy is never viewed as an asset and normally backfires for the challenger who employs it. In 1988, Michael Dukakis was attacked as being soft on defense, soft on crime, and soft on patriotism. However, George Bush was smart enough to leave direct attacks on his opponent to others and to his television advertising campaign. In 1992, Clinton attacked the policies of the president and his administration but was careful to show no disrespect to President Bush, even after the president referred to Clinton as a "bozo." However, in 1996, Bob Dole attacked President Clinton's personal character. Not only were Dole's attacks ineffective, as the president retained his double-digit lead in the polls, but the strategy actually persuaded some voters to oppose Dole and support Clinton, because they thought personal attacks were "in bad taste and removed from the issues of being the president."[82] In 2000, George W. Bush, while never actually mentioning the Clinton–Monica Lewinsky scandal or the subsequent impeachment of the president, nonetheless made Dole's argument more tactfully by focusing on how he would uphold the dignity of the presidency and his own family values. And in 2004, John Kerry, while attempting to show no disrespect for President Bush and the office of the president, nonetheless attacked or frequently talked about the president's failed economic policies.

Summary

These, then, are the strategies that comprise the challenger style. While there are fewer of them than there are incumbency strategies, they can also be powerful when used correctly. However, those who employ them, just as those who employ their counterparts, must understand the importance of image creation and maintenance. For example, it does little good if a candidate attacks the record of the incumbent but does so using demagogic language or leaves no outlet for the promise of a better tomorrow. In a similar manner, those who fail to understand the necessity of appearing to represent the values of the majority of the electorate as they call for a change in the course or direction of present policies will have little success. In short, challenger campaigning is difficult primarily because being a challenger is not nearly as advantageous as being an incumbent. Challengers win but not as often. Challengers have some advantages over incumbents but not very many. In the final analysis, challengers may be only as successful as incumbents are incompetent to employ the symbolic and pragmatic strategies their office provides.

Incumbent/Challenger: A Merger of Styles

As discussed earlier, the incumbent and challenger strategies are not absolute categories. Those candidates who are incumbents are not restricted to a specific set of incumbency strategies any more than challengers are confined to a particular set of challenger strategies. While the rhetoric of most candidates typically reflects their actual position in the race, there are instances wherein aspects of incumbency and challenger styles have been combined. It is not uncommon, for example, for challengers to assume the mantle of incumbency whenever and wherever possible; its advantages are well documented. Those who challenge must try to emphasize whatever accomplishments they have had in public life, appear to be acquainted with other leaders, and have a clear need to use whatever means available to them to gain the attention of the media. Similarly, events may, from time to time, compel incumbents to borrow strategies more frequently associated with the challenger. While we consider it unlikely that any incumbent would ever find it advantageous to drop completely the symbolic strategies or to call for a change, an incumbent may well emphasize ideological centrality or rely on surrogate speakers for overt/direct personal attacks on opponents. Such rhetorical borrowing between categories, perhaps in response to changing conditions, is only part of what we mean by the incumbent/challenger style.

The most prominent characteristics of the combined style are abandonment of the essential purpose or thrust of incumbent or challenger rhetoric and abandonment of the responsibilities each has. If the challenger does not attack or at least question the policies and actions of the incumbent, no real campaign dialogue occurs. In a similar vein, if the incumbent will not acknowledge problems, defend current policies or programs, or even suggest/offer a future course of action, no real dialogue can occur.

Although there is little question that from time to time incumbent presidents or vice presidents running for reelection have used strategies of incumbency as well as those of a challenger, perhaps the best way to understand the incumbent/challenger style is through two extended examples, one from 1984 and one from 2000. In 1984, we had two challengers, one of whom was president of the United States. Beginning with his nomination acceptance speech, Ronald Reagan's rhetoric was heavily centered around two staples of the challenger style: attacking the policies of the opposition (in this case going back to the Carter–Mondale administration) while taking the offensive position on issues, and emphasizing optimism for the future. Incumbency strategies were only to enhance his campaign as a challenger. While Reagan was not the first sitting president to try to campaign for reelection in this manner, he was the first one since Harry Truman to do so successfully.

Part of Reagan's success as an "incumbent challenger" was his ability figuratively to step out of office at crucial moments and reflect on problems—"posing as a commentator who happened to live on Pennsylvania Avenue"—never admitting that he, as the result of election, was currently more responsible than any other single individual for the federal government.[83] But there was another part to the strategy: painting the portrait of a future at once so uplifting and patriotic that all problems of the moment were dwarfed by it.

Americans are by nature optimists. We believe in people—especially heroes—and in happy endings. Successful candidates have long known that optimism is the way to the hearts of the American electorate. "At the worst of times, Franklin Roosevelt uplifted with a smile, while years later, Jimmy Carter guaranteed his defeat by telling us that we were suffering from malaise."[84] What was so effective about Reagan's use of cheer was his own appearance of amiability, an understanding of the political fact that Americans want to hear good news, as well as the way he managed to distance himself from responsibility when things went wrong. "It was as if he was a king who reigned but did not rule—a constitutional monarch whose performance was a symbol to his people while politicians did the dirty work of governing."[85] In 1984, he campaigned for reelection as a critic of federal budget deficits even while he had created the largest deficit in history.

In short, Reagan offered voters, just as he had in 1980 when he had actually been a challenger, a picture of a future that did not include hard choices or sacrifices he might ask them to make after the election. However, a strategy of optimism is possible only if a candidate has managed to avoid the defensive position on issues. This was the second overt use of the challenger style employed by the incumbent president.

Throughout the campaign, it was as if there were two challengers—both attacking, probing, questioning, but the incumbent/challenger never defending his policies. In fact, by seizing the offensive on issues, the president reduced his opponent to the most disadvantageous challenger posture, suggesting solutions for problems. Reagan did not have to make allowances for solving problems because he did not acknowledge the existence of problems. Unwilling to accept the issues presented by Mondale as problems, let alone acknowledging any responsibility for them, the president simply smiled and said that the trend is the thing and, every day in every way, things are getting better. When Mondale charged that the nuclear arms race had heated up between Washington and Moscow and that U.S.–Soviet relations were strained, the president responded by ignoring the issue and talked about America standing tall and looking to the 1980s with courage, confidence, and hope. Finally, in an absolute measure of desperation, Mondale outlined solutions—such as the inevitable raising of taxes to deal with the national deficit. When time after time Mondale tried to push Reagan on exactly what he was going to do about the deficit, the president only responded that it was a little scary to have a deficit of a $180 billion and that, even if he had "inherited the wreckage from the Democrats," he was willing to work with them to repair the problem.

From the beginning, it appeared that the challenger and the incumbent had reversed roles. The incumbent ran against "big spending demons in Washington" and "puzzle-palaces on the Potomac," and, whenever he left the White House, he talked about what a pleasure it was to be out of Washington. The challenger sought to tie the incumbent to problems the country faced, and, when there was no response, he created his own solutions. The Reagan staff had reasoned that it was unnecessary to speak to the specific issues raised by Mondale. They had determined before the campaign even began that the reelection effort would be concentrated on the president's leadership and the problems resulting from the Carter–Mondale past, without defending current programs or without proposing any new or specific programs for the future.[86] They believed their strategy would be successful because Reagan had been on the political stage for thirty years. His views were well known by the American people. As the press secretary for his reelection campaign, James Lake, said, "It would be foolish of us to let Ronald Reagan respond to Mr. Mondale . . . people don't care. They get his message. They see him on television and read the newspaper."[87] Thus, the incumbent outlined scenes and evoked symbols, leaving details—particularly unpleasant details—for later. Patriotic slogans, such as "America is back," "America stands tall," "America is too great for small dreams," or "the opportunity society," combined with the persona of the incumbent himself and his stage-managed appearances drove the 1984 presidential campaign into what one political commentator called a "collage of manufactured happiness as in an infinitely extended television commercial."[88]

In a similar manner, during the presidential campaign of 2000, Vice President Al Gore chose to ignore many of the incumbent's rhetorical strategies (which as the sitting vice president were "rightfully" his) and adopt, instead, the rhetorical posture of a challenger. From the beginning (when announcing his candidacy, in debating his only Democratic rival, Bill Bradley, during the primaries, in his nomination acceptance speech, and right through the general election), the vice president made it clear that he was "his own man." Given, however, that the country was at peace and experiencing sustained economic prosperity, it would have been reasonable (and rhetorically advantageous) for Gore to have used incumbency strategies—especially during the general election campaign when his opponent had no experience in many areas typically deemed important for presidents. It is not that the vice president seldom postured himself as an incumbent; it is that he eschewed some of those strategies that could have been important to his candidacy. For example, he failed to discuss any foreign policy experience he had had as vice president, including meeting or consulting with foreign leaders, being a member of the administration's national security team, or even being part of the administration that had achieved some progress with the Middle East peace process. In addition to not assuming the rhetorical posture of an incumbent in foreign policy issues, the vice president failed to maximize the administration's accomplishments in domestic policy issues important to the electorate. He sounded like the challenger, not the incumbent, for example, when he talked about reduced crime, welfare reform, or the turn from a national deficit to a national surplus. Instead of taking his share of the credit, he argued that "things were not good enough," "we need to do more and better," or "you ain't seen nothing yet." The point we make is simply this: By assuming an incumbent/challenger style, Vice President Gore threw out the rhetorical advantages of incumbency that may ultimately have cost him votes in a historically close election. While in 1984 President Reagan was successful in combining incumbent and challenger strategies, Vice President Gore was not. Clearly it remains a "tricky" rhetorical strategy for which there is no guarantee for success.[89]

CONCLUSION

In this chapter, we have examined an important yet frequently overlooked element of elective politics—campaign style. In so doing, we considered style as sets of communication strategies that are employed by all candidates and noted the relationship of image and advancements in transportation and communication to their creation and maintenance.

The incumbency style was defined as a blend of symbolic and pragmatic communication strategies designed to make candidates be perceived by voters as not only good enough for the office sought but appear as if they already possess the office. Fifteen different yet complementary strategies were examined. In a similar manner, we analyzed the challenger style, defining it as a series of communication strategies designed to persuade voters that change is needed and that the candidate is the best person to bring about change. Seven different yet complementary strategies were discussed.

Finally, we considered the incumbent/challenger style and noted that the combination of strategies that comprise it, at least as illustrated during the 1984 and 2000 presidential campaigns, can play a major role in the creation of empty political rhetoric.

NOTES

1. Bruce E. Gronbeck, "The Functions of Presidential Campaigning," *Communication Monographs* 45 (November 1978): 268–80.

2. Robert V. Friedenberg, *Notable Speeches in Contemporary Presidential Campaigns* (Westport, Conn.: Praeger, 2002), 1–14.

3. Friedenberg, *Notable Speeches.*

4. Irwin Silber, *Songs America Voted By* (New York: Stackpole, 1971).

5. Quoted in Kathleen Hall Jamieson, *Packaging the Presidency: History and Criticism of Presidential Campaign Advertising* (New York: Oxford University Press, 1984), 12.

6. Kenneth E. Boulding, *The Image* (Ann Arbor: University of Michigan Press, 1961), 6.

7. Allan Dean Louden, "Image Construction in Political Spot Advertising: The Hunt/Helms Senate Campaign," Ph.D. diss., University of Southern California, 1990, 1.

8. G. R. Pike, "Toward a Transactional Model of Political Images: Collective Images of the Candidates in the 1984 Elections," paper presented at the International Communication Association Convention, Honolulu, 1985. Quoted from Susan A. Hellweg et al., "Political Candidate Image: A State-of-the-Art Review," in *Progress in Communication Sciences*, vol. 9, ed. B. Dewin and M. J. Voigt, 43–78 (Norword, N.J.: Ablex, 1989).

9. Arthur H. Miller, Martin P. Wattenberg, and Oksana Malanchuk, "Schematic Assessments of Presidential Candidates," *American Political Science Review* 80 (June 1986): 521–40.

10. Dan Nimmo and Michael W. Mansfield, "Change and Persistence in Candidate Images: Presidential Debates across 1976, 1980, and 1984," paper presented at the Speech Communication Association Convention, Chicago, 1986.

11. Hellweg et al., "A State-of-the-Art Review," especially 44–53.

12. Judith S. Trent, Cady Short-Thompson, Paul A. Mongeau, Andrew K. Nusz, and Jimmie D. Trent, "Image, Media Bias, and Voter Characteristics: The Ideal Candidate from 1988–2000," *American Behavioral Scientist* 44, no. 12 (August 2001): 2109–12.

13. Judith S. Trent, Cady Short-Thompson, Paul A. Mongeau, Maribeth S. Metzler, and Jimmie D. Trent, "The Idealized Presidential Candidate: A Vision over Time," *American Behavioral Scientist* 49, no. 1 (September 2005): 130–56.

14. Jimmie D. Trent, Judith S. Trent, Paul A. Mongeau, and Gay E. Gauder, "Facial Attractiveness and Initial Choice among Political Candidates: The Effect of Sex, Race, Political Preference, and Position," paper presented at the International Communication Association, Rome, 1998.

15. Frederick Williams, *The Communications Revolution* (Beverly Hills: Sage, 1982), 37.

16. Frederick Williams, *The New Communications*, 2d ed. (Belmont, Calif.: Wadsworth, 1989).

17. Williams, *The New Communications*.

18. Edgar E. Willis, "Radio and Presidential Campaigning," *Central States Speech Journal* 20 (Fall 1969): 187.

19. Willis, "Radio and Presidential Campaigning," 191.

20. Willis, "Radio and Presidential Campaigning."

21. Michael McCurry, "The New Electronic Politics," *Campaigns and Elections* (March/April 1989): 23–32. See also Williams, *The Communications Revolution*, especially 17–39.

22. Theodore H. White, *The Making of the President, 1968* (New York: Atheneum, 1969), 154.

23. Joel L. Swerdlow, *Media Technology and the Vote: A Source Book* (Boulder, Colo.: Westview, 1988), 6–7.

24. For a discussion of the potential of what he terms "push-button government," see Williams, *Communications Revolution*, 183–99.

25. Mike Glover, "Survey Calls Dukakis Winner of TV Debate," *Cincinnati Enquirer*, January 1987, A3.

26. Michael Nelson, *The Elections of 2000* (Washington, D.C.: Congressional Quarterly, 2001), 113.

27. Robert J. Samuelson, "No More Media Elite," *Washington Post National Weekly Edition*, July 13, 1998, 26.

28. Thomas Rosenstiel, *Strange Bedfellows* (New York: Hyperion, 1993), 170.

29. Evan Thomas and Gregory L. Vistica, "Fallout from a Media Fiasco," *Newsweek*, July 20, 1998, 24–26.

30. W. Lance Bennett, "The Ritualistic and Pragmatic Bases of Political Campaign Discourse," *Quarterly Journal of Speech* 64 (October 1977): 228.

31. Keith V. Erickson and Wallace V. Schmidt, "Presidential Political Silence: Rhetoric and the Rose Garden Strategy," *Southern Speech Communication Journal* 46 (Summer 1982): 402–21.

32. R. F. Fenno Jr., *Home Style: House Members in Their Districts* (Boston: Little, Brown, 1978), 211.

33. Michael Nelson, *The Elections of 2000* (Washington, D.C.: Congressional Quarterly, 2001), 198.

34. Robert E. Denton Jr., *The Symbolic Dimensions of the American Presidency* (Prospect Heights, Ill.: Waveland, 1982), 58.

35. Theodore H. White, *Breach of Faith* (New York: Atheneum, 1975), 322.

36. Dan D. Nimmo, *Popular Images of Politics* (Englewood Cliffs, N.J.: Prentice Hall, 1974), 92.

37. John Louis Lucaites, "Rhetoric and the Problem of Legitimacy," in *Dimensions of Argument: Proceedings of the Second Summer Conference on Argumentation*, ed. George Ziegelmueller and Jack Rhodes, 799–807 (Annandale, Va.: Speech Communication Association, 1982).

38. Murray Edelman, "The Politics of Persuasion," in *Choosing the President*, ed. James David Barber, 171 (Englewood Cliffs, N.J.: Prentice Hall, 1974).

39. Denton, *Symbolic Dimensions*, 61.

40. Edelman, "Politics of Persuasion," 171.

41. Al Cross and James Malone, "Clinton Reaches Out to Heartland," *Courier-Journal*, August 31, 1996, 01A.

42. William R. Brown, "Television and the Democratic National Convention of 1968," *Quarterly Journal of Speech* 55 (October 1969): 241. For a more extensive treatment of pseudo-events, see Daniel J. Boorstin's classic *The Image* (New York: Atheneum, 1980). Originally, the book was published under the title *The Image, or What Happened to the American Dream* in 1961.

43. Edward I. Koch with William Rauch, *Politics* (New York: Simon & Schuster, 1985), 236.

44. Howard Kurtz, "White House News Leaks of Questionable Significance Unleash Publicity Deluge," *Washington Post*, July 14, 1996, A16.

45. Theodore H. White, *America in Search of Itself* (New York: Harper & Row, 1982), 296.

46. White, *America in Search of Itself*, 295.

47. "Clinton Becomes Yeltsin Fan after Early Morning Chat," *New York Times*, January 24, 1992, A24.

48. Frank Kessler, *The Dilemmas of Presidential Leadership: Of Caretakers and Kings* (Englewood Cliffs, N.J.: Prentice Hall, 1982), 313–14.

49. Ann Devroy, "The Bush Campaign, Shake and Bakered," *Washington Post*, September 21–27, 1992, 11.

50. Andrew Rosenthal, "As Polls Shift, Bush Grabs Even Small Chance of Surge," *New York Times*, October 26, 1992, A12.

51. Rae Tyson, "Farmers Rally 'Round Bush Ethanol Plan," *USA Today*, October 2, 1992, A4.

52. Edmund L. Andrews, "Bush Rejects Bill That Would Limit Rates on Cable TV," *New York Times*, October 4, 1992, A1, A17.

53. Howard Kurtz, "Ad on Christian Radio Touts Clinton's Stands," *Washington Post*, October 15, 1996, A09.

54. Kurtz, "Ad on Christian Radio," A09.

55. George Kuempel, "Bush Criticizes Federal Transfer of Border Agents to California," *Dallas Morning News*, October 17, 1996, 32A.

56. Greg Gordon, *Star Tribune*, October 1, 1996.

57. Steve Barrett, "Couple Helps Make History," *Pittsburgh Post-Gazette*, November 3, 1996, W-3.

58. Andrew Rosenthal, "Bush Sounding Like His Rivals, Tones Down His Attacks, Briefly," *New York Times*, October 27, 1992, A1, A11.

59. Devroy, "The Bush Campaign, Shake and Bakered," 11.

60. Indigo, "Shortfall in Responsibility," *Orlando Sentinel*, May 29, 1996, A12.

61. *The Gallup Organization—Congress Job Approval*, at www.gallup.com/Gallup_Poll_Data/ratecong/jobapp.htm.

62. Dan Nimmo and James E. Combs, *Subliminal Politics: Myths and Mythmakers in America* (Englewood Cliffs, N.J.: Prentice Hall, 1980), 78.

63. Barry Brummett, "Towards a Theory of Silence as a Political Strategy," *Quarterly Journal of Speech* 66 (October 1980): 289–303.

64. William Henry Harrison in 1840 and General Winfield Scott in 1852 made, at the insistence of their managers, some speeches on their own behalf.

65. "The President," *Newsweek*, August 28, 1972, 15. See also Judith S. Trent, "Image Building Strategies in the 1972 Presidential Campaign," *Speaker and Gavel* 10 (January 1973): 39–45; and for a discussion of the use of surrogate speakers, see chapter 6.

66. Robert E. Denton, Jr., and Gary C. Woodward, *Political Communication in America* (New York: Praeger, 1985), 87.

67. Ellen Reid Gold and Judith S. Trent, "Campaigning for President in New Hampshire: 1980," *Exetasis* 6 (April 1980): 7.

68. Nelson W. Polsby and Aaron Wildavsky, *Presidential Elections* (New York: Scribner's, 1976), 165.

69. David Jackson, "Campaign Financing under Attack," *Dallas Morning News*, October 24, 1996, 1A.

70. Jere Hester, "Irancon Figure Hits Dole," *Daily News* (New York), October 16, 1996, 18.

71. Remarks from the 2000 GOP Convention.

72. Remarks from the 2000 GOP Convention.

73. Ron Stodghill II, "The Motown Motormouth," *Time*, August 17, 1998, 30.

74. Judith S. Trent and Jimmie D. Trent, "The Rhetoric of the Challenger: George Stanley McGovern," *Central States Speech Journal* 25 (Spring 1974): 16.

75. "Clinton Hits Hard on Jobs, Economy," *Cincinnati Enquirer*, September 9, 1992, A8.

76. "Excerpts from Clinton Speech to National Guard," *New York Times*, September 16, 1992, A15.

77. David S. Broder, "The Lessons of Defeat," *Washington Post National Weekly Edition*, February 6–12, 1989.

78. Robin Toner, "Clinton Wins a Majority for Nomination but Perot's Appeal Is Strong in 2 Parties," *New York Times*, June 3, 1992, A1.

79. Trent and Trent, "The Rhetoric of the Challenger," 17.

80. Bill Nichols, "Clinton Agonized, the Challenger Counterattacks," *USA Today*, August 24, 1992, A5.

81. Nichols, "Clinton Agonized," A5.

82. "Dole's New Attack Style Leaves Bad Taste with Some Voters," *Arizona Republic*, October 20, 1996, A25.

83. Francis X. Clines, "Friend and Foe Cite Reagan's 'Masterful' Use of Incumbency," *New York Times*, September 18, 1983, E5.

84. Anthony Lewis, "Dr. Pangloss Speaks," *New York Times*, October 14, 1984, E19.

85. Lewis, "Dr. Pangloss Speaks," E19.

86. Jane Mayer and Doyle McManus, *Landslide* (Boston: Houghton Mifflin, 1988).

87. Howell Raines, "Reagan Appears to Succeed by Avoiding Specific Issues," *New York Times*, September 22, 1984, 14.

88. David Hoffman, "Accentuate the Positive, Put Off the Negative," *Washington Post National Weekly Edition*, March 26, 1984, 13.

89. For an excellent discussion of Vice President Al Gore's use and misuse of the incumbent/challenger style, see Craig Allen Smith and Neil Mansharamani, "Challenger and Incumbent Reversal in the 2000 Election," in *The 2000 Presidential Campaign: A Communication Perspective*, ed. Robert E. Denton Jr., 91–116 (Westport, Conn.: Praeger, 2002).

4

~

Communicative Mass Channels of Political Campaigning

No other nation in the world consumes so much mass communication. By 2004, there were over 1,456 daily newspapers, which sold for over $48 million.[1] In addition, there were approximately 11,009 commercial radio stations, and over 50 million people blog on myspace.com alone.[2] Despite the rapidly growing use of websites and blogs for all manner of news and entertainment, television remains the dominant medium. More than 98 percent of all households (260 million homes) have television sets with the average number of sets at 2.4,[3] making television more plentiful than home telephones.[4] Nearly 86 million homes subscribe to a cable service.[5] However, more striking than the number of television sets owned is the frequency of their use. Television is the major source of entertainment and information, our primary leisure time activity. For example, in 2003, Americans spent approximately 3,663 hours watching television.[6] In other words, it is a dominant force in the lives and environments of most of the public, a fact that was called to our attention by political communication scholars Dan D. Nimmo and James E. Combs in 1990. In their book *Mediated Political Realities*, Nimmo and Combs claim that, consistently since 1963, Americans have named television as their primary and most believable news medium.[7]

As we discussed in an earlier chapter and will discuss more in depth later, the widespread growth of the Internet and the increase in the number of Americans who have access to and use the Internet on a daily basis, approximately 210 million,[8] is another significant element in the utilization of mass media.

Not only is U.S. mass media consumption unequaled, in no other nation is it so inextricably linked to the electoral process. Mass communication has become the center stage for all major political events. For example, blogging, websites of 527s, campaign websites, daily newspapers, and weekly magazines keep political people and issues in our minds as they frequently report the result of the latest poll taken to measure how individuals feel about the president, governors, members of Congress, candidates, and specific issues and controversies. Radio programming is punctuated with five- and ten-minute news reports regarding some aspects of politics or with ten-, thirty-, and sixty-second spot advertisements for candidates and local "vital" issues. Moreover, by the 1992 presidential campaign, radio political talk and call-in shows had reached a zenith in popularity all over the nation. By the 2006 midterm elections, more than nine hundred shows and their hosts had become a political reality in local, state, and national races.

Even with the rapid acceleration of bloggers and blogging, it is still television that has most dramatically linked us to large-scale political campaign events such as presidential debates, national nominating conventions, primary victories and losses, candidates' gaffes, campaign trips, news conferences, election eve rituals, campaign speeches, biographies, negative commercials, and, in the late 1990s, even hearings and investigations. It was television that brought Ronald Reagan to national political attention in 1964 as he delivered one of history's most financially successful speeches; just as twenty-eight years later, Texas billionaire H. Ross Perot announced on CNN's *Larry King Live* that he would run for president if citizens would be willing to gather enough petition signatures to place his name on the ballot in all fifty states. In 1998, the public watched as the results of the Minnesota gubernatorial election made clear that Jesse "The Body" Ventura, a former professional wrestler (well known to many because of televised wrestling matches), had defeated Republican and Democratic opponents to become that state's new highest elected official, and it watched once again in 2002 as Ventura declared he would not run for reelection. And by 2006 it seemed as though any number of potential presidential contenders from both political parties were announcing on Sunday morning news talk shows about running for president. In short, the mass media and particularly television have had a profound impact on the electoral process by connecting citizens and political campaigns.

In spite of this, the influence of mass communication on political behavior remains uncertain. Although media effects is one of the most studied areas in the social sciences, after more than eighty years of intense research, there are relatively few absolutes, largely because the findings of one generation of scholars are frequently challenged by the next.

The purpose of this chapter is to sort through the major theories, perspectives, hypotheses, and models that have been advanced regarding the media's relationship to political behavior and attempt to draw at least some general conclusions. In so doing, it may be helpful to understand that, for some scholars, the "theories" are not theories at all, because they are not all unambiguous, deductive, and interrelated structures from which empirically ascertained and consistent laws or general principles have been derived. For our purposes in this chapter, however, theories come in various packages. Although most have been empirically derived, not all are unambiguously and deductively determined. Moreover, if we insisted that the theories presented here must account for or predict general principles, there would be relatively little to discuss. Few of the perspectives or hypotheses have provided the consistency needed for determining general laws or principles. In other words, when it comes to the question of the role of media in determining political behavior, there is no one grand theory. There are a number of partial theories, or what (in another context) communication scholar Frank E. X. Dance refers to as particularistic theoretical bits and pieces,[9] but no single theoretical development that can account for or predict related phenomena. It is for this reason that we discuss some of the major perspectives and approaches that have generated research. Whether or not multitheoretical conceptualizations are desirable or undesirable, the fact is that more than eight decades of research have frequently led to conclusions that contrast with one another. This is one element to which we pay special attention as we proceed through the various theoretic approaches.

We define *mass* in a standard way as consisting of people representing all social, religious, and ethnic groups, from all regions of the country. Moreover, they are anonymous (do not necessarily know one another) and therefore act not in concert but spontaneously as individuals. We use the terms *mass channels* and *mass media* interchangeably to refer to the primary means of mass communication (radio, television, the Internet, newspapers, and magazines). While we would not deny the existence of other modes of mass communication such as books, music, and motion pictures in the political campaign any more than we would refuse to recognize forms of "minicommunication" such as posters, billboards, and campaign literature, they are simply not as important. The major perspectives have been generated from studies of radio, television, newspapers, and magazines, although we believe that the Internet will be added to this list as more studies are undertaken regarding its use.

Finally, it is important to understand that the focus of this chapter is not candidates and the campaign process but *voters* and the campaign process. The principles that are analyzed center around the effect of mass communication on the political behavior of citizens. As such, we are concerned with the way researchers have answered such questions as these: (1) To what extent do the media influence cognitions and behavior? (2) What are the primary mass communication models that have guided research? (3) What have been the effects of the media on the electoral process itself? (4) How do people use the media in the political process?

The chapter is organized chronologically in that the general conceptualizations from early and contemporary research compose separate sections. Within each, major studies are examined, and any specific hypotheses or models that have been derived from them are discussed. The conclusion focuses on a summary of principles regarding the influence of the media that are most important in understanding the nature of political campaign communication.

EARLY STUDIES

The media's influence on political behavior has been a subject of scholarly investigation since the 1920s. Although readers might question the need to be aware of anything other than the most recent research findings, many of the early studies have been of tremendous importance. In fact, their impact has been so profound, they are considered "classics," and the conclusions they articulated as well as the methods they employed influenced all who followed. Thus, we discuss each of the major perspectives as well as the general models or hypotheses that were derived from them during the more than thirty-year period in which they dominated mass communication research.

Hypodermic Effect

The assumption that the press is a powerful force in shaping public opinion has been around for centuries. In 1529, fifty years after the printing press had been introduced to England, King Henry VIII seized control of the printing industry. Licensed printers held their patents only if what they printed pleased him.[10] In the mid-1600s, the Puritan establishment in Massachusetts Bay Colony maintained strict control over printing because they feared that a free press might threaten the government and promote religious heresies.[11] In 1722, the founder and editor of a Boston newspaper, the *New England Courant*, was jailed for three weeks because of his attacks on the government.[12] Years later, the press was thought to have been a powerful force in creating revolutionary fervor in the United States, in providing passion and visibility to the abolitionist movement, and in provoking Congress to go to war with Spain.

However, it was not until the 1920s and 1930s that researchers actually tried to determine the power of mass communication in shaping values and behaviors of citizens. The motivation to learn more about the ways in which media could influence the public was provided, in large measure, by Adolf Hitler's propaganda machine, which seemed to have captured the minds of the German people through movies and staged rallies, and the use of the radio by Benito Mussolini in Italy and Father Charles Coughlin in the United States to stir public support and sentiment for the fascists. The Information and Education Branch of the United States Army began recruiting social scientists to study the influence of media persuasion. As researchers analyzed the effects of propaganda film such as *The Battle of Britain* or the pro-German magazine *The Galilean*, they confirmed what had been assumed for centuries. The media really were powerful; they had the strength not only to change people's attitudes but to alter their behavior. And because citizens were often helpless to resist the persuasion of propaganda, they were easily "bamboozled." Moreover, according to the researchers, these effects occurred in all people because, despite individual attributes and characteristics, individuals responded in the same way when they received similar messages. Audiences were like mobs; there were no individual minds but only a group consciousness. Messages went directly from the media to the individual, where they were immediately assimilated. "Messages were literally conceived of as being 'injected' into the mind where they were 'stored' in the form of changes in feelings and attitudes. Eventually such feelings or attitudes produced the behavior desired by the message source."[13] This is, essentially, what researchers called the *hypodermic effect*, or the *hypodermic needle model*.

Although it may be difficult for us to subscribe to specific aspects of the hypodermic model, it must be viewed in terms of the context in which it was developed. The 1920s through the early 1940s was a time of worldwide social, political, and economic unrest, passion, and violence. Economic depression, the rise of fascism and Hitler, and the domination of the Nazis throughout much of Europe suggested irrational yet somehow controlled mass group behavior. It seemed entirely likely that people's minds were being manipulated by powerful propaganda devices. In the view of many who were studying it, the "mass media loomed as agents of evil aiming at the total destruction of democratic society. First the newspaper and later the radio, were feared as powerful weapons able to rubber-stamp ideas upon the minds of defenseless readers and listeners."[14]

By the late 1930s, the hypodermic effect was accepted widely enough (even by those social scientists not involved in the government propaganda research program) to be applied specifically to the electoral process. One of the first systematic attempts to determine the political impact of the press was undertaken in 1937. Harold F. Gosnell studied the relationship of social and economic characteristics and newspaper-reading habits to election returns in several Chicago neighborhoods and found that the endorsements of newspapers could influence the way readers voted.[15] Thus, social scientists were provided with additional proof of the seemingly unlimited power of the media to persuade.

Limited Effects, or the Social Influence Model

Although the work of many of the army's psychologists and sociologists who were studying the effects of propaganda continued to reflect the hypodermic thesis, by the early 1940s, the findings of some researchers began to challenge the idea that the media were so potent that the public was mesmerized by them. One of the most important challenges occurred when three social scientists from Columbia University's Bureau of Applied Social Research—Paul F. Lazarsfeld, Bernard Berelson, and Hazel Gaudet—studied the 1940 presidential campaign and discovered (much to their surprise) that campaign propaganda had little impact on the way the electorate had voted. This study and others that followed began to build a competing explanation for media influence, one that was in stark contrast to the presumption that people were unable to control their own destinies or the destiny of the nation. It was, of course, a much more comforting thought than the hypodermic thesis because it provided reassurance that in the United States individual rationality and society's sense of order could not be overthrown because of the seizure or control of the media by a demagogue or someone who had gone insane.

The 1940 study began to form what became known as the *social influence model*. Twenty years later, mass communication scholar Joseph Klapper, in summarizing the conclusions of the work done on the impact of the media during the 1940s and 1950s, concluded that media effects are limited and, even in cases where they do occur, are mediated by other factors.[16] He coined the term *limited effects model*, a label that obviously stands in direct contrast with the earlier hypodermic perspective.

To understand this shift, it may be best to take a closer look at those studies that are regarded as the classics and that collectively influenced generations of mass communication scholars and their view of media and politics.

The first study by Lazarsfeld, Berelson, and Gaudet was conducted in Erie County, Ohio, a section of northern Ohio fairly equally divided between a city and farmland. Lazarsfeld and his colleagues wanted to measure the repercussions of campaign press coverage during a presidential election. At the outset they divided potential political effects into three categories: First, they believed the media could arouse public interest in the campaign and encourage voters to seek out more information about the candidates and issues; second, they reasoned that the press could reinforce existing political beliefs to make them stronger and more resistant to change; and third, they hypothesized that the media were powerful enough to convert attitudes, changing voters from supporting one candidate or party to supporting the opposition.

From May to November, a member of the research team interviewed someone each month in every twentieth house or apartment in the county. In total, six hundred people were questioned about political parties, candidates, issues, and the news. Interviewers kept carefully structured records of each talk, and from these records Lazarsfeld and his colleagues were able to reconstruct how Erie County citizens made their decision between Franklin Roosevelt and Wendell Wilkie. The results were published four years later in a book called *The People's Choice*.[17]

Although Lazarsfeld and his colleagues believed that their research would confirm the prevailing thesis that the media were capable of controlling individual thought processes, they instead found that very few people changed their vote in response to the campaign propaganda and that those who changed did not attribute their conversion to media information. Specifically, they learned the following:

- People who read or listened to a substantial amount of campaign media coverage were more likely to become more interested in the election.
- Their interest and activation were selective in that they tended to seek out stories that were consistent with prior political attitudes.
- Those relative few who did change their minds did so not because of attending to the media directly but by the filtering of information to them from people in the community whom they respected. Such people were perceived to be highly active, highly informed, interested in politics, and therefore more likely than others to read or listen to media coverage of the campaign. These individuals were labeled "opinion leaders."

In the largest sense, the results of the Erie County study were not as important as the two explanations that Lazarsfeld and his colleagues offered for their findings. The explanations formed the cornerstone of the social influence theory. The researchers maintained that, if a message presented by the media is in conflict with group norms, it will be rejected. "Since groups have opinion leaders who transmit mass media information to individuals who do not attend to the media, these leaders influence whatever opinion change takes place in the followers; media messages do not have direct impact."[18] The second explanation given for their findings was that people are selective in those campaign messages to which they attend. They only listen to or read messages that are most consistent with their own beliefs, attitudes, and values. In other words, voters use the content of the media to support or reinforce the voting conclusions they would have reached because of their social predispositions. Interestingly, the concept of selective exposure was based on an analysis of only 122 persons who by August had not yet decided for which candidate they would vote. While 54 percent of those people with a Republican predisposition exposed themselves to Republican material and 61 percent with a Democratic predisposition exposed themselves to Democratic material, 35 percent of the Republicans and 22 percent of the Democrats did expose themselves to material from the other party—material that presumably was inconsistent with prior beliefs or social predispositions.

These percentages were never explained, and the concept of selective exposure became a widely accepted phenomenon not only for the sociologically oriented voter studies but also by psychologists who eventually incorporated it into a series of studies regarding involuntary and voluntary exposure to information to reduce psychological dissonance.[19]

The second of the classic studies conducted by the Columbia group was also staged in a single location. In 1948, Lazarsfeld, Berelson, and William McPhee went to Elmira, New York, to determine voter behavior during the presidential campaign. The Elmira results, published in 1954 in *Voting*, supported the Erie County findings that campaign press coverage converted few voters and that information was disseminated from opinion leaders.

The third single-location study was mounted in Decatur, Illinois, and was reported by Elihu Katz and Lazarsfeld in the book *Personal Influence*. The researchers interviewed eight hundred women regarding "four arenas of everyday decision: marketing, fashions, public affairs, and moviegoing" and for each arena asked respondents "not only about themselves and their own behavior but about other people as well—people who influence them, and people for whom they are influential."[20]

Essentially, the results of the Decatur study confirmed the social influence model, although they also produced a more precise conceptualization of "the two-step flow of communication." The idea that had been hypothesized from the Erie County data suggested that "ideas often flow from radio and print to the opinion leaders and from them to active sections of the population."[21] However, in Decatur, the Columbia group wanted to compare the media behavior of opinion leaders and nonleaders "to see whether the leaders tend to be the more exposed, and the more responsive group when it comes to influence stemming from the mass media."[22] They discovered that the women they studied were willing to admit that they were influenced by other women, that leadership varied by topic, that leaders for each topic had different social and psychological characteristics, and that no single leader exercised control over the political beliefs of others. However, their most important finding, in terms of media impact on the electoral process, was that "opinion leaders were not more likely than followers to attribute influence upon their beliefs or opinions to the mass media."[23] Thus, as a result of the third Columbia study, the role of the media was reduced even further in the minds of most social scientists. It appeared as if no group sizable enough to be measured was persuaded by media messages during a political campaign.

In 1952, another group of researchers began examining voters' behavior. Using the 1952 presidential election as their base, the University of Michigan Survey Research Center, or SRC (now called the Center for Political Studies, Institute for Social Research at the University of Michigan), soon replaced the Columbia group as the dominant research force in large-scale voting studies. Methodologically as well as conceptually, the work of the Michigan group represented a major shift in the effort to examine voters and their behavior.[24] For example, the SRC relied on panels of potential voters based on national probability samples rather than a single community. In focusing on national behaviors, they moved away from sociological explanations (the emphasis on traditions, structure, composition, and the sociological nature of major institutions within single communities), which the Lazarsfeld group had presumed were the reasons for voters' predispositions. Instead, the Michigan researchers sought cognitive and attitudinal reasons for voting decisions. They asked citizens to indicate their party affiliation (Columbia had studied parties only in terms of social predispositions that led voters to choose one candidate over another). Thus, with party identification as a key factor in explaining voters' attitudes and evaluation of candidates, the idea of interpersonal communication and the two-step flow conceptualization as the primary means of information diffusion was relegated to a "relatively unimportant position in the SRC model."[25]

However, in one important respect, the early SRC studies did not differ from their Columbia counterparts. Despite the fact that in 1952 television played a role in the presidential primaries, in the nominating conventions, and in the general advertising campaigns of at least one of the candidates, the Michigan researchers concluded that the impact of the mass media on the electoral process was minimal.[26] In fact, in *The American Voter* (a book based on the data collected in 1952 and 1956), the researchers indicated that it was party identification and not television that was the important factor in the development of political cognitions, attitudes, and behavior.[27]

Finally, in 1963, undoubtedly in an attempt to revitalize a theory that was being challenged by many, Lazarsfeld and his colleagues described a modification of the two-step flow. In the new conceptualization, information from the media was relayed from one opinion leader to another before it was passed on to followers. The revision became known as the "multistep flow," and because more people were added to the transmission process, the persuasive power of the media was viewed as even less significant than it had been before. Moreover, not only did information travel from opinion leader to opinion leader; any one of these people could act as a "gatekeeper" and thereby prevent a follower from even being exposed to part of the information. In other words, opinion leaders not only functioned as conveyers of information among each other and finally to their respective "audiences" but also determined just what information would be transmitted.

Although gatekeeping was discussed by Lazarsfeld in relationship to the multistep flow in 1963, the idea was not new. As early as 1950, one study had examined the selection and rejection of messages by gatekeepers. One of the key findings confirmed in many studies that followed was that when media gatekeepers made decisions, they did not have the audience in mind.[28]

Essentially, a *gatekeeper* is any person in the news-gathering process with authority to make decisions affecting the flow of information to the public. "The image is precisely that of a turnstile gatekeeper at a sporting event—he examines the qualifications of each person in line, and decides whether or not to let him in. The difference is that what gets let in or left out is not a person, but a piece of news."[29] One of the reasons the gatekeeping function has received so much attention is that there are a variety of people in the media who must make decisions regarding the presentation of information and news. Examples include telegraph and wire service editors, reporters, film editors, headline writers, radio and television producers, news program anchors and commentators, and even other media (small newspapers and radio and television stations frequently take their news from the larger and more established media). Thus, given the wide spectrum of people who daily determine which of the many possible news items the public will be presented, it is little wonder that gatekeeping has been the subject of scholarly investigation as well as public consternation. Undoubtedly one of the most famous attacks against media gatekeepers was leveled in 1969 by Vice President Spiro Agnew. One of the broad areas of his criticism concerned the similarities of the various media decision makers. In an address before the Midwest Regional Republican Committee in Des Moines, Iowa, Agnew charged:

A small group of men, numbering perhaps no more than a dozen "anchormen," commentators and executive producers, settle upon the 20 minutes or so of film and commentary that is to reach the public. . . . We do know that, to a man, these commentators and producers live and work in the geographical and intellectual confines of Washington, D.C. or New York City—the latter of which James Reston terms the "most unrepresentative community in the entire United States." . . . We can deduce that these men thus read the same newspapers, and draw their political and social views from the same sources. . . . The upshot of all this controversy is that a narrow and distorted picture of America often emerges from the televised news.[30]

Whether or not Agnew's charges were true, they did provoke public discussion as well as a good deal of media response. In addition, gatekeeping continued to be a subject of scholarly investigation throughout the 1960s and 1970s.[31]

In summarizing the major ideas advanced by the early studies of media influence, it is tempting to conclude that, in spite of the label of some of them as classics, almost four decades of investigation has had little relationship to contemporary theory. Researchers went from one extreme to the other; first media propaganda was the harbinger of all that was evil, and then it had little impact at all. Effects were seen primarily on a one-dimensional level—persuasion. The informational or cognitive function was largely ignored because of the dominance of selective exposure, a concept with little empirical validation then and clearly inadequate now.[32] Moreover, investigators were so intent on confirming the basic tenets of the social influence model that they ignored media effect in such important areas as voter turnout, political activation, and information seeking. The studies were conducted at a time in which home television sets were far less plentiful than they are today, and so the medium was viewed as having little direct influence on political behavior. Radio and newspapers were important only in their role as reinforcers rather than opinion formers, thus suggesting that voters were limited perceptually by their past.

However, in spite of all this, the early studies remain an important part of our media research heritage for at least four reasons. First, they pointed the way toward research methodologies that were more sophisticated than those that had been used. Moreover, the Columbia studies were the last massive single-community analysis for many years. And the Michigan studies of the national electorate continue to provide the most authoritative source of election data available. Second, the social influence model did rescue social scientists from the mass media hysteria symbolized by the hypodermic thesis. Third, although the Columbia studies may have carried the sociological explanation of voters' behavior to the extreme, they did begin the path toward the study of mass media and interpersonal relationships, obviously an important area of political campaign communication. Finally, the limited effects theory served as a catalyst for later scholars who would challenge the idea that the mass media had little impact on voters' behavior or the electoral process. Indeed, the sheer attempt to disprove the theory may well have led to the multiperspectivism that characterizes contemporary mass communication research.

CONTEMPORARY STUDIES

Just as the hypodermic thesis reflected society's turmoil and the social influence model depicted a quiet, reflective people not swayed by campaign propaganda, the mass media research of the 1960s and 1970s was a product of or at least representative of its time. If the 1950s is described by such words as *quiet, inactive,* or *dull,* the following years can be characterized as disquieting, tumultuous, and wild. While the federal bureaucracy grew in size and influence, so did citizen involvement in public affairs. Beginning with the civil rights struggle, which brought local groups together to form national organizations, a number of large-scale political and social movements appeared on the national scene. Each of them demanded new social and economic legislation to ensure equality and to guarantee their rights as citizens to help formulate national and international policy. However, each of them also needed various forms of mass communication not only to recruit, organize, and maintain their movements but to publicize their demands by drastic and frequently passionate actions.

The changes in society and the escalation of the social movements corresponded to alterations in the mass media system. It, too, was growing, largely because of the widespread use of television. More people owned television sets, and it was beginning to replace interpersonal conversations and meetings as a leisure time activity.[33] Television was becoming the most revolutionary branch of journalism. While in the 1950s television news was typically read by one person seated in front of a wall map, during the next twenty years it became a drama featuring live coverage of national and international events. The sit-ins and marches of the social movements, the urban riots and burning of U.S. cities, the funeral of a young president and the assassination of his alleged killer, the bloody battles of the war in Vietnam all contributed to the transformation of U.S. news gathering and of those social scientists who studied it.[34]

It was in this atmosphere that many mass communication scholars began to question the basic tenets of the social influence model. Although they had no one holistic theory with which to replace it, maintaining that the media had little influence on or played no major role in the electoral process appeared a direct denial of what was happening all around them. A few researchers looked to the reigning paradigm for new explanations. For example, one study in 1962 indicated that uninvolved voters are susceptible to attitude change if any new information reaches them,[35] and another showed that, under certain conditions, it is possible for large audiences to get information directly from the media without the intervention of an opinion leader, suggesting that mass communication does not always work in a two-step flow.[36] However, the most important break with the social influence model occurred when social scientists Jay G. Blumler and Denis McQuail discovered in a study of the 1964 British parliamentary election that "regular viewers of television news developed significantly different perceptions of the Liberal and Conservative parties."[37] Clearly, it was possible for media to do more than simply reinforce the status quo.

Beginning roughly about the time that the work of Blumler and McQuail appeared to suggest a new perspective for viewing media influence in politics, other theories or quasi-theories were being articulated. In the remainder of this section, we discuss the basic assumptions or tenets of four of the most important approaches undertaken during the 1960s and 1970s and reexamined, reformulated, or extended during the 1980s through the early 2000s.

Diffusion of Information

One of the approaches that bridges the gap between the limited effects model and the contemporary conceptualizations is the diffusion of information perspective. It is related to the research that characterizes social influence theory largely because it was initiated in that era and because it acknowledges the importance of interpersonal communication to the dissemination of information. However, it differs from that theory in at least two important respects. First, diffusion research maintains that, under certain conditions, media transmission of information will have a direct impact on individuals and can produce changes in their knowledge or even their behavior. Interpersonal communication occurs after the mass media transmit information about news events and is therefore only a response to media reports.[38] The second way in which diffusion research is distinct from social influence is that it does not study attitude changes in voting behavior during political campaigns but focuses instead on the influence of the mass media on the acquisition of political cognitions. In other words, diffusion research is concerned with such topics as knowledge of campaign issues, candidates, and general public affairs. It is also used to investigate possible stages of information dissemination, how specific groups within society become aware of particular political matters, what factors contribute to the acceptance or rejection of political ideas, and what conditions mediate the flow of information about events.

Although diffusion has been defined in a variety of ways, generally conceptualizations of it in communication research capitalize on the idea of movement—the spread of adoption of new ideas (innovations) through time and space from one individual or group of people to another. In spite of the fact that diffusion research and the resulting diffusion model have roots in the physical sciences, it is employed by a number of disciplines within the social sciences. In the area of our interest, much of the early important work was done by Everett Rogers. In his 1961 book *Diffusion of Innovations* and in his later work with Floyd Shoemaker, Rogers discovered a multistage process of innovation diffusion. The four stages are (1) information or knowledge, (2) persuasion, (3) decision or adoption, and (4) confirmation or reevaluation. In other words, new information is transmitted through society (or from person to person) in a particular sequential pattern. While it can be argued that these stages will not always be either separate or sequential under some conditions for some people, according to Rogers and Shoemaker, the media are important primarily in the first or information stage, where an interest in, awareness of, and understanding of the innovation can be created. Interpersonal communication is important during the last three stages as people seek confirmation or interpretation of the information they have received from the mass media.[39]

To support the view that the media were the predominant sources of information about political news events, early diffusion research in political communication was designed to measure the extent to which messages were transmitted. For example, it was discovered that the media informed most people about the death of Senator Robert Taft, President Eisenhower's decision to seek reelection, the dropping of Senator Thomas Eagleton as the Democratic vice presidential candidate, and the assassination of John Kennedy.[40] To a large extent, much of the diffusion research even during the 1970s continued to be concentrated on the extent and veridicality of information flow. Thus, researchers appeared to be more interested in the attention arousal and information-seeking characteristics of the first stage of the process rather than the later adoption or persuasion stages.[41] In fact, after reviewing the diffusion approach to political communication studies published during the 1970s, Robert L. Savage reported that, with the exception of news dissemination studies, very little use had been made of it. He urged scholars to investigate such questions as these: Are diffusing messages causes or effects of human actions? What latent and/or dysfunctional consequences follow from existing diffusion patterns? He appeared to doubt that political communication scholars had used the approach for all relevant forms of political information.[42]

In a similar vein, mass communication scholar Steven H. Chaffee acknowledged that the diffusion approach had not yet lived up to its potential when he called for research that would lead to the development of a universal scheme for categorizing different types of diffusion items according to the type of communication that transmits them, the type of person most receptive to them, and determining the way in which items are relevant from the perspective of the political system.[43] And authors Sidney Kraus and Dennis Davis suggested that the diffusion model be supplemented by stipulating specific patterns of media use and perception to understand better the conditions that mediate the flow of information.[44]

Unfortunately, those researchers who continued to use the diffusion perspective during the 1980s rarely broadened or extended the scope of the topics investigated or the ways in which human behavior was affected—especially political behavior. Studies continued to focus on crisis news events (e.g., the shootings of President Reagan and Pope John Paul II in 1981), the relative roles of interpersonal and mass communication in the dissemination process (which one is the primary source of information and under what conditions for what people), and the rate at which information is diffused through the population.[45] In short, the model was never really expanded as some political and mass communication scholars hoped that it would be.

Thus, while the diffusion of information perspective helped redirect the focus of media/political research away from the unidimensional thrust of the social influence model, its potential has yet to be realized.

Uses and Gratifications

A crucial assumption of the uses and gratifications perspective is that a wide range of motives exists for using the mass media and that an individual's media requirements are dictated by such factors as their social roles, situations, or personalities. In other words, media audiences should not be thought of as huge collectivities who watch television shows, attend movies, and read newspapers and magazines for the same reasons.[46]

In one sense, the uses and gratifications perspective is similar to some of the other research approaches discussed in this chapter in that there is really no single theory. We do not mean to imply that the perspective is atheoretical but simply that numerous theoretical bits and pieces compose the perspective. However, as one of its principal advocates, Jay G. Blumler, has argued, the various theories about the phenomena "share a common field of concern, an elementary set of concepts indispensable for intelligibly carving up that terrain, and an identification of certain wider features of the mass communication process with which such core phenomena are presumed to be connected."[47]

Although a diverse range of research has been conducted under the uses and gratifications paradigm, essentially it has been concerned with determining those uses people make of the mass media in the circumstances of their own lives as well as the gratifications they seek and receive from such consumption.

To an extent, part of the popularity of the approach is that it has served as a means of integrating ideas of massive effects (the hypodermic thesis) with limited effects (the social influence model) to form a middle-ground position where the audience is viewed as active, thinking receivers who are neither susceptible to all persuasive media messages nor impervious to them. In fact, it has been argued that it is in this role as an integrative component in an effects model "that the uses and gratifications perspective offers its greatest promise to the study of political communication."[48]

Not only, however, is the approach used for its bridge between the effects models; it has the additional benefit of allowing researchers to study more than just effects—to get at the functions mass media may provide during a political campaign. While some of these functions may be obvious (we read a newspaper account of a candidate's speech to gain more information about the candidate and the campaign), others may be latent (we watch a television commercial about a candidate so that we have enough information about the campaign to maintain our social status as an informed citizen). In other words, the functions served by the media during a campaign are not necessarily what they appear to be. Information or cognitive gain may serve many important purposes for the individual, and the uses/gratifications perspective provides a way to examine them.

Although the uses and gratifications paradigm began to be especially popular during the 1970s, research conducted under its label goes back as far as the beginning of World War II when studies were published that dealt with the use of radio for entertainment purposes. Similarly, during the following two decades, when commercial television became important, the approach was used to generate data regarding entertainment programming. It was not until the landmark Blumler and McQuail study, published in 1969, that the perspective came into major use in examining political campaigns. In fact, it was this investigation of the 1964 British election that really spelled out the basic assumptions for researchers in political communication. Other studies followed, and in 1974, Blumler and Katz summarized much of the research the perspective had stimulated in *The Uses of Mass Communication*.

Research done with the uses and gratifications paradigm in the 1990s and early 2000s has studied new communication technologies such as electronic mail and the Internet to better understand people's need for and uses of these new venues. The overwhelming conclusion from these studies indicates that computer communication is similar to traditional mass and interpersonal channels of communication. According to authors Andrew Flanagin and Miriam Metzger, Internet information-retrieving and information-giving capabilities are similar to those of television, newspapers, books, and magazines, and Internet conversation capabilities and e-mail are similar to telephone usage.[49] Interestingly, what scholars appear to be concluding is that the new communication technologies are equal in communication capabilities to traditional media because "new media are transitioning toward the roles of more traditional ones due to their capacity to improve or augment the capabilities of existing technologies."[50] In other words, "It appears that technologies meet needs and not that needs meet technologies."[51]

In spite of the fact that multiple studies have been conducted under the uses and gratifications paradigm, there remains not only the lack of one unified theory, there is still some disagreement about such basic tenets of the perspective as the meaning of an "active audience" and if media gratifications differ in any important way from one set of ideological beliefs to another or from one culture to another—in other words, the relationship of social structure to the understanding individual citizens bring to political messages/events. The question of the sociocultural bases on which or through which the meanings of political messages are constructed and responded to was not clear in the original categorical scheme used by Blumler and McQuail. The five types of gratification orientations to political television programming employed in their study of the British national election were: using the political content of the media for vote guidance, reinforcement of decisions already made, general surveillance of the political environment, excitement, and anticipation of using the information in future interpersonal communication situations. The three types of avoidance were feelings of political alienation, partisanship, and relaxation.[52] However, in more recent years, some researchers—including Blumler—have emphasized the importance of the social structure, or the culture, in arriving at any understanding of the meaning people give to messages (or their motivation to use or avoid media). For example, in 1985, Blumler and his colleagues reported that they "never meant to talk about abstracted individuals, but about people in social situations that give rise to their needs. The individual is part of a social structure and his or her choices are less free and less random than a vulgar gratificationism would presume."[53] Whether or not Blumler and McQuail simply assumed the role of sociocultural influence in their gratification and avoidance categories without specifically discussing, it is not as important as the fact that in recent years researchers have begun to more clearly acknowledge the role played by social structure.

The second area of disagreement within the uses and gratification research is closely related to the first. Not only must the social determinants of the audience's media needs and expectations be considered, so, too, must the idea or definition of an active audience be considered. As at least one theorist has argued:

If the uses and gratifications paradigm is truly to come to grips with the nature of the audience's media experience, it will have to give up the optimistic and simplistic notion that an active audience implies a powerful audience. It must be recognized that the concept of an active audience, as traditionally explicated in the literature, may in fact obscure the powerlessness of the audience. Certain audience media expectations are never voiced because they are perceived as inappropriate or as so unlikely as to make their articulation sound foolish or naïve. . . . Other expectations, for some individuals, when expressed, may be significantly modified or tempered due to the sense of powerlessness they feel with respect to the political and social system. . . . In-depth probing of individuals' media expectations may reveal more about the assumptions these individuals hold regarding their locations in the social and political system than about any true media needs. In-depth analysis of the meaning of a commonly expressed media expectation such as diversion may reveal the use of standard media fare not so much for polite relaxation but for opportunities to ridicule a presentation of reality which does not correspond to one's experience as opposed to mediated life.[54]

Thus, while the uses and gratifications perspective has been the focal point of a good deal of research, and although the paradigm itself has served a useful function by illustrating that people pay attention to the political content of the media, it is interesting to note that Denis McQuail argued in 1997 that the research emanating from the uses and gratifications theories has produced little in regard to predicting or explaining media choice. He wrote that connections between attitudes toward the media and media behavior are difficult to document because the "typologies of 'motives' often fail to match patterns of actual selection or use and it is hard to find a logical and consistent relation among the three sequentially ordered factors of liking/preference; actual choosing; and subsequent evaluation."[55] In general, he described uses and gratifications as an approach that "overestimates the rationality and activity of audience use behavior. Most actual audiences also turn out to be composed of people with varied, overlapping and not always consistent expectations and subjective motives."[56] Although the perspective continues to spark research (particularly in terms of its utility in studying the uses and gratifications of the World Wide Web),[57] we believe it may only reach its potential when researchers who employ it give full attention to the social bases of message construction and response.

Elaboration Likelihood Model

Elaboration Likelihood Model (ELM) is a theory of message processing.[58] ELM may be looked at as a mass media theory that explains how receivers perceive messages and then make attitudinal changes. Elaboration is the engagement of issue-relevant thinking. If the receiver pays close attention to a message, the receiver will carefully look at all issues and variables in the argument. However, other receivers do not put forth the effort for every persuasive topic thus showing little elaboration. Two possible routes can be taken, central route or peripheral route to persuasion. The central route is concerned with core issues of the argument and attitudes expressed are persistent and resistant to change. The peripheral route is an expression of automatic response without the effort of understanding all the information that should be considered in the argument. There are four reasons for the choice that is made. They are motivation, ability, recipient variables, and message variables. Receivers either have strong motivation to pursue an argument or they do not, due to mood, lack of concern, or lack of knowledge. Distraction or the receiver's knowledge of the issues will determine the ability of the receiver to elaborate. Recipient variables are reflections of the receiver's education level, intelligence, or the amount of understanding of the issues within an argument. Lastly, message variables can strengthen or weaken a receiver's position due to factors such as the number of people who endorse a message, the message's personal relevance, or the existence of an attached stigma.

Agenda-Setting Hypothesis

Undoubtedly, the most popular contemporary approach for studying the relationship of media and politics is the agenda-setting hypothesis. It has generated and continues to generate more research than any of the others. It clearly separates the persuasive and informational communicative functions of the media. It comes closer than any of the other approaches to reaffirming the early basic assumption that the media do have a great deal of influence on politics; the media may not always dominate, but they do have a significant impact on what we think about (our focus of attention). Finally, the perspective is important for another reason. The most frequent site for agenda-setting research has been election campaigns, which has clearly not been the case with the diffusion of information, uses and gratifications, or ELM perspectives.

The underlying assumption of agenda setting was first articulated by a political scientist, Bernard C. Cohen, in 1963. Cohen argued that the press may not be successful in telling its readers what to think, but "it is stunningly successful in telling its readers what to think about. . . . The editor may believe he is only printing the things that people want to read, but he is thereby putting a claim on their attention, powerfully determining what they will be thinking about, and talking about, until the next wave laps their shore."[59]

Just two years later, empirical verification of Cohen's ideas began to appear. In a study of the 1964 presidential campaign, researcher Jack McLeod found that the stories from two newspapers revealed clear differences in their reports of two issues in the campaign, federal spending policies and control of nuclear weapons. Specifically, the study revealed that respondents who read the paper that provided a good deal of coverage to nuclear control (the Democratic issue) ranked it higher in importance than they did the economic issue. Correspondingly, those who read the paper that focused on spending policies (the Republican issue) ranked it higher in importance than they did nuclear control.[60]

In 1972, Maxwell E. McCombs and Donald L. Shaw explored the power of the press to set the agenda by studying the 1968 presidential campaign. Specifically, they hypothesized that "the mass media set the agenda for each political campaign, influencing the salience of attitudes toward the political issues."[61] Before the election, the researchers interviewed one hundred people in five precincts in Chapel Hill, North Carolina, who had not yet decided whether they were going to vote for Hubert Humphrey, Richard Nixon, or George Wallace. The undecided voters were the only people interviewed on the presumption that they would be the most receptive to campaign information. McCombs and Shaw compared what voters said were the key issues in the campaign with the amount of space devoted to those issues in the particular medium used by the voters. They found a strong relationship between the emphasis given by the medium to specific campaign issues and the judgment of voters relating to the salience and importance of those issues.

A third study, this time a national one conducted from 1964 to 1970, compared what people identified as the most important problems facing the United States (according to data from Gallup Polls) with listings of the content of news magazines. The researcher, G. Ray Funkhouser, concluded that "the average person takes the media's word for what the 'issues' are, whether or not he personally has any involvement or interest in them."[62]

In these three studies and many others that followed them during the 1970s, the agenda-setting functions of the mass media gained wide acceptance from social scientists. In part, the perspective was well received because it did not suggest that media have the all-powerful attributes envisioned by the hypodermic thesis. Instead, the theme from the corpus of work undertaken was that the media set public priorities just by paying attention to some issues while ignoring others. They determine which issues are important and in this way play an important role in structuring our social reality. In other words, people not only learn about issues through the media but learn how much importance to give them because of the emphasis placed on them by the mass media.

Throughout the 1970s and 1980s, the perspective remained important because it illustrated "how significant communication variables" could be "operationalized and linked to concrete political processes such as election campaigns."[63] It stimulated a good deal of research (although few consistent conclusions) on such important areas as the distinct agenda-setting roles of newspapers and television, the differences between the intrapersonal agenda (operationalized in most studies in terms of what each individual considers personally most important) and the interpersonal agenda (what each individual talks about most often with others), and the length of time required for agenda-setting effects to manifest themselves in the public agenda.[64] Moreover, the approach continued to be employed in the 1990s to study, for example, public opinion during the Gulf War[65] and the relationship between public opinion in the United States about foreign countries and their visibility in our television news programs.[66]

In 1982, however, perhaps in part because the campaign of 1980 and the subsequent election of Ronald Reagan reemphasized that television had become "the single greatest mediator of political outcomes in both everyday and campaign arenas,"[67] agenda-setting research was extended, by some researchers, to include evaluation. In other words, not only did the media tell us what to think about, but they told us what to think about them, too. Evaluation was a major extension of the original formulation and, for those who subscribed to it, helped place in perspective the apparent power of such campaign tools as televised political advertising (the subject of the next chapter) during the political campaigns of the decade. Among other things, these researchers argued that news stories suggest not only the importance of the subject matter but the contextual cues or frames by which to evaluate the subject matter.[68] In one study, it was found that, when the media concentrate on a particular news story, not only do program viewers become convinced that the subject is important, but through this process they become "'primed' to evaluate the president, in part, by his apparent success in dealing with this issue."[69] The researchers, Shanto Iyengar and Donald Kinder, also sought to assess the influence of priming in elections. They found that the issues over which voters appear most concerned as they prepare to cast their ballots for president or for the U.S. House of Representatives are shaped by whatever issues have most recently been the subject of television news.[70]

In a related study, published in 1983, scholars Gladys Engel Lang and Kurt Lang argued that Watergate never really became an issue in the 1972 presidential campaign (in spite of the extensive coverage of it) because it was cast as a partisan issue, just another example of election year politics.[71] The assertions of candidate George McGovern were "balanced" by denials from the Nixon White House. The Langs found that most people did not pay much attention to Watergate until Judge Sirica was "presented by the media as a credible and presumably objective spokesperson for the cover-up scenario. Subsequently, the press abandoned its practice of balancing Watergate stories and printed news that was more or less exclusively supportive of the cover-up narrative."[72] They termed the "framing" and "balancing" media activities as agenda building.

The framing or balancing studied by the Langs in regard to Watergate and the 1972 presidential election was also the subject of a 1991 book by Shanto Iyengar titled *Is Anyone Responsible? How Television Frames Political Issues*. In this book, Iyengar develops the idea that television news frames issues in different ways, each of which affects public opinion. There are, for example, *issue-specific* news frames, which pertain to specific topics or news events, and *generic* news frames, which are applied to various news topics, including those over time and cultural contexts.[73] Generic frames include *episodic framing*, which is commonly used as event-based news reports, and *thematic framing*, which provides a broader perspective by placing an issue or event in a context or as part of a trend or public debate.[74] *Conflict* frames, which refer to tensions between individuals, institutions, or countries, focus on differing points of view and also fall under the generic frame umbrella. *Economic consequence* frames follow suit and are recognized as monetary profit and loss.[75]

Although framing has become important in understanding the influence of the media, it is important to note that less educated individuals and those who do not possess strong ties to political parties tend to receive negative consequences of exposure to frames due to a lack of understanding and learning about the issues and strategies of political campaigns and coverage.

Framing or balancing research continued throughout the 1990s and into the early 2000s. For example, building on Iyengar's work, Joseph N. Cappella and Kathleen Hall Jamieson in 1997 studied the "game" or "strategy frame" in which journalists "tell stories" that emphasize who is ahead and behind, and what strategies and tactics are necessary for the candidate to get ahead or stay ahead.[76]

Without much question, the agenda-setting perspective has generated more research than the other approaches we have discussed. Its growing volume is documented by a steady rate of publication and by its application in a variety of social science disciplines,[77] especially in political campaigns and advertising. Perhaps one of the reasons the perspective appears destined to retain its "popularity" among researchers is the more contemporary extensions emanating from it. One of the most intriguing of these extensions is the idea of agenda setting as "a process by which multiple actors construct shared meaning about the campaign."[78] In other words, "the actual agenda of the campaign results from the interaction of social actors; each actor is constrained by the others and by the flow of actual political events."[79]

Agenda setting was looked at differently in John C. Tedesco's study of the 2004 Democratic primary.[80] His study assessed candidate issue agendas and intercandidate agenda-setting during the primary campaign using press releases from Wesley Clark, Howard Dean, John Edwards, and John Kerry to "investigate prominent issues among candidates' agendas, agenda consistency, and intercandidate agenda-setting effects."[81] Tedesco found that the primary candidates "converged on a common set of issues throughout the primary campaign."[82] Many of these issues focused on incumbent president George W. Bush's policies on Iraq, health-care coverage, education, and a rising national debt. Surprisingly, no single candidate led in agenda setting. Instead of following one candidate, it seems that the four main Democratic primary candidates took turns as to which issues to focus on in the campaign. Interestingly enough, John Kerry stepped outside the prominent issues being discussed by his opponents. However, they did not follow his lead, and Kerry eventually reverted back to the main issues discussed by a majority of the candidates. This finding indicates the importance of agenda setting by the group rather than an individual in the early campaign.

Reconceptualization of the Classics

Although not a complete perspective like information diffusion, uses and gratifications, or agenda setting, we nonetheless include in this section a brief summary of the major tenets of the 1976 study that, while modeled after those of the Columbia Bureau of Applied Social Research, came to opposite conclusions. We believe that one of the reasons the study is important is because it laid a foundation for research during the 1980s and 1990s that explored the relationship between the media and political campaigns.

In an effort to provide a body of knowledge that would "contribute to an understanding of election coverage and the American voter,"[83] Thomas E. Patterson implemented the "most comprehensive panel survey ever conducted for the study of change during a presidential campaign."[84] The study and its results were described in the book *The Mass Media Election*.

Although the Patterson investigation resembles the earlier work of Lazarsfeld and Berelson, there are major differences that are important to our consideration of political campaign communication in two respects. The first concerns the overall design of the study, and the second relates to the conclusions. We will begin by comparing designs.

In each of the Columbia studies, respondents were interviewed a number of times to determine whether their attitudes were changing as the presidential campaigns were proceeding. Panel surveys were the single source of data for findings. Moreover, each of the Columbia studies interviewed six hundred to eight hundred potential voters, and each was conducted in a single community. By contrast, the design of the 1976 study was more comprehensive. First, more people were interviewed (1,236). Second, they were interviewed in seven waves (five face-to-face interviews and two over the telephone), which were timed to correspond with each of the important intervals and stages in the campaign (just before the New Hampshire primary, after the early primaries, after the final primaries, after the conventions, before the general election, after the first and second presidential debates, and after the election). Third, respondents represented two communities that had substantially different populations and media (Erie, Pennsylvania, and Los Angeles, California). Finally, data collected from repeated interviews represented only one of the sources of evidence. The other was a content analysis of election year political news stories that appeared on evening newscasts of the three major television networks, two news magazines, two national newspapers, and two local newspapers (one in each of the selected cities). The content analysis was conducted from January until after the general election in November, and the interviews began in February and also concluded when the election was over. In short, the Patterson study was not only a more ambitious undertaking than any of the Columbia efforts had been, it was the largest project attempted in the intervening years—years in which research regarding the influence of mass communication was beginning to illustrate that the media were not passive entities in the political process.

As we discussed earlier, the primary conclusion derived from the Lazarsfeld/Berelson work was that the media did not play a major role in determining voters' attitudes during a presidential campaign. In fact, media messages were far less important than the messages relayed through interpersonal communication channels. Political opinions were determined by party and social affiliations, and therefore, if the media were not absolutely powerless, they were of minor importance in influencing how people voted.

However, in reporting the results of his 1976 investigation, Patterson argued that the presidential campaign is essentially a mass media campaign. He felt that, for the "large majority of voters, the campaign has little reality apart from its media version."[85] In other words, far from being an unimportant factor, media are a significant part of the campaign process itself. As a matter of fact, virtually each of the conclusions from the 1976 study contradicted those articulated by the Columbia researchers. Among the conclusions Patterson discussed, the following three are particularly important for us:

- Although the media do not change attitudes, they do influence because people rely on them for information, thereby placing media in a position to influence perceptions.
- The stories that voters see in newspapers and watch on television "affect what they perceive to be the important events, critical issues, and serious contenders: [media] will affect what they learn about the candidates' personalities and issue positions."[86]
- Thus, the power of the press "rests largely on its ability to select what will be covered and to decide the context in which these events will be placed."[87]

Therefore, the Patterson investigation of the ways in which voters were influenced by the media in 1976 is important. First, it firmly dispelled the long-term myths created by the Columbia studies; second, it provided the comprehensive data necessary to begin updating and solidifying our knowledge of the ways in which voters, candidates, and the mass media interact with each other in contemporary political campaigns. In fact, thirteen years after the publication of *The Mass Media Election*, Patterson was even more convinced of the media's power in election campaigns. In *Out of Order*, published in 1993, Patterson's thesis is that the news media has become the "chief intermediary between voter and candidate."[88]

In support of Patterson's thesis, David Barker and Adam B. Lawrence use the direct effects model to examine "the relationship between political news reception and candidate preference in the 2000 presidential primary races."[89] They studied the relationship between media favoritism and candidate preference. Their study found that listening to talk radio was a major predictor in which candidate was preferred. Barker and Lawrence found that listening to Rush Limbaugh was associated with choosing George W. Bush over John McCain as a candidate for president among Republican voters, even though the mainstream media favored McCain.

CONCLUSION

As we have seen, beliefs regarding the political influence and power of the mass media have come nearly full circle during the almost seventy years researchers have been studying them. First, it was believed that the media were all-powerful. Then their power was seen as limited and of secondary or minor importance. In each instance, conclusions were frequently based on substantial evidence but gained prominence because they reinforced the dominant attitudes and context of the time in which they were articulated. The effective use of propaganda in the 1930s and the early 1940s convinced researchers that the power of the media was massive. Indeed, the media were virtually unlimited in the ways they could change attitudes and produce behavior modification or conformity. Whereas in the 1950s, the opposite viewpoint was held because, in the context of those years, it seemed difficult to subscribe to the belief that U.S. citizens could be reduced to puppets who would follow the ravings of any demagogue. Moreover, it must be remembered that, when the classic Columbia studies were undertaken (during the 1940 and 1948 presidential elections), television was not yet a real factor in politics or in the environment of voters. However, by the 1960 presidential campaign, television was on its way to becoming a political force. Both candidates were using the medium for spot commercials, and their precedent-setting debates broke all previously established viewing records. When over a hundred million people watched the debates and subsequently talked about their perceptions and reactions to the candidates, it became increasingly difficult for social scientists to deny that media, particularly television, had any impact.

Thus, as the context/environment changed, some researchers began to question the limited effects model just as twenty years earlier they had challenged the validity of the hypodermic thesis. Eventually, most conceded that the media possessed some influence—even if it did not create massive changes in voting behavior. Some acknowledged the media's ability in the transmission and diffusion of information regarding candidates, issues, or the campaign itself. Other researchers suggested that people use the media for a variety of political reasons: for information, entertainment, increasing the range of topics for social exchange and acceptability, meeting expectations of peer groups, or intrapersonal communication. And there were those who argued that the media are important because of their power to determine what information or news would be presented. Thus, by the middle of the 1970s, many social scientists had begun to believe that media influence in the electoral process could not be ignored. Finally, in 1976, a study was undertaken that provided enough data to confirm many of the trends evident since 1960.

But the pendulum continued to swing. During the 1980s and 1990s, when every election year appeared to bring with it an ever-increasing reliance on television to frame candidates' rhetorical and visual messages, some worried about the omnipotence of the media. Thus, when we asserted at other points in this chapter that beliefs regarding the influence of the media had come full circle, we were not exaggerating. But do these perspectives from mass media research contribute to the understanding of campaign communication? We think they can and suggest seven principles of campaign communication that can be drawn from them.

The first of these principles is that the most important effect of media influence is seldom direct persuasion but providing information that affects perception and may ultimately persuade. Persuasion theorists have consistently determined that a "one-shot" persuasive effort or message does not change attitudes—at least does not change attitudes from one extreme to the other. There may be behavior modification or conformity when conditions include threat, punishment, or even reward, but not internalized attitude change. And it is naïve to assume that it is any different in the context of a political campaign. Instead, persuasive information about a candidate, about the issues for which the candidate stands, even negative information regarding the candidate's opponent will affect perception and thus help draw attention to the candidate and campaign and may even influence later perception. Therefore, we conclude that the media are important to and powerful in a political campaign not in necessarily changing votes because of a single message but in drawing attention to candidates and thereby providing information for a full range of attitude formulations (including reinforcement, reformulation, and repositioning).

The second principle is simply that the contemporary candidate needs the mass media, in part because voters have expectations regarding the media's role in providing information about the candidate and the campaign. Citizens rely on newspapers, newscasts, websites, and televised political advertising to tell them about candidates, issues, and the campaign itself. Moreover, candidates have found that they can efficiently reach potential voters only through the mass media. And with the proliferation of cable channels and hundreds of additional channels, narrowcasting provides candidates with special challenges and opportunities in regard to communicating their messages to voters via the mass media.

The third principle is that the media have tremendous power in determining which news events, which candidates, and which issues are to be covered in any given day. Thus, a candidate's campaign must be focused, in large measure, around those sorts of issues, photographic opportunities, and events that will draw media attention and provide "sound bites" for the evening television newscasts. Whether these are pseudoevents or real, pseudoissues or real, modern candidates do those things that will "play" to the media—that will call attention to themselves and their campaigns. Perhaps more important, because of the media, candidates do not do some things and do not discuss some issues. Often what they fail to do is just as important as what they do.

The fourth principle may be less obvious. Although candidates attempt to use the media for their own purposes, they are not always able to control it. While a candidate can send a press release, its use is not guaranteed. Although an appearance at the state fair is planned, there is no assurance the event will be used in the evening newscasts. It may well be that election coverage will focus on an opponent or on yesterday's gaffe. Moreover, media have the power to penetrate even the most expertly contrived image—the newspaper reporter catches the wording of the answer to a question, or the television camera records unplanned nonverbal behavior. Our point is simply that candidates may spend most of their campaign resources on the many avenues of the mass media, they may depend on them to present persuasive information regarding their candidacies, but, with the exception of their own advertisements, they cannot control the media.

The fifth principle is that mass media influence is important to our knowledge and appreciation of the electoral process itself. The media allow us to witness political events; they teach and instruct, thereby adding to our expectations about the democratic process. Most of the crucial events of at least recent presidential elections have occurred on television. Indeed, the 2000 election was a television campaign—it was the medium through which the candidates became known to the public through such formats as ads and appearances on talk shows and news programs. While this may increase or decrease our liking for particular candidates, issues, or campaigns, it does provide a sense of involvement as we affirm (or deny) our role as citizens.

The sixth principle regards how the mass media, primarily television and the Internet, changed the way in which candidates campaign for office. As we noted in an earlier chapter, we greet candidates in the living rooms of our homes via the television screen rather than at a political rally. Moreover, the candidates' television advertising and appearances on television talk shows and town meetings, as well as their websites, are the electronic-age equivalent of the whistle-stop tours.

Finally, we believe that the influence or power of the media has contributed mightily to the many changes in the electoral process. For example, the surfacing and primary stages of the campaign have become more important to the final outcome, receive more precise and planned attention by candidates, and generate more excitement and enthusiasm from the general public than before television entered the political arena. This has happened because the media treat these preliminary events in much the same manner as they treat the later stages. In fact, because of high media involvement, the first two stages have replaced the attention-getting power of the nominating conventions and the general election, and they have also seized much of their legitimate power.

In the largest sense, we conclude this chapter as we began it—convinced that the mass media (especially television) have a tremendous impact on political campaign communication.

NOTES

1. www.census.gov/prod/2004pubs/03statab/inforcomm.pdf, Information and Communications Section 24 (accessed May 30, 2006).

2. Steven Levy and Brad Stone, "The New Wisdom of the Web," *Newsweek*, April 3, 2006, 46–53.

3. www.census.gov/prod/2004pubs/03statab/inforcomm.pdf, Information and Communications Section 24 (accessed May 30, 2006).

4. www.census.gov/prod/2004pubs/03statab/inforcomm.pdf, Information and Communications Section 24 (accessed May 30, 2006).

5. www.census.gov/prod/2004pubs/03statab/inforcomm.pdf, Information and Communications Section 24 (accessed May 30, 2006).

6. www.census.gov/prod/2004pubs/03statab/inforcomm.pdf, Information and Communications Section 24 (accessed May 30, 2006).

7. Dan D. Nimmo and James E. Combs, *Mediated Political Realities*, 2d ed. (New York: Longman, 1990), 25.

8. www.cia.gov/cia/publications/factbook/geos/us.html#Geo (accessed May 8, 2006).

9. Frank E. X. Dance, "Human Communication Theory: A Highly Selective Review and Two Commentaries," in *Communication Yearbook II*, ed. Brent D. Ruben, 7–22 (New Brunswick, N.J.: Transaction, 1978).

10. Peter M. Sandman, David M. Rubin, and David B. Sachsman, *Media* (Englewood Cliffs, N.J.: Prentice Hall, 1972), 20.

11. Sandman et al., *Media*, 23.

12. Sandman et al., *Media*, 23.

13. Sidney Kraus and Dennis Davis, *The Effects of Mass Communication on Political Behavior* (University Park: Pennsylvania State University Press, 1976), 117.

14. Elihu Katz and Paul F. Lazarsfeld, *Personal Influence* (New York: Free Press, 1955), 16.

15. Harold F. Gosnell, *Machine Politics: Chicago Model* (Chicago: University of Chicago Press, 1937).

16. Garrett J. O'Keefe, "Political Campaigns and Mass Communication Research," in *Political Communication: Issues and Strategies for Research*, ed. Steven H. Chaffee, 133 (Beverly Hills: Sage, 1975).

17. David Blomquist, *Elections and the Mass Media* (Washington, D.C.: American Political Science Association, 1981), 4–6.

18. Kraus and Davis, *Effects of Mass Communication*, 117.

19. For a discussion of the methodological difficulties of the selective exposure concept, see, for example, Lee B. Becker, Maxwell E. McCombs, and Jack M. McLeod, "The Development of Political Cognitions," in *Political Communication*, ed. Chaffee, 28–31; Kraus and Davis, *Effects of Mass Communication*, 51–54; and David Sears and Jonathan Freedman, "Selective Exposure to Information: A Critical Review," *Public Opinion Quarterly* 31 (Summer 1967): 194–213.

20. Katz and Lazarsfeld, *Personal Influence*, 138.

21. Katz and Lazarsfeld, *Personal Influence*, 309.

22. Katz and Lazarsfeld, *Personal Influence*, 309.

23. Kraus and Davis, *Effects of Mass Communication*, 120.

24. Becker et al., "Development of Political Cognitions," 32.

25. Becker et al., "Development of Political Cognitions," 33.

26. Kraus and Davis, *Effects of Mass Communication*, 53.

27. Angus Campbell et al., *The American Voter: An Abridgment* (New York: Wiley, 1964).

28. David M. White, "The 'Gate Keeper': A Case Study in the Selection of News," *Journalism Quarterly* 27 (Fall 1950): 383–90.

29. Sandman et al., *Media*, 103.

30. Sandman et al., *Media*, 109.

31. See, for example, Lewis Donohew, "Newspaper Gatekeepers and Forces in the News Channel," *Public Opinion Quarterly* 31 (Spring 1967): 62–66; Jean S. Kerrick, "Balance and the Writer's Attitude in News Stories and Editorials," *Journalism Quarterly* 41 (Spring 1964): 207–15; and G. A. Donohue, P. J. Tichenor, and C. N. Olien, "Gatekeeping: Mass Media Systems and Information Control," in *Current Perspectives in Mass Communication Research*, ed. F. G. Kline and P. J. Tichenor (Beverly Hills: Sage, 1972).

32. Studies in the late 1960s and in the 1970s have consistently indicated that voters use the media for purposes other than reinforcement of their views. Moreover, other studies have shown that there are cases wherein voters prefer messages that contradict their views. Finally, with the decline of party affiliation, there is reason to believe that voters are not holding on to preconceived political beliefs but enter a campaign season with a willingness to be persuaded on issues. Steven H. Chaffee and Michael Petrick call the concept of selective exposure "too simplistic." See their book *Using the Mass Media* (New York: McGraw-Hill, 1975), 141.

33. Kraus and Davis, *Effects of Mass Communication*, 123.

34. Blomquist, *Elections and the Mass Media*, 7.

35. Blomquist, *Elections and the Mass Media*, 7.

36. Blomquist, *Elections and the Mass Media*, 7.

37. Blomquist, *Elections and the Mass Media*, 8. See also Jay G. Blumler and Denis McQuail, *Television in Politics* (Chicago: University of Chicago Press, 1969).

38. Kraus and Davis, *Effects of Mass Communication*, 126.

39. Kraus and Davis, *Effects of Mass Communication*, 128.

40. Kraus and Davis, *Effects of Mass Communication*, 127.

41. Robert L. Savage, "The Diffusion of Information Approach," in *Handbook of Political Communication*, ed. Dan D. Nimmo and Keith R. Sanders, 104–7 (Beverly Hills: Sage, 1981).

42. Savage, "The Diffusion of Information Approach," 115.

43. Steven H. Chaffee, "The Diffusion of Political Information," in *Political Communication*, ed. Chaffee, 125.

44. Kraus and Davis, *Effects of Mass Communication*, 130.

45. See, for example, Walter Gantz, "The Diffusion of News about the Attempted Reagan Assassination," *Journal of Communication* 33 (Winter 1983): 56–66; Charles R. Bantz, Sandra G. Petronio, and David L. Rarick, "News Diffusion after the Reagan Shooting," *Quarterly Journal of Speech* 69 (August 1983): 317–27; and Ruth Ann Weaver-Tarisey, Barbara Sweeney, and Thomas Steinfatt, "Communication during Assassination Attempts: Diffusion of Information in Attacks on President Reagan and the Pope," *Southern Speech Communication Journal* 49 (Spring 1989): 258–76.

46. Jay G. Blumler, "The Role of Theory in Uses and Gratifications Studies," *Communication Research* 6 (January 1979): 21.

47. Blumler, "The Role of Theory," 11–12.

48. Jack M. McLeod and Lee B. Becker, "The Uses and Gratifications Approach," in *Handbook of Political Communication*, ed. Nimmo and Sanders, 71.

49. Andrew J. Flanagin and Miriam J. Metzger, "Internet Use in the Contemporary Media Environment," *Human Communication Research* 27, no. 1 (January 2001): 171.

50. Flanagin and Metzger, "Internet Use," 171.

51. Flanagin and Metzger, "Internet Use," 174.

52. Flanagin and Metzger, "Internet Use," 87.

53. David L. Swanson and Dan D. Nimmo, eds., *New Directions in Political Communication Research: A Resource Book* (Newbury Park, Calif.: Sage, 1990), 18.

54. Carl R. Bybee, "Uses and Gratifications Research and the Study of Social Change," in *Political Communication Research: Approaches, Studies, Assessments*, ed. David L. Paletz, 209–10 (Norwood, N.J.: Ablex, 1987).

55. Denis McQuail, *Audience Analysis* (Thousand Oaks, Calif.: Sage, 1997), 73.

56. McQuail, *Audience Analysis*, 73.

57. Diane F. Witmer, and Chutatip Taweesuk. "Flow or Function? Examining Uses and Gratifications of the World Wide Web by Mexican and U.S. Communicators," paper presented at the National Communication Association and International Communication Association Conference, July 15–18, 1998, Rome.

58. Richard E. Petty and John T. Cacioppo, "Epilog: A General Framework for Understanding Attitude Change Processes," in *Attitudes and Persuasion: Classic and Contemporary Approaches*, ed. Petty and Cacioppo (Dubuque, IA: W.C. Brown, 1981).

59. Bernard C. Cohen, *The Press and Foreign Policy* (Princeton, N.J.: Princeton University Press, 1963), 13.

60. Kraus and Davis, *Effects of Mass Communication*, 216.

61. Maxwell E. McCombs and Donald L. Shaw, "The Agenda-Setting Function of Mass Media," *Public Opinion Quarterly* 36 (Summer 1972): 177.

62. G. Ray Funkhouser, "Trends in Media Coverage of the Issues of the '60s," *Journalism Quarterly* 50 (Autumn 1973): 538.

63. Kraus and Davis, *Effects of Mass Communication*, 214.

64. Maxwell E. McCombs, "The Agenda-Setting Approach," in *Handbook of Political Communication*, ed. Nimmo and Sanders, 127–30.

65. John Mueller, *Policy and Opinion in the Gulf War* (Chicago: University of Chicago Press, 1994), 130.

66. Holli A. Semetko, "TV News and U.S. Public Opinion about Foreign Countries," *International Journal of Public Opinion Research* 4, no. 2 (Summer 1992): 126–47.

67. Bruce E. Gronbeck, "Popular Culture, Media, and Political Communication," in *New Directions in Political Communication*, ed. Swanson and Nimmo, 85.

68. Anne Johnston, "Trends in Political Communication: A Selective Review of Research in the 1980s," in *New Directions in Political Communication*, ed. Swanson and Nimmo, 336–38.

69. Johnston, "Trends in Political Communication," 337.

70. Shanto Iyengar and Donald R. Kinder, *News That Matters* (Chicago: University of Chicago Press, 1987), 110.

71. Gladys Engel Lang and Kurt Lang, "The Media and Watergate," in *Media Power in Politics*, 2d ed., ed. Doris A. Graber, 255–62 (Washington, D.C.: Congressional Quarterly Books, 1990).

72. Dennis K. Davis, "Development of Research on News and Politics," in *New Directions in Political Communication*, ed. Swanson and Nimmo, 171.

73. Claes H. De Vreese, Jochen Peter, and Holli A. Semetko, "Framing Politics at the Launch of the Euro: A Cross-National Comparative Study of Frames in the News," *Political Communication* 18 (2001): 108.

74. Shanto Iyengar, *Is Anyone Responsible? How Television Frames Political Issues* (Chicago: University of Chicago Press, 1991), 18.

75. Claes H. De Vreese et al., "Framing Politics at the Launch of the Euro," 109–10.

76. Regina G. Lawrence, "Game-Framing the Issues: Tracking the Strategy Frame in Public Policy News," *Political Communication* 17 (2000): 93.

77. Maxwell E. McCombs and Donald L. Shaw, "The Evolution of Agenda-Setting Research: Twenty-Five Years in the Marketplace of Ideas," *Journal of Communication* 43, no. 2 (1993): 59.

78. Russell J. Dalton, Paul Allen Beck, Robert Huckfeldt, and William Koetzle, "A Test of Media-Centered Agenda Setting: Newspaper Content and Public Interests in a Presidential Election," *Political Communication* 15 (1998): 465.

79. Dalton et al., "A Test of Media-Centered Agenda Setting."

80. John C. Tedesco, "Intercandidate Agenda Setting in the 2004 Democratic Presidential Primary," *American Behavioral Scientist* 49 (2005): 92.

81. Tedesco, "Intercandidate Agenda Setting," 92.

82. Tedesco, "Intercandidate Agenda Setting," 92.

83. Thomas E. Patterson, *The Mass Media Election: How Americans Choose Their President* (New York: Praeger, 1980), 8.

84. Patterson, *The Mass Media Election*, viii.

85. Patterson, *The Mass Media Election*, 3.

86. Patterson, *The Mass Media Election*, 95.

87. Patterson, *The Mass Media Election*, 53.

88. Thomas E. Patterson, *Out of Order* (Knopf: New York, 1993).

89. David Barker and Adam B. Lawrence, "Media Favoritism and Presidential Nominations: Reviving the Direct Effects Model," *Political Communication* 23 (January–March 2006): 41–59.

5

~

Communicative Types and Functions of Televised Political Advertising

During the electoral campaigns of the 1980s and continuing through the 1990s and the 2000s, it became increasingly apparent that political advertising on television is a central communication strategy for the growing numbers of those who seek our vote. While during the previous two decades those who fancied themselves president had demonstrated a willingness to explore all manner of television commercials to champion the rightness of their cause, it was the 1980s that brought the television advertising attempts of all manner of candidates to our attention. Whether running for a seat in the U.S. Senate or for a chair on the Cincinnati city council, it seemed that every candidate was using television spot advertising. Political ads came to dominate whatever portion of public attention is reserved for things political. In fact, by 1990, during the first election of the new decade, there was at least as much discussion about the number and nature of the ads being used as there was about the candidates themselves. Voter or journalist, consultant or scholar, the central focus was television advertising. Criticism of the ads and their prominent role in the campaigns of 1988 through the 1990s was broad based. However, attention centered around what appeared to be a growing reliance on negative as opposed to positive ads; replacement of campaign dialogue with television commercials; the extraordinary cost of the spots; fear that the ads, especially those that were negative, determined electoral results; and the idea that television advertising had "turned off" the public.

Televised political advertising occupies a pivotal position within a candidate's campaign. Thus, in this chapter, we take a brief look at the development of television advertising in presidential politics, explore the principles underlying different types of political commercials, and then discuss some of the most important communicative functions they perform during the campaign. In so doing, we examine the use of one kind of commercial, the attack or condemnation spot, by candidates who are women. We will conclude our discussion by reviewing the major question that has developed around the use of attack advertising. Because in chapter 10 we examine all forms of media advertising, for now our consideration is limited to the ads candidates use on television.

HISTORICAL DEVELOPMENT

Televised political spots entered presidential politics in 1952 when the Republican nominee, General Dwight D. Eisenhower, filmed forty commercials that were titled "Eisenhower Answers America." Although the twenty-eight ads that were aired in forty states revolutionized the way in which presidential candidates went about the job of getting elected, in terms of narrative and cinematography, the Eisenhower spots were but a primitive form of those we saw almost fifty years later when George W. Bush was the Republican nominee. The format for all of the spots was exactly the same: A male voice announced, "Eisenhower Answers America." A regular citizen or "person on the street" (actually a line of people waiting to get into Radio City Music Hall in New York City) would ask Eisenhower a question, and the general would respond with a one- or two-sentence answer that implied that it was time for a change. For example, "a man on the street" would say, "General, the Democrats are telling me I've never had it so good." Eisenhower would respond, "Can that be true when America is billions in debt, when prices have doubled, when taxes break our backs, and we are still fighting in Korea? It's tragic and it's time for a change."

The 1952 and 2004 spots did, however, have at least one common characteristic: Each brought the techniques used in persuading Americans to buy commercial products to the front door of the White House. One of the most interesting aspects of the application of "Madison Avenue" strategy to the 1952 campaign was that it was totally unnecessary. Eisenhower, a genuine American hero, was, according to a 1952 Roper poll, the most admired living American. Although Eisenhower used the ads, his opponent, Illinois governor Adlai Stevenson, rejected the idea of appearing in spot commercials—at least during the 1952 campaign.

By 1956, when Governor Stevenson was again the Democratic nominee for president, he changed his mind about participating in spots—largely because the experts in both political parties believed television advertising had become a necessary part of the campaign effort. In fact, as political communication scholar Kathleen Hall Jamieson has written, "The major innovation of the '56 campaign was its increasing reliance on the five minute spot."[1] The ads in 1956 and the ones that followed in 1960 frequently consisted of the candidate talking directly to the television audience (the "talking head" ads) or those that made it seem as if "the viewing audience was eavesdropping on the candidate as he addressed a rally."[2]

In spite of relatively minimal production techniques, by the time of the 1960 campaign, it was clear that, with the technology of television editing, ads could provide additional arguments for or against a candidate simply by juxtaposing a still photograph of the candidate, a name, or even part of a speech with specific visuals to create a whole range of image messages. Some of the images were positive (American flags, the Liberty Bell, waving fields of grain), others were negative (deserted factories, foreign demonstrators throwing rocks at cars, farmers standing in front of empty grain bins), but all were examples of arguments by visual association. As Jamieson notes in her chronology of the evolution of American political advertising, arguments by visual association (positive and negative) were used in the presidential campaigns of 1964 and again in 1968. Moreover, argument by positive association characterized the Ford and Carter campaigns of 1976, and it remained a staple of political advertising through the early campaigns of the 1980s.[3] Although ads that utilized negative visual images were used from at least the 1964 campaign forward, frequently those spots that directly attacked the opponent did not picture the candidate or the opponent. Attacks were left to running mates, other surrogates, or unnamed, unknown voiceovers.

Without question, the best known of the negative concept ads aired only once (because of the legal and ethical questions it raised), and it never even mentioned the opponent's name. Nonetheless, the "Daisy Girl" ad so effectively cemented perception of the Republican nominee, Senator Barry Goldwater, as a warmonger—a man who could not be entrusted with our nation's national security—that he was never able to rid himself of the negative image. The force of the following ad was its ability to engage viewers' emotions and associate their negative response with Goldwater:

Video	Audio
Camera up on little girl in field, picking petals off a daisy.	Little girl: "One, two, three, four, five, seven, six, six, eight, nine, nine—"
Girl looks up, startled; freeze frame on girl; move into her eye, until screen is black.	Man's voice, very loud as if heard over a loudspeaker at a test site: "Ten, nine, eight, seven, six, five, four, three, two, one—"

Cut to atom bomb exploding. Move into explosion.	Sound of explosion.
	Johnson: "These are the stakes—to make a world in which all of God's children can live, or to go into the dark. We must either love each other, or we must die."
Cut to white letters on black background: "Vote for President Johnson on November 3."	Announcer: "Vote for President Johnson on November 3. The stakes are too high for you to stay home."[4]

In many instances, ads were targeted to appeal to voters in the opposition political party. For example, in 1964, several of Lyndon Johnson's spots openly called to Republicans "worried" about voting for Goldwater to join him. And in 1972, Richard Nixon used negative association or concept ads whose airtime was paid for by an organization called Democrats for Nixon.

Typical of these ads was one titled "The McGovern Defense Plan":

Video	**Audio**
Camera up on toy soldiers.	Military drumbeat underneath. Announcer: "The McGovern defense plan.
Hand sweeps several away.	"He would cut the marines by one-third.
Cut to another group of toy soldiers; again, hand sweeps several away.	"The air force by one-third.
Cut to another group of toy soldiers; again, hand sweeps several away.	"He would cut the navy personnel by one-fourth.
Cut to toy planes; hand removes several.	"He would cut interceptor planes by one-half, the navy fleet by one-half, and carriers from sixteen to six.
Cut to toy ships; hand removes several.	
Cut to toy carriers. Hand removes several.	
Cut to toys in jumble.	"Senator Hubert Humphrey has this to say about the McGovern proposal: 'It isn't just cutting into manpower. It's cutting into the very security of this country.' [Music comes in: "Hail to the Chief."]
Camera pans across.	
Cut to Nixon aboard naval ship.	"President Nixon doesn't believe we should play games with our national security. He believes in a strong America to negotiate for peace from strength."
Fade to slide, white letters on black background: Democrats for Nixon."[5]	

Jamieson argues that, in 1976, two new types of attack ads replaced the association, or concept, type—personal witness and neutral reporter. These ads featured ordinary Americans (not actors) expressing their beliefs about the opposing candidate (personal witness), or they presented a list of factual statements and invited people to make a judgment call (neutral reporter). As such, they appeared less harsh than the concepts ads and somewhat removed or apart from the candidate. Typical of these ads was the following used by the Ford campaign:

Video	Audio
Camera up on slide: white letters against black background. "Those who know Jimmy Carter best are from Georgia. That's why we thought you ought to know":	Sound of teletype underneath. Announcer reads script from slide and crawl.
Photo of Gerald Ford appears and holds underneath crawl: tough, unsmiling. Script already on screen crawls upward, being replaced by new material: "The Savannah, Georgia, *News* endorses Gerald Ford for President. "The Augusta, Georgia, *Herald* endorses President Ford. "The Atlanta, Georgia, *Daily World* endorses President Ford. "The Marietta, Georgia, *Journal* endorses President Ford. "The Albany, Georgia, *Herald* endorses President Ford. "The Augusta, Georgia, *Chronicle* endorses President Ford. "The Savannah, Georgia, *Press* endorses—" The spot fades out midsentence, suggesting more papers to be named.[6]	

In 1980, the personal witness, or "man-in-the-street," ads were used once again. In addition, longer ads, in the style of the documentary (a spot designed to present a candidate's accomplishments), were utilized—especially by Ronald Reagan. But in the 1984 election, and again in 1988, the negative visual association or concept ad returned in such force that each was, at some point, termed the "year of the negative campaign."

Another element that has undergone change from campaign year to campaign year is the preferred length of commercials. There have been half-hour speeches or biographies; four- or five-minute documentaries or other special appeals squeezed between evening entertainment programs or right before or after the late night news; and there have been twenty-, thirty-, and sixty-second segments. In other words, over the years, sandwiched in between programs and product commercials, political ads have taken a variety of time frames. However, during the 1980s, the thirty-second spot became dominant—largely because research had documented that they were just as effective as longer spots in getting the message across. For the most part, campaigns have come to reserve longer ads, such as the five-minute documentaries or biographies, for specific functions such as introducing a new candidate, raising money, or conveying an election eve message.

Thus, since television's entrance into the presidential campaign arena, the form and style of televised political spots have, from election to election, undergone change. In some instances, stylistic changes were temporary and reappeared just four years later. In other cases, revisions or reformulations were more permanent. Over the years, however, political ads have reflected two patterns with some regularity. While neither is surprising, each is important enough to our understanding of televised ads as a critical tool of the campaign to spend some time discussing them. First, the style or form political ads take is frequently a reflection of the larger society of which they are a part. For example, in the two campaigns of the 1950s and even in 1960, the spots were neither hard-hitting nor very specific (particularly those in which the candidates themselves appeared), largely because Americans did not yet equate the techniques and manipulations of Madison Avenue advertising and public relations with their presidential candidates, and the candidates themselves were concerned that they not appear too "political" as opposed to "presidential." Between 1964 and 1972, we believe that the harshness of the negative associations used in commercials has to be seen within the context of the national anguish created by the escalating war in Vietnam and the civil rights movement. In the campaigns of 1976 and 1980, the number of positive ads and the "feel good" mood that was their theme, as well as the indirect and less attack-oriented negative spots, must be viewed as a reflection of public distrust and disillusionment with politics and politicians in the aftermath of Vietnam and Watergate. And the reemergence of strident and graphically explicit negative association or concept spots in 1984 and 1988 may well have occurred because the campaigns did not generate any major issues or themes. From the surfacing through the general election stage, the focus was the character and image of the candidates rather than the identification and discussion of "burning issues" facing the electorate.

Not only, however, have political spots reflected broad societal problems/ attitudes/preoccupations; they have also reflected the prevailing philosophical and stylistic "schools of thought" operant in commercial or product-oriented advertising. While we would hesitate to contend that the process

never works the other way—that is, particular strategies are used first in the
political world and then by Madison Avenue—in general, those political
consultants who work in most of the statewide to national races apply techniques that have been found successful in commercial advertising. In fact,
after studying 669 political ads made in 1984 and 1986 for candidates on all
levels, and after interviews with more than 800 campaign and media consultants, author Montague Kern wrote that during the 1980s the "world of
political advertising absorbed its commercial counterpart and became as
one."[7] Kern argues that political spots in the campaigns of the 1980s were
like their commercial counterparts in that they evoked feelings or experience, relied heavily on visual and aural effects, developed messages in
which the candidate and a single issue were blended, and frequently attempted to associate a candidate with an affect-laden symbol that already
had meaning for us.[8] And as the campaigns of the 1980s became the campaigns of the 1990s, there were no discernible differences in the ads. The attempt to develop spots that provoke strong feelings continued through the
1996 presidential campaign.

In a study of presidential advertising in the 1992 campaign, researcher
Lynda Lee Kaid found that emotional appeals were used in 52.6 percent
of the ads produced for the Perot campaign and 46.2 percent of the ads
produced for the Clinton campaign, and 56.3 percent of the spots produced for the Bush reelection campaign contained fear appeals.[9] Similarly,
Kaid's study of presidential advertising in the 1996 campaign found that
63 percent of Dole's general election ads contained emotional appeals,
while 84 percent of Clinton's ads used emotional appeals.[10] In the 2000
campaign, Kaid discovered that 26 percent of Bush's general election ads
contained emotional appeals, while 47 percent of Gore's ads utilized emotional appeals. Fear appeals were also used by both candidates. Bush used
9 percent, whereas Gore put a stronger emphasis on this style ad at 56 percent.[11] And, in 2004, television advertising took yet another turn as the Internet became a vehicle for the candidate's spots. As Kaid discovered,
over $1.7 million was spent by George W. Bush and John Kerry on Inter-
net ads.[12] In addition, the Republican and Democratic Parties spent over
$600,000 on Internet ads for their candidates.[13] Moreover, Kaid catalogued
five types of Internet ads, including (1) websites as political advertisements, (2) web ads that were originally available in other media, (3) appeals for fund-raising, (4) original web ads, and (5) blog ads.[14] Although
we do not intend to trace the historical development of commercial advertising, the ways in which its methods and techniques have been used
by a variety of candidates become obvious in the next sections as we explore the types and functions of televised political ads and the questions
and controversies they have generated.

TYPES AND FUNCTIONS OF POLITICAL ADS

As the number of televised spots used during election campaigns has increased, so, too, has the number of people writing or talking about them. Whether the report of a practitioner or the analysis of a scholar, all seem to have contributed a name to describe the ads they have studied or those they have used. For example, in their book *The Spot*, Edwin Diamond and Stephen Bates argue that political advertising goes through four phases and thus produces four types of ads. Phase 1 brings ID Spots (ads that are biographical and are intended to introduce or identify the candidate—provide a sense of the candidate in the surfacing or primary stages of the campaign). Phase 2 produces Argument Spots (ads that identify the candidate's causes, ideas, concerns—what the candidate stands for). Phase 3 is the time for Attack Spots (ads that are direct and personal attacks meant to reduce the credibility of the opposing candidate—create doubt, stir fear, exploit anxiety, or motivate ridicule). Phase 4 produces Visionary Spots (ads that are used as the campaign draws to a close to provide a reflective/thoughtful/dignified view of the candidate—create the impression that the candidate has the leadership ability and the vision to move the country/state/city forward).[15]

In his analysis of presidential television commercials used from 1952 through 1984, L. Patrick Devlin describes spots in terms of categories such as talking head ads, negative ads (those spots that tear down the opponent), cinema verité ads (those in which the candidate is filmed in a real-life setting interacting with people), documentary ads (spots that present the accomplishments of the candidate), man-in-the-street ads (those in which real people talk positively about the candidate or negatively about the opponent), testimonial ads (spots in which prominent people speak on behalf of the candidate), and independent ads (those that are sponsored by organizations separate from the candidate).[16] Montague Kern contributes two additional types of spots from her book, *30-Second Politics: Political Advertising in the Eighties*. She defines *platform ads* as those that present a candidate's commitment to a position or oppose the opponent's position and *slogan ads* as those that contain no policy statement, why statement, or any answer.[17]

In a study of political advertising and its meaning in American elections, Richard Joslyn identifies four different perspectives or approaches by which the contemporary election can be understood, and he argues that, within each perspective, specific kinds of appeals are used in the television commercials. After examining 506 of these commercials, he found that the most prevalent type of appeal is one he labeled "benevolent leader." Benevolent leader ads, according to Joslyn, focus on a candidate's personality traits rather than programmatic actions, policy positions, or political values and "attempt to accomplish a correspondence between the role expectations for a public office and the persona of the candidate."[18] For example, the benevolent leader ads might focus on such traits as the candidate's courage, honesty, strength of character, sense of fairness and justice, or compassion. The ads can be in the form of biographies or documentaries in which the candidate is shown in situations wherein the traits discussed are evident, in testimonials in which a prominent person discusses a specific characteristic of the candidate, or even in a man-on-the-street format in which several people are featured as they remark on the candidate's virtues. Whatever form the benevolent leader ad might take, its focus is the candidate's personality or character strengths.

Not only have scholars offered a classification scheme for the variety of televised commercials; some have suggested that negative ads can be divided by specific types. As mentioned earlier in this chapter, Kathleen Hall Jamieson suggests three kinds of negative spots which she terms *concept ads* (those that juxtapose unrelated visual images to suggest false inferences), *personal witness ads* (which feature regular citizens giving unscripted negative opinions about the opponent), and *neutral reporter ads* (those in which a series of informational statements is made and then the voter is invited to make a judgment or draw a conclusion about the opponent).[19] In 1985, and again in 1994, Bruce E. Gronbeck identified negative ads as *implicative* (those that operate by innuendo without attacking directly), *comparative* (ads which juxtapose the opponent's record or positions on issues with those of the candidate), and *assault* (those directly assaulting the character, motivations, associates, or actions of an opponent).[20]

Although this summary is certainly not exhaustive, it may help you appreciate the complexity of trying to understand and distinguish among the types of televised commercials that have been used since 1952. However, we have no real desire to contribute either to the proliferation of ad types or to the difficulty of describing contemporary political advertising. Rather, our goal is to reduce ambiguity by classifying spots according to their primary rhetorical purpose. Within each category, we subdivide only in terms of videostyle factors (verbal content, nonverbal content, film/video production techniques)[21] that appear to have characteristics significant enough to distinguish one from another. In some cases, you will see that at least one component of videostyle (usually film/video production techniques) overlaps from category to category, although the overall purpose of the ad is unchanged. You will also note that what we term videostyle factors, other theorists have classified as types of ads.

We suggest that the only important reason to categorize types of political commercials is to gain some understanding of their rhetorical purpose. While ads are used by candidates to fulfill a variety of functions (which we discuss shortly), they have three primary rhetorical purposes: to praise the candidate, to condemn the opponent, or to respond to charges. Although from time to time these purposes may overlap, essentially, ads can be understood in terms of their primary rhetorical purpose. Thus, we characterize televised political commercials and the communicative functions they perform in the following manner.

Ads Extolling the Candidate's Virtues

The videostyle factors available to be used in ads whose overall purpose is to praise the candidate are virtually unlimited. Over the years techniques such as testimony, documentary, talking head, cinema verité, man-on-the-street, slogan, platform, or benevolent leader have all been used. And although some election years and the campaigns of some candidates have made extensive use of a particular videostyle (e.g., in 1980, 41 percent of the Reagan campaign's television commercials were documentaries),[22] most campaigns that have the financial resources to do so use a variety of the videostyles to promote the virtues/strengths of their candidate. It is important, however, that the videostyle not detract from the ad's primary objective—extolling the candidate and ignoring the opponent.

The communicative functions performed by ads of this nature are as varied as the videostyles. Moreover, they are critical for both incumbents and challengers, although the extent to which they are used may vary in relationship to other conditions. For example, if the candidate is a relatively unknown challenger running against an entrenched incumbent, it is critically important that the campaign tell the candidate's "story" or, in other words, provide information on her background, accomplishments, positions on issues, strengths of character and personality, family, and associates—define her. And television commercials can perform this function better and more rapidly than most other campaign tools available to the candidate and her staff.

While there are countless examples of challengers running at all levels who have had some success in using commercials of this type to "define" themselves to the electorate, ones who did *not* come readily to mind. In the 1988 presidential campaign, for example, challenger Michael Dukakis did not move rapidly enough after the Democratic Nominating Convention to tell the public who he was, what he stood for, what he had accomplished, and why he should be president. Consequently, the first series of ads aired by the Bush campaign immediately following the Republican Nominating Convention provided the missing definition of Dukakis. The problem for the Democratic nominee was, of course, that the Republican definition was not very flattering.

Interestingly, the same thing happened to George H. W. Bush in 1992. In an examination of ads used in the presidential campaign, communication researcher L. Patrick Devlin argues that "the Bush Ad team was unable to emphasize a positive futuristic message."[23] Early in the campaign, there were only negative messages. When they began the positive ads, it was too late. In his study of the 1996 presidential campaign ads, Devlin reports that Bob Dole's efforts to define his character were also flawed. For example, Dole's biographic video included a good deal of black-and-white footage of Dole's war experiences, but it omitted any references to his thirty-five years in Congress. While his military accomplishments did make voters aware of the senator's service to his country during World War II, it did not convince them that he was "the right person to be president." In addition, instead of focusing on a single theme or strategy, Dole's ads communicated multiple messages about Dole as a person. As a result, the Dole camp fell behind and never caught up with Clinton's lead.[24] However, by the 2000 campaign, Republicans had learned about the value of positive messages. In fact, the Bush campaign used only seventeen negative ads throughout the campaign, while the Gore campaign used seventy-one.[25]

A second important function performed by these ads includes using commercials to develop and explain the candidate's stand or position on issues. Not only has television become the primary source of information, but political commercials have become a significant source of voter information about all aspects of the campaign. As research has demonstrated, voters can learn more about a candidate's position or stand on an issue from a commercial than they can by watching the evening newscasts.[26] Moreover, ads have a cumulative effect in that their frequent repetition during the course of a campaign helps voters learn just where the candidate stands on a given issue. During the 1996 campaign, Clinton made significant use of issue ads, especially during the general election stage when 90 percent of the commercials were issue focused. Among the issues emphasized were education, Medicare/elderly problems, the economy, crime, and children's concerns.[27] In 2000, both presidential candidates used a number of issues ads; Bush frequently focused on education, while Gore often explained his position on education as well as on the environment. And in 2004, President George W. Bush focused on the threat of terrorism while Senator John Kerry explained his position on taxes for the country's richest citizens.

Additional and related functions performed by spots that extol the candidate's virtues include reinforcing the positive feelings of supporters and partisans (just watching the ad may strengthen conviction of the rightness of one's cause or choice of candidates); redefining or softening the candidate's image (in 1968, Richard Nixon's earlier image as one of "life's losers" was redefined to "statesman," in part, by his television commercials; and in 1976 Gerald Ford's image as a well-intentioned "buffoon" was redefined to "president" by the genius of the campaign's "I'm Feeling Good about America" spots); raising money (in 1984, Democrats used a special five-minute commercial about Walter Mondale so that they could raise money from supporters to air future ads); presenting statistical or "factual" information on issues (in 1992, Ross Perot's use of sixty-second "crawls" made him appear knowledgeable and straightforward on issues important to the campaign)[28]; and focusing on shared public values (a component of Bill Clinton's ad strategy in 1996 was that "public values beat private character"—the attempt to divert attention away from character to the public values the president believed he shared with voters, such as banning cigarette ads and protecting education and the environment).[29] In short, ads whose purpose is to praise the candidate can fulfill functions important to the success of the campaign.

Ads Condemning/Attacking/Questioning the Opponent

Just as a wide variety of videostyle factors can be used in ads that emphasize the virtues of the candidate, so, too, can a number of different techniques be utilized in spots that focus on the opponent. For example, contemporary campaigns have used techniques such as personal witness, comparison, negative association or concept, talking head, assaultive, or cinema verité. Although the videostyle factors can vary and, therefore, alter the directness and strength of the attack, the primary purpose can not. These are ads designed to place the opponent in an unfavorable light or in an uncomfortable position. They focus on the shortcomings (real or imagined) of the opponent rather than the attributes of the candidate. In the largest sense, the purpose of these kind of ads—no matter the variability of techniques employed—is to increase the opponent's "negatives." As such, they have received a good deal of attention from the public, as well as from journalists and scholars.

Since the introduction of televised ads whose purpose was to attack the opponent, a wide variety of formats and strategies has been employed. Some commercials have utilized humor and ridicule, others have linked the opponent with unpopular issues or negatively perceived people (guilt by association), some have fastened labels on their opponents and then defined those labels negatively, many have relied on fear appeals, and others have sought to create a suspicion or anxiety about the opponent's beliefs or previous actions. At times, viewers are directed to make up their own minds; that is, the attack or condemnation is implied. For example, the records of the candidate and opponent are compared, and the opponent appears to have no positive attributes. But direct charges or conclusionary statements are not made. In other instances, the attack is direct and overt. For example, either in the narrative or by use of visual or aural symbols, viewers are told of the opponent's shortcomings. Clearly, depending on the videostyle and, of course, the intent, the commercials in this category can vary a good deal. Montague Kern has given names to two of the hardest-hitting spots and distinguished between them in terms of what we think of as their videostyle strategies—primarily format and production techniques. She calls them "soft-sell," ads that make "heavy use of lighter entertainment values, humor, self-depreciation, storytelling, or the unexpected turn of events"; and "hard-sell," those that utilize "dark colors and threatening voices" and create "harsh reality advertising."[30] Without question, the heavy use of emotionally laden attack or condemnation spots continued through the 1988 presidential election into the campaigns of the 1990s. In fact, during the 1992 presidential campaign, candidates Bush and Clinton established an advertising record: 56 percent of the Bush ads were negative, and 69 percent of the Clinton spots were negative; and each had "a 50/50 positive to negative ad buying ratio."[31] It was "a new high in negative advertising by two presidential candidates."[32]

However, many experts believe that negative advertising once again reached new "highs" or "lows" in the 1994 midterm election.[33] David Broder, a respected political journalist for the *Washington Post*, wrote a week before the election, "the ads are increasingly negative and personal."[34] But even these negative campaigns were outdone by the 1996 general election campaign, which was considered "the most negative campaign in the history of presidential elections." According to Kaid, 71 percent of President Clinton's ads were categorized as negative, and 61 percent of Senator Dole's were considered negative. What's more, simply looking for the inclusion of a negative attack of some kind (as opposed to categorizing the entire ad as negative) showed that 85 percent of Clinton's ads contained a negative attack, and 76 percent of Dole's ads had a negative component. In total, 81 percent of all 1996 general election campaign ads contained a negative attack.[35]

It was the New York Senate race in 1998 between incumbent Alphonse D'Amato and nine-term congressman Charles Schumer that may have been the "winner" of the ugliest and most expensive negative campaign in U.S. history. With attacks ranging from the mild "too many lies for too long" to name-calling (improperly using a Yiddish term to describe the opponent), the campaign was constantly criticized for consisting of only negative attacks. The combined total spent on this campaign was over $34 million. In campaign 2000, as noted earlier, the emphasis on negative ads changed, at least for the Republican candidate, George W. Bush, who used far fewer negative ads than did his Democratic opponent, Al Gore. But, in 2004, perhaps one of the most profound changes in presidential campaign ads occurred, when the 527 organizations began flooding the airwaves with some of the most negative ads since the 1964 Daisy Girl Ad.

Video	Audio
The camera pans over a group of men while the announcer reads the script to the right.	Announcer: They served their country with courage and distinction. They're the men who served with John Kerry in Vietnam.
	Announcer: They're his entire chain of command, most of the officers in Kerry's unit. Even the gunner from his own boat.
	Announcer: And they're the men who spent years in North Vietnamese prison camps.
	Announcer: Tortured for refusing to confess what John Kerry accused them of . . . of being war criminals.
	Announcer: They were also decorated. Many very highly. But they kept their medals.
	Announcers: Today they are teachers, farmers, businessmen, ministers, and community leaders. And of course, fathers and grandfathers.
	Announcer: With nothing to gain for themselves, except the satisfaction that comes with telling the truth, they have come forward to talk about the John Kerry they know.
	Announcer: Because to them honesty and character still matters . . . especially in a time of war.
	Announcer: Swift Vets and POW's for Truth are responsible for the content of this advertisement.

When the 2004 election was over, many scholars and journalists believed that it had been the worst the country had ever experienced because of the harshness, fear appeals, lying, and distortion in the attack spots sponsored by many of the 527 organizations. In fact, according to Kaid, both Bush and Kerry spent more time and money on commercials criticizing each other than they did talking about their own virtues.[36] Most interesting, however, were the candidates' use of fear appeals. Although Kaid found that President Bush was significantly more likely than

Senator Kerry to try to frighten the American voter, the senator also used fear appeals—especially regarding the loss of manufacturing jobs in the country and low wages for American workers.

For the most part, the communicative functions of attack ads are pretty straightforward. If the candidate uses them early enough in the campaign and if they are aired frequently, they can set the rhetorical agenda for the opponent who will, in some fashion, have to respond. Perhaps the best example of attack ads that seized the agenda were those used by a college professor, Paul Wellstone, in his successful 1990 campaign for the seat of the Minnesota incumbent, Senator Rudy Boschwitz. In a series of spots designed to paint Boschwitz as an out-of-touch, "inside-the-Beltway politician" who was concerned only with his image, Wellstone simultaneously made himself a credible candidate and taught Minnesota voters to "read Boschwitz's polished TV blitz as cynical imagemaking."[37] The spots were simple in terms of production—just the candidate and a camera. In one of the early commercials, "Looking for Rudy," Wellstone was seen "searching" for his "invisible" opponent. First he looked at Boschwitz's St. Paul Senate office where he asked to borrow a pen to leave his telephone number for the senator (one of the ideas being conveyed was the "rich" Boschwitz campaign versus the "bare-bones" Wellstone effort), and then he "searched" at the Boschwitz Minneapolis headquarters and was told by two big men in suits "that we don't like strangers walking around here."

To some extent, the late Senator Wellstone's commercials had an even greater impact than they might have had in other campaign years. Not only did they attract attention because they were different than those used by other candidates, but the press effort to scrutinize political messages resulted in media discussion of the ads and, consequently, of Wellstone's issues.

A second function of attack ads is that they may well cause a defensive posture—even in a challenger—and therefore reduce the time, thought, and money that can be allocated to presenting a positive image. Similarly, and perhaps most apparent in recent campaigns, the use of attack or condemnation ads (if the charges against the opponent take hold in the public mind) can make, by comparison, even a mediocre candidate look better than the opponent. In other words, in the parlance of the consultants, candidates attempt to reduce their negatives and build their positives by increasing their opponents' negatives. The use of attack spots can also aid candidates by contributing to the perception of them as strong or decisive. This, for example, was clearly part of the 1996 strategy designed to allow Bill Clinton to run the most negative advertising campaign in the history of presidential elections yet be perceived by voters as less negative than Bob Dole. In the 2000 election, the Republican National Committee (RNC) was accused of sponsoring an ad that used subliminal messages, now infamously known as the "RATS" ad. This spot flashed at high speed the letters *r, a, t,* and *s* from the word *bureaucrats* and accused Vice President Gore of allowing bureaucrats to lessen the effectiveness of health-care plans. When the ad was played at normal speed, the letters were not visible; but in slow motion, the message, which was declared unintentional by the RNC, became more obvious.[38] However, the results of a study conducted by Lynda Lee Kaid indicated that this subliminal message made no difference in how voters reacted to the spot,[39] as we have already discussed, primarily because of the rise of negative attack ads and fear appeal ads used not only by the two political parties and candidates but by the proliferation of independent groups (527s) whose total goal was destruction of one of the candidates.

Finally, employment of attack ads can function to divert public attention away from those issues which might threaten the incumbent or prove embarrassing for the challenger. In other words, they can serve to keep the focus of the campaign on areas of strength, avoiding areas of vulnerability. Clearly, many of these functions can block or prevent meaningful campaign dialogue.

Ads Responding to Attacks or Innuendos

Until recently, little has been written about this final category of televised advertising. But, as is the case with the other two types, a wide variety of videostyles can be and has been employed by candidates as they attempt to answer charges or attacks that have been leveled against them. The only "rule" or "law" that appears to be consistent in regard to these ads is that they must occur and occur very rapidly, as well as repeatedly, after the initial attack. In fact, most media consultants believe that some kind of a response to a televised attack spot must be aired as soon as possible after the initial attack because people are influenced by them (many are disposed to believing the worst about politicians anyway). Some theorists believe that the only instance in which a candidate can get away without responding to an attack is when the attack has been made by a weak candidate (someone with "low name recognition, no prior electoral experience, inadequate funding").[40]

Perhaps, however, it was the legacy of the 1984 senatorial campaign in Kentucky that made clear the immense peril of the unanswered charge. When the campaign began, incumbent senator Walter Dee Huddleston's approval rating was 68 percent. His challenger, Mitch McConnell, was given no real prospect of winning. However, McConnell's media adviser, Roger Ailes, designed a series of humorous ads in which he used hound dogs searching for the missing Huddleston (the senator had missed some

Senate votes while he was earning speaking honorariums). The ads were humorous but focused attention on McConnell and his campaign. More important, Huddleston never responded to the allegation that he had a "sorry record."

While a response commercial may take a variety of forms, the most frequently used are those that employ a refutation strategy (a direct rebuttal to the attack), a counterattack strategy (instead of refuting the charge, the candidate launches an attack on the character/issue positions/ motives/actions of the attacker), or a humor/ridicule/absurdity strategy. For example, Senator John Melcher used a "Talking Cows" ad in 1982 to respond to charges that he was too liberal for Montana (Melcher was one of the incumbents that the National Conservative Political Action Committee (NCPAC) had targeted for defeat). In one response, cows were talking and warned voters about outsiders in Montana who "have come to Montana to 'badmouth Doc Melcher'" and how the "cow pasture was full of material like NCPAC's."[41] There have been a number of successful response spots, and with each election campaign their use becomes more frequent—growing, obviously, in direct proportion to the increasing use of attack spots.

In subsequent elections, response ads not only became more plentiful, but they were on the air more rapidly than they had ever been in the past. Consultants frequently created and broadcast them within six hours, hastening the process by beaming the ads off satellites and sending them into television stations in specifically targeted areas. In fact, "satelliting" became a campaign buzzword. One of the reasons for focusing on a rapid response is that consultants fear the attack ads of the opponent will control the dialogue or even set the dialogue for the campaign. Although speeches given by candidates or written position papers were once the framework for dialogue, in recent years, the framework has frequently been the attack and response spot.

Nowhere was this more apparent than in the 1990 election in California between the former mayor of San Francisco, Democrat Dianne Feinstein, and Republican senator Pete Wilson. During August, Californians witnessed a month-long exchange of charges and countercharges between their two candidates for governor. He accused her of supporting quotas for appointments in state government; she denied the accusation in a counterattack. She accused him of being too close to the savings and loan industry; he countered with a charge of hypocrisy because of her husband's involvement in the industry. The only ads aired by either candidate for a solid month were attack or response.[42] In the 1992 presidential campaign, one researcher described Bill Clinton's strategy as "to let no charge stay unanswered, to let no accusation remain in the news without being refuted by Clinton, his campaign spokesman, or his ads."[43] In the 1996 presidential election, response ads were once again a major category of Clinton ads. As the president's media producer stated, "It was our strategy to be reactive. In fact, we wanted these attacks because we wanted to rebut them so that people would grow increasingly comfortable with voting for the president."[44] Even in local races in 1998, response ads played a critical role. In the First Congressional District in Ohio, incumbent Steve Chabot successfully responded to an attack ad aired by his opponent, Cincinnati mayor Roxanne Qualls. His response was worded in such a way as to belittle Qualls for the attack, even addressing her as "Roxanne" and not "Ms. Qualls" or "her honor, the mayor," which had the effect of making her seem less dignified.

Without question, the most important communicative functions of response ads revolve around attempting to contain damage resulting from the attack. Specifically, the candidate's response must function to deflect attention away from the subject of the attack/charge and onto the candidate's own safe ground. Similarly, the ad should ideally function to put the candidate back in an offensive or "one-up" position. Candidates who must continually assume a defensive position rarely win the election.

One thesis regarding the strategy and defense of attack advertising is offered by Michael Pfau and Henry C. Kenski in their book *Attack Politics: Strategy and Defense*. They argue that the most effective strategy candidates can use is to preempt attacks before opponents use them, "thus militating their effectiveness." Specifically, Pfau and Kenski contend that one kind of preemption, inoculation message strategy, is most effective because it not only anticipates and responds to an opponent's attack before it is initiated, it strengthens resistance to accepting or believing future attacks by exposing the voter to a "weak dose" of the attack. The "weak dose" is strong enough "to stimulate defenses but not strong enough to overwhelm him."[45]

Whether or not future candidates will take the advice of Pfau and Kenski in the use of response ads is difficult to forecast. In sum, we have attempted to present a complete yet uncomplicated view of the types of political commercials used by a wide variety of candidates in the television portion of their campaigns. We turn now to a consideration of one type of those commercials as they have been employed by one group of candidates.

TELEVISED ATTACK ADVERTISING WHEN THE CANDIDATE IS A WOMAN

One of the most studied aspects of televised political advertising during the political campaigns of the 1980s through the 2000s has been the use of attack spots by female candidates. In some respects, the fact that women running for political office employ spots that condemned opponents is not surprising. As we discussed earlier, attack advertising has been a prominent strategy for all manner of political candidates from 1952 to the present. Moreover, many candidates who employ it win. In addition, the phenomenon of increased numbers of women seeking and winning political office began in the 1970s and has continued into the new millennium. In fact, several months before the 2006 midterm election, eighty-one women served in the U.S. Congress—fourteen in the Senate and sixty-seven in the House of Representatives (in addition, three women served as delegates to the House from the Virgin Islands, Guam, and Washington, D.C.). The number of women in statewide elective posts was seventy-nine (including eight as governors and fifteen as lieutenant governors) while the number of women who were state legislators was 1,660, or 22.8 percent of the state legislators in the United States.[46] And, after the 2006 elections, eighty-six women served in the U.S. Congress—seventy in the House of Representatives and sixteen in the Senate (in addition, three women served as delegates to the House from Guam, the Virgin Islands, and Washington, D.C.). However, the most important milestone for women in elective politics following the 2006 midterm elections was that, for the first time in American history, a woman, Representative Nancy Pelosi from California, became Speaker of the House and thus third in the succession line to the presidency.

Despite the fact that even in the 1990s and 2000s women continued to face obstacles to their election to office, those who were credible candidates were able to garner enough financial support to run campaigns that employed media consultants and utilized television advertising as a major campaign option. For example, by 1992, women with political experience similar to those of men raised slightly more money than men.[47] In fact, Dianne Feinstein ranked fourth and Barbara Boxer ranked first among all 1992 Senate candidates in the success of their fund-raising—not least, as one scholar argues, "because large numbers of women are now putting their money where their votes (and hearts) are."[48] In 1996, Boxer ranked fourth among all Senate candidates increasing a campaign war chest, and Loretta Sanchez ranked eighth among all House candidates.[49] Hillary Rodham Clinton raise and spent over $40 million to win her first election to the United States Senate. In the first three months of 2005, she raised over $4 million, building towards her second senate run.[50] And in 2007, fully a year in advance of the presidential primaries (while she was surfacing as a potential candidate for the White House), Clinton raised $36 million, breaking the record for presidential fundraising in the first quarter of the year.[51]

Senator Blanche Lincoln is another proven fund-raiser. She raised more than $3 million for her 1998 Senate race in Arkansas and, in the final months of 2002, banked $667,000 for her 2004 reelection campaign.[52] In fact, the senator raised far more from individual contributions and PACs than did her male opponent, during her 2004 campaign. Jennifer Granholm, who won the governorship in Michigan in 2002, raised $2.84 million the year before she competed in the Democratic primary and had $2 million left to spend during the primary campaign, which was "three times the cash on hand for either of her chief rivals for the Democratic nomination."[53] Pelosi has long been acknowledged as a formidable fund-raiser. In 2002, for example, she raised more than $7 million for Democratic congressional candidates.[54] And Senator Debbie Stabenow of Michigan raised over $6 million before her 2006 reelection campaign even began.[55]

In 1983, sixteen women's political action committees had been established nationwide. But by 1996 there were fifty-eight PACs and donor networks "which either gave money predominantly to women candidates or had a predominantly female donor base."[56] Even the long-standing problem of getting the nomination of their political party in an open race was lessened in 1992, when redistricting and a record number of incumbent retirements created ninety-one open seats in the House of Representatives (although ten years later in another redistricting year there were fewer opportunities for women—or anyone—because only thirty-seven House members retired). Thus, it is possible to view the use of attack commercials by female candidates as a natural progression in the evolution of their direct participation in elective politics.

On the other hand, over the years in which women have sought elective office, there has been at least one important reason that female candidates might hesitate before employing attack ads. In spite of the fact that published research has never unequivocally supported the idea that distinct differences exist in the communication behavior of women and men, even in the early years of the twenty-first century, sex role stereotypes continue to help shape expectations regarding what is appropriate.[57] For example, traditional expectations regarding the communication behavior of men include characteristics such as strength, ambition, aggressiveness, independence, stoicism, and rationality.[58] However, the expectation for the communication behavior of women is almost exactly a polar opposite. When women speak, they are expected to exhibit characteristics such as sensitivity to the needs of others, concern for family and relationships, compassion, emotionality, affection, and nurturing.[59] They are not expected to employ harsh language or to be overtly assertive, either verbally or physically. In fact, they are expected to smile (at least smile more than men smile).[60] And a summary of over thirty empirical investigations indicated that sixteen language features distinguish the communication behavior of women and men.[61] Perhaps these differences and stereotypes were summarized most clearly by Anthony Mulac when he argued that the differences in male and female communication "provide a consistent and coherent pattern in which male style can be seen as direct, succinct, personal and instrumental," and female "preferences are at the other end of these stylistic dimensions—indirect, elaborate, and affective."[62]

Most important, however, to our discussion of women as political candidates and officeholders "is that language differences can have judgmental consequences. That is, observers perceive the female and male speakers differently based on their language use."[63] The patterns of these perceptions, the gender-linked language effect, consists of female communicators being rated more highly than males on sociointellectual status (high social status and literate) and aesthetic quality (nice and beautiful) and males being rated more highly on dynamism (strong and aggressive).[64] The conclusion that women are perceived as nicer than men but as less strong and aggressive—less tough—may well be reflected not only in a nationwide poll taken in 2006 in which, only 55 percent of those surveyed said that "the country as a whole is ready for a female president"[65] but also in the fact that, in 2006, only eight of fifty of the country's state governors are women.[66]

While we know that gender-based communication stereotypes are not universally accepted, we also know that speakers who fail to conform to expected behavior risk audience rejection of their message. One of the ways in which the impact of gender expectations on perceptions of communication effectiveness can be explained is by using Michael Burgoon and Gerald R. Miller's idea of *language expectancy theory*. According to their theory, expectations about language behaviors influence the acceptance or rejection of persuasive messages. Language that negatively violates normative expectations decreases the effectiveness of persuasive attempts, while language that conforms more closely to expectations than anticipated increases persuasive effectiveness.[67] Thus, for example, if we consider submissiveness as one of the prescriptive generalizations about appropriate language behavior for women, our expectation is that their language will be less intense than the language of males. In fact, one of the conclusions from Burgoon and Miller's research is that "females fared better when they used language of low intensity."[68] And in 1994, linguist Deborah Tannen argued in her book *Talking from 9 to 5: How Women's and Men's Conversational Styles Affect Who Gets Heard, Who Gets Credit* that our expectations "for how a person in authority should behave are at odds with our expectations for how a woman should behave."[69] In other words, "everything she does to enhance her assertiveness risks undercutting her femininity, in the eyes of others. And everything she does to fit expectations of how a woman should talk risks undercutting the impression of competence that she makes."[70]

While expectations based on gender can create problems for all professional women, in elective politics, the worry has been the very real potential for a backlash effect on the campaign efforts of those women whose communication defies or even challenges normative standards. In other words, the question is, does backlash occur when a female candidate exhibits so-called masculine communication behavior and thereby violates the traditional view of women as deferential, soft, and feminine?[71]

In 1981, Ruth B. Mandel, author of *In the Running: The New Woman Candidate*, argued that the female candidate "still must cope with centuries-old biases with perception that her image is wrong, that someone who looks like her was not made to lead a city, state, or nation or to decide questions of national well-being or international security."[72] One of the ways in which these biases are manifested is in the female candidate's communication behavior. If she does not employ the language expected, she will violate the "rules," the long-held perception of the way in which women traditionally communicate.

At first glance, it may appear that the biases or stereotypes regarding women is a concern of the past because the percentage of women holding elective office has increased in recent years. However, it is important to understand that the increased percentages do not tell the whole story. The fact is that the ratio of women to men remains small, especially as the level of office increases. For the most part, the higher the level, the less likely you are to find a woman as the elected official. Even after the 2006 elections and after eight election cycles in which women candidates had done well at the polls, only eight of the fifty states had women governors, only sixteen of the one hundred U.S. senators were women, and only seventy of 435 members of the House of Representatives were women. Thus, even with the increased percentage of women holding elective office, the ratio of men to women suggests that the biases Mandel documented in 1981 have not yet entirely disappeared.

In 1984, for example, as the vice presidential nominee of the Democratic Party, Geraldine Ferraro was questioned about her hairstyle and her recipes for baking pies. She was sometimes given a corsage to wear at rallies at which she was the principal speaker, and the size of her dress was apparently viewed as important enough to be included in a *Newsweek* story about her candidacy shortly after the Democratic Nominating Convention. A few years later, in recalling her brief campaign to "test the waters" during the surfacing stage of the 1988 presidential election, Congresswoman Patricia Schroeder noted that, when she was talking about nuclear testing, the media asked whether her "husband would donate his tuxedo to the Smithsonian Institution" and that, judging from the kind of coverage the media gave her, it was as if the "fate of all womanhood on the planet depended on whether I wore earrings."[73] In 1993, following her first election to the Senate, Kay Bailey Hutchison was "greeted after the election with a newspaper headline: 'Former University of Texas Longhorn Cheerleader

Elected.'"[74] Five years later, in 1998, when Blanche Lincoln, the mother of twins, was elected to the U.S. Senate from Arkansas, a columnist lambasted her for running for the Senate because of her sons, saying that such activity was incompatible with being a good mother to young children.[75]

And just in case we wanted to believe that with the new millennium the media changed in what they write about female candidates and officeholders, an article in a Michigan newspaper published on January 2, 2003, was as problematic as any of our previous examples. In reporting on Michigan governor Jennifer Granholm's first day in office, it was noted that, while shaking hands and greeting people, she was "wearing a purple pantsuit with black lapels and cuffs."[76] As a matter of fact, reporting on the clothes worn by Governor Granholm during the official celebration of her election victory reinforces research on the media coverage of female candidates during the first two major election cycles of the twenty-first century. In two studies of newspapers covering mixed-gender senatorial and gubernatorial races in 2002 and 2003, researchers discovered that, although female candidates received as much press coverage as male candidates and were, indeed, more likely to be the dominant focus of the newspaper reports than were males, females were much more likely than males to have their marital status, appearance, and gender mentioned. And as published in their book, *Gender and Candidate Communication*, authors Dianne G. Bystrom, Mary Christine Banwart, Lynda Lee Kaid, and Terry A. Robertson note that, in races for the United States Senate and state governorships between 1990 and 2002, Senate candidates were "often depicted in newspaper articles as wearing a certain outfit or sporting a new hairstyle."[77] In fact, "Hillary Rodham Clinton's (D-NY) suits became a major area of concern for the *New York Times* in her first race for the U.S. Senate."[78] Moreover, the children of female candidates received more attention from the media than did the children of male candidates.[79]

Thus, given the continuing pervasiveness of gender-based expectations or biases, as well as the increasing dominance of televised attack commercials, the tasks facing female candidates as they negotiate their way through a contemporary campaign continue to be formidable. If they use attack advertising, do they run the risk of being viewed as too aggressive, shrill, vicious, nagging, and "bitchy" (a metaphor or rhetorical frame that unfortunately continues to be used in regard to women leaders), thus losing the advantages of being perceived as nurturing, sensitive, and warm?[80] On the other hand, the political danger in not using attack advertising, particularly in an environment in which attacks are being used by an opponent, has been well documented.

Most researchers believe that three campaign conditions favor the use of condemnation spots: low-budget campaigns, campaigns of challengers, and campaigns in which one candidate is way behind or has suddenly begun a precipitous decline in the polls. Because female candidates have frequently found themselves in one or more of these conditions, they have been inclined to use attack spots. For example, after examining 329 ads used by twenty-five female candidates running for the United States Congress or state governorships between 1982 and 1986, Judith S. Trent and Teresa Sabourin concluded that 20 percent, or sixty-five of the 329 spots, were attack commercials.[81] However, by the 1996 and 2000 elections, studies revealed that women candidates were using more negative advertising than men.[82]

Given the fact that female candidates are using attack advertising, three questions seem important. First, have they ignored gender-based expectations or biases regarding their communication behavior? Second, have they in some way attempted to accommodate normative expectations even as they use televised condemnation spots? Third, if they have chosen to employ both strategies, how have their attack ads been packaged—that is, what has been their content and form? Perhaps most interesting are the changes that have evolved from the 1980s through the early elections of the twenty-first century.

In a study reported in 1985, James G. Benze and Eugene R. Declercq compared the television commercials of twenty-three males and twenty-three females who ran for elective office between 1980 and 1983. They learned that the females were slightly more likely than males to attack the issue stance of their opponents than to attack their opponent's character. They also discovered that the female candidates whose ads they examined did not use the ads to project an image of "toughness or aggressiveness." Instead of toughness, there appeared to be a tendency for female "candidates to stress their strengths rather than counteract their weakness."[83]

A second study, this one an examination of the "identity-building strategies" of the first two women in American history to oppose each other in a gubernatorial general election, came to a conclusion essentially similar to the one drawn by Benze and Declercq. After analyzing the television commercials used by Helen Boosalis and Kay Orr during the 1986 Nebraska gubernatorial campaign, researchers David E. Procter, Roger C. Aden, and Phyllis Japp conclude that both women attempted to "blend soft, 'womanly' images with more 'male' images of experience and leadership."[84] The authors argue that a major component of Orr's victory was that, even using attack advertising, she was able to build an image that projected compassion as well as toughness, thereby avoiding the appearance of being perceived as too strident or abrasive. In other words, the 1986 Orr campaign sought the advantages of both feminine and masculine communication stereotypes.

In an examination of the content and form of sixty-five attack ads used by women competing for elective office between 1982 and 1986, Judith

Trent and Teresa Sabourin found a clear effort to use elements of stereo-typical or expected feminine communication behavior within the confines of attack advertising. The candidates blended aspects of the female communication stereotype with masculine communication stereotypes to indicate that they were not too nurturing nor too compassionate to be successful in the office sought. To project the masculine image of strength, competence, and qualifications, the ads are infused with male voiceovers, discussion of experience or competence, and the visual picture of a candidate dressed in a highly professional/business manner. However, to maintain the feminine image, and thus preserve at least some normative expectations, candidates used strategies such as attacking issues and not character; making comparisons as opposed to harsh attacks; talking about social welfare issues; using music; picturing children or senior citizens; or ending the ad with a positive discussion of the candidate rather than continuing the attack on the opponent. In other words, attacks on opponents were embedded within a set of secondary strategies designed to mitigate against the potential negative impact of the ad on the candidate herself.[85]

In a study published in 1993, Trent and Sabourin extended their earlier research by comparing a sample of ads of male congressional and gubernatorial candidates with those of the female candidates running for the U.S. Congress or state governorships. They found that the spots used by males contained harder attacks, more frequently pictured the opponent, showed the candidate in strictly business attire, and did not typically feature the candidate live (however, when live he would be shown in close-ups generally and in every case was shown in a close-up when the attack was delivered). Trent and Sabourin conclude that the negative ads of male candidates are opponent centered. In other words, the "candidate may be distanced from the ad but the attack is 'hard and fast' and its primary focus is the opponent."[86] However, the ads used by female candidates had more variety in terms of the type of negative ad, did not picture the opponent, showed the candidate in professional clothing less frequently, and was less likely to show the candidate in a close-up at the time of the attack. The female candidates were also "more likely than males to use other people in the ad (both men and women), and to physically touch someone."[87] In other words, the negative ad style of the female candidates was candidate centered and opponent centered in that the focus of the ads were not only the "'negatives' of the opponent but the 'positives' of the candidate."[88] Trent and Sabourin conclude that the results reinforced their earlier study—that the negative ads of female candidates are composed of a blend of masculine and feminine strategies. They speculate that such blending allows female candidates to "accommodate gender-based stereotypes of femininity even while using a campaign tool that is inherently aggressive, confrontational, argumentative, or, in other words, stereotypically masculine."[89]

In a study of the television commercials of thirty-eight candidates who were running for the U.S. Senate between 1984 and 1986, it was learned that, in both their candidate-oriented and opponent-oriented commercials, female candidates spent more time on social issues such as education and health care, and male candidates spent more time on economic issues.[90]

A sixth study compared the videostyles (presentations of self through verbal, nonverbal, and production strategies) of female and male U.S. Senate candidates in 1992. It revealed that similarities as well as significant differences existed in the candidates' use of verbal, visual, and production strategies. Males and females equally emphasized stereotypical "feminine" and "masculine" issues and image characteristics and used about the same percentage of negative ads. Females, however, generally used verbal strategies such as invoking change, inviting action, and attacking their opponents on their records. They also used more language intensifiers, made more eye contact, smiled more, dressed more formally, spoke more often about themselves in the ads, pictured themselves and their opponents, appeared "head on," and used a "sound-on" candidate live audio. But males were more likely than females to stress trustworthiness, picture themselves and others, look serious or attentive, dress casually, use testimonials and other people to appear in the ads and speak on their behalf, and utilize a variety of spot lengths.[91]

Finally, Cady Short-Thompson examined televised ads, speeches, and campaign literature of the nine major party female gubernatorial candidates and the nine male major party candidates who opposed them in the 1994 election. She found limited support for the idea that gender influenced the construction of televised spots. Although there were some differences in communication styles (women smiled more frequently than men, pictured their families less frequently, used fewer language intensifiers, and dressed more formally), she noted a number of similarities. One of the most important commonalities was that both women and men used so-called masculine and feminine communication behaviors. In other words, the ads of these gubernatorial candidates were not limited to those communication behaviors or production strategies that have been traditionally associated with gender.[92]

Thus, our review of the early research on women's use of negative advertising suggests that results are mixed. There is clearly some evidence that women's ads varied in verbal, visual, or production strategies from those of men. However, there is also documentation that there had been a blending of what have been called "masculine" and "feminine" strategies or communication behaviors.

But what about the research stemming from the elections of the late 1990s and beyond? In a study of 152 spots produced for twenty-six candidates competing in mixed-gender races for U.S. Senate seats and state governorships in 1996, researchers Dianne Bystrom and Jerry Miller found that not only did female candidates use more attack ads than did their male counterparts, but also they dressed more formally, used more pictures of themselves and of their opponents, took the offensive positions on issues, emphasized an aggressive or fighter image, and discussed taxes (a campaign issue that had for years been considered "masculine"). Interestingly, the researchers found that, although women stressed their honesty, integrity, sensitivity, understanding, warmth, and compassion, men emphasized it slightly (though not statistically significantly) more. In addition, the ads of male candidates focused on their past successes and leadership experience more than did the ads of female candidates.[93] In a second study, this time of 1998 senatorial and gubernatorial races, it was learned that female candidates were significantly more likely to emphasize their aggressiveness than were male candidates.[94] In a third study that compared voter perceptions of female and male candidates using negative advertising in 1990 and again in 2000, it was found that "in both years when the female candidate received a majority of subjects' votes she was perceived as possessing higher levels of both feminine and masculine traits than the male candidate. When the female did not receive a majority of votes, the subjects perceived her as either possessing only higher levels of feminine or only higher levels of masculine traits." In other words, the female candidates needed both sets of characteristics to be successful. The male candidates had more flexibility in that they received subjects' votes whether they were perceived to have either male or both feminine and masculine traits. The female candidates who received the least support were those perceived as having primarily feminine traits.[95] In a fourth study of the television ads of female and male candidates in United States Senate and gubernatorial races from 1990 through 2002, the researchers concluded that "female Videostyle is characterized by an attention to feminine issues, balance of masculine and feminine image traits, blend of feminine style and challenger appeals, a smiling facial expression, and formal dress."[96] And in 2004, the authors of one study concluded that "successful female candidates were more likely to use fear appeals, discuss issues more frequently than their opponent, and emphasize their qualifications. Winning male candidates were more likely to use statistics, emphasize their accomplishments, and present themselves as sensitive and understanding."[97]

So, what do we conclude about the female candidate's use of negative advertising in the elections of the 1990s and into the twenty-first century? Certainly there is evidence that the attack ads of women and men continue to be a blend of stereotypical masculine and feminine styles. However, we also have reason to believe that the ads of a successful female candidate focus, at least in part, on her ability to be tough and aggressive enough to "get the job done."

The more interesting question regards public/voter response to attack ads used by female candidates. Does a woman risk more backlash than a man? The evidence here has also undergone some change. In the 1980s through the middle of the 1990s, the ads of even well-known female candidates were apparently viewed as too aggressive, too tough, and too nasty (too masculine?). Theodore Sheckels Jr., for example, after analyzing the 1986 U.S. Senate race between Barbara Mikulski and Linda Chavez, concludes that there may be a point at which ads that are perceived as particularly vicious work against a female candidate. His research suggests that, in 1986, Chavez's attack ads could well have created a type of backlash because they did not produce many Chavez votes.[98] In 1992, during the New York primary campaign, some political observers believe that Elizabeth Holtzman ruined her political career (and lost the primary) because of her harsh commercials against Geraldine Ferraro. Holtzman herself blamed her loss on the larger society and said that those who disagreed with her negative ad strategy were "simply not ready to accept a woman who campaigns like a man. Being on the cutting edge sometimes means you will be misunderstood."[99] In 1994, during the reelection campaign she lost, Texas governor Ann Richards was said to have occasionally gone "too negative," that her "sharp wit had turned acid."[100]

As we have discussed, however, more recent research conclusions have begun to suggest that women who are perceived as tough or aggressive are more likely to be successful than their less forceful female colleagues. Perhaps the lesson learned from Senator Mary Landrieu's reelection victory in Louisiana in December 2002 says it all: "Toughness wins."[101]

Whether attack or condemnation advertising is used by male or female candidates, it, more than any other strategy in the contemporary campaign, seems to have captured public, media, and scholarly attention. In the final section of this chapter, we discuss the most frequently asked question regarding this option.

A FINAL QUESTION: DO TELEVISED ATTACK ADS WORK?

Questions and concerns about the use of televised attack advertising in political campaigns have risen almost as dramatically in the last two decades as has the employment of the genre itself. Out of all of the dialogue, whether from journalists, consultants, political communication scholars, or even the public, we believe one important question emerges that has not yet been specifically addressed in this chapter: Do televised attack ads work? Although areas of uncertainty remain, we believe that the bulk of the information available indicates that the answer to the question is yes. But explanation is clearly in order.

The fact that since the 1984 election there has been a fairly consistent increase in the use of attack advertising by candidates at all levels suggests to us that political consultants who at least influence, if not make, the strategic choices in a campaign believe they are effective. Although consultants acknowledge the existence of some risks in using the option, clearly, the frequency of their choice to "go negative" suggests more advantages than disadvantages.

One of the most discussed disadvantages in employing attack ads is that they will "turn voters off" or away from the election itself. However, in spite of the fact that only a third of those eligible to vote actually do, there is really no direct evidence to indicate that people are ignoring their voting responsibilities because candidates employ attack advertising. In fact, the results of a 1990 study conducted, at least in part, to test the effect of attack advertising on the political process indicated that there is no real evidence that negative advertising has any effect on voter involvement. In fact, on the basis of their findings, the researchers observed that "perhaps negative advertising turns off some voters, yet motivates others to vote."[102]

The second concern regards what researchers and practitioners call the backlash effect.[103] Because consultants and candidates fear such an effect, attack ads are frequently sponsored by a group that is technically not a part of the campaign, frequently a political action committee.[104] However, in many of the campaigns since 1984, consultants and candidates appear to have decided that the risk of backlash is acceptable because of the research that indicates that "over time voters tend to forget the origins of political messages while retaining their content."[105]

In spite of the potential risks, most consultants believe that the advantages of using attack ads outweigh the disadvantages. And the preponderance of research suggests that voters are more influenced by attack ads than by nonattack ads, that they pay more attention to them, recall them more accurately, and remember them for a longer period of time.[106] Thus, we conclude that there is one very good reason for the increased use of attack commercials: They work.

CONCLUSION

In this chapter, we have examined an increasingly important element of contemporary campaigns: televised advertising commercials. In so doing, we have briefly discussed their historical development in presidential politics and defined three types of commercials in terms of the overall communication functions they perform in contemporary campaigns.

We have also considered televised attack advertising by female candidates. While we found mixed results, because some stereotypes regarding the appropriate communication behavior of women and men continue to exist, candidates who are women appear to be blending traits of "femininity" and traits of "masculinity" in their television advertising while simultaneously focusing on their ability to be tough and aggressive.

NOTES

1. Kathleen Hall Jamieson, *Packaging the Presidency: A History and Criticism of Presidential Campaign Advertising* (New York: Oxford University Press, 1984), 97.

2. Kathleen Hall Jamieson, "The Evolution of Political Advertising in America," in *New Perspectives on Political Advertising*, ed. Lynda Lee Kaid, Dan D. Nimmo, and Keith R. Sanders, 15 (Carbondale: Southern Illinois University Press, 1986).

3. Jamieson, "The Evolution of Political Advertising in America," 17.

4. Edwin Diamond and Stephen Bates, *The Spot: The Rise of Political Advertising on Television*, 3d ed. (Cambridge, Mass.: MIT Press, 1992), 128–29.

5. Diamond and Bates, *The Spot*, 205–7.

6. Diamond and Bates, *The Spot*, 328–29.

7. Montague Kern, *30-Second Politics: Political Advertising in the Eighties* (New York: Praeger, 1989), 23–24.

8. Kern, *30-Second Politics*.

9. Lynda Lee Kaid, "Political Advertising in the 1992 Campaign," in *The 1992 Presidential Campaign: A Communication Perspective*, ed. Robert E. Denton Jr., 118 (Westport, Conn.: Praeger, 1994).

10. Lynda Lee Kaid, "Videostyle and the Effects of the 1996 Presidential Campaign Advertising," in *The 1996 Presidential Campaign*, ed. Robert E. Denton Jr., 149 (Westport, Conn.: Praeger, 1998).

11. L. L. Kaid and A. Johnston, *Videostyles in Presidential Campaigns* (Westport, Conn.: Praeger, 2001).

12. Lynda Kaid, "Political Web Wars: The Use of the Internet for Political Advertising," in *The Internet Election: Perspectives on the Web in Campaign 2004*, ed. Andrew Paul Williams and John C. Tedesco, 67–82 (Lanham, Md.: Rowman & Littlefield, 2006).

13. Kaid, "Political Web Wars."

14. Kaid, "Political Web Wars."

15. Diamond and Bates, *The Spot*, 293–345.

16. L. Patrick Devlin, "An Analysis of Presidential Television Commercials, 1952–1984," in *New Perspectives on Political Advertising*, ed. Kaid et al., 21–54.

17. Kern, *30-Second Politics*, 51–54.

18. Richard Joslyn, "Political Advertising and the Meaning of Elections," in *New Perspectives on Political Advertising*, ed. Kaid et al., 139–83.

19. Jamieson, "The Evolution of Political Advertising in America," 17–19.

20. Arthur H. Miller and Bruce E. Gronbeck, eds., *Presidential Campaigns and American Self Images* (Boulder, Colo.: Westview, 1994), 67.

21. Lynda Lee Kaid and Dorothy K. Davidson, "Elements of Videostyle: Candidate Presentation through Television Advertising," in *New Perspectives on Political Advertising*, ed. Kaid et al., 184–209.

22. Devlin, "An Analysis of Presidential Television Commercials, 1952–1984," 32.

23. L. Patrick Devlin, "Contrasts in Presidential Campaign Commercials of 1992," *American Behavioral Scientist* 37 (November/December 1993): 282.

24. L. Patrick Devlin, "Contrasts in Presidential Campaign Commercials of 1996," *American Behavioral Scientist* 40 (August 1997): 1067.

25. John C. Tedesco and Lynda Lee Kaid, "Style and Effects of the Bush and Gore Spots," in *The Millennium Election: Communication in the 2000 Campaign*, ed. Lynda Lee Kaid, Dianne Bystrom, and Mitchell McKinney (Lanham, Md.: Rowman & Littlefield, 2003).

26. Devlin, "Contrasts in Presidential Campaign Commercials of 1992," 23.

27. Kaid, "Videostyle," 149 and 151.

28. Devlin, "Contrasts in Presidential Campaign Commercials of 1992," 288.

29. Devlin, "Contrasts in Presidential Campaign Commercials of 1996," 1060.

30. Kern, *30-Second Politics*, 94.

31. Devlin, "Contrasts in Presidential Campaign Commercials of 1992," 287.

32. Devlin, "Contrasts in Presidential Campaign Commercials of 1992."

33. Robin Toner, "Bitter Tone of the '94 Campaign Elicits Worry on Public Debate," *New York Times*, November 13, 1994, A1, A14.

34. David Broder, "Negative Costs," *Washington Post National Weekly Editor*, October 31–November 6, 1994, 4.

35. Kaid, "Videostyle," 148–49.

36. Lynda Lee Kaid, "Videostyle in the 2004 Presidential Advertising," In *The 2004 Presidential Campaign: A Communication Perspective*, ed. Robert E. Denton, Jr., 205, 283–300 (Boulder, Co: Rowman & Littlefield, 2005).

37. Charles Trueheart, "The Incumbent Slayer from Minnesota," *Washington Post National Weekly Edition*, November 26–December 2, 1990, 10.

38. Lynda Lee Kaid, "TechnoDistortions and Effects of the 2000 Political Advertising," *American Behavioral Scientist* 44, no. 12 (August 2001): 2371.

39. Kaid, "TechnoDistortions."

40. Michael Pfau and Henry C. Kenski, *Attack Politics* (Westport, Conn.: Praeger, 1990), 36.

41. Pfau and Kenski, *Attack Politics*, 22.

42. Robin Toner, "90's Politics Seem Rough as Ever Despite Criticism of Negative Ads," *New York Times*, September 9, 1990, A1, A25.

43. Devlin, "Contrasts in Presidential Campaign Commercials of 1992," 275.

44. Devlin, "Contrasts in Presidential Campaign Commercials of 1996," 1063.

45. Pfau and Kenski, *Attack Politics*, xiv.

46. Center for the American Woman and Politics, Fact Sheet Summaries, Rutgers University, 2006.

47. Clyde Wilcox, "Why Was 1992 the 'Year of the Woman'? Explaining Women's Gains in 1992," in *The Year of the Woman*, ed. Elizabeth Adell Cook, Sue Thomas, and Clyde Wilcox, 11 (Boulder, Colo.: Westview, 1994).

48. Sue Tolleson Rinehart, "The California Senate Races: A Case Study in the Gendered Paradoxes of Politics," in *The Year of the Woman*, ed. Cook et al., 39.

49. Federal Election Commission, "Top 50 Senate/House Receipts," 1998; available at www.fec.gov/finance/hserec97.htm (accessed July 25, 2003).

50. Raymond Hernandez, "Senator Clinton Piles Up a Fund-Raising Lead for 2006," *New York Times*, April 19, 2005.

51. Jill Lawrence, "Clinton Camp Reports Record Haul," *USA Today*, April 1, 2007.

52. Chris Cillizza, "Asa in the Hole?" *Roll Call Politics*, March 17, 2003, 13.

53. Mark Hornbeck and Charlie Cain, "Granholm's Fund-Raising Beats Rivals," *Detroit News*, February 1, 2002, 1.

54. David Firestone, "Reaching the Top behind a Smile," *New York Times*, November 10, 2002, 26.

55. Debbie Stabenow, United States Senator Michigan 2006, campaign website, www.stabenowforsenate.com/.

56. Center for the American Woman and Politics, National Information Bank on Women in Public Office, Eagleton Institute of Politics, Rutgers University, "Women's PACs and Donor Networks: A Contact List," 1998; available at www.rci.rutgers.edu/cawp/pacs.html.

57. Constance Courtney Staley and Jerry L. Cohen, "Communicator Style and Social Style: Similarities and Differences between the Sexes," *Communication Quarterly* 36 (Summer 1988): 192–202.

58. M. Z. Hackman and C. E. Johnson, "Leadership: A Communication Perspective," 3d ed. (Prospect Heights, Ill.: Waveland, 2000), 320–21.

59. Hackman and Johnson, "Leadership."

60. Judith A. Hall, "How Big Are Nonverbal Sex Differences? The Case of Smiling and Sensitivity to Nonverbal Cues," in *Sex Differences and Similarities in Communication*, ed. Daniel J. Canary and Kathryn Dindia, 155–77 (Mahwah, N.J.: Erlbaum, 1998).

61. Anthony Mulac, "The Gender-Linked Language Effect: Do Language Differences Really Make a Difference?" in *Sex Differences and Similarities in Communication*, ed. Canary and Dindia, 155–77.

62. Mulac, "The Gender-Linked Language Effect," 147.

63. Mulac, "The Gender-Linked Language Effect," 147.

64. Mulac, "The Gender-Linked Language Effect," 147.

65. Anne E. Kornblut, "The Ascent of a Woman: After a Fictional Female President, Are Americans Ready for the Real Thing?" *The New York Times*, Sunday, June 11, 2006, section 9, 1.

66. Center for the American Woman and Politics, Eagleton Institute of Politics, Rutgers University, "Women in Statewide Elective Executive Office," 2007, 77 (48D, 26R, 3 NP).

67. Michael Burgoon and Gerald R. Miller, "An Expectancy Interpretation of Language and Persuasion," in *Recent Advances in Language, Communication, and Social Psychology*, ed. Howard Giles and Robert N. St. Clairs, 199–229 (London: Erlbaum, 1985).

68. Burgoon and Miller, "An Expectancy Interpretation of Language and Persuasion," 210.

69. Deborah Tannen, *Talking from 9 to 5* (New York: Morrow, 1994).

70. Marjorie Williams, "He Says 'You're Fired,' She Says 'I Have to Let You Go,'" *Washington Post National Weekly Edition*, November 14–20, 1994, 35.

71. We would be remiss if we failed to note the very real "double bind" facing all female candidates. Not only must a woman avoid appearing "too tough," but she must also avoid appearing "too soft" or "too caring" for fear that such emphasis will make her appear weak.

72. Ruth B. Mandel, *In the Running* (New Haven, Conn.: Ticknor & Fields, 1981), 62.

73. Nadine Brozan, "Schroeder and Politics: The Problems of Gender," *New York Times*, November 23, 1987, B12.

74. Catherine Whitney, *Nine and Counting: The Women of the Senate* (New York: Harper-Collins, 2000), 43.

75. Whitney, *Nine and Counting*, 96.

76. Judy Putnam, "Governor Celebrates with Kids and Parents," *Grand Rapids Press*, January 2, 2003, A4.

77. Dianne G. Bystrom, Mary Christine Banwart, Lynda Lee Kaid, and Terry A. Robertson, *Gender and Candidate Communication* (New York: Routledge, 2004).

78. Kornblut, "The Ascent of a Woman."

79. Terry Robertson et al., "Gender and the Media: An Investigation of Gender, Media, and Politics in the 2000 Election," *New Jersey Journal of Communication* 10, no. 1 (Spring 2002): 104–17; Terry Robertson, "The Media and Female Candidates: An Overview of the 2002 Election," paper presented at the Central States Communication Association, Omaha, Nebraska, April 2003.

80. Karrin Vasby Anderson, "Rhymes with Rich: 'Bitch' as a Tool of Containment in Contemporary American Politics," *Rhetoric and Public Affairs* 2, no. 4 (1999): 599–623.

81. Judith S. Trent and Teresa Sabourin, "When the Candidate Is a Woman: The Content and Form of Televised Negative Advertising," paper presented at the 1989 Organization for the Study of Communication Language and Gender Conference, Cincinnati, Ohio. The paper was subsequently published in Cynthia Berryman-Fink, Deborah Ballard-Reisch, and Lisa H. Newman, eds., *Communication and Sex-Role Socialization* (New York: Garland, 1993), 233–68.

82. Dianne G. Bystrom and Jerry L. Miller, "Gendered Communication Styles and Strategies in Campaign 1996: The Videostyles of Women and Men Candidates," in *The Electronic Election*, ed. Lynda Lee Kaid and Dianne G. Bystrom, 293–302 (Mahwah, N.J.: Erlbaum, 1999); Mary C. Banwart, "Videostyle and Webstyle in 2000: Comparing the Gender Differences of Candidate Presentations in Political Advertising and on the Internet," Ph.D. diss., University of Oklahoma, 2002.

83. James C. Benze and Eugene R. Declercq, "Content of Television Political Spot Ads for Female Candidates," *Journalism Quarterly* 62 (Summer 1985): 283.

84. David E. Procter, Roger C. Aden, and Phyllis Japp, "Gender/ Issue Interaction in Political Identity Making: Nebraska's Woman vs. Woman Gubernatorial Campaign," *Central States Speech Journal* 39 (Fall/Winter 1988): 201.

85. Trent and Sabourin, "When the Candidate Is a Woman."

86. Judith S. Trent and Teresa Sabourin, "Sex Still Counts: Women's Use of Televised Advertising during the Decade of the 80's," *Journal of Applied Communication Research* 21 (February 1993): 36.

87. Trent and Sabourin, "Sex Still Counts."

88. Trent and Sabourin, "Sex Still Counts."

89. Trent and Sabourin, "Sex Still Counts."

90. K. F. Kahn, "Gender Differences in Campaign Messages: The Political Advertisements of Men and Women Candidates for U.S. Senate," *Political Research Quarterly* 46 (1993): 481–501.

91. Dianne G. Bystrom, "Candidate Gender and the Presentation of Self: The Videostyles of Men and Women in United States Senate Campaigns," Ph.D. diss., University of Oklahoma, 1995.

92. Cady Walker Short-Thompson, "Gender and Gubernatorial Candidates in 1994: A Study of Political Communication Styles and Strategies," Ph.D. diss., University of Cincinnati, 1997.

93. Dianne G. Bystrom and Jerry L. Miller, "Gendered Communication Styles and Strategies in Campaign 1996: The Videostyles of Women and Men Candidates," in *The Electronic Election*, ed. Kaid and Bystrom, 300.

94. Terry Robertson, "Sex and the Political Process: An Analysis of Sex Stereotypes in 1998 Senatorial and Gubernatorial Campaigns," Ph.D. diss., University of Oklahoma, 2000.

95. Mary Banwart, "Merging Methods: A Cross-Analysis of Campaign Advertising and the Effects in a Campaign for the U.S. House," paper presented at the Central States Communication Association, Omaha, Nebraska, 2003.

96. Dianne G. Bystrom, Mary Christine Banwart, Lynda Lee Kaid, and Terry A. Robertson, *Gender and Candidate Communication* (New York: Routledge, 2004).

97. Mary Christine Banwart and Mitchell S. McKinney, "A Gendered Influence in Campaign Debates? Analysis of Mixed-gender United States Senate and Gubernatorial Debates," *Communication Studies* 56, no. 4 (2005): 353–74.

98. Theodore F. Sheckels Jr., "Mikulski vs. Chavez for the Senate from Maryland in 1986 and the 'Rules' for Attack Politics," *Communication Quarterly* 42 (Summer 1994): 317.

99. Craig A. Rimmerman, "When Women Run against Women: Double Standards and Vitriol in the New York Primary," in *The Year of the Woman*, ed. Cook et al., 115.

100. Sue Anne Pressley, "Being Colorful and Well-Known May Not Be Enough," *Washington Post National Weekly Edition*, October 17–23, 1994, 17.

101. E. J. Dionne Jr., "Lessons from Louisiana," *Washington Post National Weekly Edition*, December 16–22, 2002, 26.

102. Gina M. Garramone, Charles K. Atkin, Bruce E. Pinkleton, and Richard T. Cole, "Effects of Negative Political Advertising on the Political Process," *Journal of Broadcasting and Electronic Media* 34 (Summer 1990): 308.

103. Gina M. Garramone, "Voter Responses to Negative Political Ads," *Journalism Quarterly* 61 (Summer 1984): 250–59. Also see Gina M. Garramone, "Effects of Negative Political Advertising: The Roles of Sponsor and Rebuttal," *Journal of Broadcasting and Electronic Media* 29 (Spring 1985): 147–59; Lynda Lee Kaid and John Boydston, "An Experimental Study of the Effectiveness of Negative Political Advertisements," *Communication Quarterly* 35 (Spring 1987): 193–201.

104. Garramone, "Effects of Negative Political Advertising."

105. Pfau and Kenski, *Attack Politics*, 158.

106. Pfau and Kenski, *Attack Politics*, 4.

II

PRACTICES OF POLITICAL CAMPAIGN COMMUNICATION

6

❧

Public Speaking in Political Campaigns

This chapter will focus on what is perhaps the most fundamental communication practice in any campaign, public speaking. In the first section, we will examine the factors that enter into a candidate's decision to speak. Decisions on where and when to speak and what to say to a given audience should not be made randomly but should be the result of considerable thought and planning on the part of candidates and their staffs. In the second section, we will inspect the use of two types of stock speeches. Virtually all candidates utilize some type of stock speech to help them meet the massive speaking demands typically placed on them. In the third section, we will discuss the practice of political speechwriting. Candidates are using speechwriters more today than ever before; any examination of public speaking practices in political campaigns must consider the use of speechwriters. Similarly, many candidates today are making extensive use of advocates or surrogates. These "substitutes" for the candidate may be heard in person by as many people, if not more, than those who actually hear the candidate. Hence, any examination of public speaking practices in contemporary campaigns that does not consider the use of surrogate speakers would be less than complete.

THE DECISION TO SPEAK

Perhaps the most important resource available to any campaign is the time of the candidate. That time must be used wisely. Decisions to use the candidates' time for public speeches are made out of self-interest, as the candidates attempt to influence the maximum number of voters. Hence, it is vital that candidates and their staffs do an effective job of analyzing voter audiences to best utilize the candidates' time. Essentially candidates face two tasks: first, to determine whom they should address and, second, to determine what messages should be presented to those they address.

Audiences

Since 1946 when Jacob Javits, then running for a seat in the House of Representatives, employed the Elmo Roper Organization to take opinion polls of his constituency to better determine what issues he should develop in his campaign,[1] political campaigns have increasingly relied on two tools to assist them in analyzing audiences. The first is studies of past voter statistics. The second is the public opinion poll. Recently, particularly in well-financed campaigns, candidates have also made use of focus groups to help develop their messages. As we have seen in earlier chapters, these tools have blossomed in recent years because of improvements in computer technology.

Local and national candidates make use of past voter statistics to analyze audiences. Yet these statistics play a more vital role in the campaigns of local candidates than they do in the campaigns of national or major statewide contenders. Indeed, there is no more valuable campaign aid to the local candidate than accurate voter statistics. Though voter statistics may serve many potential purposes, their chief function is to pinpoint, on a precinct-by-precinct basis, where candidates should be concentrating their efforts. This knowledge enables candidates to determine what speaking invitations should be accepted and in what areas of the district their staffs should attempt to arrange speaking opportunities and otherwise concentrate.

Though the same principles apply for national figures and local figures, in practicality major national or statewide figures are rarely able to aim their speeches or campaign materials to a specific precinct, as can the local candidate dealing with a smaller constituency. The local candidate, far more than counterparts seeking national or statewide office, must know precisely, down to the precinct, the nature of the constituency. Because their constituencies are smaller, in many instances the local candidate can knock on every door in the district, or at least on every door in those precincts that are deemed most valuable. When a statewide candidate like "Walking Joe" Teasdale, former governor of Missouri, walks across his state he is doing so primarily for media coverage.

Local candidates, however, will not receive the media exposure of the gubernatorial candidate. Rather, their walks in the district can put them face-to-face with a large percentage of their constituency. The act is real rather then symbolic. To be effective, the local candidate must know which areas of the district in which to walk, speak, get out the vote, and otherwise campaign. Accurate voter statistics are an acute concern for local candidates, who can meet a substantial portion of their constituency, can express their concern for voter problems face-to-face, and whose limited financial resources must be used with maximum effect.

Typically, candidates direct their efforts primarily toward precincts where their party traditionally runs well, those where elections are likely to be close, and those where ticket-splitting commonly takes place. It is in these areas that candidates should concentrate the majority of their speaking efforts. That may even mean actively soliciting speaking engagements in these areas when none are forthcoming. It means consistently giving preference to those regions when simultaneous speaking opportunities arise in two or more sections of the district. Local candidates can think in precinct terms. National and statewide candidates use the same process but must think more in media market and electoral vote terms.

Utilizing past voter records and computers to help analyze the data, state and local political organizations will often provide candidates with a precinct-by-precinct breakdown of their district. The materials a candidate receives might be similar to the two examples shown in table 6.1. These examples are modeled after materials available to Republican candidates in Cincinnati, Ohio, during recent elections.

Using the table provided, can you determine whether a Republican candidate should speak in these precincts?

The first precinct is one in which a Republican candidate should actively speak and campaign since it is a heavily Republican precinct. Note that ten of the eleven Republicans on the ballot in the last two elections have won. The only Republican who failed to win in this distract was the 2002 Senate candidate. As you can see in column ten, that candidate drew only 47 percent of the vote and lost by seventeen votes. No other Republican candidate has received less than 57 percent of the vote. Among the 418 precincts in the city of Cincinnati, in 2004 this precinct had the 16th highest average Republican percentage, and in 2002 it had the 33rd highest Republican percentage.

Moreover, Republicans in this district are not excessive ticket-splitters, although at first glance they may seem to be. In 2002 it ranked 129th of the 418 precincts in ticket-splitting, but that was because of the senatorial candidate who lost, thus creating a ticket-splitting figure of 30 percent. Without that candidate on the ballot, only 20 percent of the Republican voters would have been ticket-splitters. In 2004, when all five Republicans won, the incredibly popular incumbent congressmen drew a staggering 81 percent of the vote. This was 15 percent more than the lowest Republican, the

Table 6.1. Prior Election Results

1	2	3	4	5	6	7	8	9	10	11	12	13	14	15	16	17	18
2004 2004	U.S. Pres	U.S. Hse	St. Sen	St. Hse	Cty Comm.	2002 2002 St. Gov	St. Att.G.	St. Aud.	U.S. Sen	U.S. Hse	St. Hse	Avg. R.	Rank	Total Vote	Rank	Ticket R %	Split Rank
SAMPLE PRECINCT 1: CITY OF CINCINNATI: WARD 1 PRECINCT E																	
Rep.	294	322	280	245	286	147	148	123	119	98	185	73	2004 16	412	107	15	289
Dem.	113	76	106	130	92	80	74	94	136	69	55						
Other	5																
Total	412	398	386	375	378	227	222	217	255	267	240	64	2002 33	268	129	30	135
R.pct.	72	81	73	66	76	64	67	57	47	74	77						
D.pct.	27	19	27	34	24	36	33	43	53	26	23						
Diff.	181	246	174	115	194	67	74	29	-17	-29	130						
SAMPLE PRECINCT 2: CITY OF CINCINNATI: WARD 5 PRECINCT G																	
Rep.	205	204	192	169	184	130	137	117	99	153	112	53	2004 159	383	142	7	354
Dem.	174	149	172	162	170	114	96	109	132	90	99						
Other	4																
Total	383	353	364	331	354	244	233	226	231	243	211	54	2002 134	244	138	10	278
R.pct.	54	58	53	51	52	53	59	53	43	63	53						
D.pct.	46	42	47	49	48	47	41	47	57	37	47						
Diff.	31	55	20	7	14	16	41	8	-33	-63	13						

TOTAL PRECINCTS: CITY OF CINCINNATI—418

state House of Representatives candidate, who, it should be remembered, won with an impressive 66 percent of the vote. If the incumbent congressmen had not been on the ballot, only 10 percent of Republican voters would have been ticket-splitters. Thus, although on first glance it seems that this precinct is marked by a high incidence of ticket-splitting, a close examination of the figures indicates that the precinct is generally consistent in giving Republicans substantial victories of well over 60 percent, and the apparent high ticket-splitting is largely a function of aberrant races.

The second precinct is also one in which a Republican candidate should actively speak and otherwise campaign. It too is Republican, although not nearly so heavily as the first. The average Republican received 53 to 54 percent of the vote in the last two election cycles. The figures indicate that, although Republicans have consistently won this precinct, again losing only the 2002 Senate race, three of the 2002 races were won by sixteen votes or less. Moreover, though all five Republicans won in 2004, three of them did so by twenty votes or less. This is clearly a precinct where close elections abound. A shift of only eleven votes would have changed the outcome of six of the last eleven elections in this precinct.

This precinct is not marked by excessive Republican ticket-splitting. In 2004, 7 percent of the Republican voters split their ticket. In 2002 that figure was 10 percent. In both years this precinct ranked well within the bottom half of the district in ticket-splitting. Nevertheless, given the multitude of close elections, ticket-splitting can have an impact in this precinct. Given that the Democrats won the 2002 Senate race in this precinct, and that Democrats have frequently come within twenty votes of winning elections here, this is a precinct that is "in play" in most elections. That is, it could be won by a candidate from either party. It is likely to be targeted by both parties.

Using figures such as these, local candidates determine where they wish to speak. Typically, they will write off about 30 percent of the district as hopeless. The first precinct we just analyzed, for example, would be targeted by Republicans, but ignored as a hopeless precinct by Democratic contenders. Candidates then target the remaining 70 percent, those precincts where their party runs strong, where a close election is likely, or where ticket-splitting is common. Precinct two, for example, might well be targeted by both Republican and Democratic candidates. Though the precinct is Republican, Democrats have frequently come within eleven votes of winning it, and both sides might reasonably expect close elections in this precinct. Additionally, both of these precincts are relatively large. The vote totals rank both precincts well into the top half of the district.

National and statewide candidates operate on the same premises. They too target about 70 percent of their constituency. Typically, presidential

Column 1:

Rep.—The Republican vote in the precinct for a particular office.

Dem.—The Democratic vote in the precinct for a particular office.

Other—The vote for all other party votes in the precinct for a particular office.

Total—The total vote in the precinct for a particular office. Obtained by adding the Republican, Democratic, and other vote.

R.pct—The Republican percentage in the precinct for a particular office. Obtained by dividing the Republican vote by the total vote in the precinct.

D.pct.—The Democratic percentage in the precinct for a particular office. Obtained by dividing the Democratic vote by the total vote in the precinct.

Diff.—The difference between the Democratic and Republican vote for a particular office. A minus sign (-) indicates Republican vote is less than Democratic vote.

Columns 2–6: 2004 election results.

Columns 7–12: 2002 election results.

Column 13: Average R.% —This is the average Republican percentage in the precinct.

Column 14: Rank—This is the rank order number of the particular precinct in terms of the Republican percentage in the total district. The precinct with the highest Republican percentage in the district is number 1.

Column 15: Total vote—This is the maximum number of votes cast in the precinct since 2002.

Column 16: Rank—This is the rank order number of the precinct in the district in terms of total votes cast.

Column 17: Ticket Splitting R%—This is the percentage of ticket splitting in the precinct. It was calculated by subtracting the lowest Republican percent from the highest Republican percent in the precinct.

Column 18: Ticket Splitting Rank—This is the rank order number of the precinct in terms of ticket splitting. The precinct with the highest percentage of ticket splitting in the district is number 1.

Total Number of Precincts: City of Cincinnati Legislative Report—418.

candidates target states and media markets within states, rather than precincts, and choose to speak and campaign accordingly.[2] In recent presidential campaigns, both the Republican and Democratic candidates have targeted about ten to fourteen states and directed most of their campaign efforts, including speaking, to those states.

Messages

The second primary tool of audience analysis is the public opinion poll. Polls help candidates develop their messages. But polls are utilized differently by local and major candidates. Accurate voter statistics down to the precinct level are of acute concern to the local candidate but often of lesser concern to the major candidate. However, the public opinion poll is of more concern to major candidates but often of lesser concern to the local candidate. Typically, the explanation for this different emphasis on the use of polls involves two distinctions between local and major candidates. First, the major candidate can normally afford a polling service and may also be helped by national polls such as those of the national television networks and national newspaper chains. Candidates for Congress and statewide and national offices all utilize polling services. Most state legislative candidates and contenders for local offices in larger urban districts also use polls.

Candidates for lesser local offices, such as sheriff, county or city recorder, clerk, or engineer, particularly in less populated communities, often cannot afford polling services. Many polling consultants themselves suggest that a campaign that is budgeted at $100,000 or less probably should think twice about using a poll. Typically, the most basic benchmark poll will cost a candidate in excess of $12,000. Most pollsters themselves would suggest that, when polling eats up over 10 percent of the campaign budget, such an expense will likely reduce the ability of the campaign to communicate with the public.[3]

Second, even if the local candidate could afford polls, the essentially administrative nature, rather than policymaking nature, of most local offices tends to minimize the distinctions between the viewpoints of local candidates. Issues of policy, which sharply divide candidates for major office, often are not at stake in local elections. This is not to say that there is no opportunity for policymaking at the local level. Rather, it is to suggest that, while major campaigns almost invariably involve clashes over policy issues, many local campaigns are waged for positions with comparatively little policymaking responsibilities. For example, county sheriffs and recorders are not primarily engaged in making policy. Rather, they are primarily engaged in enforcing and carrying out policies set by legislatures, city councils, and similar policymaking agencies. Hence, there is often little distinction between candidates on the basis of issues and less need for polls.

Issue polls are designed to determine what concerns are uppermost in the minds of voters. They serve major candidates as a topoi, or topics, system. In addition to suggesting topics upon which to speak, they indicate voter opinions or beliefs. As we have noted earlier, candidates rely on polling services when they develop positions on issues.

Using polls to determine important issues makes good sense. Using polls instead of solid study, research, and good judgment to determine what to say about the public's concerns is a questionable procedure. Writing in 1954, when polling was first developing as a major campaign tool, former President Harry Truman asked:

> I wonder how far Moses would have gone if he'd taken a poll in Egypt? What would Jesus Christ have preached if he'd taken a poll in Israel? Where would the Reformation have gone if Martin Luther had taken a poll? It isn't polls or public opinion of the moment that counts. It is right and wrong leadership—men with fortitude, honesty, and a belief in the right—that makes epochs in the history of the world.[1]

Most political candidates agree with the implications of Truman's remark that, although the polls can help determine what absorbs the public's attention, they should not be used to dictate the candidate's approach to an issue.

Typically, the candidate's polls will be able to rank or order issues of concern among specific constituencies such as older voters, women voters, or middle-income voters. The degree to which the polling data are broken down and analyzed depends on the candidate's needs and the finances available. A national campaign will break down the polling data extensively, determining, for example, what issues are of concern on such bases as geography, income, race, religion, and party. As candidates speak, they can vary their subject matter to ensure they are addressing the major concerns of the groups to whom they are speaking. Polls also provide candidates with indirect feedback on messages. Candidates often reposition their stands on issues as a consequence of that feedback.

In recent years political campaigns have begun to make use of a tool that was pioneered by advertising researchers, the focus group. In 1988, George H. W. Bush's campaign team used focus groups to help them identify weaknesses in the background and statements of their opponent, Massachusetts governor Michael Dukakis. As a consequence of focus group findings, they sensed the potential impact of the governor's having furloughed a Massachusetts convict who subsequently raped a woman and assaulted her fiancé.[5]

A focus group brings together a group of eight to twenty voters. A skilled questioner leads them through a series of questions that the campaign seeks to answer. Political campaigns often use focus groups to help identify themes and issues at the outset of the campaign. Additionally, they are frequently used to help identify the best ways to structure messages on specific themes. Though polls serve the same purpose and are more reliable, focus groups have two virtues. First, they are typically less expensive than polls. Moreover, they provide, from a small group, an indication of the depth and nuance of potential messages. Focus groups are clearly not as critical in message development as good polling. However, particularly when combined with polling, they can help campaigns in message development.[6]

Competency and Format

Nearing the end of his fabled career, Texas Rangers pitcher Nolan Ryan once observed, "I would love to be governor of Texas, . . . as long as I didn't have to speak in public."[7] Most individuals who run for major public office can't pitch as well as Nolan Ryan, but, unlike the great pitcher, most candidates for public office feel comfortable in front of an audience.[8] Most have had extensive prior public speaking experience, and many have also had both formal and informal training.[9] If prospective candidates are apprehensive about the speaking demands of their races, they might well prepare by seeking the advice of competent professionals. Many candidates utilize the services of speech coaches who specialize in training political speakers. Students of speech communication will be familiar with much of the advice offered by such individuals.[10] Additionally, the Republican and Democratic national committees, as well as many state and local party committees, provide speech training in their candidates' schools.

If candidates are uncomfortable with some speaking formats, they and their staffs might attempt to place them in formats where they do not feel uncomfortable. If, for example, they are uneasy delivering formal speeches, perhaps their formal speeches could be kept brief and be followed by extensive question-and-answer periods. The type of training and formats utilized by candidates varies on an individual basis but should not be ignored. A frank and realistic assessment of the candidate's speaking abilities, no less than assessments about where and when to talk and what to talk about, must enter into the candidate's decisions to speak.

THE SPEECH

Though candidates make hundreds, in some cases thousands, of speeches in the course of a campaign, those speeches always seem new and appropriate for each audience. Nevertheless, candidates typically draw upon a well-prepared message time and time again during the campaign. This material is often called the candidate's "stock speech" and typically takes two forms. A module approach to stock speeches is the approach most frequently used by candidates, such as major national and statewide candidates, who address diverse audiences often interested in a wide variety of topics.

A second type of stock speech, used more by candidates for lower-level offices, especially administrative offices that do not involve a wide variety of topics and policies, are variations of the "Why I Am Running" speech. The demand for speeches is also one of the principal reasons used by candidates to justify the use of speechwriters. In this section, we will examine the use of both types of stock speeches, and in the next section we will examine the practices of political speechwriters.

Need and Justification

Speechmaking is fundamental to political campaigning. The politician cannot reasonably expect to campaign without continually facing audiences. Even the candidate for city council in a small community must constantly speak. Typically, such a candidate is called upon to make several major speeches during the campaign at such events as the local League of Women Voters "Meet The Candidates" nights or at the Rotary Club's monthly meeting. Moreover, these candidates must be continually speaking, often three or more times an evening throughout the final weeks of the campaign, to smaller groups of citizens. Campaign coffees, teas, church socials, and similar activities crowd the calendars of most candidates. It is not unusual for local candidates to find themselves confronting the prospect of a hundred or more speeches during the last four to six weeks of a campaign. Similarly, as we will see in the next section, candidates for more important local, state, and federal offices face situations where they must speak thirty or more times a week. Because of these demands, most candidates make use of a stock speech and, if possible, the services of speechwriters.

Stock Speeches: Utilizing Speech Modules

Although the phrase "stock speech" has entered the vocabulary of most politically aware citizens, it is a misnomer. We tend to think of it as a speech that is delivered time and time again with little change. However, candidates do not give the identical speech time after time, irrespective of the audience, occasion, or the actions of their opponents. Rather, they adapt to these factors.

How do the candidates adapt, given the heavy demands on time? The first commonly used approach is to make use of speech modules. A speech module is a single unit of a speech. Typically, candidates will have a speech unit, or module, on each of the ten to twenty issues on which they most frequently speak. Each module is an independent unit that can be delivered as a two-to-seven-minute speech on the issue. The length of each can be varied simply by adding or subtracting examples, statistics, illustrations, or other support material. Typically the organization of each module is similar and will be readily recognized by many students of public speaking.

Each module opens with some attention-gaining device, and then candidates quickly move to a discussion of a problem. Having sketched the problem, they present their policies as an appropriate solution to the problem. If more time is available, they might then vividly describe or visualize what would happen if they are elected and their policies carried out. Thus, the typical speech module is designed to (1) gain attention, (2) describe a problem, (3) present a solution, and (4) visualize the solution.[11] The first three of these steps are characteristic of virtually every speech module that the candidate presents. The final step may not be necessary. It may be implicit from the discussion of the problem and the solution and hence not warrant explicit treatment. The following is typical of a speech module used by President George W. Bush during the 2004 campaign to discuss the war on terrorism.[12]

This election will also determine how America responds to the continuing danger of terrorism. Since the terrible morning of September 11th, 2001, we've fought the terrorists across the Earth, not for pride, not for power, but because the lives of our citizens are at stake.

ATTENTION:
Dramatic language helps to describe the problem
PROBLEM:
We are in a war we must win to preserve the lives of our citizens.

Our strategy is clear. We'll defend the homeland. We will transform our military. We'll strengthen our intelligence services. We will stay on the offensive. We will defeat the terrorists abroad so we will not have to face them here at home. We will work to advance liberty and freedom throughout the world, and we will prevail.

PLAN:
We will defend homeland.
We will transform our military.
We will strengthen our intelligence.
We will stay on the offensive.

We will defeat terrorists abroad to avoid fighting them at home.

Our strategy is succeeding. Four years ago, Afghanistan was the home base of Al Qaida; Pakistan was a transit point for terrorist groups; Saudi Arabia was fertile ground for terrorist fund-raising;

We will advance liberty throughout the world.

Libya was secretly pursuing nuclear weapons; Iraq was a gathering threat; Al Qaida was largely unchallenged as it planned attacks.

Because we acted, the government of a free Afghanistan is fighting terror; Pakistan is capturing terrorist leaders; Saudi Arabia is making raids and arrests; Libya is dismantling its weapons programs; the army of a free Iraq is fighting terror; and more than three-quarters of Al Qaida's key members have been brought to justice. We've led. Many have joined. And America and the world are safer.

PLAN: Our plan was a response to the challenges presented by the hostile policies of Afghanistan, Pakistan, Saudi Arabia, Libya, Iraq, and a largely unchallenged Al Qaida terrorist organization.

VISUALIZATION: Our plan has brought about dramatic changes for the better in Afghanistan, Pakistan, Saudi Arabia, Libya, and Iraq. All are now cooperating in the war on terror.

Much of Al Qaida's leadership has been brought to justice.

My administration has led and, because of it, America is now safer.

In this module, we see an independent speech unit or module that Bush uses to discuss the war on terrorism. The passage stands by itself. It also could be linked very easily into another module with a simple transition. For example, at this point Bush could claim that, as successful as his administration has been in waging the war on terror, so to it has been successful in lowering taxes. He could then present his module on taxes. (See table 6.2)

These happen to be two modules George Bush used frequently during the 2004 election. Because the war on terror and taxes are issues that vitally affect virtually all citizens, they were appropriate to use with most audiences. But let us imagine for a moment that Bush was speaking on the campus of the University of Minnesota. He might reasonably expect, and his polls might suggest, that the war on terror was an issue that was im-

Table 6.2.

War on Terror Module	*Transition*	*Tax Module*
Attention		
Problem		
Plan		
Visualization		
		Attention
		Problem
		Plan
		Visualization

Table 6.3.

War on Terror Module	
Attention	
Problem	
Plan	
Visualization	
	Transition:
	As successful as we have
	been in the War on Terror,
	we have also been successful
	in creating jobs.
	Job Creation Module
	Attention
	Problem
	Plan
	Visualization

portant to this audience. But, suppose that his polls and the advance work done for him suggested that this audience of college students was not overly concerned with taxes. After all, relatively few of them were working full time. Rather, his polling and advance staff suggested that this immediate audience was highly concerned with job creation and employment. Having already prepared a module on job creation, it would be a rather minor adjustment for Bush to present his initial module. College students, like most Americans, are concerned about the war on terror. Then, adapting to his audience, he might choose to speak about job creation, not taxes. He could do so in the shown in table 6.3.

Most candidates will develop key modules at the outset of the campaign, occasionally adjusting them as the need arises. Additionally, they will add modules as the need arises. Then, depending on the audience, the occasion, and any other relevant factors, they will determine what modules to use for a given speech. Often, as with Bush and these modules, the same module is used in many speeches. Yet each speech is in fact tailored to the specific audience and occasion.

Speech-like Opportunities and Modular Speech

One of the principal advantages of developing a basic speech through modules is that the modules can be used by the candidate in many speech-like situations. Often candidates desire to appear on interview shows such as *Meet the Press* or talk shows such as *Larry King Live*. With the recent proliferation of all-news cable stations such as the Fox News Channel, MSNBC, CNBC, and similar channels, the opportunities for such appearances have increased dramatically for major candidates.

Candidates operating on a limited budget are especially attracted to free media. Moreover, almost every media market has local radio and television talk shows. Hence, these decisions are not unique to national contenders.

If candidates have already prepared speech modules on most major topics, they are likely to do well on these shows. The module, which can be varied in length, lends itself to use in these formats. Candidates can accept such invitations with a minimum of preparation and be confident that they are unlikely to be caught ill prepared. Moreover, they can be certain that their remarks will be consistent with those they have made throughout the campaign.

Occasionally, if a module is done especially well, it can also be turned into an effective commercial or used for other purposes. Because the module can stand alone and its length can be varied by the addition or deletion of support material such as statistics and examples, it is easy to adapt to a commercial. Often media advisors wish to show their candidate in "the real world," talking to "real people." The speech module lets them do just that. Every Republican presidential candidate since Richard Nixon in 1968 has made use of modules excerpted from their acceptance address in precisely this fashion.[13]

Stock Speeches: The "Why I Am Running" Speech

A second approach to the development of a stock speech, most commonly utilized by candidates for local administrative offices, is to utilize "Why I Am Running" speeches of varying lengths. Political consultant and commentator Ron Faucheux suggests that many candidates can meet most of their speaking demands by preparing three speeches. He recommends that the first be about two minutes in length, the second should be about five minutes in length, and the third should be about twenty minutes in length. In each speech, candidates should explain, in as much detail as the time allows, why they are running.[14]

Based on sound research on the demographic makeup of the district, the prevalent beliefs in the district, the distinctions between the candidate and the opponent, and any other pertinent information, Faucheux advises candidates to develop "a sentence or short paragraph that summarizes the reason why the voters should elect you, keeping in mind your strengths, the opposition's weaknesses, and your points of inoculation."[15] This short statement is, in effect, the essence of the candidate's message throughout the campaign. Once crafted, it should be repeated consistently throughout the campaign.

For example, in 2004, a brief version of Governor George W. Bush's "Why I Am Running" speech, drawn from the more extended version he presented in his acceptance address and throughout the campaign, would have read something like this:

> I am running for President with a clear and positive plan to build a safer world, and a more hopeful America by vigorously prosecuting the war on terror. I am running with a compassionate conservative philosophy: that government should help people improve their lives, not try to run their lives. That is why I will continue to work to reduce taxes, reduce regulations that strangle enterprise, accomplish real tort reform, and embrace educational reform. I believe this nation wants steady, consistent, principled leadership—such as that which I have provided the last four years.[16]

Depending on the audience and time available, Bush could elaborate upon virtually any part of this justification for his candidacy. He could discuss his military and foreign policies, economic policies, his education policies, or his overall aspirations for the American people.

Once a candidate has developed a concise answer to the question "Why Am I Running?" such as the Bush example, Faucheux offers several questions that can be used to evaluate and amend the answer.[17] First, Faucheux suggests asking, "From a geographic, ethnic, partisan, social, and demographic perspective, will this message appeal to the groups necessary for my winning coalition?" Utilizing the 2004 Bush example, notice that his message mentions key Republican issues, including a strong response to terror, a compassionate conservatism philosophical approach to government, tax reduction, and educational reform. It clearly appeals to Bush's basic constituency of Republicans. However, it also speaks to compassion, educational reform, and the American belief in self-reliance. Given that women might be especially responsive to appeals to education, and that all Americans were likely looking for steady leadership in a time of war, Bush's message was aimed at assembling a broad enough coalition to win the election.

Second, Faucheux suggests that the "Why I Am Running" speech should "zero-in" on both the candidate's strengths and the opposition's weaknesses. It should take full advantage of mirror opposites if they exist. Certainly this statement would do that. Kerry was a lifelong Democrat, the party often associated with big government and high taxes. Many of Kerry's principal financial supporters, and indeed his vice presidential running mate, John Edwards, were trial lawyers who abhorred tort reform. During his first years in office, Bush had secured passage of the "No Child Left Behind" Act to improve education. Kerry had served twenty-four years in the Senate without being identified with any educational reform. Throughout the campaign Kerry seemed to "waffle" back and forth on a variety of issues, including the vigor with which he would support the war on terror. In contrast, Bush no doubt hoped voters would feel he had been a "steady, consistent, principled" leader. Though Kerry might offer cogent rationales for these policy differences, clearly, a "Why I Am Running" speech such as the one above allowed Bush to "mirror" or stress the distinctions between himself and Kerry.

Third, Faucheux suggests that the "Why I Am Running" speech should be unique. It should not be so broad that other candidates could use essentially the same speech. The sample "Why I Am Running" speech offered above could not have credibly been delivered by any other candidate in 2004. The opening sentence immediately distinguishes Bush from Kerry by indicating he will continue to vigorously prosecute the war on terror. The second sentence utilizes the expression "compassionate conservative," which had come to be identified primarily with George W. Bush. The third sentence itemizes four specific policies that Bush supported. Though many candidates might agree with one or more of them, relatively few would agree with all four, much less conclude with a reference to having led the nation for the past four years.

Fourth, Faucheux suggests that the "Why I Am Running" speech should be "big enough." That is, it should treat major issues. Clearly, the above speech does that. Military and foreign policies, domestic economic issues such as tax policies, economic regulatory policies, tort reform, and educational reform, as well as leadership, are all major issues.

Fifth, Faucheux observes that the candidate must be a credible speaker for this message. Given Bush's record, he was a credible speaker for this message. He was the first president who had utilized the military in a massive way to combat terrorism abroad. Under his leadership, the federal government had been reorganized to create the department of homeland security and the "Patriot Act" had been enacted. Both of these changes were designed to help in the domestic fight against terrorism. His administration had sponsored a massive tax reform as well as educational reform through the "No Child Left Behind" Act. Clearly, he was a credible candidate for this message.

Finally, Faucheux suggests that candidates should ask whether their "Why I Am Running" speech would "inoculate" them on points where they are weak and subject to attack. The 2004 Bush speech presented above does that in several ways. First, the stress on compassion, and education, takes away issues that traditionally have been ones where Republicans do poorly and Democrats do well. Bush's use of these issues makes it difficult to portray him as a typical conservative who is out of touch with the daily concerns of Americans. Moreover, his references to tort reform and tax policies also suggest that he is in touch with the daily economic concerns of Americans. This line of attack, that he was out of touch with the daily concerns of average Americans, no doubt hurt Bush's father in the 1992 presidential election and has traditionally been used by

Democrats against Republicans. The 2004 "Why I Am Running" speech of George W. Bush presented above would help inoculate him against such charges. It meets the basic tests for such speeches. Hence, it would likely be an effective way for Bush to have met many of the speaking opportunities presented to him during the 2004 campaign.

POLITICAL SPEECHWRITING

The use of speechwriters by political figures dates back to ancient Greece and Rome when men such as Julius Caesar and Nero received aid in preparing their speeches. In the United States, the use of speechwriters has been a feature of our politics since our nation's inception. George Washington had at least four different speechwriters, including Alexander Hamilton. Amos Kendell, a former editor of the *Kentucky Argus* newspaper and a close personal confidant of Andrew Jackson, was called by one of Jackson's critics, "the President's thinking machine, and his writing machine, ay, and his lying machine."[18]

Abraham Lincoln frequently called upon his secretary of state, William Seward, for advice on public speeches. Lincoln's successor, Andrew Johnson, had grown up on the frontier and did not learn to read and write until meeting and courting his wife, a teacher. Not surprisingly, he too sought a speechwriter. This rough-hewn president found his man in George Bancroft, perhaps the most erudite and distinguished historian of the day.

Although both Presidents Calvin Coolidge and Herbert Hoover made use of the same speechwriter,[19] it was not until the administration of President Franklin Delano Roosevelt that the public at large became fully aware of the pervasive use of speechwriters by political figures. Roosevelt used a variety of individuals to provide him with aid in preparing speeches. Typically, Roosevelt drew upon both subject matter experts, often cabinet members, and stylists, such as authors Robert Sherwood and John Steinbeck. Among the most famous individuals to have ever been a speechwriter was President Dwight David Eisenhower who, early in his military career, served as a speech writer for General Douglas Macarthur.[20] While the press on occasion reported on the use of speechwriters, it was not until Richard Nixon that an American president publicly acknowledged that individuals in his employ were in fact employed primarily to help write speeches.[21] Today, it is not uncommon for speechwriters, such as Michael Gerson, George W. Bush's principal speechwriter throughout the 2000 and 2004 campaigns as well as his first term in office, or Robert Shrum, who has been a speechwriter for a wide variety of liberal Democrats including Senator Ted Kennedy and, in the 2004 campaign, Senator John Kerry, to become well-known public figures.[22]

Justification and Implications of Political Speechwriting

Since Roosevelt, the public has been aware that political figures often use speechwriters. Today no national or statewide campaign is run without them. The vast majority of candidates running for Congress utilize speechwriters, as do many candidates running for lesser office. Incumbents, whether presidents, members of Congress, mayors, state representatives, or town council members, almost invariably delegate some of their speechwriting chores to paid staff members. The staff member's title may be "assistant to," or "press secretary," but part of the job responsibility is speechwriting. Similarly, challenger candidates normally hire a "wordsmith" to help with speeches, press releases, and similar tasks right after hiring a campaign manager.

Though the public has accepted leaders who make use of speechwriters, somehow we remain vaguely troubled by the thought that those who aspire to lead us often do so by mouthing the words of others. Traditionally, there have been two basic justifications for using speechwriters.

First, candidates face such extensive demands on their time that it is impossible to fulfill those demands without speechwriters. In 1948 while governing the nation and running for reelection, President Harry Truman delivered seventy-three speeches in one fifteen-day period.[23] In 1952, during the final months of the campaign, the Republican and Democratic presidential and vice presidential candidates delivered a combined total of nearly one thousand speeches.[24] In 1960 John Kennedy delivered sixty-four speeches in the last seven days of the campaign.[25] In 1976 Jimmy Carter delivered 2,100 speeches while running for president.[26] In that same year, President Gerald Ford delivered a speech on average every six hours.[27] In 1992 Bill Clinton delivered so many speeches that he literally lost his voice and was reduced to speaking almost in a whisper toward the end of the campaign. In 1996, Robert Dole utilized a final ninety-six-hour speech blitz, which saw him fly 10,534 miles and deliver scores of speeches in twenty states.[28] Vice President Gore utilized a similar closing speech blitz in 2000, campaigning in Tampa, Florida, as late as 4:30 A.M. on the morning of election day.[29] By the time the 2004 campaign drew to a close, the candidates and their staffs had given so many speeches and were growing so exhausted that they were not only measuring the success of a rally by the size and enthusiasm of the crowd, but also by how brief it had been.[30]

These demands are not unique to presidential candidates. In 1954 Orville Freeman, running for governor of Minnesota, found himself facing over 120 speaking situations for which he felt the need for advance preparation.[31] This number does not include the many countless situations in which he spoke with little preparation. In 1970 Nelson Rockefeller delivered over three hundred speeches in his campaign for the governorship of New York.[32] A survey of candidates for Congress indicates that they spoke approximately four times a day.[33] Thus candidates at all levels simply cannot prepare for the many speeches they must make, while simultaneously fulfilling other responsibilities as candidate, breadwinner, and family member, without the help of a speechwriter. This justification is a compelling one.

Though the public is aware of speechwriters and understands the time demands that justify their use, it remains slightly troubled by the practice of one person writing the words of another. A second reason candidates use speechwriters is because they believe the writer will produce a good speech. Speechwriters possess unique skills. If their skills can be marshaled on behalf of the candidate, the result will be a stronger speech and, to that extent, an increased likelihood of election. But this justification raises troubling questions.

One critic has suggested that "the essential question is how much borrowing is ethical."[34] There is, he suggests, a continuum of help that one can provide to a speaker. On one end of the continuum, few people would find anything wrong if a candidate had a spouse or an aide listen to the rehearsal of a speech, or perhaps review drafts of a speech, in each instance making occasional suggestions to improve the language or organization. On the other end, most people might object to finding that speeches were written entirely by speechwriters who did not consult with the candidates, who in turn had no idea about what they were going to say until the moment they started to deliver the speeches that had been written for them. Where on this continuum does one draw the line between honest and dishonest borrowing and collaboration? This is an especially vexing question when candidates are using speeches to present themselves as competent to serve in a leadership position in their community, city, state, or nation.

Communication scholar Ernest Bormann finds that the point on the continuum where one must draw the line is:

> where the speech changes character. The language becomes different from what it would have been had the speaker prepared the speech for himself with some aid in gathering information and some advice from friends and associates about parts that he should consider revising. At some point the ideas are different, structure of the speech is different, the nuances of meaning change from what they would have been had this speech really been "his own."[35]

When this happens, the speech cannot achieve what should be one of its chief goals, portraying the speaker accurately to the audience, and the public clearly has reason to be troubled.

Thus, voters accept the use of speechwriters. However, we remain vaguely troubled, because the speechwriter is a skilled artisan who produces a polished product, and this too causes the candidate to hire him. To the extent that the speech reflects the writer and not the speaker, the public has cause for concern.

The very nature of political speechwriting prevents us from knowing how often "the speech changes character," becoming more a creation of the speechwriter than of the candidates. However, an examination of the job demands imposed upon political speechwriter suggests that this is probably not as frequent an occurrence as many may think. Fortunately for free societies, the demands of political speechwriting coincide with the needs of the public.

Job Demands

A veteran of over twenty-five years of political speechwriting for a wide variety of Democratic candidates, Josef Berger, claims that the most important part of a speechwriter's work is "to know his man, to know his man's ideas, not only his general philosophy and background but his thoughts on the issues that he's talking about if he's clear enough on them."[36] Similarly, virtually every political speechwriter who has commented on the job reaffirms the absolutely critical importance of knowing the candidate for whom they are writing because they seek to create a speech that is essentially that of the candidate, accurately portraying the candidate to the audience. Speechwriters must be thoroughly acquainted with the candidate's value system, for speechwriters must not present what they believe is the best justification for the candidate's policy. Rather, they must put forward the candidate's justification for a policy. William F. Gavin, a veteran political speechwriter who served on the staff of Representative Robert Michel when Michel was minority leader of the United States House of Representatives, has observed that a speechwriter should never "think he is writing speeches for himself. If you are doing that, then you're in the wrong business," he comments.[37]

Moreover, speechwriters must use language with which the candidate will feel comfortable, language that is an accurate reflection of the candidate. George H. W. Bush's principal speechwriter during the last years of the presidency watched videos of Bush speeches and news conferences, talked to Bush as much as he could given the demands on a sitting president's time, and even watched impressionists of Bush, such as comedian Dana Carvey, in order to develop an ear for how Bush sounded.[38] Similarly, Michael Gerson, President George W. Bush's principal speechwriter throughout his two campaigns for the presidency tried to discuss major addresses with Bush in advance, often using a small handheld tape recorder to capture both Bush's ideas and his language as they first discuss the speech.[39] Thus the primary demand placed on speechwriters is to gain an intimate familiarity with the candidates for whom they are working. That familiarity should include a thorough knowledge of the candidate's position on major questions, value systems, the way the candidate thinks through questions and makes decisions, as well as the candidate's manner of using language.

This information will enable the writer to produce a speech that accurately reflects the candidate. The speechwriter owes that to the public so that it might fairly judge the candidate. But what we often forget is that the speechwriter owes it to the candidate as well.

If the speechwriter does not accurately portray the candidate, the speech is likely to be a failure for several practical reasons. First, the candidate may choose to stray from the speech or ignore it altogether. In either case, the speechwriter will probably be fired for writing a speech with which the candidate felt uncomfortable or could not use. Second, if the candidate does choose to use a speech that is an inaccurate portrayal, there will likely be trouble in delivery. Unfamiliar with the basic lines of argument, the evidence, and the language, the candidate cannot be expected to do a good job in presenting the case. Third, candidates are likely to experience discomfort and nervousness in a public situation where they are liable to make some type of error as a consequence of that discomfort. Fourth, they may repudiate parts of the speech in a question-and-answer session or in subsequent public appearances. This inconsistency could create an opening for criticism. Hence, the demands on the political speechwriter to produce a message useful to the candidate create a speech that is an accurate reflection of the candidate's policies, thought processes, values, and language. Three recent examinations of the speechwriters' craft by experienced practitioners stress the importance of being faithful to the candidate and suggest that perhaps the principal function of the speechwriter is to polish the language a candidate might use, while remaining faithful to the candidate's policies, thought processes, and, for the most part, language, as well.[40] In so doing, the interests of the speechwriter and candidate coincide with the interests of the public in securing accurate information about the candidate

In addition to knowledge of the candidate, speechwriters need at least two other types of knowledge. First, they must know the subject. Occasionally, a political figure is concerned with a specific issue and calls on someone to help with speeches because of that individual's expertise on the issue. Throughout the 1980s and even after the collapse of the Soviet Union, former senator Jesse Helms took strong anticommunist positions on a host of foreign policy issues. Thus, it was not surprising to find a foreign policy specialist with a highly conservative bent, Dr. James

Lucier, on Senator Helms's staff. A U.S. senator, with a large staff, particularly concerned about one issue and perhaps having as many as six years before his next election can afford a subject-matter specialist. However, most political speechwriters are generalists because most candidates need generalists.

Campaign speechwriters must be versatile. The speechwriter for a Missouri congressional candidate in a recent election was asked to write speeches in a one-month period on such topics as international terrorism, the importance of engineering technology to the St. Louis business community, abortion laws, a federally funded lock and dam project on the Missouri River, Israel and Middle East affairs, and National Fire Prevention Week. Thus speechwriters invariably are widely read, often in literature as well as politics and current events. Moreover, they know how to do research. If they do not know about the topic, they know where to learn about it.

The final knowledge required by the good speechwriter is information regarding the audience and occasion. Speechwriters must know which audiences in the candidate's district are essential for victory. Moreover, they must know what message or impression the candidate wishes to leave with these target audiences. Is this speech being delivered exclusively to the audience in the room? If so, what is the nature of that audience? What are their interests? Is the immediate audience of secondary importance to the audience that will be reached by press accounts of this speech? How can the interest of those two audiences and the candidate be reconciled in an appropriate speech for this particular occasion? Answering these questions and then operationalizing the answers to produce a speech demands many kinds of information. It demands knowledge of the candidate's ideas, value system, reasoning process, and use of language. It demands knowledge of the subject matter, the audience(s), and the occasion.

A final demand placed on speechwriters is the trying circumstances in which their knowledge must be utilized. As one speechwriter expressed it when commenting about the type of person hired to help, "we looked for the capacity to work under harsh and often preposterous time pressures. When a speech for a particular evening calling for a ban on leaded gasoline has been co-opted by your opponent that morning, swiftness, along with eloquence, is routinely expected of the writer in coming up with a substitute."[41]

Speechwriting Teams

As the previous section has indicated, the job demands of political speechwriting are formidable. These demands grow in proportion to the office contested. Although the types of knowledge we have discussed are required by every political speechwriter, they are normally felt to a greater degree by the speechwriter working for a major national candidate because of such factors as the need to coordinate the candidate's speaking with the radio and television messages of the campaign, the need to respond to an opponent who is also constantly speaking and using media, and the constant interjection into the campaign of new issues. Hence, speechwriting in most major campaigns is done by speechwriting teams and characterized by a sharper division of labor than is found in the smaller campaign. Additionally, the team may perform functions that are not performed in other campaigns.

Firsthand accounts by members of the campaign staffs of Franklin Roosevelt, Harry Truman, Adlai Stevenson, Orville Freeman, Nelson Rockefeller, John Kennedy, Richard Nixon, Robert Michel, Gerald Ford, Hubert Humphrey, George McGovern, Jimmy Carter, Ronald Reagan, Michael Dukakis, George H. W. Bush, Bill Clinton, George W. Bush, and a wide variety of other gubernatorial, senatorial, and congressional candidates suggest that speechwriting teams exhibit similar division of labor in most larger campaigns. Craig Smith, who has been a part of several such teams and has studied many others, finds that typically speechwriting teams in larger campaigns are composed of three groups: the researchers, the stylists, and the media or public relations advisors.[42]

All these individuals should be familiar with the policies, values, and decision-making processes of the candidate. In practicality it may not be possible for each member of these teams to acquire that knowledge. Rather, key figures in each group acquire it.

The research group does basic library research. Prior to the 1990s, this was a group that frequently employed college students who were familiar with library research techniques. Pre-law and law students, college debaters, or other students interested in campaigns and with good research backgrounds often got their first experience in larger campaigns as part of the research force. While that continues to happen, more and more since 1990, well-funded candidates have turned to professional opposition research firms. The information explosion of the 1990s, fueled in part by the computer explosion, has given rise to the rapid growth of consulting firms that specialize in opposition research.[43]

The second group, the stylists, is normally composed of experienced speechwriters. They are often hired on the basis of recommendation and/or writing samples. These individuals must be able to write in any easy conversational style with which the candidate feels comfortable. They must be sensitive to the candidate's ability to tell a story, show righteous indignation, tell a joke, or use a particular jargon or group of metaphors. They use the materials presented by the researchers to produce a speech that meets high rhetorical standards and with which the candidate feels comfortable.[44]

The final group, the media and public relations consultants, are particularly concerned with the audience. More than the other groups, they tend to be familiar with survey research techniques. Their suggestions are designed to make the speeches consistent with the other messages the audience is receiving from the campaign and, given their surveys of the audience/public, to make sure that the candidate's speeches are perceived favorably by the audience.

Thus the demands put on speechwriters in large campaigns do not differ greatly from the demands put on speechwriters in smaller campaigns. The basic differences are not so much in the demands of the task, but rather in the division of labor employed to accomplish the task. Additionally, since a larger campaign is providing the audience/public with a great number of messages, most larger campaigns involve media and public relations consultants who focus on the speech from an audience's perspective, seeking to make the speech consistent with other messages the audience is receiving from the campaign.

Methods of Political Speechwriting

The literature of speech communication, as well as an examination of newspaper reports, biographies of the principals, and similar material, indicate that most speechwriters and speechwriting teams operate in a similar manner.[45] In this section we will examine the basic steps involved in campaign speechwriting.

First, the speechwriter(s), the candidate, and in some instances subject matter experts will confer. In this initial conference, the purpose of the speech will be agreed upon. The candidate will indicate positions and rationales, "talking through" the speech. Many speechwriters have noted that often the conference will be taped or a stenographer will be present. If not, the speechwriter would take copious notes. The record of the candidate's remarks would constitute a first rough draft. Michael J. Gerson, who headed President George W. Bush's staff of eight speechwriters and researchers, during his first administration, has developed an unusually close relationship with Bush. Prior to starting the preparation for a major address on terrorism or the Middle East, for example, Gerson was frequently present in the White House situation room to listen to and take notes on the discussion by Bush and his national security team. He regularly attended the daily morning senior staff meetings.[46]

From the very inception, the ideas of the speech are those of the candidate. The justification and reasoning within the speech are those of the candidate. Often, some of the language used in these conferences by the candidate is worked into later drafts and remains intact in the final speech. Speechwriters, nevertheless, in many situations have input into the development of the ideas that the speech reflects. That input is invariably secondary to that of the candidate, but as Martin Medhurst, a scholar of presidential speechwriting has recently observed, it is a "myth" to presume that speechwriters have no input into policy.[47]

At this point the speechwriters, armed with a clear understanding of what the candidate wants, do their research. If the campaign has a research staff, it is brought into the development of the speech. If the campaign is small, the research is done by the speechwriter. One of the advantages of incumbency is that incumbent office holders can often put the resources of government to work on their behalf. A speechwriter for the president might draw on the expertise of a cabinet member or someone in the appropriate department. Similarly, congressional speechwriters' efforts might be supplemented by the Legislative Reference Service of the Library of Congress, acting on a legislator's request.

At this point a draft is developed. In larger speechwriting teams, this draft is typically done by one staff member whose work may be reviewed by other speechwriters and altered. In a small operation, an equivalent process takes place as the speechwriter prepares a draft and then revises it, perhaps drawing on the suggestions of staff members or advisors who know the candidate well but have no responsibilities for speechwriting. In major campaigns it is not uncommon for the original draft to undergo five or more revisions as speechwriters revise their own work and incorporate the suggestions of others. If possible, the candidate is shown successive drafts for input. During George W. Bush's two presidential campaigns, Michael Gerson utilized fifteen or more drafts for some campaign speeches. Bush was often involved in the process and in some instances Bush retained language that did not test well in focus group research because he wanted to use it and felt comfortable with it.[48] This is typical of well-run speechwriting operations. In such operations, though the speechwriters do the bulk of the drafting and research, the candidate is periodically involved in the process and ultimately makes the final decisions.

Depending on the candidate's reaction, several actions can be taken with the version that the speechwriter believes to be close to final. Often the candidate accepts it as final, normally continuing to make minor changes, primarily stylistic, during free moments up until the time of delivery. If the speech is basically sound, but the candidate has more than stylistic concerns, these may be indicated in marginal notes or in a meeting. Subsequent drafts, better conforming to the candidate's wishes, can then be developed and resubmitted. The candidate may have an objection to one section of the speech or perhaps to some aspects of organization. Frequently when reading over the speech, the candidate may be concerned that the material will run too long or too short for the allotted time. If the speech is to be delivered over the radio or television, the media consultants will normally enter the speechwriting process during the final few drafts. Their suggestions will be geared to ensuring that the speech is appropriate for the allotted time and contains portions that can be used for brief spots on the news shows. These sound bites normally contain vivid and startling language that exemplifies the point the candidate wishes to make. In smaller campaigns, media consultants will not be available, but a conscientious speechwriter will strive to include potential sound bites in the speech in case of press coverage. Additionally, sound bites, even in smaller campaigns, might be submitted to the media in hope they will be used.

With slight variations to accommodate their own circumstances, this process is an accurate characterization of speechwriting in the vast majority of political campaigns where speechwriters are employed.[49] Several key points result from this description.

First, throughout this process the candidate is a major writer/editor/collaborator in the creative process. The final speech is a clear reflection of the candidate. The candidate accepts responsibility for what is said. It is for this reason that, as one speechwriter has noted:

> I don't think it occurs to the general public that a speech is ghostwritten. Even if someone in the audience has read somewhere that Congressman X has a ghostwriter and he knows it as the man speaks, he forgets it. He's listening to the man, and he's holding him responsible, and he's responding to him for everything that is said.[50]

Second, though the speechwriter has also contributed to the final product, the speech belongs to the person who utters it. It is the candidate, not the speechwriter, who will receive praise or blame for the speech. Thus, it is easy to understand why one experienced political speechwriter has commented that "if there is any prerequisite to ghostwriting for political figures, I suggest that it is a willingness to sublimate one's self to the figure for whom one works."[51] Though the majority of speechwriters labor in anonymity, in recent years many presidential speechwriters have breached the code of anonymity that characterized their predecessors. Emmet John Hughes and Theodore Sorensen, who wrote for Presidents Eisenhower and Kennedy, respectively, were among the first presidential speechwriters to acknowledge their roles and, in so doing, make the role of presidential speechwriter more public.[52] Today, even the speechwriters for losing presidential candidates may become public figures.[53]

Third, major campaign addresses undergo many drafts. A study on members of Congress indicates that they typically draft major campaign speeches at least three times.[54] The speeches Peggy Noonan wrote for Presidents Reagan and George H. W. Bush routinely underwent five or more drafts.[55] Mike Gerson spent over two months on the key speech of the 2000 campaign, Bush's acceptance address to the Republican National Convention. That speech ultimately went through fifteen drafts, with Bush constantly making changes to the manuscripts that Gerson and aids Karl Rove and Karen Hughes provided to him.[56] Though few candidates devote the resources to the development of one speech that the Bush campaign did for this address in 2000, every president and presidential candidate of the last fifty years has made extensive use of draft speeches prior to delivering a major address.

SURROGATE SPEAKERS

Even though most candidates make use of speechwriters, speech modules, and variants on the "Why I Am Running" speech to help them meet the demands on their time, inevitably they find that they simply cannot be in two places at once. Hence, even in smaller campaigns, it is not unusual to see a surrogate or substitute speaker filling in for an absent candidate. In large national campaigns, hundreds of people serve as surrogates for the candidate, many of whom have been trained by the campaign staff.

Selection of Surrogates

The selection of surrogate speakers is not left to chance. Candidates seek surrogates who meet certain requirements. First, they should have a proven record of competence as public speakers. In smaller campaigns, family members, lawyers, teachers, or anyone else with speaking experience may be called upon. In larger campaigns, public officials with extensive speaking experience might be used. In a governor's race, for example, members of the state legislature might serve as surrogates for their party's nominee. At the presidential level those cabinet members, members of Congress, and family members who are good speakers are often utilized as candidate surrogates.

During the 1996 campaign, Elizabeth Dole, wife of the Republican presidential candidate, was often referred to as the stronger speaker of the two.[57] Her ability as a surrogate advocate caused her husband's campaign to earmark thirty staff members, a $1.5 million budget, and a fourteen-seat jet largely in support of her speaking efforts.[58] During the 2004 campaign many members of the Bush and Kerry families served as surrogates. Many observers felt that the most effective of Bush's surrogates in

2000 was his mother, the former first lady, Barbara Bush.[59] Similarly, many observers felt that the most effective of Bush's surrogates in 2004 was his wife, Laura. Relatives are perceived as being unusually close to the candidate, as are cabinet members and legislative allies.

If surrogate speakers do not have an obvious connection to the candidate, they should make their connection clear to the audience early in the speech. Perhaps they grew up with the candidate, previously worked with the candidate, or have simply been long-time supporters of the candidate. In 1976 Jimmy Carter made heavy use not only of his relatives, but also of many other long-time supporters from Georgia who became known as the "Peanut Brigade." In 2004 many of Senator Kerry's most effective surrogates were men who had served with him in Vietnam.

Third, the surrogate should have some clearly identifiable connection to the audience. Since the substitute is just that, a substitute, the candidate or the staff should select a substitute who is appropriate for the audience. In local campaigns, the surrogate may be a member of the organization sponsoring the speech or a native of the geographic area. In national campaigns, the surrogate may be the cabinet member with responsibilities for the area of government that most affects the sponsoring group, as when the secretary of labor represents the president at union affairs. Again, surrogates should make clear reference to this connection early in their speeches if it is not obvious.

As the candidate is not present, it is clear that whoever is speaking on the candidate's behalf is not the audience's first choice. Hence that individual may have to overcome the resentment of the audience. It is for this reason that the speaker should be able to stress a connection to the candidate. In effect, the surrogate is saying "I'm the next best thing" and reminding the audience that, like Hallmark cards, this candidate cares enough to send the very best.

Utilization of Surrogates

Surrogates should have attempted to familiarize themselves with the candidate's positions. Indeed, one reason that some candidates like to use their speechwriters for surrogates is that they are uniquely adept at putting themselves in the candidate's shoes. Nevertheless, surrogate speakers should consider using two guidelines. First, particularly in smaller campaigns, surrogates should acknowledge why the candidate is not there. Most people understand the demands placed on a candidate, and a frank statement of where the candidate is will be better received than an attempt to hide the fact that the candidate has chosen to speak elsewhere. Depending on the audience being faced, most surrogates can indicate why their principal is not present in a tactful or humorous way. One rather rotund surrogate we are acquainted with often opened his after-dinner or after-luncheon addresses by saying that his candidate wanted to maintain his weight, and it was difficult to do so during the campaign when he was constantly out attending breakfast meetings, luncheons, dinners, coffees, teas, beer busts, and the like.

> So he's out rounding up some votes tonight in _____ where they are not serving food. Since I am the one member of the staff who clearly does not have a weight problem, he sent me here to guarantee that your food would be appreciated. Well, I certainly appreciated this fine meal, and I hope that when I am finished this evening you will have a better appreciation of why _____ ought to be elected to the Congress.

An introduction like this one acknowledges that the candidate is campaigning elsewhere but does so in a humorous and tactful fashion, which reduces audience resentment.

Second, surrogates should not hesitate to remind the audience that they are not the candidate. Hence, they may not know all of the answers or precisely what the candidate thinks. If the surrogate is well prepared, there should not be many occasions for this to happen. However, the speaker may confront a difficult question. When this occurs, the surrogate should simply acknowledge that to be the case, rather than guess. Arrangements should then be made for the candidate or staff to respond later.

Benefits of Surrogates

The use of surrogate speakers can provide a variety of benefits to campaigns. In some instances, the surrogate may be a more credible speaker for a given audience than the candidate. Additionally, surrogates can say things that the candidate feels uncomfortable saying. Finally, surrogates can often aid candidates in fund-raising.[60]

Surrogates who have a unique connection to the audience may, on occasion, be more effective with that audience than the candidate. In both 2000 and 2004, Laura Bush spoke to many groups with which she had more in common than her husband. A former librarian, Laura Bush was identified with libraries and programs aimed at learning to read. Hence, her husband's campaign frequently used her with school groups and educators where she would extol the importance of reading education and what her husband might do for such programs.

Frequently, candidates may wish to say something but find that it is not politically expedient. A surrogate may be able to make the statements for the candidate. For example, 1992 George H. W. Bush surrogate Mary Matalin, who served as deputy campaign manager and political director for the Bush-Quayle campaign, gave speeches and interviews in which she suggested that Clinton was "a philandering, pot-smoking, draft dodger." She referred to some of Bush's critics as "sniveling hypocritical Democrats." Matalin, not Bush, referred to the Clinton staff member assigned to refute and minimize the charges of Clinton's womanizing as being "in charge of bimbo eruptions."[61] Similarly, it was Clinton surrogate Congresswoman Maxine Waters, not the candidate himself, who called George H. W. Bush "a racist."[62] Typically, surrogates deliver the harshest criticism of the foe. Surrogates, like Matalin and Waters, can deliver the candidate's message, but they are not the candidate. Hence, surrogates may be able to make remarks that are not politically expedient for the candidate to make.[63] Similarly, it is for this reason that vice presidential candidates are often characterized as the "attack dogs" of the campaign, while the presidential candidate stays "above the fray," appearing presidential at all times.

A classic example of the desire of the presidential candidate to stay "above the fray" and let his surrogates do the "dirty work" was evident in the first 2004 political debate when moderator Jim Lehrer questioned Senator Kerry. "You've repeatedly accused President Bush—not here tonight, but elsewhere before—of not telling the truth about Iraq, essentially of lying to the American people about Iraq. Give us some examples of what you consider to be his not telling the truth." Kerry responded by claiming, "Well, I've never used the harshest word, as you did just then. And I try not to. I've been—but I'll nevertheless tell you that I think he has not been candid with the American people."[64] Clearly, Senator Kerry was attempting to distance himself from the charge that the president was a liar. Yet, repeatedly his surrogates used that term to describe the president, particularly in discussing the president's justifications for going to war in Iraq. Surrogates can call their opponents liars. Candidates, like Kerry, often prefer to suggest that their opponent lacks candor.

Finally, surrogates are often able to help candidates raise money. Many candidates feel that it is unbecoming for them to personally ask for money. Three recent examples illustrate the use of surrogates for this purpose. In February of 1994 George Bush, no longer an officeholder and having previously announced his retirement, broke his self-imposed year-long silence on political matters by addressing a major fund-raising dinner held on behalf of one of his former White House aids, Representative Rob Portman of Ohio. Bush raised $120,000 with that one address for Portman.[65] In 1996 the Clinton campaign scheduled many of Hillary Clinton's speeches to highly sympathetic audiences where she proved to be among the most successful fund-raisers of all of President Clinton's surrogates.[66] In 2002 Al Gore chose to briefly reenter the political arena by keynoting a massive fund-raising effort on behalf of the Tennessee Democratic Party. Many political figures feel that it is unbecoming for them to ask for money personally. Surrogates are not embarrassed or compromised because they are not asking for themselves.

In sum, the use of surrogate speakers can provide many benefits. Their primary function is to spread the candidate's messages to audiences that might otherwise not hear them. However, as Martha Kessler stresses, this is by no means the only advantage to using surrogates.[67] Indeed, the benefits of using surrogate speakers are so important in larger campaigns, where candidates cannot possibly address all the audiences that wish to hear them, that most national and many state and regional campaigns actively recruit surrogate speakers, provide them with training, and schedule them through a speaker's bureau.

CONCLUSION

Although, as we have seen in chapter 4, the media have come to play an increasingly important part in contemporary political campaigns, the public speaking of candidates and their surrogates nevertheless is at the core of any campaign. In small campaigns, public speaking may be the principal form of persuasion utilized. In this chapter, we have seen that the decisions to speak are not left to chance in well-managed campaigns. Rather, the campaign identifies the audiences to whom it wishes to speak and the messages it wishes to send and then arranges situations that conform to those wishes. Moreover, we have observed how candidates make use of speech modules and variants on the "Why I Am Running" speech to create a basic speech that can be used, with some adjustments, repeatedly during the campaign. Additionally, we have examined the reasons for the growing use of speechwriters, the demands placed on such individuals, and the methods they use to meet those demands. Finally, we have observed the use of surrogate speakers, focusing on the criteria for selecting such speakers, the techniques such speakers commonly employ, and the benefits surrogate speakers provide to a campaign. In spite of changes that have occurred in technology and the way campaigns are managed, all candidates, whether incumbents or challengers, whether speaking at a rally, a press conference, or on television or radio, utilize the ideas we have discussed in this chapter. Clearly public speaking remains a fundamental practice of political campaign.

NOTES

1. Jacob Javits, "How I Used A Poll in Campaigning for Congress," *Public Opinion Quarterly* 11 (Summer 1947): 222–26.

2. See Martin Schramm, *Running for President: A Journal of the Carter Campaign* (New York: Pocket Books, 1977), 428–31, for insight into a national campaign's targeting strategies.

3. See Robert V. Friedenberg, *Communication Consultants in Political Campaigns: Ballot Box Warriors* (Westport, Conn.: Praeger, 1997), 42–43. Some candidates are finding it helpful to take a "mini-benchmark" poll very early, and delay their major benchmark. Such a poll, involving approximately twenty-five to thirty questions, surveying three hundred people, is currently costing candidates around $3,500–$4,000. See, for example, the advertisement for such a poll by the RTNielson Company, *Campaigns and Elections* 21 (August 2000): 3.

4. Quoted in "Out of the Past," *People*, February 16, 1981, 74.

5. Pamela Hunter, "Using Focus Groups in Campaigns: A Caution," *Campaigns and Elections* 21 (August 2000): 38.

6. See Friedenberg, *Communication Consultants in Political Campaigns*, 51–54.

7. Ryan is quoted in "Off the Record," *Campaigns and Elections* 15 (December/January 1994): 82.

8. Perry Sekus and Robert Friedenberg, "Public Speaking in the House of Representatives: The 97th Congress Speaks," unpublished study, Miami University, 1982, 2–4.

9. Sekus and Friedenberg, "Public Speaking in the House of Representatives."

10. See, for examples, Jacob Maor, "Writing Campaign Speeches That Connect," *Campaigns and Elections* 22 (August 2001): 35–37; James T. Snyder, "7 Tips for Writing a Great Campaign Speech," *Campaigns and Elections* 21 (February 2000): 68–70; Jeanette Alexander, "Presentation Makes the Difference," *Campaigns and Elections* 14 (October/November 1993): 53–54; and Mary G. Gotschall, "The Lost Art of Speechmaking," *Campaigns and Elections* 14 (June/July 1993): 48–49.

11. Organizing a persuasive message by gaining attention and then presenting a need, satisfying the need, and visualizing that satisfaction are recommendations that date at least as far back as the earliest editions of Alan Monroe's classic public speaking text, *Principles and Types of Speech Communication*, which first appeared in 1935. Yet those very terms are currently being used by political speech coaches. See Michael Shadow and Greg Peck, "Politically Speaking," *Campaigns and Elections* 12 (May 1991): 54.

12. This module was excerpted from the text of the speech Bush delivered at his largest 2004 campaign rally, held in West Chester, Ohio, September 27, 2004. For the text of the entire speech Bush delivered see the Weekly Compilation of Presidential Documents at frwebgate.access.gpo.gov/cgi-bin/getdoc.cgi?dbname=2004_presidential_documents.

13. In 1992 Democratic candidates Clinton and Gore put together a book that was little more than their speech modules. See Bill Clinton and Albert Gore, *Putting People First* (New York: Time Books, 1992).

14. Ron Faucheux, "Public Speaking and Doing Press Interviews," presentation to *Campaigns and Elections* 12th Annual National Campaign Training Seminar and Trade Show, Washington D.C., June 17, 1995. Also see Ron Faucheux, "The Message," *Campaigns and Elections* 15 (May 1994): 46–49

15. Faucheux, "The Message," 49.

16. This "Why I Am Running" statement is based on George W. Bush, "Acceptance Address to the Republican National Convention," September 2, 2004, retrieved from his web site at www.georgewbush.com/news/read.aspx?ID=3422.

17. The next few paragraphs utilize the questions that Faucheux suggests. See Faucheux, "The Message," 49.

18. Quoted in William Norwood Brigance, "Ghostwriting before Franklin D. Roosevelt and the Radio," *Today's Speech* 4 (September 1956): 11

19. Robert Bishop, "Bruce Barton—Presidential Stage Manager," *Journalism Quarterly* 33 (Spring 1956): 85–89.

20. Discussed in Peggy Noonan, *What I Saw at the Revolution: A Political Life in the Reagan Era* (New York: Random House, 1990), 92.

21. Bernard K. Duffy and Mark Royden Winchell, "'Speak the Speech I Pray You': The Practice and Perils of Literary and Oratorical Ghostwriting," *Southern Speech Communication Journal* 55 (Fall 1989): 105.

22. President George W. Bush made his principal speechwriter, Michael Gerson, available to the media almost immediately upon taking office, never hiding the fact that Gerson played a major role in developing his speeches.

23. Irwin Ross, *The Loneliest Campaign* (New York: New American Library, 1968), 89.

24. Walter J. Stelkovis, "Ghostwriting: Ancient and Honorable," *Today's Speech* 2 (January 1954): 17.

25. John F. Kennedy, *The Speeches of Senator John F. Kennedy: Presidential Campaign of 1960* (Washington, D.C.: Government Printing Office, 1961), 840–1267.

26. Jimmy Carter, *A Government as Good as Its People* (New York: Simon and Schuster, 1977), 7.

27. George F. Will, "A Weird Sincerity," *Newsweek*, November 13, 1995, 94.

28. Dole used a tea called "Throat Coat" to help him through the last two days of his final four-day marathon. See Evan Thomas and *Newsweek*'s Special Projects Team, "Victory March," *Newsweek*, November 18, 1996, 124.

29. On Gore's last minute speaking efforts, see Evan Thomas and *Newsweek*'s Special Projects Team, "The Inside Story: What a Long Strange Trip," *Newsweek*, November 20, 2000, 124–28.

30. Evan Thomas and the staff of *Newsweek*, "How Bush Did It," *Newsweek*, November 15, 2004, 124.

31. Donald K. Smith, "The Speech-Writing Team in a State Political Campaign," *Today's Speech* 20 (Spring 1972): 16.

32. Joseph Persico, "The Rockefeller Rhetoric: Writing Speeches for the 1970 Campaign," *Today's Speech* 20 (Spring 1972): 57.

33. Sekus and Friedenberg, "Public Speaking," 9.

34. Ernest Bormann, "Ethics of Ghostwritten Speeches," *Quarterly Journal of Speech* 47 (October 1961): 266.

35. Bormann, "Ethics of Ghostwritten Speeches," 266–67.

36. Thomas Benson, "Conversations with a Ghost," *Today's Speech* 16 (November 1968): 73

37. Quoted in Martin Medhurst and Gary X. Dreibelbis, "Building the Speechwriter-Principal Relationship: Minority Leader Robert Michel Confronts His Ghost," *Central States Speech Journal* 37 (Winter 1986): 242.

38. "The Man behind the President's Lips," *Cincinnati Enquirer*, April 28, 1991, A1.

39. Gregg Zoroya, "'Scribe' Is a Man of Bush's Words," *USA Today*, April 11, 2001.

40. James T. Snyder, former speechwriter for New York governor Mario Cuomo offers seven suggestions for aspiring speechwriters. Three of them deal directly with language and style. See Snyder, "7 Tips," 68–70. Melvin Helitzer's discussion of political speechwriting focuses around characteristics of language that facilitate good delivery. See Melvin Helitzer, "Political Speeches," in *The Practice of Political Communication*, ed. Guido H. Stempel, 71–88 (Englewood Cliffs, N.J.: Prentice Hall, 1994). Peggy Noonan, in perhaps the most informative recent discussion of the craft of speechwriting, stresses that political speechwriters are dealing with policy. But her discussion of her years in the Reagan White House indicates that as a speechwriter she largely followed the policy directives of others and made most of her important contributions by providing Reagan with language that helped persuade audiences to support his policies. Especially see chapter 5, "Speech! Speech!" in Noonan, *What I Saw at the Revolution*, 49–67.

41. Persico, "Rockefeller Rhetoric," 58.

42. Craig R. Smith, "Contemporary Political Speech Writing," *Southern Speech Communication Journal* 42 (Fall 1976): 52–68; Craig R. Smith, "Addendum to Contemporary Political Speech Writing," *Southern Speech Communication Journal* 43 (Winter 1977): 191–94.

43. See Friedenberg, *Communication Consultants in Political Campaigns*, 72–73.

44. On the matter of candidate comfort with the writer and the speech, see Medhurst and Dreibelbis, "Building the Speechwriter-Principal Relationship," 242–46.

45. The speech communication literature utilized in this section includes Robert F. Ray, "Ghostwriting in Presidential Campaigns," *Central States Speech Journal* 8 (Fall 1956): 8–11; Benson, "Conversations with a Ghost," 71–81; Persico, "Rockefeller Rhetoric," 57–62; Howard Schwartz, "Senator 'Scoop' Jackson Speaks on Speaking," *Speaker and Gavel* 5 (November 1968): 21–31; Robert Friedenberg, "The Army of Invisible Men: Ghostwriting for Congressmen and Congressional Candidates," *The Forensic* 62 (May 1977): 4–8; Sara Arendall Newell and Thomas King, "The Keynote Address of the Democratic National Convention 1972: The Evolution of a Speech," *Southern Speech Communication Journal* 39 (Summer 1974): 346–58; Smith, "Contemporary Political Speech Writing," 52–68; Smith, "Addendum," 191–94; Lois J. Einhorn, "The Ghosts Unmasked: A Review of Literature on Speechwriting," *Communication Quarterly* 30 (Winter 1981): 41–47; Medhurst and Dreibelbis, "Building the Speechwriter-Principal Relationship," 239–47; Robert V. Friedenberg, "Jesse Alexander Helms: Secular Preacher of the Religious Right," *Speaker and Gavel* 24 (Fall/Winter/Spring 1987): 60 68; Lois J. Einhorn, "The Ghosts Talk: Personal Interviews with Three Former Speechwriters," *Communication Quarterly* 36 (Spring 1988): 94–108; Duffy and Winchell, "'Speak the Speech I Pray You'," *The Southern Communication Journal* 55 (Fall 1989): 102–15; and Noonan, *What I Saw at the Revolution*, 68–92. The best detailed account of the composition of a George W. Bush speech does not involve a political race. However, the speechwriting process in his White House no doubt closely resembled that used during the campaign. See Dan Balz and Bob Woodward, "A Presidency Defined in One Speech," *Washington Post*, February 2, 2002, A-1. Also available at www.washingtonpost.com/wp-dyn/articles/a11062-2002Feb1.html.

46. Mike Allen, "For Bush's Speechwriter, Job Grows beyond Words," *Washington Post*, October 11, 2002, A35. Also available at www.washingtonpost.com/wp-dyn/articlesa9575-2002Oct10.html.

47. See Martin J. Medhurst, "Presidential Speechwriting: Ten Myths That Plague Modern Scholarship," in *Presidential Speechwriting: From the New Deal to the Reagan Revolution and Beyond*, ed. Kurt Ritter and Martin J. Medhurst, 12–14 (College Station: Texas A&M University Press, 2003).

48. This description of the Bush operation is based on Larry Powell and Joseph Cowart, *Political Campaign Communication Inside and Out* (Boston: Allyn and Bacon, 2003), 159. Powell and Cowart cite Frank Bruni, "For Bush, An Adjustable Speech of Tested Themes and Phrases," *New York Times*, November 1, 1999, A1, A14.

49. An extremely brief description of the ghostwriting process, which coincides with this one, can be found in Einhorn, "Ghosts Unmasked," 42. Also see Medhurst and Dreibelbis, "Building the Speechwriter-Principal Relationship," 242–45.

50. Benson, "Conversations with a Ghost," 79–80.

51. Friedenberg, "Army of Invisible Men," 4.

52. Medhurst, "Presidential Speechwriting," 9–10.

53. Robert Shrum, a veteran Democratic political consultant and speechwriter, has worked for a host of losing Democratic presidential candidates including John F. Kerry in 2004. Shrum is frequently interviewed and quoted. Though his presidential candidates often lose, he is acknowledged to be among the finest liberal Democratic speechwriters.

54. Sekus and Friedenberg, "Public Speaking," 6.

55. Noonan, *What I Saw at the Revolution*, 74.

56. On the development of this speech, see Robert V. Friedenberg, *Notable Speeches in Contemporary Presidential Campaigns* (Westport, Ct.: Praeger, 2002), 234–35.

57. Elizabeth Dole is now serving as a United States senator from North Carolina. While she had a distinguished record of public service, virtually all of her prior service was in appointive positions. Her abilities as a campaigner were not proven until she served as a surrogate for her husband in 1996.

58. Denise M. Bostdorff, "Hillary Rodham Clinton and Elizabeth Dole as Running 'Mates' in the 1996 Campaign: Parallels in the Rhetorical Constraints of First Ladies and Vice Presidents," in *The 1996 Presidential Campaign: A Communication Perspective*, ed. Robert E. Denton Jr., 210 (Westport, Ct.: Praeger, 1998).

59. Barbara Bush was especially popular among Republican voters and was used heavily by her son's campaign during the final days of the campaign to help turn out the Republican base vote.

60. On the functions of surrogates, see Martha Stout Kessler, "The Role of Surrogate Speakers in the 1980 Presidential Campaign," *Quarterly Journal of Speech* 67 (May 1981): 148–50.

61. See Jack W. Germond and Jules Witcover, *Mad as Hell: Revolt at the Ballot Box, 1992* (New York: Warner Books, 1993), 419–21. Also see "Unleashing the Campaign Attack Dogs," *Newsweek*, August 17, 1992, 30.

62. Waters is quoted in "Unleashing the Campaign Attack Dogs," 30.

63. On several occasions in the final days of the 1992 presidential campaign, George H. W. Bush took to calling Bill Clinton and Al Gore "a couple of bozos" and tried to suggest that Gore was overly concerned with the environment by calling him "Ozone." Bush suggested, "If I want foreign policy advice, I'd go to Millie (his dog) before I'd go to Ozone and Governor Clinton." Intemperate comments of this sort, far more characteristic of surrogates than principals, particularly sitting presidents, according to some Clinton advisors, hurt Bush more than anything Clinton was saying at that time. Certainly that lesson was not lost on Bush's son. In 2000 George W. Bush avoided such remarks, as did his opponent, Vice President Gore. See Germond and Witcover, *Mad as Hell*, 496–500.

64. The quoted material in this paragraph is drawn from the text of the first presidential debate of 2004. See the text found on the site of the Commission for Presidential Debates at www.debates.org/pages/trans2004a_p.html.

65. *Cincinnati Enquirer*, February 9, 1994, B2.

66. George J. Church, "Hillary Clinton—Hushed on the Stump," *Time*, October 7, 1996, available at www.time.com/time/magazine/article/0,9171,985261,00.html (accessed January 21, 2007).

67. Kessler, "The Role of Surrogate Speakers in the 1980 Presidential Campaign."

7

∾

Recurring Forms of Political Campaign Communication

In his classic article *"The Rhetorical Situation,"* Lloyd Bitzer defines a rhetorical situation as "a complex of persons, events, objects and relations presenting an actual or potential exigence which can be completely or partially removed if discourse, introduced into the situation, can so constrain human decision or action as to bring about the significant modification of the exigence."[1] Bitzer's work has served as the basis for many studies of rhetoric that are based on the premise that comparable rhetorical situations produce comparable rhetorical responses.[2] While such studies have been subject to criticism, we find that the basic premise that some rhetorical situations are relatively analogous and hence produce relatively analogous discourse is a valuable premise for the study of much political campaign communication.

In this chapter, we suggest that most political campaigns tend to produce several similar, comparable, or analogous situations. Moreover, these situations tend to create similar, comparable, or analogous discourse. Four such comparable situations, found in most campaigns, are the rhetorical situations created by the need of candidates to:

- announce formally their candidacies to the public,
- accept publicly the nomination of their party,
- seek media coverage of their views, and
- make public apologies for their statements or behavior.

In this chapter, we also examine the discourse to which these situations traditionally give rise: announcement speeches, acceptance addresses, press conferences, and political apologies. We study these recurring forms first by describing the situations that create the need or exigence for their use. Second, we discuss the purposes that these four recurring forms of political campaign communication traditionally serve. Third, we consider the strategies most frequently and successfully employed by candidates delivering these forms of communication.

ANNOUNCEMENT SPEECHES

Candidates normally announce that they are seeking public office through a formal address to the public. However, this formal address is rarely the first act of the campaign. Rather, it has been preceded by considerable work. The effort in which candidates and their associates have engaged during the surfacing stage helps shape the rhetorical situation in which the announcement address is made.[3]

Preannouncement Situation

At least three activities typically precede any announcement address, regardless of the office being sought or the candidate who is announcing. First, an assessment must be made of the likelihood of winning. This will include an assessment of the candidate's ability to attract sufficient voter and financial support and to develop an organization capable of winning the office. The results of this analysis may enter into the announcement address itself. In any event, it gives the candidate a clearer understanding of the situation.

Second, most candidates tend to inform key individuals personally, prior to their public announcement. Typically these are politically, financially, or personally significant individuals whom the candidate wishes to flatter. If the office being contested is statewide or national in scope, often the candidate may inform a small group of individuals personally and then send a personal letter of announcement, in advance of the candidate's public statement, to several dozen, hundred, or even thousands of others. The point is that these individuals are significant, and the candidate wishes to flatter them.[4]

However, the advance announcement in person to a few key figures fulfills a second purpose. It serves as a means of providing the candidate with feedback regarding the rhetorical situation to be faced. These key, well-placed individuals may be able to help shape strategy, better understand the concerns of the constituency, or identify possible obstacles. For example, a judge with a group of six family members and close friends decided to run for Congress. After having assessed his opportunity for

winning, the judge personally set about contacting twenty-five key individuals whom he wanted to inform of his decision to run. He anticipated that all would be encouraging and would pledge their support.
Among those contacted were three elected officials, several party leaders, five prospective financial contributors, the director of a prominent
local political action committee, three journalists who were contacted
entirely off the record, and officers of several organizations whose members the judge felt might be sympathetic to his candidacy. While those
contacted pledged their support, over half indicated that they believed
the incumbent would prove much more difficult to defeat than the
judge's initial planning group had anticipated. Many mentioned aspects
of the judge's record that might work against him in an election. Moreover, they pointed out characteristics of the incumbent that would make
him much harder to defeat than he had been two years earlier, when he
won election by under five thousand votes. Thus, through a tentative exploration of candidacy with key individuals, the judge became more
aware of the situation that confronted him.

Finally, the announcement should conform to any preconceived expectations that the public might have about it. Hence, the third preliminary
activity of the candidate is to determine public expectations about the announcement. For example, have prior candidates conditioned the public
to expect that an announcement of candidacy for the office sought should
be made from the state capital rather than from the candidate's home?
Does the public have any expectations about what the candidate should
say? Does the public have expectations about the qualifications necessary
for this position, which might be mentioned in the announcement speech?

In recent years, at the presidential level, public expectations for a candidate announcement have changed to some degree. In the past, voters expected candidates to give major speeches announcing their candidacy and
generating considerable press coverage. Then the candidates would campaign. Today, considerable coverage is not automatic. Moreover, the coverage is likely to center on the horse race aspects of the coming campaign—
the chances the candidate has of winning, and the tactics the candidate will
employ to win—rather than the message of the candidate to voters. Consequently, in recent years, at the presidential level, candidates have often
revealed their intentions gradually. The public has come to expect that a serious presidential candidate will likely go through several steps before ultimately delivering an announcement speech. The 2000 announcement
"trek" of former vice president Dan Quayle is illustrative.

First, Quayle went on CNN's *Larry King Live*, in February 1999, to announce that he was going to "file the papers" necessary to run for the
presidency. Second, the following week he held a news conference in his
home state of Indiana to announce that he was forming a committee to ex-

plore the possibility of running for president. Third, he returned to Phoenix, where he resided, to announce that he was setting up a campaign headquarters. Fourth, he then made campaign trips to Iowa and New Hampshire, in both cases strongly suggesting he was likely to announce his candidacy shortly. Finally, on April 14, in his hometown of Huntington, Indiana, Quayle officially announced that "I will seek and win the presidency of the United States."[5] Though Quayle's public trek toward his eventual announcement was more extensive than most, the public has been conditioned to expect that contemporary presidential candidates will typically explore the possibility of running for the presidency, before they actually do so. Moreover, explorations of the feasibility of a campaign are starting to be used by candidates for lesser office. Hillary Clinton's spring of 2000 listening tour of New York and Jerry Springer's summer of 2002 tour of Ohio, done ostensibly to enable them to determine what was on voters' minds prior to determining whether they would run for the Senate, are recent well-publicized examples.

Clearly the rhetorical situation for every announcement address differs. Yet, typically, the candidate has, first, to analyze prospects for the campaign, second, to share impending candidacy with a group of significant associates, and, third, to consider public expectations concerning the announcement address.

Purpose of the Address

The announcement address should serve several purposes. Depending on the situation that the candidate confronts, one or more of the purposes discussed here may be minimized or underplayed, while others are stressed. Nevertheless, a sound announcement address may serve several purposes. First, it clearly signals the candidate's intention to run. Second, it may serve to discourage the competition. If the announcement address alludes to the candidate's strengths, such as the ability to articulate the issues, raise money, or wage an aggressive campaign, it may discourage other potential candidates from contesting for the party nomination or the office itself. As we will see in our discussion of strategies, typically the content of the address must be accompanied by actions that successfully discourage the competition. Nevertheless, one of the purposes of an announcement address, particularly if there is liable to be a primary, may be to discourage potential competition.

The third purpose that announcement addresses often serve is to indicate why the candidate is running. Candidates may want to stress what they can bring to the office that others cannot—how they can uniquely serve the public. For example, in his 2004 address announcing his candidacy for the presidency, Connecticut senator Joe Lieberman linked unique aspects of his biography to the issues that he wished to focus on as president.

> Today I am ready to rise above partisan politics to fight for what's right for the American people. . . . I want to talk with them about the tough fights I have waged before. As a young man I marched in Washington with Dr. King and I went to Mississippi to fight for the right of African-Americans to vote. As my state's Attorney General, I stood with single moms to go after deadbeat dads—and fought against oil companies that were trying to gouge consumers and corporate polluters who were spoiling our water and our air. As a member of the Armed Services Committee, I have consistently supported a strong defense, our men and women in uniform, and the use of our mighty American military to protect our security and advance our values—in the Gulf War, Bosnia, Kosovo, and now in Iraq. As a father and now a grandfather, I have taken on the entertainment industry for peddling sex and violence to our children—and spoken up for parents who feel they are in competition with the popular culture to raise their children and give them the right values.[6]

Lieberman's life experiences, as an early crusader for civil rights, attorney general of Connecticut, staunch advocate of a strong national defense, and sharp critic of Hollywood and the entertainment industry, clearly distinguished him from other Democratic candidates for their party's nomination.

A fourth purpose frequently served by the announcement address is to initiate the themes of the campaign. As the candidate's first major campaign address, it is appropriate to initiate any important themes that may run throughout the campaign. For example, in his 2000 announcement address, George W. Bush claimed, "I'm running because my party must match a conservative mind with a compassionate heart."[7] As he concluded his discussion of his conservative policy positions, Bush declared, "I'll be guided by conservative principles. Government should do a few things, and do them well." Then he turned to his second major point, that the next president must rally the "armies of compassion" that exist in every community. Speaking of the nation's churches, synagogues, mosques, and charities, Bush claimed that he would "lift the regulations that hamper them. I will involve them in after-school programs, maternity group homes, drug treatment, prison ministries."

In 2004 Democratic presidential candidates were faced with the prospect of running against an incumbent wartime president. Democratic senator John F. Kerry used his announcement address to stress his experiences in Vietnam and develop the theme that, as a combat veteran, he was the candidate best prepared to lead the nation in time of war. He likely hoped to use his service as a means of contrasting himself to both the other candidates vying for the Democratic nomination, and President Bush. Speaking in front of an aircraft carrier, surrounded by individuals with distinguished military records, Kerry made repeated references to his own military background, and that of those from whom he had learned. His father had enlisted "even before Pearl Harbor." Referencing his Vietnam experience, Kerry observed that "as I look around at my crewmates and the veterans here today, I am reminded that the best lessons I learned about being an American came in a place far away from America—on a gunboat in the Mekong Delta with a small crew of volunteers." Throughout the speech Kerry was critical of President Bush's wartime actions, and developed his overarching campaign theme that he would be an effective wartime leader.[8]

In sum, the announcement address may serve several purposes in addition to the obvious one of officially signaling the candidate's intent to run. It may serve to discourage possible competitors, indicate why the candidate has chosen to run, and initiate major campaign themes.

Strategies of the Address

In preparing to announce their intention to run, candidates are confronted by a variety of choices. They must consider the timing, location, who should be with them, speech content, and finally the means by which they follow up on their announcement.

Timing the announcement speech may be difficult. Often the first candidate to announce receives more coverage and, by virtue of being first, may be perceived as being more serious, credible, or legitimate. Though an early announcement may attract media coverage, content of the coverage might well focus on the candidate's potential to win, the funds raised, and the staff that has been recruited. Obviously, by announcing early to gain coverage, the candidate runs the risk that the announcement will not be taken seriously because there are few other overt trappings of a campaign.

The press treatment of Delaware senator Joseph Biden, among the first Democrats to announce for his party's presidential nomination in 2008, illustrates the problem. While Biden's early announcement did generate press coverage, it was not favorable coverage. In June of 2005, Biden announced his intention to seek the 2008 Democratic nomination on the CBS show *Face the Nation*, claiming that "my intention now is to seek the nomination." His use of the qualifier "now" suggested the underdog nature of his candidacy. Typical of the coverage his announcement received was the *Cincinnati Enquirer* syndicated story that stressed Biden's failed presidential campaign in 1988, reminding readers that it ended when it became evident that he had plagiarized parts of a speech.

Moreover, the article observed that the week before his announcement Biden finished fourth in a straw poll of likely Democratic candidates. It went on to quote Biden, who acknowledged that he might have trouble raising sufficient money to campaign effectively and that several of his positions were not popular among his fellow Democrats.[9] In sum, Biden's early exposure focused on the negatives his campaign faced in what would be an uphill battle to win the nomination.

Timing is also vital because of the effect that it may have on others who are politically important, both other candidates and potential supporters. Evidence suggests, for example, that Michael Dukakis was not anxious to run for the presidency in 1988 but was forced to do so because he feared that, in 1992, Massachusetts senator Edward Kennedy would be a presidential candidate.[10] By running in 1988, Dukakis could start with the support of his own home state, which could not be taken for granted if he delayed until 1992. In races for lesser offices, timing of the announcement can also be important. Obviously it may not receive the publicity that is associated with a presidential candidate's announcement, but it will be noticed and considered by other crucial decision makers in the constituency: potential opponents, potential contributors, volunteers, staff members, and supporters.

Where to deliver the announcement address is a second strategic consideration that candidates must confront. In so doing, they must consider voter expectations and tradition, as well as the issues they hope to develop in the upcoming campaign.

As rhetorical scholar Bert Gross has observed, all of the Democratic challengers in 1992, running as outsiders and seeking to indict Washington as the source of our national problems, announced their candidacies outside Washington.[11] The same thing happened in 2004, when once again the Democratic challengers ran as outsiders and sought to indict Washington and incumbent President Bush as the source of our national problems. Most of the Democratic candidates announced in places that had personal meaning for them or, in the case of Senator Kerry, underscored a major campaign theme. Senator Kerry, who would stress his ability to lead a nation at war, announced while standing in front of the aircraft carrier USS *Yorktown*, docked at Mount Pleasant, South Carolina.[12]

Virtually all of the remaining Democratic candidates utilized announcement settings that had symbolic meaning for them. Three used schools or other buildings. Senator Joe Lieberman spoke from the high school from which he had graduated, Stamford High School, in Stamford, Connecticut. He observed that "I wanted to come back home to Stamford today to make this announcement, because it is here that I came to appreciate the miracle of America." He went on to discuss how America, and Stamford, had been so important in the lives of his immigrant parents and himself.[13] Similarly, Congressman Dick Gephardt announced his 2004 candidacy for the presidency at Mason Elementary School, in St. Louis, Missouri, claiming that "I can't tell you what it means to me to be back at Mason Elementary School, the place where I was educated and raised with the people whose love and kindness has sustained me all my life."[14] Ohio congressman Dennis Kucinich used the Cleveland city council chamber as the scene of his announcement address. Kucinich had first come to political prominence in Cleveland, where he served as mayor and spent considerable time in the room from which he spoke.[15]

Three others announced from communities that had special meaning for them and also emphasized campaign themes. Former Vermont governor Howard Dean utilized the main street of one of Vermont's most picturesque lakeside towns, Burlington, as the setting for his announcement. Facing a field largely dominated by experienced Washington politicians, Dean utilized a bucolic Vermont setting to help emphasize that he was an outsider.[16] General Wesley Clark announced his candidacy from the Little Rock Boys and Girls Club. Clark was introduced by Congressman Marion Berry of Little Rock, Arkansas, who claimed that "it is significant that we're at the Penick Boys and Girls Club—inspiring responsibility in General Clark's life." Moreover, Clark acknowledged the importance of his Little Rock roots at the outset of his speech.[17] Similarly, Florida senator Bob Graham spoke from Miami Lakes, Florida, and claimed that he was pleased to do so because it is places like Florida that will lead the way into the future. "This land at the southern tip of the United States," claimed Graham, "has lured people for centuries with the promise of a better future." He then developed his vision for a better future.[18]

Though most candidates strive to announce their candidacies at a location that has unusual meaning, several presidential candidates have taken other approaches. At the outset of the 2000 presidential campaign, conservative activist Gary Bauer, head of the Family Research Council and a former Reagan administration official, as well as Ohio Republican congressman John Kasich, no doubt anticipated that the announcement of their candidacies would not attract the media attention of the leading Republican contenders, such as Texas governor Bush and Arizona senator John McCain. Consequently, they went to the media. On January 31, Bauer announced his candidacy on the NBC public affairs show *Meet the Press*.[19] Two weeks later, Kasich used the same venue to announce his candidacy.[20] In 2004 the relatively unknown senator from North Carolina, John Edwards, first used the media and then immediately followed up by traveling to a personally significant location. Edwards told many friends and supporters that he was running for the presidency the day before he made his announcement. He then made his announcement from his home in Raleigh, North Carolina, but he did so on a remote feed to NBC's *The*

Today Show. Shortly thereafter, Edwards again announced his candidacy at the Milliken mill, where his father had worked for many years, in Robbins, North Carolina.[21]

Among the most unusual means of announcing a candidacy was the one used by publisher Steve Forbes to announce his 2000 bid for the Republican presidential nomination. Claiming that the Internet is "a combination of cutting edge technology and a return to having individuals participate directly in the American political process," on March 17, 1999, publisher Steve Forbes became the first presidential candidate to formally announce his candidacy on the Internet. After posting his announcement of candidacy on the Web, Forbes held a traditional rally on the steps of the state capitol in Concord, New Hampshire, where the first presidential primary would take place.[22]

Two recent presidential candidates, Bill Clinton in 1996 and George W. Bush in 2004, did not deliver formal announcement addresses of any sort. Both were incumbent presidents who clearly were going to seek second terms. Neither felt it was necessary to give an announcement address, no doubt in part because as incumbent presidents so much of what they said was widely covered. Bush did post a brief statement on his campaign website on August 18, 2003, in which he thanked visitors for their interest and encouraged their involvement in his forthcoming campaign, thus signaling that he would run.[23]

A third question candidates consider when making their announcement addresses is with whom they might wish to share the spotlight. That is, who else should be present and in a prominent position? Traditionally, most candidates have announced their candidacies while surrounded by family, close friends, admirers, and supporters. However, exactly who should be invited, who should sit with the candidates, and who might also make a few brief remarks are matters that candidates must address as they plan their announcement event. Often the presence of prominent individuals in the community, city, or state, supportive remarks from party leaders, and similar visible signs of support for the candidate at the very outset of the campaign can help establish credibility and discourage potential competitors for the nomination or the office itself.

In 1960, John Kennedy's staff was in close contact with Ohio governor Michael DiSalle. The Kennedy announcement was made with the full knowledge that, immediately thereafter, DiSalle would be the first governor to endorse Kennedy. In doing so, DiSalle could guarantee that the large Ohio delegation to the Democratic convention was committed to Kennedy.[24] DiSalle's actions, immediately after the Kennedy announcement, made it clear to prospective challengers that the Kennedy campaign was not to be underestimated and may well, as the Kennedys hoped, have slowed down or discouraged the challenges of other possible contenders.

In contrast, in 1996, virtually no one besides his wife Gayle was on the podium with California governor Pete Wilson when he announced for the presidency. This fact was observed and commented on in press reports, which suggested that Wilson had little support. For example, the widely syndicated *New York Times* account of Wilson's announcement observed that "he faces a tough fight. . . . In New York state, for instance, most major party leaders have endorsed Dole. So Wilson appeared alone Monday on the podium, except for members of his family and a few friends."[25]

On occasion, as in John Kerry's announcement address in 2004, the candidate may wish to share the stage with individuals whose very presence may signal a major theme of the campaign. While opening his campaign in Mount Pleasant, South Carolina, with the USS *Yorktown* looming in the background, John Kerry shared the stage with eight of his Vietnam War swift boat crewmates, and was introduced by former Georgia senator Max Cleland, a triple amputee as a result of his Vietnam War injuries.[26] The presence of these individuals was designed to underscore a major campaign theme, that Kerry was uniquely fit for leadership in a time of war.

The announcement address itself is yet a fourth strategic consideration with which candidates must deal. The content of this speech is, in part, dictated by its purposes. Typically, three themes are present in most announcement addresses. Candidates announce that they are, in fact, running. Additionally, they offer an explanation of why they are running. Finally, they also suggest the likelihood of their victory.

Unless candidates can provide some cogent reasons for running, their candidacy may end very early. Senator Edward Kennedy experienced this difficulty in 1980 when he announced his intention to run for the presidency. In his announcement speech and in the speeches and interviews that followed, he had difficulty in offering cogent reasons for running. He chose to challenge an incumbent president of his own party. Yet, analysis of his positions on major issues, compared to those of President Carter, revealed very few significant differences at the outset of the campaign.[27] Kennedy's failure to offer a clear explanation of why he was running hurt his candidacy. The public expects candidates to have rational reasons for running and to share those reasons at the outset of the campaign. Candidates who fail to provide them in the announcement speech, or very shortly thereafter, tend to generate public distrust of their motives.

In 2000, both George W. Bush and Al Gore used their announcement addresses to provide the public with reasons for electing them. Bush had the easier task. He was running for the nomination of the party that had been out of the White House for eight years. Claiming that "an old era of American politics is ending," Bush observed that he and his supporters would prove "that someone who is conservative and compassionate can win without sacrificing principle. We will show that politics, after a time of tarnished ideals, can be higher and better. We will give our country a fresh start after a season of cynicism." Moreover, Bush's speech indicated a variety of shifts in policy emphasis that he would bring to the White House.[28] Vice President Gore argued that he would continue the prosperity of the Clinton administration. On economic issues he clearly identified himself with the administration, as when he claimed that "under the policies President Clinton and I have proposed, instead of the biggest deficits in history, we now have the biggest surplus in history." He implied that Republican policies would not continue this prosperity. Moreover, he suggested no fewer than fifteen proposals for new or expanded government action.[29] Clearly, both men were attempting to offer the public good reasons for their election.

Similarly, in 2004, John Kerry claimed that the nation needed courage and that he had the courage to "change what is wrong and do what is right." He claimed that Bush's foreign policy was wrong and needed to be changed. Moreover, he indicted a host of Bush administration domestic policies, including Bush energy, environmental, and tax policies. In each instance he suggested that he had better solutions and as a consequence there was good reason for his election.

In announcing candidacy, most office seekers also stress the likelihood of their victory. In so doing, they often focus on their strengths and on the weaknesses of potential opponents. Implicit in this discussion is their fitness for the office. The candidate claims to be better able to manage the office, better able to represent the constituency, and of course better able to attract funds and wage an effective campaign than anyone else.[30] Essentially, the actual content of the candidate's announcement address varies with the situation. However, most candidates, perhaps conditioned in part by public expectations, will formally declare their candidacy, attempt to explain why they are running, and suggest that they will win.

The strategies involved in the announcement address must also include the immediate follow-up to the address. The candidate should not simply announce that he or she is running and then seemingly disappear from public view. Rather, the timing of the address, perhaps its location, the other people invited to the announcement, and the discourse itself might all contribute to and be climaxed by the means in which the candidate follows up on the announcement. For example, many cash-starved candidates in recent years have followed up their announcement addresses with a practice introduced by Florida senator Richard Stone but forever associated with Missouri governor "Walking Joe" Teasdale. Immediately upon concluding their announcement addresses, these candidates start on a walking tour of their district or state. Such a method of following up may allow the candidate to stress key issues and begin to live up to announcement address promises. It enables the candidate to express concern for all constituencies within the district, evidencing the ability to unify people. At various points in the walk, the candidate can be greeted by prominent supporters, discuss the campaign with them, and of course get extensive media coverage of all this activity.

Regardless of the specific method used—a walk, follow-up mailings, the endorsement of prominent citizens, announcing staff appointments, or the like—it is sound strategy to coordinate the announcement address with some type of follow-up activity illustrating that the candidate is serious about seeking office and is already gaining support. In the 2000 and 2004 presidential campaign, the candidates used a host of follow-up activities, though the activities of Senator Bill Bradley were the most elaborate. After his announcement, Bradley gave the media a walking tour of his hometown. The next morning he held a press conference in the backyard of the home in which he was raised and then led a caravan of friends and supporters up the Mississippi River to Keokuk, Iowa, where he began a three-day campaign tour of the Hawkeye State, the first state to select delegates to the party nomination conventions.[31]

One of the more elaborate follow-ups to any 2004 announcement address was that of Ohio congressman Dennis Kucinich who, after his "first announcement," at noon on October 13, 2003, in the chambers of the Cleveland city council, then departed for a three-day eleven-state "announcement tour." Flying on a private plane, Kucinich spent three days reannouncing his candidacy in eleven other cities. He traveled as far north as Minneapolis, Minnesota, as far south as Austin, Texas, as far west as Albuquerque, New Mexico, and concluded in the East with an announcement banquet in Washington D.C. Throughout the three days, Kucinich supporters held house parties to raise money and celebrate his candidacy.[32]

Summary

The announcement address is not as simple as it may at first appear. Considerable thought must be given to the timing of the address, to its location, to the other parties who may share the spotlight with the candidate, to what the candidate will actually say, and to how the candidate will immediately follow up on the announcement. The announcement address is the centerpiece of a rhetorical situation created by the candidate's need to formally announce his or her candidacy to the public. Though the address may be the first public indication of candidacy, it should not be the first political activity the candidate attempts. Rather, the announcement speech should be preceded by considerable thought and preparation to ensure that the candidate's campaign is opened effectively.

ACCEPTANCE ADDRESSES

In the 1830s, national candidates nominated by the Democratic Party began to respond to their nominations with letters of acceptance. By the 1850s, Democratic candidates began to respond to their nominations with informal speeches. In 1868, Horatio Seymour delivered the first formal nomination acceptance address, but, like most such addresses in the latter portion of the nineteenth century, it was a perfunctory speech indicating gratitude at receiving the nomination and promising a full formal letter of acceptance. It was not until 1892, when Grover Cleveland accepted his nomination for the presidency by speaking at a large public meeting in Madison Square Garden, that acceptance addresses began to assume their current importance. Cleveland, William Jennings Bryan in 1896, and subsequent national candidates have used acceptance addresses as a means of thanking their supporters, seeking party unity, and dramatizing the issues. In 1932, Franklin Delano Roosevelt flew to the Democratic National Convention and became the first presidential candidate to accept personally his nomination at the convention.[33]

Situation during the Address

The situations faced by candidates delivering acceptance addresses have often varied, but typically they share several key characteristics. Most important, candidates have successfully attained their party's nomination for office. This success may be the consequence of running in primaries throughout the nation, as it is with current presidential candidates. It may be the consequence of persuading a majority of party voters in a statewide or local primary. It may be a consequence of persuading a majority of key party officials in a local, regional, or state party caucus or committee. It may even be a consequence of default, because no one else chooses to run. Regardless of how it was achieved, the important point is that candidates have obtained the nomination of their party and the legitimacy and attention accompanying that nomination.

Acceptance addresses are given to audiences as varied as the massive television audience that watches the major party presidential nomination conventions or a small group of highly partisan political activists who form the Republican, Democratic, or third party central or executive committee for a small town. The acceptance address may be given after a long, exhausting, and bitter fight, or it may be given after a placid and uncontested nomination. Clearly, the nature of the audience and the nature of the struggle preceding the nomination are situational factors that must be accounted for in the candidate's acceptance address.

A final situational factor that heavily affects acceptance addresses is the fact that they must be considered as part of what many scholars have called "a legitimization ritual."[34] In full view of those who have nominated them, candidates lay claim to their nomination and attempt to justify their supporters' faith and belief. Both their nominators and the public have come to expect such a ritual. Both nominators and the public will judge the candidate's effort and begin to accord the nominee legitimacy in part based on their judgments of the candidate's success at fulfilling the demands of acceptance address ritual.

Purpose of the Address

Acceptance addresses should satisfy four closely related purposes. First, the address is the means through which the candidate publicly assumes the role of a candidate/leader of the party. Second, the address should generate a strong positive response from the immediate audience. Third, it should serve to unify the party. Finally, it is a partisan political address, which in some instances may be the most important such address the candidate makes throughout the campaign. Hence, it should also serve as a strong persuasive message.[35]

The candidate typically spends very little time formally assuming the role as a party leader. In his 2004 acceptance address, President George W. Bush accepted the nomination of his party within twenty-seven words of starting his speech.[36] In 2004 Senator John Kerry opened his acceptance address to the Democratic National Convention by announcing that "I'm John Kerry and I'm reporting for duty."[37] However, he delayed formally accepting the nomination of his party until he was about 25 percent through his speech. Prior to formally accepting the nomination, Kerry expressed his gratitude to family, weaving in biographical information and several issue positions, before claiming that "with great faith in the American people, I accept your nomination of president of the United States."

Even at the national presidential nominating conventions, where the delegates are essentially simply ratifying the decisions made in the primary elections, delegates expect the candidate to acknowledge their efforts by explicitly accepting the nomination. Audiences would likely find something lacking, something incomplete, something unfulfilling, if the ritual of accepting the nomination was not observed. The rhetorical situation demands that the candidate acknowledge obtaining the party's nomination.

The immediate audience for an acceptance address is normally composed of those individuals who have affirmed the candidate's nomination. Hence, it is imperative that they respond positively to the candidate's remarks. These individuals, be they national, state, or local party officials, should constitute a nucleus of solid and vigorous support for the candidate in the forthcoming election. A second major purpose of the acceptance address is to arouse these individuals and properly motivate them for the responsibilities that will be falling upon them as the campaign progresses. This may be particularly difficult if large numbers of them have supported other candidates for the party nomination.

The third major purpose of acceptance addresses is to reaffirm and, if necessary, reestablish party unity. If the most active members of the party, its delegates to local, state, and national nominating conventions, leave the proceedings divided and with mixed attitudes toward the candidate, the base that most candidates count on for election—their party support—is of little value. In acceptance addresses that have been delivered by candidates who won bitterly contested nominations, it is not uncommon to see major segments of the acceptance address aimed at restoring party unity.

Finally, the acceptance address is a partisan political speech. David Valley has pointed out how each new advance in communications technology has brought national presidential acceptance addresses to larger and larger audiences.[38] Similarly, at least portions of the acceptance address of state and local figures, delivered at state and local nominating proceedings, are often read or heard by a large portion of the public. Consequently, acceptance addresses present the candidate with a unique opportunity to speak not only to party partisans but also to the general public. Valley concludes that, as early as 1896, William Jennings Bryan was tailoring his acceptance address not to the immediate audience but to the hundreds of thousands of citizens who might read his speech.[39] Similarly, even state and local candidates must consider that their acceptance addresses may be carried in full, or quoted in part, by a variety of media outlets, and placed on Internet sites. Additionally, the campaign may choose to use segments of the address in advertisements. Through such exposure, even local acceptance addresses may acquire broad audiences, while the audiences for the acceptance addresses of national figures number in the tens of millions. Hence, acceptance addresses serve partisan political purposes.

Strategies of the Address

A variety of strategies have been utilized by campaigners to satisfy the purposes associated with acceptance addresses. Traditionally, acceptance addresses are characterized by:

- simplified partisan statements,
- laments about the present and celebrations about the future,

- stress on the crucial nature of this election, and
- attempts to seek support from the entire constituency.

In recent years, as the importance of political parties has declined, and as decision making has shifted from nominating convention delegates to the will of party voters as expressed in primary elections, the functions of acceptance addresses have changed. As communication scholar Kurt Ritter has argued, candidates giving acceptance addresses today "face a voting public who will judge them not so much on the basis of their political party as on their personal appeal on television." As a consequence, Ritter continues, acceptance addresses "must persuade audiences who are less inclined to vote on the basis of party affiliation, and more inclined to vote on the basis of the individual candidate and his or her general orientation as liberal, moderate or conservative."[40] Hence, Ritter suggests that acceptance addresses are now less distinct from other campaign speeches and exhibit two additional characteristics not readily apparent in such addresses earlier. First, candidates are increasingly utilizing their biographies as "important sources of material for acceptance addresses." Second, acceptance addresses are increasingly "likely to reflect a personal comparison between the leading candidates."[41]

Which of these six strategies will dominate an acceptance address is largely a function of the specific situation in which that address is being delivered. All six strategies are common in current acceptance addresses.

Using Simplified Partisan Statements

In an attempt to attain a strong positive response from the immediate audience, as well as deliver a frankly partisan political address to the large secondary audience, candidates often use simplified partisan statements. Such statements characteristically suggest that the nominees and their parties are necessary to solve any problems confronting the constituency and/or that opponents and their parties will exacerbate any problems confronting the constituency. Typically, in harsh and uncompromisingly partisan language, candidates suggest that there is no real choice in this election—that their position and party are clearly right and their opponents are clearly wrong. Though simplified partisan statements are still common in acceptance addresses, Ritter cogently argues that, as party affiliation becomes less important to voters, such statements are likely to be found less and less in acceptance addresses.[42] A comparison of the 1992 and 2004 acceptance addresses of the Republican and Democratic candidates suggests that Ritter is correct in suggesting that simplified, harsh partisan statements are growing less important in these addresses.

In his 1992 acceptance address, George H. W. Bush reviewed the soul-searching decisions he made as commander in chief during the Persian Gulf conflict and then sarcastically asked, "Well, what about the leader of the Arkansas National Guard, the man who hopes to be commander in chief? Well, while I bit the bullet, he bit his nails." He spoke of Bill Clinton as a "con man" and claimed that, as governor, Clinton had raised taxes "128 times and enjoyed it every time."[43] Similarly, in his 1992 acceptance address, Bill Clinton claimed that the Bush administration had "hijacked" government for the "privileged, private interests." He went on to claim that the Bush administration represented "forces of greed" and that it was "brain-dead."[44] Both Bush and Clinton used harsh and uncompromising language to suggest that there was no real choice.

In contrast to his father, George W. Bush's criticism of his 2004 opponent, Senator John Kerry, was muted. In a text of nine single-spaced pages, Kerry was only mentioned in three brief passages, with a total length of about one page. In only one passage was Kerry mentioned by name. In two of these instances, Bush introduced the passage by observing that "my opponent's policies are dramatically different from ours," and "again my opponent and I have different approaches." In each instance he then simply contrasted his policies with those of Kerry. Obviously Bush spun the contrast to suggest the merit of his own policies, but he never demeaned Kerry personally or insulted him in a manner such as his father employed in discussing Clinton in 1992.

Similarly, John Kerry's 2004 acceptance address was not as harsh as Clinton had been in 1992. There are no passages whatsoever in Kerry's 2004 address comparable to Clinton's 1992 claims that the Bush administration had "hijacked" the government for the rich, represented the "forces of greed," and was "brain-dead." Rather, most of Kerry's criticism of Bush and his administration was by implication. Like Bush, he focused largely on policy differences, suggesting what he would do and, by implication, where Bush was in error. Kerry avoided the demeaning and insulting approach that Clinton utilized in 1992 with more restrained criticism such as:

- I will be a commander in chief who will never mislead us into war.
- I will have a vice president who will not conduct secret meetings with polluters to rewrite our environmental laws.
- I will appoint an attorney general who will uphold the Constitution of the United States.
- And on my first day in office, I will send a message to every man and woman in our armed forces: You will never be asked to fight a war without a plan to win the peace.

- As president I will not privatize Social Security. I will not cut benefits. And together we will make sure that senior citizens never have to cut their pills in half because they can't afford lifesaving medicine.

Remarks such as these certainly implied criticism of President Bush, but they were focused primarily on policy differences and avoided the bitter tone of Clinton's 1992 remarks. The harsh partisan statements so characteristic of prior acceptance addresses were not nearly so evident in the addresses of the 2004 nominees. Moreover, the muted criticisms of 2004 are an extension of a characteristic that began to manifest itself in the 1996 acceptance addresses of Senator Robert Dole and President Clinton, and was continued in the 2000 addresses of then Governor Bush and Vice President Al Gore.[45]

Though it might well be argued that the reduction in partisan statements is unique to these few candidates in these particular elections, it seems likely that the more temperate language we saw in 2004, as Ritter claims, is a recognition on the part of the candidates that harsh partisan attacks are not likely to be well received by contemporary audiences, which have less party affiliation than ever before. Though simplified partisan statements that in the past caused one critic to call acceptance addresses the "apotheosis of political oratory"[46] are likely to remain a characteristic of these speeches, it is also likely that their prominence is declining.

The work of communication researchers William L. Benoit, William J. Wells, P. M. Pier, and Joseph R. Blaney points to yet another manifestation of the reduction of purely partisan statements. These researchers find that, since 1980, the acceptance addresses of major party presidential candidates have focused far more on candidates than on parties. In the five earlier campaigns they studied (1960–1976), Benoit and his colleagues found that acceptance addresses acclaimed or attacked individual candidates almost exactly as often as they did the parties. However, since 1980, over four times as many remarks were aimed at candidates than were aimed at parties.[47] Clearly, acceptance addresses are partisan statements, but in recent years the diminishing stature of parties and the growing candidate-centeredness of campaigns have produced a corresponding shift in the targets of that partisan rhetoric.

Lamenting the Present while Celebrating the Future

A second strategy characteristic of acceptance addresses is that they tend to lament the present while celebrating the future. As Ritter has illustrated, challengers lament the present, claiming that incumbents have abandoned the abiding principles of the American Dream and, hence, have contributed to the nation's problems. Challengers offer to lead the people back to fundamental American values, thereby resolving our problems and giving rise to a bright future.[48]

In 2004 challenger John Kerry utilized this approach during his acceptance address. He claimed that "we have it in our power to change the world, but only if we're true to our ideals." He then suggested that the Bush administration had abandoned fundamental American values which he would restore. Specifically, he claimed that as commander-in-chief, Bush had "misled us into war." By so doing, he had broken the fundamental trust that the American people have with their president. He indicted other Bush administration figures for also having abandoned fundamental American values. He claimed that Vice President Richard Cheney had conducted "secret meetings with polluters to rewrite our environmental laws." He claimed Secretary of Defense Donald Rumsfeld had refused to listen "to the best advice of our military leaders." He found that Attorney General John Ashcroft had refused to "uphold the Constitution of the United States." By having misled the people into war, conducting secret meetings, refusing to listen to advice, and violating the Constitution, the Bush administration had repeatedly violated fundamental American values. A new Kerry administration would restore those values, never engaging in this type of behavior. Kerry, a Vietnam War veteran, made frequent reference to his military background, suggesting that he had fought for American values in battle and would continue to do so if elected president. He opened his speech by reminding the audience of his military service, claiming that "I'm John Kerry, and I'm reporting for duty." At other points in the speech he wrapped himself in the flag and American values.

- You see that flag up there. We call her Old Glory, the stars and stripes forever. I fought under that flag, as did so many of you here and all across the country. That flag flew from the gun turret right behind my head and it was shot through and through and tattered, but it never ceased to wave in the wind. . . . That flag doesn't belong to any president. It doesn't belong to any ideology. It doesn't belong to any party. It belongs to all the American people.
- We believe in the family value expressed in one of the oldest Commandments. "Honor thy father and thy mother." As president I will not privatize Social Security. I will not cut benefits. And together, we will make sure that senior citizens will never have to cut their pills in half because they can't afford lifesaving medicine.
- We believe that what matters most is not narrow appeals masquerading as values, but the shared values that show the true face of America; not narrow values that divide us, but the shared values that

unite us: family, faith, hard work, opportunity and responsibility for all, so that every child, every adult, every parent, every worker in America has an equal shot at living up to their God-given potential. That is the American dream and the American value.

Thus Kerry lamented an administration that, among other things, had misled "us into war," conducted secret meetings with polluters," ignored the best advice of the military, violated the Constitution, attempted to suggest that the flag somehow uniquely belonged to them and their partisans, wished to privatize Social Security, and followed policies that divided the nation. All of the ills of the Bush administration that Kerry lamented would be corrected by his new administration, which would return to basic American values.

Kerry concluded by celebrating America's future under his leadership. After reaffirming America's values, he utilized a series of rhetorical questions to dramatize the future, consistent with American values, that he would create.

And now it's our time to ask, "What if?" What if we find a breakthrough to cure Parkinson's, diabetes, Alzheimer's and AIDS? What if we have a president who believes in science, so we can unleash the wonders of discovery like stem-cell research and treat illness for millions of lives? What if we do what adults should do, and make sure that all of our children are safe in the afternoons after school? What if we have a leadership that's as good as the American dream, so that bigotry and hatred never again steal the hope or future of any American? I learned a lot about these values on that gunboat patrolling the Mekong Delta with Americans—you saw them—who came from places as different as Iowa and Oregon, Arkansas, Florida, California. No one cared where we went to school. No one cared about our race or our backgrounds. We were literally all in the same boat. We looked out, one for the other, and we still do. That is the kind of America that I will lead as president: an America where we are all in the same boat. . . . It is time to reach for the next dream. It is time to look to the next horizon. For America, the hope is there. The sun is rising. Our best days are still to come.

While lamenting the past and celebrating the future appears to be a strategy uniquely suited to challenger nominees, Ritter points out that it is also used, with slight adaptation, by incumbents.

The "in-party" version of the acceptance speech places the speaker at the later stages in the sequence of the rhetorical form. Instead of citing immediate difficulties, the incumbent cites the national decline immediately prior to his arrival at the White House. The incumbent typically describes the sorry state of America when he took office and then points out how he has brought the nation back to its historical purpose. . . . Each incumbent is quick to add that our work is not yet done. In fact, the opposing party threatens the restoration.[49]

Hence, this strategy of lamenting the past and celebrating the future is one that incumbents may also utilize in their acceptance addresses. George Bush follows this strategy in his 2004 acceptance address. He opens the speech observing that "tonight I will tell you where I stand, what I believe, and where I will lead this country in the next four years." As he does so, he simultaneously illustrates problems that clearly predate his administration. For example, he claims that "we passed the most important federal education reform in history," but the problem is long-standing and much more remains to be done. Similarly, he observes that "I brought Republicans and Democrats together to strengthen Medicare. Now seniors are getting immediate help buying medicine; soon every senior will be able to get prescription drug coverage, and nothing will hold us back." In addition to citing the national decline prior to his arrival at the White House, Bush describes the sorry state of America that would exist if Kerry were elected.

> Senator Kerry opposed Medicare reform and health savings accounts. After supporting my education reforms he now wants to dilute them. He opposes legal and medical liability reform. He opposed reducing the marriage penalty, opposed doubling the child credit, and opposed lowering income taxes for all who pay them. He's proposed more than $2 trillion in federal spending so far, and that's a lot, even for a senator from Massachusetts. And to pay for that spending he's running on a platform of increasing taxes, and that's the kind of promise a politician usually keeps.

In addition to indictments of Kerry's domestic policies, Bush strongly indicted Kerry's foreign policy, finding that Kerry's past record suggested that he could not be trusted to lead the war on terror. Throughout his speech, Bush laments both the past under the prior administration of Bill Clinton and the future, if Kerry were to be elected.

Bush's remedy for the problems of the past or the problems of a Kerry presidency was to return to basic American values with himself as president. Bush concludes by using his perceptions of military families who had recently experienced death, and with whom he had visited during recent weeks as a means of reaffirming American values.

> How can people so burdened with sorrow also feel such pride? It is because they know their loved one was last seen doing good, because they know that liberty was precious to the one they lost. And in those military families, I have seen the character of a great nation, decent, idealistic, and strong. . . . We see America's character in our veterans who are supporting military families

in their days of worry. We see it in our young people, who have found heroes once again. We see that character in workers and entrepreneurs, who are renewing our economy with their effort and optimism. And all of this has confirmed one belief beyond doubt: Having come this far, our tested and confident nation can achieve anything. . . . This young century will be liberty's century. By promoting liberty abroad, we will build a safer world. By encouraging liberty at home, we will build a more hopeful America. Like generations before us, we have a calling from beyond the stars to stand for freedom. This is the everlasting dream of America, and tonight, in this place, that dream is renewed. So we go forward, grateful for our freedom, faithful to our cause, and confident in the future of the greatest nation on earth.

Hence, Bush found that, although there was much to lament in the past, and there might be much to lament should Kerry be elected, his own administration had done much to remedy the problems of the past and his own reelection would eliminate the threat of a Kerry presidency. "So tonight," he concluded, "in this place, our American values will endure and prosper." Like most candidates before him, Bush lamented the past and celebrated the future. Unlike most candidates before him, Bush also lamented the hypothetical future if his opponent won, and celebrated the real future, that would no doubt feature his own victory. In both cases, the problems were caused by his opponents turning away from basic American values, and the successes he had and would achieve were a consequence of his adherence to basic American values.

Stressing the Crucial Nature of the Election

A third common strategy found in acceptance addresses is to stress the urgency and crucial nature of this election. In his study of presidential acceptance addresses, David Valley reports that 74 percent of all the words in the acceptance speeches of Democratic nominees he studied "have been used to discuss contemporary issues."[50] Ritter similarly concludes that "although incumbent and challenging candidates have found different lessons from the American past, they all find that their election represents a key moment in American history."[51] With the nation both peaceful and prosperous in 2000, neither Al Gore nor George W. Bush chose to stress the urgency of the election. The closest either of them came to doing that was a brief passage early in Bush's speech in which he claimed, "This is a remarkable moment in the life of our nation. Never has the promise of prosperity been so vivid. But times of plenty, like times of crisis, are tests of American character."

In 2004, with the nation at war, both Senator Kerry and President Bush stressed the crucial nature of the election. Though Kerry made repeated references to the importance of this election, none were more forceful than his claim that "this is the most important election of our lifetime. The stakes are high. We are a nation at war—a global war on terror against an enemy unlike any we've ever known before." Bush too acknowledged the crucial times in which we live and the importance of this election. "This election will also determine how America responds to the continuing danger of terrorism, and you know where I stand. Three days after September 11th, I stood where Americans died, in the ruins of the Twin Towers. Workers in hardhats were shouting to me, 'whatever it takes.' A fellow grabbed me by the arm and he said, 'Don't let me down.' Since that day, I wake up every morning thinking about how to better protect our country. I will never relent in defending America, whatever it takes." Both Bush and Kerry perceived the 2004 election to be among the most critical in our national history.

Calling for Unity

A fourth strategy characteristic of acceptance addresses is to call on all audience members, immediate and secondary, to unify behind the nominee to secure victory in the upcoming general election. Calls of this sort may be exceptionally important if the nomination has been bitterly contested. Because of the highly divisive primary campaign in 1980 between Senator Edward Kennedy and President Carter, the latter made a special point of including a passage in his acceptance address in which he addressed Kennedy by name:

> Ted, your party needs—and I need—you and your idealism and dedication working for us. There is no doubt that even greater service lies ahead of you— and we are grateful to you and to have your strong partnership now in the larger cause to which your own life has been dedicated. I thank you for your support. We'll make great partners this fall in whipping the Republicans.[52]

Carter was trying to unify his party by beckoning to his Democratic opponent and inviting his support.

Both Kerry and Bush targeted their base party loyalists as they attempted to build unity with their acceptance addresses. Typical of Kerry's remarks were his many comments aimed at middle-class America.

- And let's not forget what we did in the 1990s: We balanced the budget. We paid down the debt. We created 23 million new jobs. We lifted millions out of poverty. And we lifted the standard of living for the middle class.
- I am proud that at my side will be a running-mate whose life is the story of the American dream, and who's worked every day to make

that dream real for all Americans. . . . And next January Americans will be proud to have a fighter for the middle class to succeed Dick Cheney as vice president of the United States.
- We value an America where the middle class is not being squeezed but doing better.

Perceiving the base of his party to be lower- and middle-class America, Kerry included passages in which he discussed a host of economic issues such as tax policy, job creation, Social Security reform, pension reform, health care, childcare, and air pollution. All of these passages were no doubt designed to unify his support among the Democratic Party's perceived lower- and middle-class base.

George Bush also targeted his base voters. The Republican Party has oriented itself around philosophical issues. In the past, Republicans have stressed policies that limit the growth of government and encourage individual and entrepreneurial growth. In 2000, George W. Bush ran as a "compassionate conservative." Rhetorical critic Ray D. Dearin, who has studied every Republican acceptance address between 1980 and 2000 suggests that "the rhetorical situation facing Governor George W. Bush in Philadelphia [2000] enabled him to articulate what appears to be a more expansive concept of the American community than his predecessors had set forth."[53] In 2004, Bush continued to target both those who were philosophically in agreement with him, as well as the broader electorate that Dearin claimed he attempted to target in 2000. Hence, like Kerry, Bush spoke to the broader electorate, including the middle- and lower-class base of the Democratic Party, when he spoke of education reform, tax reform, health-care reform, job creation, and Social Security reform. But, Bush also spoke directly to millions of Americans he perceived animated by the entrepreneurial spirit and concerned about the growth of government.

- I believe in the energy and innovative spirit of America's workers, entrepreneurs, farmers, and ranchers, so we unleashed that energy with the largest tax relief in a generation.
- I'm running with a compassionate conservative philosophy, that government should help people improve their lives, not try to run their lives.
- To create jobs, my plan will encourage investment and expansion by restraining federal spending, reducing regulation, and making the tax relief permanent.

Thus, Bush attempted to build unity within his base by frequently stressing that his policies would limit government and foster individual initiative and the entrepreneurial spirit. Moreover, to a greater extent than

Kerry, Bush attempted to grow his base, as he did in 2000, with his comments about a host of government programs that reflected the "compassionate" portion of his "compassionate conservative philosophy."

Using Biography

The final two strategies that are commonly utilized in acceptance addresses are outgrowths of the increasingly candidate-centered nature of campaigning. As Ritter and Wayne Fields have argued, the candidate-centered, rather than party-centered, nature of recent campaigns is reflected in acceptance addresses by the stress recent candidates have placed on elements of their own biography.[54] Additionally, it has caused candidates to compare themselves with their opponents to a greater degree than ever before. The stress candidates have placed on elements of their biography is clearly evident in the acceptance addresses of John Kerry and George W. Bush.

The first 25 percent of Kerry's speech is biographical in nature. Kerry speaks about his childhood, detailing the influence of his father, a WWII pilot, who as a diplomat helped him to learn the value of freedom and what it "meant to be an American." Kerry also speaks of his mother, claiming she "was the rock of our family" and "gave me her passion for the environment." He discusses his experiences as a prosecuting attorney and young senator. He stresses what he perceives to be the high points in his senate career, including breaking with the leadership of his party to vote for a balanced budget, and working with Republican John McCain to "find the truth about our POWs and missing in action and to finally make peace in Vietnam."

Woven implicitly throughout the biographical section of this speech is Kerry's effort to be perceived as patriotic and strong on national defense. He starts by observing that "I'm John Kerry, and I'm reporting for duty." He follows that applause-generating line immediately with the observation that: "We are here tonight because we love our country. We're proud of what America is and what it can become. My fellow Americans, we're here tonight united in one purpose: to make American stronger at home and respected in the world." He then talks about his parents stressing their respective activities during WWII and concluding that "mine were Greatest Generation parents," and thanking his parents and their entire generation for winning WWII and the Cold War. Clearly Kerry was giving America a chance to become acquainted with him, and in the process using his biography to illustrate that he would be an appropriate wartime president.

As the incumbent president, George W. Bush was well known to most members of his audience. Hence, he used less than 5 percent of his acceptance address to focus on his biography. He uses this 5 percent to indicate the key individuals who will help him in a second term, and to praise them for their help in his first term. He mentions Vice President Dick Cheney's "calm and steady judgment in difficult days." He acknowledges his gratitude to his wife Laura, claiming that "Americans have come to see the goodness and kindness and strength I first saw 26 years ago." He acknowledges his "two spirited, intelligent and lovely" daughters and "a sister and brothers "who are my closest friends." He claims that "I will always be the proud and grateful son of George and Barbara Bush." Though Bush has worked with, and/or is related to, everyone he mentions, he saves his last reference for someone with whom he has had little firsthand experience. He concludes this section of the speech by observing, "my father served 8 years at the side of another great American, Ronald Reagan. His spirit of optimism and good will and decency are in this hall and are in our hearts and will always define our party." Thus, while Kerry uses 25 percent of his speech to acquaint the audience with basic biographical details of his life, Bush finds it necessary to use only 5 percent of his speech to accomplish the same task.

Bush virtually ignores his prior public service in the overtly biographical section that starts the speech. Unlike challenger Kerry, the key elements of Bush's biography were thoroughly aired in the 2000 presidential election, and he could likely assume that most audience members knew that he had graduated from Yale, earned an MBA from Harvard, served in the National Guard, been involved in the oil industry, been part-owner of a major league baseball team, and was twice elected governor of Texas before being elected president. In the body of the speech Bush reflects on some of his major accomplishments as president, but this is in the context of setting the stage for what he wishes to accomplish in the next four years, not acquainting the audience with salient biographical characteristics. Nevertheless, both Kerry and Bush open their speeches with sections devoted to acquainting or reacquainting the audience with aspects of their biographies. Kerry's needs are greater and he spends more time than the president. He is also able to utilize his biography to help make the point that he would be an appropriate wartime leader. Bush has been the national leader throughout the first three years of the war on terror, and has no equivalent need.

Using Biography to Go Negative

In their 2000 acceptance addresses, Vice President Albert Gore and Texas governor George W. Bush broke with many of their contemporaries, including Senator Robert Dole and President Bill Clinton in 1996, by not using the biographical elements of their 2000 acceptance addresses to go negative.[55] But, in 2004, Kerry used the biographical elements of his speech to go negative. Bush did not. One of the most discussed characteristics of American campaigns in the last twenty years has been negative advertising. But candidates can "go negative" not simply in their ads, but also in their speeches. Often, the biographical sections of their acceptance addresses are used to contrast themselves with their opponents, and hence to make implicit, if not explicit, attacks on their foes.

Kerry opened his speech by proclaiming that "I'm John Kerry, and I'm reporting for duty." On one level that was a simple observation. But the language "I'm reporting for duty" was no doubt calculated to remind the audience that Kerry had seen combat duty in Vietnam, while Bush had served in the National Guard.

Kerry continued to contrast himself to Bush and by so doing implicitedly attacked the president.

- We have it in our power to change the world, but only if we're true to our ideals. And that starts by telling the truth to the American people. As president that is my first pledge to you tonight. As president, I will restore trust and credibility to the White House. . . . I will be a commander-in-chief who will never mislead us into war.
- I will have a vice president who will not conduct secret meetings with polluters to rewrite our environmental laws.
- I will have a Secretary of Defense who will listen to the best advice of the military leaders.
- I will appoint an Attorney General who will uphold the Constitution of the United States.

Though elsewhere in his acceptance address Senator Kerry was much more explicit in his criticisms of President Bush, in the biographical section he chose to use a series of contrasts. These contrasts tended to blend attacks on Bush the person and Bush's policies. In several cases such as those above, Kerry implied that Bush did not have the good judgment necessary to appoint competent people. Clearly, this was an attack on Bush the person. But those people were also charged with carrying out Bush's policies; hence the attack was also on policy. In at least one case he directly attacked Bush personally, all but claiming that he had lied when he led us into war.

Bush did not use the short biography section of his speech to launch attacks, implicit or explicit, on Kerry. Rather, when he attacked Kerry, Bush was very explicit. He directly denounced Kerry's position on a host of policies. As he and Gore had done in 2000, Bush shied away from any biographical comparisons of himself to Kerry that might have been seen as attacks on the Democratic candidate.

Summary

Acceptance addresses are often among the most important speeches of a campaign. They are responses to a unique rhetorical situation that serve a variety of purposes beyond simply accepting a nomination. They may utilize at least six common strategies to fulfill those purposes.

NEWS CONFERENCES

Candidates universally complain of their lack of media coverage. But some events or statements that occur during the campaign are perceived by candidates and their staffs as uniquely important and especially deserving of media coverage. Such occasions often cause candidates to call news conferences.

Situations for a News Conference

News conferences are normally occasioned by events or statements that the candidate feels warrant special attention. Ostensibly, they provide a means of making statements that will be passed on, through the media, to the public at large. During the last half century, technology has dramatically impacted news conferences. Perhaps the two most dramatic effects of technology on news conferences occurred in 1954 and 1992. In 1954 Eastman Kodak perfected a new type of fast film. This film allowed press conferences to be televised without the use of high intensity lights. Immediately following this breakthrough, President Dwight David Eisenhower began delivering televised press conferences on a monthly basis. Televised press conferences soon became far more common for political figures, and campaigns could be far more flexible in selecting the times and places of the conference.[56]

The manner in which candidates communicate with the public at large underwent a second substantial change in 1992. The growth of cable television in the late 1980s and early 1990s created many new news and talk programs. In 1992, to a far greater extent than ever before, candidates bypassed the traditional news media and spoke directly to the public, primarily through television talk shows such as *Donahue, Oprah, Nightline, Good Morning America, The Today Show, The Tonight Show,* and the many shows on cable outlets. Though this was most evident in the presidential campaign, widespread use of local television and radio shows in lower-level races was also common. In the election cycles since that time, including those of 2004 and 2006, many candidates have utilized talk shows to address voters directly. Moreover, the growth of twenty-four-hour news/talk stations on both radio and television provides candidates more opportunities than ever before. Hence, the traditional importance of press conferences may be diminishing, as new technology and programming formats facilitate candidates bypassing the press to speak directly to the public.

Nevertheless, although their importance may be diminishing somewhat, news conferences remain an important and reoccurring means of campaign communication. Part of that importance is derived from the fact that, although the public is one audience in the news conference situation, at least four other audiences also exist. They include the candidates' rivals, their own staffs, political elites, and journalists. These five potential audiences exist for every news conference.[57] Moreover, on occasion, the candidate's remarks at a news conference are not meant primarily for the general public but for one or more of the other four audiences. It is through a news conference, ostensibly held for the public, that the candidate may also choose to address these other audiences.

News conferences are an exceptionally effective means of addressing an opponent. Candidates can exchange challenges, promises, or threats in private and by using third parties. But, if such messages are conveyed through a news conference, they take on a different dimension. A message to one's rival, made publicly in the midst of a news conference, clearly implies a degree of commitment, which the same message conveyed privately lacks. By deliberately going on public record and calling unusual attention to the message, the candidate is telling the opponent that this is no idle challenge, promise, or threat but rather a deadly serious message. The use of a news conference, more than virtually any other form of communication, conveys that seriousness and hence is occasionally used by candidates as a means of addressing one another.

Candidates may also use news conferences as a means of addressing their own staff. As political scientist Leon Sigal has observed, "campaign organizations tend to combine decentralization at the bottom with inaccessibility at the top."[58] The decentralized group of supporters at the bottom of the campaign has infrequent and short contact with the candidate. A news conference presents the candidate with a forum to which the campaign organization will no doubt be attentive. Hence, messages aimed primarily at the candidate's organization may be transmitted through the news conference.

News conferences also serve the candidate by providing a means of addressing political elites. In prior years, as discussed in chapter 1, campaign decisions were often made by relatively few individuals, often in private meetings to which the public had little access. The decline of political parties and changes in campaign financing have tended to increase the number of politically elite. In the past, candidates might have used a few meetings and phone calls to put out the word that they needed money, had dramatically spurted in the last poll, or had found a new campaign issue. Today, it would be difficult to contact all of those with whom a candidate might want to share this news. Hence, candidates may choose to use news conferences as a means of reaching political elites with information.

The use of news conferences to reach multiple audiences can be seen in the press conference held on the evening of November 2, 2000, by George W. Bush. This may well be the most significant press conference called during an American presidential general election during the last twenty years. Earlier in the day, while Bush was campaigning in Wisconsin, a story broke that Bush had been arrested in 1976 for driving under the influence (DUI) of alcohol and had pleaded guilty. With only four days remaining before the election, Bush clearly wanted to address multiple audiences in the hastily called press conference. His awareness of those audiences is apparent in several exchanges between Bush and the press.[59]

QUESTION: Why wait until now [to comment on the arrest]?

BUSH: Well, it came out now because a TV station in Maine broke the story. But I made the decision that, as a dad, I didn't want my girls doing the kinds of things I did and I told them not to drink and drive. It was a decision I made. I have been very up front with the people of the state of Texas that, you know, that I had been drinking in the past, that I had made mistakes. And the story broke.

QUESTION: Why now?

BUSH: I think that's an interesting question, why now four days before an election?

QUESTION: Did the girls know before today?

Bush: No, the girls did not know until tonight. I talked to them.

QUESTION: Why didn't you come out with this sooner?

BUSH: I just explained why. I wanted to make—I didn't want to talk about this in front of my daughters. I've told my daughters they shouldn't be drinking and driving. It's the decision I made. I have been very candid about my past. I've said I've made mistakes in the past. People know that. They've thought about that. They're making their minds up now. And they've seen me as the governor of the state of Texas. I've upheld the honor and integrity of my office. And it's a regrettable incident that I find interesting that four or five days before the election is coming to the surface. And the only thing I can tell you is that I told the people in my state I used to drink. I quit drinking. I'm not going to drink and I haven't had a drink in 14 years.

In these exchanges, Bush links his refusal to disclose that he had been arrested for DUI with his responsibilities as a father. It is a linkage with which many in the public might empathize. Moreover, he points out that he has been "up front with the people of the state of Texas," and indeed the entire nation, about his prior drinking. These remarks were likely designed to reassure the public, Bush's own staff, and political elites that this was, essentially, an old and not very newsworthy story. Elsewhere in this conference, on two occasions when the questions enabled him to do so, Bush made it clear that there "were no more mistakes of this kind or similar awaiting to be discovered" in his past. Such observations may have been reassuring to many, but they were no doubt in large part aimed at Bush's staff throughout the country from whom he needed maximum effort in the remaining few days of the campaign, and political elites from whom he no doubt sought last-minute support. Moreover, in these passages and on three other occasions during this brief press conference, Bush comments about the timing of this story, observing that he had his "suspicions" about why it broke that day and urging the press to investigate why, so late in the campaign, this had become a story. Bush was clearly laying this story at the doorstep of his rival and suggesting it was dirty politics. It was a serious charge, but one that was likely inevitable given the timing of the story. As the campaign drew to a close, Bush was telling Gore and the American people that he had been victimized by "dirty tricks."

Finally, candidates use news conferences as a means of influencing journalists. Those journalists who attend the news conference comprise the immediate audience. The candidate clearly seeks to influence what they disseminate and by so doing influence the many secondary audiences already discussed. Additionally, many news organizations may choose not to be represented at the news conference and fail to cover it. If candidates are newsworthy at the conference and if their remarks get good play in the media that are represented at the conference, the likelihood of increased media coverage of their campaign will be enhanced.

In sum, rhetorical situations in which candidates perceive the need to seek media coverage of their views for the purpose of better expressing them to the public, to rivals, to their own staffs, to political elites, and to journalists may frequently give rise to news conferences.

Purposes of News Conferences

New conferences serve three basic purposes. First, they enable the candidate to get the attention of a variety of audiences. News conferences often serve this purpose better than alternatives, such as news releases. However, they should not be abused. National candidates and major regional and state candidates can often be assured of reasonable media attendance at any news conference they call, simply because of the importance of any statement being made by a potential president, senator, or governor. Incumbents also have an advantage in attracting the media, simply because news organizations routinely assign someone to cover state senators, state representatives, members of city council, and administrative offices. Other candidates frequently have trouble getting media coverage of their campaigns. There are three reasons why properly used news conferences can increase coverage.

The first reason is novelty. The conference must be a reasonably unusual event. Candidates who are not overtly newsworthy cannot expect the media to respond to daily announcements of press conferences. On the other hand, if they call conferences only a few times during the campaign, the very novelty may cause some news organizations to send representatives.

Second, the conference should be called with a clear newsworthy issue in mind. As former vice presidential spokesman David Beckwith has observed, "having a press conference is a good idea when you have something to announce or something to say."[60] News organizations should be made aware of what the candidate will discuss. Unless the candidate has hard news and hopefully the data to support statements, news organizations may choose to ignore the conference. But if candidates are prepared to really make news that will be of interest to the readers, listeners, and viewers of the news organizations in their area, the news conference may be well covered.

For example, a St. Louis–area congressional candidate, concerned about excessive government spending and what he believed to be unfair government intervention in strikes, linked these two issues together when workers struck at a major employer in his district during the campaign. He pointed out that federal government benefits would be given to these strikers. He noted that the strikers all had well-paying skilled labor jobs and that they had voluntarily, by their own vote, given up those jobs to strike. The candidate questioned whether people who were voluntarily unemployed should be subsidized by the government. He cited federal employees and federal laws to explain in detail the benefits that these strikers would receive from the federal government, noting that it could well approach half a million dollars. This portion of his presentation was made with visually interesting aids for the benefit of television. He contrasted the government help that these strikers were receiving with the benefits received by people of his district who were physically disabled, could not work, and hence also received government aid. He claimed that people with physical disabilities should receive more money as they clearly needed it, while those who had voted to strike should not receive any government subsidy. Unlike individuals with physical disabilities, they had well-paying jobs to which they could return at a moment's notice. He concluded by criticizing his opponent who had voted for much of the legislation that provided help to strikers.

This news conference was one of only three that the candidate called throughout the campaign. It was directly related to an important news story—a large strike that affected thousands of people in the district. It related this strike to a major difference in the position of the two candidates. Moreover, the candidate provided hard information by way of facts and figures on government programs, quotes from government officials, and the voting record of his opponent. The material was presented orally but also with an awareness of the needs of television. The novelty and newsworthiness of this conference resulted in extensive coverage for the candidate.

A final reason why news conferences can effectively serve to focus widespread attention on the candidate's message is that reporters consider them reliable. Reporters often express doubts about the reliability of press releases or political advertisements. But the reliability of news conferences, witnessed by many reporters, with the candidate's statements captured on both audio and videotape, cannot be doubted.

For example, incumbent Missouri senator Jean Carnahan's 2002 campaign ran ads in which she took credit for saving the jobs of TWA pilots and other airline industry workers in the St. Louis area. Her opponent, Congressman Jim Talent, countered in part with a press conference. He appeared with TWA pilots who had lost their jobs. He discussed the plight of the over five hundred St. Louis–area pilots who had lost their jobs and the many others dependent on the airline industry and TWA.[61] With the pilots visibly supporting Talent and the factual information Talent presented, the widely covered press conference seemed far more believable than the claims in Carnahan's advertisements.

Thus, the news conference can serve as a means through which the candidate is able to reach many audiences. Even candidates whom news organizations judge to be unworthy of much attention can gain some attention if they use news conferences properly.

A second important purpose served by news conferences is to allow the candidate to focus attention on one issue or a limited number of issues. As we discussed in chapter 2, a major function of the press is to help set the campaign agenda. But the candidate also wants to help shape the agenda. By focusing remarks on one issue, the candidate is able to influence strongly what issue the media will cover. Using a press conference, but focusing the issues treated and stressed in that conference, is an effective means utilized by many candidates to help set the campaign agenda.

A final purpose served by news conferences is to establish and improve relationships between the candidate and individual members of the media. The more efficiently run the conference is, the more prepared and responsive the candidate is, the easier the job of the reporter becomes. Press conferences are one means by which candidates can make the job of reporters easier and in so doing improve relationships between themselves and the media.

The chief purpose of news conferences—to allow candidates to bring their views to the attention of many audiences—may be readily apparent, but we should not ignore the other purposes served by press conferences: to allow the candidate to focus attention on one or a limited number of issues, presumably selected by the candidate to be of advantage to the candidate, and to enhance candidate–press relationships.

Strategies of News Conferences

Candidates attempt to use news conferences to their own advantage. One of the reasons they are used is to foster the illusion that the candidate is not in control. C. Jack Orr has suggested that presidential news conferences can be thought of as "counterpoised situations" in which the reporters have competing obligations. They must both confront the president, and they must give deference to him.[62] To a lesser extent, the same counterpoised situation exists when reporters interview any office seeker. The candidate must be shown some deference as a responsible individual running for a responsible job. Moreover, the conference is, after all, the candidate's proceeding. Yet, reporters also may seek to confront, challenge, and criticize.

The candidate's control extends beyond the deference that may be extended by reporters. The control is real. The candidate decides when and where to hold a news conference. The candidate decides what format will be used. The candidate decides who will ask questions, and, of course, the candidate provides the answers. Scholars who have examined news conferences, such as Robert Denton and Dan Hahn, have concluded that, while the situation may appear to be one in which the press has considerable control, ultimately it is the skilled respondent who controls the news conference.[63] Candidates exercise their control by utilizing one or more of at least ten common strategies.

As it is the candidates who call news conferences, they will do so to suit their own needs. Decisions by the candidate about the timing of news conferences are important, and determining when to call a conference is the candidate's first strategic decision. As indicated earlier, typically the fewer conferences called, the more attention the press will extend to those that are called. Calling a news conference to deal with a topic is a clear means not only of signaling that the candidate attaches major importance to this topic but also of increasing the treatment it receives in the media.

In addition, the candidate must consider the media that will attend and the deadlines with which they operate. Typically, candidates vary the time of day that they hold press conferences, so that they are not slighting any of the media organizations serving their constituency. However, this matter, too, is a strategic decision. The candidate, by determining the time of day to hold the conference, can play favorites with the media.

A second consideration is where to hold a news conference. Candidates may make their conferences visually interesting to audiences and hence especially appealing to television news organizations by holding them in visually appealing settings. The candidate who has promised to repair the roads and eliminate dangerous potholes might choose to hold the conference at the site of a recent fatal accident caused by poor roads. The need for a visually appealing setting should also be balanced with consideration of the accessibility of the site and the technical requirements of the media.[64]

Although George H. W. Bush held relatively few press conferences during the 1988 election, he used site selection to the utmost advantage when he attacked Michael Dukakis. In his attempt to claim that Dukakis was weak on environmental issues, Bush visited the most polluted harbor in the nation, which just happened to be Boston Harbor, in Dukakis's home city. Similarly, Bush subsequently discussed the environment and pollution with the press while visiting the New Jersey coast, off of which Governor Dukakis had proposed dumping sewage from Massachusetts. By selecting these sites, Bush provided the media with visually appealing settings and focused the media's attention on his opponent's weaknesses.

Candidates should keep in mind that sometimes a site might be highly visual, lending itself to television news, but it might be difficult and time-consuming to reach. Such sites may cause radio and print media representatives to feel that a news conference is hardly worth their effort. Typically, candidates seek to balance their news conference site selections. Some are held with television in mind, while others are held in the campaign headquarters or some highly accessible central location. Whatever decision is made, the candidate can use the selection of a news conference site strategically, to help fulfill overall purposes.

However, sometimes, as in George W. Bush's 2000 campaign, a candidate must choose between the timing of the conference and the site of the conference. Bush held what was likely the most important press conference of his 2000 campaign with nothing more than the brick wall of a building in West Allis, Wisconsin, a suburb of Milwaukee, in the background and his wife at his side.[65] It was simply a convenient place at the end of a long day of campaigning. His organization did not have time to set up an elaborate press conference, for he was responding to news released earlier in the day that he had pleaded guilty to a drunk driving charge in 1976. With only four days left in the campaign, Bush and his organization felt that timing was more important than site selection. They wanted to provide Bush an opportunity to answer press questions immediately, hoping that the controversy over a twenty-four-year-old incident would pass quickly if he responded immediately.

These first two strategic concerns involving news conferences, where and when to hold them, relate primarily to the candidate's goal of increasing news coverage. The second group of strategies can help focus the topic of the conference on the areas that the candidate wants covered and stressed in the media.

Candidates utilize at least five strategies to guarantee that the agenda-setting function of the media works in their favor when news organizations cover their press conferences. Perhaps the most commonly used of these strategies is to make an opening statement at the outset of the conference. Based on her studies of presidential press conferences and her experience as director of political coverage for ABC News, Carolyn Smith has suggested that opening statements are an exceptionally effective means of setting a press conference agenda if they are used at press conferences that involve reacting to a single major event or treating a single major policy.[66] Though this tactic seems commonplace today, fifty years ago it was not frequently used. Dwight Eisenhower was the first president who regularly made opening statements at his news conferences.[67] The opening statement should, in itself, be newsworthy. If it is, it will generally prompt questions on the issue it treats and be the focus of most reports of the news conference. Moreover, as Catherine Collins has illustrated in her examination of former secretary of state Henry Kissinger's press conferences, if the interviewee assumes the role of the expert, defines the topic of immediate concern, develops a perspective from which events should be viewed, utilizes data to depict the event, and warns the media that other perspectives will not be considered acceptable, the chances are greatly increased that the interviewee's perspective will be reflected clearly in media accounts of the conference.[68]

In his November 2, 2000, press conference, George W. Bush made a brief opening statement in which he observed that the DUI arrest took place twenty-four years earlier; that he had frequently indicated to voters that in the past he had made mistakes, including drinking too much; that he had fully cooperated with the police who arrested him; and that he had not had a drink in fourteen years. The main points in Bush's opening statement were typically repeated in subsequent news stories.

Similarly, candidates may not only present opening statements but also restructure questions. In restructuring a question, candidates are again generally attempting to focus attention onto key issues, from certain perspectives, in order to make their points better.

A third strategy frequently utilized by candidates to ensure that news conferences focus on their agenda is to follow the advice of former Republican political consultant Roger Ailes, who recommends that candidates use the formula Q = A + 1 when responding to questions. Ailes explains that, when asked a question (Q), his clients "reply briefly and directly with an answer (A). Then if it will help, add a point or points (+1) preferably from your agenda."[69] Bush illustrated this strategy in responding to questions about his DUI arrest:

QUESTION: Governor, do you believe this [DUI arrest] is relevant to your candidacy in any fashion?

BUSH: No. I think the people knew that I had been straightforward, that I had made mistakes in the past. This happened 24 years ago. I do find it interesting that it's come out four or five days before the election. But I have been straightforward with the people, saying that I used to drink too much in the past. I'm straightforward with people saying that I don't drink now.

Bush answers the question with one word: *no*. The bulk of his answer is designed to introduce the points he wants to make. Bush wants people to know that this took place twenty-four years ago. He wants them to suspect the timing, which suggests that this story is little more than a dirty political trick. Perhaps most important, Bush wants to stress that he has been consistently straightforward with the public. In this instance, Bush's formula is Q = A + 3.

A fourth strategy utilized to make sure candidates are able to focus the conference on their topics and from their perspective is to plant questions. This tactic became commonplace in the presidential press conferences of Eisenhower and Johnson.[70] It has since been used by many candidates for public office. Typically, a staff member approaches a reporter and suggests a question that might be asked, noting that it will no doubt produce a newsworthy response. Obviously, many reporters may not choose to be used in this fashion. But others will, perceiving the suggested question as a means of drawing attention to something that is newsworthy, which is just what the candidate also wants. The ethics of restructuring questions and planting questions is certainly open for debate. But clearly they are strategies that are utilized by many interviewees, including political candidates, who wish to limit the focus of news conferences.

The final strategy, used primarily to focus the news conference, is selective recognition of reporters. Candidates recognize those who question them, but they can fail to recognize those who wish to question them. Most of the time, recognition is haphazard. But it can also be done in a deliberate fashion. A survey of the White House press corps found that "the random selection of questioners by the President" was among the most serious problems associated with White House news conferences.[71] News conferences held by candidates for lesser office will not draw the massive number of reporters that a White House news conference attracts. But any conference that draws a reasonable sample of the media is one in which a candidate might selectively recognize reporters.

Candidates normally hold news conferences when they seek extensive coverage of their views. Typically, they have a limited number of issues on which they wish to focus in the news conference and that they hope the public will learn of through the efforts of the journalists in attendance. To ensure that these topics are clearly the centerpieces of the news conference, candidates often assume the role of the expert, utilizing an opening statement that spells out their position on issues and indicates the perspective on the issue that they find satisfactory. They may also choose to restructure questions, consistently add comments from their agenda to answers (Q = A + 1), plant questions, and selectively recognize reporters. All these strategies are done primarily to enable candidates to stress their issues and prevent the conference from dealing with other issues. However, as Smith points out, reporters attend press conferences to address their own agendas of what is newsworthy, not to serve as a foil for the individual holding the conference.[72]

Three final strategies can be utilized by most candidates holding news conferences. The first is to prepare. Candidates differ in the manner of their preparation for news conferences. However, most attempt to anticipate questions that might be asked and prepare responses. Presidents, such as Truman and Kennedy, typically rehearsed for news conferences by reviewing forty to seventy-five possible questions that might arise in their press conferences.[73] Most candidates follow similar procedures. They rely on their staffs to generate possible questions and then prepare responses.

Though George W. Bush's press conference on the evening of November 2, 2000, in West Allis, Wisconsin, was called hastily in response to breaking news events, Bush's press secretary, Karen Hughes, met with reporters prior to the press conference. Among the questions that were directed to her were the following:

- Is this the only time this has happened?
- Did he ever drive while his license was suspended?
- Are there any other arrests of this nature of any kind?
- Was any accident involved in this?
- Did he appear in court on this charge?
- Did he spend the night in jail?[74]

We do not know definitively whether Bush discussed these questions with Hughes prior to his facing the press. However, it certainly seems like a reasonable possibility that she could have briefed him on what was on the mind of the press and how her responses were greeted. Bush himself received, virtually word for word, about two-thirds of the questions asked his press secretary earlier in the day. Even on short notice, he might have had some time to prepare for the questions that Hughes's appearance had generated. Clearly, even on short notice, candidates can anticipate questions and, at least to a limited extent, prepare their answers.

Second, if the conference starts to go bad, the candidate can filibuster. Typically, press conferences are called for specific time periods. The press has deadlines and the candidate has a full schedule. Hence, if their conferences are going poorly, some candidates will take considerable time in answering questions, particularly those that they are comfortable with and deal with topics they wish to address. By so doing, they reduce the opportunity the press has for further questioning.

Finally, candidates often attempt to appear vulnerable in press conferences. Given the many controls and strategies available to candidates who utilize news conferences, it may be easy to forget that there are other actors in this situation. President Carter's television adviser noted that, even though the news conference was in effect a theater in which the president called on reporters to play their supporting roles, "it is important that the President appear vulnerable."[75] Similarly, most candidates wish to appear vulnerable in news conference situations. The desire to appear vulnerable often motivates the use of the news conference. It is one of the reasons that candidates will utilize "risky" news conferences, rather than safer press releases or other forms of communication with the public. The appearance that the candidate is taking a chance and is vulnerable is one that most candidates believe the public admires. The news conference situation suggests openness and honesty, as well as confidence in one's ability. Candidates are not readily able to suggest these qualities through the use of other forms of communication.

The symbiotic relationship that exists between candidates and journalists is, perhaps, nowhere more evident than in the news conference. News conferences are called by candidates seeking widespread coverage of their views. They are attended by representatives of news organizations who sense that the conference may produce newsworthy material. Both the candidate and the reporter have an interest in aiding one another. But candidates are desirous not only of creating news but also of influencing and persuading. Hence, most candidates utilize a variety of strategies, attempting to ensure that their conferences are indeed covered and that the conferences focus on those issues on which the candidates wish to focus. Moreover, though they prepare in order not to be vulnerable and weak, they recognize that a format that suggests their vulnerability may be desirable.

APOLOGIAS

An increasingly recurring form of speech that many candidates have recently found necessary to deliver is the apologia. In this section, we examine the situations that create apologias and in so doing perhaps also gain an understanding of why they have been on the increase in recent years. We also consider the major purposes of such speeches and the strategies utilized to attain those purposes.

The Situation for an Apologia

Apologias are speeches made by candidates who find it necessary to apologize for some statement or behavior. Typically, the statement or behavior implies a serious flaw in the candidate's character, one that if widely accepted by the public would prevent the candidate from winning office. In 1984, Jessie Jackson's anti-Semitic remarks, characterizing Jews as "Hymies" and New York City as "Hymietown," not only were offensive to Jews but also suggested that Jackson could not equitably and fairly govern a racially, ethnically, and religiously diverse nation such as the United States.

Similarly, in 1992, Bill Clinton was the subject of widespread rumors that he engaged in numerous extramarital affairs while governor of Arkansas, the most infamous of which was alleged to have lasted for twelve years and been with a former Little Rock newswoman, Gennifer Flowers. If such rumors and accusations proved true, Clinton, at that time simply one of several candidates for the Democratic Party nomination, was in grave trouble. With relatively few people familiar with Clinton and his candidacy, charges of this sort would suggest to many that Clinton lacked the integrity, honesty, and other qualities of character desired in national leaders.

Apologias have become a feature of recent campaigns for two reasons. First, the news media seem more prone then ever before to report on the candidate's weaknesses and flaws. Gone are the days when Franklin Delano Roosevelt could dictate that he never be photographed wearing leg braces or being carried by his aides. Gone are the days when the candidate's private life was not discussed. The press is far more unsparing of candidates today. Additionally, one of the legacies of Watergate has apparently been to sensitize the public to the personal integrity of candidates. During both of his campaigns for the presidency, as well as his administration, Bill Clinton's personal integrity came under frequent attack, and his vice president, Al Gore, suffered throughout the 2000 campaign from the perception on the part of many that he often lied. In 2004, accusations that both Senator Kerry and President Bush had at the least embellished, if not lied, about their Vietnam service permeated the presidential campaign.

Purposes of an Apologia

Apologias serve to enable the candidate to explain some statement or behavior that casts doubt on the candidate's suitability for office. To accomplish this explanation with the least amount of damage to their image, candidates often have three purposes in mind when they deliver apologias.

First, they hope to explain the behavior or statement in a positive light. In so doing, they hope to minimize damage to their character and image. If the incident that triggered the need for the apologia cannot be explained positively, the second purpose of the apologia may be considered. The candidate can at least justify behavior. Again, by so doing, the candidate hopes to minimize damage to character and image.

The final purpose of an apologia is to remove the topic from public discussion. Ellen Reid Gold has pointed out that, at least with major national figures, frequently reporters repeat the charges against a candidate so often that it is difficult for the candidate not to appear guilty.[76] Day after day, the candidate is seen denying the charge. The proliferation of media has compounded this problem. With twenty-four-hour cable news networks, the growth of all-day talk radio stations, and a host of new politically oriented Internet sites, the "feeding frenzy" of the press is greater today than ever before. To the extent that an apologia can put an end to questioning and allow the campaign to move on to other issues, it has served a vital purpose.

Strategies of an Apologia

Rhetoricians have identified six strategies commonly utilized by speakers delivering apologias. Not every strategy can be used in every apologia, but all six have been used frequently.

Control of the Apologia Setting

First, apologias are often best delivered in settings where individuals other than the candidate seem in control.[77] Many early apologias were delivered in settings where the candidate seemed to be in complete control. For example, Richard Nixon's 1952 "Checkers" address, following charges that Nixon benefited from a slush fund set up by wealthy supporters, and Ted Kennedy's 1969 "Address to the People of Massachusetts," following the incident at Chappaquiddick, in which Kennedy's car went off a bridge and a young woman died, were both made by men who had purchased airtime and were in complete control of what was said. However, as Sherry Butler points out in contrasting these two addresses, by 1969, mass media viewers were "more sophisticated, less likely to place automatic belief in magic power of the television tube, more likely to question."[78] Additionally, the legacies of Vietnam, Watergate, and the Clinton scandals include voter disenchantment with less-than-honest officials. Both of these facts, growing voter sophistication in using media and growing voter disenchantment with public figures, have contributed to changes in the early apologia, typified by Nixon's "Checkers" address.

Rather than an address such as Nixon's in which the candidate is in complete control of the setting, candidates today often deliver their apologias in settings that appear to be controlled by others. For example, among the best-known and most successful political apologias of recent years is no doubt the interview granted by Bill Clinton in response to the accusations that he had conducted a twelve-year affair with Gennifer Flowers. Significantly, Clinton's apologia was delivered on a special edition of CBS's *60 Minutes*, one of the nation's most respected investigative TV shows. Viewers no doubt were aware that Clinton and his wife were not in control of the situation as they responded to questions from correspondent Steve Kroft, who appeared to control the interview. When Clinton saw the broadcast, he is reported to have been "furious," claiming that the interview was "a screw job."[79] As Clinton's appearance on *60 Minutes* illustrates, appearing in a setting where one does not have complete control involves risk. However, many contemporary candidates choose to take this risk, believing that public sophistication with media and alienation from leaders makes this an acceptable risk that must be taken if their message is to be appreciated.

Denial

A second strategy utilized by candidates delivering apologias is to simply deny the "alleged facts, sentiments, objects, or relationships" that give rise to the charge.[80] If the candidate cannot deny the substance of the charge, one can deny the intent, arguing that the statement or action has been misunderstood.[81] Kroft opened his *60 Minutes* interview by observing that Flowers "is alleging and has described in some detail in a supermarket tabloid what she calls a 12 year affair with you."[82] As Kroft finished his statement, Clinton jumped in: "That allegation is false." He went on to suggest that, although as a public figure in Little Rock he had known Flowers when she was a TV reporter in the same city, her story was a total fabrication that she no doubt had made up for the payment she received from the tabloid.[83] As the interview progressed, Kroft again offered Clinton an opportunity to deny the alleged affair. "I am assuming from your answer," said Kroft, "that you are categorically denying that you ever had an affair with Gennifer Flowers." The camera showed Clinton nodding his head affirmatively as Kroft spoke and then declaring, "I said that before."

Though Clinton clearly denied having an affair with Gennifer Flowers, he did not deny the possibility of other infidelities. At one point he acknowledged, "I have caused pain in my marriage." Kroft responded by stating, "Your answer is not a denial, is it?" Clinton responded, "Of course it is not." Thus, while Clinton's denial might resolve the charges of Gennifer Flowers, he did not attempt to deny all of the rumors about his infidelity. Clinton's response to the broader issue of infidelity utilized several additional strategies common to apologias.

Bolstering

A third strategy frequently used in apologias is what B. L. Ware and Wil Linkugel characterize as "bolstering strategies." These are attempts by the candidate to identify "with something viewed favorably by the audience."[84] Clinton made use of bolstering when he attempted to make a virtue out of his inability to deny totally the accusations of marital infidelity. "I have acknowledged wrongdoing. I have acknowledged causing pain in my marriage. I have said things tonight and to the American people from the beginning that no American politician ever has." Repeatedly Clinton and his wife claimed that they had "leveled" with and had been "candid" with the American public. Clearly Clinton was attempting to bolster his case by claiming to display character traits viewed favorably by the audience—candor and honesty. To the extent that Clinton might make his candor and honesty in dealing with charges of infidelity the focus of audience attention, rather than the infidelity itself, he was likely to bolster his case successfully.

Clinton's apologia was unusual because of the presence and statements of a second individual, his wife Hillary. Throughout the interview the couple was seated side by side, and, as one spoke, the camera, for the most part, remained focused on both of them. Both Hillary Clinton's presence at her husband's side and her statements in defense of him may have fulfilled bolstering functions for the governor. Her presence and active defense of her husband suggested a solid marriage that had endured stress. Clinton observed that "my wife and I are still in love with each other; we have a stronger marriage than most people who have never had to survive the trials and tribulations of a challenging marriage. As most married Americans will acknowledge, marriage is a hard institution. But it is a better alternative to divorce that is prevalent in our society." To the extent that Americans associated the Clintons with people who had successfully resolved troublesome issues in their marriage, they bolstered their own case by identifying themselves with a second set of qualities typically admired by most Americans: the determination and ability to work through a troubled relationship, rather than abandon it.

Differentiation

A fourth strategy frequently used in political apologias is differentiation. Ware and Linkugel define *differentiation* as "separating some fact, sentiment, object, or relationship from some larger context within which the audience presently views that attribute."[85] As Gold notes, "in political campaigns, the candidate may try not only to redefine the larger context for the audience, but to separate himself symbolically from the accusation by attacking the source."[86]

Attacks on the source have become increasingly common in political apologias. Kathryn M. Olson offers us an incisive explanation of why this tactic has become widely used, though, as she observes, it is a "strategy near last resort."[87] Olson claims that in recent years, in part because of the growing dominance of television as a news media, the blending of journalism and entertainment, and the economic realities of the contemporary news media, journalists have faced growing tension between "objective" reporting and "adversarial" reporting. Candidates can exploit that tension to their advantage by utilizing what Olson has characterized as role imbalance attacks. That is, candidates can suggest that journalists have crossed the line between objective reporting and treated them in a harshly adversarial fashion, thereby exacerbating, exaggerating, or otherwise inappropriately reporting the charges against the candidate.

The Clintons repeatedly utilized differentiation and role imbalance attacks as they attempted to differentiate the questions of infidelity from the context of Clinton's fitness for office and to place it within the context of the right to privacy. If the public viewed infidelity as an issue pertinent to the right of privacy, rather than one pertinent to presidential fitness, then Clinton's role imbalance attacks on the press were also pertinent and potentially persuasive.

Olson claims that, for role imbalance attacks to succeed, the accused "must not appear totally self-serving" and hence must suggest "that the news media's role imbalance has negative implications for someone in addition to him- or herself." Clinton's strongest attempt to do this was his last remark in the interview. He claimed that "this will test the character of the press. It is not only my character that is being tested." Clearly he was suggesting that the press coverage of him is really a test of the press's objectivity and that both the press and the entire public will suffer if the press continues its nonobjective, imbalanced, and adversarial treatment of him.

Similarly, Olson claims that, for role imbalance attacks on the press to succeed, the accused must indicate that press coverage "threatens the democratic system and/or hurts innocent individuals." Both Clinton and his wife made accusations of this type during their interview. Clinton claimed that "the press has to decide if it is going to engage in a game of 'got you'" and went on to add that the excessively imbalanced adversarial attacks he had already endured made it impossible for him to defend himself. "No matter what I say," asserted Clinton, "to pretend the press will then let this die, we are kidding ourselves. This has become a virtual cottage industry." Clinton portrayed the press as engaging in unfair, imbalanced adversarial reporting from which it profited. His wife suggested that many innocent individuals, not simply the Clintons, would suffer if the press continued in this type of behavior, observing, "I think it is real dangerous in this country if we don't have some zone of privacy for everybody."

Thus, the Clintons used differentiation strategies to move questions about his infidelity out of the context of presidential fitness and into the context of the right of privacy. Placing the charges against him in the context of the right of privacy then facilitated the Clintons' use of role imbalance attacks on the press.

Transcendental Strategy

The fifth type of strategy found in political apologias is what Ware and Linkugel have called the "transcendental strategy." This kind of strategy "cognitively joins some fact, sentiment, object, or relationship with some larger context within which the audience does not presently view that attribute."[88] Such strategies "psychologically move the audience away from the particulars of the charge at hand in a direction toward some more abstract, general view of his character."[89] The combined effect of the Clintons' strategies, if successful, would serve this purpose. That is, if the Clintons were able to get the public thinking about the courage they had in appearing on *60 Minutes*, their candor and honesty in "leveling" with the American public about the difficulties they had experienced in their marriage, their perseverance in working through the troubles of their marriage, and the press abuses of their rights to privacy, then these more abstract general issues, not Clinton's character, as reflected specifically in charges of infidelity, would be the focus of attention.

Confession

The final strategy that political figures have utilized in their apologias is to confess. If the candidate is guilty, a quick confession may put the unwinnable issue generating the apologia behind the candidate and let the campaign progress to other issues. In 1984, Jessie Jackson's attitudes toward Jews became the focal point of fourteen days' worth of news coverage about his campaign, at the very outset of the critical first primary in New Hampshire. Finally, on the fourteenth day, rejecting the advice of his staff, Jackson spoke to a Jewish audience at Temple Adath Yeshurun in Manchester, New Hampshire, confessed to making the derogatory statements that had given rise to the controversy, and observed that "however innocent and unintentional, it was insensitive and it was wrong. In part, I am to blame, and for that I am deeply distressed."[90] With that confession, Jackson was finally able to put the controversy behind him and return to other issues. Moreover, the issue never surfaced again in Jackson's 1988 campaign.

Similarly, though Clinton denied a long-standing affair with Gennifer Flowers, he never flatly denied having had extramarital affairs. Most Americans, including moderator Steve Kroft, interpreted his remarks about having caused "pain" in his marriage essentially as a confession of infidelity.[91] Having so confessed, there was little more that the press could pursue on this story. Moreover, combined with the other attempts discussed earlier to put the most favorable light on Clinton's extramarital affairs, and combined with his criticism of the press, this confession helped cause this story to drop out of the campaign early in the Democratic primaries.

The situation Clinton faced in 1998, when he was accused of having had an affair with a twenty-one-year-old White House intern, Monica Lewinsky, was substantially more complex than the situations that typically give rise to campaign apologias. First, the accusations were not made in the context of a political campaign. Clinton was president at the time of the affair, and much of the affair took place in the White House. Second, campaign apologias rarely involve statements or behavior that can provoke legal action. Clinton lied about his affair, which he ultimately acknowledged, under oath, while testifying in the sexual harassment case brought by Paula Jones. The legal dimensions of this situation distinguish it from most occasions that give rise to campaign apologias. Third, many of the strategies associated with apologias presume that the candidate is innocent or that, at the least, there is doubt about guilt. Those strategies were essentially denied to Clinton with the presence of physical evidence of his affair in the form of Lewinsky's famed semen-stained dress and his subsequent statements on August 17, 1998, acknowledging his affair.

Summary

Apologias seem to be characterized by the use of one or more of six strategies. Increasingly, candidates are making their apologias in situations over which they do not have full control. Moreover, they are using denial, bolstering, differentiation, transcendental, and confessional strategies to carry out their apologias.

In recent years, apologias have become a common, often recurring form of political speech. Contemporary stress on the character of candidates and the aggressiveness of contemporary journalists seem, in recent years, to have created far more situations calling for apologias than ever before. It is likely that apologias will be a feature of American political rhetoric for years to come.

CONCLUSION

In this chapter, we have observed that most campaigns are marked by similar, comparable, or analogous situations that require a rhetorical response. The responses to four such situations take the form of announcement of candidacy speeches, nomination acceptance addresses, news conferences, and apologias. We have examined the situations that give rise to these types of presentations, the purposes of such presentations, and the major strategies employed in each type of presentation.

NOTES

1. Lloyd Bitzer, "The Rhetorical Situation," *Philosophy and Rhetoric* 1 (January 1968): 6.

2. Karlyn Kohrs Campbell and Kathleen Hall Jamieson, "Form and Genre in Rhetorical Criticism: An Introduction," in *Form and Genre: Shaping Rhetorical Action*, ed. Karlyn Kohrs Campbell and Kathleen Hall Jamieson (Falls Church, Va.: Speech Communication Association, 1977), 15.

3. Judith S. Trent, "Presidential Surfacing: The Ritualistic and Crucial First Act," *Communication Monographs* 45 (November 1978): 281–92.

4. See, for example, Hamilton Jordan, "Memo of August 4, 1974 to Jimmy Carter," in *Running for President: A Journal of the Carter Campaign*, ed. Martin Schram (New York: Pocket Books, 1977), 416.

5. On Quayle's preannouncement activities, see Faye Fiore, "In Announcing Presidential Runs, Candidates Take Many Small Steps"; available at www.latimes.com/HOME/NEWS/POLITICS/NATPOL/lat-run990325.htm (accessed March 25, 1999). Also see Terry M. Neal, "Quayle Begins White House Quest," *Washington Post*, April 15, 1999, A-4.

6. This and all other quotes from Senator Lieberman's announcement address are taken from Joe Lieberman, "Announcement Address," retrieved on June 1, 2003, from www.joe .2004.com/site/News2?page=NewsArticle7id=5075&news_iv-ctrl=1002.

7. This and all other quotes from George W. Bush's announcement address are taken from the speech text found on his home page at www.georgewbush.com/speeches/6–12–99TheSpeech.htm (accessed June 12, 1999). Hereafter, it is referred to as Bush, "Announcement Address, 2000."

8. John F. Kerry, "Announcement Address," retrieved on September 2, 2003, from www.johnkerry.com/news/speeches/spc_2003_0902.html.

9. Jennifer Brooks, "Biden to Run for President in 2008," *Cincinnati Enquirer*, June 20, 2005, A-3.

10. Shortly before Dukakis announced his 1988 candidacy, *Boston Globe* political columnist David Nyhan claimed that Kennedy might well be ready to run for the presidency again in 1992 and that Massachusetts's junior U.S. senator, John Kerry, was looking to 1996. If one believes this scenario, and certainly Dukakis and his advisers were aware of it, then 1988 loomed as the only year in which Dukakis could run and be assured of the unified support of the Massachusetts Democratic organization from the outset. See Donald Morrison, ed., *The Winning of the White House* (New York: Time, 1988), 125–26.

11. Bertram W. Gross, "The Announcement Speeches of Democratic Candidates for the 1992 Presidential Nomination," paper presented at the National Communication Association Annual Convention, October 29, 1992, 25.

12. Jim VandeHei, "Kerry Opens Campaign on War Theme," retrieved on September 3, 2003, from www.washingtonpost.com/ac2wp-dyn/A13394-2003Sep2?language=printer.

13. Joe Lieberman, "Announcement Address."

14. Dick Gephardt, "Announcement of Presidential Candidacy," retrieved June 1, 2003, from www.dickgephardt2004.com/release/sp021903html.

15. Edward Walsh, "Kucinich Makes Presidential Bid Official," retrieved on October 14, 2003, from www.washingtonpost.com/ac2/wp-dyn/A21231-2003Oct13?language=printer.

16. Michael Powell, "Ex-Vermont Governor Comes Out Swinging," retrieved June 24, 2003, from www.washingtonpost.com/wpdyn/articles/a24333-3003Jun23.html?nav=hptoc_p.

17. Berry's remarks as well as Clark's can be found in Wesley K. Clark, "Announcement Speech," retrieved on September 19, 2003, from www.clark04.com/speech_01.php.

18. Bob Graham, "Declaration of Candidacy for President of the United States," retrieved on July 1, 2003, from www.grahamforpresident.com/own-words/030506-announcement.html.

19. On Bauer's announcement, see "Gary Bauer Enters Race for Presidency"; available at www.msnbc.com/news/meetpress_font.asp (accessed January 31, 1999).

20. On Kasich's announcement, see "*Meet the Press* Transcript, Sunday, Feb. 14 1999"; available at www.msnbc.com/news/meetpress_font.asp (accessed February 14, 1999).

21. On Edwards's announcement, see Kevin Begos, "Edwards Announces Candidacy," retrieved on May 26, 2005, from www.journalnow.com/servelet/Satellite?pagename-wsj%2FMGArticle%2FWSJ_ba. Also see "Edwards to Hold Announcement in Front of Robbins Mill," retrieved on May 26, 2005, from blog.4president.org/2004/2004_presidential_campaign/.

22. On the Forbes announcement, see Richard L. Berke, "Forbes Declares Candidacy on Internet and the Stump"; available at www.crab.rutgers.edu/gertz/forbes.htm (accessed March 17, 1999).

23. George W. Bush, "A Charge To Keep," retrieved on March 22, 2004, from www.georgewbush.com/News/read.aspx?ID=1947.

24. Kenneth P. O'Donnell and David F. Powers, *Johnny, We Hardly Knew Ye* (New York: Pocket Books, 1977), 416.

25. B. Drummond Ayres, "Wilson in Presidential Race," A-2. This article was written for the *New York Times*, which then syndicated it to other papers such as those in Cincinnati.

26. On those who shared the spotlight with Kerry, see VandeHei, "Kerry Opens Campaign," and William Saletan, "The Thin Man: The Mystery of John Kerry's Missing Courage," retrieved on September 2, 2003, from slate.msn.com/toolbar.aspx?action=print%id=2087839.

27. See the Kennedy and Carter responses in *The Candidates 1980: Where They Stand* (Washington, D.C.: American Enterprise Institute, 1980). Also see Robert V. Friedenberg, "Why Teddy Wasn't Ready: An Examination of the Speaking of Senator Edward Moore Kennedy during the 1980 Presidential Primaries," paper presented at the Ohio Speech Association, October 1980, 3–4.

28. Bush, "Announcement Address, 2000."

29. All the quotations in this paragraph are drawn from Albert Gore, "Announcement of Candidacy," June 16, 1999, Carthage, Tennessee. Retrieved June 16, 1999, from Gore's official home page, www.gore2000.org/speeches/speeches-announce-061699.html.

30. Perhaps because of a sense that the public expects modesty from candidates, often this theme is not as directly stated as the other two. Rather, candidates speak of "our administration," as though they have already been elected. They speak of the inspiration they have received from their families, their supporters, the people, and God. In so doing, candidates obliquely suggest that no opponent could defeat them. See Robert V. Friedenberg, "Form and Genre in Announcement of Candidacy Addresses," paper presented at the Temple University Fourth Annual Conference on Discourse Analysis: Form and Genre in Political Discourse," March 1983, 13–14.

31. See "Bradley to Make Official Announcement," retrieved September 8, 1999, from www.CNN.COM/allpolitics/stories/1999/09/07/president.2000/bradley.

32. Details concerning his announcement activities can be found at "Kucinich Announcement Tour," retrieved on October 16, 2003 at www.kucinich.us/schedule_announceme.htm.

33. For a thorough history of Democratic acceptance addresses, see chapters 2 and 3 of David B. Valley, *A History and Analysis of Democratic Presidential Nomination Acceptance Speeches to 1968* (Lanham, Md.: University Press of America, 1988). A more concise history can be found in David B. Valley, "Significant Characteristics of Democratic Presidential Nomination Acceptance Speeches," *Central States Speech Journal* 25 (Spring 1974). 56–60.

34. Thomas B. Farrell, "Political Conventions as Legitimation Ritual," *Communication Monographs* 45 (November 1978): 293–305; and Kurt W. Ritter, "American Political Rhetoric and the Jeremiad Tradition: Presidential Nomination Acceptance Addresses, 1960–1976," *Central States Speech Journal* 31 (Fall 1980): 153–71.

35. For discussions of these purposes, see Robert O. Nordvold, "Rhetoric as Ritual: Hubert H. Humphrey's Acceptance Address at the 1968 Democratic National Convention," *Today's Speech* 18 (Winter 1970): 34; Valley, "Nomination Acceptance Speeches," 60; and Ritter, "American Political Rhetoric," 155.

36. This and all subsequent quotations and references to the Bush acceptance address are taken from the text of the address as retrieved on May 31, 2005, from the Weekly Compilation of Presidential Documents, frwebgate.access.gpo.gov/cgi-bin/getdoc.cgi?dbname-2004_presidential_documents. Hereafter cited as "Bush Acceptance Address, 2004."

37. This and all subsequent quotations and references to the Kerry acceptance address are taken from the text of the address as retrieved on July 30, 2004, from www.washington post.com/ac2wp-dyn/a256778-2004Jul20?language=printer. Hereafter cited as "Kerry Acceptance Address, 2004."

38. Valley, "Nomination Acceptance Speeches," 61.

39. Valley, "Nomination Acceptance Speeches," 61.

40. Kurt Ritter, "The 1996 Presidential Nomination Acceptance Addresses: What Do the Speeches by Dole and Clinton Tell Us about the Genre of Acceptance Speeches?" paper presented at the annual meeting of the Speech Communication Association, San Diego, November 1996, 2.

41. Ritter, "The 1996 Presidential Nomination Acceptance Addresses," 1.

42. Ritter, "The 1996 Presidential Nomination Acceptance Addresses," 1–3.

43. George H. W. Bush, "Transcript of Bush Accepting the Nomination for Another Four Years," *New York Times*, August 21, 1992, A-14.

44. William Jefferson Clinton, "Acceptance Address at the 1992 Democratic National Convention: A New Covenant," in Bill Clinton and Albert Gore, *Putting People First* (New York Times Books, 1992), 218–22.

45. See the fourth edition of this book, 220–21, for examples of how Dole and Clinton treated one another in their 1996 acceptance addresses and the fifth edition of this book, 234–35, for examples of how Governor Bush and Vice President Gore treated one another in their 2000 acceptance addresses.

46. Nordvold, "Rhetoric as Ritual," 34.

47. On this and other differences between contemporary and earlier acceptance addresses, see William L Benoit, William J. Wells, P. M. Pier, and Joseph R. Blaney, "Acclaiming, Attacking, and Defending in Presidential Nominating Acceptance Addresses, 1960–1996," *Quarterly Journal of Speech* (August 1999): 247–67.

48. Ritter, "American Political Rhetoric," 157–64.

49. Ritter, "American Political Rhetoric," 161–62.

50. Valley, *A History and Analysis*, 60.

51. Ritter, "American Political Rhetoric," 162.

52. Jimmy Carter, "Acceptance Speech," Democratic National Convention, August 14, 1980," in *The Pursuit of the Presidency 1980*, ed. Richard Harwood (New York: Berkley, 1980), 402.

53. Ray D. Dearin, "George W. Bush in the Tradition of Republican Acceptance Speeches," paper presented at the Central States Speech Association, Cincinnati, Ohio, April 4, 2001.

54. Wayne Fields, *Union of Words: A History of Presidential Eloquence* (New York: Free Press 1996), 72.

55. On Dole and Clinton's use of biography as a vehicle for attack, see the fourth edition (2000) of this book, 224–25. On Gore and Bush's refusal to use biography as a vehicle for attack see the fifth edition (2004) of this book, 240–41.

56. Rick Shenkman, "Presidency: What George W. Bush and William Howard Taft Have in Common," 1–2, retrieved on June 8, 2005, from the History News Network, at hnn.us/articles/221.html.

57. This analysis of news conference audiences is adapted from Leon V. Sigal, "Newsmen and Campaigners: Organization Men Make the News," *Political Science Quarterly* 93 (Fall 1978): 466–67.

58. Sigal, "Newsmen and Campaigners," 466.

59. All quotations from this press conference found in this and subsequent paragraphs are drawn from "Governor George W. Bush (R-TX) Presidential Candidate Holds News Conference about His Arrest Record." This transcript of the news conference was retrieved on May 17, 2001, from www.elibrary.com/s/edumark/getdoc.cgi?/1d=19611552x12/y39914w0.

60. Beckwith is quoted in the United States Department of State's Bureau of International Information Programs "Press Conferences," retrieved on June 8, 2005, from www/wasjito,es/cp,/commentary/20020829-2125840htm.

61. For an account of this press conference, see Donald Lambro, "Incumbent Lacks Depth in Missouri," *Washington Times*, August 29, 2002; available at www.wasjto,es/cp,/commentary/20020829–21258404htm (accessed August 29, 2002).

62. C. Jack Orr, "Reporters Confront the President: Sustaining a Counterpoised Situation," *Quarterly Journal of Speech* 66 (February 1980): 17–21.

63. Most such examinations have focused on presidential news conferences, but the rationales for the conclusions, as well as the conclusions themselves, seem appropriate for most political candidates. See Robert E. Denton and Dan F. Hahn, eds., *Presidential Communication* (New York: Praeger, 1986), 252; Michael Grossman and Martha Kumar, *Portraying the President: The White House and the News Media* (Baltimore: Johns Hopkins University Press, 1981), 243–44; Orr, "Reporters Confront the President," 31–32; and Delbert McQuire, "Democracy's Confrontation: The Presidential Press Conference," *Journalism Quarterly* 44 (Winter 1967): 638–44.

64. United States Department of State, "Press Conferences," 2.

65. "Bush Acknowledges 1976 DUI Charge," retrieved November 3, 2000, from CNN at www.3.cnn.com/2000/allpolitics/stories/11/02/bush.dui.

66. Carolyn Smith, *Presidential Press Conferences: A Critical Approach* (New York: Praeger, 1990), 81.

67. Peter M. Sandman, David M. Rubin, and David B. Sachsman, *Media: An Introductory Analysis of American Mass Communications* (Englewood Cliffs, N.J.: Prentice Hall, 1972), 344.

68. Catherine Ann Collins, "Kissinger's Press Conferences, 1972–1974: An Exploration of Form and Role Relationship on News Management," *Central States Speech Journal* 28 (Fall 1977): 190–93.

69. Roger Ailes, *You Are the Message: Secrets of the Master Communicators* (Homewood, Ill.: Dow Jones–Irwin, 1988), 154–55.

70. Grossman and Kumar, *Portraying the President*, 248.

71. McQuire, "Democracy's Confrontation," 640.

72. Smith, *Presidential Press Conferences*, 89. Though Smith's observations deal directly with presidential press conferences, many of her comments on agendas seem entirely appropriate for press conferences held in the course of political campaigns.

73. A. L. Lorenze Jr., "Truman and the Press Conference," *Journalism Quarterly* 43 (Winter 1966): 673–75; Harry P. Kerr, "The President and the Press," *Western Speech* 27 (Fall 1963): 220–21.

74. "A Last Minute Revelation: Bush's Site of TV Rundown," a site devoted to examining "TV DUI Record," found at the treatment of major news events. It can be found at www.tvrundown.com/polgbdui.htm (accessed November 10, 2000).

75. Barry Jogoda, quoted in Grossman and Kuman, *Portraying the President*, 243.

76. Ellen Reid Gold, "Political Apologia: The Ritual of Self Defense," *Communication Monographs* 45 (November 1978): 311–12.

77. Gold, "Political Apologia," 311.

78. Sherry Devereaux Butler, "The Apologia, 1971 Genre," *Southern Speech Communication Journal* 37 (Spring 1972): 283.

79. The morning after the interview broadcast, Clinton is reported to have claimed that it "was a screw job. They [*60 Minutes* producers/editors] lied about how long it was going to be. They lied about what was going to be discussed. They lied about what the ending would be. It couldn't have been worse if they had drawn black X's through our faces." Quoted in "How He Won: The Untold Story of Bill Clinton's Triumph," *Newsweek*, Special Election Issue (November/December 1992): 34.

80. B. L. Ware and Wil A. Linkugel, "They Spoke in Defense of Themselves: On the General Criticism of Apologias," *Quarterly Journal of Speech* 59 (October 1973): 25.

81. Gold, "Political Apologia," 308.

82. This and all other direct quotes drawn from this *60 Minutes* have been transcribed directly from the videotape of the *60 Minutes* broadcast of January 28, 1994.

83. Flowers was reported to have received $150,000 for her story from *The Star*.

84. Ware and Linkugel, "General Criticism of Apologias," 277.

85. Ware and Linkugel, "General Criticism of Apologias," 278.

86. Gold, "Political Apologia," 308.

87. This and all subsequent references are to Kathryn M. Olson, "Exploiting the Tension between the News Media's 'Objective' and Adversarial Roles: The Role of Imbalance Attack and Its Use of the Implied Audience," *Communication Quarterly* 42 (Winter 1994): 36–56.

88. Ware and Linkugel, "General Criticism of Apologias," 280.

89. Ware and Linkugel, "General Criticism of Apologias," 280.

90. Quoted in Jack Germond and Jules Witcover, *Wake Us When It's Over: Presidential Politics of 1984* (New York: Macmillan, 1985), 159.

91. In January 1998, giving a sworn deposition in the Paula Jones case, Clinton acknowledged having had a sexual relationship on one occasion with Gennifer Flowers. Clinton's defenders observed that in 1992 he had denied a twelve-year affair, and they claimed that his statement made under oath did not contradict his 1992 claim.

8

~

Debates in
Political Campaigns

In the summer of 1858, one of the most remarkable local political campaigns in U.S. history was being waged on the plains of Illinois. The
1858 Illinois Senate race was remarkable for many reasons. Few races, regardless of office, bring together two such outstanding public servants as
those competing for the Senate seat from Illinois in 1858. Few races, regardless of office, have had as profound an impact on our national history
as did this one. Few races have produced such masterpieces of campaign
oratory as those produced on the plains of Illinois in the summer of 1858.
For in that year, Abraham Lincoln and Stephen Douglas vied for the Senate seat from Illinois.

On July 24, Lincoln challenged Douglas to a series of debates. Douglas
accepted. As the front-runner in what was anticipated to be a close election, Douglas dictated the terms. He suggested seven debates and demanded the opportunity both to open and to close four of the debates.
Lincoln would open and close only three. Lincoln accepted, and thus en-
sued what the *New York Tribune* called "a mode of discussing political
questions which might well be more generally adopted."[1]

Though the Lincoln–Douglas debates were the first significant political
campaign debates in U.S. history, as Kathleen Hall Jamieson and David S.
Birdsell remind us, they were not the first American political campaign
debates.[2]

Moreover, unlike their successors, they were real debates rather than
joint speeches or joint press conferences. Most authorities would agree
with J. Jeffery Auer when he argues that there are five essential elements
for a true debate. "A debate," claims Auer, "is (1) a confrontation, (2) in

equal and adequate time, (3) of matched contestants, (4) on a stated proposition, (5) to gain an audience decision."[3] Auer points out that "each of these elements is essential if we are to have true debate. Insistence upon their recognition is more than mere pedantry, for each one has contributed to the vitality of the debate tradition."[4]

The Lincoln–Douglas debates were not followed by many other debates. It was not until a century later, in 1960, that we next had "Great Debates" of comparable significance. However, the 1960 presidential debates between Senator John F. Kennedy and Vice President Richard M. Nixon gave rise to political debating as we now know it in the media age.

Yet most contemporary political debaters, including Presidents Jimmy Carter, Ronald Reagan, George H. W. Bush, Bill Clinton, and George W. Bush have not engaged in political debates. Based primarily on the Kennedy–Nixon model of 1960, most contemporary political debates can be characterized as "counterfeit debates."[5] This is not to say that contemporary political debating is, like a counterfeit bill, of little value. As we will see later, contemporary political debates are extremely valuable. But in large part because of the influence of media, they involve different formats and strategies than those of the Lincoln–Douglas era.

Perhaps the counterfeit nature of contemporary political debates can best be understood by using Auer's five essentials of debate to compare the Lincoln–Douglas debate with the prototypical contemporary media political debate, that of Kennedy and Nixon in 1960.

First, the Kennedy–Nixon debate and most political debates since do not involve direct confrontation. Lincoln and Douglas confronted one another. They met on the same platform, questioned one another, and refuted one another. Indeed, the highlight of the seven debates came in the second debate, at Freeport, when Lincoln confronted Douglas with a series of four questions to set up what became known as "The Freeport Dilemma."

Lincoln claimed that Douglas had to repudiate the Supreme Court's *Dred Scott* decision (which made it illegal for voters to prohibit slavery in the territories and hence was enormously popular in the South) or repudiate his own program of popular sovereignty. As chairman of the Senate Committee on Territories, Douglas had argued that each of the western territories should be allowed to choose by popular vote whether it would enter the Union free or slave. Repeatedly in the debates after Freeport, Lincoln confronted Douglas with this dilemma. Lincoln demanded that Douglas choose between a fundamental tenet of U.S. democracy—the sanctity of Supreme Court decisions—or his own proposal. If Douglas supported the *Dred Scott* decision, he was admitting that he had labored in the Senate on behalf of a policy that was illegal. If he supported popular sovereignty, he was admitting Supreme Court decisions were not the highest law of the land and was isolating himself from the southern wing of the Democratic Party. Lincoln confronted, questioned, followed up, and harangued Douglas. Douglas responded, claimed the dilemma was false, and argued that Lincoln ignored a third alternative.

In contrast, it was not Richard Nixon but a journalist who suggested to John Kennedy, "you are naïve and at times immature." Nor was it John Kennedy but rather a journalist who suggested to Richard Nixon that his experience as vice president was as an observer, not as a participant or initiator of policy.[6] Kennedy and Nixon did not talk to each other, as did Lincoln and Douglas. Kennedy and Nixon did not question and pursue one another, nor did they respond to one another. Rather, if Kennedy, Nixon, and most political debaters since are confronted at all, it is by the media, not by one another.[7] Some of the debate formats utilized since 1960 have allowed for somewhat more direct confrontation between candidates than those of 1960.

Second, the Kennedy–Nixon debate, and most political debates since, did not involve equal and adequate time. The key, of course, is adequate time. Lincoln and Douglas dealt almost exclusively with one issue, the future of slavery in the territories. Each man spoke for one and a half hours in each of seven debates. Kennedy and Nixon each spoke half an hour in each of four debates. The subject matter for the first Kennedy–Nixon debate was domestic affairs, for the last foreign affairs, and no restrictions whatsoever existed for the middle two debates. It is entirely fair to say that Lincoln and Douglas spent up to twenty-one hours debating one issue, while Kennedy and Nixon spent eight minutes on any one issue. Formats like the Kennedy–Nixon format typically allow candidates three to five minutes to deal with an issue.[8] Kennedy and Nixon, and most political debaters since, did not have adequate time to deal with major public issues.

Political debates do typically meet the third criterion for debates. The contestants are closely matched. If one contestant is vastly brighter, more fluent, more poised, more knowledgeable, and better prepared, no real debate can take place. Typically, this is not the case in political debates, where both candidates must agree to debate and hence are probably able debaters, having merit enough to secure major party nominations to the office.

However, political debates frequently do not meet the fourth criterion of debates. The Kennedy–Nixon debate and most political debates since did not involve one stated proposition. Rather, depending on format, ten or more topics are discussed in a single debate. In the first Kennedy–Nixon debate, the two men dealt with such diverse questions as who was most fit and prepared to lead the country, how would each man handle the farm subsidy programs, what policies each would advocate for reducing the federal debt, what would each man do about improving the nation's schools, and what policies would each pursue with respect to medical aid to the aged and with respect to a comprehensive minimum hourly wage program. Moreover, each was asked how serious a threat to national security he believed communist subversive activity in the United States was and how he would finance public school construction. In sum, Kennedy and Nixon had under an hour to deal with nine totally diverse topic areas.

Finally, the Kennedy–Nixon debates did not really gain an audience decision of the issues. Debates, as Auer suggests, are "clashes of ideas, assumptions, evidence, and argument."[9] They secure from audiences a decision of the issues. The 1858 Lincoln–Douglas debates revealed the inadequacies of Douglas's program of popular sovereignty for the territories and the inconsistency of that program with existing institutions. It was because he illustrated the inadequacies and inconsistencies of Douglas's position, while justifying and defending his own belief in restricting slavery's spread into the territories, that Lincoln emerged from the debates a national figure, and Douglas's national aspirations were shattered. Those debates were a true clash of ideas, assumptions, evidence, and argument. The 1960 Kennedy and Nixon debates did not facilitate the audience's making a decision about the issues. Contemporary political debates that are heavily oriented toward the broadcast media audience are not in the tradition of issue-oriented debates.

Political debating is widespread in this country. It is almost a ritualistic aspect of campaigns for one candidate to challenge the other to a debate. Yet, as we have seen, contemporary media-oriented debates, regardless of what office is sought, are vastly different from earlier political debates. Although they typically involve matched candidates, they rarely if ever entail direct confrontation, equal and adequate time, one stated proposition, and a clear decision on the issues. In the next section, we trace how political debates evolved from the Lincoln–Douglas debates to the media-oriented debates we have today.

HISTORY OF POLITICAL DEBATES

During the nineteenth century, debating was an important aspect of campaigning, though perhaps not as widespread as it is today. However, a few debates of local or statewide interest did take place.[10]

Although Lincoln and Douglas had gained national attention, figures of comparable stature did not engage in campaign debates in the years that followed. Rather than debating their opponents, in the nineteenth century many candidates utilized surrogate debaters. This practice was especially widespread in nineteenth-century presidential elections.[11] Nevertheless, relatively few nineteenth-century debates received attention beyond their own constituencies, and none attained national prominence.[12]

By the mid-1920s, due to the growth of radio, national debates began to seem feasible. In 1924, testifying before a congressional committee investigating broadcast regulations, William Harkness, an executive of the American Telephone and Telegraph Company, made what is generally believed to be the first suggestion for broadcasting political debates.[13] At the time of Harkness's suggestion, such a broadcast would have probably been local or regional in scope, but within two years, with the birth of the National Broadcasting Company (NBC) in 1926, nationwide political broadcasts became feasible. NBC's first programs were carried over a twenty-four-station hookup serving twenty-one cities from the East Coast to as far west as Kansas City. Other networks soon followed.

The implication of national radio networks for political campaigns was not lost on Congress. In 1927, Congress included a section in its radio broadcast regulations dealing with political broadcasts. Those regulations were modified in 1934, and section 315 of the Communications Act of 1934 affected political broadcasts for years. This "equal time" provision required that, if any licensed radio or television station allowed a legally qualified candidate for any public office to use its station, it must "afford equal opportunities to all other such candidates for that office in the use of such broadcasting station."[14] This provision, designed to provide equal access to the public's airwaves to all candidates, tended to inhibit political debates. It required that, if major party candidates received airtime from a station, that station would have to provide airtime to every other candidate, regardless of the extent of their following. Few broadcasters were willing to make time for the many minor party candidates, and hence little time went to any campaign activities. Although this act was modified in 1959 to ensure that broadcasters could cover the normal newsworthy activities of major political candidates without being subject to harassment by lesser candidates,[15] throughout the period 1934–1976, section 315 inhibited political debates in any race where more than two candidates were involved.

Nevertheless, political debating did not come to a complete standstill during this period. On October 17, 1936, during the presidential election between Governor Alfred Landon and President Franklin Roosevelt, Republican senator Arthur Vandenberg of Michigan produced a "fake" debate over the Columbia Broadcasting System (CBS) network by editing recordings of Roosevelt's speeches. The live Vandenberg naturally bested the edited Roosevelt. The nature of this debate was not made clear to stations until shortly before the broadcast. Of the sixty-six stations scheduled to broadcast the debate, twenty-three did so without interruption. Clearly

Vandenberg had edited Roosevelt's speeches to produce a partisan one-sided program. However, perhaps more than anything that had preceded it, this program focused attention on the possibilities of nationally broadcast political debates between major figures.[16] Four years later, in 1940, Republican Wendell Wilkie opened his campaign by challenging President Roosevelt to debate. Polls found the public almost evenly divided in their response to Wilkie's challenge.[17] Apparently much of the opposition stemmed from the public's perceptions of the risks that might be involved in having an incumbent president debate. Roosevelt suffered no significant political consequences in declining to debate.

In 1948, the first broadcast debate between two major presidential candidates took place. The candidates were Governor Harold Stassen of Minnesota and Governor Thomas Dewey of New York. They were seeking the Republican nomination to challenge President Harry S. Truman. In the midst of the Oregon primary, Stassen challenged Dewey to debate. Dewey accepted but specified the terms. As Dewey wished, the debate was held in private, with only a small audience of journalists. Stassen had suggested that it might be held in a ballpark with a large public audience. Dewey spoke last, as he wanted. Dewey selected the topic: that the Communist Party should be outlawed in the United States. Moreover, Dewey chose to defend the negative. The debate was broadcast nationally by all four major radio networks and was well received by audiences and political observers.[18]

Among the first suggestions that 1952 presidential candidates General Dwight David Eisenhower and Illinois governor Adlai Stevenson engage in a televised debate were those made by Michigan senator Blair Moody and Democratic media specialist J. Leonard Reinsch.[19] Both NBC and CBS immediately offered to provide the airtime, if Congress would suspend or revoke the equal time provision. However, nothing came of the network's offer, since both Eisenhower and Stevenson were reluctant to debate.[20] Not so reluctant were the two Massachusetts senatorial candidates, Henry Cabot Lodge and John F. Kennedy, who debated that year in Waltham, Massachusetts.

By 1956, virtually the entire country had access to television. Televised political programs of every sort were commonplace. Candidates at all levels—presidential, senatorial, congressional, as well as scores of local candidates—were routinely appearing on television. But with one significant exception, broadcast debates between political candidates were not seen on the nation's television screens.

In 1956, the contest for the Democratic presidential nomination became a fight between Tennessee senator Estes Kefauver and Adlai Stevenson. Kefauver had become a well-known political figure in 1951 when, as chair of the Senate Crime Investigating Committee, he had presided over nationally televised hearings investigating organized crime. Kefauver challenged Stevenson to debate during the primaries. Stevenson, reluctant to debate Eisenhower in 1952, was again reluctant. However, after losing the Minnesota primary, Stevenson agreed to debate Kefauver in the Florida primary. The debate was nationally televised, and, though it apparently helped Stevenson, he came away unimpressed with political debates.[21] As in 1952, neither Stevenson nor Eisenhower wished to be involved in broadcast debates during the general election in 1956.

In 1960, John Kennedy was challenged to debate in the primaries by Senator Hubert Humphrey. During the West Virginia primary, both men agreed to a televised debate. Observers agreed that Kennedy did well in the debate, which was televised throughout the East Coast as well as throughout West Virginia. Perhaps this experience and his 1952 debate with Lodge contributed to Kennedy's acceptance of an NBC offer for free time during the general election if he would agree to a series of joint appearances with the Republican nominee. This offer had been made feasible by a joint resolution of Congress suspending the equal time law until after the election. Like Kennedy, Richard Nixon quickly accepted the NBC offer but noted that, since the other networks had issued similar invitations, the networks should coordinate their proposals. The networks had lobbied earlier in the year to suspend the equal time law for just this opportunity. They perceived televised presidential debates as providing them with enhanced credibility as a news medium. As we will see in more detail in the next section, 1960 was one of those years where the selfish interests of both candidates seemed best served by involvement in political debates. Hence, in 1960, for the first time since 1858, the United States was absorbed by a political debate or at least a joint appearance, national in scope and significance.

Political debates at the presidential level were not held for the sixteen years following the Kennedy–Nixon debate, for reasons that will be discussed in the next section. However, they became commonplace in campaigns for almost all other offices. In the years immediately following the Kennedy–Nixon debate, there were political debates between candidates for statewide office in Michigan, Massachusetts, Connecticut, Pennsylvania, and California. Races for lesser offices frequently included debates. For example, two short years after the Kennedy–Nixon debates, debates were held between the candidates for all six congressional seats in Connecticut.[22] Although presidential candidates frequently utilized debates during the primaries that were held after 1960, it was not until 1976 that presidential debates were held during the general election. However, unlike their presidential counterparts, local, regional, and statewide candidates made increasing use of debates during the 1960s and 1970s. One such debate, which took place between the two candidates for governor of Tennessee in 1970, indirectly led to the 1976 presidential debate between Governor Jimmy Carter and President Gerald Ford and resolution of the impediment to political debates caused by the equal time provision.

In 1970, Winfield Dunn, Republican, and John J. Hooker Jr., his Democratic opponent for the governorship of Tennessee, decided to debate. Aiding Dunn was a University of Virginia law student, Stephen A. Sharp, who found several Tennessee stations reluctant to carry the debates for fear that they would have to provide equal time to all other minor candidates for the governorship. Sharp's involvement in the Tennessee race caused him to prepare a law school paper on the history and interpretation of section 315. He found that political debates between major candidates might well be considered "bona fide" news events under the 1959 changes to section 315. If so, they could be reported on by stations as normal newsworthy activities, and those stations would not be subjected to providing equal time to all other candidates.

Sharp was subsequently hired by the Federal Communications Commission (FCC), where his work with section 315 became known. The FCC had previously ruled that candidate appearances not "incidental to" other news events were not newsworthy and hence not exempt from the equal opportunities requirement. Political debates by major candidates that were not incidental to any other activity were not exempt. But a political speech incidental to a rally or a dinner was exempt.

After considerable legal maneuvering by a variety of interested parties, including the Aspen Program for Media and Society, CBS, and others, the FCC ruled in 1975 that debates that were covered live and in their entirety and not sponsored by broadcasters (and hence presumably legitimate news events that would take place with or without the press) could be covered without fear of having to provide time to all minor candidates.[23]

This 1975 FCC ruling, known as the Aspen decision, made nationally televised presidential debates feasible from the network's standpoint. But debates do not take place without willing debaters. In 1960, Kennedy and Nixon had both been willing to debate for reasons that will become evident in the next section. Republicans and Democrats in Congress, following the lead indicated by their presidential candidates, had suspended section 315. After the Aspen decision, an act of Congress was no longer necessary for presidential debates, but willing debaters were.

The League of Women Voters, responding to the Aspen decision, took it upon itself to become the sponsoring organization for presidential debates in 1976. In 1976, both major candidates perceived that their own self-interest might be well served by political debates. In every election since 1976, both major presidential candidates have been willing to debate. Today, political debates are widespread at all levels.

DECIDING WHETHER TO DEBATE

At virtually every level of politics, candidates and their advisers strategically address themselves to six questions in determining whether to engage in political debates.[24] Public expectations that serious candidates for the nation's highest office should be willing to debate their ideas have grown steadily stronger since 1976. Today, presidential candidates risk the possibility of severe backlash if they decline to debate. Candidates for other high offices, such as most statewide offices and congressional seats, also face strong public expectations that they will debate. Candidates for lesser offices are not likely to face as much public aversion to their failure to debate. Consequently, since 1976 these six factors have grown less important for many major office candidates, though they remain factors for consideration in many other races.

1. *Is this likely to be a close election?* Expectations about the outcome of the election are vital to the decision to engage in debates. If the election seems as though it will be close and both candidates are in doubt about the outcome, the likelihood of political debates is greatly increased. If either candidate has a strong conviction that he or she can win the election without engaging in debates, the likelihood of debates taking place is dramatically reduced.

2. *Are advantages likely to accrue to me if I debate? Will I suffer for not debating?* No candidate willingly engages in counterproductive activity. Consequently, both candidates must have good reason to expect that the debates will be advantageous to them. Conversely, as public expectations that candidates will debate have grown, especially since 1976, candidates who feel they are unlikely to be advantaged by a debate must also consider to what degree they might suffer in the public's mind, and be handing their opponent an issue, by not debating.

3. *Am I a good debater?* No candidate willingly puts themselves in a position where their foe will clearly appear to be stronger. Consequently, when measuring against the opponent, each candidate must be confident about his or her debating ability.

4. *Are there only two major candidates running for the office?* Typically, our political system produces two serious candidates for each office. On those occasions where a third candidate seems to have a possibility of drawing a respectable share of the vote, the likelihood of political debates taking place is reduced. Third party candidates are not predictable. They are not bound by the same "rules" as candidates who anticipate election. Often they speak to make a point or to dramatize a single issue, rather than to win an election. Moreover, the presence

of a third candidate provides the possibility that two candidates may "gang up" on one. These variables reduce the likelihood that political debates will take place in races where a third candidate is on the ballot and appears to have a possibility of drawing a respectable share of the vote.

5. *Do I have control of all the important variables in the debate situation?* Candidates cannot be expected to place themselves in positions where they cannot reasonably anticipate what will happen. Consequently, each candidate must feel comfortable with all the major variables in the debate situation: the dates, location, formats, topics, and other participants (moderators and questioners). Unless candidates are satisfied with all of the major variables in the debate, they are unlikely to consent to debating.

6. *Is the field clear of incumbents?* If either candidate is an incumbent seeking reelection, the probability of debates taking place is reduced, especially for lower-level races. Incumbency is a much greater obstacle to political debating in lower-level races than it is in upper-level races for at least four reasons.

First, most incumbents reason that their credibility is unquestioned by virtue of prior service. The credibility of their opponents is often an issue in the campaign. This is more apt to be true in lower-level races where challengers may be virtually unknown, than in more prominent races where challengers have probably held other offices or attained prominence in their chosen fields.

Second, incumbent officeholders are frequently better able than challengers to make their views known to the public. Hence, they are reluctant to provide their opponents with a platform from which to be heard. Again, this is more apt to be true in lower-level races, where the overall press coverage of the race is not as great as the coverage for major races and challengers have an especially difficult time of getting coverage.

Third, almost any incumbent will necessarily be placed on the defensive in a political debate. The incumbent's record will probably be a major topic of discussion. Typically, no incumbent will hand an opponent the opportunity to attack vigorously, much less in a well-publicized situation. Again, this is more apt to be true in a lower-level race. In major races, challenger candidates have generally held offices and established political records that may lend themselves to attack by an incumbent. But in lower-level races, challengers may have not held office in the past and may not have an established political record for an incumbent to attack.

Finally, since 1976 when President Ford became the first incumbent president to engage in a debate, the public has grown to expect candidates for major office to engage in debates. By 1984, public expectations had grown so strong that some have argued that incumbent Ronald Reagan, holding a commanding lead in all the polls, nevertheless risked debating because he felt that not to do so would create a greater problem for him than any possible error he might make in debating.[25] In recent years, incumbents have come to fear that their failure or obvious reluctance to debate will be interpreted extremely negatively by the public to mean that they are weak and unable to defend their own positions and policies.[26] Candidates for lower-level offices do not generate quite the same expectations in the public and hence are unlikely to suffer as greatly if they fail to debate. Nevertheless, public expectations that candidates debate have grown to the point where virtually any candidate refusing to debate is likely to suffer for doing so.

APPLYING THE CONDITIONS REQUISITE FOR POLITICAL DEBATES

The importance of these conditions can be illustrated by analyzing virtually any campaign. However, in the next few pages we examine three presidential campaigns to better illustrate the ways in which candidates and their managers determine whether they should debate. We have chosen to focus on select presidential campaigns first because they are especially instructive and also because readers are probably more acquainted with the circumstances and events of presidential campaigns than with those of any other campaigns. However, keep in mind that public expectations that presidential candidates will debate have grown so strong since 1976 that today for a major presidential candidate to refuse would likely be a serious mistake. Such a refusal would likely have some damaging effect on candidates for many other top-of-the-ballot offices, such as state governor and many statewide offices, as well as U.S. senator and U.S. representative. Candidates do not choose to debate by chance. Rather, their decisions are based on self-interest.

1960: Kennedy–Nixon Debates

From the outset, most observers expected a close election.[27] As the campaign progressed, public opinion polls confirmed expectations. Neither candidate ever led by more than six points in the major polls. Clearly, both camps anticipated a close election.

In 1952, vice presidential candidate Richard Nixon gave one of the most successful political speeches in U.S. history. Using the new medium of television, he had saved his position on the ballot as Dwight Eisenhower's running mate with his "Checkers" speech. His 1960 advisers considered him a "master" of television.

His own extensive background as a college debater and his recent "kitchen" debates with Soviet premier Nikita Khrushchev also contributed to Nixon's confidence in his ability to debate Kennedy. Nixon's strategists were so confident that their candidate would gain in the debates that they initially argued for only one debate. They believed that Nixon could virtually eliminate Kennedy in one debate and that it would be disadvantageous to give Kennedy any opportunity to recover. Clearly, Nixon's camp believed that advantages would accrue to him from debating and that he was a good debater.

The optimism of the Nixon camp was curious in light of the fact that Nixon and Kennedy had debated to a standoff in 1947. In that year, Pennsylvania congressman Frank Buchanan had been asked to bring two outstanding young political figures to McKeesport, Pennsylvania, a town in the midst of the Pennsylvania steel belt, to debate the controversial Taft–Hartley labor bill. Buchanan had asked freshmen congressmen Richard Nixon and John Kennedy. They accepted. Nixon had defended the bill, and, speaking to an audience that included many who were sympathetic to labor, he argued that big labor had grown too powerful. Kennedy had acknowledged merit in the bill but felt it was unnecessarily restrictive on labor. Perhaps foreshadowing 1960, Nixon seemed to have won the debate itself, but Kennedy seemed to have won the audience.[28]

Moreover, while many observers recalled Nixon's successful 1952 Checkers speech, few 1960 observers recalled what most of Kennedy's inner circle best remembered about 1952. John Kennedy had run for the Senate against a heavily favored, vastly more experienced, incumbent Republican, Senator Henry Cabot Lodge. Kennedy debated Lodge at Waltham, Massachusetts. From that point forward, Lodge's assertions about his superior experience, maturity, and judgment—the same issues Nixon was using in 1960—were no longer viable. At least two of Kennedy's inner circle, his brother Robert and close adviser Kenneth O'Donnell, anticipated that the Kennedy–Nixon debates might well be a "rerun" of the Lodge debate. Clearly, Kennedy's strategists felt that their man was an able speaker and that his presence on the same platform as Nixon, as well as what he said, would prove advantageous. Thus, both candidates felt that they were good debaters and hence would be advantaged by debates.

Kennedy and Nixon were the only major candidates for the presidency. After fifteen negotiating sessions, which included discussions of virtually every detail of television production—camera angles, staging, lighting, and backdrops—both camps felt that no unexpected variable would confound the situation.

Thus, Nixon and Kennedy had every reason to debate. It was not an accident that they became the first presidential candidates to engage in an extensive series of public debates. It was at their bidding that both Republican and Democratic members of Congress voted to suspend section 315 of the Communications Act to allow national coverage of the debates.

1992: Clinton–Bush–Perot Debates

In 1987, at the recommendation of a variety of experts, a nonprofit, nonpartisan corporation was established to sponsor presidential and vice presidential debates. The Commission on Presidential Debates sponsored all of the 1988 debates. In the years since 1988, the commission has worked with a variety of organizations, including the National Communication Association, to promote and study political debates. Charged with developing a schedule and format for the 1992 debates, the commission ultimately proposed a series of three presidential debates and one vice presidential debate for 1992. Importantly, the commission proposal was for ninety-minute debates to be conducted by a single moderator.[29]

The Democratic candidate, Governor Bill Clinton, accepted the commission proposal, but incumbent Republican president George H. W. Bush did not. The Bush campaign was widely reported to object to the single-moderator format, preferring instead the use of a panel of questioners, as had been used in his 1988 debates with Governor Michael Dukakis. The single-moderator format had been offered by the commission as the format most conducive to following up questions and probing the candidates. It was widely believed to be the format that best provided viewers with information.

This seemingly simple detail of format, the use of a single moderator or a panel of questioners, almost prevented debates in 1992. The date of the commission's proposed first debate, September 22, came and passed with no debate. With one debate canceled and the election only six weeks distant, the Commission on Presidential Debates offered the candidates another proposal. Clinton again immediately accepted. The Bush campaign refused, observing that it had sent a proposal for debates directly to the Clinton campaign and awaited a response.

Bush no doubt favored the format in which a group of reporters rotated in asking questions for several reasons. First, it was the format in which Bush had excelled four years earlier. Second, it was likely to yield questions on a wide variety of topics. If the debate remained focused on one or a limited number of topics, as might happen with a single moderator asking a series of follow-up questions on a limited number of issues, the Bush economic record was most assuredly going to be discussed at length, with little discussion of Clinton or his policies. However, the use of a panel of reporters might facilitate questions about many of Clinton's costly campaign promises, as well as the controversial aspects of his life such as his reputed womanizing and draft dodging.

Bush's refusal to accept the offers of the nonpartisan Commission on Presidential Debates, in light of Clinton's acceptance, continued to cause Bush discomfort. Clinton's attacks on Bush for not debating were resonating well with the public, and, by late September and early October, Bush himself was getting fed up with the negative image his refusal to debate was creating, telling his staff, "I'm tired of looking like a wimp."

With time running short, hoping to change growing negative public opinion about his refusal to debate, Bush challenged Clinton to a series of six debates. The Bush challenge quickly resulted in direct negotiations between the two campaigns. After extensive discussions, the campaign staffs announced their agreement. A series of four debates, three presidential and one vice presidential, would be held. The sponsoring organization would be the Commission on Presidential Debates. The overall package of formats for the four debates was an equitable settlement of the major format differences between the two campaigns.

Thus, after having resolved the issues between themselves regarding the important variables in the debate situation, both candidates were willing to debate. Though Clinton held a lead in all the polls, the president's natural advantages as an incumbent and the continued attacks on Clinton's character suggested the likelihood of a close election. Both candidates saw advantages to debating. The debates offered Bush what many thought might be his last strong opportunity to catch up. For Clinton, they offered the opportunity to go before the entire American public and prove himself worthy of the office, dispelling many of the charges raised about him during the primaries and surfacing periods. Both men perceived themselves to be good debaters. Bush had successfully debated as both a vice presidential and a presidential candidate. Clinton had been successful throughout the Democratic primary season.

Though Bush was an incumbent, the public expectation that presidential candidates debate was so great that Bush was suffering in the polls for his failure to debate. Indeed, Bush's own tracking polls indicated that he was paying a price in public opinion for this failure. Hence, the president was willing to debate.

Though the details of the debates were worked out by negotiators representing only President Bush and Governor Clinton, at the very time the Clinton and Bush camps were negotiating the details of the debates, wealthy businessman H. Ross Perot, candidate of the "United We Stand,

America" movement, reentered the race. Typically, as we have seen, the presence of a third-party candidate discourages political debate. Perot had entered the race, initially captured the support of upwards of 30 percent of the voters, and then withdrawn. Now, six weeks later, he again entered the race.

The Commission on Presidential Debates—recognizing that within days of reentering Perot seemed to be attracting the support of 7 to 10 percent of the public, that during the spring he had actually at one point been the front-runner when his support surged to about 30 percent, and that he would be waging an exceedingly well-financed campaign—determined that he warranted an invitation to debate. Neither the Clinton nor the Bush campaigns wanted to offend the Perot supporters by keeping their candidate out of the debates. Both major party candidates hoped that eventually the Perot support would fade and turn to them. Consequently, neither objected to the commission's invitation to Perot. Typically, third party candidates reduce the likelihood of debates. Though neither Clinton nor Bush were likely to be happy with the presence of Perot in the debates, neither felt that they could afford to engender ill will from the Texas businessman or his supporters.

2004: Bush–Kerry Debates

Well before the major parties had determined their candidates, the Commission on Presidential Debates had established criteria for debate participation. In addition to evidence of constitutional eligibility, the commission criteria required a candidate "to have his/her name appear on enough state ballots to have at least a mathematical chance of securing an Electoral College majority." Moreover, "the CPD's third criterion requires that the candidate have a level of support of at least 15% (15 percent) of the national electorate as determined by five selected national public opinion polling organizations, using the average of those organization's most recently publicly-reported results at the time of the determination."[30] The only two candidates who qualified, as might be anticipated, were Republican president George W. Bush and his Democratic challenger, Senator John F. Kerry.

The commission subsequently announced a schedule of three presidential debates and one vice presidential debate, all to be held in what were proving to be battleground states, and all four to be held within a two-week window, between September 30 and October 13. The debates would have a variety of formats, presumably providing each candidate with at least one debate in a format that he liked. The Kerry campaign accepted the commission proposal on July 15. But the president's campaign simply announced that it looked forward to debating Senator

Kerry "at an appropriate time," but had not reached any decisions about the details of the debates.[31]

Throughout the summer public opinion polls indicated that the nation was almost evenly divided between the two candidates and that the 2004 election would be very close. The election seemed as though it would be so close that many speculated it would turn on who got the greatest number of their own supporters to the polls on election day. The debates provided both candidates with an opportunity to reinforce their base voters, who would be critical in a close election.

Moreover, both candidates could perceive other advantages accruing to themselves if they debated. Kerry was a former college debater, a prosecuting attorney, and a long-time member of the United States Senate. His entire career had centered around positions that demanded verbal dexterity. His optimism about his ability to defeat President Bush in debates was well evidenced in August, when he made headlines by challenging the president to a series of weekly debates from late August to election day.[32]

President Bush's malapropisms had been the source of much humor during his first term of office. But he and his supporters knew that he had never lost a political debate. In 1994 Bush won his first term as governor in part by defeating one of the preeminent speakers of the Democratic Party, Governor Ann Richards, in a debate. Four years earlier, he had defeated Vice President Al Gore, at the time perceived as the most experienced and likely the finest political debater in the country. Bush was accustomed to being perceived as an underdog in political debates and seemed able to turn that to his advantage. From his vantage point, 2004 might well prove to be another example of his opponents underestimating George W. Bush's abilities as a political debater. Bush's reluctance to immediately accept the commission proposals, as did Kerry, helped contribute to the impression that Bush would be a reluctant debater and, hence, played into the perception that he was an underdog. Yet it was this very perception that had aided him when he exceeded expectations against Governor Richards and Vice President Gore. Hence, though Bush was slower than Kerry to accept the commission recommendations, it may have been part of an overall debate strategy to lower expectations. Regardless, ultimately the Bush and Kerry campaigns agreed to a memorandum of understanding that essentially accepted the Commission on Presidential Debates recommendations on dates, locations, and formats for the 2004 presidential debates.[33]

Though Bush was an incumbent, the public desire for debates, especially among presidential candidates, is now so great that the negative political consequences of refusing to debate seem to far outweigh any advantages that an incumbent president might obtain by not debating. Indeed, today it might be argued that an incumbent has more to lose by refusing to debate than a challenger. For incumbents, refusing to debate would suggest an inability to defend their records in office. After seven straight elections with debates, six of which involved incumbent presidents, President Bush's incumbency was not a deterrent to his debating.

Thus, in 2004, both candidates no doubt anticipated a close election. Additionally both candidates perceived possible advantages accruing to them if they debated, and both candidates were experienced and successful political debaters. Both candidates accepted the Commission on Presidential Debates recommendations which involved a variety of formats. The commission criteria had effectively limited the debate to just the two major party candidates.[34] Moreover, the public expectations of debates had, by 2004, largely negated the early obstacles to an incumbent's debating. All of these reasons contributed to the 2004 agreement by both President George W. Bush and challenger Senator John F. Kerry to participate in presidential debates.

POLITICAL DEBATE STRATEGIES

Political debate strategies can best be understood if we recognize that they involve three stages. First are those strategies that take place prior to the debate itself. Second are those the candidate attempts to implement during the debate. Finally are those following the debate. Each is important. A political debate can be won or lost before it takes place, as it takes place, or after it is held. In this section, we examine all three stages of political debating strategies.

Predebate Strategies

Lowering Public Expectations

The perception as to which candidate won the debate is often a function of what people expected. Hence, many candidates seek to lower public expectations of their performance. If prior expectations are low, then it may not take a strong effort on the part of the candidate to appear to have done well. Moreover, if a candidate is expected to be outclassed but does well, it may be regarded as a major victory.

Goodwin F. Berquist and James L. Golden have noted that the media tend to establish public expectations regarding the probable outcome of political debates.[35] Observing the 1980 Reagan–Carter debate, Berquist and Golden point out that, prior to the debate, the media alerted the public to what might take place by discussing expected candidate strategies, interviewing campaign staff, and presenting guidelines for successful debating to which the candidate might adhere.[36]

The interaction between the candidate and campaign staff, on the one hand, and the media, on the other, can be crucial during the predebate period. As the media go about their job, they will seek comments from the campaigners. Campaigners will normally tend to downplay the potential outcome of the debate. By minimizing expectations, campaigners feel they are putting themselves in the best possible position to capitalize on a strong performance and to rationalize for a weak one.

The importance of minimizing expectations was made exceptionally clear in the 2000 debates between Governor George W. Bush and Vice President Al Gore. Almost immediately after the Commission on Presidential Debates announced its proposal for a series of debates, the Gore team accepted and posted a section on its home page called "Bush Debate Duck." Day after day, hour after hour, throughout the primaries and beyond, the Gore home page indicated how long Bush had avoided accepting Gore's offer to debate him.[37] The implication was clear. The weak debater Bush was afraid of the strong debater Gore. Gore's campaign staff was foolishly minimizing expectations on Bush.

During the early summer, Gore appeared on NBC's *Meet the Press* and CNN's *Larry King Live*. On both shows, he challenged Bush, claiming that he would be delighted to debate the Texas governor "anywhere, anytime," suggesting to the hosts of both shows that their shows would be good places for such a debate. On September 3, Bush held a press conference rejecting the first two debates recommended by the commission. He did not care for their formats. Rather, he accepted Gore's challenge to debate him on the two television shows, and then he added that he would accept the third debate recommended by the commission. Once more, the Gore staff denigrated Bush's ability to debate.

Gore spokesman Mark Fabiani claimed, "George Bush is trying to do everything he can to avoid primetime presidential debates that will be seen on all three networks." Again, the implication was clear. The weak debater Bush was afraid of the strong debater Gore. Once more, the Gore staff was playing right into the hands of the Bush campaign, by reinforcing the perception that Bush was a weak debater and Gore a strong one. But, while Gore's staff was portraying the vice president as the Superman of presidential debates, Superman himself was feeling more like Clark Kent. Gore told his staff that he would never be able to win the debates. The expectations for Bush, he claimed, were just too low.[38] By the time of the first debate, Bush had effectively minimized expectations on himself, with inadvertent help from the Gore staff, and raised expectations on Gore. Gore proved correct. Expectations on him were exceedingly high, and though neither he nor Bush made serious errors in the debates, for a variety of reasons, clearly including public expectations created in part by the two campaigns, Bush was perceived to have benefited more from the debates than Gore.

Similarly, in 2004 both the Bush and Kerry campaigns attempted to minimize expectations on their candidate. Democratic National Committee Chairperson Terry McAuliffe for example, called Bush "a great debater," and echoed a frequent refrain of the Kerry campaign, that four years earlier Bush had bested Albert Gore, perceived to be the best political debater the Democratic Party had to offer. Similarly, Bush spokesperson Dan Bartlett called Kerry "a seasoned debater," and cautioned Bush supporters that, at best, Bush would merely "hold his own" against Kerry. "Kerry," Bartlett went on to observe, "has been preparing his whole life for this moment. He was an all-star debater in school and an all-star debater in the Ivy League. He was 20 years in the most august debating society, the United States Senate."[39]

Typically, it is easier for a challenger to minimize expectations than it is for an incumbent. The incumbent already commands respect and has fulfilled the job responsibilities for several years. Incumbents may have debated about the demands of the very offices being contested just a few years earlier. But, though Bush was the incumbent in 2004, relative to the debates, it was Kerry who behaved like a confident incumbent. It was Kerry, not Bush, who challenged his opponent to a series of weekly debates. It was Kerry, not Bush, who accepted all three of the presidential debates recommended by the commission immediately, while Bush initially wished to have only two debates and eliminate the one utilizing audience questions in a town-hall meeting format. Consequently, Kerry's behavior tended to undercut the comments of his staff designed to lower expectations on him. Ultimately, as in 2000, in 2004 the public likely had lower expectations for George Bush's performance during the presidential debates than it did for his opponent.

Determining the Target Audience

A second predebate strategy is to determine clearly the target audience. Political debates typically draw the largest audiences of any single communicative event of the campaign. The candidates must determine who their target audiences are for the debate. Typically, they will be the same as the normal campaign target audiences. However, due to the unusual size of the audience, it is possible that the candidate may choose to go after a new target group of voters during a debate. The debate may be the first time that this group has been exposed to the candidate. Most practitioners would not suggest using the debate to attract massive numbers of new and different voters to the candidate. But the unusual nature of debate audiences—their size, the presence of many adherents of the opponent, the propensity of both the college educated and women to watch debates—means that the candidates must clearly determine whether they wish to maintain their campaigns' targeted audiences for the debate or whether they wish to make some changes, normally in the form of adding targeted groups.

Devising and Rehearsing Possible Answers

Finally, with a clear conception of targeted audiences in mind, candidates must work out answers to possible questions and practice them. This is the third predebate strategy. The firsthand reports of many participants in political debates suggest several successful approaches to practice.[40] First, in a relaxed atmosphere the candidate and a limited number of aides should work through possible questions and answers, consistently keeping in mind overall themes and target audiences. Second, the candidate should practice the answers in a situation as similar to the real one as possible. For nationally televised presidential debates, this has meant simulating the television studio or auditorium to be used and often utilizing a stand-in for the opponent. Some candidates have reviewed the speeches and tapes of their opponent's past performances. In the case of opponents who have debated in the past, an examination of their past debates has proven helpful.[41]

Preparing for a debate may well mean curtailing other campaign activity for several days, but, given the attention normally focused on debates, this sacrifice would seem worthwhile. In each of the last three presidential elections, all four participants in the presidential and vice presidential debates took time out from their schedules to engage in mock debates and other methods of preparation.[42]

Debate Strategies

Relating Issues to an Overall Theme

As the debate progresses, candidates must constantly respond to specific questions on the issues of the day. While those issues vary from campaign to campaign, most successful political debaters have been able to integrate the specific issues into an overall framework. For example, when Senators John Kennedy and Hubert Humphrey debated in the 1960 West Virginia primary, Kennedy developed the overall thesis, just as he did months later when debating Nixon, that, while the United States was a great nation, it could and should be greater. As he dealt with specific issues concerning West Virginia and the nation, he integrated many of them into his overall thesis, that the United States could do better.[43]

Skilled political debaters will first present their overall theme in the introductory statement, if the opportunity to make such a statement is allowed in the debate format being used. Then they will reinforce it with answers to as many specific questions as possible. Finally, they will return to it in their concluding statement.

In the 1988 presidential debates, the format did not include opening statements. However, George H. W. Bush concluded the first debate by observing that "it gets down to a question of values. . . . We've got a wide array of differences on those [values]. But in the final analysis, in the final analysis, a person goes into that voting booth, they're going to say, who has the values I believe in?"[44] Bush's overarching thesis throughout the evening had been that his conservative values were more acceptable to the nation than Dukakis's liberal values, and he used his concluding statement, as well as his responses to many questions, to emphasize his thesis.

In 1996, Clinton and Gore seemed more coordinated than any two debaters in the history of national political debating. Indeed, they utilized virtually identical language in presenting their overall thesis. In his opening statement of the first debate, Clinton claimed that, if reelected, he and Gore would "balance the budget and protect Medicare, Medicaid, education, and the environment." Gore claimed that "we have a plan to balance the budget while protecting Medicare, Medicaid, education, and the environment." Both men repeated this refrain throughout their debates.[45]

In the first debate of 2004 the candidates were not allowed to make opening statements. But both used the answer to the first question asked them to indicate their overarching theme. Kerry opened his first answer by observing "I can make America safer than President Bush has made us. . . . I believe America is safest and strongest when we are leading the world and we are leading strong alliances. . . . This president has them [our alliances] in shatters all across the globe."[46] Repeatedly, he related his answers to the specific questions he was asked to his overall theme. He used his answers to try to illustrate how he could make America safer than it was under President Bush and how he could repair our alliances.

President Bush also used the first question he was asked to present his overall theme. "I know how to lead. I've shown the American people I know how to lead. I have—I understand everybody in this country doesn't agree with the decisions I've made. And I made some tough decisions. But people know where I stand. People out there listening know what I believe. And that's how best it is to keep the peace." Bush's overarching thesis for the evening was that he knew how to keep the peace and how to lead. When answering specific questions he often utilized his answers to support his claim that he was an effective leader.

Issues serve skilled debaters by allowing them to develop an overall thesis. We know that most people forget much of what they hear in as little as twenty-four hours. Any response to an opponent or a panelist on a specific issue is liable to be forgotten by most of the audience. But, by making the response to a specific issue part of a theme that is consistently repeated, issues can be used to best advantage. Strategies on specific issues, of course, cannot be generalized. They vary depending on the candidate and the situation. But developing an overall thesis, which can be presented in opening and closing statements and repeatedly reinforced by the responses to many specific issues, is a highly effective strategy employed by many political debaters.

Developing an Image

Issues are one of the two major concerns of the candidate during the debate. The other is image. As Robert O. Weiss has argued, in political debates issues and images "intertwine in all manner of convolutions and mutually affect one another in countless ways."[47] Weiss calls this relationship the "issue–image interface."[48] Though issues and images are closely intertwined, several image strategies can be employed in political debates.

The principal image strategies that can be utilized in political debating include the development of a leadership style, personification, and identification.[49] As Dan Nimmo points out, political figures can develop an *activist* leadership style or a *passive* leadership style. The activist is just that. In a debate, activists consistently refer to their actions, their initiatives, their effect on events. Passive leaders are cautious. They do not speak of their initiatives but rather portray themselves as reacting to events.

During the 2004 debates Senator Kerry and President Bush both presented themselves to the public as energetic active leaders. During his very first answer, in the first debate, Kerry made eleven references to actions he or his administration would take. On average, every eleven seconds he suggested an action that he or his administration would take. Consistently through the debates he made references to his new plans for addressing an issue. During the course of the second debate, Kerry made reference to fourteen different new plans he had for treating a wide variety of the nation's ills. Clearly, Kerry was suggesting that his would be an activist presidency. Like Kerry, President Bush presented himself as an activist as well. During his very first answer, in the first debate, he made nine references to actions that he would take during his second term. On average, he suggested an action every thirteen seconds. Throughout the debates Bush constantly referenced his prior actions as president, suggesting he would continue them, or referenced new actions that he would take. Both candidates presented themselves as activists who would impact and shape events, not wait for events to impact and shape them.

Similarly, throughout the 2000 debates, Al Gore consistently presented himself to the public as a vigorous and active leader. For example, during his first answer, which was only two minutes long, he used the word *I* or variants of it (*I'll*, *I'm*) twenty times, on average once every six seconds. In what served as his opening statement, Gore made reference to no fewer than thirteen programs he would implement as president.[50] He was clearly presenting himself as an activist president. He continued to do so from this answer forward in the first debate and those debates that followed.

Bush, too, portrayed himself as an activist in the 2000 debates. Throughout the debates, he consistently stressed the five basic issues on which he had focused during the entire campaign. During the first debate, for example, he concluded by stressing the activist reforms he wished to implement in the nation's Medicare, Social Security, and education programs. Moreover, he claimed that he would try to implement changes in prescription drug programs and rebuild the military. Clearly, both men were suggesting that they would be activist presidents.

The second image strategy that lends itself to political debating is *personification*, the effort of the candidate to personify a definite role. In 2004, with the war on terror being waged, President Bush attempted to portray himself as a strong wartime leader. At one point he observed, "I believe that I am going to win [the election] because the American people know I know how to lead. I've shown the American people I know how to lead. I have—I understand everybody in this country doesn't agree with the decisions I've made. And I made some tough decisions. But people know where I stand. People out there listening know what I believe. And that's how best it is to keep the peace." Bush's observations not only suggested that he was an accomplished leader, but denigrate the leadership qualities of his opponent. Senator John Kerry was plagued throughout the campaign by charges that he was a "flip flopper" who changed his positions on a host of issues, including the war in Iraq, based on political expediency.

In 1980, concerned about President Carter's attempts to characterize him as a warmonger who might have an itchy trigger finger on the nuclear button, Ronald Reagan worked to counter that image in the debate. He did so in part by personifying a kind, statesmanlike, religious family man, seeking peace. For example, at various points in the debate, he observed that "I believe with all my heart that our first priority must be world peace . . . I am a father of sons; I have a grandson. . . . I'm going to continue praying that they'll [the Iranian hostages] come home."[51] In sum, Reagan was attempting to personify himself, to play a role, as a gentle statesman and devout family man. This personification would clearly distance him from charges of being a warmonger.

The final image strategy is *identification*. Debaters attempt to identify themselves with what they believe are the principal aspirations of their audience. Governor Clinton was exceptionally effective at this throughout the 1992 campaign as he identified himself with the nation's aspirations for economic improvement. In 1996, in a strategy no doubt geared to one of his principal target audiences, women, Clinton accented his education policies at the end of his opening statement. Clinton was skillfully appealing to that most basic of human aspirations, the desire to pave the way for great success by their children. Clinton sketched a picture of eight-year-olds reading, twelve-year-olds surfing the Internet, and eighteen-year-olds in college.

As these examples make clear, there is a close relationship between a candidate's response to specific issues and the image that the candidate projects. Nevertheless, as the debate is in progress, the candidate should have a clear idea of an overall issue strategy or thesis to which specific answers can be related. Moreover, candidates should be cognizant of the image they may be projecting and develop appropriate strategies, such as a leadership style, personification, and identification, to create the persona they want.

Postdebate Strategies

Political debates are not over when the last word is uttered. Who won? Who made a grievous error? Who seemed best in control? Questions like these immediately follow the debate, and their answers are often as important as the debate itself. After all, it is what the audience perceives to have happened in the debate that is of consequence. Therefore, the well-prepared campaign will be ready to try to influence audience perceptions of the debate as soon as it concludes.

The importance of postdebate strategies was dramatized in the second Ford–Carter debate of 1976, perhaps best remembered because President Ford seemed to be unaware of the Soviet domination of Eastern Europe. Yet, at the time that Ford made his unfortunate statement, it was barely noticed. It was not until the next day, after continual publicity of his remark, that Ford was perceived as having erred badly. Frederick T. Steeper has studied this debate and concludes:

> The volunteered descriptions of the debate by the voters surveyed immediately after the debate included no mentions of Ford's statement on Eastern Europe. Not until the afternoon of the next day did such references appear, and by Thursday night they were the most frequent criticism given Ford's performance. Similarly, the panelists monitored during the debate gave no indication of an unfavorable reaction at the time they heard Ford's Eastern European remarks. The conclusion is that the preponderance of viewers of

the second debate most likely were not certain of the true status of Eastern Europe, or less likely, did not consider Ford's error important. Given the amount of publicity given Ford's East European statements the next day by the news media and the concomitant change that took place, it is concluded that this publicity caused the change.[52]

Most students of political debate believe that the effects often lag behind the debate itself. Frequently, audience members do not reach final judgment until they have discussed the debate with others and have observed the media reaction.[53] It is during these hours, when interpersonal influence and media influence are often operating, that the campaign engages in the postdebate strategy of favorably influencing perceptions of the debate.

The first presidential debate of 2000 well illustrates the importance of favorably influencing public perceptions of the debate and how that perception often lags a day or so behind the debate itself. At first glance this was a close debate, with perhaps a slight edge going to Vice President Gore, who seemed more fluent and conversant with the issues. Immediately after the debate, Gore bested Bush in three of the four "instant polls" taken.[54] Press accounts stressed the clash between the two candidates, while also observing that both candidates were attempting to move their parties to the center of the political spectrum.[55]

However, though the first accounts portrayed a close debate with a slight edge going to Gore, the following day three stories were developing from the debate, and all of them clearly favored Bush.

First, Gore had not proven to be a substantially stronger debater than Bush. Bush had challenged Gore sharply on critical issues such as tax policy, Social Security reform, prescription drugs for the elderly, education, and rebuilding the military. Moreover, he had repeatedly questioned Gore's use of statistics. The initial perception, fostered during the predebate period deliberately by the Bush camp and inadvertently by the Gore camp, was that Gore was clearly the better debater, in large part because he was so much more familiar with the issues. Hence, Gore failed to live up to expectations. He did not appear substantially more fit for the office than Bush. Bush exceeded expectations. He seemed to be approximately as well prepared and able to assume the office as Gore.

Second, Gore's statements in the debate were examined, and on three occasions it appeared as though he had exaggerated his accomplishments.[56] This problem had plagued Gore throughout the campaign. By the day after the debate, the first debate was being interpreted as yet another example of Gore's propensity to exaggerate his own accomplishments. Gore's exaggerations, for many observers little more than a euphemism for lies, became the second major story to come out of the debate.

Gore's arrogant and bullying attitude was the third major story to come out of the debate. Viewers found him condescending toward Bush. As the debate progressed, Gore could be heard sighing into his microphone when Bush spoke. His facial expressions as Bush spoke also suggested to many viewers that he had little respect for his foe. Also adding to this negative impression of Gore were his constant attempts to interrupt both Bush and moderator Jim Lehrer. Gore consistently exceeded his time limits and attempted to have the last word on a topic, often in violation of the ground rules for the debate. He came across to many as simply not a very nice person.

In the twenty-four to forty-eight hours that followed the debate, these three story lines dominated coverage and discussion. During that time period, Bush pollster Matthew Dowd told the Bush high command that his polling indicated that viewers judged the debate a draw, but they "had focused on Gore's grimace, his sighs, his mannerisms."[57] Dowd claimed that Gore was hurting himself. Similarly, Gore pollster Stan Greenberg was unhappy with Gore's performance in the first debate. He urged Gore to defend his ideas more and attack Bush less.[58] Clearly, as these three story lines were being developed, the initial reaction to the debate as one in which Gore had won a close debate was turning around. Within little more than twenty-four to forty-eight hours, the first debate was being considered a Bush triumph. Bush had exceeded expectations and seemed equal to both his opponent and the job. Gore had continued to exaggerate and shown himself to be arrogant and bullying.

Offering a Large, Well-Coordinated Surrogate Effort

The principal postdebate strategy is to provide a massive and well-coordinated surrogate effort. Typically, campaigns will make available to the press a host of surrogate spokespersons who will claim their candidate won the debate. Moreover, these surrogates will be briefed in advance, so that they will all be speaking about the same few issues that their candidate used to defeat the opponent. After both the 2004 and 2000 debates, both campaigns did this. For example, immediately following the 2004 debates, a host of campaign officials and other surrogates were in "spin alley," the room near the site of the debate where the press could interview experts and partisans for reaction. Among those available in "spin alley" after the debate who told reporters that Bush was the decisive winner were Bush campaign aids Karl Rove, Karen Hughes, Dan Bartlett, Mathew Dowd, and Ken Mehlman. Mere feet away, in the same room, reacting to the same debate, Kerry aids Tad Devine, Joe Lockhart, Mike McCurry, and Kerry swiftboat crewmate Del Sandusky were extolling the debate victory of John Kerry.[59]

But the surrogate efforts that followed the 2004 and 2000 debates were not as successful as they had been in the past.[60] First, the press, having "been used" in this fashion in the past, was more resistant. Second, in recent years, the debate schedule has been compressed, the second and later debates all taking place within a few days of each other. Hence, the press does not have several days or perhaps a week or more between debates in which to look back and examine a completed debate. Such a situation provides the press with an opportunity to interview party leaders and other candidate allies who serve as surrogates. When a series of three presidential debates and a vice presidential debate all take place within about a two-week period, as has happened in each of the presidential campaigns since 1996, the press has little time to examine a debate. Rather, after a day or two of examining the just concluded debate, the press typically starts to write about the upcoming debate.

Using Ads to Underscore Debate Themes

Though the use of surrogates does remain the primary postdebate strategy, a second postdebate strategy is to utilize advertising that capitalizes on the major theme and points made by a candidate during the debate. If the major points of a candidate can be reinforced in the days immediately following the debate, they are likely to stick better in the public mind.

In the first of the 2000 debates, Bush had repeatedly questioned Gore's "fuzzy numbers" and used gentle humor to remind the public of Gore's exaggerations. The day after the first debate, the Bush team began to air an ad they called "Trust." This sixty-second spot featured Bush talking about personal responsibility. Bush told voters that he would keep his promises and by implication suggested that Gore would not. Moreover, Bush went on to claim that he would trust people to spend their money wisely, but evidently Gore did not trust the people. Rather, he had a host of programs on which to spend their money. In light of the stories about Gore's exaggerations in the debate and in light of the perception people had of Gore's arrogance during the debate, it was an exceptionally well-timed message that reinforced many perceptions of the first debate. This ad was originally designed to run in the closing days of the campaign, but the Bush team went with it right after the first debate.[61]

Using Audience Members to Project a Positive View

The use of prominent spokespersons to present a positive view of the debate is the most common postdebate strategy. It is used in all levels of campaigns. In well-financed campaigns, paid advertisements may be used to reiterate and stress a key idea made in the debate.

Other strategies are less common and often depend on the circumstances and formats of the specific debate. Often, if an audience is present, campaign staff members will work to "load" the audience with partisans. Not only will they provide positive responses during the debate, but, as they are interviewed later, they may well do the same thing. Community leaders, known to be sympathetic to the candidate, can be urged to write letters to the editors of local papers, commenting favorably on the candidate's performance.

In every instance, postdebate strategies such as the use of surrogates, advertisements, audience members, and letters are designed to influence public perception in the crucial hours and days that immediately follow the debate.

EFFECTS OF POLITICAL DEBATES

Any discussion of the effects of political debates must be tempered with an awareness that it is difficult to draw strong conclusions about them. This difficulty arises for several reasons. First, each debate is different. It involves different candidates, different offices, different issues, different audiences, different press coverage, different formats, and a host of other differences. Hence, to talk about the specific effects of debates is virtually impossible, for no two will be identical, nor will their effects be identical.

Second, debate effects cannot be isolated from the effects of all the other communication that voters receive during the campaign. Individuals may be exposed to a dozen messages about the candidates on the very day of the debate. Distinguishing the effects of the debate from all the others is difficult.

While there have been hundreds, if not thousands, of political debates in the last forty years, by and large, researchers have only studied the presidential debates in detail. Hence, our discussion of effects must necessarily be limited to a consideration of the effects of presidential debates. We cannot be certain that the effects of nationally televised political debates are similar to those of the vast majority of political debates held in campaigns for lesser offices. Most debates are not nationally televised. They are not well publicized in advance. They are not subjected to endless speculation, examination, and evaluation for days afterward. However, while findings concerning the effects of presidential debate are not necessarily valid for other debates, there is reason to suspect a broad similarity in the pattern of effects produced by political debates. But, we cannot be absolutely certain.

Finally, unlike laboratory experiments, scientists cannot control political debates. Hence, those debates that have been examined are often subject to studies that, of necessity, are prepared under less than ideal conditions, including little advance planning and an inability to control fully all of the variables in the study.

Despite each of these problems, at this time there appear to be some striking findings about the effects of political debates, which are subject to revision as debating becomes an even more widely studied communication event.

Effect 1: Increased Audiences

Political debates, even at the local or state level, attract large audiences. Debates create conflict, the essence of drama. Hence, it should not surprise us that presidential debates attract huge audiences. Similarly, we might well hypothesize that debates attract larger audiences than virtually any other activity that takes place during the typical campaign. While research on audiences for nonpresidential debates is not yet widely available, the basic element of conflict exists and might operate as it evidently does in presidential debates—to attract a large audience.

In 1960, CBS estimated that over one hundred million people in the United States watched at least part of the Kennedy–Nixon debates.[62] Numerous other surveys also suggested that the Kennedy–Nixon debates drew an immense national audience. In fact, the debates drew the largest audience for any speaking event in history up to that time.[63]

Similarly, every measure of audience size conducted in connection with the 1976 debates also suggests a massive audience. Most measures of the 1976 debates claim that over 70 percent of the nation watched at least part of the first Carter–Ford debate. While viewing fell off somewhat as the series of debates progressed, it never fell below 60 percent.[64]

In 1960 and again in 1976, debates between presidential candidates were novelties. However, such debates have been a feature of every election since. Moreover, debates between the vice presidential candidates have also become common. This may, in part, account for the fact that, between 1980 and 2000, the audiences for national political debates diminished. Nevertheless, they attracted the largest audiences of any campaign activity.

The 2000 presidential debates attracted audiences of approximately thirty-seven to forty-seven million viewers. The 28.5 million viewers who watched the vice presidential debate were the smallest audience of any nationally televised presidential or vice presidential debate since 1960.[65] Moreover, by 2000, two of the four major networks, NBC and Fox, chose not to air the debates. NBC had a contractual obligation to show a divisional baseball playoff game. It did air the debate on its cable network MSNBC. Fox decided to show its regular entertainment programming, though, like NBC, it did air the debate on its cable network, Fox News Channel.

The audience for presidential debates in 2004 rebounded. The first debate between Bush and Kerry attracted an audience of 62.4 million voters, up 34 percent from the audience for the first Bush–Gore debate four years earlier. The second debate attracted an audience of 46.7 million. The final debate attracted an audience of 51.1 million. The total audience size for the 2004 presidential debates exceeded 160 million, in contrast to 2000 when 121 million Americans watched the Bush–Gore debates.[66]

A variety of reasons likely contributed to this increase. The fact that the nation was at war no doubt increased the interest in the election of the commander-in-chief. The extensive voter contact efforts and "get out the vote" efforts of both major parties may have also peaked the interest of many Americans who had rarely, if ever, been contracted by the parties in the past. Though the public seems to have become accustomed to debates between presidential candidates, those debates continue to draw by far the largest audiences of any campaign activity, though over time the audience size seems to be diminishing.[67] Whether the upward trend witnessed in 2004 was unique to that election, or continues, remains to be seen.

Effect 2: Audiences Reinforced

Comedian Lenny Bruce unwittingly summarized a host of research studies about the effects of political debates when he observed that:

> Everybody hears what he wants to hear. Like when they were in the heat of the 1960 election campaign I was with a group who were watching the debate and all the Nixon fans were saying "Isn't he making Kennedy look like a jerk?"—and all the Kennedy fans were saying "Look at him make a jerk out of Nixon." Each group really feels that their man is up there making the other man look like an idiot.
>
> So then I realized that a candidate would have had to have been that blatant—he would have had to look at his audience right in the camera and say, "I am corrupt. I am the worse choice you could ever have for President."
>
> And even then his followers would say, "Boy, there's an honest man. It takes a big guy to admit that. That's the kind of man we should have for a President."[68]

As Bruce's comment suggests, most research has concluded that political debates tend to reinforce the positions of a candidate's partisans. After the 1960 debates, most researchers did not find substantial shifts of voter opinion. Rather, they found that Kennedy and Nixon partisans became more strongly committed to their candidate. As *Newsweek* reported, the debates "merely stiffened attitudes."[69]

Research since the 1960 debates tends to confirm these early findings. Examining data pertinent to all of the presidential debates held prior to 1987, George Gallup Jr. claims that presidential debates "have caused few people to change their minds."[70] Similarly, the debates held since 1988 seem to have served primarily to reinforce existing attitudes.[71] In 2004, the electorate seemed very closely divided throughout the campaign period. A consensus of public opinion polling immediately prior to the first debate suggested that President Bush was ahead of Senator Kerry by a 49.5 percent to 43.5 percent margin. At the conclusion of the first debate, that consensus of public opinion polling found that President Bush was ahead of Senator Kerry by only .2 percent. However, after the second and third debates, the president's margin grew. In sum, after the entire series of debates in 2004, the president's original 6 percent lead had been reduced to a 3.8 percent lead.[72] Clearly the vast majority of Americans who watched the debates had not changed their mind. On balance, Bush was favored by virtually the same percentage before and after the debate, while Kerry's popularity had gone up slightly.

The reason for this effect is explained by David Sears and Steven Chaffee, who claim that "the information flow stimulated by debates tends to be translated by voters into evaluations that coincide with prior political dispositions. They perceive their party's candidate as having 'won' and they discuss the outcome with like-minded people." Sears and Chaffee continue, noting that since the Democratic Party is substantially larger than the Republican Party, the net effect of the cumulative reinforcement stimulated by the debates probably benefits Democratic candidates.[73] Nationally, the Democratic Party is no longer substantially larger, as it was when Sears and Chaffee first wrote. However, their reasoning remains valid. Consequently, in a very evenly divided nation, the cumulative reinforcement stimulated by the debates probably benefits Republican and Democratic candidates almost equally. The logical outgrowth of these conclusions, applied to local campaigns, would be that debates, because they tend to reinforce prior political dispositions, generally work to the advantage of the party that is dominant in the district, city, or state.

Effect 3: Shifting Limited Numbers of Voters

Political debates do not normally result in massive shifts of votes. As indicated earlier, most audience members have their existing predispositions reinforced by the debate. However, some voters may shift. In a close election, the number who shift as a consequence of debates might be decisive.

The Kennedy–Nixon debates were widely perceived at the time as having affected massive numbers of voters. President Kennedy helped foster this impression by attributing his election to the debates. Yet evidence on this point suggests that, while they may have been decisive due to the extremely close nature of the election, the debates did not shift massive numbers of votes. The highest estimate of voter shift is pollster Elmo Roper's guess that four million voters, about 6 percent of the vote, changed as a consequence of the debates.[74] However, most researchers are far more cautious. Elihu Katz and Jacob Feldman, after examining thirty-one studies of the 1960 debates, typify the conclusions of most when they write, "Did the debates really affect the final outcome? Apart from strengthening Democratic convictions about their candidate, it is very difficult to tell."[75] Evidence on the 1976 presidential debates,[76] as well as those of 1980, tends to confirm this limited effects paradigm.[77]

In their perceptive analysis of the effects of the 1984 presidential debates, Craig Allen Smith and Kathy Smith observe that, although some polls reported that Walter Mondale had clearly beaten Ronald Reagan in their first debate, this victory did not translate into a shift in votes.[78] Similarly, in 1996, Clinton continually polled 51 to 53 percent of the vote during the portion of the campaign shortly before, during, and shortly after the debates. During this same period, Senator Dole remained consistently at 34 to 36 percent, and Ross Perot trailed with 12 to 14 percent.[79]

The 2000 debates did give Governor George W. Bush a slight increase in his poll standings. However, as Jamieson has illustrated, that increase was not a direct consequence of the debates. Indeed, as we have seen, immediately after the debates, Gore bested Bush in three of the four instant polls. Rather, Bush's increase in the polls came as the three story lines developed by the press took hold. As Jamieson and Paul Waldman point out, those who actually watched the debate remained consistent to their first impressions. Those voters who shifted their judgments in favor of Bush were, for the most part, those who had not watched the debate but rather relied on media accounts.[80] As we have seen, throughout the 2004 debates Bush's support remained firm at 49 percent. The slight shift towards Kerry was likely the result of undecided voters making up their minds in somewhat greater numbers for Kerry.

Effect 4: Debates Help Set Voters' Agenda

As we have discussed in chapter 4, much recent research has stressed the importance of the agenda-setting function of mass communication. In essence, this research holds that "we judge as important what the media judge as important. Media priorities become our own."[81] If the considerable body of evidence that supports the agenda-setting function of mass media is correct, then it would stand to reason that those issues stressed in mass media political debates, and mass media coverage of those debates, should also become issues of high priority for voters who watch the debates and attend to the media coverage of them.

Linda Swanson and David Swanson offer strong evidence in support of the agenda-setting function of political debates.[82] They attempted to determine whether those issues of primary concern to voters changed as a consequence of watching political debates. Based on research done at the University of Illinois during the 1976 campaign, they concluded that "the first Ford–Carter debate exerted an agenda-setting effect on our subjects who viewed it, although that effect was tempered by enduring personal priorities of subjects."[83] As Swanson and Swanson subsequently observed, "to the extent that citizens base their voting choices on their assessment of campaign issues, this is surely an effect of some political importance."[84]

The agenda-setting function of political debates seems to remain strong. However, as campaigns become more and more sophisticated and candidates attempt to work into their debates the very lines that permeate their speeches and paid advertising, it grows increasingly difficult to isolate the agenda-setting effects of political debate from the overall agenda-setting effects of media coverage of the entire campaign.

The importance of the potential agenda-setting effects of debates has been implicitly acknowledged in the format of every series of presidential debates since 1992. At least one debate in each campaign since 1992 allowed an audience of undecided voters either to question the candidates directly or to write questions from which the moderator selected those that were asked of the candidates. Allowing voters, rather than journalists, to question the candidates is, in part, an attempt to provide that the public's agenda is served by the debates. Nevertheless, critics of the presidential debates claim that the debates focus on narrow policy issues and never treat major systemic issues that are critical to the democratic process and which would resonate with a public that is growing increasingly disenchanted with the entire political process.[85]

Effect 5: Debates Increase the Voters' Knowledge of Issues

A wide variety of studies has attempted to determine whether political debates increase the voters' knowledge of the issues. These studies seem to point to three conclusions. First, voters do seem more knowledgeable as a consequence of watching political debates. Second, debates are particularly helpful to voters in local elections. Tempering these conclusions is the final conclusion: Often voters do not learn about the very issues that most concern them.

That voters clearly learn about the issues as a consequence of watching debates seems to have been well established by research.[86] Moreover, it would appear that debates serve as a more important source of information in local elections, which receive comparatively little media coverage, than for major national or statewide races. One study suggests that 80 percent of the viewers of debates between local candidates report that they had learned about the candidates by viewing the debates, whereas only 55 percent made the same claim about the presidential debates.[87]

Although voters apparently learn about issues by watching debates, often they do not learn about the issues that most concern them. Michael Pfau has cogently argued that "a political debate ought to match—to the extent possible—the agendas of the candidates and the public." However, after studying several presidential debates he concluded, "the journalists' questions have virtually ignored the public's agenda."[88] The problem is well illustrated in the remarks of one of the journalists who helped set the agenda of the 1980 debates with her questions. She claimed that she "felt under enormous pressure to try forming a single question that would somehow catch the well-briefed candidates by surprise on a subject of importance."[89] More appropriately for the public, she might have attempted to ask a question dealing with those issues that were of greatest public concern. But far too often, the public's concerns are not reflected in the journalists' questions.[90] Indeed, one critic of the 1988 debates has characterized many of the questions asked in that year's presidential debates as "trite."[91]

It should be recalled that in 1960, when the precedents that have since been largely followed were established, the impetus for a panel of journalist-questioners came from the candidates, not the press.[92] Hence, for a variety of reasons, not the least of which was the intrusion of journalistic panels, the public agenda was frequently poorly served in earlier political debates. Since 1992, the Commission on Presidential Debates has attempted to accommodate this concern by including at least one debate in which undecided voters ask questions. Additionally, in 1996, the traditional use of a panel of journalists was abandoned. Rather, one journalist served as the moderator and questioner. The use of only one questioner was designed to allow follow-up questions. Multijournalist panels tended to skip from one topic area to the next, as each of the journalists asks a question about a different topic. The use of one questioner meant that the questioner could repeat a question and follow up on evasive answers, thus providing greater information to the public.

While debates do increase the voters' knowledge of issues, particularly debates in local campaigns, their formats often prevent them from being as informative as the public might wish. The Commission on Presidential Debates has attempted to be responsive to this concern and changed the formats used at the presidential level in recent years. Nevertheless, critics of the debates have argued that, regardless of format, the debates persist in excluding issues.

Moreover, the issues discussed seem to be those aimed at voters in a limited number of "battleground states" where the election will be decided. Hence, major issues of interest to voters in the rest of the country are often excluded. So, for example, during the 2004 debates the candidates were asked seven questions on health care. Moreover, on several occasions health care was discussed in responding to other questions. For example, in the second debate Senator Kerry was asked about creating new jobs for American workers but answered by discussing the shrinking number of American workers who had health-care coverage. Kerry's answer then caused Bush to also deal with health care in his answer. Thus the candidates views on health care, an issue of critical importance in a battleground state like Florida, with an aging population, were repeatedly explored. Yet, there was only one question allowing the candidates to discuss their views on illegal immigration, an overwhelming concern in states like Texas, Arizona, and California, where the outcome of the election was virtually never in doubt.[93]

Effect 6: Debates Modify Candidate Images

Debates apparently affect the images of candidates. In their evaluation of the impact of the 1976 debates, Paul Hagner and Leroy Rieselbach suggest that debates affect candidate images primarily when the candidate is not well known and hence the candidate's public image is not well developed.[94] When the public is unfamiliar with the candidate, perception of the candidate's general character, personality attributes, and general competency seems to be affected by political debates and their subsequent media coverage.

Most accounts of the 1960 debates note that Kennedy, the comparative unknown, improved his image as a consequence of the debates. He was able to convey a sense of competency and familiarity with major issues, as well as a charming personality. Similarly, Sears and Chaffee summarize a number of studies of the 1976 debates and conclude that the public's image of the candidates was affected by the debates.[95]

In his perceptive study of the 1976 vice presidential debates, Kevin Sauter observes that both Walter Mondale and Robert Dole hoped to impress the voters with their presidential potential. Sauter concluded that Mondale was successful in this effort, and his strong image contributed appreciably to his subsequent nomination to the presidency. Conversely, Sauter finds that a variety of circumstances, many beyond his control, contributed to Dole's failure to impress the voters with his presidential potential. His failure in 1976, Sauter suggests, may have contributed to Dole's difficulty in obtaining the Republican nomination, for which he was a candidate repeatedly prior to his 1996 nomination.[96]

In 1992, the least-known figure on any of the tickets was James Stockdale. Though many in the public were aware that he was the senior American officer captured in Vietnam and had been an inspiration to other American prisoners while suffering enormously at the hands of his Vietnamese captors, comparatively little else was known about him. The vice presidential debate afforded him an opportunity to allow America to become acquainted with him. Yet, the image he projected was remarkably unpresidential. Often unable to answer questions and frequently admitting his lack of knowledge, Stockdale projected an image of incompetence. Moreover, in contrast to the much younger Gore and Quayle, his hearing difficulties and limp, both largely a consequence of his treatment while a prisoner of war, no doubt concerned voters who were evaluating his ability to step into the presidency if the need arose. Though in many respects the most praiseworthy of the three vice presidential candidates, Stockdale projected the least presidential image. He appeared unable to grasp the complexities of many public issues. He appeared passive and frail. He was characterized in the press as "clueless," "an embarrassment," and "not ready for prime time."[97] Given that Stockdale had a distinguished career as both a military figure and as a scholar but that his accomplishments were little known by the public, it is clear that the debate created a dramatically negative image of him.

Though the general public was likely somewhat more familiar with President Bush by 2004 than it was with Senator Kerry, both men were well known. Hence, they were unlikely to dramatically change their images. But, during the first debate, Bush seemed ill at ease, while Kerry seemed comfortable and in command of the situation. Much of the favorable reaction to Kerry after that debate, which resulted in a modest surge in the public opinion polls for Kerry, likely reflected the fact that for many viewers he was projecting an image of greater assurance and strength than Bush, more consistent with their expectations of what they wanted in a president. During the second and third debates Bush seemed much more at ease and both men projected strong images, consistent with public expectations about the office of president. The stronger image Bush projected helped account for the modest surge in the polls that he received after the last two debates.[98]

In sum, debates can affect public perception of a candidate's image—general competency, personality attributes, and character traits. The potential for affecting image seems to be inversely related to public knowledge of the candidate. The better known the candidate, the less likely the debate will greatly affect that candidate's image. Hence, the potential for improving one's image is generally greater for the lesser-known candidate. Well-known candidates will have difficulty changing their images during debates, but they can reinforce preexisting audience perceptions of their image. Moreover, it is likely that in races for lesser offices, among lesser-known candidates, the impact of a debate on the image of the candidates is potentially great.

Effect 7: Debates Freeze the Campaign

The timing of the 1992 debates, all four of which came in a twelve-day period, and those of 1996, all three of which came in a ten-day period, emphasized a previously little-noticed effect of debates. As Dan Hahn has observed, once debates are announced, "there will be an electoral flat-line until after the debates."[99] Once debates are announced, most voters tend to harden their positions until after the debates. Partisans see no reason to consider changing until after the debates, and, as we have observed earlier, the debates rarely provide them with sufficient cause to change. Undecided voters tend to reserve judgment in the days immediately preceding the debates and throughout the debates, preferring to utilize the debates in making their judgment.

The tendency to schedule debates in a short window of time (all the 2004 debates were held within thirteen days) is likely to continue. This effect of debates, to largely freeze the campaign in place until their conclusion, works to the advantage of the leading candidate. It makes the leader more difficult to catch by effectively shortening the time the trailing candidates have to catch up. Presidential debates are likely to be scheduled within a short window of time both because of pressure from the leading candidate, and because of the contractual considerations of the television networks, some of whom have contracts to televise sporting events such as the baseball playoffs and the Olympics during the closing weeks of the campaign.

Effect 8: Debates Build Confidence in U.S. Democracy

A wide variety of studies has attempted to evaluate the effects of political debates on American political institutions. Do debates result in greater confidence and support of political institutions and office holders? Do debates facilitate political socialization? While individual studies differ, and continued research will no doubt shed greater light on questions such as these, current research does offer some tentative answers.

First, as Sidney Kraus and Dennis Davis argue, debates are consistent with democratic theory, which stresses the importance of rational decision making by an informed electorate.[100] Second, as Samuel Becker and colleagues point out, debates provide voters with greater exposure to information about candidates, which "probably resulted in a certain degree of commitment to the election process and to the candidate selected through that process."[101] Third, as Chaffee illustrates, debates apparently have a positive impact on people's confidence in government institutions and play a positive role in political socialization or the recruitment of new members into the body politic.[102]

In recent presidential elections, the candidates have largely targeted their media effort at about one-third of the nation, the battleground states. Consequently, much of the nation is never directly exposed to the media campaign of the candidates. Debates are virtually the only aspect of a contemporary presidential campaign to which the entire nation is now exposed. They serve as one of the few campaign experiences the entire nation has in common.

In sum, it appears that political debates contribute to voter satisfaction with the democratic process. Though much has been written about growing voter apathy, increasing voter disenchantment with the political process, and rising voter skepticism of politicians, it would appear that this overall trend of disaffection with the political process is not fostered by debates. Quite to the contrary, as Kraus has claimed, "televised presidential debates may be unparalleled in modern campaigning as an innovation that engages citizens in the political process."[103] Indeed, current research suggests that political debates might be a step in the direction of remedying current disaffection.

CONCLUSION

In sum, it would appear that political debates have at least eight distinct effects. Typically they attract large audiences. Second, they seem to reinforce many of the preexisting attitudes and beliefs of audience members. Third, they seem to shift a limited number of voters. Though the number of voters whose opinions are shifted by the debates is limited, it should be kept in mind that, as discussed earlier in this chapter, debates are much more likely to be held in close elections, where the shift of a limited number of voters might well prove crucial to the outcome. Fourth, debates help set the political agenda. Fifth, debates contribute to the education of audience members. Voters who watch the debates apparently are more knowledgeable as a consequence of their watching. This educational benefit of debates must be tempered somewhat by the recognition that current debate formats often preclude the viewers' really learning about the issues that most concern them. Sixth, debates seem to affect the images of candidates. The image of the lesser-known participant is normally affected more by a political debate. Seventh, debates tend to freeze the campaign in place until their conclusion. Finally, debates seem to contribute to the public's confidence in government institutions and leaders.

NOTES

1. Quoted in *The Lincoln–Douglas Debates*, ed. Robert W. Johannsen (New York: Oxford University Press, 1965), 3.

2. Kathleen Hall Jamieson and David S. Birdsell note that since as early as 1788, when two future presidents, James Madison and James Monroe, debated for a seat in the new House of Representatives, debates have been a part of American election campaigns. See their *Presidential Debates: The Challenge of Creating an Informed Electorate* (New York: Oxford University Press, 1988), 34.

3. J. Jeffery Auer, "The Counterfeit Debates," in *The Great Debates: Kennedy vs. Nixon, 1960*, ed. Sidney Kraus, 146 (Bloomington: Indiana University Press, 1962).

4. Auer, "Counterfeit Debates," 146.

5. This term was first used by Auer in his essay "The Counterfeit Debates" to describe the 1960 debates. It has since been used to describe many political debates, most notably by Lloyd Bitzer and Theodore Rueter in their work *Carter vs. Ford: The Counterfeit Debates of 1976* (Madison: University of Wisconsin Press, 1980).

6. The statements in this paragraph were made by panelists Robert Flemming and Stuart Novins during the opening minutes of the first Kennedy–Nixon debate. See *The Joint Appearances of Senator John F. Kennedy and Vice-President Richard M. Nixon: Presidential Campaign of 1960* (Washington, D.C.: Government Printing Office, 1961), 78.

7. See Bitzer and Reuter, *Carter vs. Ford*, especially chapter 3, for an excellent analysis of the adversarial nature of the press in the 1976 debates. The press's adversarial quality remains a characteristic feature of campaign debates. Susan A. Hellweg and Anna M. Verhoye's "A Comparative Verbal Analysis of the Two 1988 Bush–Dukakis Presidential Debates," paper presented to the Speech Communication Association, November 1989, 17–18, details the extent of adversarial questioning in the 1988 presidential debates. The only contemporary national political debate that afforded the candidates an opportunity to directly question and clash with one another was the 1992 vice presidential debate between Senator Albert Gore and Vice President Dan Quayle. With this lone exception, all other contemporary national political debates have utilized journalists to stimulate clash.

8. Formats of the presidential debates are fairly well known. For examinations of the formats used in presidential primary debates, see Susan A. Hellwig and Steven L. Phillips, "Form and Substance: A Comparative Analysis of Five Formats Used in the 1980 Presidential Debates," *Speaker and Gavel* 18 (Winter 1981): 67–76; Michael Pfau, "A Comparative Assessment of Intra-Party Debate Formats," paper presented at the Speech Communication Association Convention, Chicago, November 1984. Examinations of debate formats at the nonpresidential level can be found in Jack Kay, "Campaign Debate Formats: At the Non-Presidential Level," paper presented at the Speech Communication Association Convention, Anaheim, California, November 1981; and Michael Pfau, "Criteria and Format to Optimize Series," paper presented at the Speech Communication Association Convention, Anaheim, California, November 1981. Ironically, Patrick Caddell noted that the 1980 presidential debate format used by Reagan and Carter, which allowed for nine to ten minutes of discussion on a single topic, was "exhaustive." See his "Memo of October 21, 1980," reprinted in Elizabeth Drew, *Portrait of an Election: The 1980 Election* (New York: Simon & Schuster, 1981), 426.

9. Auer, "Counterfeit Debates," 148.

10. Perhaps the debate with the most significance for the subsequent development of political debating was the one held between the Tennessee gubernatorial candidates in 1886. For an explanation of the subsequent impact of this debate, see Herbert A. Terry and Sidney Kraus, "Legal and Political Aspects: Was Section 315 Circumvented?" in *The Great Debates: Carter vs. Ford, 1976*, ed. Sidney Kraus, 44–45 (Bloomington: Indiana University Press, 1979).

11. See Jamieson and Birdsell, *Presidential Debates*, 35–36, for a discussion of this feature of nineteenth-century campaigns.

12. When debates were held, they were frequently the centerpieces of the campaigns. For an especially informative example of this, see Cal M. Logue, "Gubernatorial Campaign in Georgia in 1880," *Southern Speech Communication Journal* 40 (Fall 1974): 12–32.

13. Samuel L. Becker and Elmer W. Lower, "Broadcasting in Presidential Campaigns," in *The Great Debates: Kennedy vs. Nixon, 1960*, ed. Sidney Kraus, 29 (Bloomington: Indiana University Press, 1962).

14. Quoted in Sidney Head, *Broadcasting in America* (Boston: Houghton Mifflin, 1976), 331.

15. For a full discussion of these changes, see Edward W. Chester, *Radio, Television and American Politics* (New York: Sheed & Ward, 1969), 247–65. Also see Head, *Broadcasting in America*, 330–32.

16. Chester, *Radio, Television and American Politics*, 37. Also see Becker and Lower, "Broadcasting in Presidential Campaigns," 35.

17. Chester, *Radio, Television and American Politics*, 42.

18. An excellent description of this debate can be found in Robert F. Ray, "Thomas E. Dewey: The Great Oregon Debate of 1948," in *American Public Address: Studies in Honor of Albert Craig Baird*, ed. Loren Reid, 245–70 (Columbia: University of Missouri Press, 1961).

19. Lee M. Mitchell, *With the Nation Watching* (Lexington, Mass.: Heath, 1979), 28, claims that Moody made his suggestion while being interviewed on the CBS radio network show *The People's Platform* in July 1952. J. Leonard Reinsch, a media consultant to Presidents Roosevelt and Truman, also made an early effort to get Stevenson and Eisenhower to debate. See Goodwin Berquist, "The 1976 Carter–Ford Presidential Debates," in *Rhetorical Studies of National Political Debates: 1960–1988*, ed. Robert V. Friedenberg, 29 (New York: Praeger, 1990).

20. In 1952, neither man felt comfortable with the idea of televised debates. Both candidates were also advised not to debate.

21. Mitchell, *With the Nation Watching*, 30.

22. Chester, *Radio, Television and American Politics*, 133–35, provides a brief account of the stimulus that the 1960 presidential debates had on political debating.

23. For a complete and far more thorough account of this change in the equal time provisions, see Terry and Kraus, "Legal and Political Aspects," 41–49.

24. This section is based primarily on two articles by Robert Friedenberg. Full citations for all quoted material and fuller explanations of all major points can be found in those two articles. See Robert V. Friedenberg, "'We Are Present Here Today for the Purpose of Having a Joint Discussion': The Conditions Requisite for Political Debates," *Journal of the American Forensic Association* 16 (Summer 1979): 1–9; Robert V. Friedenberg, "'Selfish Interest,' or the Prerequisites for Political Debate: An Analysis of the 1980 Presidential Debate and Its Implications for Future Campaigns," *Journal of the American Forensic Association* 18 (Fall 1981): 91–98.

25. Reagan's 1984 advisers have been quoted as claiming that "they did not think it would be politically acceptable" for the president to refuse to debate. Apparently well in command of the election, Reagan and his strategists nevertheless evidently feared the negative reaction his refusal to debate might prompt. See J. Jeffery Auer, "Presidential Debates: Public Understanding and Political Institutionalization," *Speaker and Gavel* 24 (Fall 1986): 5; Auer cites a conversation between Reagan advisers and reporter Elizabeth Drew. Similarly, see Craig Allen Smith and Kathy B. Smith, "The 1984 Reagan–Mondale Presidential Debates," in *Rhetorical Studies of National Political Debates: 1960–1988*, ed. Friedenberg, 96.

26. On the evolution of public attitudes toward incumbent presidential debating, see Robert V. Friedenberg, "Patterns and Trends in National Political Debates: 1960–1996," in *Rhetorical Studies of National Political Debates*, ed. Robert V. Friedenberg, 62–64 (New York: Praeger, 1998).

27. The following account of the 1960 debates is based primarily on Theodore White, *The Making of the President: 1960* (New York: Pocket Books, 1961); Kenneth P. O'Donnell and David F. Powers, *Johnny, We Hardly Knew Ye* (New York: Pocket Books, 1973); and Friedenberg, "Conditions for Political Debates."

28. For a more complete account of this debate, see Christopher Matthews, *Kennedy and Nixon: The Rivalry That Shaped Postwar America* (New York: Simon & Schuster, 1996), 51–53.

29. The sources used for this paragraph and throughout the remainder of this section on the 1992 debates include the appropriate sections of Peter Goldman and Tom Mathews, *Newsweek*, Election Special Edition (November/December 1992); Jack Germond and Jules Witcover, *Mad as Hell: Revolt at the Ballot Box, 1992* (New York: Warner, 1993); and the continuing campaign coverage of the *New York Times*, the *Washington Post*, and the *Cincinnati Enquirer* for September and October 1992.

30. Commission on Presidential Debates, "Commission on Presidential Debates' Nonpartisan Candidate Selection Criteria for 2004 General Election Debate Participation," retrieved February 23, 2004, at www.debates.org/pages/candsel2004.html.

31. Cable News Network, "Kerry Accepts Proposed Debate Schedule," found at www.cnn.com/2004/ALL POLITICS/07/15/prez.debate.

32. Mary Dalrymple, "Kerry Challenges Bush to Weekly Debates." This Associate Press story was retrieved online on August 26, 2004, at news.yahoo.com/news/?tmpl=story&u=/ap20040826/ap_onel_pr/kerry-18.

33. For a copy of the full memorandum of understanding see "Bush–Cheney/Kerry–Edwards Campaigns, Memorandum of Understanding, 2004," which can be found at www.gwu.edu/~action/2004/deb04main/deb09204st.ht.

34. The commission has frequently been criticized by those who feel that their criteria for participation are designed to deliberately rule out third-party candidates. For an insightfully critical examination of the policies developed by the Commission on Presidential Debates see George Farah, *No Debate: How the Republican and Democratic Parties Secretly Control the Presidential Debates* (New York: Seven Stories Press, 2004).

35. Goodwin F. Berquist and James L. Golden, "Media Rhetoric, Criticism, and the Public Perception of the 1980 Presidential Debates, *Quarterly Journal of Speech* 67 (May 1981): 125–26.

36. Berquist and Golden, "Media Rhetoric," 127–28.

37. Gore 2000, "Bush Debate Duck," found daily throughout the spring of 2000 at www.algore2000.com.

38. Howard Kurtz, "Leaks, Rats and Blackberries," *Washington Post*, December 17, 2000, C1.

39. The quotations from McAuliffe and Bartlett found in this paragraph are drawn from Deb Riechmann, "Campaigns Aim to Lower Debate Expectations." This Associated Press story was retrieved on September 28, 2004 at apnews.myway.com/article/20040927/d85c07j00.html.

40. One of the authors, Friedenberg, has been involved in a variety of political debates. Also see for examples Dale Hardy-Short, "An Insider's View of the Constraints Affecting Geraldine Ferraro's Preparation for the 1984 Vice Presidential Debate," *Speaker and Gavel* 24 (Fall 1986): 8–22; Myles Martel, "Debate Preparations in the Reagan Camp: An Insider's View," *Speaker and Gavel* 18 (Winter 1981): 34–46; Martin Schram, *Running for President* (New York: Pocket Books, 1977), 326–31, 348–64, 370–89; Caddell, "Memo of October 21, 1980," 410–39; White, *Making of the President 1960*, 335–55; Theodore Otto Windt, "The 1960 Kennedy–Nixon Presidential Debates," in *Rhetorical Studies of National Political Debates: 1960–1988*, ed. Friedenberg, 9–10; and Judith S. Trent, "The 1984 Bush–Ferraro Vice

Presidential Debate," also in *Rhetorical Studies of National Political Debates: 1960–1988*, ed. Friedenberg, 135–36.

41. By all accounts, Ronald Reagan's preparation for his 1980 debates with John Anderson and Jimmy Carter was the most thorough in this regard. Reagan practiced in a garage converted to resemble the actual television studios used in the debates. His staff went to great lengths to simulate and anticipate his opponents, including studying tapes of prior debates involving Anderson and Carter. Eventually David Stockman, a former administrative assistant to John Anderson, based in large part on his study of tapes, played both Anderson and Carter in Reagan's practices. The 1980s proliferation of candidate forums and candidate debates during the primary season has meant that by the general election, at least at the presidential level, candidates have been in a variety of debates or debate-like situations, and an opponent will normally have access to tapes of their prior performances.

42. See the sections on preparation in Kathleen Kendall, "The 1996 Clinton–Dole Debates: Through Media Eyes," in *Rhetorical Studies of National Political Debates: 1996*, ed. Robert V. Friedenberg (Westport, Conn.: Praeger, 1997); and Gaut Ragsdale, "The 1996 Gore–Kemp Vice Presidential Debate," in *Rhetorical Studies of National Political Debates: 1996*, ed. Friedenberg, 34. In 2000, press accounts indicated that the candidates also practiced this way. Bush and Gore both spent much of their practice time in Florida.

43. An informative account of this frequently overlooked precursor to the 1960 general election debates can be found in Goodwin F. Berquist, "The Kennedy–Humphrey Debate," *Today's Speech* 7 (September 1960): 2–3.

44. "Transcript of the First TV Debate between Bush and Dukakis," *New York Times*, September 26, 1988, A19.

45. Transcripts of the 1996 presidential and vice presidential debates can be found at www.debates.org/.

46. This and all subsequent quotes to the 2004 presidential debates are taken from the transcripts of the debates provided by the Commission on Presidential Debates through their Internet site, which can be found at www.debates.org/.

47. Robert O. Weiss, "The Presidential Debates in Their Political Context: The Issue–Image Interface in the 1980 Campaign," *Speaker and Gavel* 18 (Winter 1981): 22–27.

48. Weiss, "The Presidential Debates," 22.

49. This threefold analysis of image strategies is based on Dan Nimmo's discussion of the techniques that can be used by a political figure. The terminology and definitions are Nimmo's. See Dan Nimmo, *Popular Images of Politics* (Englewood Cliffs, N.J.: Prentice Hall, 1974), 100–2.

50. These figures concerning Gore's activism and all other references and quotations to the 2000 debates are based on the transcripts of the debates provided by the Commission on Presidential Debates through its website: www.debates.org/index.html.

51. Quoted passages from the 1980 presidential debate are taken from the NBC-verified transcript record of the debate found in Richard Harwood, ed., *The Pursuit of the Presidency 1980* (New York: Berkley, 1980), 359–400.

52. Frederick T. Steeper, "Public Response to Gerald Ford's Statements on Eastern Europe in the Second Debate," in *The Presidential Debates: Media, Electoral and Policy Perspectives*, ed. George F. Bishop, Robert G. Meadow, and Marilyn Jackson-Beeck (New York: Praeger, 1978), 101.

53. Steeper, "Public Response." Also see Roger Desmond and Thomas Donohue, "The Role of the 1976 Televised Presidential Debates in the Political Socialization of Adolescents," *Communication Quarterly* 29 (Fall 1981): 306–8; and George A. Barnett, "A Multidimensional Analysis of the 1976 Presidential Campaign," *Communication Quarterly* 29 (Summer 1981): 156–65.

54. Thomas Ferrano, "Gore Buoyed by Polls, Raises Fists in Victory," found at Excite News.com., October 4, 2000. This Reuters news service story is not archived by Excite News or Reuters, but a hard copy is available from the authors. Also see Will Lester, "Gore Fares

Better in 3 of 4 Polls," which ran on the Associated Press Wire, October 4, 2000. The Associated Press does not archive old stories. A hard copy is available from the authors.

55. See, for example, Dan Balz and Terry Neal, "Gore and Bush Clash Sharply on Policy Issues," *Washington Post*, October 4, 2000, A-1.

56. Gore claimed to have visited Texas to help with federal emergency relief efforts after a series of severe brushfires. In fact, though he had visited Texas after weather-related emergencies, he had not visited on this occasion. He used as an example of a crowded and poorly equipped high school a school that was not crowded and among the best equipped in the state of Florida. More seriously, he claimed that a Bush recommendation on getting Russia involved in Kosovo was terribly risky, when in fact that was precisely the policy that President Clinton and Secretary of State Madeline Albright were attempting to follow.

57. Thomas and Newsweek's Special Projects Team, "The Inside Story," 103–4. Also see Dowd's remarks made after the campaign in Kathleen Hall Jamieson and Paul Waldman, *Electing the President, 2000: The Insider's View* (Philadelphia: University of Pennsylvania Press, 2001), 22–23.

58. Thomas and Newsweek's Special Projects Team, "The Inside Story," 104.

59. Chris Suellentrop, "Scenes from Spin Alley," found at politics.slate.msn.com/toolbar .aspx?action=print&id=2107516. Suellentrop is the deputy Washington bureau chief for the Internet magazine *Slate*.

60. Steven Brydon's study suggests that the networks were becoming sensitive to being "used" in this fashion by as early as 1988. Hence, in recent elections, the networks have relied more heavily on their own news staffs and political or debate consultants for analysis. See Steven R. Brydon, "Spinners on Patrol: Network Coverage in the Aftermath of Presidential and Vice Presidential Debates," paper presented to the Speech Communication Association Convention, November 1989.

61. Thomas and Newsweek's Special Projects Team, "The Inside Story," 103.

62. Cited in Harry P. Kerr, "The Great Debates in a New Perspective," *Today's Speech* 9 (November 1961): 11.

63. Susan A. Helleg and Steven L. Phillips, "A Verbal and Visual Analysis of the 1980 Houston Republican Presidential Primary Debate," *Southern Speech Communication Journal* 47 (Fall 1981): 24.

64. John P. Robinson, "The Polls," in *The Great Debates: Carter vs. Ford, 1976*, ed. Kraus, 262–63.

65. These figures are drawn from the history section of the Commission on Presidential Debates Internet site, www.debates.org/pages/his_2000.html.

66. The figures used in this paragraph are drawn from the history section of the Commission on Presidential Debates Internet site, www.debates.org/pages/his_2004.html.

67. One of the more ominous signs for not only debate audiences, but political participation of all types, was made evident immediately prior to the 2000 debates, when a Pew Research Center poll found that over half of those surveyed over age sixty-five were very likely to watch the debate. In contrast, only about one-third of those aged eighteen to twenty-nine reported that they were very likely to watch the debate. See Howard Kurtz, "Despite Close Race, Many Uninterested in Debates," *Washington Post*, October 3, 2000, A10.

68. Bruce is quoted in Kitty Bruce, *The Almost Unpublished Lenny Bruce* (Philadelphia: Running Press, 1984), 91.

69. "'The Silent Vote': The Debates," *Newsweek*, October 17, 1960, 27.

70. George Gallup Jr., "The Impact of Presidential Debates on the Vote and Turnout," in *Presidential Debates: 1988 and Beyond*, ed. Joel L. Swerdlow, 34 (Washington, D.C.: Congressional Quarterly, 1987).

71. For example, the debates seemed to have very slight effect in 1996. Typical of many polls were the findings of the Gallup organization, which had conducted polls for several

media outlets. Gallup found that, during the week prior to the first debate, Clinton was favored by 52.42 percent of the voters. In the week after the last debate, Clinton was favored by 52.71 percent of the voters. In the week prior to the debates, Dole was favored by 36.85 percent of the voters. In the week after the debates, Dole was favored by 34.14 percent. See "Daily Tracking Poll," retrieved on November 1, 1996, at www.usatoday.com/elect/eq/eq/127.html. The Gallup figures are highly consistent with those of other polling groups. See, for example, the results of the ABC News Poll, "The Data," accessed November 1, 1996, at www.politicsnow.com/news/Oct96/31/abc1031data/.

72. These figures are the consensus figures used by RealClear Politics, a widely quoted Internet site. RealClear Politics utilizes all of the major public opinion polls and averages them to arrive at their consensus figure. Though their statistical procedures are not perfect, the RealClear Politics consensus figures involve far more polls and samples than other sources and hence were often relied upon by both the press and political professionals in 2004. See "RealClear Politics Poll Average," retrieved on September 30, 2004, from RealClear Politics at www.realclearpolitics.com/polls.html, and "RealClear Politics Poll Average," retrieved on October 13, 2004 from RealClear Politics at www.realclearpolitics.com/bushvskerry.html.

73. David O. Sears and Steven H. Chaffee, "Uses and Effects of the 1976 Debates: An Overview of Empirical Studies," in *The Great Debates: Carter vs. Ford, 1976*, ed. Kraus, 255.

74. Elmo Roper, "Polling Post-Mortem," *Saturday Review* (November 1960): 10–13.

75. Elihu Katz and Jacob Feldman, "The Debates in Light of Research: A Survey of Surveys," in *The Great Debates: Kennedy vs. Nixon, 1960*, ed. Kraus, 211.

76. Jack M. McLeod et al., "Reactions of Young and Older Voters: Expanding the Context of Effects," in *The Great Debates: Carter vs. Ford, 1976*, ed. Kraus, 365–66; Paul R. Hagner and Leroy N. Rieselbach, "The Impact of the 1976 Presidential Debates: Conversion or Reinforcement?" in *The Presidential Debates*, ed. Bishop et al., 178.

77. David Leuthold and David Valentine, "How Reagan Won the Cleveland Debate: Audience Predispositions and Presidential Debate Winners," *Speaker and Gavel* 18 (Winter 1981): 60–66.

78. Smith and Smith, "The 1984 Reagan–Mondale Presidential Debates," 102.

79. See "Daily Tracking Poll," and "The Data."

80. Jamieson and Waldman, *Electing the President 2000*, 5, 75.

81. Maxwell McCombs, "Agenda Setting Research: A Bibliographic Essay," *Political Communication Review* 1 (Summer 1976): 3.

82. Linda L. Swanson and David L. Swanson, "The Agenda Setting Function of the First Ford–Carter Debate," *Communication Monographs* 45 (November 1978): 347–53.

83. Swanson and Swanson, "The Agenda Setting Function," 353.

84. Swanson and Swanson, "The Agenda Setting Function," 353.

85. This is one of many indictments of the current system of presidential debates leveled by George Farah. On agenda setting in the debates see Farah, *No Debate*, 125–39.

86. Lee B. Becker et al., "Debates' Effects on Voter Understanding of Candidates and Issues," in *The Presidential Debates*, ed. Bishop et al., 137–38; Steven H. Chaffee, "Presidential Debates—Are They Helpful to Voters?" *Communication Monographs* 45 (November 1978): 336; Jian Huazhu, J. Ronald Milawsky, and Rahul Biswas, "Do Televised Debates Affect Image Perception More Than Issue Knowledge? A Study of the First 1992 Presidential Debate," *Human Communication Research* 20 (March 1994): 302–32.

87. Allen Lichtenstein, "Differences in Impact between Local and National Televised Political Candidates' Debates," *Western Journal of Speech Communication* 46 (Summer 1982): 296.

88. Pfau, "Criteria and Format," 5–6.

89. Soma Golden, "Inside the Debate," *New York Times*, September 24, 1980, A30.

90. For an examination of the differing agendas of voters, reporters, and candidates, see Marilyn Jacson-Beeck and Robert Meadow, "The Triple Agenda of Presidential Debates," *Public Opinion Quarterly* 42 (Summer 1979): 173–80.

91. Ryan, "The 1988 Bush–Dukakis Presidential Debates," 160.

92. Windt, "The 1960 Kennedy–Nixon Presidential Debates," 4.

93. The examples and numbers used in this paragraph are based on analysis of the text of the 2004 debates. For a more extensive elaboration of the entire problem of issue exclusion, see George Farah, *No Debate*, 125–39.

94. Hagner and Rieselbach, "Impact of 1976 Presidential Debates," 172.

95. Sears and Chaffee, "Uses and Effects of 1976 Debates," 246–47.

96. Kevin Sauter, "The 1976 Mondale–Dole Vice Presidential Debate," in *Rhetorical Studies of National Political Debates: 1960–1988*, ed. Friedenberg, 45–68.

97. These characterizations are representative of a wide variety of press reactions cited in L. Patrick Devlin, "The 1992 Gore–Quayle–Stockdale Vice Presidential Debate," in *Rhetorical Studies of National Political Debates: 1960–1992*, ed. Friedenberg, 229–30.

98. On the slight surge in Bush's standing after the second and third debates, see the discussion on the reinforcing effects of political debates.

99. Dan Hahn, "The 1992 Clinton–Bush–Perot Presidential Debate," in *Rhetorical Studies of National Political Debates: 1960–1992*, ed. Friedenberg, 208.

100. Sidney Kraus and Dennis Davis, "Political Debates," in *Handbook of Political Communication*, ed. Dan Nimmo and Keith Sanders (Beverly Hills, Calif.: Sage, 1981), 273–98.

101. Samuel L. Becker et al., "Information Flow and the Shaping of Meanings," in *The Great Debates: Carter vs. Ford, 1976*, ed. Kraus, 396.

102. Chaffee, "Presidential Debates," 343–45.

103. Kraus, *Televised Presidential Debates and Public Policy*, 123.

9

~

Interpersonal Communication in Political Campaigns

This chapter examines the place of interpersonal communication in political campaigns. We perceive interpersonal communication to be transactional. When people communicate, they define themselves and simultaneously respond to their perceptions of the definitions being offered by others. This transactional perspective, which we share with most communication scholars, has several implications that have unusual importance for political communication.

First, interpersonal communication is contextual. Part of the context in which any communication takes place is the other person. You behave differently when you are with your parents than when you are with your employer. Each participant affects the other. Similarly, candidates behave differently when they visit with small groups of bowlers in neighborhood bowling alleys than when they visit with a few large financial contributors in someone's home. The physical setting of the two transactions, the differences in background music and noise, the differences in clothing worn by the bowlers and the contributors, the differences in the language used by the two groups, and countless other stimuli help define the bowlers and the contributors to the candidate. Simultaneously, the presence of the candidate in the bowling alley or at a contributor's home, the clothing and language of the candidate, and countless other stimuli that the candidate emits enable the bowlers and the contributors to define the candidate. As each party to the transaction shapes and refines definitions of the other, their own behavior will be affected, thus continually changing the communication context.

Second, this perspective suggests that each party to the transaction is simultaneously both a sender and a receiver of verbal and nonverbal messages. When you meet the candidate at a neighborhood coffee and criticize a local bond issue that the candidate supports, you are simultaneously watching facial expressions, observing the tightening of the candidate's fist, and noting that the candidate's face is becoming flush. As candidates emit these communicative stimuli, they are defining themselves to you. You sense better that candidate's support for this bond issue and the irritation your criticism provokes, even though that candidate may have said nothing.

Clearly, as you observe candidates listening to your criticism, they appear affected by your statements. Similarly, as you see the candidate's face flush and fist tighten, you begin to temper your criticism. You gradually lower your voice and use more moderate language. You have been affected by this communication transaction, and so has the candidate. This is the third major implication that the transactional perspective has for political communication; that is, each participant affects and is affected by the other.

In addition to noting our transactional perspective, before beginning our discussion of interpersonal communication and political campaigning, we want to note two other characteristics of the interpersonal communication studied in this chapter. They deliberately narrow the expanse of interpersonal communication, limiting it to interpersonal communication utilized in political campaigns. First, one party to the interpersonal transactions discussed in this chapter is either a candidate or the surrogate/advocate of a candidate. The surrogate/advocate may be a formal representative of the candidate, such as a member of the campaign staff, or an informal representative, such as a voter who is not in any way affiliated with the candidate but nevertheless discusses the candidate. The final characteristic of the interpersonal transactions examined is that the overt, normally verbal, messages either directly or indirectly involve a campaign for public office.

In this chapter, we discuss crucial areas of interpersonal communication in political campaigns: interpersonal communication between the candidate and voters, interpersonal communication between the candidate and potential financial contributors, interpersonal communication between voters, interpersonal communication and the Get Out The Vote effort of campaigns, and finally, behavioral characteristics of successful interpersonal campaigners.[1]

INTERPERSONAL COMMUNICATION
BETWEEN CANDIDATES AND VOTERS

As indicated in chapter 5, no resource is more vital to the campaign than the candidate's time. This is a finite resource. Once the time is lost, it cannot be replaced. Consequently, if candidates are spending time meeting individuals or small groups of individuals, they must be sure that there is an unusually high chance that these meetings will be productive. For candidates to spend an hour or more with two, four, or ten people and come away with nothing is a loss that cannot be recovered. More money cannot buy lost time, nor can more volunteers produce it. Hence, decisions on where candidates should spend time and with whom they should meet are critical.

The use of the candidate's time is especially critical in local campaigns. Over half a million public offices are filled by election.[2] Lynda Lee Kaid points out that the tendency of researchers to study highly visible national and statewide campaigns has caused us often to neglect what is the most effective channel of political persuasion in vast numbers of races—the interpersonal communication of the candidate.[3] As Kaid notes, the channels of communication available to the candidates in thousands of campaigns below the national and statewide levels are often severely limited.

In many campaigns, the geographic makeup of the district precludes the effective use of mass media such as radio and television. For example, the Eighth Congressional District of Ohio, located between Cincinnati and Dayton, includes about ninety-five thousand residents of suburban Cincinnati. It also includes Hamilton (a city of eighty thousand); Middletown (a city of sixty thousand); all of Preble County (a prosperous agricultural county with no town over twenty-five thousand); and parts of Darke, Green, and Montgomery Counties, including portions of suburban Dayton. To use traditional broadcast television effectively in this district, the candidate would have to purchase time on both Dayton and Cincinnati stations. Yet the approximately 70 percent of the district receiving Cincinnati television constitutes less than 20 percent of the Cincinnati media market. The remaining 30 percent of this district, within the Dayton media market, constitutes less than 10 percent of the Dayton media market. To cover this district adequately with broadcast television, candidates would have to pay for an audience approximately ten times larger than the one they want. Similarly, to pay for other mass media such as radio and newspapers may not be cost-effective either. As discussed in chapter 10, in recent elections the growth of cable television has facilitated the use of television in some districts such as these. Nevertheless, this is a congressional district where mass media is often not cost-efficient.

Moreover, within this single congressional district, there are hundreds of other elected public officials: county commissioners in Butler, Preble, Darke, Green, Hamilton, and Montgomery Counties; county prosecutors, treasurers, sheriffs, and the like, in each county; and city council members, mayors, and a variety of other officials in at least forty communities. The point should be abundantly clear: Geographic and financial considerations make television, radio, and other mass media at best extremely costly and at worst simply impractical for hundreds of races in this area alone and for hundreds of thousands of races nationally. The targeting provided by mass media is often simply not narrow enough for many lower-ballot races. Additionally, messages on behalf of most local candidates, delivered through the mass media, are liable to be ignored or ineffective when those media are saturated with information concerning many major candidates running for federal and state offices. Although it may not be as widely appropriate as when she first wrote, Kaid's conclusion that "the interplay of some or all of these limitations may create an environment in which interpersonal communication, particularly communication between the candidate and the voters, may be a crucial factor in the outcome of an election"[4] is still true for many races, particularly those for lesser offices and those in rural areas.

Given the importance of the candidate's time and given that in many races its waste cannot be offset by purchasing media time, it is essential that the candidate's interpersonal communication be utilized effectively.[5] This means that candidates must know where to campaign. Consequently, in local races especially, the most valuable materials that a campaign can have are often the precinct analysis of recent voter statistics, such as those illustrated in chapter 6. The thoroughness of such analysis is a direct function of the amounts of money spent on obtaining them. In most states, party organizations will prepare voter statistics for candidates. Hence, even in areas where the local organization is weak, candidates should not have trouble obtaining a complete analysis of prior voting statistics for their district. Moreover, if the various party organizations do not provide an analysis of statistics, candidates can obtain the statistics themselves and perform their own analysis, as all vote totals are a matter of public record and kept on file by the appropriate election boards.

Once they have access to prior election results, particularly a precinct-by-precinct analysis, candidates can determine which precincts are essentially Republican, Democratic, or marked by a high incidence of ticket splitting. As we observed in chapter 6, the candidates should direct the campaign primarily at those precincts where the party traditionally runs well and those precincts where ticket splitting commonly takes place. It is in these precincts that most of the candidate's interpersonal communication should take place.

Far more than national figures, local candidates must know precisely where to spend their time. Because their constituencies are smaller, in many instances local candidates can knock on every door in their district or at least on every door in those precincts that are deemed most important. The door-to-door campaigning of candidates for major offices is most often done for media coverage, rather than for any direct impact. It allows the major candidate to appear in the media while walking through a barrio or a cornfield, presumably illustrating concern for Hispanics or farmers. Local candidates will not receive media exposure of their door-to-door campaigning. Rather, their efforts will put them face-to-face with a large percentage of their constituency. Interpersonal campaigning is not symbolic for the local candidate, as it is for the major candidate. Rather, it is often the major thrust of the campaign, an essential means of compensating for the lack of media exposure.

It is often difficult for an inexperienced candidate or campaign staff to recognize the critical importance of targeting voters, even in interpersonal campaigning. Candidates and campaign staffs are frequently tempted to meet the most people, not necessarily targeted people. But just as duck hunters must go where the ducks are, regardless of where the deer or the turkeys may be, so too, candidates must go to where their targeted voters are, not simply where there are a lot of people. Candidates for lower-ballot races especially will often want to campaign at the county fair, the Little League game, the municipal pool, the factory gate, or the busy intersection. Typically, the people whom the candidate may meet in these situations are often not those targeted by the campaign. Indeed, a good deal of the candidate's precious time might well be wasted dealing with people who are not even registered to vote or not registered in their district. The candidate's interpersonal communication should always be targeted to potential voters and supporters. If this allows the campaign to utilize the candidate or other affiliated spokespersons at the factory gate or the busy street corner, fine. But campaigns, particularly local campaigns, must keep in mind that their interpersonal communication efforts must be aimed not at communicating with the most voters but rather at communicating with *targeted* voters.[6]

Though major candidates do not rely as extensively on interpersonal campaigning as do local candidates, it does often serve an important place in their campaigns. Clearly, because of the size of the constituency, major candidates, as well as many local candidates, will utilize surrogates/advocates to represent them in door-to-door canvasses of a community. The door-to-door canvass is often especially effective in the primary campaigns of major candidates. Such races typically involve substantially fewer voters than the general election. Candidates and their representatives can often reach a high percentage of those voters who are eligible to vote in the primary. George McGovern's effective use of the principles of interpersonal communication in door-to-door canvassing in small state primaries that occurred early in 1972, such as New Hampshire, Massachusetts, and Rhode Island, played a substantial role in his success that year. It has been emulated, with changes often driven by technology, in every primary season since.[7]

The most typical methods of interpersonal campaigning by candidates or their representatives are coffees and door-to-door canvasses. Each method allows the candidates or their representatives to interact for brief periods of time with a smaller number of voters. Done repeatedly, they may serve as an effective means of supplementing media campaigning or, as in the case of many local candidates, almost entirely replacing it.

The Coffee

Keeping in mind the precinct analysis of voters, the campaign organization will arrange a schedule of coffees. The events can be as casual or formal as the hosts wish. Some hosts will keep it very informal, serving coffee, tea, soft drinks, perhaps beer. If, as might happen on occasion, the event is also to serve as a fund-raiser, the refreshments will typically be somewhat more elaborate. But these details are for hosts/hostesses to arrange. Once they have agreed to host the event, the campaign may provide them guidance, but it is, after all, their party for the candidate.[8]

The organization should arrange the coffees so that the candidate is able to meet with two groups. First, the candidate should meet with "those people residing in areas which are generally independent" and in which considerable ticket splitting takes place. Second, "coffees should be scheduled in areas where the candidate and his [or her] party can be expected to run well."[9] In these areas, coffees give "the candidate an opportunity to pay personal attention to those who are working for him [or her, and] it gives the campaign organization an opportunity to recruit new workers."

Keeping in mind our transactional viewpoint of interpersonal communication, we can readily see why campaigners seek to hold coffees and similar events that promote interpersonal transactions with neutral and friendly voters. Such events provide the candidate with much more than the opportunity simply to meet voters. They offer an opportunity to establish a relationship, to affect the other parties in the transaction.

In virtually any election, but perhaps more so in local elections, candidates will often meet constituents in countless small social gatherings early in the campaign. They can then follow up on the relationships initiated at these meetings by remaining in contact with short notes, letters, calls, or e-mail. People are affected by the candidates they meet this way, and subsequently those people often prove helpful to the candidates.

Conversely, candidates are also affected by interpersonal transactions such as coffees. As we have seen in chapter 2, promises made during the surfacing and primary stages of a campaign tend to be kept more than those made later. Part of the reason for this seems to be that promises made early in the campaign are frequently made in small interpersonal contexts, where the candidate is more prone to be affected by voters. Later in the campaign, crowded candidate schedules often prohibit the types of interpersonal transactions that frequently take place early in the campaign.

Candidates "should never attend" coffees by themselves. They should always have another person with them. The function of this other individual is to get the candidate away from the coffee gracefully if the host/hostess fails to do so. The candidate's associate, not the candidate or the host/hostess, can take the blame for rushing the candidate away if that becomes necessary. The candidates should avoid making speeches at coffees. Rather, a candidate "need give only brief informal remarks." After the candidate's brief remarks, a short question-and-answer period is appropriate.

Four rules should govern every coffee. First, "optimum size of the gathering is twenty to thirty people." This includes the host and hostess, candidate, and those traveling with the candidate. Second, name tags should be provided for each guest. The affair is essentially social, and the candidate wants to establish a first-name relationship with the guests. One consultant who has been involved in arranging a large number of meetings of this sort advises candidates to "obtain a list of the attendees prior to the event and become familiar with your audience."[10] The individual traveling with the candidate might also help in this regard. Third, the host or hostess should "never permit a guest to buttonhole the candidate or enter into arguments." Finally, it should always be remembered that the coffee "is an excuse for getting together, and the stress should be on easy informality and comfort."

This description of an ideal coffee clearly indicates that the simple act of being present and interacting with a number of voters is as important, if not more so, as what the candidate actually says. A well-run coffee maximizes the opportunities for fruitful interpersonal transactions. Time is devoted to establishing personal friendships. The group is small enough for the candidate to interact with everyone, and the candidate's aide as well as the host/hostess of the coffee should facilitate the candidate's interaction with everyone.

Laura Peck, vice president of a large political consulting firm, says that, in situations such as these, eye contact is essential. She tells candidates, "Give your full attention, even if for just a few seconds, to the person in front of you. If someone is anxious to meet you, you will feel positively encouraged and reinforced. Once the connection is sealed, you can then move on."[11]

Peck also stresses the importance of handshakes. She claims "with a handshake, you touch your audience physically for the first time. This tactile presentation will be remembered." She adds that "if you wish to make the connection especially heart-felt, place your other hand on top of the handshake."[12]

Local candidates often run for administrative positions that do not involve issues of policy. The county recorder, engineer, prosecutor, and sheriff, for example, provide administrative service, but they rarely set policy. Hence, interpersonal communication opportunities, where candidates can establish relationships illustrating their concern, personality, and character, are vital. Given that many local races lack real issues between the candidates and that the candidates are relatively unknown, often the candidates who are best known in the district, who have visited the neighborhoods, who seem to make themselves available and accessible, and who have worked at establishing relationships are the candidates who most appeal to the voter.

Good campaigns can effectively arrange three coffees an evening for their candidate, several evenings a week, through the last months of the campaign. Such programs, particularly in local races, enable candidates to interact with a significant percentage of their constituency. Moreover, the candidate's presence in the neighborhood will be rapidly reported the next day over backyard fences, in beauty and barber shops, markets and restaurants, as those invited to the coffee discuss their experience.

Major candidates will not be able to devote several evenings a week to a program of campaign coffees. But, thanks to technology, major candidates can approximate the effect of such a program. During the 2004 campaign all of the major presidential candidates attempted to do so. Typical was the "Parties for the President" program. These small personal gatherings were a basic staple of the president's reelection campaign in such states as Ohio.[13] People went online and signed up to host a party. They were sent a packet of supplies for the party. Included in the packet were personal postcards that guests filled out and mailed to unregistered neighbors. The parties helped the president's campaign recruit voters and new workers. They were often conducted like a coffee, with light refreshments, name tags, and a considerable amount of talk, both political and neighborly. The parties culminated with a conference call, where all of the many parties being hosted simultaneously across the country heard from a distinguished guest such as Vice President Cheney, First Lady Laura Bush, or the president. Though the contact was not interpersonal, as is the case with a lower ballot candidate and a coffee, the many parties held on behalf of major candidates in 2004 enabled campaign activists to mix with potential voters, donors, and volunteers on an interpersonal basis. It allowed prominent candidates to at least simulate an interpersonal moment with thousands of potential supporters. Among the most effective candidates at using the Internet to simulate the interpersonal moments often found in the coffees of lower-level campaigns was Vermont governor Howard Dean. His "MeetUps" were critical to the early growth of his presidential bid.[14]

Door-to-Door Canvass

The use of small social gatherings, such as coffees, serves primarily to foster interaction between the candidate and voters. A second major form of interpersonal communication between the candidate and voters, the door-to-door canvass, typically serves several additional purposes. Like the coffees, candidates meeting voters while doing canvasses will be perceived as accessible and concerned, leaving a positive image with the voters they meet. Presumably, the same impressions should be left with voters who meet the candidates' representatives.

The canvass can serve additional functions and is often utilized in major races, where coffees play a lesser role. When utilized in major races, most of the canvassing is done by representatives of the candidate. Regardless of who is canvassing, the canvass can identify voters who are favorable, neutral, or hostile to the candidate. Depending on their attitudes, these voters can subsequently be contacted. The canvass also is an excellent means of distributing information about the candidate. A conversation between the canvasser and the voter can provide information about the candidate. Additionally, the canvasser can leave materials, and, if the voter has a specific concern, the canvasser can arrange to have additional information sent later.[15]

If they are doing their jobs well, canvassers will follow several important principles of interpersonal communication. The instructions given to those who canvass on behalf of a candidate "will typically exhibit sensitivity to psychological principles important in interpersonal communication."[16] Instructions such as these are representative of what most campaigns will encourage:

1. Speak with enthusiasm and sincerity.
2. Be a good listener. Let the voters speak. Do not interrupt or argue.
3. Be open-minded. Whenever possible, express your agreement with the voter.
4. Family members make good surrogates. It impresses voters that the candidate's husband, wife, mother, father, or sibling came to their

door. When unrelated strangers canvass, people sometimes wonder what the canvasser is getting out of it.

5. Don't knock on doors after dark.[17]

Pennsylvania state legislator Mike Hanna adds several additional guidelines that candidates should use when they are doing the canvassing. When candidates canvass themselves, Hanna advises them to dress in normal business clothing. He observes that "people will take you seriously if you look the part of a serious candidate." Additionally, he advises that candidates always end their interaction in a canvass by "explicitly" asking for the citizen's vote. Most important, Hanna observes that, when candidates are going door-to-door, they should avoid long conversations. "Civics lessons aside," claims Hanna, "your job is not to bring voters over to your point of view. Your objective is to show yourself at their door for a brief and shining moment and leave them with an impression that you are a nice, trustworthy person and that you care."[18]

These guidelines focus primarily on the actual canvass itself. Peck adds several suggestions that campaigns might follow to prepare for the canvass. She suggests that, prior to canvassing a neighborhood, the campaign should provide advance warning by utilizing yard signs announcing the impending canvass or sending out a mailing that lets voters know that the candidate will be visiting their neighborhood. Similarly, she recommends that candidates might ask neighborhood residents to accompany them on canvasses and brief them on the neighborhood in which the canvass is taking place.[19] Peck also suggests that the neighborhood canvass might be made into a memorable neighborhood event by creating a miniparade. As the candidate canvasses door to door, one or more campaign vehicles with signs can accompany the candidate down the street, and several campaign volunteers wearing campaign shirts could also be on the street.[20]

Canvassers who follow instructions such as these can accomplish much. They can leave literature, determine voting intentions, or question for other information that the campaign desires.[21] Additionally, when done by well-prepared canvassers, particularly the candidate and members of the candidate's family, the door-to-door canvass leaves voters with a positive feeling about the candidate that will not be readily forgotten.

In sum, interpersonal communication between the candidate and the voter is, for most people, a unique event. The details of the coffee or the door-to-door canvass meeting will no doubt fade from an individual's memory, but the fact that the candidate cared enough to come to the neighborhood or send a representative or family member and followed up the initial coffee or canvass will often remain and loom far larger in the voter's mind than the specifics of what may have been said.

The Internet

Campaigns in recent years have made growing use of the Internet. Though the Internet is clearly not interpersonal campaigning, in some respects it approximates interpersonal campaigning to a greater degree than any other media. The characteristic that most distinguishes the Internet from other mass media and makes it most analogous to interpersonal exchanges is the fact that both parties can be sources-receivers of messages. The print, radio, and television media are media that facilitate one-way communication. Candidates and their staffs send messages to audiences who receive those messages. But the Internet allows audience members to respond. It is this characteristic, the fact that both parties can be senders and receivers of messages, that makes the Internet analogous to interpersonal communication. Hence, in this section, though we acknowledge that the Internet is not interpersonal communication, it is appropriate to discuss it as a medium that facilitates a sense of interpersonal communication between candidate and voter.

In the chapter on advertising, the Internet is treated as an advertising medium. In this section, we wish to consider it as an interpersonal medium. One of the primary differences between the Internet and other forms of media is the level of candidate involvement.[22] To voters, the Internet seems to offer an opportunity to interact directly with candidates and their principal advisers. Primarily through e-mail, voters can provide feedback to candidates. Other media do not offer this opportunity, which is more characteristic of interpersonal communication. However, as Laura Woolsey has observed, radio and television often involve candidates themselves communicating through the media. Hence, candidates using them should have some level of proficiency in using these media.[23] However, the Internet, like the print media, is primarily a text- and graphics-based medium that requires only that someone controls a candidate's site. Hence, the candidate is not required to use the Internet effectively.

Nevertheless, candidates have attempted to utilize the Internet in such a fashion as to appear to be communicating directly with voters. The principal means that candidates have developed for this purpose are e-mail newsletters and responding to e-mail. Campaigns utilizing e-mail newsletters typically offer the visitor to the campaign website an invitation to sign up to receive the e-mail newsletter on the home page of their website. Once voters leave their address, the campaign can send an introductory e-mail. It should be brief but simulate the remarks the candidate would make when first meeting a voter during a canvass or coffee. For example, visitors to Senator Hillary Clinton's Senate Campaign website in 2000 who signed up to receive her e-mail newsletter automatically received the following initial greeting: "I'm so pleased to know you are keeping up with our committee by e-mail. As I travel through New York listening to New Yorkers, I will also use this e-mail network to stay in touch and bring you news of our activities. Hillary."[24]

The first and all subsequent e-mail newsletters should be sent by the candidate or the campaign so that the candidate's name appears in the voter's in-box. The candidate's name should always appear in the in-box, not the name of a staffer or consultant. Moreover, thought should be given to the subject line of the e-mail. Just as first impressions are unusually important in interpersonal communication, so, too, the first impression created by the name of the sender and the subject line are exceedingly important when individual voters confront a mailbox full of messages.

The style of e-mail newsletters should reflect the normal conversations the candidate has with voters. The candidate's personality and background should come through in the language that is used. A candidate like George W. Bush, a lifelong baseball fan who once owned a baseball team, might occasionally be expected to talk about a program that "touches all the bases" or is a "grand slam." Additionally, the campaign should be sensitive to the reading level of the language used. Research suggests that a seventh- to eighth-grade reading level is an appropriate reading level for Internet users.[25]

Those in charge of the candidate's e-mail newsletter must decide how often to send their newsletter. Clearly, they do not want to send a newsletter too often, for it will soon prompt people to delete the newsletter before reading it. Moreover, excessive newsletters will likely provoke a negative reaction to the candidate. One way of handling this is to indicate in the first newsletter how often the voter should expect to receive them from the campaign. Campaigns will often send them once a week, or once every two weeks, or once a month. Just as you wish to talk to a good friend on a relatively regular basis, so, too, the candidate wishes to talk to voters on a relatively regular basis.[26] If the candidate makes clear how often the newsletter will be sent and provides a convenient means for voters to end their subscription, there should not be a problem with excessive newsletters.

A second way, evident in the Clinton newsletter quoted previously, is to send them when campaign events warrant a newsletter. Just as a friend might contact you with good news, a newsletter might be sent with news of a favorable poll, a prominent endorsement, or favorable press coverage. Just as a friend might notify you if she is going to be visiting your community, if the candidate's website has gathered subscriber ZIP codes, an e-mail newsletter can be sent to subscribers in communities the candidate is visiting. Just as a friend might notify you in advance if he is going to be on television, a candidate's e-mail newsletter might indicate upcoming media appearances.

Care should be given to any material that is included in an e-mail newsletter. A mistake in a print story or on radio or television may be seen by tens of thousands, hundreds of thousands, or even millions of voters. Using more conventional media, the candidate can issue a correction or an apology in the same media and be reasonably confident that most people who saw the original statement will also have an opportunity to see the correction. However, because it is easy for information to be passed along from one site to another on the Internet, there is far less guarantee that those exposed to an error on the Internet will also be exposed to the candidate's attempt to correct that error.[27] Finally, e-mail newsletters should make it convenient for recipients to unsubscribe. Just as you would not want to communicate to someone who no longer is attentive, so, too, a candidate should not bother voters with e-mail newsletters they no longer wish to receive.

In addition to newsletters, many campaigns will make use of e-mail by sending brief e-mails to voters, often asking for money or other types of support. Many of us have received unwanted e-mails, spam, from a wide variety of sources, including political figures. Congress tried to eliminate many forms of spam with the CAN-SPAM Act of 2003, which limited types of commercial e-mail. However, the act deliberately excluded political messages from its provisions. Hence, the nation's e-mailboxes likely received well in excess of a billion unsolicited political e-mails prior to the 2004 election.[28] Unlike newsletters, which voters typically request by signing up to receive them, brief unsolicited e-mail, which is often regarded by the recipient as spam, is of questionable value. By virtue of their brevity and, most importantly, the fact that the recipient has not indicated a desire to receive the message, unsolicited e-mail messages lack the interpersonal quality that an effective newsletter can create over the Internet.

INTERPERSONAL COMMUNICATION BETWEEN THE CANDIDATE AND PROSPECTIVE FINANCIAL CONTRIBUTORS

Before examining interpersonal communication designed to solicit campaign contributions, we must first answer two fundamental questions about fund-raising. First, who currently contributes to political campaigns? Second, who is likely to contribute in the future? The 2004 election was the first held under the McCain-Feingold Campaign Finance Law of 2002. That election illustrates several patterns of political giving that are likely to continue in the immediate future.

First, candidates and, to a lesser extent, political parties are raising massive amounts of money through small contributions from exceedingly large numbers of small donors. Second, big money contributions are alive and healthy in American politics, in large part as a consequence of massive contributions by limited numbers of donors to 527 groups, named after the tax code section that governs them. These patterns have implications for the interpersonal communication between candidates and prospective financial contributors.

First, political parties and the candidates themselves are raising immense sums of money through small contributions from exceedingly large numbers of donors. Democracy 21, a nonprofit, nonpartisan organization that is among the foremost observers of political financing, claims that "the most important long-term campaign finance development of the 2004 elections" was the breakthrough in Internet fundraising, which energized thousands of new small donors to political campaigns of both parties and both leading presidential candidates.[29] By April of 2004, the Republican National Committee received donations from more than a million first-time contributors during George W. Bush's first term. The average contribution was $29.80, causing former Republican National Committee Chairman Ed Gillespie to observe that during these years "our donor base has just mushroomed."[30] Similarly, the candidates vying for the Democratic nomination had stimulated a massive growth in the number of small donors to their party. Then Democratic National Committee Chairman Terry McAuliffe estimated that 70 percent of the people who gave money to the DNC during Bush's first term were first-time small contributors. Both parties experienced a dramatic increase in the number of donations under $200.[31]

Moreover, spurred largely by Internet donors, candidates themselves saw an increase in small donations. Immediately after the election, the political finance division of the Center for Responsive Politics, a nonprofit, nonpartisan research group that tracks money in politics, claimed, "the largest chunk of money in this year's elections—by far—is coming from individuals giving to federal candidates and political parties." The center estimated that these contributions, none of which could exceed $2000 with the passage of McCain-Feingold, accounted for $2.5 billion or about 63 percent of the total $4 billion spent on the 2004 presidential and congressional elections.[32] Clearly, individual donors giving relatively small amounts of money are the principle source of political financing in the country today.

Second, big money still plays a crucial role in the financing of political campaigns. The intent of the McCain-Feingold legislation of 2002 was to reduce the effect of large contributions. However, one of the unintended consequences of that legislation is that it gave rise to 527 groups. These advocacy groups, the best known of which are the Democratic groups America Coming Together and MoveOn.org Voter Fund, can accept donations of unlimited size. In 2004 they raised and spent just short of $400 million on federal elections.[33] Their contributions came in any size from anyone who wished to contribute. But because there is no limit on the contribution size, 527 groups are typically financed primarily by a highly limited number of donors, giving exceedingly large amounts of money. Indeed, $300 million of the $400 million raised by these groups came from fifty-two people. The biggest single contributors were Democratic contributors George Soros and Peter Lewis, who each gave $23 million.[34]

Most observers of American politics are concerned about the impact of 527 groups for two major reasons. First, they allow a wealthy individual to have unprecedented influence in an election. Second, in the past most advertisements were run by candidates or parties. Both candidates and parties ultimately are responsible to the public whose support they seek. Consequently, fear of offending the general public often restrained parties and candidates from their harshest, most offensive, and most negative advertisements. In contrast, 527 groups are responsible to only the person who writes the check. So they are free to be as negative as they wish. No doubt they have contributed appreciably to the harsh, uncompromising tone of contemporary politics.

The Role of PACs

Political action committees were the third principal source of money for federal elections in 2004. They contributed $384 million to political campaigns in 2004.[35] Among the major PACs are such groups as the National Rifle Association Victory Fund, EMILY's List (pro-choice Democratic women candidates), the American Federation of State County and Municipal Employees, the International Brotherhood of Electrical Workers, Committee on Political Education, the National Education Association Fund for Children and Public Education, and the Association of Trial Lawyers of America Political Action Committee.

Political action committees may make large independent expenditures on behalf of a candidate, as long as there is no contact between the PAC and the candidate's organization. Moreover, they may contribute the legally acceptable amounts to each campaign. Though PACs raise and contribute large sums of money, they often derive that money from small individual contributors. Some organizations, such as AARP, the National Education Association, and many unions, have PACs that are often financed, at least in part, out of member dues. Collectively, because of the large membership, this money can be used for large political expenditures on behalf of candidates the group supports. Though PACs often make large independent expenditures on behalf of candidates they favor, their money often comes from relatively modest donations from large numbers of people.

The Importance of Individual Contributors

As the above sections indicate, while exceedingly large political contributions by a relatively few wealthy individuals play an important role in financing political campaigns, most money comes from large numbers of smaller donations. This was true prior to the McCain-Feingold legislation of 2002 and, if anything, the patterns of giving evident in the 2004 elections suggest that smaller contributions will grow increasingly important in the future. Campaign finance legislation, and the growing use of the Internet as a means of fund-raising are both likely to continue this trend in the future. Moreover, the need for candidates to solicit money from larger and larger numbers of small contributors will no doubt increase as the cost of campaigning spirals higher and higher.

The Role of Attraction

People do not contribute to a political campaign unless they are attracted to the candidate. Political fund-raising is largely interpersonal in nature. Typically, the candidate, finance director, and members of the finance committee seek contributions from individuals they believe would be receptive to such an appeal. Similar in conception, though obviously less personal in execution, are direct mail and Internet fund-raising. Here again, the campaign seeks contributions from individuals believed to be receptive to the candidate. Invariably, the key is to determine who would be attracted to the candidate and thus receptive to financial appeals.

Students of interpersonal communication identify at least five principles of human attraction.[36] First, we are attracted to people who are in close physical proximity to us. Second, we are attracted to people who are similar to us. Third, we are attracted to people who provide us with positive feedback. Fourth, if we find ourselves in an anxiety-producing situation, we tend to have a greater need for human interaction and hence are more prone to be attracted to other people. Fifth, if we have already extended some type of supportive behavior to an individual, we are more likely to be attracted to that individual than if we had never provided such behavior. Each of these five principles of human attraction has major implications for conducting political fund-raising.

The first determinant of attraction is *proximity*. That is, all things being equal, the more closely two people are located, the more likely they are to be attracted to each other. Far too often, campaigns tend to neglect this simple fact. Rather than seek fiscal support from the most likely sources—people within the district—they seek financial support out of the district. Doing so creates two potential problems. First, and most serious, it rarely works. Just as charity begins at home, just as most of us contribute to our own United Way, our own church, our own schools and colleges, most of us will be more prone to contribute to candidates who will directly affect us.

This simple fact was illustrated by the efforts of a recent congressional candidate who was a Christian Scientist and a graduate of Principia College, the only Christian Science institution of higher education in the country. The candidate made an extensive fund-raising effort among Principia alumni. But he was running for a Missouri congressional seat and Principia is in Iowa. Additionally, as the only Christian Science school in the nation, Principia has a national flavor, attracting students from throughout the country, and its alumni have settled throughout the country. The candidate's efforts failed to produce any significant results because so few of those he contacted were located in close proximity to him and his district. Indeed, he received a number of responses indicating that some people were annoyed by his soliciting them, as they did not live in his district.

The importance of proximity is also illustrated by the guidelines both the Republican and Democratic National Committees use to determine which candidates will receive financial support. One of those guidelines is that candidates must demonstrate fund-raising ability *within* their districts. The assumption is that, if they cannot raise money among people in close proximity, they cannot raise money from anyone.[37]

The second determinant of human attraction that is of exceptional importance for political fund-raising is *similarity*. We are attracted to people who are similar to us. Potential donors should always be approached by people who are highly similar to them. A carefully selected and highly motivated fund-raising committee working through their own social networks (the people with whom they are most similar) and drawing on the candidate's presence when necessary is perhaps the most effective means of utilizing the concept of similarity. The key to a successful interpersonal fund-raising effort is in the selection of the individuals who will head the fund-raising effort by endorsing the candidate and seeking contributions for the candidates from their friends and associates. Political consultant Cathy Allen calls the use of these interpersonal fund-raising networks "peer pressure politics" and observes that, in selecting key fund-raisers, candidates must remember that they "are soliciting an endorsement which will translate into thousands of dollars in contributions from the endorser's peers."

She observes that the key fund-raiser in each group (Lawyers for Smith, Nurses for Smith, Environmentalists for Smith, etc.) should be a highly credible and influential member of the group—someone, in other words, whom group members will perceive favorably in large part because of their similarity.[38] If the candidate selects good fund-raisers, each new fund-raiser in a congressional race should produce $5,000 to $15,000 from her colleagues, family, and friends.[39]

When the candidate is making the solicitation calls, the principle of similarity is still critical. Allen suggests that, immediately after establishing rapport, candidates who are phoning for contributions should explain what they have in common with the prospective donor.[40] Even if the prospective donor rejects the candidate's request for money, the candidate's response should utilize the concept of similarity. Allen suggests that, virtually regardless of the reason for the turndown ("I'm supporting someone else"; "I don't have any money right now"; "I really don't know you well"; "I want to learn about all the candidates first"), the candidate should respond with "feel, felt, found." That is, the candidate should indicate similarity to the donor by observing that "I know how you feel; I've felt that way myself, but I have found that . . . ."[41] Notice that prior to directly responding to the prospective donor's rationale for refusing a donation, the candidate attempts to establish similarity by speaking about mutual feelings.

The third principle of attraction that has import for political fund-raising is that we are attracted to and respond favorably to people who like us and validate us with *positive feedback*. Candidates and their surrogates must keep this fact uppermost in their minds as they seek funds. This does not mean the fund-raiser must be overly compliant. If fund-raisers feel compelled to do that, then they are not dealing with equals. They should not be attempting to get donations from persons with whom they do not feel similar and equal. Rather, it means that fund-raisers must do their research. They should be able to make reference to the potential contributor's family by name, to make reference to recent accomplishments of the potential contributor's business, schools, family, and friends. In many fund-raising meetings, it is fair to say that topics such as politics, current events, and making political contributions do not take up more than two to three minutes of a ten-minute conversation. Fund-raising situations are so patently obvious that often they do not need any belaboring. Rather, such meetings stress the similarities among the candidates, their supporters, and the prospective contributors, as the candidates or their supporters attempt to provide positive feedback to the prospective contributors. Often this is done by focusing comments on the contributor's role in mutual projects of a nonpolitical nature, such as charitable, social, educational, or civic projects.

Once the similarities among the candidate, fund-raiser, and potential contributor have been established, the fund-raiser can make his pitch on behalf of the candidate, stressing the philosophical or issue similarities between the candidate and the potential contributor. If the fund-raiser has done a good job of establishing similarities, his final pitch on behalf of the candidate should convince the contributor that the question is not so much whether to give to the candidate but rather how much to give.

A fourth principle of human attraction enters into political fund-raising. Research suggests that we experience a *heightened need for human attraction during moments of anxiety.*[42] This point should be noted by the competent political fund-raiser. As the campaign develops, the good fund-raiser will keep in mind who might be made anxious by current events. As opponents make statements and develop their campaigns, the good fund-raiser will follow them closely, seeking to determine who might be made anxious by the opponents' statements and positions. And as current events take place and receive publicity, the well-run campaign will have the appropriate person seeking funds from the individuals most likely to be made highly anxious by these events, at the very moment that they may be causing anxiety. For example, in a St. Louis–area congressional race, one candidate announced that he was in favor of a controversial Army Corps of Engineers construction project that involved erecting several dams and flooding thousands of acres of lowland to create a large lake and recreational area to be utilized primarily by St. Louis residents. His opponent opposed this project as an unnecessarily wasteful and extravagant use of federal funds that would prove utterly disruptive to much of the Missouri environment and wildlife. Within three days of the first candidate's announcement, the second candidate or his representatives had contacted over 120 members of the St. Louis chapter of the Sierra Club, as well as similar environmental organizations. This effort produced almost $8,000 of unexpected contributions and many new enthusiastic workers for the campaign.

The final basis of human attraction that warrants the attention of the political fund-raiser is the concept of *supportive behavior.* Research suggests that our own behavior greatly influences our perception of other people. If, for example, you perform a favor for another person, you tend to like that person better as a consequence.[43] Hence, good fund-raisers, if unsuccessful in getting what they want—large contributions—should always have backup requests. If the car dealer will not contribute any money to the Smith for City Council campaign, will the dealer at least let candidate Smith use that beautiful yellow car in the showroom for three hours during the Labor Day parade? If worse comes to worst, at least the car dealer can look over some of Smith's campaign literature.

The practice of consistently seeking some type of supportive behavior, minimal as it may be, has at least two beneficial effects. First, the tangible benefit requested will be honored. Candidate Smith does ride in the most attractive car in the parade. Second, now that the car dealer has provided some sort of supportive behavior to the candidate, the dealer is more likely to respond favorably to a second fund-raising appeal. Importantly, once people have made an initial contribution to the candidate, they are prone to make a second or third contribution. Effective fund-raisers are aware of the positive effect that supportive behavior has on subsequent behavior and consistently strive to obtain some type of supportive behavior from everyone they approach. As Robert Kaplan, president of one of the most successful political fund-raising firms in the country, has observed, "At its core, a successful fund-raising philosophy is based on asking, asking again and asking one more time."[44]

These principles of interpersonal communication should guide candidates and fund-raisers as they seek contributions. Moreover, they clearly have implications for other forms of fund-raising. They can help determine, for example, both the mailing list and the message content of direct mail solicitations, phone solicitations, and Internet solicitations on behalf of the candidate. Ultimately, all of the principle means of fund-raising involve asking for money. Whether the candidate is asking others for contributions, whether the candidate's supporters are asking their friends and associates for contributions, whether the candidate and the candidate's supporters are asking others to organize fund-raising events and sell tickets, or whether the asking takes place through direct mail, telephone appeals, or Internet appeals, the principles of interpersonal communication invariably come into play.[45] In sum, candidates and fund-raisers who are skillful interpersonal communicators, clearly sensitive to and aware of the determinants of human attraction, are far more prone to achieve success than those who ignore these important variables of interpersonal communication.

INTERPERSONAL COMMUNICATION BETWEEN VOTERS

Voters talk among themselves about politics, campaigns, and candidates. Interpersonal communication between voters is an important aspect of virtually every campaign. In this section, we will try to answer four questions about interpersonal communication between voters. First, in what campaigns is it likely to be of unusually high importance? Second, what do voters typically discuss? Third, what is the relationship between interpersonal communication and mass media in political campaigns? Fourth, how do campaigns use relationships between voters to turn out their supporters in large numbers?

Importance

Interpersonal communication between voters is normally of greatest importance in those campaigns that receive little media attention. When information about the campaign and the candidates is lacking in the media, voters rely more heavily on interpersonal communication. Consequently, several types of campaigns characteristically lacking in media coverage often must rely heavily on interpersonal communication. First are campaigns for lesser offices and local offices; second are primary campaigns. L. Erwin Atwood and Keith Sanders have found that communication with other people was the most credible source of information for 32 percent of the voters in a primary election, but that it was the most credible source of information for only 12 percent of the voters in a general election.[46] Though there has been little research since the work of Atwood and Sanders on this point, and the exact figures may have changed, their basic conclusion that people learn more about primary elections from other people, where other sources of information are limited, and less about general elections, where other sources of information are more plentiful, continues to make sense. Often, as when three or more candidates seek a single office in a primary, the media coverage received by any single candidate tends to be more limited than in a general election. Moreover, the media budgets of most primary campaigns are lower than those of general elections. The reduced media coverage of individual candidates and campaigns in some primaries likely causes voters to rely more heavily on interpersonal communication in these elections than in general elections. Knowing little about a candidate, the opinion of a friend or relative may take on added importance in lower ballot and primary elections.

The third group of campaigns where interpersonal communication between voters seems to play an unusually important role are those campaigns in which the constituency has a relatively high educational level. Research on this point is limited, and much of it has been done primarily on school-age populations. Nevertheless, it does tend to suggest that voters with good educational backgrounds are less affected by the media, more prone to discuss current events, and more likely to be influenced by those discussions.[47]

Discussion Topics

Voters discuss virtually everything that is pertinent to a campaign. However, three subjects tend to dominate their conversations. First, interpersonal communication is often the means by which people initially learn of a newsworthy development in the campaign. In one of the first studies to focus on how people learn about campaign events, Wayne Danielson found that knowledge of news events in a presidential campaign was most rapidly spread throughout the population by radio and interpersonal communication. Television and newspapers, according to Danielson, did not transmit knowledge of news events as rapidly.[48] Though

Danielson's findings may have since been altered by the widespread growth of television and the Internet, it nevertheless seems safe to conclude that many people do frequently discuss and often first learn of news events through interaction with one another.

Second, William Kimsey and Atwood found that voters tend to "talk most about the things they like least about candidates."[49] Conversations between voters are not subject to libel laws, equal time laws, and other legal constraints that may affect the various mass media. Media coverage of the negative aspects of a candidate may be tempered by considerations such as these, but interpersonal communication is not.

Additionally, Kimsey and Atwood found that voters tend to use interpersonal communication selectively to reinforce their ballot decisions.[50] This finding makes good sense because of our tendency to be attracted to, and communicate primarily with, those who are similar to us. Hence, we are prone to be exposed to messages congruent with our own ideas. Moreover, we do not equally attend to all the messages we receive. We are prone to attend selectively to those messages that conform to our existing attitudes and beliefs. Kimsey and Atwood's findings, that we use interpersonal communication selectively to reinforce prior decisions, seem to be very much in accord with our existing knowledge of interpersonal communication.

Thus, interpersonal communication is used by voters to deal with virtually everything that happens in a campaign. However, in contrast to other forms of campaign communication, it may be especially important as a medium of news transmission, as a medium by which negative information about a candidate is transmitted, and as a medium that serves to reinforce attitudes and beliefs.

INTERPERSONAL COMMUNICATION AMONG VOTERS, MASS MEDIA, AND VOTING BEHAVIOR

As early as 1948, students of mass media realized the relationship and importance of interpersonal communication. John P. Robinson provides us with a critique of the relationships among voting behavior, mass media, and interpersonal communication.[51] Robinson, like prior researchers, finds that, when interpersonal communication is in conflict with media information, "interpersonal sources wield greater influence."[52] The explanation for this no doubt rests in large part on the feedback and adaptation that one voter can provide to another as they discuss politics. Mass media messages cannot adapt and react to feedback, as can interpersonal communication. However, Robinson also finds that interpersonal influence attempts are not that pervasive in elections. More people seem to be exposed to media attempts to influence their votes than to interpersonal attempts to influence their votes.[53] Those people who receive media messages attempting to influence their votes, but no interpersonal messages, seem much more receptive to direct influence from the media.[54]

Silvo Lenart argues for what he calls "an integrated model." He claims that candidates and campaigns utilize the mass media to communicate to voters but that these efforts are often affected by such interpersonal influences as the characteristics of individual voters, the one-to-one individual discussions between voters, and the group interactions that voters have. Lenart concludes, "Once a campaign is underway in the media, the entire communication process is best characterized as a dynamic interplay among media, interpersonal interactions, and opinion climate pressures."[55]

Though most candidates make special efforts to facilitate interpersonal communication between themselves and voters and between themselves and financial contributors, few candidates make concrete efforts to facilitate interpersonal communication between voters that might have a favorable impact on their candidacy. However, at least one political consultant has long attempted to stimulate interpersonal communication among voters to benefit his clients. Stephen Shadegg, who advised Barry Goldwater and whose son currently serves in Congress, recommends that candidates develop "social precincts" as crucial elements of their campaigns.[56] *Social precincts*, as Shadegg employs the term, are simply enthusiastic and knowledgeable supporters of the candidate. They are not members of special organizations or groups, nor are they in any way prominent in their communities. Initially, members of social precincts are recruited from among friends and associates of the candidate, and gradually the number of members is increased. Many of these people may not even know the candidate well. Members of social precincts are provided "inside" information. As the campaign progresses, they get key press releases a day in advance, and their opinion is solicited before the candidate makes a key speech. They are made to feel that they are insiders whose opinions and advice are valued by the candidate. And indeed they are just that. By using the Internet, faxes, and other technology, the candidate is able to develop a large group of people who look upon the candidate as someone with whom they have a special relationship. Based on extensive experience with social precincts, Shadegg claims that, if he can enlist 3 to 5 percent of the constituency in these social precincts, he will win the election. For if 3 to 5 percent of the constituency believe they have a special interest in a candidate, Shadegg feels that, in their normal day-to-day social interactions, they will prove influential on a significantly large enough number of voters to win most elections.

Shadeggs's approach is one of the few clear attempts to mobilize interpersonal communication among voters on behalf of a candidate. His success with social precincts, as well as research evidence on the relationship among voting behavior, mass communication, and interpersonal communication, speaks to the importance of interpersonal communication between voters.

INTERPERSONAL COMMUNICATION AND GETTING OUT THE VOTE EFFORTS

GOTV or Get Out The Vote efforts are a vital part of every campaign. But they have changed in at least two rather dramatic ways in recent elections. First, they have simply become much more critical to the success of campaigns, particularly upper ballot campaigns such as those for the presidency and statewide offices. Second, interpersonal communication is becoming more and more widely recognized as the key to a successful effort.

The 1990s witnessed a decline in ticket splitting. A few figures illustrate that, at least at the federal level, there seems to be relatively little ticket splitting. In 1996, President Clinton was reelected with 49 percent of the vote. Democratic candidates for the House of Representatives received 48.51 percent of the vote that year. In 1998 Democratic House candidates received 48 percent of the vote while their Republican counterparts received 49 percent of the vote. In 2000 both Democrat Gore and Republican Bush received 48 percent of the popular vote, at the same time that 48 percent of voters cast their ballot for Democratic House candidates and 49 percent cast their ballots for Republican House candidates. In 2002 Republican House candidates received 51 percent of the vote while Democratic candidates for the House of Representatives received 46 percent of the vote. This pattern led many political consultants to conclude that the number of truly independent voters had declined, by 2004, to no more than 7 percent of the electorate.[57]

As a consequence, with far fewer voters subject to persuasion, the Republican campaign in 2004 was geared not to persuading weakly committed Democratic voters and independents, but was consciously designed to reinforce committed Republican voters and get them out to the polls on election day. Similarly, the Democratic Party focus was primarily on voters already committed to that party. Getting Out The Vote, or GOTV, efforts are largely matters of interpersonal communication. They place a premium on interpersonal contact, rather than on persuasive media advertising. Both parties were successful in turning out large numbers of their voters in 2004. But the Republicans were significantly more successful at increasing their turnout than were Democrats. President Bush won 23 percent more votes in 2004 than he did in 2000. His vote total increased from 50 million in 2000 to 62 million in 2004. Senator Kerry won

16 percent more votes in 2004 than did Vice President Gore in 2000. Gore won 51 million votes in 2000 compared to Kerry's 59 million in 2004.[58] A key to the Republicans' success was their interpersonal communication with the voters, especially in their GOTV efforts.

In 2004 the Democrats built their GOTV effort on the backs of union labor and the well-funded efforts of 527 groups such as Moveon.com. These groups relied on paid workers. They organized heavily in black neighborhoods and university towns. These were the types of communities that had exceedingly strong Democratic voting histories. The numbers suggest their success. As Steve Rosenthal, chief executive officer of America Coming Together and the former political director of the AFL-CIO, wrote about the turnout in the critical state of Ohio, "When it came to getting out the Democratic vote in Ohio during the presidential election, we hit our target numbers. My organization, America Coming Together, along with our 32 America Votes partner organizations, the Democratic National Committee and the Kerry–Edwards campaign not only exceeded our turnout goals for the Buckeye State, but far exceeded anything the Democrats have done in the past."[59] But they lost Ohio, and of course the Democrats lost the presidency, lost the Senate, and lost the House of Representatives. Why?

One important key to the Republican victories was the interpersonal nature of the Republican GOTV effort. As two participants in the Ohio Republican GOTV effort observed, "the Bush–Cheney '04 campaign was built around the concept of personal contact. Everything was geared around one human being talking to another, be it by telephone or in person."[60] Moreover, all the efforts in the weeks and months prior to the election were designed to facilitate a final seventy-two-hour GOTV effort. First, throughout the nation, for months in advance of the election, Bush–Cheney supporters were being identified. A variety of means were used to identify Republican-leaning voters. They were all interpersonal in nature: door-to-door neighborhood canvasses, millions of phone calls, and Internet responses to Republican websites. As we have noted, although the Internet is not explicitly interpersonal, the fact that a typical citizen can be both a sender and receiver of messages to and from the campaign gives it an interpersonal nature that is lacking in most other mass media. In mid-2003, as Vermont governor Howard Dean moved to the front of the pack of Democratic contenders, his campaign manager Joe Trippi was given much credit for his creative use of the Internet. Trippi deserved the credit, and political observers were impressed with the fact that the Dean campaign had amassed a list of six hundred thousand e-mail addresses. But few reporters bothered to see what the Republicans were doing on the Internet. At the same time that Dean and Trippi were being lauded for their six hundred thousand addresses, the Bush campaign had quietly collected six million e-mail addresses.[61]

For over two years, the Bush campaign built an organization of 1.4 million active volunteers. The size of this organization dwarfs the volunteer organizations of the past. The Democratic National Committee, by contrast, claimed the services of 223,000 volunteers.[62] Importantly, as potentially sympathetic names were amassed by the campaign, the organization followed up and prepared for their GOTV effort. These follow-ups and many initial contacts were not by paid workers, who might have little in common with those they were contacting. Rather, the Republicans tried to match their volunteers with people with whom they had something in common. The Bush campaign used existing connections to recruit volunteers, identify voters, and, perhaps most importantly, get out the vote.

Reminiscent of Shadegg's social precincts, the Republican effort was built on allowing their millions of volunteers to network. Their effort was based on occupational networks, ethnic networks, religious networks, hobby networks, and similar points of commonality between their volunteers and voters. A volunteer who was an accountant who also advised her daughter's Girl Scout troop would be directed to contact other accountants, or Girl Scout leaders and parents. A volunteer who was a Hispanic nurse would be utilized to contact other nurses and Hispanics. These were not paid professionals contacting strangers. They were volunteers contacting people with whom, in many instances, they had at least one or more things clearly in common. This facilitated, at least to some small degree, the building of an interpersonal bond between the Bush organizational volunteer and the persons being contacted. Moreover, the Bush volunteers brought an enthusiasm to their task which was hard to duplicate with paid workers. For example, one volunteer in Ohio, Doug Corn, took the week before the election off, at considerable financial sacrifice to his business, and worked twelve-hour days. "The core values Bush holds are very important to me," he explained.[63] He conveyed that importance and his dedication to those with whom he was in contact. That kind of enthusiasm and effort is hard to duplicate with paid workers, and it likely communicated itself to many of those whom the Bush volunteers were contacting in the critical GOTV effort. It is likely that this interpersonal bond helped secure the large Republican turnout on election day.

In sum, it would appear that, as partisanship becomes more pronounced in our society, fewer and fewer voters are amenable to persuasion. Consequently, perhaps to a greater degree than in the past, parties and candidates are striving to "gin up the base." That is, they are striving to get their strong supporters excited about candidates and committed to voting for those candidates. As we have seen, perhaps the most effective way of accomplishing that is through interpersonal communication.

Behavioral Characteristics of Successful Interpersonal Campaigners

As we know from our own personal experience, some people are more interpersonally successful than others. Some people seem able to establish more and stronger interpersonal relationships than others. Clearly, that ability would be a major asset for an individual seeking elected office. Yet, until recently, little research has focused on the ways in which political candidates might behave that would enhance their interpersonal attractiveness. One team of researchers has attempted to focus on desirable interpersonal communication behavior for political candidates. Their work warrants our attention because clearly it is among the few studies that offers practical behavioral suggestions to candidates seeking to increase their interpersonal attractiveness to voters.

Timothy Stephen, Teresa M. Harrison, William Husson, and David Albert have focused their work on the interpersonal communication styles of political candidates. Specifically, in their most recent study, they have attempted to distinguish between the interpersonal behaviors of winning and losing candidates in three recent presidential elections.[64] These researchers find that there are "clear and consistent" differences between the interpersonal behavior characteristics of winning and losing political candidates. In general, they find that winners "communicate in a more self-contained, secure, relaxed, and interpersonally functional manner" than losers. Compared to winners, losers are perceived in "ways that appear to be somewhat overbearing, tense, contentious, histrionic, and serious."[65]

Breaking these overall observations down, Stephen, Harrison, Husson, and Albert identify a number of behavior characteristics that are perceived in successful presidential candidates. To a greater degree:

- Winners are perceived to more frequently tell jokes and use humor than losers.
- Winners are perceived to laugh more frequently than losers.
- Winners are perceived to smile more frequently than losers.
- Winners are perceived to explain by using examples, analogies, and stories.
- Winners are perceived to make frequent and appropriate eye contact.
- Winners are perceived to be calm and relaxed in manner.

Moreover, losers are perceived to behave differently than winners. To a greater degree:

- Losers are perceived to control what gets talked about.
- Losers are perceived to dominate others in conversation.

- Losers are perceived to have loud voices.
- Losers are perceived to insist that terms be carefully defined.
- Losers are perceived to disagree frequently.
- Losers are perceived to be more likely to blame or accuse.[66]

Stephens, Harrison, Husson, and Albert also identify a variety of interpersonal behaviors where the differences between winning and losing candidates are relatively slight. Their work is unusual because it represents an effort to identify specific interpersonal behavioral differences among candidates. To some degree, it provides candidates with explicit interpersonal communication behavioral objectives to be used throughout the campaign.

CONCLUSION

In this chapter, we have found that interpersonal communication between the candidate and voters is exceptionally important in local campaigns, in campaigns where the use of media may not be feasible, and in primary campaigns. In such campaigns, the interpersonal communication between the candidate and voters through programs of informal coffees and canvasses can be extremely valuable. Moreover, we have found that political fund-raising lends itself to interpersonal communication and that current interpersonal communication research on attraction has major implications for interpersonal fund-raising by political candidates and their advocates.

Moreover, we have examined the often-neglected interpersonal communication between voters. We have seen in which campaigns such communication is most important; what voters tend to discuss among themselves; and the relationship among voting behavior, media, and interpersonal communication. Additionally, we have observed how critical Get Out The Vote efforts have become in recent years, and how interpersonal communication plays a vital role in those efforts. Finally, we have observed that the perceptions of the interpersonal behavioral characteristics of winning and losing candidates differ and we have offered some of the characteristics of both winning and losing candidates.

NOTES

1. For a discussion of some of the mechanics involved in implementing the first two of these types of interpersonal communication, see Robert Agranoff, *The Management of Election Campaigns* (Boston: Holbrook, 1976), 411–54.

2. Herbert E. Alexander, *Financing Politics: Money, Elections and Political Reform* (Washington, D.C.: Congressional Quarterly, 1980), 1.

3. Lynda Lee Kaid, "The Neglected Candidate: Interpersonal Communication in Political Campaigns," *Western Journal of Speech Communication* 41 (Fall 1977): 245.

4. Kaid, "The Neglected Candidate," 245.

5. The following analysis of the importance of interpersonal campaigning in local political campaigns is based heavily on Robert V. Friedenberg, "Interpersonal Communication in Local Political Campaigns," *Ohio Speech Journal* 12 (1974): 19–27.

6. Daniel M. Shea, *Campaign Craft: The Strategies, Tactics, and Art of Political Campaign Management* (Westport, Conn.: Praeger, 1996), 243, 249.

7. See Patrick L. Devlin, "The McGovern Canvass: A Study in Interpersonal Political Campaign Communication," *Central States Speech Journal* 24 (Summer 1973): 83–90, for an account of some of the McGovern techniques that have been widely copied.

8. See Nancy Bocskor, "No Place Like Home," *Campaigns and Elections* (April 1998): 28–29. Bocskor stresses the fund-raising potential of coffees and similar events hosted by supporters of the candidate in their own homes.

9. This statement and all quotations in this section, unless otherwise explicitly footnoted, are drawn from "Coffee: The Campaign Beverage," a pamphlet issued by the Republican State Central and Executive Committee of Ohio to candidates for state and local offices. No date or place of publication is available.

10. Laura Peck, "Face to Face Campaigning: How to Work a Room," *Campaigns and Elections* (April 1996): 47.

11. Peck, "Face to Face Campaigning," 47.

12. Peck, "Face to Face Campaigning," 47.

13. Adam Carrington and James Kresge, "In the Midst of History: The Ground Game in Ohio," publication of the John M. Ashbrook Center for Public Affairs, Ashland University, retrieved on February 17, 2007 at www.ashbrook.org/publicat/onprin/v13n1/carrington-kresge.html.

14. Though the Bush program described in this paragraph was among the most effective modification of coffees used by major candidates in 2004, virtually all the top of the ballot candidates were indebted to Governor Howard Dean of Vermont, and his campaign staff headed by Joe Trippi, for pioneering the use of the Internet as a means of bringing together supporters. See Joe Trippi, *The Revolution Will Not Be Televised: Democracy, The Internet, and The Overthrow of Everything* (New York: Regan Books, 2004).

15. See Devlin, "The McGovern Canvass," 82–90, for an excellent description of a highly effective canvassing operation that served all of the functions described in these paragraphs.

16. Devlin, "The McGovern Canvass," 89.

17. These guidelines are modeled after those provided to McGovern canvassers during the 1972 presidential primaries, which have been widely copied ever since, and the guidelines recommended by Pennsylvania Democratic state representative Mike Hanna, whose upset 1990 election with 65 percent of the vote in a district where Republicans had dominated was largely attributed to his successful utilization of door-to-door canvassing. See Devlin, "McGovern Canvass," 84–85, and Mike Hanna, "The Campaign Door Knocking Game," *Campaigns and Elections* (September 1991): 52–53.

18. See Hanna, "The Campaign Door Knocking Game," 52.

19. Laura Peck, "Going Door-to-Door: 10 Tips for Success," *Campaigns and Elections* (July 1996): 45.

20. Peck, "Going Door-to-Door," 45.

21. See Agranoff, *Management of Election Campaigns*, 411–54, for a discussion of the many purposes of canvasses as well as illustrations of the material used in canvasses.

22. Laura Woolsey, "Web Usability: The Development and Application of a New Instrument for Objective Usability Inspection," master's thesis, Miami University, 2001, 41.

23. Woolsey, "Web Usability," 41.

24. Clinton is quoted in Mary Clare Jalonick, "E-Mail Newsletters: Getting Your Campaign Message Out—Fast and Cheap," *Campaigns and Elections* (June 2001): 48.

25. Woolsey, "Web Usability," 67.

26. While many candidates will send out e-mail newsletters on a regular basis, this is most typical of the newsletters sent by news organizations, party organizations, and special interest groups. See Adam Graham-Silverman, "E-Mail Newsletter Sites: The Strongest Link," *Campaigns and Elections* (July 2001): 42–43.

27. Woolsey, "Web Usability," 43.

28. Ari Pinkus, "Politics Goes E-mail Crazy," *Campaigns and Elections* (September 2005): 11. Pinkus cites Andrew Klein, antifraud product manager at Mailfrontier, an e-mail security and antispam company as the source of this figure.

29. Democracy 21, "A Democracy 21 Report: Campaign Finance Successes and Problems in the 2004 Elections," 4. Retrieved on November 29, 2004 from www.democracy21.org/index.asp?Type=B_PR&SEC={A8B4DE.

30. Paul Farhi, "Small Donors Grow into Big Political Force," retrieved on May 3, 2004, from www.washingtonpost.com/ac2wp-dyn/A61480-2004May2?language=printer.

31. Farhi, "Small Donors Grow into Big Political Force."

32. Center for Responsive Politics, "2004 Elections Expected to Cost Nearly 4 Billion," 1–4. Retrieved on November 17, 2004 from www.opensecrets.org/pressreleases/2004/04spending.asp.

33. Center for Responsive Politics, "2004 Elections."

34. Democracy 21, "A Democracy 21 Report," 5.

35. Center for Responsive Politics, "2004 Elections," 3.

36. Many researchers have attempted to establish the major determinants of human attraction. Two of the better summaries of current research, on which this analysis is based, are Joseph Devito, *The Interpersonal Communication Book* (New York: Longman, 2003), 253–56; and Stewart L. Tubbs and Sylvia Moss, *Human Communication* (New York: Random House, 1987), 66–75.

37. This guideline is a long-standing one used by Republican and Democratic National Committee field staff to help determine which candidates are the most viable and hence warrant aid from their respective national committees.

38. Cathy Allen, "Peer Pressure Politics: Getting Your Money's Worth from Friends and Colleagues," *Campaigns and Elections* (June/July 1990): 49.

39. Robert P. Odell Jr., "The Money Pit," *Campaigns and Elections* (November 1992): 51.

40. Cathy Allen, "How to Ask for Money," *Campaigns and Elections* (April 1998): 25.

41. Allen, "How to Ask for Money," 27.

42. Tubbs and Moss, *Human Communication*, 72–73.

43. William Wilmot, *Dyadic Communication: A Transactional Perspective* (Reading, Mass.: Addison-Wesley, 1975), 73–74.

44. Robert Kaplan, "Psychology of Silence: Raising More Money by Psyching Out Donors," *Campaigns and Elections* (November 1991): 54.

45. Ron Faucheux, "Ask and You Shall Receive," *Campaigns and Elections* (April 2005): 25–27. Faucheux suggests that political fund-raising simply comes down to asking.

46. L. Erwin Atwood and Keith R. Sanders, "Information Sources and Voting in a Primary and General Election," *Journal of Broadcasting* 20 (Summer 1976): 298.

47. John P. Robinson, "Interpersonal Influence in Election Campaigns: Two-Step Flow Hypotheses," *Public Opinion Quarterly* 40 (Fall 1976): 312; and Marilyn Jackson-Beeck, "Interpersonal and Mass Communication in Children's Political Socialization," *Journalism Quarterly* 56 (Spring 1979): 53.

48. Wayne A. Danielson, "Eisenhower's February Decision: A Study of News Impact," *Journalism Quarterly* 33 (Fall 1956): 437.

49. William D. Kimsey and L. Erwin Atwood, "A Path Model of Political Cognitions and Attitudes, Communication and Voting Behavior in a Congressional Election," *Communication Monographs* 40 (August 1979): 429.

50. Kimsey and Atwood, "A Path Model," 430.

51. Robinson, "Interpersonal Influence in Election Campaigns," 304–19.

52. Robinson, "Interpersonal Influence in Election Campaigns," 315.

53. Robinson, "Interpersonal Influence in Election Campaigns."

54. Robinson, "Interpersonal Influence in Election Campaigns," 316.

55. Silvo Lenart, *Shaping Political Attitudes: The Impact of Interpersonal Communication and Mass Media* (Thousand Oaks, Calif.: Sage, 1994), 110–12.

56. This discussion of social precincts is based on Stephen C. Shadegg, *The New How to Win an Election* (New York: Tapplinger, 1976), 103–19.

57. All of the figures used in this paragraph are drawn from Michael Baron, "American Politics in the Networking Era," retrieved on February 25, 2005, at nationaljournal.com/scripts/printpage.cgi?/about/njweekly/st., 1–2. Baron cites the 7 percent figure as the figure that Bush strategists Karl Rove and Ken Mehlman used on the basis of prior elections and polling done in late 2003 and repeated in early 2004.

58. Baron, "American Politics," 2.

59. Steven Rosenthal, "O.K., We Lost Ohio. The Question Is, Why?" retrieved on December 6, 2004, at www.washingtonpost.com/ac2/wp-dyn/a34157-2004Dec3?lan.

60. Carrington and Kresge, "In the Midst of History: The Ground Game in Ohio."

61. These figures are drawn from Baron, "American Politics," 2.

62. Baron, "American Politics," 2.

63. Peter Bronson, "Bush's Secret: Doug Corn's Loyalty, Work," *Cincinnati Enquirer*, November 4, 2004, B2.

64. Timothy Stephen, Teresa M. Harrison, William Husson, and David Albert, "Interpersonal Communication Styles of Political Candidates: Predicting Winning and Losing Candidates in Three U.S. Presidential Elections," in Kenneth L. Hacker, ed. *Presidential Candidate Images* (Lanham, Md.: Rowman and Littlefield, 2004), 177–196.

65. Stephen, Harrison, Husson, and Albert, "Interpersonal Communication Styles of Political Candidates," 185.

66. Stephen, Harrison, Husson, and Albert, "Interpersonal Communication Styles of Political Candidates." This list reflects modifications of wording in Stephen, Harrison, Husson, and Albert's list of variables, as presented in table 8.1, 186. The changes do not alter the meaning.

10

~

Advertising in
Political Campaigns

Many campaigns are waged essentially through advertising, primarily over radio and television. These campaigns tend to be high-profile races, such as those for national and statewide office. In many urban
areas, lower races such as those for city offices are also waged heavily
through the use of radio and television. However, in lower-level races,
where budgets preclude the extensive use of radio and television or
where local demographic conditions make it impractical, other forms of
advertising remain dominant. Moreover, even high-profile media campaigns cannot forsake the more traditional, often preelectronic media
means of campaigning and advertising. If they do so, they run a serious
risk of incurring consequences that so badly damage their efforts, even a
highly effective media campaign cannot win the election.

Three thoughts should always be kept in mind when considering the
uses of political advertising: (1) that political advertising is enormously
costly, not only in dollars but also in time and effort; (2) that as appealing
as television commercials may be, rarely can a campaign be waged successfully by relying exclusively on television; and (3) that advertising media are simply vehicles for conveying the images and ideas of candidates,
and it is the images and ideas, not the size of the commercial buy and the
placement of the commercial buy, that ultimately are of the most consequence. The remainder of this chapter focuses first on factors that affect
the selection and use of various advertising media available to political
campaigners. Second, we consider what have become key figures in many
contemporary campaigns, professional political consultants, with emphasis on those who specialize in media.

DEVELOPING A MASTER PLAN FOR POLITICAL ADVERTISING

The array of advertising media that has been used in political campaigns is staggering. A partial listing includes brochures, newsletters, questionnaires, letters, billboards, yard signs, bumper stickers, newspaper advertisements, magazine advertisements, matchbooks, buttons, pencils, computer bulletin boards, faxes, Internet home pages, and, of course, radio and television commercials. This list does not even include one of our all-time favorites, cans of "GOLD WATER," the delightful drink for all right-thinking supporters of the 1964 Republican standard bearer! Indeed, the list is endless. Political campaigners have used virtually every technological advance in communication to facilitate getting their messages to the public. However, almost every campaigner pays homage to the adage that the good campaign dominates the dominant media. If the dominant medium in the school board election is yard signs, the good campaign will have the best and most yard signs. If the dominant medium in the congressional race is television, the good campaign will have the best and most television commercials.

Among the first responsibilities of any campaign is to develop a master plan that should include a section on expected advertising. Typically such a plan should be developed fifteen to eighteen months before election day[1] and should serve to coordinate all of the paid media activities of the campaign. Not only must all the paid media activities of the campaign be coordinated with one another, but the paid media component of the campaign must also be coordinated with other components of the campaign, including the overall strategy and targeting, the budget and fundraising, and the earned media.[2] Obviously occasions will arise when events make it necessary to deviate from the overall plan. However, well-run campaigns plan their media activities early and then stick as closely as possible to their overall blueprint, adjusting as events make it necessary.

The advantages of advance planning cannot be overestimated. Decisions that are made as the campaign is beginning tend to be made more dispassionately and are typically based on greater objectivity, thought, and research. Decisions made on the spur of the moment in response to campaign events are typically subject to less thought, less research, less analysis, and hence are prone to be less successful.

The many advantages of advance planning can be best illustrated by example. Let us imagine that we are involved in planning a congressional primary race. Our candidate is only moderately known in the district. However, our opponent is also known only moderately in the district. They are both vying for the nomination to succeed a popular incumbent who is retiring after twenty-four years in Congress. We will imagine that our candidate is a university professor who has served on local school boards and subsequently was elected mayor of a small college town of twenty-one thousand within the district, a position she currently holds. She is also highly active in supporting the arts and has been a longtime supporter of the local symphony orchestra. Our opponent is a young lawyer who has just completed his second term in the state House of Representatives, representing a district of about eighty thousand, located in the suburbs of a large city. His district comprises about one-fourth of the congressional district; the town in which our candidate serves as mayor comprises only about 6 percent of the district. Another 25 percent of the district is composed of suburbs, such as the one our opponent has represented, and about half the district is rural, though the rural area includes several towns of about fifteen thousand to twenty-five thousand, such as the one our candidate has served as mayor. For the sake of illustration we will imagine that traditionally candidates wait until January before announcing their candidacy for the May 1 primary.

Using the surfacing period during the summer of the year preceding the election, we draft our first master plan. We decide to run a series of radio and television commercials for ten days immediately after declaring candidacy in January. Moreover, we decide to take out large advertisements in the three daily papers that serve the district and in each of the district's ten highest circulation weekly papers in the week immediately following our candidate's announcement. Our advertising master plan then calls for three direct mail efforts in February and March. The first two mailings (in February) are to target groups that may be expected to be highly supportive of the candidate. We might imagine a master plan that calls for a mailing on February 12 to individuals concerned with education, such as members of teacher groups, PTAs, and similar organizations. The master plan then calls for a mailing on February 25 to members of a variety of groups concerned with culture and music, such as season ticket purchasers to local theater groups, symphony, and ballet. The master plan we develop further calls for a mailing on March 25 to all voters eligible to participate in the primary. In addition to mailings, we develop a master plan that calls for the distribution of five hundred yard signs during the first two weeks of March and a major push to distribute five hundred yard signs on each of the last two weekends of March.

Since the primary election is scheduled for May 1, we decide that our radio advertising should start on April 1, doubling in quantity every ten days. That is, for every commercial run between April 1 and 10, two radio commercials will be run between April 11 and 20. For every commercial run between April 11 and 20, two radio commercials will be run between April 20 and May 1. Moreover, we decide to use a second and final round of television commercials to start on April 1, and their number is to double on April 21.

Additionally, the master plan calls for running large advertisements in each of the three daily papers and in each of the ten largest weekly papers in the district during the last phase of the campaign. Advertisements will be placed on each of the last three days in the three dailies and in each of the last two editions for the ten weekly papers. Finally, the master plan calls for a final mailing to all eligible voters to be sent on April 25 so as to be received by voters within three days of the election.

Notice what developing this relatively simple advertising plan has forced us to do and how it impacts on and governs much of the rest of the campaign. The first advantage to developing this plan early is that it forces us to identify our basic goal in the campaign. In this example, we have one basic goal: acquiring name recognition as a prominent member of our party. Since this is a primary, there may not be major differences between the candidates. Moreover, since the candidate of our party has won this congressional seat for the last twenty-four years, securing the party nomination may in itself be the critical step necessary for our candidate's ultimate election. In most campaigns, the first advantage to developing an initial advertising program is that it forces the campaign to develop and prioritize its overall objectives or goals for the campaign.

Since our goal is recognition, we have decided to campaign vigorously from the moment of our announcement. If we are going to use newspapers, radio, and television all in the first weeks of the campaign, as our plan calls for, then clearly we need money early in the campaign. Our master plan for advertising must be coordinated with our fund-raising. For example, if we cannot raise money for ten days' worth of radio and television at the outset of the campaign, what can we do? Perhaps we should curtail the radio and television and use yard signs earlier in the campaign. Yard signs, however, may call for considerable use of volunteers. Yards have to be solicited; signs have to be made and distributed. We can estimate the cost of producing commercials and buying time. We can estimate the number of volunteers needed to produce and place yard signs. The second advantage to planning our advertising campaign early is that it forces us to work closely with those involved in fund-raising and volunteer efforts, making sure the entire campaign is well coordinated.

In this example, we may conclude that, since name recognition is clearly an early problem for us, we are best served, given our limited initial finances, by using radio, billboards, and yard signs, early in the campaign. These forms of media can all be used effectively to help establish early name recognition. Moreover, they are typically less expensive than newspaper advertisements and television commercials. Hopefully, early in the campaign when we are laying out our positions, we may be able to supplement advertising with free media, such as newspaper stories and stories and interviews on local radio and television shows. Later, when we have more money, and when we may need to communicate more than our name and party, billboards and yard signs will be of little help. Using them in March, as we originally planned, may not make as much sense as using them earlier, which also enables us to save money for newspaper and television advertisements that we might need later in the campaign to explain our positions. Moreover, if we use yard signs early, it forces our volunteer coordinators to amass a large number of volunteers early, and those people may be vital to our later efforts to put out a variety of mailings, and mount a strong get-out-the-vote effort. Thus, as we plan early, we are able to refine our advertising program in those ways that best enable us to blend the efforts of all elements of the campaign.

Additionally, as we begin to recognize our financial problems, we may choose to divert a greater effort in that area. We may be forced to have our candidate spend a greater percentage of her time on fund-raising. We may have to develop extra fund-raising activities. Regardless of our situation, by giving ourselves ample time to plan we can make the most of whatever resources we have available to us. Among the factors that our advance media planning should consider are the following:

- Relative costs in dollars of available media
- Relative costs in candidate time/volunteer effort or other campaign resources of available media
- Ability of media to target specific audiences
- Ability of various media to accomplish specific goals of advertising
- Sequential development of advertising
- Coordinating advertising with the remainder of the campaign

We can best understand many of these factors by examining the various media that campaigners can choose to employ.

BASIC CONSIDERATIONS IN THE SELECTION OF POLITICAL ADVERTISING MEDIA

Political campaigns make use of seven types of advertising media: display graphics, direct mail, telephone, print, radio, television, and the Internet. Each of these options has virtues, and each has liabilities. Advance planning that evaluates those virtues and liabilities in relation to the factors listed above facilitates a skillfully developed campaign advertising program. Hence, this discussion focuses on each of the seven types of advertising media in relation to the factors that must be considered as the campaign's advertising program is developed.

Display Graphics

Display advertising, also called *graphic advertising*, most commonly includes such items as billboards, posters, yard signs, bumper stickers, and buttons. Such advertising has been a part of American campaigning virtually from our nation's inception. As technology has changed, so, too, has display advertising. For example, campaign buttons were virtually unknown until the late nineteenth century. But by 1896, the celluloid button process had been patented, and, in the 1896 campaigns of William McKinley and William Jennings Bryan, buttons assumed their place in the arsenal of the campaign persuader. In the 1920s, technological changes allowed for the lithographed production of buttons on tin. This process did not allow for the elaborate artwork and use of photographs that celluloid buttons did, but brought the cost of buttons down dramatically.[3]

Display advertising can be instrumental in helping (1) create and reinforce name recognition, (2) give a very quick impression of the candidate, (3) serve as a reminder medium when other campaign activity is limited, such as between a primary and the outset of the general election period, and (4) reach markets that other media cannot reach, such as rural areas.[4] If these are among the goals of the advertising campaign, and often early in the campaign they are, the use of display advertising should be considered. Such advertising normally carries an exceedingly brief message, often not more than the candidate's name or the name and a brief slogan.

For example, in the recent national elections, billboards, posters, yard signs, bumper stickers, and buttons have carried such messages as "Forward with KENNEDY," "Nixon Now, Re-elect the president," "PRESIDENT MUSKIE Don't You Feel Better Already?" "Leaders for Change— CARTER Mondale," "The Time is Now REAGAN & BUSH," "Geraldine Ferraro America's First Woman Vice Pres.," "JACKSON for President— Follow the Rainbow," "Ross for Boss," "Clinton–Gore—Out in Four," "Go Pat Go! Buchanan for President," "No Child Left Behind—Bush For President," "Show Bush the Door in 04," "Restore Honor to the White House—WESLEY K. CLARK," "BUSH CHENEY 04," "The Winning Team: Kerry Edwards," "Re-Elect George W. Bush." Typical of the similarly brief messages used on display media in recent state and local campaigns are messages such as "DEWINE for OHIO," "I Gave a Buck for YOUNG for Congress," "Run RABBIT Lt. Governor," "ROCKY!" "FRANKE for CONGRESS," "Kinky for Governor Why the Hell Not?" "I'll Be Back—The Governator."[5]

Display advertising such as that cited here clearly contributes to enhancing name recognition. Additionally, as several of these examples illustrate, display advertising may reinforce a major campaign theme. For example, in 2000, Republican George W. Bush continually stressed his educational accomplishments as governor of Texas and his concern for education, a traditionally Democratic issue. Hence a major theme of his campaign was "No Child Left Behind."

Display graphics, the format of which does not allow for an extended message, can serve two additional important, yet often overlooked, functions. They are particularly useful in reinforcing partisans who are already committed to the candidate. When distributed at campaign meetings, rallies, and similar activities, they often enhance the spirit of the staff and volunteers, serving as a visible link between the candidate and the worker. Indeed, many campaigns will purchase a few hundred pins, bumper stickers, or yard signs, simply to keep up the morale of the staff. One candidate with whom the authors are acquainted complained so much about his lack of yard signs that the campaign manager assigned a volunteer to post fifty yard signs on the mile and a half route that the candidate took into his headquarters every morning, and then to check once a week to replace any signs that had come down. The manager reported an immediate improvement in the candidate's outlook and performance! On occasion, the cost for a small amount of display graphic advertising is well worth the improved staff and volunteer morale that it provides.

Finally, if handled well, display graphics can be used to impress voters with the candidate's strength and help to create a bandwagon effect. For example, most consultants would advise that yard signs or bumper stickers not be given out in a small trickle, a few every day. Rather, a well-coordinated effort should be made to distribute a massive number of them simultaneously. So, for example, on September 9 there are virtually no yard signs in the district. All of a sudden, on September 10, there seems to be one on every block. Though there is not a sign on every block, the startlingly sudden appearance of many signs multiplies their effectiveness, making the casual voter highly aware of them and often suggesting to that voter that the candidate must have a large organization behind him to get up so many signs so quickly. Putting up massive numbers of yard signs all at once makes their impact far stronger, suggests massive support for the candidate, and helps create a bandwagon effect among casual voters. A similar effect can be achieved by distributing bumper stickers throughout the district all at once. Many campaigns will post volunteers in every high school football field parking lot one Friday night in early October, and in that fashion they distribute thousands of bumper stickers simultaneously. The same effect can be achieved by using shopping mall parking lots.

In recent years, the quantity and variety of display graphic advertising in political campaigns has been diminished. This is a direct function of cost. As recently as twenty-five years ago, it was not uncommon for a voter to be able to walk into the campaign office of a candidate and be given pins, bumper stickers, and similar materials, not only of that candidate but also of other candidates of the same party. Today, voters seeking such material are often asked to leave a contribution for every button or bumper sticker they take.

Display graphics are expensive, in terms of dollars as well as time and effort. Costs vary from community to community, though national suppliers that specialize in campaign materials tend to be exceedingly competitive. The cost for one thousand 2.25-inch celluloid buttons that allow the use of photographs, other elaborate artwork, and a variety of colors will be about $330, or thirty-three cents each, from most national suppliers. Most suppliers offer quantity discounts for orders of twenty-five hundred, five thousand, or more, which will bring the per-button price down. Large-quantity orders will reduce the costs by at least two to four cents per button.[6]

In recent years, many campaigns have saved on the cost of buttons by utilizing adhesive lapel stickers. These stickers will adhere to clothing, serving the same name recognition function as a button. Unlike a button, though, they cannot be readily reused from day to day. The current cost for 2.5-inch round lapel stickers, utilizing one color on a solid contrasting background, is $99.95 per thousand, about ten cents each. Most suppliers will offer substantial discounts for volume purchases, bringing the costs down to approximately six cents for each label when five thousand labels are ordered and five cents a label when twenty-five thousand such labels are ordered. Additionally, some suppliers will offer reduced rates for labels if they are purchased simultaneously with buttons.[7]

In addition to buttons or stickers, perhaps the most popular small form of display graphic is the bumper sticker. The current cost for a thousand of the simplest, standard 3 by 11.5–inch bumper stickers, one color printed on a standard background color, will range from $230 to $320, or twenty-three to thirty-two cents each. Most vendors offer a substantial discount for volume. Thus, twenty-five hundred of the same bumper stickers will cost $375 to $650, or fifteen to twenty-six cents each. An order for five thousand of the same bumper stickers will cost $600 to $1200, which brings the cost down to about twelve to twenty-four cents each.[8]

A wide variety of other smaller forms of display graphics has been used by campaigns. They include such products as emery boards, car litterbags, pocket combs, pens, pencils, and balloons—always with the candidate's name prominently displayed. Prices for these smaller forms of display advertising vary, but most can be obtained for between $120 and $200 per thousand.[9]

Larger forms of display advertising such as billboards and yard signs are also costly. In Cincinnati, Ohio, the thirty-first largest media market in the nation, the 2006 cost of renting sufficient billboard space on large highway-size billboards to provide that 25 percent of the Cincinnati population will see your message at least once daily was $9,500 a month. Additionally, the printing cost for those boards will normally run approximately $1,700. Thus, the total cost for a modest billboard effort running only one month in duration would be approximately $11,200.[10] Purchases to cover more of the market or for longer durations of time will typically be discounted.[11]

Yard signs are also costly. Their price will vary depending on such factors as the size and quality of the material used. However, because they are designed to remain outside, and must be weather resistant, many campaigns are opting to use corrugated plastic yard signs. The current cost for one thousand professionally printed corrugated plastic yard signs, measuring a standard 18 by 24–inch size, using one-color printing on a standard background color with the same copy and color on both sides, ranges from $1946 to $2,640 from national suppliers.[12] It should be remembered that typically some expense will be incurred in transporting and erecting yard signs throughout the district.

Over the last twelve years, in excess of sixteen million polyethylene bags or sleeves have replaced or supplemented the materials used by thousands of campaigns for their yard signs. These signs are printed on a heavy-duty polyethylene plastic bag or sleeve that fits over a wire frame, provided and included in the cost. Patriot Signage, the leading supplier of this alternative to traditional yard signs, prices a 26 by 16–inch sign utilizing one color plus white at $2,100 per thousand, including the metal frames over which the bag or sleeve is spread. As with the suppliers of most display graphics, purchases in larger quantity will result in substantial price reductions.[13]

Direct Mail

Direct mail advertising provides campaigns with one enormous advantage that cannot be readily duplicated by any other form of political advertising. It allows the campaign to be highly selective in targeting audiences. The wise use of radio and television commercials or of newspaper and magazine advertisements also allows for some degree of targeting. However, direct mail allows the campaign to target an audience more precisely than virtually any other form of advertising. The only comparable media, in terms of precise targeting, is the telephone.

Unlike many other forms of campaign communication, direct mail can be considered "high-interest, low-backlash communication."[14] That is, a direct mail piece can be tailored to reflect the interests of a specific constituency. For example, the candidate's views on reestablishing the draft might be featured in a mailing sent to a large section of the district near a university, where many residents are young. However, the candidate's views on social security policy can be featured in a mailing sent to an immediately adjacent retirement community in the district where the residents are older. Such mailings focus on topics of high interest to the recipients. However, they create low backlash. If the candidate spoke about reestablishing the draft or social security on radio or television, or in the print media, it is possible that many viewers or readers would have little interest in the topic of the ad and hence react negatively to the candidate for boring them by failing to address their concerns. By using direct mail to target audiences, the likelihood of high recipient interest is increased and the risk of backlash is largely eliminated.

Not only does direct mail allow for precise targeting of audiences, but it allows for an extended message. It is a vehicle that enables candidates to fully express themselves on a given issue. It is not uncommon for candidates to use letters and mailings that run four or more pages in length to treat one specific issue or a group of closely related issues. For example, a candidate may wish to fully explain her position on real estate taxes. To do so might require considerable radio and television time or considerable newspaper space and hence be extremely expensive. However, by using a mailing piece directed at property owners, the candidate can explain her position more fully than would be possible by using other media, to an audience of individuals precisely targeted because of their interest in property taxes. The candidate might actually save money because her direct mail is targeted more narrowly and she will not be paying for audience members who might not be affected by her comments on property taxes.

Because it allows for precise targeting and because it can be used to convey a long message, political campaigns have used direct mail both to persuade voters and raise money from contributors. In the 1970s, direct mail became the principal means of fund-raising for a variety of candidates, most notably George McGovern, who harnessed the direct mail team of Morris Dees and Tom Collins to find approximately 250,000 supporters who financed his presidential campaign largely by responding to his repeated direct mail solicitations.[15] Since that time, direct mail has served as the principal means of fund-raising for at least two other presidential campaigns, the 1980 campaign of independent candidate John Anderson and the 1980 Republican campaign of Congressman Philip Crane. Many specialists in the use of direct mail suggest that it is most effective in raising funds among older voters and hence is best suited to use with contributor lists that are oriented toward older voters.[16] Indeed, recent research suggests that the person who responds to direct mail is at least fifty-five years old.[17] In contrast, in recent years, the Internet has often been mentioned as a medium that is unusually well suited to raising funds among younger voters.[18] Though direct mail is an expensive way of raising funds, with 60 to 70 percent of every dollar collected often going to offset the cost of the mailing, it has been the principal means of fund-raising for many candidates.[19] Though direct mail's fund-raising use may be declining, in part as a consequence of the use of the Internet for this purpose, it nevertheless remains a valuable tool for conveying both persuasive messages and fund-raising appeals to voters.

The dollar costs of direct mail are difficult to talk about because mail pieces can be as simple as a mimeographed flyer or as elaborate as a multicolor, multipage letter and brochure with pictures produced on high-quality stock. As with most display graphics, quantity orders yield considerable discounts. Starting in 2002, Picture Perfect Campaigns, a major national distributor, began to offer an extra large, 22 by 12–inch, prefolded, four-color mailer on high-quality, seven-point stock that allows for a built-in reply card. Picture Perfect will provide design, printing, and mail-house services to its clients. This mailer is 40 percent larger than the traditional 11 by 17–inch size. Currently, when clients order five thousand such mailers, the price runs sixty-four cents each. An order for fifty thousand such mailers will cost only twenty-four cents each. An order for one hundred thousand such mailers will reduce the cost to eighteen cents each, and larger orders will continue to reduce the per-mailer cost. Similarly, larger orders will reduce price per-mail-piece cost on smaller-sized mailers as well. For example, a more traditionally sized 11 by 17–inch, four-color mailer on a high-quality stock will cost sixty cents each in quantities of five thousand. But, an order for fifty thousand such mailers will bring the cost down to twenty-two cents each, and an order for one hundred thousand will lower the cost further to eighteen cents each. The quantity discount is also evident in postcard-size mail pieces. Picture Perfect Campaigns will provide five thousand postcard-size mail pieces on a high-quality card, with four-color printing, for fifty-five cents each, but an order of fifty thousand such cards will reduce the price to eighteen cents each and an order of one hundred thousand will cut the price to thirteen cents each.[20]

While costs for the mailing piece itself normally diminish as the number of pieces purchased increases, the larger the mailing, the larger the costs of postage and the larger the costs in the use of volunteer time or payment to a direct mail house that arranges the mailing.

By controlling the costs of the mail piece itself, as well as the size of the mailing, the cost of direct mail can generally be managed to conform to the campaign's needs, enabling most campaigns to use mailings. Direct mailings are the major form of campaign advertising in many lower-level races. Often, the advertisements that the lower-level campaign might use in newspapers or on radio and television are likely to be lost in the large number of political advertisements that flood those media in the weeks before election. Moreover, often the costs of purchasing sufficient radio or television time, or newspaper space, are simply beyond the ability of small local campaigns. Direct mail, which can be made to fit most campaign budgets, can be targeted to specific voter blocs, and allows candidates to explain themselves thoroughly, is often critical in lower-level races.

Indeed, while most laypersons think of television as the principal medium of political campaigns, more money is actually spent on direct mail than on any other campaign medium. When every race from the bottom of the ballot to the top of the ballot is counted, and when all the expenses involved in direct mailings (including list rentals, database management, labeling, printing, and of course postage) are included, political candidates and their committees spent more money on direct mail—over $3 billion—than on any other advertising medium in the 1994 and 1996 election cycles.[21] With constant calls to reduce the costs of campaigning, it has been pointed out that, ironically, the largest single recipient of money spent on campaigns may be the United States Postal Service.[22]

As with any form of campaign communication, some principles have proven successful in the use of direct mail. Hal Malchow, creative director of The November Group, a well-respected political direct mail firm, has recently suggested a variety of guidelines for designing direct mail. Among them are:

- *Give the voter a reason to read your mailing.* Begin the mail piece in a dramatic and compelling way. The opening panel of the mail piece should attract attention through the use of a dramatic headline or an interesting photograph.
- *Localize your message.* Because direct mail facilitates very precise targeting, it should be used accordingly. If a neighborhood in your district is concerned about a school issue or a proposed highway, be sure that the mail sent to that community reflects your interest in their concern and does not ignore local issues in favor of simply treating issues of more general concern throughout your constituency.
- *Use the twenty-second test.* Malchow claims that the average voter will give a mail piece between twenty and sixty seconds. "They will look at the cover, the headlines, the pictures and often the captions under the photographs. But few people will actually read your literature." Consequently, "to be effective, you have to tell your story in a 20-second glance. Can someone in 20 seconds read the headlines, look at the pictures and maybe read the captions and come away with the basic points of your message? If not, you have not designed a good piece of campaign literature."

- *Use a letter shop.* Malchow is an advocate of using a professional mailing organization. He claims that "we all want to save money, but don't be a dunce. A letter shop is cheaper than pizza and beer for your volunteers." Malchow has found that, for two to five cents per piece, a letter shop will automatically label your pieces, sort and bag the mail, and fully prepare it for the post office in a manner that qualifies for full postal discounts for presorted mail. He claims that "even the poorest campaign should avoid" hand labeling and sorting third-class mail. He finds such a task to be both so difficult and so time-consuming that the costs of having it done professionally are well worth the expense.[23]

Since 75 percent of all direct mail is not opened, Malchow and others focus not only on the content of the direct mail piece, but also on the envelope. Malchow has suggested not even utilizing an envelope. To both save money, and more importantly to gain attention, he recommends using oversized postcards, unusual shapes, and folded pieces that bear no resemblance to a letter or traditional campaign brochure.[24] Other direct mail specialists focus on using the envelope itself to attract attention. Todd Meredith, co-owner of the Direct Mail Marketing Group, who has worked on behalf of forty members of Congress, claims that varying envelope color and size are the most basic ways of gaining voter attention.[25]

Telephone Contact Services

Growing sophistication in the application of computer technology to campaigning has resulted not only in the growth of direct mail but also in the growth of telephone contact services. Companies providing such services, in many instances, will work from voter lists that they have prepared and will sell or lease to candidates, as well as from lists that the campaign itself provides. Campaigns will use telephone contact for a variety of purposes. Most commonly, it will be used to deliver persuasive messages, raise money, and get out the vote on election day.

When persuasion is the goal, voters can be targeted by demographic characteristics, and a persuasive message can be scripted for members of each group being called. Similarly, fund-raising solicitations can also be narrowly targeted and a precise script developed to use with various types of potential contributors. Telephone contact, like direct mail, allows for precise targeting. Telephones are frequently used on election day to get out the vote. As the day progresses, voters previously identified as supportive can be contacted to remind them, and if necessary help them, get to the polls.

Telephone contact firms will provide several services to a campaign. First, they will often script the phone conversation. Second, they will provide professionally trained callers to actually make the calls. Third, they will provide state-of-the-art equipment to facilitate efficient use of the phone. Predictive dialing systems, used by most major national telephone contact services, which utilize sophisticated dialing equipment and computer software, can provide the campaign with major savings in time and cost. Typically, by filtering out all busy signals, answering machines, disconnected lines, and other useless responses, such systems allow the campaign to deliver as many as thirty to forty messages of ninety seconds in length each hour from each phone being used. Non-computerized phone banks will average about fifteen calls per phone, per hour, of the same length. Moreover, these systems can reduce the per-call cost of reaching voters by 30 percent or more, often bringing the costs down to under a dollar a call for persuasive messages and as little as thirty-five cents or less for election day get-out-the-vote calls. In addition, a sustained effort can reach a large number of voters. With good equipment, a fifty line phone bank, using a ninety-second script, operating three hours an evening, can place approximately five thousand calls per night.[26] One growing concern of telephone contact services is the growing reliance of Americans on cell phones. Cell phone numbers are not listed in directories. Hence, those Americans who rely on them exclusively, a growing number in recent years, are difficult for political phone contact firms to reach.

Print Advertisements

Print advertisements in newspapers and magazines have been a part of American campaigns from our nation's inception.[27] Newspaper and magazine advertisements, the two types of print advertisements on which this section focuses, offer political advertisers several advantages. First, they provide for timeliness. Not only can the campaign plan well in advance to determine precisely when it wants an advertisement to run, but normally the campaign can make changes, both in the advertisement content and in the advertisement size, relatively quickly. Consequently, utilizing the daily paper may be an effective means of quickly countering an opposition argument.

Typically, if advertisement space has been purchased in advance, the copy can be changed on short notice in most metropolitan dailies. Additionally, a new advertisement can be purchased on short notice.[28] Since skilled writers can normally produce a political advertisement extremely quickly, the daily paper is an efficient means of responding to opponents. Radio commercials offer a similar advantage, but television is normally not as advantageous. Though television stations can accommodate changes in commercials, it normally takes a greater effort to produce a television commercial than to produce a newspaper or radio spot, making it more difficult for the candidate to respond rapidly through television. This is not to say that television commercials cannot be changed, for frequently they are. However, typically, the process is either slower or entails more hardship on the campaign.[29]

Newspapers and magazine advertisements also offer the opportunity for candidates to express themselves more fully than do most other types of paid advertising. Candidates can present a considerable amount of material about themselves in a full-page or even a half- or quarter-page advertisement. Speaking at the normal rate of speed, a sixty-second radio or television commercial forces the campaign to reduce its message to one hundred and fifty words or less.[30] By adjusting the size of both the advertisement and the type used in the advertisement, candidates can easily present a print message that is three times longer or more and still create a physically appealing advertisement. If the message being sent is complex and needs considerable explanation, newspapers and magazines are often exceptionally good vehicles for getting the message to voters.

The liabilities of print advertising involve targeting and cost. First, according to most estimates, over 12 percent of adult Americans are functional illiterates.[31] Clearly, this substantial group of citizens cannot be effectively reached by print media. Second, it is frequently difficult to target specific audiences with newspaper and magazine advertisements.

However, in recent years targeting messages to specific magazine and newspaper audiences has become easier. Many larger daily papers that have readerships located in large geographical areas have special sections or editions that are used in the appropriate geographic area. For example, both of the daily newspapers in Cincinnati, Ohio, have special northern Kentucky editions. While the paper is largely the same, the northern Kentucky editions focus the local news coverage more heavily on northern Kentucky than on Ohio. These editions are distributed to Kentucky subscribers and used on newsstands in Kentucky, facilitating some geographical targeting. The use of special editions aimed at specific geographic segments of the market has become commonplace for many larger metropolitan newspapers.

Smaller newspapers, because their circulation is limited, may also lend themselves to targeting. Candidates running for offices that include the entire voting populations of smaller towns may do well to advertise in the weekly papers that service most smaller communities or suburban communities. Candidates who have targeted a specific religious, ethnic, or occupational group might also do well to consider advertising in the smaller, often weekly, newspapers that are aimed at these audiences.

Additionally, today many magazine advertisements can also be bought on a regional or even a ZIP code basis. This type of magazine purchase facilitates rather precise targeting. For example, a congressional candidate might choose to advertise in a special interest magazine that she feels is read heavily by a group she has targeted. Moreover, the candidate can limit her purchase to subscribers who live in those ZIP codes within her congressional district.

An additional advantage to this type of purchase is that it may give a local, regional, or statewide candidate additional stature to be associated with a national publication. The degree to which specific magazines can accommodate this type of advertising varies, as of course does price. In recent years, primarily as a function of the growth of computerization within the newspaper and magazine industry, the use of magazines and newspapers for targeted audiences has become more feasible. However, they are still considered "mass media" and cannot be as narrowly focused as direct mail.

Precisely because they are mass media, read by massive numbers of people, newspaper and magazine costs are often high. For example, a full-page weekday black-and-white advertisement in the *Cincinnati Enquirer*, the dominant daily paper in the thirty-first largest market in the country, would cost a political campaign $11,033. Smaller advertisements are sold at the rate of $85.53 per column inch; hence, a quarter-page ad would cost $2,758. A similar ad, run on a Sunday, when the other daily paper in Cincinnati does not print, costs $14,436. The costs of smaller Sunday advertisements are calculated at the rate of $111.91 per column inch; hence, a quarter-page ad would cost $3,609. These costs are for black-and-white advertisements. Adding color increases the prices by approximately $5000 for a full-page advertisement and corresponding amounts for smaller ads.[32]

Radio

Radio is an often-underestimated vehicle for political advertisements. Surveys suggest that the typical American household has four radios, not including those in cars.[33] Radio also allows for a moderate degree of targeting. While radio is not as precise as direct mail, the wide variety of radio stations found in most areas tends to segment the audience and provides campaigns with the means to target some audiences.

For much of the first half of the twentieth century, radio was ranked with the print media as the dominant media of political advertising. However, beginning in the 1950s, radio was utilized less and less frequently. The 1952 presidential campaign between General Dwight David Eisenhower and Governor Adlai Stevenson was the last national campaign in which expenditures on radio advertising were roughly equal to those on television.[34] Since 1952, television has superseded radio as the dominant electronic media. By 2004, political campaigns were spending only about 7 percent of their budgets on radio.[35] Nevertheless, radio has a place in many campaigns, and is often a critical medium in bottom of the ballot races and races in rural areas.

Radio retains an important place in the arsenal of political advertising weapons available to candidates for at least three reasons. First, radio lends itself to advertisements that can vary greatly in length and hence can serve a variety of functions. Second, radio can be targeted. Third, radio is not perceived as an expensive medium.

Radio commercials can be bought in a variety of time lengths, ranging from ten or fifteen seconds, through the more common thirty- and sixty-second spots, to longer time slots, such as five minutes, fifteen minutes, or half an hour. Consequently, radio can serve a variety of functions. For example, a fifteen-second spot might consist of nothing more than a brief jingle in which the candidate's name is repeated several times. Constant use of this jingle can quickly help to establish name recognition. Since 80 percent of radio users are using it to hear music, jingles are often suggested as especially appropriate for use on radio.[36] The effect of political jingles can be enhanced by designing a jingle that fits the overall format of the station on which it is being played. A jingle that sounds like music from the 1950s and '60s might, for example, be used effectively on an oldies station.

Traditional thirty-second and sixty-second radio advertisements might be used for jingles and other commercials to establish name recognition, but can also provide some insight into the candidate and the candidate's beliefs. A five-minute commercial allows the candidate to present a reasonably complete analysis of one or perhaps more questions. Purchasing such time slots on television is often either costly or impractical.

Radio can be targeted because certain stations tend to attract certain demographic groups. Easy listening stations, religious stations, foreign language stations, hard rock stations, news talk stations, and oldies stations all appeal to different demographic groups. Contrary to popular belief, the appeal of talk radio cuts across the entire political spectrum and is not limited to conservatives. According to Arbitron studies done during 2004, political independents make up the largest segment of talk radio listeners, accounting for about 41 percent of the talk radio audience. Republicans account for 31 percent of the talk radio audience, and Democrats account for 26 percent of the talk radio audience.[37] Though these are overall figures, clearly some talk radio stations and shows will likely be more appealing and attract more listeners from one party than the other. Radio gives the campaign an opportunity to target specific audiences and prepare messages aimed at those audiences. It is impossible to say whether radio allows for better targeting than, for example, newspapers and magazines. Every campaign has to evaluate the media available to it and the audiences it wishes to target. Nevertheless, in many communities, radio can be used to reach targeted audiences and often lends itself to this use better than many other forms of advertising.

Radio is often perceived as an inexpensive advertising medium. Most political campaigns seek to advertise during drive times—5:00 to 9:00 a.m. and 2:00 to 6:00 p.m.—when commuters on their way to and from work help create the largest radio audiences. During the 2006 elections, a thirty-second political commercial during morning drive time on the most popular talk radio station in Cincinnati cost $110. The same commercial run during the same time period on the most popular music station, which appeals to a relatively youthful audience, sold for $250. The same commercial run on the highest-rated morning radio show in Cincinnati sold for $300.[38] Clearly the differences in audience size and audience demographics will enter into their attractiveness to political advertisers.

Thirty-second advertisements on popular nationally syndicated radio talk shows, such as those of Laura Ingram or Michael Savage, cost $115 and $30, respectively, in the Cincinnati market. A $40 fee would have bought the political advertiser their choice of a thirty-second or a one-minute advertisement on the Al Franken show. Similar advertisements on the Rush Limbaugh show would cost $150 for a thirty-second spot and $175 for a one-minute spot during the 2006 election cycle. None of these shows airs during the prime drive-time advertising hours.[39]

As evident in the next section, in some areas the cost of a single television commercial on a local nightly news program may be the equivalent of a week's worth of drive-time radio advertising on a highly rated station, or two weeks or more of drive-time advertising on a station that may not attract a broad audience but that appeals to a group targeted by the campaign.

Radio is particularly popular among political advertisers who are campaigning in rural areas and those who are campaigning for lesser offices. Rural areas may be reliant on papers from larger nearby cities or on more urban areas for television. Advertising in the larger papers or on television forces the campaign to purchase an audience that cannot vote in its election. This is often simply not cost-effective for the rural election. Utilizing the small-town paper provides an appropriate audience but that audience can only be addressed once per week. Hence, many rural campaigns find local small-town radio stations an attractive option to include in their media mix. Similarly, lower-level elections, often poorly financed and often covering a smaller geographical area than that served by television stations and large circulation metropolitan area papers, find radio a viable option.

Indeed, radio stations in some areas have been forced to put a limit on the number of political commercials they will accept. In past election cycles such stations limited political campaigns to one drive-time advertisement each morning and one each afternoon during the workweek. It is also common for stations to prefer federal candidates and place more restrictive limits on state and local candidates.[40] Such limits are often necessary because the demand of political advertisers during the few weeks preceding the election are often so great that stations could not accommodate their normal advertisers and honor their long-term advertising contracts to those advertisers if they accepted all of the political commercials that campaigns wish to air.

Though radio has many virtues as a vehicle for political commercials, it also has drawbacks. Chief among them is the fact that, among all of the major forms of media, radio demands the least amount of attention. Most radio is listened to by individuals simultaneously engaged in other activities. Consequently, campaigns are paying for audiences that are not giving them full attention.

Television

Television offers the political advertiser a variety of advantages. First, it is the only advertising medium that appeals to two of our senses—seeing and hearing. As a consequence, television is able to convey more in a short time, and typically it has a greater impact on the viewer who is getting "twice the message."

Second, of all the mass media, television is often able to produce the largest audiences. The viewership for a popular show often far exceeds the readership for the largest circulation papers in a community. If the candidate seeks widespread exposure, television is unmatched as an advertising medium. However, many television programs attract audiences that are politically apathetic, thus somewhat diminishing their value. Because news programs tend to attract audiences that are attentive to current events and more prone to vote, political advertisers normally seek to place their advertisements on news programs and other shows such as *60 Minutes, Prime Time Live, Dateline, Today, Good Morning America*, and local newscasts that attract individuals with an interest in current events. Somewhat related to the fact that television can provide a large audience is the third advantage of television. In our media-oriented society, television lends a degree of credibility. Imagine how seriously a presidential candidate would be taken if he or she never used television. Indeed, this was one of the problems that Jesse Jackson faced in 1984. In part because his campaign did not make extensive use of television, he was not viewed as a viable candidate. The legitimacy that television conveys to a candidate has also been recognized by candidates running for lesser offices. Today, in many areas, it is not uncommon to see television commercials on behalf of candidates for every federal and statewide office, and for many local offices such as mayor, city council member, county prosecutor, judge, or sheriff. Candidates for offices that voters have come to associate with television commercials run a real risk of losing credibility if they do not include television in their media mix.

A final advantage of television is that it does allow for some degree of targeting. As indicated earlier, certain shows tend to attract audiences composed of individuals who are concerned with current events and prone to vote. Other shows attract audiences that are heavily weighted toward a given demographic group that the campaign may have targeted. For example, *Monday Night Football* is more prone to attract a heavily male audience, while *General Hospital* is more prone to attract a heavily female audience. Even local news shows often attract audiences with different demographic makeups, often depending on the nature of the anchorpersons and the manner in which the news is presented.

In sum, television has become the dominant media of political advertising for a variety of reasons. Because it allows the viewer to use two senses, it is often able to convey more than other media. Television can provide wide exposure, helping unknown candidates become known rapidly. Moreover, it lends a sense of credibility to candidates and allows for some degree of targeting. However, like all political media, television is not without its liabilities.

The most obvious disadvantage of television is the enormous expense associated with it. For the growing number of campaigns that utilize television, it almost invariably is the principal expense that these campaigns incur. Many campaigns budget 75 to 80 percent of their money for television.[41] By April 28, 2006, still early into the 2006 election cycle, the 1,018 candidates running for the House of Representatives had already raised $390,061,491 or an average of approximately $383,100. Similarly, by April 28, 2006, still early into the 2006 election cycle, the 124 candidates running for the United States Senate had already raised $266,426,948 or an average of approximately $2,143,600.[42] In many states it has become impossible to be a serious candidate for the United States Senate without the prospect of raising ten million dollars or more. In many congressional districts, it has become impossible to be a serious candidate without the prospect of raising one million dollars or more. In 2004, candidates running for the presidency raised a total of $880 million dollars. Of that, George W. Bush raised $367 million, John Kerry raised $326 million, and third-party candidates or candidates who dropped out during the primaries accounted for the remainder.[43] Today, it has become impossible to be considered a serious candidate for the presidency without the prospect of raising tens of millions of dollars just to compete in the major party primaries. And, of course, these figures continue to increase. Importantly, for this discussion, virtually every explanation for this staggering increase in the cost of campaigning focuses partially, if not primarily, on the increased costs of television.[44]

Several examples will make clear how quickly television costs escalate. During the 2006 election cycle, a single thirty-second political spot on highly rated news-like morning shows such as *Today* cost $750 in the medium-sized market of Cincinnati. Lesser-rated competitors commanded $450 for the same thirty-second spot.[45] Shows such as these tend to attract audiences concerned with current events who are prone to vote. Hence, they are popular with political advertisers. The cost of a thirty-second spot on a moderately rated syndicated talk show, such as those of Montel Williams or the more popular Martha Stewart, broadcast throughout the morning on the network affiliates in Cincinnati ranged from $250 to $450. A thirty-second spot on the afternoon soap operas, whose demographics make them appealing to campaigns that are targeting women, cost $500 in the Cincinnati market.[46]

A thirty-second ad on the syndicated early-evening quasi-news show that leads into Cincinnati's CBS network's prime-time schedule, *Entertainment Tonight*, cost $2,400 for political advertisers. An ad on the information/entertainment syndicated shows that lead into the NBC network prime-time schedule, such as *Access Hollywood* and *Extra*, cost $1,400 for political advertisers in the Cincinnati market during the 2006 election cycle. These shows are often popular with political advertisers since they command large audiences as they lead into the prime evening viewing hours.

The costs of a thirty-second political ad run during a popular prime-time show, in the Cincinnati market during 2006, could quickly mount up. For example, such an ad run on *Law and Order* cost $9,250. A similar ad run on *Will and Grace* sold for $9,000. A thirty-second spot aired during *Survivor* would have cost a campaign $12,000 and a similar spot aired during *C. S. I.* would have cost $15,000. A thirty-second spot on *Deal or No Deal* cost $4,200, while a similar spot on *King of Queens* cost $6,000. Representative rates on prime-time newsmagazines, often popular with political advertisers because they tend to attract viewers with a high interest in the news and a propensity to vote, were the $2,800 fee charged for a thirty-second spot on *Dateline NBC*, and the $3,500 fee charged for a thirty-second spot on *60 Minutes*. The cost of a thirty-second spot on the 11 p.m. local newscasts ranged from about $2,500 to $2,800.[47]

Thus, a very limited television campaign in 2006 consisting of a daily thirty-second spot on a soap opera, a daily thirty-second spot on an early-evening quasi-news show such as *Entertainment Tonight*, two prime-time ads in an entire week on moderately rated shows such as *Deal or No Deal* and *King of Queens*, and a single daily spot on the mid-rated late evening news would cost slightly over $37,000 a week. Keep in mind, this would be an exceedingly limited advertising campaign. It includes only three regularly scheduled commercials a day, and then they are only scheduled for a five-day week. These daily commercials are supplemented with only two commercials a week on modestly priced prime-time shows. Moreover, Cincinnati is not among the largest thirty media markets in the nation. A campaign that advertised on two or more newscasts, which is common in political campaigns; that advertised in the morning, as many campaigns seeking to target older voters and women commonly do; that included several more prime-time commercials; that advertised on weekends, as most campaigns do; or that was waged in a larger media market would quickly escalate the costs. Clearly, television advertising can be expensive; moreover, that expense is growing exceedingly rapidly.[48]

In addition to the cost of purchasing time, television involves more elaborate production costs than other media. Most political consultants who specialize in television currently suggest that a good rule of thumb is to estimate the cost of television production at 5 to 10 percent of the cost of air time. Many political spots are produced for $10,000 or less. The more expensive political spots rarely exceed $30,000 in production costs. While this is substantially higher than the production costs for other forms of political media, it is exceedingly modest when compared to the production cost of other television commercials.[49]

A second difficulty with television is one that is a function of geography. In many parts of the nation, targeting with television is difficult and candidates may be forced to pay for audiences that cannot vote in their elections. For example, the media markets served by stations in such cities as St. Louis, Kansas City, Philadelphia, New York City, Louisville, Washington, D.C., and Boston, to name just a few, are composed of residents of more than one state. Thus, candidates running for any local office, and even state offices, are forced to pay for audiences who cannot participate in their election. While this problem also exists for other media serving communities such as these, the expenses of television heighten the problem.

A third potential problem with television is that many candidates do not project well using television. Though some candidates like President Ronald Reagan, Senator Jessie Helms, and Arizona congressman J. D. Hayworth entered politics after first working in radio and television, and others such as former Florida congressman Joe Scarborough and former Cincinnati mayor Jerry Springer had such an affinity for television that when they left elected office they became television personalities, many candidates are not comfortable with television. This does not by any means preclude the use of television, but it does mean that a realistic assessment of the candidate's abilities must be made and, if the candidate is found wanting, the campaign may have to change its advertising strategy.[50]

In sum, just as with any other advertising medium, television offers political candidates both advantages and disadvantages. Television commercials often have a strong impact on viewers who must utilize two of their senses as they attend to the commercials. Television can also provide a massive audience for the campaign's messages, contribute to the candidate's credibility, and allow for limited targeting. However, the costs of television are extremely high, especially in many races where candidates find themselves paying for audiences that cannot participate in the election. Moreover, production costs for television are also high, and many candidates do not perform well on television. All of these factors must be weighed as the campaign develops its own unique media mix.

Videocassettes and Cable Television

By 1994, over ninety-two million videocassette recorders (VCRs) could be found in over seventy-five million American households. Over 90 percent of the households that included regular voters owned a VCR.[51] Thus, in the last decade, political campaigns, always on the cutting edge of technology, have not ignored the explosive growth in VCR popularity.

Traditionally, the use of a customized videocassette to distribute the candidate's message has been perceived as either excessively expensive or ineffective. But improved technology in the production of the cassettes themselves, as well as improved methods of packaging and mailing, have brought the cost of a customized videocassette to under $2 each, including mailing costs.[52] Cost figures of this sort, which might also include accompanying literature and a mailer that typically has a printed message on it, are gradually making customized videos price-competitive with direct mail. Improved technology and the economies of size suggest that, though customized cassettes will likely remain more expensive than most mail pieces, that gap will continue to diminish in the near future.

Moreover, evidence suggests that customized videocassettes are exceptionally effective. According to some studies, as many as 40 percent of those who receive an unsolicited video will watch it, a far higher rate than unsolicited mail typically generates. Moreover, studies suggest the response rates, whether the video is simply seeking voter support or seeking volunteers and/or money, typically run 20 percent higher than direct mail.[53]

As discussed in the preceding section, television is a powerful medium. A cassette typically provides the candidate with more time to persuade and inform the voter than the normal thirty- to sixty-second television spot. Cassettes can be better targeted to more specific voters than typical television spots. Moreover, customized videos can be adapted for a variety of uses. As we discussed earlier, they can be shown as part of a coffee or tea, both in place of the candidate or as a supplement to the candidate's message. They can be used with surrogate speakers. They can be used for both persuading voters and seeking contributions.

Like customized videocassettes, the use of cable television also allows political figures to capitalize on the power of television as a medium, while providing better targeting than can typically be done through the use of network and local affiliate programming. As recently as the 1988 and 1990 election cycles, political campaigns made little use of cable television. But as the industry grew, so too did its attractiveness to political candidates. By 1992, cable billings to political campaigns totaled $4.5 million. By 1996, some estimates suggest that 36 percent of political media budgets was spent on cable, and 80 percent of all congressional candidates used cable.[54] Today, not only major federal office seekers like these, but a host of state and local figures are also making use of cable. It has become a tool in the paid media package of a wide variety of political campaigns.

The rise of the cable industry, whose sales forces were aggressive in seeking political business, and the decline in network viewership are altering the political time-buying strategies of many campaigns. The availability of national advertising on the cable networks, local advertising on cable networks and local cable shows, and even regional advertising on "cable interconnects," which link cable systems into regional networks, facilitates voter targeting by geography.

Moreover, cable stations segment the audience by interest and background. Stations such as ESPN, CNN, Arts and Entertainment, Lifetime, the History Channel, USA, the Nashville Network, the Comedy Channel, and many others each appeal to a unique segment of the population. Thus, cable advertising facilitates voter targeting by both geography and demography, often in many areas to a greater extent than the broadcast networks allow.

In sum, the enormous costs of television advertising are driving political campaigners to seek the most bang for their buck. Consequently, political campaigns, seeking to harness the power of television with better ability to target and reduce costs, now utilize alternatives to the traditional over-the-air television advertisements—most notably, customized videocassettes and, particularly, cable television.

The Internet

In 1993, Ted Kennedy became the first U.S. senator to have a website, while, in 1994, Dianne Feinstein established the first candidate website.[55]

By the 1996 elections, some studies suggest that as much as 20 percent of the public utilized the Internet for politically related activities.[56] In 1998, Jesse Ventura won the governorship of Minnesota, and observers, as well as Ventura staff, claimed that he could not have done so without his effective use of the Internet. Moreover, by the late 1990s, a website was more of a campaign necessity than a campaign novelty. During the 2000 and 2002 election cycles, the Internet was used by candidates for a wide variety of reasons, and by the 2004 election cycle political candidates were raising large amounts of money through their websites.[57]

The principal effect of the Internet is to provide candidates a means of dispensing information directly to the public. The implications of this are considerable. The Internet is a high-return, low-cost means of dispensing information. Campaigns can establish an Internet presence for a very modest amount, compared to the costs of many other forms of advertising. As a consequence, it can be utilized by even poorly funded campaigns.

Currently, political Internet sites serve a variety of functions. They serve to:

1. Provide information to voters about the candidate.
2. Raise money.
3. Provide information to voters about candidate views on policy issues.
4. Provide political information and news about the campaign.
5. Communicate with supporters and endorsing groups.
6. Provide election information to voters (polling place, registration information, etc.).
7. Recruit campaign volunteers.
8. Provide information and news about the community.
9. Seek voter opinion on issues.
10. Attack the opposition.

The functions that Internet sites serve for candidates, as listed here, seem to coincide well with the purposes voters have in mind when they access political sites on the Internet. Researchers Marion Just, Ann Crigler, and Montague Kern have found that voters tend to use the Internet for what they term "surveillance" and "solidarity" reasons. By *surveillance*, they refer to the desire of voters to survey or gain information about the campaign. By *solidarity*, they refer to the desire of voters "to experience the gratifications of reinforced, shared political identification or orientation."[58]

Candidate sites are not the only places on the Internet where users can get political information. Virtually every major news organization in the nation has a website. Moreover, there are political news sites that are not affiliated with any candidate or party. Many voters seeking to survey the campaign scene, Just et al. claim, rely on these sites more than on candidate or party sites.[59] Nevertheless, candidates and party sites contribute to the surveillance function and clearly serve the solidarity function.

As with other media, the quality of political Internet sites varies. The best candidate Internet sites share several characteristics. First, the home page identifies the candidate, utilizes the candidate logo, and offers at least one clear indication of what the candidate is about. Frequently that indication may be a slogan or a brief phrase or sentence synopsis of the candidate's position on a key issue.

Second, the home page clearly indicates what content is available throughout the candidate's site. Typically, the viewer can click on a series of icons that will take the viewer to such things as the candidate's biography, the candidate's issue positions, a message or story of the day, news of upcoming campaign events, and information about key staff members. Moreover, again by clicking on an icon found on the home page, viewers can get involved in the campaign by indicating their willingness to volunteer on behalf of the candidate. Additional icons can offer viewers an opportunity to receive e-mail or make a contribution to the campaign.[60]

Third, a good site will be constantly updated by the campaign. Users who indicate strong interest in the campaign by volunteering should be contacted immediately. E-mail should be sent out regularly to voters who put themselves on receiver lists. The story or message of the day should be just that and changed on a daily basis.

Finally, throughout the site, large blocks of text should be broken up by frequent use of subheads, photos, links to other sites, or white space. Strong graphics should be used, but a good website will also keep the graphics to a manageable size so that each area of the site can be accessed quickly and the viewer is not delayed, waiting for a large graphic.[61]

In sum, the use of the Internet as an advertising medium by political candidates has come of age. Internet sites are a vital advertising tool in most campaigns. As the entire medium matures, no doubt political candidates will develop increasingly sophisticated ways of using it to communicate with voters. However, already it has become a source of information for many voters, and it provides the campaign a means of interacting with voters, particularly supporters.

CAMPAIGN ADVERTISING STRATEGIES

The circumstances of the campaign normally dictate the use of one of four basic patterns in the purchase of radio and television time. Since radio and television constitute a major portion of the advertising of most campaigns, the strategies used for purchasing radio and television time typically characterize the entire campaign's advertising strategy. Time buyers aim at reaching targeted voters the maximum number of times the campaign budget allows. To do so, they utilize the standard audience measure, gross rating points. A gross rating point represents 1 percent of the TV viewing audience. Theoretically, a purchase of one hundred points means that the entire TV audience will see the commercial once. Since most consultants estimate that a commercial needs to be seen at least three to five times before it makes an impression, a buy of five hundred points is considered "saturation." However, by the 2000 and 2002 election cycles, many consultants were recommending that their clients buy even more TV time. They did so because of the growing "clutter" of political commercials. With soft money enabling many groups to utilize television, it was becoming harder and harder for the candidates' ads to register with the public. Moreover, the growing use of VCRs often meant that ads were skipped by many audience members. Hence, currently, many consultants advocate a purchase of seven hundred to one thousand ratings points for "saturation."[62]

Buying backward from election day, campaigns will seek purchases of at least five hundred points. In markets where costs are low and perhaps where a large number of highly targeted voters can be expected to see the advertisements, or in exceedingly well financed campaigns, it is not unheard of for a campaign to purchase twenty-five hundred points in the last weeks of the campaign, thus providing that theoretically voters will see the commercial twenty-five times. Computerization of such things as program schedules, demographic audience data, and pricing information has facilitated more and more sophistication in the purchasing of airtime.[63]

The purchase of commercial time reflects a campaign's overall strategy. With some differences that are reflected in the unique virtues of each form of media, the basic radio and television strategy is often commonly extended to the use of display graphics, direct mail, and print media. In this section, we briefly examine the four most common overall campaign advertising strategies.[64]

The Spurt Strategy

This strategy is often used by candidates who are not well known at the outset of the campaign. The strategy is to "spurt" early in the campaign, often four to six months before the election, purchasing a large amount of radio and television time for one to two weeks. The use of radio and television is often supplemented with an early round of newspaper advertisements and an early effort at distributing a large number of yard signs, bumper stickers, buttons, and other display graphics. The point of this early spurt is to build name recognition and help establish the candidate as a credible contender for the office.

The campaign, having now utilized a reasonable amount of its resources early, then typically eliminates or drastically reduces its use of radio and television for a long period of time. During this period, the campaign may well focus on the Internet and direct mail efforts, often using these media both to target specific audiences for persuasive messages and to help raise funds to replenish the monies spent on the early spurt deemed necessary to establish name recognition. Moreover, the campaign may do a considerable amount of neighborhood canvassing, leaving literature throughout the district.

Finally, the campaign makes a final spurt, purchasing considerable radio and television time from the morning of the election backward as far as it can, hopefully at least a week or more. As with the original spurt, the final radio and television spurt is accompanied by the use of other media.

The point of this strategy is to allow the candidate to open strongly and close strongly. While all candidates seek to close strongly, those who start at a disadvantage often utilize the spurt strategy to get them into the race. The candidate who starts out with little name recognition typically has many problems. The initial spurt in advertising spending will hopefully create a spurt in the candidate's standing in the polls, enhance the candidate's credibility, facilitate greater fund-raising, encourage more people to volunteer support, and, in sum, simply get the campaign moving.

The Fast Finish Strategy

This strategy goes by a variety of names, including the Silky Sullivan strategy, the Miracle Braves strategy, or the '51 Giants strategy. Just as Silky Sullivan, the famous California-bred racehorse, and those famous baseball teams started very slowly, only to close with a rush and win, some candidates choose to start slowly and close with a rush, expecting to win on election day.

Typically this strategy is implemented by buying a complete schedule of radio and television advertisements for the last portion of the election. Buying backward from election day, the campaign purchases a complete schedule of radio and television time for as many days as it can afford, normally at least a week, and further back if it can afford it. Then, depending on what the campaign can afford, still buying backward, the campaign gradually diminishes the amount of commercials it purchases each day. The effect of this type of purchase is that voters see the campaign starting very slowly, with a scattering of commercials. Gradually, the advertising increases until voters are completely saturated in the week immediately preceding the election. Similarly, other media efforts are intensified as the election draws closer.

Most campaigns will use some variation of this strategy. Clearly, candidates want their messages to have the greatest impact and feel that this is best achieved by surrounding the voter with their message in the days immediately preceding the election. Candidates who start from a position of strength find this strategy particularly appealing, since they often feel that their initial strength allows them to husband their resources until near the end of the campaign. By then, concentrating their advertising in a limited time, they can purchase so much airtime in the last days of the campaign that they are confident their messages cannot be missed by voters.

The Really Big Show Strategy

This strategy is designed to capitalize on free news coverage. Named after the expression frequently used by 1950s and 1960s television variety show host Ed Sullivan to describe his program, this strategy is built around several major events that are scheduled periodically throughout the campaign. For example, in a congressional race, the candidate holds a press conference and immediately follows it up with several speeches making a major accusation about the shortcomings of her opponent. Second, the candidate has a debate with her opponent. Third, a major national figure comes to town to speak on behalf of the candidate. Each of these three occurrences is a major event in the campaign. Moreover, the candidate has considerable control over their timing.

Using the "really big show" strategy, the candidate will focus her advertising around those events that are likely to receive considerable free media coverage on the news. She will increase her paid advertising at the time of the press conference and speeches, reinforcing through advertising what she is saying in the conference and speeches. She will increase her advertising at the time of the debate, reinforcing positions she takes in the debate or perhaps using cinema verité and testimonial commercials to emphasize how effective she was in the debate and reinforce the points she made during the debate. She will increase her advertising immediately preceding, during, and after the visit by the major national figure, better linking herself to that figure and basking in that figure's prominence and credibility.

By increasing her advertising at the time she is naturally receiving greater free coverage in the news, the candidate turns a campaign event into a "really big show." Often, because of the proximity in timing between the news coverage and the commercials, and depending on how her advertisements are handled, the paid media blends with the free news coverage in the mind of the voter. Candidates using this strategy will generally provide that at least one major event takes place within a few days of the election so that they can combine elements of this approach with the fast finish strategy. Moreover, this strategy can also be blended with the spurt approach by coordinating the early media effort with an important campaign event.

The Cruise Strategy

This strategy is particularly appealing for candidates who are clearly ahead and are striving to maintain their lead. Just as the cruise control of a car allows the driver to drive at a steady speed, this approach calls for the campaign to advertise at a steady rate. The campaign makes what the media industry calls a "flat buy," purchasing a constant number of commercials each day during the stages of the campaign when media will be used.

Often this strategy is combined with the fast finish approach, so that the campaign makes a flat buy for several weeks or even a month or more prior to the last week or two of the campaign, when it then increases its advertising. This strategy allows the candidate who is ahead to remain constantly visible for a long period of time and then finish strongly. In sum, the overall advertising strategies of political campaigns can be characterized by the way they purchase radio and television time. Most campaigns utilize one of four approaches, or some combination of them. Though such factors such as the availability of funds, poll results, and the strategies of opponents may force modifications, part of the initial campaign plan should be to develop an overall advertising strategy.

MEDIA AND OTHER TYPES OF POLITICAL CONSULTANTS

As part of the 1986 U.S. Senate race in Georgia, an Atlanta television station arranged a debate between Frank Greer and Mike Murphy. Yet, neither man was a candidate for the Senate. Rather, they were the respective media consultants for U.S. Senate candidates Wyche Fowler Jr. and Mack Mattingly.[65] This debate dramatically illustrates the growing importance of political consultants, especially media consultants, in contemporary politics. While political consultants provide a variety of services to their candidates, most of those services are advertising and media related. Hence, we will conclude this chapter on the practices of political advertising by briefly examining the rise and growth of political consulting and the functions of political consultants.

History of Political Consulting

Virtually every political candidate, from George Washington's day forward, has turned to a group of advisers for advice on getting elected and often for advice on governing. Perhaps the most outstanding of America's early political consultants was John Beckley, a close personal friend and key political adviser to Thomas Jefferson. During Jefferson's bids for the presidency, Beckley wrote campaign material on his behalf, arranged for its distribution in key states, and organized a speaker's bureau on behalf of Jefferson.[66]

Throughout the nineteenth and early twentieth centuries, the growth of political parties, improvements in communication and transportation technology, and the need to deal with rapidly growing constituencies all contributed to the professionalization of political campaigning. The presidential campaigns of 1828, 1840, and 1896 were especially notable for advances in political campaigning and served as precursors to the consultant-driven campaigns of today.[67]

However, it was not until the 1920s when Calvin Coolidge turned to Edward Bernays that political figures began to seek the advice of individuals with extensive backgrounds and expertise in advertising, public relations, and polling. Few political figures listened to Bernays, a public relations counselor who was far ahead of his time in advising candidates to make better use of the media and polling. Nevertheless, his ideas foreshadowed much of what political campaigning has become at the outset of the twenty-first century.[68]

In 1934, Californians Clem Whitaker and his wife, Leona Baxter, founded the public relations firm of Whitaker and Baxter, which from its inception took on political clients, normally California Republicans. In that year, the firm helped defeat the popular writer Upton Sinclair, the Democratic candidate for governor. From that point on, political candidates sought their services. Whitaker and Baxter was a pioneer firm, and, though they eventually diversified to handle a wide variety of accounts, they were still helping candidates as late as 1967, when they handled Shirley Temple's unsuccessful congressional race.[69]

In 1952, television was first used as an advertising medium in a presidential campaign. The 1952 campaigns of both General Dwight David Eisenhower and Illinois governor Adlai Stevenson made use of television. Although both candidates had reservations about television, both campaigns secured the services of advertising agencies to help produce television commercials and serve in a variety of other functions.[70]

The fact that media consultants, whether in the employ of political consulting firms or advertising agencies, were in politics to stay was evident in 1956 when Stevenson again challenged Eisenhower. Accepting the

Democratic nomination, Stevenson decried the use of mass media advertising techniques, claiming that "the idea that you can merchandise candidates for high office like breakfast cereal—that you can gather votes like box tops—is, I think, the ultimate indignity in the democratic process." Yet, Stevenson made this very remark from a platform that had been redesigned by an advertising agency, to a national convention whose activities were being orchestrated in no small part by that same agency, for the benefit of the television audience.[71]

By the 1960s, campaigns were being waged more and more in the media, and political consultants were becoming more and more conspicuous in the conduct of those campaigns. Stuart Spencer, Bill Roberts, David Garth, Tony Schwartz, and a host of other consultants began to bring high technology to political campaigning throughout the 1960s.

In recent years, two factors have combined to make political consultants essential players in virtually every major political campaign. First, getting elected has become a perpetual job. Thus, helping candidates has become a perpetual job. In the past it was difficult to work as a political consultant, simply because, during nonelection years, the political consultant had no clients.

But the 1970s witnessed the advent of the perpetual candidate.[72] In the footsteps of the perpetual candidate has come the perpetual political consultant. As Burdett Loomis has incisively illustrated, since 1974, a "new breed" of politicians has encouraged the growth of administrative staffs, subcommittee and committee staffs, campaign staffs, political action committees and their staffs, a variety of political caucuses and their staffs, a variety of task forces and their staffs, a host of party organizations and their staffs, as well as the expansion of lobby groups and the dramatic growth of political action committees. Though the surge of these enterprises is perhaps most evident in Washington, it is also apparent in virtually every state capital as well. Political consultants can work on a campaign, which today might well start eighteen months to two years prior to the election, and when the campaign ends they can move to another campaign or to an organization such as those mentioned above, which utilize many of the skills of political consultants. As soon as the next campaign opening is available, they can then move to that opening, with very little "down" time.

In addition to the increased opportunities for employment of those with the skills of political consultants, political consulting itself has now become a full-time job for many consultants. As more and more campaigns are able to afford consultants, campaigns that once would not have used consultants are today often doing so. In sum, since the 1970s political consulting has become a viable career for a large number of individuals.

The rapid growth of the political consulting profession is a consequence of a variety of changes in our political system during the last decades of the twentieth century. From the standpoint of candidates, political consultants provide two big advantages over a candidate's own campaign staff and the efforts of party professionals. First, they provide a bigger bang for the buck, a greater return on the money spent in the campaign. Consultants are specialists in designing media messages and ensuring that those messages are transmitted most effectively. Whether it is the consultant who specializes in setting up phone banks, coaching political debaters, or producing television advertisements, consultants provide the campaign with a better return on its dollars. Second, political consultants provide campaigns with public opinion polling designed and executed specifically to help the campaign locate voters and prepare messages for those voters. Hence, the consulting profession has grown rapidly in the last three decades because it has provided candidates with highly desired services.[73]

Moreover, the growth of political consulting services has made the field one in which growing numbers of people are able to make a living. Though fees vary from consultant to consultant, currently it is not unusual for media consultants to charge a straight fee of $50,000 to $100,000 for a statewide race. Frequently the fee of the media consultants will be based on the size of the media buy. In the 2004 presidential campaign, Democratic media consultants working for Senator Kerry received fees that varied from 9 percent to 4.5 percent of the cost of the media buy, and President Bush's Republican media consultants received fees that represented 4.5 percent or less of their media buy.[74] In large market states and national campaigns, fees such as this can quickly amount to hundreds of thousands of dollars.

The "elite" political consultants, a group of about forty firms, have focused most of their efforts on statewide races. Working for presidential candidates, while potentially bringing prestige to a firm, is risky from a business standpoint. Only two of perhaps ten or more candidates will make it through the primaries. A consulting firm whose clients lose primaries has little to boast about when it seeks additional clients. Moreover, a presidential campaign is so demanding that a consulting firm handling a presidential campaign normally has to sacrifice other candidates or neglect them. Hence, a firm that opts to work for a presidential candidate typically turns away business during the primary season and may find itself lacking clients for the general election if its candidate loses the primaries.[75]

The typical consulting fee for a variety of political services, such as setting up a precinct organization or a phone bank operation, had reached $1,000 per day by the 1990s and continues to rise.[76] An all-purpose consulting firm that will develop a campaign strategy and offer advice on implementing that strategy will typically charge base fees of approximately $7,500 to $15,000 for a congressional race and $20,000 to $30,000 for a statewide race. Additional fees will depend on the specific services provided. Most consultants or consulting firms are also available on a monthly retainer fee of $4,000 to $8,000, which allows client candidates and their staff unlimited phone contact with the consultant and also provides that the consultant will be in the campaign several days a month. Though overhead and expenses for consulting are high, for a growing number of people, political consulting has become a viable way to make a living.[77]

It should be remembered, however, that as with the time of any professional—plumber, electrician, lawyer, or doctor—the time of political consultants is limited. Most consultants shy away from taking on more than four or five races simultaneously.[78] Hence, political consulting is no longer the province of enthusiastic amateurs, perhaps occasionally taking leaves from their other positions to help the candidate of their choice. While that type of individual is still a feature of some campaigns and may provide valuable services, today political consulting is a fast-growing profession.

Though this discussion has focused on the economic aspects of consulting, because it was not until the field became an economically viable one that people could enter it on a full-time basis, virtually everyone involved in political consulting will note that monetary rewards are a secondary motivation. The primary motivation of most consultants is to have an impact on the political process. Most consultants have strong political beliefs. They work for like-minded candidates. And, invariably, consultants will claim that the most satisfying aspect of their job is to "win one you're not suppose to win."[79]

FUNCTIONS OF POLITICAL CONSULTANTS

Political consultants can provide candidates with virtually any service necessary in the conduct of a campaign, including help in targeting voters, establishing a precinct organization, setting up and utilizing phone banks, polling the electorate, preparing and utilizing direct mail, preparing and using radio and television commercials, writing and preparing to deliver a speech, preparing for a debate, mounting a fund-raising campaign, and establishing and utilizing an Internet website. A full-service political consulting firm can provide clients with virtually all of these services, though it may well specialize in a more limited number. Smaller firms will limit their work to providing a group of related services. It would be impossible to discuss all of the services provided by consulting firms in the remainder of this chapter.[80] Rather, we will briefly focus on four services that are directly related to the campaign's efforts to communicate through advertising.

Writers

The preparation and communication of messages are at the heart of any campaign. Hence, virtually all consultants are involved in some form of writing. In the chapter on public speaking, we discussed political speechwriting. Consultants who specialize in writing can often handle virtually all of the advertising writing chores in the campaign: radio and television scripts; press releases; and copy for all printed materials such as brochures, mail pieces, or newspaper and magazine advertisements. There are techniques unique to writing each of these types of advertisements well, and often in larger campaigns different individuals will handle each. In small and midsized campaigns, the writer who often also serves as the press secretary and speechwriter is generally involved in the preparation of scripts for commercials.

Speech Coaches

One of the basic services frequently provided to candidates at the schools for candidates run by the Republican and Democratic Party organizations is speech coaching. Many consulting firms will coach candidates in public speaking and, if necessary, in debate. Most speech coaches would agree with Democratic consultant Michael Sheehan, who has worked with President Clinton and former Texas governor Ann Richards, among others, when he describes his job by claiming that "I bring out their [the candidates'] strengths; I try to bring out the best qualities in candidates that they already have."[81]

Although he is currently involved primarily in television production, Republican Roger Ailes, who coached both Ronald Reagan and George H. W. Bush for many of their major addresses and debates, is also among the best-known consultants to have specialized in coaching candidates for speeches and debates. Based on his experiences, Ailes has identified what he calls the ten most common communication problems. Depending on the individual candidate's strengths and weaknesses, speech coaches will normally work to help the candidate overcome one or more of the following problems Ailes identifies:

1. Lack of initial rapport with listeners
2. Stiffness or woodenness in use of body

3. Presentation of material is intellectually oriented, forgetting to involve the audience emotionally
4. Speaker seems uncomfortable because of fear of failure
5. Poor use of eye contact and facial expression
6. Lack of humor
7. Speech direction and intent unclear due to improper preparation
8. Inability to use silence for impact
9. Lack of energy, causing inappropriate pitch pattern, speech rate, and volume
10. Use of boring language and lack of interesting material[82]

Direct Mail Specialists

Preparing direct mail pieces, and in many instances providing the lists of individuals to whom such pieces are sent, has become a critical political consulting specialty. Such firms are typically involved in utilizing direct mail both for voter persuasion and for fund-raising. Perhaps the best-known early consultant to specialize in direct mail was Richard Viguerie, and his story is highly illustrative of how direct mail specialists operate.

In 1960–1961, Viguerie worked in the Houston campaign offices of Texas senator John Tower. Soon after, he was employed by Young Americans for Freedom (YAF), a group of conservative young people, and was placed in charge of the organization's fund-raising. Recalling his early experiences, Viguerie states:

> I'm basically a pretty shy person and I did not feel comfortable asking for money directly. So I began writing letters instead, and they seemed to work. So I wrote more and more letters and before many months, direct mail was my whole focus—for fundraising, subscriptions for *The New Guard* [a YAF publication], YAF membership, everything.[83]

Quickly recognizing the power of direct mail, Viguerie used the most obvious means to begin to develop a mailing list. After the 1964 election, he simply copied the names and addresses of those who had given $50 or more to the Goldwater campaign from the contributor records that, by law, were on file with the clerk of the House of Representatives. This effort provided him with over twelve thousand names, which became his first mailing list.[84]

Direct mail consultants like Viguerie are continually building their lists, adding new names after each campaign in which they are involved. The use of sophisticated computers and printers enables them to handle thousands of pieces of mail quickly and further enables them to tailor lists to the geographic and demographic needs of a client.

Political consultants who specialize in direct mail typically provide two services for their clients. First, they can help in designing and producing the actual mail pieces. Second, they can create lists of individuals to whom such pieces should be sent. This second service is highly valuable for major national campaigns and other larger races.

However, in smaller races, often the candidate and campaign staff can develop a good mailing list, based on their associates, the lists of other candidates who have run in the same area, or the lists of the local party. Candidates who contract to utilize the lists of consulting firms must be certain that the lists are likely to be of help to them and almost invariably will want to supplement those lists. One of the principal ways in which direct mail firms increase the size and value of their lists is by constantly adding names from the campaigns in which they work.

Specialists in Television Commercial Production and Placement

Because of the large expense involved and the technical expertise necessary, today few campaigns will attempt to produce and air television commercials without the advice of political consultants who specialize in such work. Some campaigns will supplement the efforts of such consultants by also employing local advertising agencies that are familiar with local media. Nevertheless, political media consultants have come to dominate the business of producing and buying time for televised campaign commercials.

Clearly, the candidate and campaign staff must make the final decisions. Typically, the campaign staff, the polling firm, and the television consultants will all work closely together, with the campaign having the final authority. Aware of the issues in their particular campaign, the campaign will certainly be receptive to the advice of consultants, but they must make the final decisions on what they want to accomplish with the commercials. Well-financed campaigns test ads in focus groups and never air the ones that don't work. At one time the standard approach was to begin the campaign with biographical ads and continue with issue ads, followed by endorsement and attack ads, before ending with inspirational commercials, in the belief that voters want something positive as they enter the voting booth.[85] While all of these types of ads are still utilized in contemporary campaigns, there is really no longer a standard approach or sequencing of the ads. Moreover, use of attack or negative ads, or "comparison" ads in which the candidate or her ideas are contrasted to the opponent or the opponent's ideas, has grown to dominate many recent campaigns.

Political consultants can help in a variety of ways. They can suggest types of commercials that can implement the candidate's goals. They may be able to point out how other campaigns successfully, or unsuccessfully, handled similar problems. They are aware of what approaches are working or failing in other parts of the country and hence might or might not work in the relevant region. Depending on their background, they will help script and produce the commercial, utilizing their skills in every phase of production, including casting, shooting, and editing. In well-financed campaigns, using focus groups and electronic advertising-testing techniques that facilitate monitoring voter responses to individual sentences, phrases, and split-second visual images contained within the ad, some commercials are rejected; others are improved before they are finally accepted for broadcast. In many campaigns, the consultant takes personal control over creating the commercials.

The consulting firm will also purchase airtime. A good firm knows the demographics of the local media market, is experienced in dealing with the local media, and is familiar with the candidate's strategy. Using all of this information, it purchases airtime to maximize the impact of the candidate's messages among those voters that the campaign has targeted.

Until ten to fifteen years ago, most consultants would suggest that the campaign purchase three hundred to five hundred rating points of time per week for television advertisements. If the campaign could not afford to do this, many consultants would suggest that they consider dropping television from their advertising strategy. Rating points are the percentage of television sets tuned to a specific show. If *60 Minutes* has a 35 rating in the Boston market, 35 percent of the television sets in Boston are tuned to *60 Minutes*. As recently as a decade ago most consultants felt that the message of a political spot would not really register until the audience has seen the message at least three to five times—hence, the desirability of purchasing three hundred to five hundred rating points, which should enable 100 percent of the audience to see the commercial three to five times.[86]

By 1996, the guideline of three hundred to five hundred rating points was being questioned, as most consultants urged larger purchases than in prior years. They did so largely because of the proliferation of remote controls, which facilitates channel surfing by viewers during ads, and the proliferation of VCRs, which enable viewers to totally skip advertisements.

Since 1996, additional technology and voter apathy and insensitivity to political commercials are frequently mentioned as reasons that political advertisers have had to purchase larger quantities of time than in past years.[87] While consultants are often paid a percentage of the cost of the television time they purchase and hence have a self-interest in purchasing larger quantities of time, it is hard to deny that traditional viewing habits have been changed by technology and that voter indifference to politics is widespread.

Summary

Clearly, campaigns can make use of a wide variety of political consultants. In this section, we have treated those consultants who we feel impact most directly on political advertising. It is significant to note that, although we have not treated such consulting specialties as the public opinion pollster, the fund-raising specialist, the precinct organizer, or the database manager, it could well be argued that even these consultants impact on political communication and political advertising. We would not dispute that argument in the least, for it gives further credence to the principal thesis of this book—that communication is at the heart of political campaigning.

CONCLUSION

This chapter has illustrated some of the practical concerns that must be confronted when using political advertising. We have first noted the importance of advance planning in the development of the campaign's use of political advertising. Second, we have examined the seven principal advertising media used in political campaigns: display graphics, direct mail, telephone, print, radio, television, and the Internet. We have illustrated the virtues and liabilities of each medium for political advertising. Third, we have examined the four principal overall advertising strategies commonly utilized in political campaigns: spurt, fast finish, really big show, and cruise control. Fourth, we have discussed political consultants, who have, largely because of their mastery of advertising media, become key players in contemporary political campaigns. We have considered the history of political consulting in the last three decades. Moreover, we have examined the functions of those political consultants who are most directly concerned with communication and advertising: writers, speech coaches, direct mail specialists, and television specialists.

NOTES

1. Frank Luntz, "Preparing Your Campaign Playbook," *Campaigns and Elections* 12 (July 1991): 40–46.

2. For valuable insight into the components of a campaign plan, see Ron Faucheux, "Writing Your Campaign Plan," *Campaigns and Elections* (April 2004): 26–29.

3. Smithsonian Institution, National Museum of American History, "Campaign Buttons" (Washington, D.C.: Smithsonian Institution, 1989). This small flyer on the history of campaign buttons is included with a variety of reproductions of campaign materials available through the Smithsonian.

4. The four functions discussed in this paragraph are mentioned primarily as the functions of billboard advertising by Craig Varoga of Varoga and Rice, a California consulting firm. However, virtually all display graphics serve one or more of these functions. See Craig Varoga, "Hiring Fundraisers, Using Billboards," *Campaigns and Elections* (May 2001): 69.

5. Campaign materials, buttons, and bumper stickers using all of these slogans are in the collection of one of the authors, Robert V. Friedenberg.

6. The figures in this paragraph are drawn from the online catalogues of several suppliers. They include Signelect, the Promoplace, and The Button King. Those catalogues were retrieved on May 9, 2006, at www.signelect.com/buttons.htm; www.promoplace.com/ws/webstore.d11; and www.thebuttonking.com/yard_signs_and_buttons_magnets.htm.

7. The figures in this paragraph are drawn from the online catalogue of Dr. Don's Buttons, Badges & More, retrieved on May 9, 2006, at www.buttonsonline.com/political.

8. The figures in this paragraph are drawn from the online catalogues of PC Signs and Political Sign Express, retrieved on May 10, 2006, at www.pcsigns.com/indexphp?page=ProductViewPage&idx=11 and www.politicalsignexpress.com/political-bumper-stickers.html.

9. For example, as of the spring of 2002, Advertising and Supply would provide 1,500 emery boards for $176 to $195 depending on the style and imprint. Similarly, PC Signs would provide a thousand nine-inch round balloons with the name in one color on a contrasting standard balloon color for $108. A two-inch-larger version of the same balloon costs $122 per thousand.

10. These figures were provided by Larry Steir of Norton Outdoor Advertising, Cincinnati, Ohio, in a phone interview with Robert V. Friedenberg, April 10, 2006. While there are a variety of ways to purchase billboards, costs reflect the percentage of the metropolitan area that will see the board on a daily basis and the size of the board.

11. Billboard advertising firms much prefer to sell for longer periods of time. Depending on the firm and the market, discounts for three-, six-, and twelve-month-long purchases can sometimes be negotiated. These figures represent the most common way that billboards are currently purchased by political figures in the Cincinnati area. Due to limits on the locations of billboards, and the preference of billboard advertising firms to sell for longer periods of time, arrangements for billboard advertising should be made well in advance.

12. These figures are drawn from the online catalogues of several larger firms, including PC Signs, the Victory Store, and SS Graphics Inc. The prices quoted were retrieved on May 10, 2006, at www.pcsigns.com/index.php?page=Product; www.victorystore.com/signs/corrplast.htm; and www.ssgraphicsco.com/en-us/dept_198.html.

13. The cost figure used in this paragraph comes from the online catalogue of Patriot Signage. It was retrieved on May 10, 2006, at patriotsigns.com/political.asp.

14. Direct mail has often been called a "high interest, low backlash, communications vehicle" in campaign seminars conducted by the Republican National Committee and in the literature that the committee has produced for candidates and their staffs. See, for example, Republican National Committee, *Campaign Seminars: Campaign Graphics, Direct Mail and Outdoor Advertising* (Washington D.C.: Republican National Committee, n.d.), 5.

15. See Richard Viguerie, *The New Right: We're Ready to Lead* (Falls Church, Va.: Viguerie Company, 1980), 125–26. Viguerie, the principal direct mail fund-raiser of the conservative movement throughout the 1960s and 1970s, credits the McGovern campaign with making political figures aware of the enormous potential of direct mail as a medium of political fund-raising.

16. Ron Kanfer, "Direct to the Bank," *Campaigns and Elections* (July 1991): 22. Kanfer is president of Response Dynamics, Inc., a political direct mail fund-raising firm.

17. Todd Meredith, "Open the Envelope: Getting People to Look at the Direct Mail They Receive," *Campaigns and Elections* (December 2004/January 2005): 27. Todd Meredith is co-

owner of the Direct Mail Marketing Group, and has worked with more than forty members of Congress.

18. Joe Trippi notes that fully one-fourth of the contributors to Howard Dean's campaign were under thirty years old and claims that "this is an amazing number, given that we are living in an age when political involvement among young people is at a historic low." See Joe Trippi, *The Revolution Will Not Be Televised: Democracy, the Internet, and the Overthrow of Everything* (New York: Regan Books, 2004), 190.

19. See both Kanfer, "Direct to the Bank," 24, and Viguerie, *The New Right*, 124. Viguerie argued that in the 1960–1980 era direct mail fund-raising was exceptionally useful for underdog, nonestablishment candidates, much as Trippi has more recently argued that the Internet is exceptionally useful for underdog, nonestablishment candidates.

20. These prices are drawn from the Picture Perfect Campaigns rate card, retrieved on May 12, 2005, at ppc2win.com/prices/general_rates.html. These prices are consistent with most display graphics rates which typically provide quantity discounts.

21. See Kate McKeown, Richard Schlackman, Jamie Douglas, Jason Ercole, Eric Jayne, Michael Terris, Eva M. Campbell, and Mark Campbell, "Direct Mail," *Campaigns and Elections* (May 1997): 22. The authors have been unable to find a comparable figure for more recent election cycles. Nevertheless, given that it likely remains used in so many bottom of the ballot races that do not utilize television, it would not be surprising to find that campaigns continue to spend more on direct mail than on television.

22. Jan Crawford of Crawford Communications made this observation at a session of the American Association of Political Consultants Annual Meeting, Washington, D.C., January 17, 1997.

23. Hal Malchow, "10 Ways to Design In-House Voter Mail That Works," *Campaigns and Elections* (June/July 1990): 50–51. The cost figures that Malchow mentions in connection with the services of a letter shop have gone up slightly since he first wrote. However, so too have the costs of everything, including beer and pizza, so that his point that such shops are a bargain likely remains true.

24. Malchow, "10 Ways," 50.

25. Meredith, "Open the Envelope," 77.

26. For good overviews of telephone contact services, see Roger S. Conrad, "Winning Votes on the Information Super Highway," *Campaigns and Elections* (July 1994): 22–25 and 52–54; Robert V. Friedenberg, *Communication Consultants in Political Campaigns: Ballot Box Warriors* (Westport, Conn.: Praeger, 1997), 112–18. On the cost of voter contact services, Friedenberg provides representative figures for the 1996 election cycle; the reader can obtain current costs by contacting the firms directly. Most major firms are listed under "Telephone Contact Services," in the *2006 Political Pages*, a special edition of *Campaigns and Elections*, published in February of 2006.

27. Newspaper advertisements played a role in the nation's earliest elections. See Robert J. Dinkin, *Campaigning in America: A History of Election Practices* (Westport, Conn.: Greenwood, 1989), 3–4, 14–16. Also see Kathleen Hall Jamieson, *Packaging the Presidency* (New York: Oxford University Press, 1984), 5.

28. This information was provided by Shawn Savage of the *Cincinnati Enquirer* advertising sales department. Phone interview with Robert V. Friedenberg, April 26, 2002.

29. Typical of many major market stations, in the Cincinnati market most television stations must be provided the television commercial by noon of the workday prior to when it will first air.

30. Studies have repeatedly indicated that Americans usually speak at a rate of between 120 and 150 words per minute. See Stephen E. Lucas, *The Art of Public Speaking* (New York: Random House, 2004), 300.

31. This figure is drawn from "Bush, Governors Set Goals," *Facts on File: World News Digest with Index*, March 2, 1990, 141.

32. The cost figures used throughout this paragraph were provided by Chad Gordczyca of the *Cincinnati Enquirer* advertising sales staff in a phone interview with Robert V. Friedenberg, May 12, 2006.

33. Republican National Committee, *Campaign Seminars: Media Advertising* (Washington, D.C.: Republican National Committee, n.d.), 12.

34. Dinkin, *Campaigning in America*, 167.

35. This figure is based on the TNS Media Intelligence figures found in Curtis Green, "A Good Radio Jingle Goes a Long Way," *Campaigns and Elections* (April 2005): 37. TNS reports that during the period from January to October 2004, political campaigns spent $89 million on radio and $1.4 billion in total. It should be kept in mind that, as with virtually all advertising media, some campaigns will rely very heavily on radio and others will barely use it.

36. Green, "A Good Radio Jingle," 37–38.

37. These Arbitron figures are cited in Green, " A Good Radio Jingle," 37.

38. These figures were provided by Toni Smith, who handled political sales for the Clear Channel stations in Cincinnati during the 2006 election cycle. Interview with Robert V. Friedenberg, May 15, 2005. In addition to her discussion with the author, Ms. Smith provided the political rate cards for many of the Clear Channel stations, including those whose rates are cited in this paragraph, WKRC Talk Radio; WEBN, the rock station; and "700 WLW," a talk and information station whose morning host, Jim Scott, attracts the city's largest audience. These figures are all for nonpreemptible purchases, which are typically utilized by political figures advertising on Cincinnati radio.

39. These figures were also provided by Smith, as described in the preceding note. All of these shows, with the exception of the Al Franken show, air on WKRC radio in Cincinnati. Franken airs on WCKY. All of the rates quoted in this paragraph are for nonpreemptible ads.

40. These have been the practices of many Cincinnati stations, and, according to members of their sales departments, similar practices are widespread in most larger media markets. For example, these practices were noted on the political rate cards of several Cincinnati stations during the 2002 and 2006 election cycles.

41. While figures such as these have long been commonplace for major national and statewide races, David Wells's article on campaign expenses in one metropolitan area during 1988 elections, "If You Run, Bring Money," indicates that since the late 1980s, figures such as these are becoming commonplace even in many lower ballot races. Examining a wide variety of 1988 Cincinnati-area races, including judicial contests, Wells found candidates consistently spending 70 to 80 percent of their money on television commercials. Moreover, the number of races utilizing television has steadily moved down the ballot, as more and more candidates purchase television time.

42. These figures were retrieved on May 16, 2006, from www.opensecrets.org. Opensecrets obtained these figures directly from the Federal Election Commission.

43. These figures were retrieved on May 16, 2006, from www.opensecrets.org.

44. Charles Green, "Congress for Sale?" *Cincinnati Enquirer*, October 8, 1989, p. B1. While a variety of other factors including the greater use of polling services, the wider use of direct mail, and the general lengthening of campaigns has undeniably contributed to increasing campaign costs, no authority would deny that the increased use of television is a primary factor causing the dramatic increase in campaign expenses. Moreover, this increase has far exceeded increases in the consumer price index. Nor does it seem to be leveling off. While inflation has risen at a modest 2 to 4 percent during most of the last decade, Robert V. Friedenberg's informal discussions with individuals in the advertising industry suggest that the costs of television advertising have increased by 40 to 50 percent during that same period.

45. These figures and the cost figures utilized in this and the following paragraphs are drawn from a series of phone interviews Robert V. Friedenberg held with the specialists in political advertising sales at several of the network affiliate stations in Cincinnati between May 15 and 17, 2006. In addition, several of them provided the author with their political advertising disclosure statements and their political rate cards. The author is particularly grateful to Jerry Imsicke of WLWT, the NBC affiliate in Cincinnati, Randi Near of WKRC, the CBS affiliate in Cincinnati, and Tom Reardon of WCP, the ABC affiliate in Cincinnati, for their help.

46. Because the demographics of the CBS afternoon soap operas—*The Young and the Restless, The Bold and the Beautiful, As the World Turns,* and *The Guiding Light*—were so similar in the Cincinnati market, advertisers simply bought time on this block of shows, rather than on a specific show.

47. All of the prices presented in this and the preceding paragraphs are for nonpreemptible ads. These ads cannot be bumped by later buys by other advertisers (commercial or political) and hence tend to be favored by most campaigns in the Cincinnati area. Preemptible ads, which are often sold at 50 percent to 66 percent of the cost of nonpreemptible ads can be bumped by the station at the last minute if the station receives a contract for a higher-paying ad. Most political campaigns will buy their time backward from election day and rarely use anything but nonpreemptible ads for the ten days immediately preceding the election. Some campaigns will purchase preemptible ads further out from the election, though more and more campaigns are sticking to nonpreemptible purchases.

48. In the last edition of this book, the authors priced out a very comparable media buy, based on television advertising rates for political advertisers in the Cincinnati market during the 2002 election cycle. The cost of that buy was $22,000, compared to the $37,000 figures cited here, a mere four years later. See Trent and Friedenberg, *Political Campaign Communication: Principles and Practices,* 5th edition (Lanham, Md.: Rowman & Littlefield, 2004): 360–61.

49. See Friedenberg, *Communication Consultants in Political Campaigns,* 158–60, for an examination of political television production costs. It should be noted that the production of political commercials is typically accomplished at a small fraction of the cost of product commercials. As of 1997, the average thirty-second product spot cost producers $278,000, according to a survey conducted by the American Association of Advertising Agencies. See "Production Costs Rise for TV Ads," *Cincinnati Enquirer–TV Week,* September 21, 1997, 2.

50. Typically, the change will be to a form of commercial that does not require the candidate to be on the camera. One of the most successful such adjustments was engineered by New York governor Nelson Rockefeller's 1966 reelection campaign managers. At the outset of the campaign, Rockefeller had several major political liabilities; moreover, his deep, gravely bass voice was not appealing. These factors caused his management team to conclude that putting him on television was counterproductive. Instead, they produced a series of advertisements featuring a puppet fish that focused on his many accomplishments as governor. Later in the campaign, when his standing had increased, Rockefeller appeared in his own advertisements. See Edwin Diamond and Stephen Bates, *The Spot: The Rise of Political Advertising on Television* (Cambridge, Mass.: MIT Press, 1984), 318–19, for an account of this campaign.

51. These figures are from "Push Play to Win," a promotional video available through West Coast Video Duplicating Inc., the largest American video duplicator. They may be contacted at 11755 Wilshire Boulevard, Suite 2400, Los Angeles, Calif. 90025.

52. This is the benchmark figure cited by both West Coast Video Duplicating and Promotional Video Duplicators, the two largest players in the political cassette market. Both firms use this figure in their promotional videos. West Coast Video can be reached at the address cited in the preceding note. Promotional Video Duplicators can be reached at 900 Second Street, NE, Washington, D.C. 20002. Typically, for mailings of one hundred thousand cassettes

or more, the price per cassette can be held to approximately $1.50, which includes duplication, labels on the cassette itself, a color printed sleeve, shrink-wrap, addressing, and postage.

53. Paula Tati, "Eight Myths of Video Cassette Campaigning," *Campaigns and Elections* (December/January 1994): 34.

54. The 36 percent estimate was made by Robin Roberts of National Media Inc., one of the largest Republican media consulting firms, in an interview with Robert Friedenberg, Alexandria, Virginia, January 17, 1997. The 80 percent estimate was made by Ondine Fortune of Creative Cable TV in an interview with Robert Friedenberg, Washington, D.C., January 16, 1997.

55. Laura Woolsey, "Web Usability: The Development and Application of a New Instrument for Objective Usability Inspection," master's thesis, Miami University, 2001, 40.

56. James Katz, Philip Aspden, and Warren Reich, "Elections and Electrons: A National Opinion Survey on the Role of Cyberspace and Mass Media in Political Opinion Formation during the 1996 General Election," paper prepared for the Telecommunications Policy Research Conference, Washington, D.C., October 1997, cited in Marion Just, Ann Crigler, and Montague Kern, "Citizens and the Internet: Diversifying Information Sources in Cyberspace," paper prepared for the annual meeting of the National Speech Communication Association, Chicago, November 1997, 2.

57. During the primaries, the campaign of Howard Dean was funded primarily by contributions made over the Internet. The Dean campaign's breakthrough use of the Internet as a fund-raising tool was quickly emulated by other candidates. See Andrew Chadwick, *Internet Politics* (New York: Oxford University Press, 2006), 164. Chadwick claims that "probably the most significant element of the primaries was the genuine emergence of the Internet as a fund-raising weapon."

58. Just, Crigler, and Kern, "Citizens and the Internet," 17–19.

59. Just, Crigler, and Kern, "Citizens and the Internet," 12–21.

60. Mike Connell, "Internet Survival Guide: Designing Lively Web Sites," *Campaigns and Elections* (September 1998): 29–32 and 41. Connell offers an analysis of the characteristics of good websites based on his examination of a wide variety of 1998 sites; however it is highly unlikely that they would have changed in the last decade.

61. Connell, "Internet Survival Guide." Also see Michael Cornfield, Shabbir Safdar, and Jonah Seigler, "The Top 10 Things We're Tired of Seeing in Candidate Web Sites," *Campaigns and Elections* (September 1998): 26.

62. See Friedenberg, *Communication Consultants in Political Campaigns*, 173–83, for a detailed analysis of political time-buying practices.

63. The explanation of buying found in this paragraph is based on Jerry Hagstrom, *Political Consulting: A Guide for Reporters and Citizens* (New York: The Freedom Forum, 1992), 22–23.

64. These strategies are adapted and in some cases renamed from those presented in Republican National Committee, *Campaign Seminars: Media Advertising*, 21–22.

65. "What's in a Name? For Consultants, Much Cash," *Congressional Quarterly Guide to Current American Government* (Fall 1988): 28.

66. The best readily available source of information on Beckley is Nobel E. Cunningham Jr., "John Beckley: An Early American Party Manager," *William and Mary Quarterly* 13 (January 1956): 40–52.

67. See Friedenberg, *Communication Consultants in Political Campaigns*, 2–15, for an overview of the growth of political consulting during the nineteenth and early twentieth centuries. For detail on the 1840 campaign, also see the prologue in Robert V. Friedenberg, *Notable Speeches in Contemporary Presidential Campaigns* (Westport, Conn.: Praeger, 2002).

68. On Bernays, see Friedenberg, *Communication Consultants in Political Campaigns*, 16–17; Sidney Blumenthal, *The Permanent Campaign: Inside the World of Elite Political Operatives*

(Boston: Beacon, 1980), 11–26; and, for the last interview Bernays gave prior to his death, see chapter 1 of Stuart Ewen, *PR! The Social History of Spin* (New York: Basic Books, 1996).

69. Blumenthal, *The Permanent Campaign*, 143–47.

70. On Eisenhower's and Stevenson's television consultants in 1952, see Friedenberg, *Communication Consultants in Political Campaigns*, 153–56; and chapter 2 of Jamieson, *Packaging the Presidency*.

71. For a brief discussion of the rise of political advertising and media influence on the 1956 campaign, which includes the quotation from Stevenson, see Stan Le Roy Wilson, *Mass Media/Mass Culture* (New York: Random House, 1989), 309.

72. In his remarkably incisive study, Burdett Loomis claims that the huge freshman class of "Watergate" congressmen elected in 1974 changed the face of American politics by combining ambition and entrepreneurship to work perpetually at acquiring resources to guarantee their reelection and to push their favorite policies. Since 1974, the "new breed" politician, Loomis argues, approaches Congress as an enterprise and seeks to develop a group of personnel resources, such as those discussed in this paragraph, which can be relied on to further the politician's own election and policy aspirations. See Burdett Loomis, *The New American Politician: Ambition, Entrepreneurship, and the Changing Face of Political Life* (New York: Basic Books, 1988), 1–52 and 181–208.

73. This paragraph is based largely on the analysis of Charles Press and Kenneth VerBurg, *American Politics and Journalists* (Glenview, Ill.: Scott, Foresman, 1988), 155–56.

74. On the fees paid to Kerry's and Bush's media consultants in 2004, see Joe Klein, *Politics Lost: How American Democracy Was Trivialized by People Who Think You Are Stupid* (New York: Doubleday, 2006), 205.

75. Hagstrom, *Political Consulting*, 6.

76. These figures are based on interviews with a wide variety of political consultants, among them Ken Kling, of S.K.C. and Associates, a lobbying and consulting firm; Jim Weber, of Eddie Mahe and Associates, an all-purpose consulting firm; and Gary Koops, a press secretary and campaign manager in a variety of Republican congressional races.

77. Larger political consulting firms that contract to handle a variety of races during a single election period are normally headed by one or more individuals with exceptional reputations. These individuals serve as "magnets" to attract clients. Often they are heavily involved in the formulation of basic strategies and subsequently turn much of the work over to their associates and/or the local campaign staff to implement, returning periodically to help the candidate with major events such as filming commercials or preparing for a debate. Like any business, the consulting firm must judge the often considerable costs of doing business (e.g., labor, materials, travel, etc.) when establishing fees.

78. Most consultants recognize that, if they spread themselves too thin, they run the risk of being involved in losing races and hence jeopardizing future employment. Additionally, today most candidates, expecting their consultants to provide them with considerable time and service, shy away from those who have already committed to a large number of other races. The exceptions to this rule are polling consultants who can deal with many campaigns at once.

79. This sentiment is constantly voiced when consultants are asked about the satisfaction of their job. It has come up in virtually every consultant interview Friedenberg has conducted for this chapter and related writings.

80. Perhaps the best way to get a sense of the wide variety of political consulting services now available to candidates is to simply examine a few recent editions of *Campaigns and Elections*, the "trade paper" of the industry. *Campaigns and Elections* publishes a special edition each winter, normally the March edition, called *The Political Pages*, which is a directory of political consulting firms organized by consulting specialty. The current edition of *The Political Pages*, which is in effect *Campaigns and Elections* (March 2006), is organized

around forty-five campaign consulting specialties and thirteen public affairs and grass-roots lobbying specialties.

81. Morgan Stewart, "Michael Sheehan: Coaching Clinton," *Campaigns and Elections* (June/July 1993): 54.

82. Roger Ailes, *You Are the Message: Secrets of the Master Communicators* (Homewood, Ill.: Dow Jones–Irwin, 1988), 9.

83. Viguerie, *The New Right*, 26.

84. Viguerie, *The New Right*, 26–27.

85. Hagstrom, *Political Consulting*, 14.

86. The explanation of rating points in this paragraph is based on Pat Beall, "Buy Your Own Time," *Campaigns and Elections* (July 1991): 48. Also see Chris Meyer and Phil Porado, "Hit or Miss: Your Guide to Effective Media Buying," *Campaigns and Elections* (August/September 1990): 37–41.

87. These reasons were remarked on by a variety of political television consultants interviewed by Robert Friedenberg in December 1996 and January 1997, shortly after the 1996 elections. Among those citing the growing need for time were Robert Tannenbaum of HMS Associates, Columbus, Ohio; Joseph Mercurio of National Political Services, Inc., New York, New York; John Franzen of John Franzen Multimedia, Washington, D.C.; and Robin Roberts of National Media Inc., Alexandria, Virginia.

11

~

The Internet and Political Campaigns

At least since the mid-1990s, the Internet has had a growing role in political campaigns at all levels. In this chapter we will examine candidate websites, the functions of websites, and the breadth and future of the
Internet and its tools in elective politics.

CONTENT OF CANDIDATE WEBSITES

In little more than a decade, candidate websites have become a requirement for virtually any political campaign that hopes for success. Indeed,
just as it was once difficult for a presidential candidate to be considered
credible without the use of television, today it is difficult for virtually any
major office candidate to be considered credible without the use of the Internet. As recently as 2002, only 55 percent of all candidates for the United
States Senate utilized a website. By 2006, that figure had grown to 97 percent.[1] When they were first used, in the 1990s, candidate websites were little more than electronic leaflets with biographical text, pictures of the candidates and their families, and perhaps a few speeches or comments
about the issues. Today, candidate websites are far more complex.

A 2006 survey of the websites of seventy-seven candidates running unopposed in the primaries or in a primary for the United States Senate indicates the complexity of current political websites. The Blivins Group survey
concluded that by 2006 candidate website content reflected three tiers.[2] The
first-tier content consists of basic information that could be found on many
early candidate websites, such as the candidate's biography, campaign

news, and forms to enable the website visitor to volunteer to help the campaign or to donate to the campaign. First-tier content also included some clear means to facilitate contact between the visitor and the campaign. The Blivins group found that at least 80 percent, and in some instances 94 percent, of all surveyed candidate websites provided this content to visitors. Volunteer forms were found on 80 percent of all campaign websites surveyed, while a means to contact the campaign and a means to donate to the campaign were provided on about 94 percent of all the surveyed candidate websites.[3] Moreover, four of these five content components of a candidate website—candidate biography and means to volunteer for the campaign, donate to the campaign, or contact the campaign—were found on all of the candidate websites involved in the eleven key 2006 Senate races. The only first-tier component not to be utilized by all of the key Senate race candidate websites was campaign news. Campaign news was available on all of the Republican sites, but only on about 88 percent of the Democratic sites.[4] Clearly, these five first-tier features are becoming virtually standard on candidate websites.

Second tier content consists of (1) multimedia, (2) blogs, (3) RSS (Rich Site Summary, or Really Simple Syndication), and (4) downloads. Multimedia content allows the user to access audio and video files. Blogs are frequent, chronological publications of personal thoughts and website links. Political blogs are, in effect, a cross between the blogger's personal thoughts and a guide to many of the items on the Internet that help shape those thoughts.[5] RSS feeds are a means used by some campaigns to keep interested parties and news sites up-to-date on the campaign by enabling them to retrieve summaries of the latest content from the candidate site. Downloads provide the visitor with materials, such as handouts about the candidate, which they can download and reprint on their own.

These features were found on between 14 percent and 55 percent of the Senate websites surveyed in 2006.[6] As with first-tier content, second-tier content was used more heavily on the websites of key races.[7] In light of the dramatic growth of blogs on the Internet since the 2004 election cycle, it is perhaps surprising to note that only 23 percent of the 2006 senatorial websites used blogs.[8] At least two factors may contribute to the relatively limited use of blogs by candidates, at a time when blogging itself is a rapidly growing phenomenon. First, candidates are busy people who simply may not have the time to engage in blogging. Given that those who come to the candidate's website are, as we will see in the next section, often already committed to the candidate, blogging may be perceived as a wasteful use of the one resource that the campaign can never increase, the candidate's time. Moreover, many candidates are not overly computer literate and may shy away from such activities. Finally, bloggers tend toward the political extremes. Hence, a candidate who is actively blogging may be perceived as drawn toward the extreme left or right and risk losing support from the more moderate middle.

The most commonly used of the second-tier content is multimedia. By 2006, 55 percent of senatorial candidates made audio and video files available on their websites.[9] For example, the website of Maryland congressman Ben Cardin, running to succeed retiring Maryland senator Paul Sarbanes offered visitors a "multimedia" option to click on. When visitors clicked they were presented with two choices: photos or multimedia. The multimedia section provided viewers with tapes of two speeches by Cardin, one dealing with Iraq and the other his announcement address, as well as highlights from his first campaign events.[10] Many candidates, such as Maryland Republican senatorial candidate Michael Steele, running against Cardin, put their television and/or radio ads on their website.[11] Since most Senate races involve radio and television advertisements, it should not be surprising to find that many candidates will attempt to increase the reach of their ads by placing them on their websites.

The remaining second-tier content features of candidate websites are downloading, and RSS feeds, also called webfeeds. About 28 percent of all challenger candidates used RSS feeds, though only 3 percent of incumbents did so, according to the Blivins Group survey.[12]

An RSS feed can be thought of as a "Headline News" approach. It is a way for online venues such as candidate sites to continuously "feed" you announcements of their latest content. As a new item is added to a candidate site, a headline, normally a summary, and a link back to the full and original source (the candidate site) is fed to all the subscribers to the RSS feed. In effect, the campaign site RSS feed serves several roles. It provides announcements of what is new on the campaign site to online audiences. It makes it easy for those audiences to access the full content of the feed. Moreover, it makes it easy for other sites to republish a site's content. In effect it is a syndication channel.[13]

The final second-tier content features of campaign websites, according to the Blivins Group survey, are downloads. A campaign using downloads provides the visitor to the campaign site with a means of downloading and printing their own fliers, pictures, banners, or other campaign materials. The Blivins Group survey found that 20 percent of incumbents used downloads, compared to 11 percent of challengers.[14]

The third tier of candidate website content is the least frequently used, perhaps because for the most part it involves the most advanced technologies. Third-tier content includes such things as what the Blivins Group called "en español," providing a Spanish-language version of the candidate site, providing the ability of voters to organize their own fund-raising campaigns, providing for volunteers to organize and track their activities, providing help to volunteers setting up house parties for the candidate, and offering podcasts. Only 3 to 12 percent of all campaigns surveyed made these services available on their websites.[15]

FUNCTIONS OF CANDIDATE WEBSITES

From the earliest students of rhetoric forward, questions about the artificiality of the division between informing and persuading have been raised. Often it is argued that by simply informing, presenting an audience with new information, one is also persuading. To a large extent, that viewpoint seems to underlie how many candidates have treated their Internet sites. Much of what could be found in candidate websites during the 2004 and 2006 election cycles was informative. For example, common features of many candidate websites were sections in which the candidate's biography was presented, the candidate's votes or position statements on key issues were presented, and the candidate's major speeches were presented. Similarly informative in nature were sections of candidate websites that provided visitors with a schedule of the candidate's forthcoming appearances, or information about the candidate's family members and staff. All of this information was put on the websites of candidates who were clearly hoping that it would help persuade visitors.

In this section we will analyze three fundamental functions of candidate websites. First, we will examine the use of candidate websites to affect visitor opinions. Second, we will examine the use of candidate websites as a means of fund-raising. Third, we will examine the use of candidate websites as a means of developing a body of candidate volunteers. Just as the line between informing and persuading is not always a clear one, so too the line between these three functions is not always clear.

Candidate Websites and Affecting Visitor Opinions

Though many of the early advocates of the use of the Internet in political campaigns believed that it could provide voters with a wealth of information upon which to base their decisions, by 2000, political professionals involved with the Internet did not perceive informing voters to be the major purpose of candidate websites. Based on their research, which included interviews with the webmasters of national, statewide, and local campaigns during the 2000 election cycle, Bruce Blimber and Richard Davis concluded:

Campaigns just do not see the Internet in this way—or at least they do not see their own Web sites this way. They figure that voters' choices about which candidate to support would for the most part already have been made by the time they arrived at the site. The campaign staff instead hope to influence a different set of decisions: whether to volunteer, whether to donate, whether to vote or stay at home.[16]

This is not to say that campaigns assume that all of their website visitors will have determined whom they favor by the time they visit the candidate website. But the websites are not constructed primarily for undecided voters or voters who are strictly seeking information.

Several sections of most candidate websites would be of value to both undecided voters and decided voters. For example, during the 2000 and 2004 presidential primaries, the websites of all seventeen Democratic and Republican candidates contained sections that would provide the visitor with information on the candidate's position on issues. Similarly, with the exception of Al Sharpton's 2004 website, the websites of the remaining sixteen candidates who ran during one of those two primary seasons all provided the visitor with sections devoted to the candidate's biography and texts of major speeches.[17] Clearly material such as this would be of value to the undecided voter attempting to learn about the candidates and make a decision among them, as well as the committed voter, seeking information to help reinforce existing attitudes.

Other sections of the websites can also serve the dual purposes of informing voters who are not well acquainted with the candidate, and providing information that can reinforce those who are acquainted with the candidate. For example, the 2006 candidate websites of Hillary Clinton, running for reelection to the Senate from New York, and Ken Blackwell, running for governor of Ohio, both provided visitors the opportunity to view current television commercials run by the candidates and to read recent press releases issued by the campaign. Some candidate websites, such as that of Maryland congressman Steny Hoyer and California congressman Wally Herger, included sections devoted to the candidate's accomplishments and record of leadership.[18]

Sections of the candidate website such as these, which might serve to both persuade the uncommitted voter and reinforce the committed voter, have long been a feature of candidate websites. But as the political use of the Internet has evolved, candidate websites have also evolved. By the 2004 election cycle, it is fair to say that the observations that Blimber and Davis first made about the 2000 election websites were, if anything, more accurate in 2004. Candidate websites are currently designed to influence a host of potential voter decisions, most of them likely to be made by website visitors who are already sympathetic to the candidate.

Candidate Websites and Fund-raising

Between the presidential campaigns of 2000 and 2004, the Internet emerged as a potent tool for fund-raising. The 1996 campaign of President Bill Clinton raised about $10,000 over the Internet. By the 2000 election, the amounts of money raised over the Internet had increased substantially. During the 2000 cycle, the most impressive Internet fund-raising was that of Senator John McCain, who received $1.4 million in online contributions during the course of three days immediately following his victory in the New Hampshire presidential primary. Candidates used events in the campaign to help jumpstart Internet fund-raising. For example, the Gore campaign used the Republican nomination of Dick Cheney for vice president to point out a number of his more conservative votes in e-mails to their supporters. By doing so the Gore campaign enjoyed several days during which their Internet fund-raising reached $125,000–150,000 a day. Similarly, the 2000 Bush campaign used e-mails to stimulate online donations, often gearing their requests to statements or activities of the Democratic candidates. The Bush donations eventually averaged $200,000–$300,000 per e-mail. Ultimately, the Gore campaign raised approximately $2.7 million over the entire primary season, and the Bush campaign raised approximately $1.6 million during the same period.[19]

Nevertheless, Blimber and Davis concluded of the 2000 election cycle, "in the end, Internet fundraising proved no substitute for traditional mechanisms of shaking the money tree."[20] They point out that lower-level races likely raised even less on the Internet than did the high-profile presidential races. For example, Jim Talent's 2000 gubernatorial campaign in Missouri raised $10,000 via the Internet, a figure which pales compared to the $8 million he raised through more traditional means. Thus, by the 2000 election cycle, the Internet had arrived as a potential vehicle for fund-raising, but, when compared to the traditional means of fund-raising, it was a motorcycle in a garage full of Jaguars.

The 2004 election cycle saw the use of the Internet for fund-raising purposes come of age. Two factors no doubt contributed to the growth of Internet fund-raising between 2000 and 2004. The first was the growing reliance and familiarity of Americans with the Internet. By 2004, approximately 75 million adults, 37 percent of the adult population, used the Internet to get political news and information or in some more direct fashion participate in the political process. Clearly more and more Americans are growing reliant and comfortable with Internet usage, including usage that relates to political campaigning.[21]

Second, in addition to the increase of Internet usage between 2000 and 2004, Americans seem more comfortable with using the Internet for a host of activities, including financial transactions. No doubt part of the explanation for this is the growing experience Americans have with the Internet. By 2004, more than 80 percent of American Internet users had at least three years of experience using the Internet and over 50 percent had over six years of experience using the Internet.[22] Moreover, improved security has made Americans more at ease with "doing business" over the Internet. The widespread growth of online shopping, and online banking, illustrate the public acceptance of the security of engaging in financial transactions online. Hence, the lack of familiarity and the security fears that might have at one time inhibited the use of the Internet as a fund-raising tool had been dramatically reduced by 2004.

These two factors help to account for the dramatic increase in Internet contributions to political campaigns between 2000 and 2004. The number of Americans who contributed to political campaigns by using the Internet doubled between 2000 and 2004, from 2 million to 4 million.[23] The first big recipient of those contributions was former Vermont governor Howard Dean. Though his campaign faded after the Iowa caucus, Dean raised over $20 million online, about 40 percent of his total receipts.[24]

Joe Trippi, Dean's campaign manager, wanted to run a race in which Dean would be identified as the candidate of personal empowerment, the candidate who would return power to the people. Consequently, the Dean campaign relied heavily on the Internet for a host of campaign functions, including fund-raising.[25] Key to the success of Dean's online fund-raising was his use of what Michael Cornfield has called "news-pegged fundraising appeals."[26] These appeals capitalized on the ability of the Internet to enable large numbers of supporters to provide a swift reaction to fund-raising appeals. To illustrate news-pegged fund-raising, Cornfield cites the Dean campaign's usage of July 2003 news reports about a $2,000-a-plate Republican luncheon featuring Vice President Cheney. Learning of the Cheney luncheon shortly before it was scheduled, the Dean campaign issued the "Cheney Challenge." Using the Internet, they challenged their supporters to raise more money than the luncheon. Their appeal featured a picture of Dean lunching on a three-dollar turkey sandwich to mock the big-ticket Republican affair. The Cheney luncheon raised $250,000 from 125 supporters. The Cheney Challenge raised $500,000 for the Dean campaign from 9,700 people.[27] Cheney's contributors had paid $2,000 each. In contrast, contributors to the Cheney Challenge made an average contribution of $52.

Though Dean may have been the first of the 2004 candidates to fully exploit the Internet, others soon followed. Among the two major party presidential candidates, Kerry supporters were more prone to give money over the Internet than Bush supporters. Fully 9 percent of Kerry voters who used the Internet made contributions online, while only 2 percent of Bush voters who used the Internet made contributions online.[28] Consequently,

Kerry ultimately raised $89 million, about 33 percent of his total receipts, over the Internet. Bush raised $14 million, about 5 percent of his total receipts, over the Internet. Most of the money raised by Bush and Kerry during the general election was in the form of small donations of $200 or less.[29]

In sum, a 2006 survey of seventy-seven senatorial candidates, thirty of whom were incumbents and forty-seven of whom were challengers, suggests that the Internet fund-raising breakthrough pioneered by Howard Dean in the 2004 Democratic primaries, and continued by George W. Bush and John Kerry into the 2004 general election, will be a feature of virtually all future campaigns. That survey found that 92 percent of all senatorial candidate websites were providing visitors a means of donating on the Internet, with very little difference between the fund-raising strategies of Republican and Democrats, or incumbents and challengers.[30] Clearly, the Internet has become a key weapon in the arsenal of political fund-raisers.

Developing a Core of Campaign Activists

Until relatively recently, the typical approach of Republican presidential candidates was to run somewhat to the right of center to appeal to their base and hence secure the nomination, while Democratic presidential candidates would run somewhat to the left of center to appeal to their base and hence secure their nomination. Then having secured the nomination by appealing to the base, the candidates would typically attempt to expand on their base by moving toward the center during the general election. However, in recent years, with the country so evenly divided, presidential candidates, and many candidates lower on the ballot, have focused their general election efforts not on persuading new supporters, but rather on reinforcing those who are naturally inclined to support them, and making sure that those individuals vote on election day. The Internet is an exceptionally valuable tool for these types of enterprises.

Scholars of interpersonal communication tell us that we expose ourselves primarily to messages that will confirm our existing beliefs. This phenomenon of selective exposure suggests that a large number of the visitors to a candidate website are likely to be predisposed toward that candidate.[31] In the 2004 election cycle, Governor Howard Dean was the first to take advantage of that fact, though ultimately it may have been President Bush who exploited it most effectively on election day.

Dean's campaign manager, Joe Trippi, had come across Meetup.com before he took over the Dean campaign. On his first day on the job, he recalls, "I offered up the closest thing I had to a strategy: 'We need to put a link to this web site, Meetup.com., on our campaign web site.'"[32] Meetup.com allows people of similar interests to, literally, meet up. The site would then match people with similar interests—writing, baseball,

Howard Dean—and give them a time and place to meet. Meetup.com initially even reserved the place.[33] Typically, new members to Meetup.com would register, indicating their interest, in this case in Howard Dean. They would be given information about the next "meetup" in their area, and could then send a message to the group leader, post a message on the group bulletin board, and tell the group a little about themselves. When Trippi made his suggestion, 432 people had expressed an interest in meeting up with others who were interested in Howard Dean's candidacy. Ultimately, Meetup.com became the key way that the 190,000 members of the Dean meetups could stay in touch with one another.

The Dean meetups provided the campaign with a growing body of campaign activists who might be called upon to serve a variety of functions. The Dean campaign built support by linking to Meetup.com and utilizing e-mails to encourage supporters to join a Dean meetup in their community. People with a common interest in Howard Dean simply met one another, and determined what they wanted to do on his behalf. Initially, this was largely a bottom-up operation. However, as the campaign realized that they had tapped into an enormous potential source of campaign activists who could often be mobilized on short notice, the Dean campaign began to provide direction. Zephyr Teachout, director of Internet Organizing for Dean for America, likens the campaign's use of Meetup.com to a network with a hub. He observed that:

> An unbidden Meetup group—i.e. one that is running on its own momentum with little input from the campaign HQ and little lateral contact with cousins—is less likely to organize a campaign to write letters to the editor about the war, say, if they don't know whether the Meetup 10 miles away is doing the same thing, something different, or at cross purposes. To feel nationally powerful, local groups need a connection to a national campaign and, to grow, local groups need a constant evangelist.
>
> To call this "bottom-up" isn't exactly right, because what I'm talking about is a productive tension between leaders and end users. Just as eBay is better than a thousand separate auction sites, and each auctioneer on eBay is happy that eBay advertises and improves its user interface and sets good rules for all to follow, the most powerful political network needs a center and something of an ideology. But if it's built right, the imagination, language and work can all come from the edges. Not just individuals on the edges, but groups and communities on the edges. [34]

The Dean campaign broke new ground in its use of the Internet both for fund-raising purposes and for developing a body of campaign activists. As we have seen, during the general election Senator Kerry raised substantially more money online than did President Bush. However, President Bush's campaign was contacting individual voters and ultimately encouraging them to vote for Bush. To that end, it focused on the Internet as a means of developing an organization of campaign activists who would work their neighborhoods on behalf of the president.

Bush was using the Internet to build an organization that would serve him well. Once a volunteer had committed to help the president's campaign, the volunteer could enter his or her zip code on a webpage and the campaign would generate a list of targeted voters in the volunteer's own neighborhood. The Bush campaign generated the lists by integrating mapping technology with the party's databases. Not only would the list of targeted voters be generated for the volunteer, but a map of those voters' residences would be generated, and the volunteer would be provided with an estimate of the time it would require to visit those neighbors and distribute talking points. The Internet allowed Bush volunteers to make their own arrangements at any hour, to canvass in their own neighborhoods where they might build on personal relationships, and to fit their volunteer work into their own schedule with knowledge of how long it would take. As each canvasser found support, the Internet could be used to encourage those supporters to in some fashion become part of the Bush organization.[35] Moreover, as the Bush campaign used the Internet to recruit volunteers to canvass neighborhoods, they were also building an organization that would prove exceedingly useful in getting out the vote on election day.

Computer mediated communication has many elements of interpersonal communication. Though it is not face-to-face, neither is it one-way, as are the mass media. As we have seen, by utilizing feedback, whether through sites like Meetup.com or extensive use of e-mails, in 2004 better than ever before, campaigns were able to develop a body of campaign activists. Thus, the Internet became a major media in the 2004 elections, serving such critical functions as reinforcing voter opinion and perhaps persuading some voters, proving a means of fund-raising from large numbers of small contributors, and providing a means of developing a body of campaign activists.

THE BREADTH AND FUTURE OF THE INTERNET AND INTERNET TOOLS IN ELECTIVE POLITICS

As we have discussed throughout this and other chapters, there is little doubt that the effect of the Internet and Internet tools on political campaigns at all levels will grow exponentially. Without question, the Internet has already played many important roles in a number of campaigns—all the way from helping candidates who, for some reason, "catch fire and raise millions in small donations practically overnight,"[36] to providing in-

formation about candidates to previously uninformed voters and reinforcing the opinions of those already informed, to developing a core of
campaign activists who interact with each other in their support and pro-
motion of specific candidates. But the most interesting questions are really
not about the use and effect of the Internet in past campaigns but about its
future in electoral politics. While there are enthusiasts who predict an Internet revolution that will change the face of American politics by ending,
for example, the "stranglehold" of media consultants over candidates and
their campaigns or by the purposeful redesign of the presidential nominating process,[37] we believe that the "revolution will be markedly different than the pie-in-the-sky predictions made just a couple of short years
ago."[38] Yes, of course, there will continue to be major changes in the way
campaigns of the future will be run that will be markedly different from
even those in the first decade of the twenty-first century. Given the successes of Internet usage in campaigns from the 1990s through the midterm elections of 2006, it seems clear that "successful campaigns will incorporate whatever technologies are available and affordable into
traditional campaign structure."[39] And whether or not these changes will
be "revolutionary" may be only a matter of definition. In fact, we suggest
that "E-campaigning"[40] in the years to come will realistically yield four advantages or benefits for candidates and their campaigns.

Before discussing some of the most important benefits E-campaigning
will bring, it is important to understand why they will occur—why the
potential for such breadth exists. On March 26, 2006, the Federal Election
Commission unanimously voted "not to regulate political communication
on the Internet, including e-mails, blogs and the creation of Web sites."[41]
The e-mail exemption was pushed by bloggers who sought to convince
the commission "that their writings should not be considered for the purposes of regulation the same as campaign contributions. In the end, they
won. Only paid political ads placed on Web sites were ultimately subjected to campaign finance limitations."[42] Thus, as one political consultant
explained, with this loophole in election spending regulations in place, all
types of political entrepreneurs, including political consulting groups,
campaign staffs, wealthy individuals, unions, and any and all interest
groups are able to purchase, for example, "all of the e-mail addresses for
registered voters in a congressional district . . . produce an Internet video
ad, and e-mail it along with a link to the campaign contribution page" and
not have any of it "count against any contribution limits or independent
expenditure requirements; it would never even need to be reported."[43] In
other words, not only can campaigns put unlimited amounts of money
into Internet communication but individuals or groups not even affiliated
with a particular campaign can "use e-mailings to alter the outcome of
key congressional races and still remain anonymous."[44]

While the website funding exemption has the potential for abuse, it also has the very real potential of benefiting candidates and their campaigns. And, although some of the four benefits are somewhat futuristic, others were put into use even in the 2004 election cycle.

E-campaigning Benefits

The first benefit of E-campaigning is especially interesting because of the effect that it could have on reducing the cost of one of the most expensive elements of a candidate's campaign, paid television advertising. According to political communication scholar Lynda Lee Kaid, more money was spent by the presidential candidates on television advertising ($547 million) during the 2004 presidential campaign than in any other presidential campaign in the nation's history.[45] In her study of the use of the Internet for political advertising in the 2004 presidential election, Kaid points out that, while web advertising was used by many of the presidential hopefuls and independent groups during the second (primaries) stage of the campaign, its utilization was a good deal less than the use of televised ads. In fact, although by the end of the general election stage, the Bush and Kerry campaigns and the Republican and Democratic National Committees spent $4.2 million on online advertising, it was, nonetheless, far removed from the $547 million they spent on televised ads.[46] Thus, we predict that, beginning with the 2008 presidential campaign, Internet advertising will become an extensively used venue for political advertising—frequently taking the place, or at least changing the dynamic, of hugely expensive televised ads. As journalist Jonathon Alter has suggested, "in 2008, any presidential candidate with half a brain will let a thousand ad ideas bloom (or stream) online and televise only those that are popular downloads. Deferring to 'the wisdom of crowds' will be cheaper and more effective."[47] We agree.

A second benefit of E-campaigning is closely related to our earlier discussion in this chapter of ways in which the Internet contributes to developing a core of campaign activists. "True believers" may argue that the Internet's place in campaigns of the future will be the "central organizing force" that allows "campaigns to assemble themselves, with passionate supporters signing up on a Web site, assigning tasks to themselves, completing them, and returning to the Web site to claim new tasks, with the candidate enjoying the fruits of these anonymous worker bees all the while."[48] Although we suggest that such a "utopian" claim is probably unrealistic, we have no doubt that social networking data (the kind of thing we discussed earlier in terms of the 2004 Howard Dean primary campaign) will be incredibly important to campaigns at all levels. Websites that ask individuals to "volunteer publicly a list of their hobbies, professional interests, close friends, geographic ties, deepest fears and greatest aspirations"[49] will provide relevant and critical metadata, thus allowing campaigns to move beyond "such crude aggregation as households and walk lists"[50] and directly target the specific location of those potential volunteers and supporters most receptive to the candidate and his/her message. In other words, random telephone calls, candidate literature, and videos mailed to "all" Republicans or Democrats in a neighborhood or congressional district, and knocking on strangers' doors, will be replaced by highly focused campaigning that is able to map social networks because of the metadata that has been collected.

The third benefit of E-campaigning is somewhat controversial, although it was used by some pollsters during the 2004 presidential election. In fact, political pollster John Zogby views online polling as "a ship that has already sailed and is proving itself as the vessel of choice for quickly, cheaply, and accurately handicapping campaigns," arguing that "anyone in this business who has not yet caught the Internet wave is missing the boat, like the naysayers who were slow to embrace telephone polling 35 years ago."[51] Zogby's enthusiasm for online polling is based on his experience using it during the 2004 presidential campaign when his firm, Zogby Interactive, called seventeen of twenty states correctly and in 2005 when the firm not only correctly predicted who would win governors' races in Virginia and New Jersey but projected numbers that were very close to the actual results. In spite of Zogby's success, other political pollsters argue that online polling is a problem because it underrepresents blacks, Hispanics and senior citizens (not all Americans have Internet access) and feel that, at least in the immediate future, the telephone "will remain the gold standard of political polling" because it is more accurate and allows for more scientifically selected population samples to survey public opinion.[52] However, even with its problems, most pollsters believe that in the years to come telephone polls will have to be replaced by online polling. As one pollster suggested, "the phone is going to go away" because "the ability to find phone numbers for people is waning, the willingness of people to take polls on the telephone is decreasing and the quality of your samples is declining. The internet is the obvious replacement. What's left unclear is exactly what Internet methodology will work."[53]

A fourth benefit of E-campaigning is, we believe, especially important because of its potential to communicate with voters. Earlier in this chapter we discussed the dramatic rise of political blogs on the Internet during the 2004 presidential election. But blogs, as Kaye D. Trammell has noted, have been around since the 1990s, although only "since the terror attacks on September 11, 2001, did blogs really start to gain mainstream popularity and did the world start to consider their use in the information process."[54] In her study of the blogs used by the campaigns of George W.

Bush and John Kerry in 2004, Trammel argues that blogging can be an important addition to campaign communication strategies because of its ability to humanize the messages of candidates and their campaigns, providing a more "personalized approach to presenting news and information" that allows "people to discuss thematic, big-picture issues in a very episodic and anecdotal way."[55] Not only, however, did the use of blogs to gain information increase during the 2004 election, one study found that people rated them as more credible than other information sources such as online newspapers and television broadcasts.[56] And although more research during future election campaigns is necessary to draw firm conclusions, it may well be that the "explanation" or the "breaking down" of a candidate's issue or political statement—the interaction of blogger and online reader—is viewed as a more comfortable and personable way to understand campaign messages. If that is the case, that is, voters better understand a campaign and its candidate—feel more interpersonally involved—when receiving the campaign message from blogs, there is little doubt that the medium will play an even more important role in campaigns of the future than it did in 2004 and 2006.

CONCLUSION

In this chapter, we have examined an increasingly important player in contemporary political campaigns: the Internet. In so doing, we have discussed the content of candidate websites as well as the multiple functions or roles they have assumed in a campaign—all the way from fund-raising to developing a core of campaign activists. We have also analyzed some of the benefits of E-campaigning for candidates and their campaigns and for the American voter. Clearly, the Internet has not only become a fundamental element in political campaigns, it may well assume an even more dominant role in years to come.

NOTES

1. Blivins Group, "The Internet's Role in Political Campaigns: Utilization by 2006 United States Senatorial Candidates," 3. Retrieved June 5, 2006, from www.blivins.com.
2. Blivins Group, "The Internet's Role in Political Campaigns," 3.
3. Blivins Group, "The Internet's Role in Political Campaigns," 9.
4. Blivins Group, "The Internet's Role in Political Campaigns," 10. The Blivins group used a *Washington Post* analysis of key races to determine that the eleven key Senate races in 2006 were those in Maryland, Minnesota, Missouri, Montana, Nebraska, New Jersey, Ohio, Pennsylvania, Rhode Island, Tennessee, and Washington. Hereafter, any reference to websites in key races will be to these races.
5. Blogs are also often called weblogs. On their definition see the dictionary of marketing terms found at www.marketingterms.com/dictionary/blog/.

6. Blivins Group, "The Internet's Role in Political Campaigns," 3.

7. Blivins Group, "The Internet's Role in Political Campaigns," 4.

8. Blivins Group, "The Internet's Role in Political Campaigns," 5.

9. Blivins Group, "The Internet's Role in Political Campaigns," 5.

10. This description is based on the authors' visit to www.bencardin.com on July 10, 2006.

11. See www.michaelsteeleformaryland.com. The authors found television ads when they visited this site on July 10, 2006.

12. Blivins Group, "The Internet's Role in Political Campaigns," 4.

13. The explanation of RSS feeds found in this paragraph is drawn from Amy Gahran, "News and Musings on How We Communicate in the Online Age: Part 1: "Webfeeds (RSS): What's New Online?" 1–2; and Amy Gahran, "News and Musings on How We Communicate in the Online Age: Part 2: "How Most Webfeeds (RSS) Work," 1. Retrieved on July 12, 2007, at blog.contentious.com/archives/2004/05/04/part1-webfeeds-rss-whats-new-online and blog.contentious.com/archives/2004/05/04/part-2-how-most-webfeeds-rss-work. Also see "What is RSS? RSS Explained," retrieved on July 12, 2007, at www.whatisrss.com/.

14. Blivins Group, "The Internet's Role in Political Campaigns," 4.

15. Blivins Group, "The Internet's Role in Political Campaigns," 3.

16. Bruce Blimber and Richard Davis, *Campaigning Online: The Internet in U.S. Elections* (New York: Oxford University Press, 2003), 67.

17. For a helpful overview of what candidate websites contained during the 2000 and 2004 primaries, see Steven M. Schneider and Kirsten A. Foot, "Web Campaigning by U.S. Presidential Primary Candidates in 2000 and 2004," in *The Internet Election: Perspectives on the Web in Campaign 2004*, ed. Andrew Paul Williams and John C. Tedesco, 26 (Boulder, Colo.: Rowman & Littlefield, 2006).

18. All of these websites were visited by the authors on June 23, 2006. See hillaryclinton.com; www.kenblackwell.com; hoyerforcongress.com; and www.wallyherger.com.

19. All of the figures found in this paragraph are drawn from Blimber and Davis, *Campaigning Online*, 38, 61.

20. Blimber and Davis, *Campaigning Online*, 61. Blimber and Davis found that, in 2000, Internet fund-raising increased for virtually all levels of campaigns but, regardless of the office being sought, never seriously threatened the more traditional means of fund-raising. Blimber and Davis note that the Talent campaign is one of the few that kept reliable records of the fraction of contributions that came in via the Internet. Federal election rules do not require such information.

21. All of the figures used in this paragraph are drawn from Lee Rainie, Michael Cornfield, and John Horrigan, *The Internet and Campaign 2004* (Washington, D.C.: Pew Research Center, 2005), i, iv. Retrieved on June 5, 2006, at www.pewinternet.org/.

22. Rainie, Cornfield, and Horrigan, *The Internet and Campaign 2004*, 1.

23. Rainie, Cornfield, and Horrigan, *The Internet and Campaign 2004*, iv.

24. Monica Postelnicu, Justin D. Martin, and Kristen D. Landreville, "The Role of Campaign Web Sites in Promoting Candidates and Attracting Campaign Resources," in *The Internet Election: Perspectives on the Web in Campaign 2004*, ed. Andrew Paul Williams and John C. Tedesco (Boulder, Colo.: Rowman & Littlefield, 2006), 105.

25. See Joe Trippi, *The Revolution Will Not Be Televised: Democracy, The Internet, and The Overthrow of Everything* (New York: Regan Books, 2004) for discussions of many of the ways that the Dean campaign pioneered in the use of the Internet. Trippi was quick to see the interpersonal elements of computer-mediated communication and try to utilize them on behalf of his candidate.

26. Michael Cornfield, "The Internet and Campaign 2004: A Look Back at the Campaigners." Retrieved on July 28, 2006 at www/[ewomtermet/prg/pdfs/Cornfield_commentary.pdf.

27. Cornfield, "The Internet and Campaign 2004," 2.

28. Rainie, Cornfield, and Horrigan, "The Internet and Campaign 2004," 1.

29. Postelnicu, Martin, and Landreville, "The Role of Campaign Web Sites," 105.

30. Blivins Group, "The Internet's Role in Political Campaigns," 19–21. Those campaigns that had not provided website visitors an opportunity to donate were almost exclusively in races that were not considered "key races," and hence likely not to be heavily contested.

31. On selective exposure, see Joseph A. Devito, *The Interpersonal Communication Book* (New York: Pearson, 2007), 81.

32. Trippi, *The Revolution Will Not Be Televised*, 83.

33. A current visitor to meetup.com will notice that they do not select the meeting place, but rather leave that to the individual who starts the meetup.

34. Zephyr Teachout is quoted in Ann Hubert, "What Lessons Can Internet Businesses Teach Political Movements?" found in "Briefing Materials: Internet and Society 2004: Votes, Bits and Bytes," 15. This conference was sponsored by the Berkman Center for Internet and Society of Harvard Law School, December 9–11, 2004. Retrieved on June 5, 2006, at anya.law.harvard.edu/is2k4/.

35. John Palfrey, "The Internet's Effect on Politics: A Working Hypothesis," found in "Briefing Materials: Internet and Society 2004: Votes, Bits and Bytes," 4. This conference was sponsored by the Berkman Center for Internet and Society of Harvard Law School, December 9–11, 2004. Retrieved on June 5, 2006, at anya.law.harvard.edu/is2k4/.

36. Jonathon Alter, "A New Open-Source Politics," *Newsweek*, June 5, 2006, 35.

37. Alter, "A New Open-Source Politics," *Newsweek*, 35.

38. Chad Dotson, "No Revolutions," *Campaigns and Elections* (August 2006): 51.

39. Dotson, "No Revolutions," 51.

40. Andrew Chadwick, *Internet Politics: States, Citizens, and New Communication Technologies* (New York: Oxford University Press, 2006), 144.

41. Jeffery Birnbaum, "The Political Spam Floodgates Open," *Washington Post*, June 19–25, 2006.

42. Birnbaum, "The Political Spam Floodgates Open."

43. Birnbaum, "The Political Spam Floodgates Open."

44. Birnbaum, "The Political Spam Floodgates Open."

45. Lynda Lee Kaid, "Political Web Wars: The Use of the Internet for Political Advertising," in *The Internet Election*, ed. Andrew Paul Williams and John C. Tedesco, 67–82 (New York: Rowman & Littlefield, 2006).

46. Kaid, 68.

47. Alter, "A New Open-Source Politics," 35.

48. Waldo Jaquith, "Friends Telling Friends," *Campaigns and Elections* (August 2006): 50.

49. Jaquith, "Friends Telling Friends," 50.

50. Jaquith, "Friends Telling Friends," 50.

51. J. Todd Foster, "Is Online Polling: a. Representative, b. Accurate, c. Efficient, d. Don't Know Yet," *Campaigns and Elections* (September 2006): 30–34.

52. Foster, "Is Online Polling . . .," 32.

53. Foster, "Is Online Polling . . .," 34.

54. Kaye D. Trammell, "The Blogging of the President," *The Internet Election*, ed. Andrew Paul Williams and John C. Tedesco (New York: Rowman & Littlefield, 2006), 134.

55. Trammell, 134.

56. Thomas J. Johnson and Barbara K. Kaye, "Wag the Blog: How Reliance on Traditional Media and the Internet Influence Credibility Perceptions of Weblogs among Blog Users," *Journalism and Mass Communication Quarterly* 81, no. 3 (2004): 622–42.

Political Campaign Communication: An Epilogue

The central thesis of this book has been that communication is the heart of the modern political campaign. It is, as we argued in chapter 1, the epistemological base. Without it, there would be no campaign. With this as our premise, we explored many principles of contemporary political campaigning including the communicative functions, styles, and media channels. We have also examined a number of the communicative practices in the contemporary campaign, including speechmaking, debating, interpersonal communication, and the Internet. Moreover, as we analyzed technological advancements in the modern campaign, we were talking about techniques of communication. While we have not denied the importance of such variables as political parties, voter demographics, philosophical questions, or even economic considerations, we have consistently maintained that understanding the principles and practices of campaign communication is the only way to come to grips with the reality of the modern campaign.

We have striven to present a realistic picture of the way in which candidates and their consultants go about their tasks, implementing the techniques of communication. In so doing, we have attempted to be descriptive. We have not attempted to make judgments, to cast praise or blame on candidates or their methods. We do not intend to do so now. However, we would be remiss (or at the least not very observant) if we failed to acknowledge some of the most important questions or concerns that have been raised regarding modern political campaigning.

In 1983 when this book was first written, we raised six questions or concerns about political campaigning. Those concerns still remain and in some instances have grown alarmingly more disturbing than they were twenty-four years ago. Moreover, those six questions or concerns have, we believe, in the past twenty-four years given rise to an overarching question that both subsumes and transcends our original six concerns. In this epilogue, we wish to review our original six questions, examining them in light of recent developments. Moreover, we wish to address a final and substantially more meaningful question that Americans of all walks of life have been asking with increasing frequency. Finally, while we scarcely presume to be able to resolve many of the questions and concerns generated by contemporary political campaigning, we wish to conclude by examining some of the many proposals that thoughtful citizens, academicians, and practitioners have offered in response to the questions and concerns being raised by contemporary political campaigns.

The first question we and others were asking in 1983 about political communication was simply, Will these trends continue? Will the new techniques of communication continue to play a dominant role in the campaigns of the future? While we do not have the benefit of a political crystal ball, our answer is yes. Twenty-four years ago, we observed that it seemed unlikely that the methods of campaigning would revert to those of an earlier day. Since 1983, the technological changes in campaigning have been as far reaching as in any comparable period in our history. This is unlikely to change. People have consistently embraced technology, and we have every reason to believe that they will continue doing so. This is especially true of political candidates and consultants. As new methods of transportation and communication were developed, they were incorporated into political campaigns, often before they were widely employed in other situations.

We see little prospect that candidates or their staffs will shun current technology or turn their backs on the future. However, the very fact that new tools of communication have changed the nature and methods of campaigning has resulted in more calls to alter campaigns. After every election, political parties, political scientists, candidates, and legislators call for such things as shorter primary seasons, national primaries, more stringent finance reforms, reducing the power of the Iowa caucus and the New Hampshire primary, provision to candidates of free television time, significant changes to the negative tone of campaigns, and a host of other changes. Moreover, as we have detailed earlier, often changes take place. But, in the largest sense, the trends we have indicated throughout the book, trends that have made communication the preeminent factor in the waging of contemporary political campaigns, will continue.

A second question that has been raised by many is basic to the thrust of this book: Does campaigning make a difference? Apparently those who ask the question do so because they see such trends as low voter turnout, diminished party affiliation, and the growth of citizen distrust and apathy as clear signs that political campaigns have little or nothing to do with election results. Obviously, we disagree with this point of view. Any number of examples illustrate that campaigns have indeed made a difference in winning and losing elections. If we cite only a few contemporary instances, they would surely include the 2000 election of Senator Debbie Stabanaw of Michigan and Senator Hillary Rodham Clinton; the 2002 elections of Governor Robert Ehrlich of Maryland, Senators Mary Landrieu of Louisiana, Jim Talent of Missouri, Susan Collins of Maine, and Elizabeth Dole of North Carolina; the 2004 elections of President George W. Bush, Senator Barack Obama of Illinois, and Governor Linda Lingle of Hawaii; and the 2006 elections of Governor Ted Strickland of Ohio and Senator Sherrod Brown of Ohio.

Indeed, if campaigning makes no difference to election returns, why, then, are there more and more candidates, including those on state and local levels, who spend enormous amounts of time and energy, to say nothing of money, planning and implementing campaigns? Political campaigning has become a growth industry. It is difficult to believe this would have happened if the candidates doubted its worth.

Finally, and from our point of view, most important, we believe that, beyond helping determine winners and losers, political campaigns serve many useful functions for voters and candidates. While some of these functions are important symbolically, others have instrumental value. Taken collectively, what all of this suggests is that campaigning does make a difference to citizens and candidates alike.

The third question raised by the growing emphasis on political campaigns as communication phenomena is related to the whole area of ethics. This book has dealt with several ethical questions that are conspicuous in contemporary campaigns, including the appropriate use of speechwriters, public opinion polls, and media advertising. Throughout this study, we have chosen to describe, not evaluate. But anyone interested in political campaign communication cannot fail to be concerned with its ethical dimensions. "Dirty politics" had been around long before the advent of "unfair" or "unethical" television spot commercials. In fact, it was a part of political life in our nation's first political campaigns. Though campaign principles and practices may change from election to election, practitioners do not. Office seekers and their advisers are human beings. They remain subject to the foibles and temptations that have always confronted people. We see no evidence that contemporary candidates and their advisers are inherently less ethical than those of prior generations. The new communication-oriented politics, in which candidates and media have focused on the negative, have doubtlessly brought questions regarding political ethics into sharper focus.

The fourth question raised by the growing emphasis on communication in political campaigns is that of cost. Many have expressed concern, if not outrage, about the high costs of political campaigning. In recent years, the expenses associated with effective campaigning have increased dramatically. In the election cycle of 2000, candidates at all levels were spending unparalleled amounts of money. The two New York senatorial candidates spent over $80 million. One of the New Jersey senatorial candidates spent $60 million. Three people running for a seat in the U.S. House of Representatives spent over $19 million on their campaigns.[1]

The overall total for the 2000 election cycle was over $3 billion, or about 50 percent higher than it had been a mere four years earlier.[2] And by the 2004 election cycle, the two major party presidential candidates' individual expenditures reached over $600 million and the overall cost of just the presidential election was $1 billion. The 2006 campaign was another record breaker with more than $2.6 billion spent in a nonpresidential year.[3] As costs escalate, there are those who feel that we have reached, or are fast reaching, the point where access to money will become the chief determinant of a candidate's success. This is, of course, a principal advantage for incumbent candidates who most generally win their elections.

Similarly, campaigns are becoming more expensive in terms of human resources. Candidates and their associates are spending enormous amounts of time and effort to win office. Three of our last five presidents, George H. W. Bush, Ronald Reagan, and Jimmy Carter, have made running for president into full-time jobs lasting several years, as have many of their competitors such as Pat Buchanan, Lamar Alexander, Bill Bradley, Carol Moseley-Braun, and Howard Dean. Others, such as Senators Joseph Lieberman, John McCain, John Kerry, John Edwards, and Bob Graham; Congressmen Richard Gephardt and Dennis Kucinich; and Governors Bill Clinton and George W. Bush, have found it difficult to campaign and simultaneously hold responsible positions. In 1996, Senator Bob Dole gave up his seat in the Senate to campaign for the presidency. Though the demands of presidential campaigning are unusually high, these same demands are often placed on those who seek lesser offices. Members of Congress or members of many of the state legislatures, for example, take extended recesses during the election period. Challengers find it necessary to abandon their professions temporarily, often taking leaves of absence. Because time demands are high, it grows increasingly difficult for many citizens seriously to consider running for public office, particularly those who are not financially secure.

Moreover, as we have seen, candidates are not the only individuals who face high costs in money and time when they choose to run. Often responsibilities must be borne by their spouses, children, business associates, and close friends. The use of family and friends as surrogates, fund-raisers, and aides in other campaign-related activities places heavy burdens on all. These demands grow even greater as campaign seasons lengthen. The 2004 presidential campaign, for example, with the first primaries moved up to January, was the longest presidential campaign in history, although, the 2008 presidential campaign will clearly be even longer. In sum, the length of current campaigns and the demands they make on the financial and time resources of candidates and associates are costs that have grown so dramatically in recent years that many concerned individuals are calling for change.

The fifth question raised by the growing emphasis on communication in political campaigns involves the extent to which public expectations are being affected. Many political observers have commented on the growing cynicism of voters. Voters feel that their opinions do not count, that governments in Washington and the state capitols do not understand either their problems or their aspirations, and that candidates do not keep their campaign promises. One manifestation of these feelings is low voter turnout. Beginning with the 1992 election and continuing until 2004, it seemed as though Americans were staying home on election day in record numbers. In 2004 the heavy vote of younger Americans increased voter turnout, with 60.3 percent of eligible Americans voting.[4]

At least two campaign phenomena contribute to unfulfilled public expectations. The first is the pervasiveness and ugliness of negative advertisements. As Charles Krauthammer has observed:

Delta Airlines, you might have noticed, does *not* run negative TV ads about USAir. It does not show pictures of the crash of USAir flight 427 with a voice-over saying: "USAir, airline of death. Going to Pittsburgh? Fly Delta instead."

And McDonald's, you might also have noticed, does not run ads reminding viewers that Jack in the Box hamburgers once killed two customers. Why? Because Delta and McDonald's know that if the airline and fast food industries put on that kind of advertising, America would soon be riding trains and eating box-lunch tuna sandwiches.

Yet every two years the American politics industry fills the airwaves with the most virulent, scurrilous, wall-to-wall character assassination of nearly every political practitioner in the country—and then declares itself puzzled that America has lost trust in its politicians.

Voters declare a burning desire to throw the bums out. Polls show an aversion to politicians that can only be called malignant. And the sages pull on their beards stumped.

Why? No need for exotic theories. The simplest explanation is always the best. Politics is the only American industry whose participants devote their advertising budgets to regular, public savage undermining of one another. It is the only American industry whose participants devote prodigious sums to destroying whatever shred of allegiance any of them might once have with customers.[5]

Thus, as Krauthammer illustrates, negative advertising has had a deleterious effect on public perception of the process, the candidates, and the institutions of government. This perception has been reflected in a retreat from political activities—"precinct work, communication with Congress and federal agencies—and from voting itself."[6]

The second campaign phenomenon contributing to unfilled public expectations is voters' belief that they are being manipulated by political consultants, pollsters, advertising wizards, and maybe bloggers. Voters believe that the purpose of campaign consultants is to elect candidates by using words and images that manipulate with "inflammatory messages and insinuations that often are totally false or grotesquely misleading."[7] This growing alienation was exacerbated by the problems surrounding the 2000 presidential election. Since the 2000 election cycle, voting irregularities have frequently been charged. This too contributes to the dissatisfaction of the American public.

The sixth issue raised by contemporary campaigns focuses on the candidates. The skills of advocacy necessary for election are not necessarily the skills of compromise and deliberation required for effective governing. Moreover, today the closest advisers of many elected officials are their pollsters and other communication specialists, not issue experts or party liaisons. Can a nation, even a county, be adequately, much less skillfully, governed by officials and advisers whose skills reflect the demands of successful political campaigning?

Since we first expressed these concerns twenty-four years ago, none have been remedied. Indeed, many of our concerns have grown more serious. Like many Americans, we sometimes grow exasperated by the effectiveness of modern campaign methods; repeated revelations about campaign and campaigner ethics; the skyrocketing costs of campaigning, which consistently work to the advantage of the incumbent; growing evidence of the public's disillusionment with our political process; and similar evidence of our citizenry's dissatisfaction with the caliber of our national, regional, and local political leaders.

These growing concerns all contribute to a fundamental question that both subsumes and transcends the six concerns we expressed in 1983. Put bluntly: Is contemporary political campaigning failing the nation?

The very fact that a question such as this must be asked, and is being asked, not simply by us but by countless Americans, both politically sophisticated and politically naïve, is disturbing. We would not have asked it thirty years ago, nor would most other Americans. Yet, today it cannot be escaped. Virtually all retiring officeholders lament the election process and celebrate that they will no longer be subject to it. Columnists from across the political spectrum bemoan our election system. Two relatively recent retirees from public office, President Bill Clinton and Senator

Robert Dole, agree on few things other than the need to reform our election system.

If contemporary political campaigning is failing our nation, what might be done? The list of suggested reforms is lengthy. Among the most frequent suggestions are limiting the number of terms that officeholders such as members of Congress can serve, providing candidates for major statewide and federal offices free television time, offering additional public financing for candidates, and limiting PAC contributions.

We have reservations about all of these suggestions. This is not to say that they may not have merit. But it is to say that they do not strike to the heart of the question. If contemporary political campaigning is failing the nation, it does so because it does not enable the nation to select its best leaders.

Most of the concerns being expressed about our election systems and about contemporary campaigning center on congressional, senatorial, and presidential elections. Several observations are in order.

First, we have no evidence that the losing candidates in recent years would be better officeholders than the winning candidates. Obviously, judgments such as this often reflect the highly subjective and partisan feelings of the individuals making judgment.

Second, we have no compelling evidence to suggest that hordes of extraordinary candidates and officeholders are out "there," refusing to run because of the demands of political campaigning. If contemporary political campaigning is failing our nation, presumably it is doing so by providing us with a lesser quality of leadership. It strikes us as virtually impossible to prove such a contention.

Third, the indictments of contemporary political campaigning often seem to miss the point. In one fashion or another, most of the complaints about current campaigning hinge around the charge that campaigns cost too much money. It is this charge that gives rise to most major suggestions for reform: public financing, shorter election periods, and free television. But the problem is not that campaigning costs too much money. It is that incumbents have blatant financial advantages over challengers. The monies spent on campaigning are not excessive given the significance of campaigning. Each year more money is spent on advertising snack food and soft drinks than on political advertising. What is excessive is the disproportionate share of money that flows to the coffers of incumbent officeholders.

Although voter desire for change propelled the 1992 Clinton defeat of an incumbent president, the 1994 Republican victories over a host of incumbent Democratic officeholders, and the 2006 takeover by the Democrats of the House of Representatives and the Senate, incumbents, as we suggested earlier, win more often than they lose. And, frankly, we are not optimistic that incumbents will approve legislation that will diminish their chances of winning. However, any serious attempt at reforming our system of electing public officials must come to grips with this problem.

Questioning political campaign principles and practices is not unique to Americans of our generation. Dissatisfaction has always existed, and our system has evolved to accommodate those complaints that seemed warranted. Dissatisfaction with methods of campaigning and electing officials has prompted a host of changes over the years, many of which we chronicle earlier in this book. A change we have implied but not commented on explicitly is that an ever-increasing number of women and underrepresented minorities are running for and winning offices at all levels.

Contemporary political campaigning is by no means perfect. It has never been perfect in the past, and we see no reason to expect perfection in the future. Critics will always have questions about our election procedures and practices. And they should. Surely no activity is more central to our way of life than the establishment, maintenance, and transfer of leadership through free elections. Political campaign communication is the apotheosis of the democratic experience. It warrants our constant reexamination and reappraisal.

NOTES

1. On the expenses associated with Senate and House seats such as these, see Michael Barone and Richard E. Cohen, eds., *The Almanac of American Politics, 2000* (Washington, D.C.: National Journal Group, 2001), 1729–30.

2. Robert E. Denton, Jr., ed., *The 2000 Presidential Campaign: A Communication Perspective* (Westport, Conn.: Praeger, 2002), xiv.

3. Chuck Raasch, "Campaign Money Likely to Top Record." *Cincinnati Enquirer,* October 25, 2006, A4.

4. Michael P. McDonald, "5 Myths about Turning Out the Vote," *Washington Post,* October 29, 2006.

5. Charles Krauthammer, "Either Way, We Get Brand X," *Cincinnati Enquirer,* October 30, 1994, E-2.

6. Richard Harwood, "The Ugly Elections of '94," *Washington Post National Weekly Edition,* November 14–20, 1994, 29.

7. Harwood, "The Ugly Elections of '94."

Selected Bibliography

Anderson, Karrin Vasby, and Kristina Horn Sheeler. *Governing Codes*. Lanham, Md.: Rowman & Littlefield, Inc., 2005.

Barone, Michael, and Richard E. Cohen, eds. *The Almanac of American Politics, 2002*. Washington, D.C.: National Journal Group, 2001.

Beasley, Vanessa B. *You, the People: American National Identity in Presidential Rhetoric*. College Station: Texas A&M University Press, 2004.

Bennett, W. Lance. *The Governing Crisis: Media, Money, and Marketing in American Elections*. New York: St. Martin's, 1992.

Blimber, Bruce, and Richard Davis, *Campaigning Online: The Internet in U.S. Elections*. New York: Oxford University Press, 2003.

Brareton, Charles. *First in the Nation: New Hampshire and the Premier Presidential Operatives*. Portsmouth, N.H.: Randall, 1987.

Brock, Bernard L., Mark E. Huglen, James F. Klumpp, and Sharon Howell. *Making Sense of Political Ideology*. Lanham, Md.: Rowman & Littlefield, Inc., 2005.

Bystorm, Dianne G., Mary Christine Banwart, Lynda Lee Kaid, and Terry A. Robertson. *VideoStyle, WebStyle, NewsStyle: Gender and Candidate Communication*. New York: Routledge, 2004.

Campbell, Karlyn Kohrs, and Kathleen Hall Jamieson, eds. *Form and Genre: Shaping Rhetorical Action*. Falls Church, Va.: Speech Communication Association, 1977.

Chadwick, Andrew. *Internet Politics: States, Citizens and New Communication Technologies*. New York: Oxford University Press, 2006.

Cook, Elizabeth Adell, Sue Thomas, and Clyde Wilcox, eds. *The Year of the Woman: Myths and Realities*. Boulder, Colo.: Westview, 1994.

Darcy, R., Susan Welch, and Janet Clark. *Women, Elections, and Representation*. 2d ed. Lincoln: University of Nebraska Press, 1994.

Davis, Richard, ed. *The Press and American Politics: The New Mediator*. New York: Longman, 1992.

Denton, Robert E., Jr., ed. *The 2000 Presidential Campaign: A Communication Perspective*. Westport, Conn.: Praeger, 2002.

——. *The 2004 Presidential Campaign: A Communication Perspective.* Lanham, Md.: Rowman & Littlefield, 2005.

Denton, Robert E., Jr., and Rachel L. Holloway. *Images, Scandal, and Communication Strategies of the Clinton Presidency.* Westport, Conn.: Praeger, 2003.

Devlin, Patrick L. *Political Persuasion in Presidential Campaigns.* New Brunswick, N.J.: Transaction, 1987.

Diamond, Edwin, and Stephen Bates. *The Spot: The Rise of Political Advertising on Television.* 3d ed. Cambridge, Mass.: MIT Press, 1992.

Edelman, Murray. *The Symbolic Uses of Politics.* Urbana: University of Illinois Press, 1985.

Foote, Joe S. *Television Access and Political Power: The Networks, the Presidency, and the Loyal Opposition.* New York: Praeger, 1990.

Friedenberg, Robert V. *Communication Consultants in Political Campaigns: Ballot Box Warriors.* Westport, Conn.: Praeger, 1997.

——, ed. *Rhetorical Studies of National Political Debates: 1960–1992.* Westport, Conn.: Praeger, 1994.

——, ed. *Rhetorical Studies of National Political Debates—1996.* Westport, Conn.: Praeger, 1997.

Hahn, Dan F. *Political Communication: Rhetoric, Government, and Citizens.* 2d ed. State College, Pa.: Strata, 2003.

Hause, Gerard A., and Amy Grim, ed. *Rhetorical Democracy.* Mahwah, N.J.: Lawrence Erlbaum, 2004.

Herrnson, Paul S., ed. *Guide to Political Campaigns in America.* Washington, D.C.: CQ Press, 2005.

Hoff, Paul S. *Beyond the 30-Second Spot: Enhancing the Media's Role in Congressional Campaigns.* Washington, D.C.: Center for Responsive Politics, 1988.

The Institute of Politics, John F. Kennedy School of Government, and Harvard University, eds. *Campaign for President: The Managers Look at 2004.* Lanham, Md.: Rowman & Littlefield, 2006.

Iyengar, Shanto, and Richard Reeves, eds. *Do the Media Govern? Politicians, Voters, and Reporters in America.* Thousand Oaks, Calif.: Sage, 1997.

Jamieson, Kathleen Hall. *Packaging the Presidency: A History and Criticism of Presidential Campaign Advertising.* New York: Oxford University Press, 1984.

Jamieson, Kathleen Hall, and David S. Birdsell. *Presidential Debates: The Challenge of Creating an Informed Electorate.* New York: Oxford University Press, 1988.

Jarvis, Sharon E. *The Talk of the Party.* Lanham, Md.: Rowman & Littlefield, 2005.

Jones, Jeffrey P. *Entertaining Politics: New Political Television and Civic Culture.* Lanham, Md.: Rowman & Littlefield, 2005.

Kaid, Lynda Lee, and Dianne G. Bystrom, eds. *The Electronic Election: Perspectives on the 1996 Campaign Communication.* Mahwah, N.J.: Erlbaum, 1999.

Kaid, Lynda Lee, John C. Tedesco, Dianne G. Bystrom, and Mitchell S. McKinney, eds. *The Millennium Election: Communication in the 2000 Campaign.* Lanham, Md.: Rowman & Littlefield, 2003.

Kendall, Kathleen E. *Communication in the Presidential Primaries: Candidates and the Media, 1912–2000.* Westport, Conn.: Praeger, 2000.

Kern, Montague. *30-Second Politics: Political Advertising in the Eighties.* New York: Praeger, 1989.

Kraus, Sidney. *Televised Presidential Debates and Public Policy.* Hillsdale, N.J.: Erlbaum, 1988.

Lordan, Edward J. *Politics, Ink: How America's Cartoonists Skewer Politicians, from King George III to George Dubya.* Lanham, Md.: Rowman & Littlefield, 2006.

Martel, Myles. *Political Campaign Debates: Images, Strategies, and Tactics.* New York: Longman, 1983.

Mayhead, Molly A., and Brenda Devore Marshall. *Women's Political Discourse.* Lanham, Md.: Rowman & Littlefield, 2005.

McQuail, Denis. *Audience Analysis*. Thousand Oaks, Calif.: Sage, 1997.

Mickelson, Sig. *From Whistle Stop to Sound Bite: Four Decades of Politics and Television*. New York: Praeger, 1989.

Miller, Arthur H., and Bruce E. Gronbeck, eds. *Presidential Campaigns and American Self Images*. Boulder, Colo.: Westview, 1994.

Morris, Dick. *Behind the Oval Office: Winning the Presidency in the Nineties*. New York: Random House, 1997.

Nelson, Michael, ed. *The Elections of 2004*. Washington, D.C.: CQ Press, 2005.

Nimmo, Dan D., and James E. Combs. *Mediated Political Realities*. 2d ed. New York: Longman, 1990.

Noonan, Peggy. *What I Saw at the Revolution: A Political Life in the Reagan Era*. New York: Random House, 1990.

Paletz, David L. *The Media in American Politics: Contents and Consequences*. New York: Longman, 1999.

———, ed. *Political Communication Research: Approaches, Studies, Assessments*. Norwood, N.J.: Ablex, 1987.

Payne, Gregory J., ed. *American Behavioral Scientist* (March/April 1989; November/December 1993; August 1997; August 2001; September 2005).

Pfau, Michael, and Henry C. Kenski. *Attack Politics: Strategy and Defense*. New York: Praeger, 1990.

Reichley, A. James, ed. *Elections American Style*. Washington, D.C.: Brookings Institution, 1987.

Sabato, Larry J. *Feeding Frenzy: How Attack Journalism Has Transformed American Politics*. New York: Free Press, 1993.

Sabato, Larry J., and Glenn R. Simpson. *Dirty Little Secrets: The Persistence of Corruption in American Politics*. New York: Random House, 1996.

Scher, Richard K. *The Modern Political Campaign: Mudslinging, Bombast and the Vitality of American Politics*. Armonk, N.Y.: Sharpe, 1997.

Selnow, Gary. *High-Tech Campaigns: Computer Technology in Political Communication*. Westport, Conn.: Praeger, 1994.

Swanson, David L., and Dan D. Nimmo, eds. *New Directions in Political Communication Research: A Resource Book*. Newbury Park, Calif.: Sage, 1990.

Thurber, James A., and Candice J. Nelson. *Campaigns and Elections American Style*. Boulder, Colo.: Westview, 1995.

Trippi, Joe. *The Revolution Will Not Be Televised: Democracy, the Internet, and the Overthrow of Everything*. New York: Regan Books, 2004.

Valley, David B. *A History and Analysis of Democratic Presidential Nomination Acceptance Speeches to 1968*. Lanham, Md.: University Press of America, 1988.

White, Theodore H. *The Making of the President, 1960*. New York: Pocket Books, 1961.

———. *The Making of the President, 1964*. New York: Atheneum, 1965.

———. *The Making of the President, 1968*. New York: Atheneum, 1969.

———. *The Making of the President, 1972*. New York: Bantam, 1973.

Whitney, Catherine. *Nine and Counting: The Women of the Senate*. New York: HarperCollins, 2000.

Williams, Andrew Paul, and John C. Tedesco, eds. *The Internet Election: Perspectives on the Web in Campaign 2004*. Lanham, Md.: Rowman & Littlefield, 2006.

Williams, Frederick. *The New Communications*. 2d ed. Belmont, Calif.: Wadsworth, 1989.

Wilson, Dizard, Jr. *Old Media New Media*. 3d ed. New York: Addison Wesley Longman, 2000.

Windt, Theodore Otto, Jr. *Presidents and Protesters: Political Rhetoric in the 1960s*. Tuscaloosa: University of Alabama Press, 1990.

Woodward, Bob. *The Choice*. New York: Simon & Schuster, 1996.

Index

acceptance addresses, 238–53
Adams, John Quincy, 79
Aden, Roger C., 177
advertising in political campaigns, 353–97;
    consultants and, 382–91; developing a
    master plan for, 354–58; direct mail and,
    361–66; display graphics and, 358–61;
    Internet and, 376–78; print and, 366–71;
    radio and, 368–71; strategies of, 378–82;
    telephones and, 365–66; television and,
    371–76
agenda setting, 140–144
Agnew, Spiro, 132
Ailes, Roger, 169, 261–62, 387
Alexander, Lamar, 29, 34–35, 46, 418
Allen, Cathy, 338–39
Anderson, John, 362
announcement speeches, 28–30, 227–37
apologias, 265–72
Atwood, L. Erwin, 342–43
Auer, J. Jeffery, 277, 280

Babbitt, Bruce, 34
Baker, Howard, 5
Bancroft, George, 207
Bates, Stephen, 161, 396
Bauer, Gary, 233
Baxter, Leona, 383
Bayh, Birch, 12, 50
Bayh, Evan, 26

Beatty, Warren, 25
Becker, Samuel L., 46
Beckley, John, 383
Bennett, William, 62
Benoit, William L., 243
Benze, James G., 177
Berelson, Bernard, 127–29, 144–45
Berger, Josef, 210
Bernays, Edward, 383
Berquist, Goodwin, 293, 318
Biden, Joseph, 85, 231–32
Bitzer, Lloyd, 71, 226, 315
Blaine, James G., 80
Blaney, Joseph R., 243, 275
Bloomberg, Michael R., 8
Blumenthal, Sidney, 13
Blumler, Jay, 134, 136–38
Bono, Sonny, 33
Boosalis, Helen, 177
Bormann, Ernest, 209
Boschwitz, Rudy, 168
Boulding, Kenneth E., 75
Boxer, Barbara, 172
Bradley, Bill, 23–24, 33, 117, 237, 418
Brinkley, David, 82
Broder, David, 166
Brown, Edmund G. "Jerry," 14, 34, 44,
    62, 104
Brown, Ron, 61–62
Brown, Sherrod, 417

Bruce, Lenny, 306
Bryan, William Jennings, 79, 103, 238, 240, 358
Buchanan, Frank, 288
Buchanan, Pat, 25, 62, 418
Burgoon, Michael, 174
Bush, Barbara, 225, 251
Bush, George H. W., 23–25, 27–28, 34–35, 44, 51, 61, 64, 90–91, 95, 97, 108, 110–13, 160, 163–64, 199, 211, 213, 217, 219–20, 387, 418; acceptance address of, 242–43; campaign styles and strategies of, 90, 91, 95, 108, 110–13; debates, 289–91; nominating convention and, 61, 64; primaries and, 43–44, 51; surfacing stage and, 24, 27, 33–35
Bush, George W., 5, 7, 8, 9, 11, 15, 28–29, 33, 36–37, 41, 43, 50–51, 60, 63–65, 84, 87–88, 91, 93–96, 98, 101, 107, 110, 112–13, 146, 155, 160, 164, 166–67, 201–7, 210, 213–15, 333, 335, 350, 370, 387, 401–8, 410, 412; acceptance address of, 239, 243–45, 247–52; announcement address of, 230–36; campaign styles and strategies of, 84, 87–88, 91, 93–94, 96–98, 101, 106, 110, 112–13; debates, 291–93; Internet and, 404, 406–7, 410–12; news conferences and, 255–56, 261–62, 265; nominating convention and, 60, 63–65; political ads of, 358, 372, 385; primaries and, 41, 49, 51; speeches of, 201, 204, 206–7, 211, 213, 215–16; surfacing stage and, 25, 28–29, 34, 36–37
Bush, Laura, 219, 329
Butler, Sherry, 267
Byrne, Jane, 95
Bystrom, Dianne, 180

Campbell, Carroll, Jr., 24
Cappella, Joseph N., 143
Carnahan, Jean, 258
Carter, Jimmy, 13–14, 27, 35, 235, 264, 418; acceptance address, 248; campaign styles and strategies of, 91, 94, 103, 108–09, 111; nominating stages, 50, 59, 61, 64; political debates of, 278, 284
Carvey, Dana, 210
Chabot, Steve, 171
Chaffee, Steven H., 136, 307, 311, 314
challenger campaign style and strategies, 105–114

Chavez, Linda, 181
Cheney, Richard B., 91, 94, 110, 244, 249, 329, 346, 358, 404, 405
Church, Frank, 12
Clay, Henry, 79
Cleveland, Grover, 80, 238
Clinton, Hillary Rodham, 26, 64, 81, 173, 417, 403
Clinton, William Jefferson "Bill," 8, 12, 208, 213, 220, 333, 345, 417–18, 420–21; acceptance address of, 242–43, 251; announcement addresses, 234–36; apologias, 265, 267–71; campaign styles and strategies of, 84, 88, 90, 92–93, 95–97, 99, 107–13; debates, 278, 289–91, 297, 300, 308; nominating convention and, 59, 62–64; political ads of, 160, 164–65, 168, 170–71; primaries and, 38, 44–45, 48–49, 51; surfacing stage and, 24, 29, 35
coffees (campaign event), 31–32, 45, 200, 219, 327, 328–30, 349
Cohen, Bernard C., 141
Collins, Catherine, 261
Collins, Susan, 417
Collins, Tom, 362
Combs, James E., 122
Commission on Presidential Debates, 289–94, 310
Connally, John, 7, 51
Coolidge, Calvin, 207, 383
Coughlin, Charles (father), 126
Cox, James, 102
Crane, Phillip, 362
Crigler, Ann, 377
Cronkite, Walter, 55, 82
Culver, John, 12
Cuomo, Mario M., 34

D'Amato, Alphonse, 166
Dance, Frank E. X., 124
Danforth, John "Jack," 28
Danielson, Wayne, 342
Davis, Dennis, 136, 313
Davis, John W., 52, 80
Davis, Richard, 402, 403, 405
Dean, Howard, 15, 25, 33, 40, 51, 144, 233, 330, 347, 405–7, 410, 418
Dearin, Ray D., 249
debates in political campaigns, 277–321; conditions required for, 287–93;

deciding whether to debate, 285–87; effects of, 304–15; history, 280–83; strategies, 293–304
Declercq, Eugene R., 177
Dees, Morris, 362
Denton, Robert, 259
Devlin, L. Patrick, 161, 164
Dewey, Thomas, 282
Diamond, Edwin, 161
diffusion of information theory, 134–36
Dionne, E. J., Jr., 38
direct mail, 358–65
DiSalle, Michael, 234
display graphics, 358–61
Dole, Elizabeth, 29, 36, 96, 217, 417
Dole, Robert, 51, 64, 208, 235, 243, 251; campaign styles and strategies, 85, 93, 107, 109, 112–13; debates and, 308, 311–12; political ads of, 160, 164, 166, 168; primaries and, 45, 48, 49, 51; surfacing stage and, 24, 29, 34–36
door-to-door canvass, 330–31
Douglas, Stephen, 100; debates and, 277–80
Dowd, Matthew, 301–2
Dreyfus, Lee, 43
Dukakis, Michael, 35, 198, 213, 232, 260; campaign styles and strategies, 109, 112–13; debates and, 289, 297; nominating convention and, 60–61, 64; political ads of, 163; primaries and, 51
Dunn, Winfield, 284
DuPont, Pierre, 34

Eagleton, Thomas, 135
Eastwood, Clint, 33
Edelman, Murray, 28, 90
Edwards, John, 25, 26, 51, 64, 65 108, 110, 144, 205, 233, 234, 346, 418
Ehrlich, Robert, 417
Eisenhower, Dwight David, 14, 90, 108, 155, 207, 216, 268, 283; debates, 282–83; news conferences of, 253, 261–62
Engler, John, 107

Fabianai, Mark, 294
Faucheux, Ron, 204–6
Feiger, Geoffrey, 107
Feingold, Russell, 335–37
Feinstein, Dianne, 170, 172, 376
Fenno, R. F., 87
Ferraro, Geraldine, 59, 76, 175, 181, 358

Fields, Wayne, 250
Flanagin, Andrew, 137
Flowers, Gennifer, 44, 265, 267, 268, 271
Forbes, Malcolm S. "Steve," Jr., 7, 28, 33, 35, 36, 96; announcement address of, 234
Ford, Gerald, 25, 56, 64, 101, 103, 106, 156, 158, 165; debates, 284, 286, 300, 301, 305, 309; speeches and, 208, 213
Fowler, Wyche, 382
Freeman, Orville, 208, 213
Frist, Bill, 26
fund-raising, interpersonal, 334–36
Funkhouser, G. Ray, 141

Gallup, George, Jr., 307
Gallup Poll, 6, 99, 141
Gaudet, Hazel, 127
Gavin, William F., 210
general elections stage of campaigns, 47, 50, 66–68, 159, 164, 410
Gephardt, Richard, 23, 25, 33, 51, 233, 418
Gerson, Michael J., 207, 210, 214–15, 217
Gingrich, Newt, 45
Glenn, John, 33, 42, 108
Gold, Ellen Reid, 266, 269
Golden, James L., 293
Goldwater, Barry, 60, 109, 112, 156–57, 289, 344
Gore, Al, Jr., 8, 18, 160, 164, 166, 169, 208, 220, 256, 265, 345–46, 404; acceptance address of, 247, 251–52; announcement address of, 235–36; campaign styles and strategies, 85, 91, 93, 107, 117; debates and, 292, 294–95, 297, 299, 301–3, 306, 308, 312; nominating stage and, 62, 64; primary stage of campaigns and, 41, 49, 51; surfacing stage and, 24–25, 28–29, 34
Gore, Tipper, 25, 63, 85
Gosnell, Harold, F., 127
Graham, Bob, 36, 37, 46, 233, 418
Gramm, Phil, 28–29
Granholm, Jennifer, 173, 176
Greenberg, Stan, 302
Greer, Frank, 382
Gronbeck, Bruce, 30, 67, 73, 161
Gross, Bert, 232
Gumpert, Gary, 55

Hagner, Paul R., 311
Hahn, Dan, 259, 313
Haig, Alexander, 34

Haldeman, H. R., 81
Hamilton, Alexander, 207
Hanna, Mike, 331
Harding, Warren, 52, 80, 102
Harkin, Tom 27, 39, 51
Harkness, William, 281
Harrison, Benjamin, 102
Harrison, William Henry, 74–75
Hart, Gary, 34, 51, 76
Hatch, Orin, 36
Hayakawa, S. I., 42
Helms, Jesse, 211–12, 274
Hitler, Adolf, 113, 126
Hoffa, Jimmy, 98
Holzman, Elizabeth, 31, 181
Hooker, John J., Jr., 284
Hoover, Herbert, 80, 90, 207
Huddleston, Walter Dee, 169–70
Hughes, Karen, 217, 263–64, 302
Humphrey, Hubert, 60, 141, 157, 213, 283, 298
Huntley, Chet, 82
Hutchinson, Kay Bailey, 175
hypodermic effect, 125–27

Iacocca, Lee, 34
imagery and campaigning, 74–78
incumbent and campaign style and
    strategies, 9, 11, 12, 86–105, 402, 406
Internet, 376–78, 399–412
Internet and political campaigns, 399–412;
    contents of websites, 399–402; functions
    of websites, 402–8; future of the
    Internet, 408–12
interpersonal communication and political
    campaigns; 322–49; between candidates
    and financial contributors, 334–36;
    between candidates and voters, 324–31;
    between voters 341–43
Iyengar, Shanto, 142–43

Jackson, Andrew, 79, 207
Jackson, Henry, 50
Jackson, Jesse, 34, 61, 371; apologia, 265,
    271
Jamieson, Kathleen Hall, 143, 156, 158, 162,
    277, 308
Japp, Phyllis, 177
Javits, Jabob, 192
Jefferson, Thomas, 383
John Paul II, 136

Johnson, Andrew, 207
Johnson, Lyndon, 90, 103, 157; news
    conferences and, 262
Jones, Paula, 84, 271
Joslyn, Richard, 161
Just, Marion, 377–78

Kaid, Lynda Lee, 160, 166–67, 169, 176,
    324–25, 410
Kaplan, Robert, 341
Kasich, John, 233
Katz, Elihu, 129, 137, 308
Kefauver, Estes, 56; debate and, 283–83
Kendell, Amos, 207
Kennedy, Edward "Ted," 31, 32, 34, 51, 62,
    65, 94, 95, 103, 109, 113, 208, 232, 263,
    266, 376; announcement address, 236,
    248; apologia, 266
Kennedy, John F., 14, 63, 79, 98–99, 108–10,
    135, 208, 213, 216, 234, 264; debates and,
    278–80, 282–84, 287–89, 296, 305–7, 311
Kennedy, Robert F., 288
Kenski, Henry, 171
Kern, Montague, 160–61, 166, 378
Kerry, John, 5, 8–9, 11–13, 84, 101, 107–8,
    110, 114, 144, 160, 165, 167–68, 205–7,
    217–18, 220, 265, 346, 372, 385, 405–7,
    410, 412, 418; acceptance address, 239,
    242, 244–52; announcement speech,
    230–32, 235–36; debates, 291–93, 295,
    297–99, 302, 306–8, 311–12; nominating
    convention, 58, 60, 64–65; primaries, 39,
    51; surfacing, 25
Kessler, Frank, 97
Kessler, Martha, 221
Khrushchev, Nikita Sergeyevich, 288
Kimsey, William D., 343
Kinder, Donald, 142
King, Larry, 123, 203, 228, 293
King, Martin Luther, Jr., 61, 230
King, Martin Luther, Sr., 61
kingmakers, 5
Kinnock, Neil, 85
Kissinger, Henry, 261
Klapper, Joseph, 127
Kling, Ken, 397
Koch, Edward I., 92
Kraus, Sidney, 136, 313–14
Krauthammer, Charles, 419–20
Kroft, Steve, 267–68
Kucinich, Dennis, 33, 233, 237, 418

Lake, James, 116
Landon, Alfred, 282
Landrieu, Mary, 181, 417
Lang, Gladys Engel, 142
Lazarsfeld, Paul F., 127–31, 144–45
League of Women Voters, 200, 284
Lehrer, Jim, 220, 302
Lenard, Silvo, 344
Leno, Jay, 27, 28
Lewinsky, Monica, 113, 271
Lieberman, Joseph, 25, 91, 93, 229, 230, 232, 418
Limbaugh, Rush, 146
Lincoln, Abraham, 52, 207; debates and, 277–80
Lincoln, Blanche, 172, 176
Linkugel, Wil, 268–70
Lodge, Henry Cabot, 282–83, 289
Louden, Allan, 75
Lucier, James, 212
Lugar, Richard, 35, 46

MacArthur, Douglas, 208
Magnuson, Warren, 12
Malchow, Hal, 364–65
Mallory, Mark, 8
Mandel, Ruth B., 175
mass media and political campaigns, 122–53; agenda setting and, 140–44; diffusion of information and, 134–36; elaboration likelihood model and, 139–40; hypodermic effect and, 125–27; social influence and model and, 127–33; uses and gratifications, 136–39
Matalin, Mary, 219–20
Mattingly, Mack, 382
McAdoo, William, 80
McAuliffe, Terry, 37, 41–42, 295, 335
McCain, John, 9, 15, 26, 33, 34, 36, 51, 65, 147, 334–35, 337, 418; announcement addresses and, 234, 250; Internet fundraising and, 404
McCarthy, Eugene, 34, 48
McCombs, Maxwell E., 141
McConnell, Mitch, 169–70
McGovern, George, 12, 14, 54, 56, 60, 61, 101, 109, 111–13, 142, 157, 213, 327, 362
McKinley, William, 102, 358
McLeod, Jack, 141
McPhee, William, 129
McQuail, Denis, 137–39

Meehan, Martin, 9
Melcher, John, 170
Metzger, Miriam, 137
Michel, Robert, 210, 213
Mikulski, Barbara, 181
Miller, Gerald R., 174
Mondale, Walter, 112, 113, 115, 116, 165, 308, 311
Moody, Blair, 282
Morris, Richard, 45, 54, 362
Moseley-Braun, Carol, 418
MoveOn.org, 12, 335
Murphy, Mike, 382
Mussolini, Benito, 125

Nader, Ralph, 15
National Communication Association, 1, 289
Nimmo, Dan, 57, 122, 298
Nixon, Richard, M., 57, 64, 79, 81, 82, 97, 98, 101, 108, 111, 141, 143, 157, 164, 204, 207, 213, 266–67; debates, 279–80, 283–84, 287–89, 296, 298, 305–7
nominating conventions, 51–65
Noonan, Peggy, 217
Nunn, Sam, 23

Obama, Barack, 64, 417
O'Donnell, Kenneth, 288
Olson, Kathryn, M., 269–70

PACs (political action committees), 9–13, 173, 336; 527s, 12, 123, 169
Patterson, Thomas E., 46–49, 144–46
Peck, Laura, 328, 329, 331
Pelosi, Nancy, 172–73
Perot, H. Ross, 7, 44, 82, 123, 160; debates, 289–91, 308
Pfau, Michael, 171, 310
Phillips, Susan C., 81
Pier, P. M., 243
Pierce, Franklin, 52
Plumb, J. H., 4
political campaigns: advertising strategies of, 378–81; changes in, 5–16; communication functions, 22–71; communication styles, 72–121; importance of, 3–5; primaries and, 38–51; stages of, 22–71; technology and, 13–16, 78–85

political consultants, 382–91; functions and types, 386–91; history of, 383–86
political speeches, recurring forms of, 226–76; acceptance addresses, 238–53; announcement speeches, 227–38; apologias, 265–72; news conferences, 253–64
Portman, Rob, 221
Proctor, David E., 177
public speaking in political campaigns, 191–225; audiences and, 192–97; competency and format, 199–200; decision to speak and, 191–92; political speechwriting and, 207–17; speech modules, 200–207; stock speeches, 200–207; surrogate speakers and, 217–21; use of polls and, 197–99

Qualls, Roxanne, 171
Quayle, J. Danforth "Dan," 28, 91, 228, 229; debate and, 312, surrogate speakers and, 220
Quayle, Marilyn, 62

radio, 368–71
Rather, Dan, 27
Reagan, Ronald, 14, 19, 34, 123, 136, 142, 158, 163, 213, 217, 234, 251, 418; campaign styles and strategies, 88, 90, 108–12, 115–17; debates and, 287, 293, 299, 308; nominating stage and, 51, 55–56; political advertisements and, 374, 387; primaries and, 43–45
Reinsch, J. Leonard, 282
Reston, James, 132
Rice, Donna, 51
Richards, Ann, 387, 181, 291
Rieselbach, Leroy N., 311
Roberts, Bill, 384
Robertson, Marion G. "Pat," 7, 30, 34, 62
Robinson, John P., 343
Rockefeller, John "Jay," 24
Rockefeller, Nelson, 60, 208
Rogers, Everett, 134
Roosevelt, Franklin Delano, 63, 79, 80, 94, 108, 110, 115, 127, 238, 265; acceptance address of, 207, 208, 213; debates and, 281, 282
Roper, Elmo, 191, 155
Rove, Karl, 217, 302
Ryan, Nolan, 199

Sabourin, Teresa, 177–78
Sanchez, Loretta, 172
Sanders, Keith R., 342
Sasso, John, 109
Sauter, Kevin, 311–12
Savage, Michael, 370
Savage, Robert L., 135
Schroeder, Patricia, 175
Schumer, Charles, 166
Schwartz, Tony, 384
Schwarzenegger, Arnold, 33, 65
Sears, John, 43, 44
Seward, William, 207
Seymour, Horatio, 238
Shadegg, Stephen, 344, 347
Sharp, Stephen A., 284
Sharpton, Al, 25, 403
Shaw, Donald, 141
Shays, Christopher, 9
Sheckels, Theodore, Jr., 181
Sheehan, Michael, 007
Shepherd, Cybil, 24
Sherwood, Robert, 207
Shoemaker, Floyd, 135
Short-Thompson, Cady, 179
Sigal, Leon, 254
Sinclair, Upton, 383
Smith, Alfred, 52
Smith, Carolyn, 261
Smith, Craig Allen, 338
Smith, Craig R., 213, 308
Smith, Kathy B., 308, 341
Smith, Larry David, 56
social influence model, 127–33
speeches, political. *See* political speeches, recurring forms of
speechwriting, 191–225; job demands of, 210–12; justification for, 200, 208–12; methods of, 214–17; uses of teams in, 212–17
Spencer, Stuart, 384
Springer, Jerry, 228, 374
Stassen, Harold, 281
Steeper, Frederick T., 301
Steinbeck, John, 207
Stevenson, Adlai, 155, 212, 368, 383; debates and, 282–83
Stewart, John, 27
Stockdale, James, 312
Stone, Richard, 236
Strauss, Robert, 61

styles of political campaigns, 72–121; challenger style, 105–14; incumbency style, 86–106; merger of challenger and incumbency styles, 114–17; technology and, 78–85
Sullivan, Ed, 381
surfacing, 22–39
surrogate speakers, 217–21; benefits of, 219–21; selection of, 217–18; utilization of, 218–19
Swanson, David L., 309
Swanson, Linda L., 309
Swift Vets, 167

Taft, Robert, 136
Talent, Jim, 258, 417
Tannen, Deborah, 174
Taylor, Maurice Manning "Mory," Jr., 8
Taylor, Zachary, 80
Teasdale, "Walking Joe," 192, 237
telephones, 365–66
television, 154–87, 371–77; advantages/disadvantages as political media, 181–82; historical use in politics, 155–60; history of political debates, 281–82, 288, 294, 296, 313; types and functions of political ads on, 161–71; women candidates and, 172–81
Thatcher, Margaret, 97
Tower, John, 388
Trent, Jimmie, 78; "The Rhetoric of the Challenger: George Stanley McGovern," 121
Trent, Judith, 77, 78, 177–78; "The Rhetoric of the Challenger: George Stanley McGovern," 121

Truman, Harry, 63, 90, 106, 115, 198, 208, 263; debates and, 282
Trump, Donald, 24–25
Tsongas, Paul, 51

Udall, Morris, 54
uses and gratifications model, 136–39

Valley, David, 240, 247
Van Buren, Martin, 74
Vandenberg, Arthur, 281–82
Ventura, Jesse "The Body," 123, 377
videocassettes, 375–76
Viguerie, Richard, 388

Wallace, George, 141
Ware, B. L., 268–70
Washburn, Wilcomb E., 75
Washington, George, 78, 86, 100, 207
Waters, Maxine, 220
Weiss, Robert O., 298
Wells, William J., 243
Wellstone, Paul, 168
Whitaker, Clem, 383
White, Theodore H., 81, 88
Wilkie, Wendell, 128; debates and, 282
Williams, Frederick, 79
Wilson, Gayle, 235
Wilson, Pete, 170, 235
Wilson, Woodrow, 52, 101
women candidates and advertising, 171–81
Woolsey, Laura, 332

Yeltsin, Boris, 96

About the Authors

Judith S. Trent is a professor of communication at the University of Cincinnati. She is the author of numerous books and book chapters, including "Surfacing in 2004: The Democrats Emerge," in *The 2004 Presidential Campaign: A Communication Perspective* (Robert Denton Jr., ed.; 2005); "And They All Came Calling: The Early Campaign of Election 2000," in *The 2000 Presidential Campaign: A Communication Perspective* (Robert E. Denton Jr., ed.; 2002); and "The Beginning and the Early End," in *The 1996 Presidential Campaign: A Communication Perspective* (Robert E. Denton Jr., ed.; 1998). She has also served as editor of the books *Included in Communication: Learning Climates That Cultivate Racial and Ethnic Diversity* (2002) and *Communication: Views from the Helm for the 21st Century* (1998). She has written and spoken widely on the subject of political campaign communication and is a frequent commentator and analyst on political campaigns and candidates for the ABC, NBC, and CBS television affiliates in Cincinnati, as well as Ohio/Cincinnati newspapers. In 1997, she served as the president of the National Communication Association.

Robert V. Friedenberg is a professor of communication at Miami (Ohio) University. He is the author of numerous books, book chapters, and articles including "The 2004 Presidential Debates" in *The 2004 Presidential Campaign: A Communication Perspective* (Robert Denton Jr., ed.: 2005). He is the author of *Notable Speeches in Contemporary Presidential Campaigns* (2002), *Communication Consultants in Political Campaigns: Ballot Box Warriors* (1997), and *Theodore Roosevelt and the Rhetoric of Militant Decency*

(1989). He is the editor of *Rhetorical Studies of National Political Debates—1996* (1997) and *Rhetorical Studies of National Political Debates: 1960–1992* (1994). In 1989, he received the Outstanding Book of the Year Award from the Religious Speech Communication Association for *"Hear O Israel": The History of American Jewish Preaching, 1654–1970.* He has served as a communication consultant for the Republican National Committee and has been involved in more than seventy political campaigns.